EMPRESS DOWAGER CIXI

by the same author

WILD SWANS: THREE DAUGHTERS OF CHINA

MAO: THE UNKNOWN STORY
(with Jon Halliday)

EMPRESS DOWAGER CIXI

The Concubine Who Launched
Modern China

Jung Chang

JONATHAN CAPE
LONDON

Published by Jonathan Cape 2013

2 4 6 8 10 9 7 5 3 1

First published in Great Britain in 2013 by
Jonathan Cape
Random House, 20 Vauxhall Bridge Road,
London SW1V 2SA

Map by Darren Bennett

www.vintage-books.co.uk

Addresses for companies within The Random House Group Limited can be found at:
www.randomhouse.co.uk/offices.htm

The Random House Group Limited Reg. No. 954009

A CIP catalogue record for this book is available from the British Library

ISBN 9780224087438 (cased edition)
ISBN 9780224087445 (trade paperback edition)

The Random House Group Limited supports the Forest Stewardship Council® (FSC®),
the leading international forest-certification organisation. Our books carrying the FSC
label are printed on FSC®-certified paper. FSC is the only forest-certification scheme
supported by the leading environmental organisations, including Greenpeace. Our paper
procurement policy can be found at www.randomhouse.co.uk/environment

Typeset in Bembo by Palimpsest Book Production Limited,
Falkirk, Stirlingshire
Printed and bound in Great Britain by
Clays Ltd, St Ives PLC

To Jon

Contents

List of Illustrations

About the Sources

This book is based on historical documents, chiefly Chinese. They include imperial decrees, court records, official communications, personal correspondence, diaries and eye-witness accounts. Most of them have only come to light since the death of Mao in 1976, when historians were able to resume working on the archives. Thanks to their dedicated efforts, huge numbers of files have been sorted, studied, published, some even digitalised. Earlier publications of archive materials and scholarly works have been reissued. Thus I have had the good fortune to be able to utilise a colossal documentary pool, as well as consulting the First Historical Archives of China, the main keeper of the records to do with Empress Dowager Cixi, which holds twelve million documents. The vast majority of the sources cited have never been seen or used outside the Chinese-speaking world.

The Empress Dowager's Western contemporaries left valuable diaries, letters and memoirs. Queen Victoria's diary, Hansard and the copious international diplomatic exchanges are all rich mines of information. The Archives of the Freer Gallery of Art and the Arthur M. Sackler Gallery, in Washington DC, is the only place that possesses the original negatives of the photographs of Cixi.

Author's Note

The 'tael' was the currency of China at the time. One tael weighed about 38 grams and was valued at roughly a third of a pound sterling (£1 = Tls. 3).

Chinese (and Japanese) personal names are given surname first, except for those who chose to render their names differently.

The *pinyin* system is used where transliteration is needed. Thus there are non-*pinyin* Chinese names, e.g. Canton, Tsinghua (University).

The dates and ages of people are given according to the Western system (which is used in China today). The exceptions are stated.

In the Bibliography, the publication dates are of the editions which this author consulted. Many very old books may therefore give the appearance of having been published quite recently.

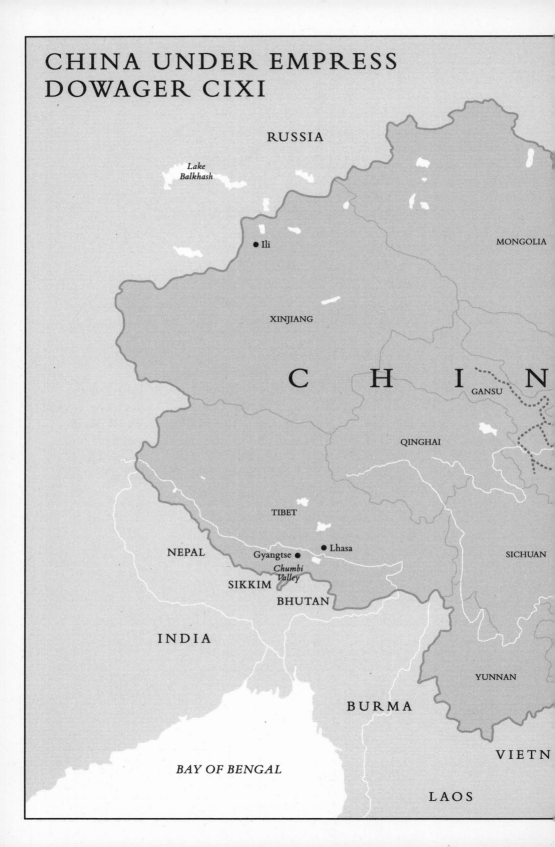

CHINA UNDER EMPRESS DOWAGER CIXI

RUSSIA

Lake Balkhash

MONGOLIA

• Ili

XINJIANG

C H I N

GANSU

QINGHAI

TIBET

• Lhasa

NEPAL

Gyangtse •

Chumbi Valley

SICHUAN

SIKKIM

BHUTAN

INDIA

YUNNAN

BURMA

VIETN

BAY OF BENGAL

LAOS

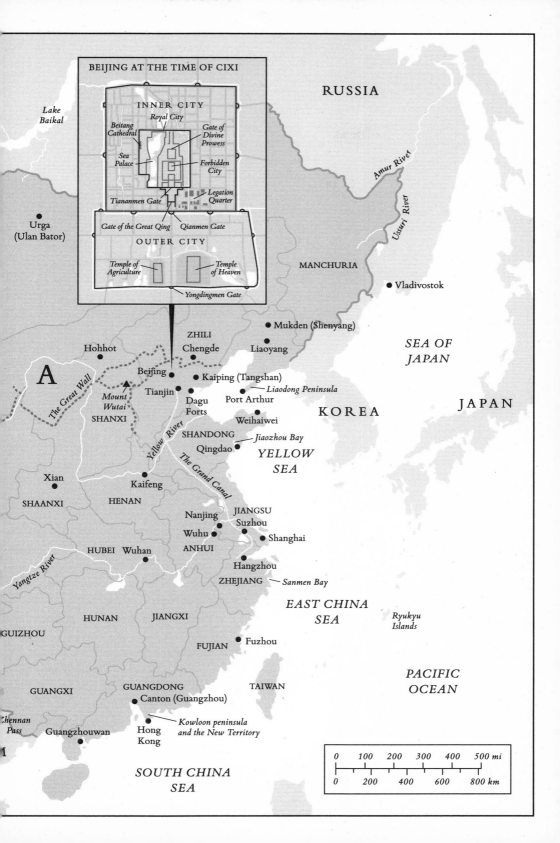

BEIJING AT THE TIME OF CIXI

INNER CITY

Beitang Cathedral

Royal City

Sea Palace

Gate of Divine Prowess

Forbidden City

Tiananmen Gate

Legation Quarter

Gate of the Great Qing   *Qianmen Gate*

OUTER CITY

Temple of Agriculture   *Temple of Heaven*

Yongdingmen Gate

RUSSIA

Lake Baikal

Amur River

Ussuri River

Urga (Ulan Bator)

MANCHURIA

Vladivostok

• Mukden (Shenyang)

ZHILI
Chengde   Liaoyang

SEA OF JAPAN

Hohhot

The Great Wall

Beijing   • Kaiping (Tangshan)

Mount Wutai   Tianjin

Liaodong Peninsula

Dagu Forts   Port Arthur

KOREA

JAPAN

SHANXI

Weihaiwei

Yellow River

SHANDONG   *Jiaozhou Bay*

Qingdao

YELLOW SEA

Xian

Kaifeng

The Grand Canal

SHAANXI   HENAN

JIANGSU

Nanjing   Suzhou

Wuhu   Shanghai

HUBEI   Wuhan   ANHUI

Hangzhou

Yangtze River

ZHEJIANG   *Sanmen Bay*

EAST CHINA SEA

Ryukyu Islands

HUNAN   JIANGXI

GUIZHOU

FUJIAN   • Fuzhou

PACIFIC OCEAN

GUANGXI   GUANGDONG
Canton (Guangzhou)

TAIWAN

Zhennan Pass

Guangzhouwan

Hong Kong

Kowloon peninsula and the New Territory

SOUTH CHINA SEA

| 0 | 100 | 200 | 300 | 400 | 500 mi |

| 0 | 200 | 400 | 600 | 800 km |

EMPRESS DOWAGER CIXI

PART ONE

The Imperial Concubine in Stormy Times (1835–1861)

1 Concubine to an Emperor
(1835–56)

IN spring 1852, in one of the periodic nationwide selections for imperial consorts, a sixteen-year-old girl caught the eye of the emperor and was chosen as a concubine. A Chinese emperor was entitled to one empress and as many concubines as he pleased. In the court registry she was entered simply as 'the woman of the Nala family', with no name of her own. Female names were deemed too insignificant to be recorded. In fewer than ten years, however, this girl, whose name may have been lost for ever,* had fought her way to become the ruler of China, and for decades – until her death in 1908 – would hold in her hands the fate of nearly one-third of the world's population. She was the Empress Dowager Cixi (also spelt Tzu Hsi). This was her honorific name and means 'kindly and joyous'.

She came from one of the oldest and most illustrious Manchu families. The Manchus were a people who originally lived in Manchuria, beyond the Great Wall to the northeast. In 1644, the Ming dynasty in China was overthrown by a peasant rebellion, and the last Ming emperor hanged himself from a tree in the back garden of his palace. The Manchus seized the opportunity to smash across the Great Wall. They defeated the peasant rebels, occupied the whole of China and set up a new dynasty called the Great Qing – 'Great Purity'. Taking over the Ming capital, Beijing, as their own, the victorious Manchus went on to build an empire three times the size of the Ming

---

* There has been an assumption that her maiden name was *Lan*, meaning 'magnolia' or 'orchid'. This was in fact the name assigned to her when she entered the court. Her descendants suggest that her own name was *Xing*: 'almond', which has the same pronunciation as the character for 'good fortune'.

empire, at its peak occupying a territory of 13 million square kilometres – compared to 9.6 million today.

The Manchu conquerors, outnumbered by the indigenous Chinese, the Han, by approximately 100:1, imposed their domination initially by brutal means. They forced the Han males to wear the Manchu men's hairstyle as the most visible badge of submission. The Han men traditionally grew their hair long and put it up in a bun, but the Manchu men shaved off an outer ring of hairs, leaving the centre part to grow and plaiting it into a trailing queue. Anyone who refused to wear the queue was summarily beheaded. In the capital, the conquerors pushed the Han out of the Inner City, to the Outer City, and separated the two ethnic groups by walls and gates.* The repression lessened over the years, and the Han generally came to live a life no worse than that of the Manchus. The ethnic animosity diminished – even though top jobs remained in the hands of the Manchus. Intermarriage was prohibited, which in a family-oriented society meant there was little social intercourse between the two groups. And yet the Manchus adopted much of the Han culture and political system, and their empire's administration, extending to all corners of the country like a colossal octopus, was overwhelmingly manned by Han officials, who were selected from the literati by the traditional Imperial Examinations that focused on Confucian classics. Indeed, Manchu emperors themselves were educated in the Confucian way, and some became greater Confucian scholars than the best of the Han. Thus the Manchus regarded themselves as Chinese, and referred to their empire as the 'Chinese' empire, or 'China', as well as the 'Qing'.

The ruling family, the Aisin-Gioros, produced a succession of able and hard-working emperors, who were absolute monarchs and made all important decisions personally. There was not even a Prime Minister, but only an office of assistants, the Grand Council. The emperors would rise at the crack of dawn to read reports, hold meetings, receive officials and issue decrees. The reports from all over China were dealt with as soon as they arrived, and rarely was any business left undone for more than a few days. The seat of the throne was the Forbidden City. Perhaps the largest imperial palace complex in the world, this rectangular compound covered an area of 720,000 square metres, with a moat of proportional size. It was surrounded by a majestic wall some 10 metres high and nearly 9 metres thick at the base, with a magnificent gate set into each side, and a splendid watchtower above each corner. Almost

---

* The Han people who had been in the Manchu army in Manchuria counted as Manchus.

all the buildings in the compound displayed glazed tiles in a shade of yellow reserved for the court. In sunshine, the sweeping roofs were a blaze of gold.

A district west of the Forbidden City formed a hub for the transportation of coal, bound for the capital. Brought from the mines west of Beijing, it was carried by caravans of camels and mules, wearing tinkling bells. It was said that some 5,000 camels came into Beijing every day. The caravans paused here, and the porters did their shopping from stores whose names were embroidered on colourful banners or gilded on lacquered plaques. The streets were unpaved, and the soft, powdery dust that lay on top in dry weather would turn into a river of mud after a downpour. There was a pervasive reek from a sewage system that was as antiquated as the city itself. Refuse was simply dumped on the side of the roads, left to the scavenging dogs and birds. After their meals, large numbers of vultures and carrion crows would flock into the Forbidden City, perching on its golden roofs and blackening them.

Away from the hubbub lay a network of quiet, narrow alleys known as *hu-tong*. This is where, on the tenth day of the tenth lunar month in 1835, the future Empress Dowager of China, Cixi, was born. The houses here were spacious, with neatly arranged courtyards, scrupulously tidy and clean, in sharp contrast to the dirty and chaotic streets. The main rooms had doors and windows open to the south to take in the sun, while the north was walled up to fend off the sandy storms that frequently swept the city. The roofs were covered with grey tiles. The colours of roof tiles were strictly stipulated: yellow for the royal palaces, green for the princes, and grey for all others.

Cixi's family had been government employees for generations. Her father, Huizheng, worked as a secretary and then a section chief for the Ministry of Officials. The family was well-off; her childhood was carefree. As a Manchu, she was spared foot-binding, a Han practice that tortured their women for a millennium by crushing a baby girl's feet and wrapping them tightly to restrict their growth. Most other customs, such as male–female segregation, the Manchus shared with the Han. As a girl of an educated family, Cixi learned to read and write a little Chinese, to draw, to play chess, to embroider and to make dresses – all deemed desirable accomplishments for a young lady. She was a quick and energetic learner and developed a wide range of interests. In the future, when it was the ceremonial duty of the empress dowager, on a certain auspicious day, to cut the pattern for a dress of her own – as a symbol of womanhood – she would perform the task with tremendous competence.

Her education did not include learning the Manchu language, which she neither spoke nor wrote. (When she became the ruler of China, she had to issue an order for reports written in Manchu to be translated into Chinese before she was shown them.) Having been immersed in Chinese culture for 200 years, most Manchus did not speak their own original tongue, even though it was the official language of the dynasty and various emperors had made efforts to preserve it. Cixi's knowledge of written Chinese was rudimentary, and she may be considered 'semi-literate'. This does not mean that she lacked intelligence. The Chinese language is extremely hard to learn. It is the only major linguistic system in the world that does not have an alphabet; and it is composed of numerous complicated characters – ideograms – which have to be memorised one by one and, moreover, are totally unrelated to sounds. At Cixi's time, written texts were completely divorced from the spoken form, so one could not simply write down what one spoke or thought. To qualify as 'educated', therefore, learners had to spend about a decade in their formative years imbibing Confucian classics, which were severely limited in range and stimulation. Fewer than 1 per cent of the population were able to read or write the bare minimum.

Cixi's lack of formal education was more than made up for by her intuitive intelligence, which she liked to use from her earliest years. In 1843, when she was seven, the empire had just finished its first war with the West, the Opium War, which had been started by Britain in reaction to Beijing clamping down on the illegal opium trade conducted by British merchants. China was defeated and had to pay a hefty indemnity. Desperate for funds, Emperor Daoguang (father of Cixi's future husband) held back the traditional presents for his sons' brides – gold necklaces with corals and pearls – and vetoed elaborate banquets for their weddings. New Year and birthday celebrations were scaled down, even cancelled, and minor royal concubines had to subsidise their reduced allowances by selling their embroidery on the market through eunuchs. The emperor himself even went on surprise raids of his concubines' wardrobes, to check whether they were hiding extravagant clothes against his orders. As part of a determined drive to stamp out theft by officials, an investigation was conducted of the state coffer, which revealed that more than nine million taels of silver had gone missing. Furious, the emperor ordered all the senior keepers and inspectors of the silver reserve for the previous forty-four years to pay fines to make up the loss – whether or not they were guilty. Cixi's great-grandfather had served as one of the keepers and his share of the fine amounted to 43,200 taels – a colossal sum, next to which his official salary had been a pittance. As he had died a long time ago, his son, Cixi's grandfather, was obliged to pay half the sum, even though he worked in the Ministry of Punishments and had nothing to do with the state coffer. After three years of futile struggle to raise money, he only managed to hand over 1,800 taels, and an edict signed by the emperor confined him to prison, only to be released if and when *his* son, Cixi's father, delivered the balance.

The life of the family was turned upside down. Cixi, then eleven years old, had to take in sewing jobs to earn extra money – which she would remember all her life and would later talk about to her ladies-in-waiting in the court. As she was the eldest of two daughters and three sons, her father discussed the matter with her, and she rose to the occasion. Her ideas were carefully considered and practical: what possessions to sell, what valuables to pawn, whom to turn to for loans and how to approach them. Finally, the family raised 60 per cent of the sum, enough to get her grandfather out of prison. The young Cixi's contribution to solving the crisis became a family legend, and her father paid her the ultimate compliment: 'This daughter of mine is really more like a son!'

Treated like a son, Cixi was able to talk to her father about things that were normally closed areas for women. Inevitably their conversations touched on official business and state affairs, which helped form Cixi's lifelong interest. Being consulted and having her views acted on, she acquired self-confidence and never accepted the common assumption that women's brains were inferior to men's. The crisis also helped shape her future method of rule. Having tasted the bitterness of arbitrary punishment, she would make an effort to be fair to her officials.

As he had raised a sizeable sum of money to pay the fine, Cixi's father, Huizheng, was rewarded in 1849 with an appointment from the emperor to be the governor of a large Mongolian region. That summer he travelled there with his family, setting up home in Hohhot, today's provincial capital of Inner Mongolia. For the first time Cixi journeyed out of crowded Beijing, beyond the decaying Great Wall and along a stony route that led to the Mongolian steppes, where uninterrupted open grassland extended to a very distant horizon. Throughout her life Cixi would feel passionate about fresh air and unrestricted space.

In his new job as governor, Cixi's father was responsible for collecting taxes and, in line with prevailing and age-old practice, he fleeced the local population to make up for the family losses. That he should do so was taken for granted. Officials, who were paid low salaries, were expected to subsidise their income with whatever extras they could make – 'within reason' – from the population at large. Cixi grew up with corruption of this kind as a way of life.

In February 1850, months after the family settled in Mongolia, Emperor Daoguang died and was succeeded by his son, Emperor Xianfeng. The new emperor, then nineteen years old, had been born prematurely and had been in poor health since birth. He had a thin face and melancholy eyes, as well as a limp, the result of a fall from a horse in one of the hunting expeditions that were obligatory for the princes. As an emperor is referred to as a 'dragon', gossips in Beijing nicknamed him 'the Limping Dragon'.

After his coronation, an empire-wide operation began to select consorts for him. (At this point, he had one consort, a concubine.) The candidates, teenage girls, had to be Manchu or Mongol; the Han were excluded. Their families had to be above a certain rank, and had been obliged by law to register them when they reached puberty.

Cixi was on the list and now, like other girls from all over China, she travelled to Beijing. She settled back into the family's old house and waited for the occasion when all the candidates would parade in front of the emperor. After he had made his pick, some of the girls would be given to the princes and other royal males as consorts. Those who failed to be chosen were free to go home and marry someone else. The inspection in the Forbidden City was scheduled for March 1852.

The procedure for the inspection had been passed down over the generations. On the day before the fixed date, the candidates were taken to the palace in mule-drawn carts – 'taxis' of the day – which were hired by their families and paid for by the court. These carts were like a trunk on two wheels, and were hooded with woven bamboo or rattan that had been soaked in tung-oil to become rain- and snow-proof. Curtains of bright blue were draped over it, and felt and cotton mattresses and cushions were piled inside. This was a common conveyance even for the families of princes, in which case the inside would be lined with fur or satin, depending on the season, while the outside bore markers of its owner's rank. On seeing such a vehicle passing by silently and disappearing into the gathering darkness, Somerset Maugham (later) mused:

you wonder who it is that sits cross-legged within. Perhaps it is a scholar . . . bound on a visit to a friend with whom he will exchange elaborate compliments and discuss the golden age of Tang and Sung which can return no more; perhaps it is a singing girl in splendid silks and richly embroidered coat, with jade in her black hair, summoned to a party so that she may sing a little song and exchange elegant repartee with young blades cultured enough to appreciate wit.

The cart that seemed to Maugham to be carrying 'all the mystery of the East' was singularly uncomfortable, as its wooden wheels were secured by wire and nails, without springs. The occupant was bounced up and down on the dirt-and-stone roads, banging on all sides within. It was particularly challenging for Europeans, who were not used to sitting cross-legged without seats. The grandfather of the Mitford sisters, Algernon Freeman-Mitford, soon to be an attaché in the British Legation in Beijing, remarked: 'After ten hours of a Chinese cart a man is fit for little else than to be sold at an old rag and bone shop.'

Walking at a sedate pace, the carts of the candidates converged outside the back gate of the Royal City, the outer enclosure that cradled the Forbidden City. As the Forbidden City itself was already enormous, this gigantic outer area was similarly encircled by broad crimson-red walls under roof tiles glazed with the same royal yellow colour. It housed temples, offices, warehouses and workshops, with horses and camels and donkeys coming and going, providing services for the court. On this day, at sunset, all activities stopped and a passage was left clear for the carts bearing the candidates, which entered the Royal City in a prescribed order. Passing by the artificial hill Jingshan, and crossing the moat, they arrived outside the north gate to the Forbidden City, the Gate of Divine Prowess, which had an imposing and ornate two-tiered roof over it.

This was the back entrance to the Forbidden City. The front, south gate, was prohibited to women. In fact, the entire front – and main – section was for men only. Constructed for official ceremonies, it consisted of grand halls and vast, empty, stone-paved grounds, with a most noticeable absence: plants. There was virtually no vegetation. This was by design, as plants were thought to convey a feeling of softness, which would diminish the sense of awe: awe for the emperor, the Son of Heaven – 'Heaven' being the mystic and formless ultimate god that the Chinese worshipped. Women had to stay well within the rear part of the Forbidden City, the *hou-gong*, or harem, where no men were permitted except the emperor, and the eunuchs, who numbered many hundreds.

The potential entrants for the harem now stopped outside the back entrance for the night. Under the towering gate, the carts parked on an enormous paved ground as darkness descended, each lantern casting its own dim circle of light. The candidates would spend the night cooped up in their carts, waiting for the gate to open at dawn. They would then alight and, directed by eunuchs, walk to the hall, where they would be scrutinised by the emperor. Standing before His Majesty, several in a row, they were specifically exempted from performing the obligatory kowtow: going down on their knees and putting their foreheads on the ground. The emperor needed to see them clearly.

Apart from the family name, 'character' was a key criterion. The candidates must demonstrate dignity as well as courteousness, graciousness as well as gentleness and modesty – and they must know how to behave in the court. Looks were secondary, but needed to be pleasing. In order for them to show their pure selves, the candidates were not allowed to wear richly coloured clothes: the gowns they wore had to be simple, with just a little embroidery along the hems. Manchu dresses were usually highly decorative. They hung from the shoulders to the floor and were best carried with a straight back. Manchu women's shoes, daintily embroidered, had the elevation at the centre of the soles, which could be as high as 14 centimetres and compelled them to stand erect. Over their hair, they wore a headdress that was shaped like a cross between a crown and a gate tower, decorated with jewels and flowers when the occasion demanded. On such occasions, a stiff neck was needed to support it.

Cixi was not a great beauty; but she had poise. Though she was short, at just over 1.5 metres, she looked much taller, thanks to the gown, the shoes and the headdress. She sat erect and moved gracefully, even when she was walking fast, on what some described as 'stilts'. She was blessed with very fine skin and a pair of delicate hands, which, even in old age, remained as soft as a young girl's. The American artist who later painted her, Katharine Carl, described her features thus: 'a high nose . . . an upper lip of great firmness, a rather large but beautiful mouth with mobile, red lips, which, when parted over her firm white teeth, gave her smile a rare charm; a strong chin, but not of exaggerated firmness and with no marks of obstinacy'. Her most arresting feature was her brilliant and expressive eyes, as many observed. In the coming years during audiences she would give officials the most coaxing look, when suddenly her eyes would flash with fearsome authority. The future – and first – President of China, General Yuan Shikai, who had served under her and had a reputation for being fierce, confessed that her gaze was the only thing that unnerved him: 'I don't know why but the sweat just poured out. I just became so nervous.'

Now her eyes conveyed all the right messages, and Emperor Xianfeng took notice. He indicated his liking, and the court officials retained her identification card. Thus being shortlisted, she was subjected to further checks and stayed one night in the Forbidden City. Finally she was chosen, together with several other girls, out of hundreds of candidates. There can be no doubt that this was the future she wanted. Cixi was interested in politics and she had no knight in shining armour awaiting her return. Segregation between male and female precluded any romantic liaison, and the threat of severe punishment for any family who betrothed their daughter without her first having been rejected by the emperor meant that her family could not have made any marital arrangement for her. Although, once admitted to the court, Cixi would rarely see her family, it was officially stipulated that elderly parents of royal consorts could obtain special permission to visit their daughters, even staying for months in guest houses in a corner of the Forbidden City.

A date was set for Cixi to take up her new home: 26 June 1852. This followed the formal ending of the mandatory two-year mourning for the deceased Emperor Daoguang, signalled by the new emperor visiting his late father's mausoleum west of Beijing. During that mourning period he had been required to abstain from sex. Upon entering the palace, Cixi was given the name *Lan*, which seems to have derived from her surname Nala, which was sometimes written as Nalan. *Lan* was also the name for magnolia or orchid. To name a girl after a flower was a common practice. Cixi did not like the name, and as soon as she was in a position to ask the emperor for a favour, she had it changed.

The harem she entered on that summer day was a world of walled-in courtyards and long, narrow alleyways. Unlike the all-male front section, this quarter had little sense of grandeur, but quite a lot of trees, flowers and rockeries. Here the empress occupied a palace, and each of the concubines had a mini-suite. The rooms were decorated with embroidered silk, carved furniture and bejewelled ornaments, but little display of individual personality was permitted. The harem, like the whole of the Forbidden City, was governed by rigid rules. Exactly what objects the girls could have in their rooms, the quantity and quality of the textiles for their clothes, and the types of food for each day's consumption were meticulously determined in accordance with their rank. For food, an empress had a daily allowance of 13 kilos of meat, one chicken, one duck, ten packages of teas, twelve jars of special water from the Jade Spring Hills, as well as specified amounts of different kinds of vegetables, cereals, spices and other ingredients.★ Her daily allowance also included the milk produced by no fewer than twenty-five cows. (Unlike most of the Han, the Manchus drank milk and ate dairy products.)

Cixi was not made the empress. She was a concubine, and a low-rank one at that. There were eight rungs on the ladder of imperial consorts, and Cixi was on the sixth, which put her in the lowest group (the sixth to the eighth). At her rank, Cixi had no private cow and was only entitled to 3 kilos of meat a day. She had four personal maids, while the empress had ten, in addition to numerous eunuchs.

The new empress, a girl named Zhen, meaning 'chastity', had entered the court with Cixi. She had also started as a concubine, but of a higher rank, the fifth. Within four months and before the end of the year, however, she had been promoted to the first rank: the empress. It was not on account of her beauty, for Empress Zhen was quite plain. She was also of poor physique, and the gossip that had dubbed her husband 'the Limping Dragon' named her 'the Fragile Phoenix' (phoenix being the symbol of the empress). But she possessed the quality most valued in an empress: she had the personality and skill to get on with the other consorts, and manage them, as well as the servants. An empress's primary role was to be the manageress of the harem, and Empress Zhen fulfilled this role perfectly. Under her, the harem was remarkably free of the backbiting and malice that were endemic in such places.

There is no evidence that Cixi was favoured as a concubine by her husband. In the Forbidden City the emperor's sex life was diligently recorded. He picked his sexual partner for the night by marking her name on a bamboo tablet presented to him by the chief eunuch over dinner, which he mostly ate alone. He had two bedrooms, one with mirrors on all sides, and the other with silk screens. The beds were

---

★ The 'leftovers' were not wasted. A previous emperor had dictated that they should be given to servants, and their leftovers be fed to cats and dogs. Even the remnants were not to be thrown away: they must be dried and made into bird feed.

draped with silk curtains, inside which hung scent bags. The bed-curtains in both rooms were lowered when the emperor went into one of them. This was apparently for reasons of security, so that even intimate serv-ants did not know for certain which bed he went to. Court rules forbade the emperor to sleep in his women's beds. They came to his, and if legend were to be believed, the chosen one was carried over by a eunuch, naked and wrapped in silk. After sex, the woman went away; she was not permitted to stay overnight.

The Limping Dragon loved sex. There are more stories about his sexual activities than about any other Qing emperor. His consorts soon increased to nineteen, some of whom had been elevated from among the palace maids, who were also chosen from all over China, mostly from low-class Manchu families. In addition, women were brought to his bed from outside the court. Rumour had it that most of them were well-known Han prostitutes, who had bound feet – for which he apparently had a penchant. As the Forbidden City had strict rules, they were said to have been smuggled into the Old Summer Palace – the *Yuan-ming-yuan*, Gardens of Perfect Brightness – a gigantic land-scaped complex some 8 kilometres to the west of Beijing. There, the rules were more relaxed, and the emperor could indulge in sexual ventures more freely.

For nearly two years, a sexually active – even frenetic – emperor showed no particular fondness for Cixi. He left her at Rank 6, while elevating those lower in status to her rank. Something put him off her. And it seems that the teenage Cixi, in her eagerness to please her husband, made the mistake of trying to share his worries.

Emperor Xianfeng faced monumental problems. As soon as he ascended the throne, in 1850, the biggest peasant rebellion in Chinese history, the Taiping, broke out in the southern coastal province of Guangxi. There, famine drove tens of thousands of peasants into a desperate last resort – armed rebellion – though they risked the most horrific conse-quences. For their leaders, the mandatory punishment was *ling-chi*, 'death by a thousand cuts', during which the condemned was sliced piece by piece in public. Even this was not enough to deter the peas-ants who faced the slow death of hunger, and the Taiping rebel army quickly grew into hundreds of thousands. By the end of March 1853, it had swept into the old southern capital, Nanjing, and set up an opposing state, the Taiping Heavenly Kingdom. The day he received the report, Emperor Xianfeng wept in front of his officials.

And this was not the emperor's only woe. Most of the eighteen provinces inside the Great Wall were thrown into turmoil by numerous other uprisings. Countless villages, towns and cities were devastated. The empire was in such a mess that the emperor felt obliged to issue an Imperial Apology, in 1852. This was the ultimate form of contrition from a monarch to the nation.

It was just after this that Cixi entered the court. Her husband's problems could be felt even in the depths of the Forbidden City. The empire's state silver reserve fell to an all-time low of 290,000 taels. To help pay for his soldiers' upkeep, Emperor Xianfeng opened the purse of the royal household, in which, eventually, only 41,000 taels remained, barely enough to cover daily expenditure. Treasures in the Forbidden City were melted down, including three giant bells made of pure gold. To his consorts he wrote stern admonitions like these in his own hand:

No big ear clips or jade earrings.
No more than two jewelled flowers for the hair, and anyone who wears three will be punished.
No more than one *cun* [roughly 2.5 cm] for the elevation of the shoes, and anyone whose shoes are more than one and a half *cun* high will be punished.

The disasters of the empire also directly affected Cixi's family, with whom she maintained contact. Prior to her entry into the court, her father had been transferred to the east-central province near Shanghai, Anhui, to be the governor of a region that administered twenty-eight counties, with its seat in Wuhu, a prosperous city on the Yangtze. But this was close to the Taiping battleground, and a year later her father was forced to flee when the rebels attacked his city. Terrified of the emperor's wrath – some officials who fled their office had been decapitated – and exhausted by the flight, Huizheng fell ill and died in summer 1853.

The death of her father, to whom she was very close, made Cixi feel she really must do something to help the empire – and her husband. It appears that she tried to offer him some suggestions as to how he might deal with the upheavals. Coming from a background in which her advice was sought and acted on by her own family, it seems that she assumed that Xianfeng too would appreciate her counsel. But it only annoyed him. The Qing court, following ancient Chinese tradition, strictly forbade royal consorts from having anything to do with state affairs. Emperor Xianfeng told Empress Zhen to do something about Cixi, using derogatory words to describe her advice – 'crafty and cunning'. Cixi had violated a basic rule and risked deadly punishment.★ A well-known story has it that Emperor Xianfeng later gave a private edict to Empress Zhen, saying that he worried Cixi would try to interfere in state affairs after he died and, if she ever did so, Empress Zhen was to show the edict to the princes and have her 'exterminated'. As it happened, or so the story goes, Empress Zhen showed the lethal piece of paper to Cixi after the death of their husband, and then burned it.

Empress Zhen was a brave woman, and her contemporaries also praised her for her kindness. When the emperor was angry with a concubine, she always mediated. Now, it seems, she put in a good word for Cixi. And her argument might well have been that Cixi was only trying – perhaps trying too hard – to express her love and concern for His Majesty. At this most vulnerable time for Cixi, Empress Zhen protected her. This helped lay the foundation of Cixi's lifelong devotion to the empress. The feelings were mutual. Cixi had never been underhand in her dealings with Empress Zhen. Although she must have been dissatisfied with her position at the bottom of the consort ladder, while Zhen rose to be empress, Cixi never did anything to undermine Zhen. Even her worst enemies did not accuse her of such scheming. If there was any jealousy, which in Cixi's position would seem to have been unavoidable, Cixi kept it well under control and never let it poison their relationship. Cixi was not petty – and she was wise. So, instead of being rivalrous, the two women became good friends, with the empress addressing Cixi intimately as 'Younger Sister'. She was actually a year younger than Cixi, but this indicated her seniority as the empress.

Empress Zhen may well have been instrumental in persuading the emperor to promote Cixi in 1854 from Rank 6 to 5, lifting her out of the bottom group. To accompany this elevation, he gave her a new, carefully considered name, *Yi*, which means 'exemplary'. A special edict in the emperor's own hand, in crimson ink that signalled the authority of the monarch, publicly announced Cixi's new name, together with her promotion. A ceremony was held for her to receive the honour formally, during which eunuchs from the Music Department of the court played congratulatory compositions.

For Cixi, the whole episode taught her that to survive at court she

---

★ It is sometimes asserted that Cixi helped her husband read official reports and write instructions. There is no evidence of this.

must hold her tongue about state affairs. This was difficult, as she could see that the dynasty was in trouble. The victorious Taiping rebels not only consolidated their bases in southern China, but were sending military expeditions with a view to attacking Beijing. Cixi felt that she had practicable ideas – in fact it was under her rule that the Taiping rebels were later defeated. But she could not say a word, and could only share non-political interests with her husband, such as music and art. Emperor Xianfeng was an artistic man. His paintings from his teenage years (figures, landscapes and horses with endearing eyes) were remarkably accomplished. Cixi too could draw. She designed embroidery when she was a young girl, and her painting and calligraphy would blossom in older age. For now, at least, she could talk about this common interest with her husband. Opera provided a closer bond. Emperor Xianfeng not only loved to watch operas, but also composed tunes, wrote lyrics and directed performances. He even put on make-up and took part in acting. Keen to improve his skills, he got actors to teach eunuchs while he looked on, and learned by watching. His favourite instruments were the flute and drum, which he played well. As for Cixi, her lifelong love affair with the opera would one day help to create a sophisticated art form.

On 27 April 1856, Cixi gave birth to a son. This event was to change her destiny.

2 From the Opium War to the Burning of the Old Summer Palace (1839–60)

THE birth of Cixi's son, the emperor's firstborn male, was a monumental event for the court. Emperor Xianfeng had had only one daughter by this time, the Grand Princess, by a concubine who had entered the court with Cixi; but, as a female, the princess was not entitled to carry the dynastic line. With the arrival of Cixi's son, a palace file was opened with the title 'Imperial Concubine *Yi* Gave Joyous Birth to a Grand Prince'. It shows that several months earlier, in accordance with a sensible royal household rule, Cixi's mother had been invited into the Forbidden City to look after her daughter. On an auspicious date determined by the court astrologer, a 'Hole of Joy' had been dug behind Cixi's apartment, in a ceremony during which 'Songs of Joy' were recited. Into the hole were placed chopsticks wrapped in red silk next to eight treasures, including gold and silver. Chopsticks have the same pronunciation, *kuai-zi*, as the expression 'to produce a son quickly'. The hole was to be used for burying the placenta and the umbilical cord.

Silks of all kinds, the finest cotton and muslin, for baby clothes and bedding, were readied. Scores of women with childbirth experiences were interviewed. Together with doctors from the Royal Clinic, these mature women would stay by Cixi's side when her pregnancy entered the seventh month. Actually, court rules specified the eighth month, but an anxious Emperor Xianfeng decreed special treatment. He was kept closely informed about the development of Cixi's condition, and the moment the child was born, the chief eunuch rushed over and reported that 'Imperial Concubine *Yi* has just given birth to a prince', and that the royal doctors had found 'the pulses of the mother and the son are both peaceful'. (The pulse is regarded as a crucial indicator of health.) All cried: 'Oh great rejoicing to our Master of Ten Thousand Years!'

Overjoyed, Emperor Xianfeng instantly elevated Cixi to a higher rank. The whole court was swept into a frenzy of celebration over the baby, who was named Zaichun. On the third day he was given a thorough wash, in a large bowl of pure gold, with the date, time (noon) and position (facing south) painstakingly calculated by the court astrologer. Soon, to great fanfares, the baby was formally placed in a cradle. More festivities took place when he was one month old, during which he had his first haircut. On his first birthday, a pile of objects was laid out for him to grasp: his choice was supposed to indicate his future disposition. The first item he grabbed was a book – for which he would in fact develop a phobia. On all these and other occasions he received lavish presents. Gift-giving was carried to extraordinary lengths at the time, and no occasion was thought proper without it. At the court, scarcely a day went by without presents being brought in or sent out, or exchanged by those within. By the end of his first year, Cixi's son had received some 900 objects made of gold, silver, jade and other precious stones, as well as more than 500 pieces of clothing and bedding in the finest textiles.

Thanks to her son, Cixi quickly became the undisputed No. 2 consort, second only to Empress Zhen. Her position was made even more secure when the emperor's second son, born two years later to another concubine, lived only a few hours and died before he was given a name. The strength of her position enabled Cixi to persuade her husband to marry her eighteen-year-old sister to one of his younger half-brothers, the nineteen-year-old Prince Chun. Consorts for the princes had to be chosen by the emperor, from the candidates presented for the selection of his own consorts. Cixi had seen quite a lot of the prince at the opera shows. Although on such occasions male and female were separated by a screen, the curious ones always found a way to size up a member of the opposite sex. From the boxes in which they were seated, cross-legged on cushions, the royal women could observe the royal males without being seen. The American missionary physician Mrs Isaac Headland, who (later) treated many aristocratic ladies, including Cixi's mother, noted: 'these gentle little ladies have their own curiosity, and some means of finding out who's who among that court full of dragon-draped pillars of state; for I have never failed to receive a ready answer when I inquired as to the name of some handsome or distinguished-looking guest whose identity I wished to learn'. Cixi would have made it her business to find out about the character of Prince Chun, and indeed he would be of enormous service to her in the future.

Meanwhile, Cixi devoted herself to her son. Court rules forbade her to breast-feed him, and doctors prescribed herbal medicine to stop her milk. A wet nurse from a lower-class Manchu family who met the court requirements was engaged and, to facilitate her milk, one instruction enjoined her to eat 'half a duck every day, or pigs' knuckles, or the front part of pigs' lungs'. The royal household also paid for the wet nurse to employ a wet nurse for her own child.

Empress Zhen was the official Mother to the child, and took precedence over Cixi. This did not lead to animosity between the two women, and the child grew up with two doting mothers. When he was older, he had a playmate, his elder sister, the Grand Princess. Court painters captured the two children playing together in the palace gardens, the little boy in an indigo robe tied round the waist with a red sash and the girl in green with a red waistcoat, with flowers in her hair. They are shown fishing from a pavilion under a willow tree open to a lake of blooming lotuses. In another picture, set in early spring, with white magnolias next to an evergreen pine, both the boy and the girl have little caps on, the prince's robe thick with pale-blue lining. They seem to be looking for insects that were perhaps waking from a long hibernation, among the gaunt roots of old trees and rockeries. In the pictures, the younger boy always appeared twice as big as his elder sister.

Behind these peaceful and idyllic scenes of the early childhood of Cixi's son, the empire continued to be convulsed by the Taiping rebellion in the south and by violent unrest elsewhere. In fact it was facing another gigantic problem: foreign powers had invaded.

The origin of the Anglo-French war against China in 1856–60 can be traced back 100 years earlier. In 1757, the then-emperor, Qianlong, who ruled China for sixty years (1736–95) and is often referred to as 'Qianlong the Magnificent' for his achievements, closed the door of the country, leaving only one port open for trade, Canton. The emperor's paramount concern was the control of the vast empire, and a closed door made control much easier. But Britain was hungry for trade. Its main imports from China were silks and teas, the latter cultivated only in China at that time. Each year, through import duty, teas alone brought more than £3 million into the Exchequer, enough to cover half the expenses of the Royal Navy. To persuade Emperor Qianlong to open more ports for trade, a British mission arrived in Beijing in 1793. Its leader, Lord Macartney, did his best to accommodate Chinese demands and accepted that the boats and carts conveying his mission bear banners inscribed with Chinese characters: 'The English Ambassador bringing tribute to the Emperor of China'. In order to be granted an audience with Qianlong, he even performed the obligatory *san-gui-jiu-kou* – that is, kneeling three times to the emperor and touching the ground with his forehead nine times. Macartney did so with great reluctance and after much resistance, knowing that otherwise Emperor Qianlong would not see him.★

Emperor Qianlong treated Lord Macartney with what the Englishman called 'every external mark of favour and regard', but he would absolutely not consider more trade. To show him what Britain could offer, Lord Macartney had brought with him, among other gifts, two mountain-howitzers, complete with carriages, limbers and ammunition. The emperor left them untouched in storage in the Old Summer Palace. In his reply to a letter from King George III, he carefully rejected the British king's requests point by point. To open up more ports for trading was 'impossible'; Britain acquiring a small island off China's coast for its merchants to stay and store goods was not allowed; and the stationing of an envoy in the capital, Beijing, was 'absolutely out of the question'. Lord Macartney had also requested that Christian missions be allowed into the country, to which the emperor's answer was: 'Christianity is the religion of the West, and this Celestial Dynasty has its own beliefs bestowed by our sacred and wise monarchs, which have enabled our 400 million subjects to be led in an orderly fashion. Our people's minds must not be confused by heresy . . . The Chinese and the foreigners must be strictly separated.'

The emperor claimed that his 'Celestial Dynasty possesses all things in prolific abundance and lacks no product within its own borders', and that it therefore had no need for anything from the outside world. He asserted that he only allowed trade at one port out of generous consideration for the foreigners, who could not do without Chinese goods. These swaggering words were neither true, nor what the emperor really thought. Customs duty from Canton contributed

★ This is according to Chinese records. Some suggest that Lord Macartney did not perform this ritual. But Emperor Qianlong specifically told his court he would see Lord Macartney 'now that he has agreed to follow the rules of this Celestial Dynasty' on this matter. For other arguments suggesting that Lord Macartney did perform the detested 'three kneelings and nine head knockings', see Rockhill, p. 31.

substantially to the state coffers – more than 1.1 million taels of silver in 1790, three years before Lord Macartney's mission. A large tranche of the money went to the court, whose annual expenses stood at 600,000 taels. Emperor Qianlong was well aware of this, as he regularly went through the books of transactions. Nor was he ignorant of the advancement of European science and technology. As vital a thing as the Chinese calendar, which guided agricultural production of the empire, had been definitively devised in the seventeenth century by European Jesuits – notably Ferdinand Verbiest – who had been employed by Emperor Kangxi (1661–1722), Qianlong's grandfather. Since then, European Jesuits had been continuously manning the Imperial Observatory in Beijing, using European equipment. Currently they were working for Emperor Qianlong himself. Even the map of China under Qianlong (as well as under Kangxi) was drawn up by missionaries who surveyed the territory of the empire using European methods.

It was in fact his sense of insecurity regarding the control of China that prompted Qianlong's emphatic rejection of the Macartney mission, just like his closing the door of the country. The emperor's control over his vast empire was built on total and unquestioning submission from the population. Any foreign contact that might disturb this blind obedience was dangerous to the throne. From Qianlong's point of view, the empire could well run out of control if it was not sealed off and if foreign elements were near the population – especially when the grass roots were already restive. The Qing dynasty, which had been enjoying considerable prosperity, blessed by good weather for long stretches of time (some fifty years under Emperor Kangxi) was beginning to decline by the late eighteenth century. This was largely due to population explosion, partly the result of the introduction to China of high-productivity foods like potato and corn from the American continent. By the time of Lord Macartney's visit, China's population had more than doubled in half a century and exceeded 300 million. Another fifty years later, it was well over 400 million. The country's traditional economy was unable to sustain this dramatic population growth. Lord Macartney observed: 'Scarcely a year now passes without an insurrection in some of their provinces. It is true they are soon suppressed, but their frequency is a strong symptom of the fever within. The paroxysm is repelled, but the disease is not cured.'

Virtually throwing out Lord Macartney, Emperor Qianlong wrote aggressively to King George III, threatening to use force to repel British cargo ships, should they come to his coast, ending his letter with: 'Don't blame me for not serving you proper warnings!' He was behaving like an animal raising its hackles at the smell of danger. Emperor Qianlong's closed-door policy was born of alarm and calculation, not ignorant conceit, as is so often claimed.

His successors, his son and grandson, stuck to this closed-door policy, as the empire grew increasingly weak. Then, half a century after Lord Macartney's failed mission, the closed door was pushed ajar by Britain through the Opium War (1839–42), China's first military clash with the West.

The opium was produced in British India and was smuggled into China by (mainly) British merchants. Beijing had prohibited the import, cultivation and smoking of opium since 1800, as it was well aware that the drug was doing tremendous damage to its economy as well as to the population. A contemporary description of addicts painted a vivid picture: 'Their shoulders hunched, eyes watering, nose running, and breath short, they look more dead than alive.' There was great fear that if this went on, the country would run out of fit soldiers and labourers, not to mention silver, its currency. In March 1839, Emperor Daoguang, Cixi's future father-in-law, sent a crusading drug fighter, Lin Zexu, as the Imperial Commissioner to Canton, along whose shore foreign ships anchored. Commissioner Lin ordered the merchants to hand over all the opium in their possession and, when his order was resisted, he had the foreign community cordoned off and declared that it would only be released when all the opium in Chinese waters was surrendered. In the end, 20,183 chests of opium, containing more than one million kilos, were delivered to Commissioner Lin, who then lifted the cordon. He had the opium destroyed outside Canton, first melting it and then pouring it into the sea. Before releasing the drug, the Commissioner performed a sacrificial ritual to the God of the Sea, begging him to 'tell the fishes to swim away for the time being to avoid the poison'.

Commissioner Lin knew that 'the head of England is a woman, and quite young, but all orders come from her'. He penned a letter to Queen Victoria, who had been on the throne since 1837, asking her for cooperation. 'I hear that opium-smoking is strictly banned in England,' Lin wrote. 'And so England knows the harm the drug does. If it does not allow it to poison its own people, it should not allow it to poison the people of other countries.' Emperor Daoguang approved the letter. It is unclear to whom the Commissioner entrusted it, but there is no record of Queen Victoria receiving it.★

Major trading companies and Chambers of Commerce from London to Glasgow were up in arms. Lin's action was said to be 'injurious' to British property, and there were calls for going to war to seek 'satisfaction and reparation'. Foreign Secretary Lord Palmerston, an exponent of 'gunboat diplomacy', was in favour of war. When the matter was debated in Parliament on 8 April 1840, the then-young Tory MP and future Prime Minister, William Gladstone, spoke passionately against it:

. . . a war more unjust in its origin, a war more calculated in its progress to cover this country with permanent disgrace, I do not know, and I have not read of. The right hon. Gentleman opposite spoke last night in eloquent terms of the British flag waving in glory at Canton . . . but now, under the auspices of the noble Lord, that flag is hoisted to protect an infamous contraband traffic . . . No, I am sure that Her Majesty's Government will never upon this motion persuade the House to abet this unjust and iniquitous war.

But a vote of censure moved by the Opposition – the Tories – was defeated by 271 to 262, a majority of nine. During the next two years, scores of British warships and 20,000 men (including 7,000 Indian troops) attacked the Chinese coast in the south and east, occupying Canton and, briefly, Shanghai. Without gunboats and with a poorly equipped army, China was defeated and was forced to sign the Treaty of Nanjing in 1842, and to pay an indemnity of US $21 million.†

Thus encouraged, opium-smuggling flourished. Shipments of the drug from Calcutta and Bombay nearly doubled straight away, and

★ It is not in the Royal Archives at Windsor, and there is no sign of the letter reaching London. It was, however, published in the contemporary English press in Canton, the *Canton Press*, and the February 1840 issue of the *Chinese Repository*, a periodical for the Protestant missionaries.
† Demanding an indemnity was not a standard European practice at the time. Later, under fire and defending himself, Palmerston told Parliament that 'what the late Government demanded was satisfaction for the injured honour of the country, and that one of the ways in which satisfaction was to be given was payment for the opium so extorted . . .' For China to pay 'the expenses of the war' was, conceded Palmerston, 'certainly unusual in European warfare', but 'in order to make the Chinese sensible of the extent of the outrage they had committed, and that they might sufficiently feel the exercise of the power of Britain in vindication of their honour, it was thought expedient and proper to make them pay the expense of the war, in addition to compensating the injured parties.'

more than tripled before the next decade ended – from 15,619 chests in 1840 to 29,631 in 1841, and to 47,681 in 1860. Bowing to the reality that its battle against the drug was futile, China made the opium trade legal in October 1860. At the time called 'the foreign drug' (*yang-yao*), it was inextricably associated with the West. The American missionary physician Mrs Headland recalled: 'When calling at the Chinese homes, I have frequently been offered the opium-pipe, and when I refused it the ladies expressed surprise, saying that they were under the impression that all foreigners used it.'

The Treaty of Nanjing compelled China to open four more ports for trade, in addition to Canton. These ports, known as Treaty Ports, were Western settlements and were subject to Western, rather than Chinese, laws. One of them was Shanghai. A separate item in the Treaty 'gave' the island of Hong Kong to Britain for its ships and cargo. Sun-scorched and barren, with a few trees tucked amid rugged hills, Hong Kong at the time contained only a scattering of fishermen's huts, while the foreign settlement in Shanghai was little more than a stretch of marshland next to some fields. Two spectacular international metropolises were to rise out of these inconspicuous soils, with Chinese hard work and foreign, mainly British, investment and governance. Later, at the beginning of the twentieth century, a leading diplomat under Cixi, Wu Tingfang, wrote of Hong Kong:

> the British Government spent large sums of money year after year for its improvement and development, and through the wise administration of the local Government every facility was afforded for free trade. It is now a prosperous British colony . . . the prosperity of that colony depends upon the Chinese who, it is needless to say, are in possession of all the privileges that are enjoyed by the British residents . . . I must admit that a great deal of good has been done by the British Government in Hongkong. It has provided the Chinese with an actual working model of a Western system of government which . . . has succeeded in transforming a barren island into a prosperous town . . . The impartial administration of law and the humane treatment of criminals cannot but excite admiration and gain the confidence of the natives.

The Opium War forced China to accept Western missionaries. By then, they had been banned for more than 100 years. After the war, the French, who had little trade with China and were only interested in propagating Catholicism, rode on a European victory and lobbied hard for the lifting of the ban. Emperor Daoguang resisted the demand. But then, already bewildered, and as a character prone to dithering, he gave in under the relentless pressure of the French, conveyed by his Commissioner in charge of dealing with Westerners, Qiying, who advised acceptance. A historic edict on 20 February 1846 lifted the ban on Christian missions, although this only applied to the Treaty Ports; the ban remained in force for the rest of China.

But missionaries could not be contained. With footholds thus secured, they at once began to penetrate the vast interior, defying the prohibition. Unlike the early Jesuits, who had been individual court employees and had never sought to disobey the emperor, missionaries were now bold and defiant, backed as they were by gunboats. Throwing themselves into this ancient land with zeal, they spread Western ideas and practice and helped modernise China, bringing down the Qing dynasty along the way, whether or not this was their intention. Their role in the transformation of China was vital, even though they won relatively few converts.

Emperor Daoguang may not have foreseen the future, but he certainly realised that he had unleashed a monumental and ominous force – and this unsettled and weighed on him. His unsuccessful dealings with the British had already caused him intense regret and despair. 'Hounded by such unspeakable bullying, so much anger and hate bottle up inside me,' he had written. Now he felt: 'I can only blame myself and feel utterly ashamed of myself' and 'I just want to strike and strike my chest with clenched fists.' Months after the fateful edict, alarms were raised in the provinces about the arrival of missionaries and the problems this was causing. The emperor's agony intensified, and it was now that he wrote his will and designated his successor. It was imperative to leave the empire in the hands of a son who would be more determined and more able to resist the West. He chose his fourth son, the later Emperor Xianfeng, Cixi's husband. This son had grown up fervently loathing Westerners.

The Qing dynasty did not practise the system of the eldest son automatically inheriting the throne, but rather left the reigning emperor to make a will in secret appointing his successor. Emperor Daoguang made his in a private and yet solemn manner. He wrote it in both Chinese and Manchu, as an official document of such magnitude required. Then he folded it, enfolded it within two layers of the royal yellow paper, and signed and dated the envelope. This he put inside a cardboard folder, which had a white lining and yellow cover. With another piece of yellow paper he wrapped up the cardboard folder, and on top he signed again and wrote in the Manchu language the words 'Ten Thousand Years', to signal the finality of the will. He then placed the will inside a box made of the most precious wood, *nan-mu*, with a yellow silk lining and a yellow wool cover. This box had been used by the previous emperors to contain their succession wills. The lock and key of the box were carved in the auspicious pattern of bats flying amidst clouds. (Bats enjoy the same pronunciation as the word for 'good fortune'.) Emperor Daoguang did not seal the box immediately: he waited for a day, to allow second thoughts, and to be quite sure of his decision. Then, still with his own hands, he locked the box and sealed it with paper strips, signing each of them and adding the date on the front. This box was then carefully placed behind the giant plaque that hung over the entrance to a major hall in the Forbidden City. On the plaque were inscribed four enormous characters – *zheng-da-guang-ming* – 'upright, magnanimous, honourable and wise', an imperial motto.

Emperor Daoguang had nine sons from different consorts, but only the fourth and the sixth were of the right age and were qualified to be candidates.★ The sixth son was emphatically ruled out by the emperor, who exceptionally conferred on him the title *qin-wang*, the highest of all princes. Charming and popular in the court, the sixth son was not viscerally anti-foreign like his half-brother, the designated heir. Their father was worried that he could be pliable in the face of foreign demands and would allow the door of China to be pushed open still wider.† The father knew his sons well. In the future, they behaved exactly as he had anticipated.

The emperor-to-be, Cixi's future husband, was eight when the Opium War broke out and he saw in the ensuing years how it had broken his father, leaving him tormented. When he succeeded to the throne in 1850, one of his first acts was to write a long edict condemning Qiying, the conciliatory Imperial Commissioner who had signed the Treaty of Nanjing and had persuaded his father to lift the ban on Christian missions. In the edict, Emperor Xianfeng denounced Qiying for 'always

★ The first, second and third sons had died, and the seventh (Prince Chun, who was to marry Cixi's sister), eighth and ninth princes were too young. The fifth had been given away by his father to be an adopted son to a (deceased) brother, thus disqualifying him from the succession.
† A common explanation for Emperor Daoguang's choice of heir is that one day he discovered that the fourth son could not bear to hurt animals in spring in case they were pregnant. This is plainly sentimental tosh.

caving in to foreigners at the cost of the country', 'extreme incompetence' and 'having not a shred of conscience'. Qiying was demoted, and was later ordered to commit suicide.

Once, the emperor was told that the roof of a church in Shanghai had collapsed in a thunderstorm, and the big wooden cross bearing the figure of Christ had been destroyed. He saw this as Heaven doing the job that he ought to be doing, and wrote on the report: 'I am so awed and moved, and feel all the more ashamed.' His loathing of Christianity and Westerners was made yet more intense by the fact that the Taiping rebels who were rocking his throne claimed to believe in Christianity, and their leader, Hong Xiuquan, declared that he was the younger brother of Jesus Christ. Emperor Xianfeng would fight tooth and nail, every inch of the way, to keep Westerners out of China.

Meanwhile, the British wanted even more ports to be opened for trade and their representatives to be stationed in Beijing. The man Emperor Xianfeng designated to deal with them, Viceroy Ye Mingchen of Canton, was a kindred spirit of the emperor and turned a deaf ear to all their requests. In the end, the British decided that 'ships of war are absolutely necessary'. An incident involving a boat called *Arrow* triggered what is often called 'the Second Opium War' in 1856 – the year Cixi's son was born. Next year Lord Elgin (son of the 7th Earl, of Elgin Marbles repute) was dispatched to China with a fleet of warships. The French went along as an ally, wanting to gain unlimited access to the interior for their missionaries. The allies occupied Canton and carted Viceroy Ye off to Calcutta, where he soon died. The Europeans sailed north. In May 1858 they seized the Dagu Forts, which lay some 150 kilometres southeast of Beijing, and entered the nearby city of Tianjin. With enemy troops on his doorstep, Emperor Xianfeng still categorically rejected their requests. Eventually, as Lord Elgin threatened to march on Beijing, he was forced to send in negotiators, who accepted all the demands: envoys to station in Beijing, more ports to open for trade and missionaries to be admitted to the interior. After a few agonising days, Emperor Xianfeng succumbed to what the French envoy Baron Gros called a 'pistol at the throat' and gave his endorsement. The allies were satisfied and left the Dagu Forts in their gunboats.

Emperor Xianfeng hated the new deal that had been forced on him. Racking his brain to find a way out, he even proposed that Britain and France be exempt from all import duties, if they would agree to its annulment. But the two countries said that while they would be glad to be exempt from import duties, they wanted to stick to the agreements. The emperor kept berating his representatives who were in Shanghai talking to the Europeans – but to no avail.

A year passed and, as had been stipulated, it was time for the agreements to be ratified in Beijing. Lord Elgin's younger brother, Frederick Bruce, headed for the city in June 1859 accompanied by British troops and a small French force. (France at this time was busy fighting to colonise Indochina.) Emperor Xianfeng created all sorts of hurdles in an attempt to thwart Bruce and his colleague. He required that the envoys' ships had to dock at a small coastal town; they must then 'travel to Beijing with an entourage of no more than 10 men, no arms . . . no sedan-chairs or processions . . . and leave Beijing the moment the ratification is done'. Sedan-chairs were the prestigious means of transport. The alternative for the envoys was to take the singularly uncomfortable mule-cart on potholed country roads, which was highly humiliating. Bruce refused to oblige the emperor and instead launched an assault on the Dagu Forts. To his great surprise he was repelled: the Chinese had been strengthening the forts for a year. The emperor's confidence was enormously boosted, and he immediately gave orders to back out of the agreements.

But the allies returned a year later, in 1860, with a much larger force, headed by Lord Elgin as the British ambassador-extraordinary and Baron Gros as the French ambassador. The two men first reached Hong Kong, then Shanghai, before pushing north by sea. They had between them 20,000 land forces, including a Cantonese coolie transport corps. This allied force seized the Dagu Forts, with heavy casualties on both sides. Lieutenant Colonel G. J. Wolseley commented: 'England has never before opened a campaign with such a well-organised or a more efficient force.' In contrast, most Chinese troops were 'ill-clad, and wretchedly mounted and equipped, some having nothing but bows, others spears, and the rest, rusty-looking, old matchlocks'. Chinese war resolve was equally wanting to the European eye. 'Had the Chinese adopted the plan of campaign which Wellington did in defence of Portugal in 1809, or of the Russians in 1812 in defence of Moscow, we could not have reached Pekin [Beijing] in 1860. They had only to lay waste the country, burn the standing crops, drive away all cattle and destroy the boats upon the Peiho, to have completely checkmated us . . .' Wolseley also noted that when he landed, 'people were most obliging, and seemingly gave every information in their power'. He observed that 'they seemed to hate all the Tartar troops [the defending army was

Mongolian], whom they described as "a horrible race, speaking an unknown tongue, feeding chiefly upon uncooked mutton"; and . . . "stinking more than you (the English) do" . . .' The Lieutenant Colonel added good-humouredly: 'highly complimentary to our national feelings, particularly as John Bull is prone to think himself the cleanest of mankind . . .'

It is true, indeed, that the war was the business of the throne and not that of the average man. The emperor was infinitely remote from the common people. Even the average official was not particularly concerned. This was not surprising, as the regime's policy was to discourage political participation from even its educated class, the literati. So the allies marched to Beijing with little hindrance. They were now not merely seeking ratification of the agreements signed two years earlier, but had added new demands, including opening up Tianjin as an additional trading port and the payment of war indemnities. Emperor Xianfeng, beside himself with fury, resorted to undignified sarcasms and abuses when counselled to accept the allies' demands so that they would leave. To induce his army to fight, he offered a bounty: '50 taels of silver for each black barbarian head' – meaning the Indians in the British force – and '100 taels for each white barbarian head . . .'

Lord Elgin wanted negotiation and sent his forward representative, Harry Parkes, to a town near Beijing under a flag of truce. Parkes and his escorts were seized and thrown into the prison of the Ministry of Punishments. The emperor personally ordered 'harsh incarceration'. So the captives were bound and cuffed in the most painful possible manner, the *kao-niu*, which was likely to prove fatal. In Chinese warfare, to harm the enemy's messengers was the ultimate way of sending the message: we will fight you to the death. The Mongolian army commander, knowing that he could not win in a showdown, urgently pleaded for the captives to be treated more gently and provided with comfortable accommodation and good food. He was so anxious that he took it upon himself to write an emollient letter to Lord Elgin, expressing his wish for peace and conciliation. An irate Emperor Xianfeng reprimanded him. The emperor's inner circle, a group of princes and high officials, urged him to be uncompromising. One of them, Jiao, said that 'Parkes should be put to death in the extreme manner', which meant death by a thousand cuts. Emperor Xianfeng liked the idea; he wrote: 'You are absolutely right. Only we have to wait for a few days.'

The emperor's optimism came from the men in his inner circle whom he had appointed to 'handle the barbarians'. They told him: 'The barbarian Parkes is the one man good at military manoeuvre, and all the barbarians take orders from him. Now that he is captured, the morale of the barbarian troops is bound to collapse, and if we seize the opportunity to carry out our extermination campaign, victory will be ours.' Three days after this counsel of bizarre self-delusion, on 21 September 1860, the Chinese army was roundly beaten on the outskirts of Beijing. Emperor Xianfeng learned the news in the Old Summer Palace; all he could do was flee. That night, the court was packing amidst chaos and panic. The next morning, when his officials came for their audiences, they found that the emperor had disappeared. Most of the court had to leave later, separately, as the roads were jammed by fleeing crowds, the residents of Beijing, who had heard that the emperor himself had gone.

On 6 October, the French troops burst into the Old Summer Palace. On the 8th, Parkes and some other captives were released. More were returned over the next few days – most only as dead bodies. Of the thirty-nine men seized, twenty-one had been killed by the way they had been bound, as the emperor had ordered. Their comrades saw that their captors had 'tied their feet and hands together behind their backs as lightly [tightly] as possible, afterwards pouring water on the cords to increase the tension, and they were kept in this terrible position until the condition of their hands and wrists became too horrible for description'. Their deaths had come after days of lacerating agony. Parkes and the other survivors only lived because sensible officials in the Ministry of Punishments had quietly protected them.

Lord Elgin was much affected by what he saw and heard. He wrote to his wife, 'My dearest, we have dreadful news respecting the fate of some of our captured friends. It is an atrocious crime – and not for vengeance but for future security ought to be seriously dealt with.' Europeans were now coming to China. In order for them not to be treated in this way, he decided to serve a warning, something that would really hurt the emperor, and he settled on razing the Old Summer Palace. General Grant wrote in his dispatch that, without such a punitive act, 'the Chinese Government would see that our countrymen can be seized and murdered with impunity. It is necessary to undeceive them on this point.' Lord Elgin had contemplated other options, but rejected them: 'I should have preferred crushing the Chinese army which is still in this neighbourhood, but as we go to work we might have followed them round the walls of Peking [Beijing] till doomsday without catching them.' He was keen to finish his job and leave, rather than get bogged down in China, where the weather was turning cold and Chinese reinforcement armies might be coming. A quick fire was the easiest option.

The Old Summer Palace was in fact a complex of palaces begun in the early eighteenth century and added to over the next 100 years. Covering an area of 350 hectares, it housed grand European edifices, designed by the Jesuits Giuseppe Castiglione and Michel Benoist, who had been employed by Qianlong the Magnificent, as well as hundreds of buildings in the Chinese, Tibetan and Mongolian styles. Architectural designs from all over China were represented. Landscaped gardens celebrated the diverse sceneries of the empire, among them rice paddies of the Yangtze Valley, noted for the peach flowers and bamboo groves and meandering brooks in their midst. Images from great poems were reproduced. In one, after a poem by the eighth-century poet Li Bai, a waterfall was created, falling into a pond of chiselled stones, making music as the force of the water varied. When the sun was in the right place a rainbow appeared in the waterfall, matching the sharp arch of a bridge that dropped from the top of the waterfall down to the pond. To gaze at the rainbow and listen to the water-music in a dainty pavilion perched on the bridge was a favourite pastime of the court. In this pleasure palace, grandeur was of no concern – beauty was everything. Priceless art and treasures that had been accumulated for more than 100 years filled every cranny.

Before Lord Elgin set fire to this colossal treasure-trove, the palace had been looted by the French, who arrived first. Their commander, General de Montauban, wrote upon seeing the palace: 'nothing in our Europe can give any idea of such luxury, and it is impossible for me to describe its splendours in these few lines, impressed as I am especially with the bewilderment caused by the sight of such marvels'. His troops fell on their prey with little inhibition. Lieutenant Colonel Wolseley was an eye-witness: 'Indiscriminate plunder and wanton destruction of all articles too heavy for removal commenced at once . . . Officers and men seemed to have been seized with a temporary insanity; in body and soul they were absorbed in one pursuit, which was plunder, plunder.' The British troops, arriving later, soon joined in, as 'the General now made no objection to looting', wrote Robert Swinhoe, staff interpreter to General Grant. 'What a terrible scene of destruction presented itself!' Grant wrote:

One room only in the palace was untouched. General de Montauban informed me he had reserved any valuables it might contain for equal division between the English and the French. The walls of it were covered with jade-stones . . . The French general told me that he had found two . . . staves of office, made of gold and green jade-stone, one of which he would give me as a present to Queen Victoria, the other he intended for the Emperor Napoleon.

Among the presents that Queen Victoria received was a little dog. An elderly imperial concubine, who did not flee with the court, had died of fright when the allies arrived. Her dogs, five Pekinese, were brought to Britain and became the origin of the Pekinese breed outside China. One came back with Captain Hart Dunne of the Wiltshire Regiment, who named it 'Lootie' and presented it to Queen Victoria. In his letter presenting the dog, the Captain wrote, 'It is a most affectionate and intelligent little creature – it has always been accustomed to be treated as a pet and it was with the hope that it might be looked upon as such by Her Majesty and the royal family that I have brought it from China.' The little dog caused a little frisson at Windsor. The housekeeper, Mrs Henderson, wrote to her superior, 'It is very dainty about its food and won't generally take bread and milk – but it <u>will</u> eat boiled rice with a <u>little chicken</u> and <u>gravy</u> mixed up in it and this is considered the best food for it.' Her superior seemed somewhat annoyed and scribbled on the back of another, similar letter, 'A Chinese dog that insists on chicken in its dietary!' Mrs Henderson was instructed: '. . . after a little fasting and coaxing he [*sic*; Lootie was female] will probably come to like the food that is good for him . . .' In Windsor, Queen Victoria had Lootie painted by the German artist Friedrich Keyl, and she specially requested through her personal secretary, Miss Skettett, that 'When Mr Keyl sketches the dog he must put something to shew its size it [*sic*] is *remarkably* small . . .' Lootie lived in the kennels at Windsor for another decade.

When Lord Elgin decided to burn the Old Summer Palace, the French refused to take part, calling it an act of vandalism against a '*site de campagne sans défense*'. Nonetheless, the burning was carried out, methodically. General Grant described the scene in his letter to the Secretary of State for War in London:

On 18th October, Sir John Michel's division, with the greater part of the cavalry brigade, were marched to the palace, and set the whole pile of buildings on fire. It was a magnificent sight. I could not but grieve at the destruction of so much ancient grandeur, and felt that it was an uncivilised proceeding; but I believed it to be necessary as a future warning to the Chinese against the murder of European envoys, and the violation of the laws of nations.

The fire, fuelled by more than 200 opulent and exquisite palaces, pavilions, temples, pagodas and landscaped gardens, raged for days, enveloping west Beijing in black and ashen smoke. Wolseley wrote, 'When we first entered the gardens they reminded one of those magic grounds described in fairy tales; we marched from them upon the 19th October, leaving them a dreary waste of ruined nothings.'

Lord Elgin achieved his goal to some extent. Future Chinese authorities would treat Westerners with special care, quite differently from the way they treated their own people. But any thought of comfort for Westerners must be overshadowed by the potent seeds of hate stirring in the ashes of the Old Summer Palace. Charles Gordon, who later acquired the sobriquet 'Chinese Gordon', was then a captain in the invading army and took part in the devastation. He wrote home: 'The people are civil but I think the grandees hate us, as they must after what we did to the Palace. You can scarcely imagine the beauty and magnificence of the places we burnt. It made one's heart sore to burn them . . .' Victor Hugo wrote a year later: 'This wonder has disappeared . . . We Europeans are the civilized ones, and for us the Chinese are the barbarians. This is what civilization has done to the barbarian.'

The Old Summer Palace was in its full glory when Cixi left it with her husband and son in September 1860. Autumn is Beijing's best season, when the sun is no longer scorching, the biting cold has yet to descend, and no sandstorms from the northwestern desert are whipping the city, as they habitually do in spring. Just days before the allies landed on the coast, her husband had celebrated his thirtieth birthday,★ and tradition had allowed the opera-loving monarch, besieged though he was by troubles, to indulge his passion for four days. The large stage, built on three levels, stood in the open air by a vast lake, and Cixi watched the operas with him in a pavilion across a courtyard. At

★ By the traditional way of calculating age, according to which newborns start at one year old.

the climax, crowds of actors – men playing the parts of both sexes and of the gods – sang and danced on all three levels, congratulating the emperor on his birthday. Under a clear autumn sky, the music was borne by the wind into every latticed window on the scented palace grounds. The splendour of the Old Summer Palace was etched in Cixi's mind and would often return to haunt her. To rebuild it would become her obsession.

Travelling 200 kilometres to the northeast, the court crossed the Great Wall and arrived at the royal Hunting Lodge on the edge of the Mongolian steppes in the hilly region of Chengde. This 'lodge' was in fact even larger than the Old Summer Palace, though less lavishly crafted. It had been the major base for hunting expeditions for earlier emperors. Emperor Kangxi, who had first built the Lodge in 1703, had been a master hunter and apparently once killed eight tigers in one week. In the evenings, the emperors and their men had lit bonfires and roasted their kill, drinking and singing and dancing, in all-male company. There had been wrestling bouts and rowing competitions on the long, serpentine lake. One of the buildings was a replica of the Potala Palace in Lhasa and, elsewhere, in a martial-looking Mongolian yurt, Lord Macartney had had a futile audience with Emperor Qianlong in 1793. Cixi had never been here before. Her husband had had to cope with mounting mayhem throughout his reign, and they were only here now as refugees.

During this unprecedented dynastic crisis, Cixi played no political role. She was confined to the harem, where it was dangerous for her even to hint at her views. Her job was to look after her son, then four years old. Half a century later, in 1910, after she had died, an Englishman, Sir Edmund Backhouse, wrote a much-quoted biography of her, *China under the Empress Dowager*, in which he faked a diary, depicting Cixi as a very hawkish figure who urged her husband not to flee and not to talk peace with the foreigners, but to kill their messengers. This was sheer invention.* As events would show, Cixi

---

* Backhouse has since been exposed as a literary forger. In this case, what he seems to have done was to fake five passages about Cixi, and insert them into a well-known published diary by a Beijing official named Wu Kedu. As Backhouse published his biography first in English, the five faked passages melt into the English translation of the diary he quoted. When his book was then translated into Chinese, the forged passages, thus laundered, became part of the diary. The fake has puzzled historians, as the editions of the diary that exist in China contain no such references to Cixi. In the faked passages, residents in Beijing were seen to be hanging on Cixi's every word about the fate of the empire. This may have been the case when Backhouse was in China decades later, but not in 1860, when she, as an imperial concubine, was a non-person to the public.

was indeed opposed to the foreign policy of her husband and his inner circle – but for very different reasons. Silently observing from close quarters, she in fact regarded their stubborn resistance to opening the door of China as stupid and wrong. Their hate-filled effort to shut out the West had, in her view, achieved the opposite to preserving the empire. It had brought the empire catastrophe, not least the destruction of her beloved Old Summer Palace. She herself would pursue a new route.

3 Emperor Xianfeng Dies
(1860–61)

JUST before he fled to the Hunting Lodge, Emperor Xianfeng ordered his younger half-brother, Prince Gong, to remain in the capital and deal with the invaders. Prince Gong, twenty-seven years old, was the sixth son of their father, the one who had specifically been ruled out as successor to the throne because of his lack of visceral hatred for Westerners and his tendency to accommodate. Now, thanks to these qualities, he quickly settled with the allies – by accepting all their demands, including paying indemnities of eight million taels of silver to each European country. The Treaty of Beijing with Britain was signed on 24 October 1860 and the Treaty with France the following day. The allies left and peace was restored. Western powers began to install their representatives in Beijing, where they dealt with Prince Gong.

The prince, pockmarked like most men of his time who had caught smallpox in childhood, was nonetheless good-looking. John Thomson, the celebrated photographer who later took photos of him, said that Prince Gong 'had what phrenologists would describe as a splendid head. His eyes were penetrating, and his face, when in repose, wore an expression of sullen resolution.' When he sat, it was in the posture dictated for Manchu aristocrats: legs slightly apart and feet positioned at ten-past-ten. His robe embroidered with dragons in gold thread, his hat adorned with a plume in a jade holder with a coloured button that denoted his rank, he was the picture of a high prince. Whenever he held up his long-handled pipe, a flame would appear instantly at its tiny bejewelled bowl, struck by an attendant dropping on one knee. The prince's pipe was held in his lined black satin boot, in an inside compartment – the gentleman's 'pocket' in those days. These pockets held a variety of items, from tobacco to state papers, from sweets to pieces of tissue with which the aristocrats wiped their mouths and their ivory chopsticks after dining out. (They usually took their own chopsticks with them.) The prince's chopstick-case, and a profusion of bejewelled objects including a fan-case, dangled from his girdle. When he travelled in the capital, his sedan-chair would be under a canopy, surrounded by a showy entourage on horseback. All traffic would make way for him. Nearer his destination, a horseman would ride ahead and alert people to his imminent arrival so that they would line up to greet him.

Prince Gong's half-brother, the emperor, enjoined that, as a great prince, he must not lower himself by receiving the Europeans in person, even though they were the victors. But the prince was practical and knew his brother's order was unrealistic. He signed the treaties himself with the British and French, even arriving at the venue early to wait for Lord Elgin. When Elgin arrived, with an escort of 400 infantry, 100 cavalry and two bands playing at the head of the procession, Prince Gong advanced to greet him with his hands closed together in front of his chest, a gesture that he would use with an equal. Lord Elgin, according to General Grant, 'returned him a proud contemptuous look, and merely bowed slightly, which must have made the blood run cold in poor Kung [Gong]'s veins. He was a delicate gentlemanlike-looking man . . .' Elgin soon toned down his show of hauteur. 'Both of the national representatives . . . appeared willing to treat each other as equals, but not as superiors.' Prince Gong's conciliatoriness won him sympathy from the Europeans. Elgin wrote a friendly letter of farewell when he departed, in which he expressed the wish that future foreign affairs in China be put in the hands of Prince Gong.

Emperor Xianfeng authorised the treaties, telling Prince Gong he had done well. The emperor then had the treaties announced throughout the empire, by sending them to all provinces and having posters put up in Beijing. 'Those who are thinking of taking advantage of the war to start a revolt will now think twice when they know peace has been restored,' he said. One diarist saw the notice and wept: the Chinese emperor was listed on an equal footing with the British and French monarchs, which the man regarded as 'an utterly unheard of thing, ever, and an unbelievable fall in our status'.

The country that gained most from the war was a third party, Russia, China's neighbour to the north. On 14 November, Prince Gong signed a treaty with the Russian envoy, Nicholas Ignatieff, which ceded to Russia hundreds of thousands of square kilometres of territory north of the Amur River and east of the Ussuri, defining the border to this day. This area, which was commonly held to be 'a great wilderness', had been surrendered to Russia back in 1858 by the Manchu garrison chief of the territory, General Yishan, apparently in a moment of panic when the Russians made warlike noises. The General had in fact proven himself a lying and hopeless coward during the Opium War. Consisting of three paragraphs and filling less than a page, the document was never endorsed by Emperor Xianfeng.

But now this highly irregular piece of paper was accredited by Prince Gong, who had its contents incorporated in the Treaty of Beijing with Russia. Nicholas Ignatieff claimed to the prince that it was he who had persuaded the British and French to accept a peaceful settlement and that his country therefore deserved to be rewarded. Prince Gong told the emperor that Ignatieff did nothing of the sort; in fact he had 'nudged the British and the French to invade'. Now he was only 'taking advantage of their presence in Beijing to exact what he wants'. But regarding Ignatieff as 'an exceedingly cunning and immovable character', the prince was worried that he would 'make mischief' and 'stir up unpredictable troubles' with the allies, and so he counselled accepting his demands. Emperor Xianfeng cursed Ignatieff, calling him 'the most loathsome', but gave his consent – even though it is hard to imagine what trouble could have been stirred up, given that the allies were impatient to go home. And so the Qing dynasty suffered the biggest loss of territory in its history. 'With this treaty in his pocket,' writes Nicholas's great-grandson, Michael, 'Ignatieff and his Cossacks saddled up for Petersburg', and:

> having traversed the whole of Asia on horseback in six weeks . . . he was received by the Tsar, decorated with the Order of St Vladimir, promoted to general and shortly thereafter made head of the Asian department of the Foreign Office. Without firing a shot, he had secured for Russia a wild terrain the size of France and Germany combined and the hinterland of Vladivostok, the new empire's port on the Pacific.

The fact that Prince Gong yielded without a fight indicates a lack of nerve in his character, which his father had foreseen, and which was to manifest itself in other critical circumstances. As for Emperor Xianfeng, his preoccupation at the time was how to avoid an audience with the Western envoys in Beijing, who had been asking to present their credentials to him. He found the prospect of being face-to-face with his enemies unbearable and told Prince Gong to refuse their request, in such a way that the issue would never arise again. Otherwise, the emperor threatened, somewhat petulantly, 'if I get back to Beijing and they come and ask again, I will hold you responsible and punish you'. Prince Gong argued that the Europeans had no malevolent designs, but the emperor was adamant. Lord Elgin had carried to China on his two trips in 1858 and 1860 handwritten letters from Queen Victoria to Emperor Xianfeng, professing good-will. These letters were brought back to Britain, undelivered and unopened.

In the north, in the Hunting Lodge beyond the Great Wall, Emperor Xianfeng maintained contact with Prince Gong in Beijing, and continued his administrative routine, dealing with dozens of reports from all over the empire each day. The documents were delivered through an ancient, but efficient system, with messengers riding on horses whose speed was specified, depending on the urgency of the message. The most urgent took two days to arrive from Beijing. At first, the emperor was keen to return to the capital once the British and French had pulled out. The weather at the Lodge was getting very cold and worse with each passing day. Having not been inhabited for decades, the palaces were not equipped to cope with the severe winter. But then he hesitated: several times, after announcing that he was departing, he cancelled the trip. Officials urged him to go, anxiously pointing out that the country risked instability if the emperor was not on the throne in the capital. But the argument did not move the monarch; nor did the thought of his own health. He finally chose to spend the grim winter in the northern wilderness, knowing it was bad for his delicate physique. The emperor, it appears, was determined not to be in the same city as the Western legations. He seems to have been living out the Chinese idea of ultimate hatred: 'Not under the same sky!' (*bu-gong-dai-tian*). Or he could not bear being near the ravaged Old Summer Palace. His self-imposed exile was prolonged, and became permanent. Spending the interminable harsh winter in the ill-equipped Hunting Lodge, he fell ill and coughed blood. Eleven months after arriving, on 22 August 1861, he died.

In the last months of his life, although he still dealt with state matters diligently, stopping working only on the days he was confined to bed, he no longer wrote the same kind of detailed instructions as before. He allowed himself to indulge in his real passions, opera and other music, which were performed almost every day. The performers had been summoned from Beijing to the Lodge as soon as he had settled down there, and the moment they arrived they had been rushed to him, given no time to change into their costumes. Well over 200 singers, dancers and musicians eventually crowded the Lodge, and the place ran out of habitable rooms. The emperor spent a lot of time with them, selecting the repertoires and picking the cast, watching rehearsals and arguing with the performers about interpretations. He listened to the singing of music that he himself had composed. The performances, which usually lasted for hours, were sometimes staged on an islet in the middle of a lake, in a courtyard theatre poetically named a 'Touch of Cloud'. At other times they were held in the quarters where he lived, or where Cixi and their young son lived. In the last sixteen days of his life the emperor watched operas on eleven days, each day for several hours. Two days before he died, he listened to opera from 1.45 to 6.55 p.m., with a break of only twenty-seven minutes. The next day's scheduled performance had to be cancelled. The emperor was feeling extremely sick, and then he lost consciousness.

When he became conscious again that night, Xianfeng summoned to his bedside the men closest to him, his old inner circle, eight princes and ministers, and announced his will to them. His only son, by Cixi, now five years old, would be the next emperor, and the eight men were to form a Board of Regents, to be jointly in charge. They asked him to write the will down in his own hand in crimson ink, to give it unquestioned authority, but he was unable to hold the brush. So one of the men wrote it for him, making it clear that this had been the emperor's wish. Emperor Xianfeng died a few hours later, with these men by his side. China was now in the hands of the Regents.

These were the same men who had ordered the capture and abuse of Elgin's messengers, which had resulted in some of them dying horribly – and had led to the burning of the Old Summer Palace. These were the same men who had helped Emperor Xianfeng make all his disastrous decisions, which ended with his own death. Cixi could see that with these men in charge, stumbling along the same self-destructive road, there would be no end to catastrophe, which promised to destroy her son as well as the empire. She made up her mind to act, by launching a coup and seizing power from the Regents.

4 The Coup that Changed China
(1861)

THOUGH her son succeeded to the throne, Cixi had no political power. In fact, as a concubine, she was not even the new emperor's official mother. That was the role of Empress Zhen, who immediately assumed the title of dowager empress — *huang-tai-hou* (interchangeable with empress dowager). No title was given to Cixi. Nor was she with her son when he was conducted by a Regent to bid goodbye to his late father, acting out a ritual in which he held a gold cup containing liquor over his head, then emptied it on the ground, before placing the cup on a gold-cornered table in front of the bier. Cixi belonged to the unnamed 'others' in court records, who, 'headed by the dowager empress', namely Empress Zhen, performed a similar ritual.

Cixi needed the title of a dowager empress. Only then would she acquire the status of the mother of the emperor. Without it she was a mere concubine. A clash with Empress Zhen seemed inevitable, and the two women had an emotional row for the first time in their relationship. But they soon found a solution. Court records were trawled and it was discovered that there had been a similar case. Almost exactly 200 years previously, when Emperor Kangxi succeeded to the throne in 1662, his mother had also been a concubine, but had been given the title of dowager empress, so there had been two dowager empresses simultaneously. With this precedent, the Board of Regents awarded Cixi the title. The friendship of the two women was unscathed, and they were referred to as the Two Dowager Empresses. In order to distinguish between them, they decided on different honorific names. Empress Zhen took 'Ci'an', which means 'kindly and serene',★ and Cixi, hitherto called Imperial Concubine Yi, took Cixi, meaning 'kindly and joyous'. It was from now on that she became known as Empress Dowager Cixi.

The two women did more than resolve a major problem, they went on to form a political alliance and launch a coup. Cixi was twenty-five years old and Empress Zhen a year younger. Facing them were eight powerful men in control of the state machine. The women were well aware of the risk they were taking. A coup was treason, and if it failed the punishment would be the most painful *ling-chi*, death by a thousand cuts. But they were willing to take the risk. Not only were they determined to save their son and the dynasty, but they also rejected the prescribed life of imperial widows – essentially living out their future years as virtual prisoners in the harem. Choosing to change their own destiny as well as that of the empire, the two women plotted, often with their heads together leaning over a large glazed earthenware water tank, pretending to be appraising their reflections or just talking girls' talk.

Cixi devised an ingenious plan. She had noticed a loophole in her late husband's deathbed arrangements. The Qing emperors demonstrated their authority by writing in crimson ink. For nearly 200 years, beginning with Emperor Kangxi as a young adult, these crimson-inked instructions had always been written strictly by the hand of the emperor. Now, however, the monarch was a child and could not hold the brush. When the decrees were issued by the Board of Regents in the child's name, there was nothing to show authority. There was the official seal, but it was only used on very formal occasions, and not on everyday communications. This deficiency was pointed out to the Board after it issued the first batch of decrees. It was told, then, that the late emperor had given one informal seal to the child, which was kept by Cixi, and another similar seal to Empress Zhen. It was suggested to the Board that these seals could be stamped on the decrees as the equivalent of the crimson-ink writing, to authenticate them. It was undoubtedly one or both of the women who pointed out the deficiency and made the suggestion. Such informal seals, numbering in the thousands in the Qing court, were not political items, but objects of art commissioned by the emperors for their pleasure, which they sometimes stamped on their paintings and books – or gave as presents in the privacy of the harem.

★ In order not to confuse readers, this book will continue to refer to Dowager Empress Ci'an as Empress Zhen.

The Board of Regents accepted the solution and announced that all future edicts would be stamped with the seals. They made the announcement as a postscript on a decree that had already been written and was about to be issued – a sign that the idea had only just been put to them, that they had approved it and had hurriedly put it into practice. The postscript also stated that they were issuing the current edict without the seals, as there was no time to stamp it. Clearly they had not known about the existence of the seals until then and had to have them fetched from the harem.* A formal proclamation followed, making the use of the two seals obligatory on all edicts: one at the beginning and the other at the end.

The authority of the seals was thus established, an accomplishment that would be vital in the forthcoming coup. It is possible that the seal allegedly given to the child and kept by Cixi was actually a present to Cixi herself, which she attributed to the child emperor, to give it more weight. The Board of Regents readily agreed to the use of the seals because they regarded them as mere rubber stamps. The women had given them the illusion that 'all is in harmony, and all is fine', and 'everything is following old rules . . .' The Regents felt 'very pleased' about the compliance of the Two Dowager Empresses and had no idea what was in their minds.

Next the women tried to secure Prince Gong as an ally. The prince was the foremost nobleman in the land and was held in high esteem. There was a consensus among top officials and generals that he should have been made the Regent. Whereas the appointed Board had only brought disaster to the empire, the prince had succeeded in getting the allied troops out of Beijing and in restoring peace. The army and the Praetorian Guards listened to him. It was also clear to Cixi that the prince, too, wanted a different approach to foreign policy.

Prince Gong was in Beijing at this moment. He had stayed on after concluding the treaties the year before, on the express order of Emperor Xianfeng. When he had begged to come to the Hunting Lodge to visit his half-brother, who had fallen ill, Emperor Xianfeng had replied: 'If we saw each other, we could not avoid recalling the past, and that would only make us feel sad, and would really not be good for my health . . .

* It is a common assumption that Emperor Xianfeng had intended Empress Zhen and Cixi to use the seals as a counterbalance to the Board of Regents. There is no evidence for this. In fact, he left power only to the eight men. It is also improbable that he should have intended the two women to have political power.

I therefore order you not to come.' On his deathbed, the emperor had again sent instructions specifically telling Prince Gong to remain in the capital. He had not wanted the prince around because he had intended to exclude him from the Board of Regents – for the same reason as their father had kept the prince off the throne. Prince Gong was no hardline hater of the West; he was pliable towards Westerners, as the signing of the treaties had proven. The prince felt no bitterness for any of Emperor Xianfeng's decisions, however apparently unfair they had been. He had a reputation for being honourable. Ever since his half-brother had ascended the throne, he had shown no resentment – only a complete absence of personal ambition. He had composed eulogies to his half-brother, as befitted a prince to an emperor, and had written poetic lines on his brother's paintings, which was something done between close friends. The prince's character had won him the trust of his half-brother. Emperor Xianfeng had left him alone in the capital to deal with the Europeans, who he knew preferred the prince to him and were entertaining plans to put Prince Gong on the throne in his place. Prince Gong's impeccable record of loyalty, his lack of interest in supreme power and in intrigue were also important factors to Cixi as she prepared to make herself his boss.

So, within days of her husband's death, Cixi quietly extracted an edict out of the Regents allowing Prince Gong to visit the Hunting Lodge to bid his late half-brother farewell – in spite of the late emperor's order. Not to allow the prince to come would simply be unseemly.

When Prince Gong arrived, he threw himself to the floor in front of the bier and cried out in floods of tears. An eye-witness observed that 'no one had shown so much grief as he did'. Those present in the hall were moved and started sobbing themselves. After this show of sorrow, a eunuch came with a message from Cixi and Empress Zhen, summoning the prince to the harem. Some grandees were against the meeting, pointing out that tradition dictated that brothers and sisters-in-law should be kept apart, especially when the sister-in-law had just lost her husband – even if there was the obligatory screen to separate them. But the Two Dowager Empresses insisted, sending more eunuchs to deliver their request. Prince Gong, always anxious to behave correctly, asked the Regents to go in with him. But the two women sent out a firm 'No'. He went in alone, and did not re-emerge for two hours.

This was a very long audience, much longer than any the Regents had been given. But it rang no alarm bells with them. They believed Prince Gong's explanation that he had to spend a great deal of time trying to persuade the women to return to Beijing as soon as possible, and to reassure them that there would be no danger from the foreigners. The Regents had total confidence in Prince Gong's probity, and had been lulled by the two women into a relaxed and complacent frame of mind.

Knowing how prudent the prince was, Cixi, it seems, did not broach the idea of a coup at this first meeting. Overturning the late emperor's solemn will was not something he would readily contemplate. What the conversation seems to have achieved was an acceptance from Prince Gong that the empire should not be left entirely in the hands of the Board of Regents, who, after all, had such a woeful track record. On this basis, the prince agreed to get someone in his camp to petition for the Two Dowager Empresses to take part in decision-making, and for 'one or two close princes of the blood to be selected to assist with state affairs'. The petition would not mention Prince Gong by name. He clearly wanted to avoid the impression that he coveted power, even though he had solid ground to stake a claim.

This idea was secretly conveyed to Prince Gong's camp in Beijing, and a relatively junior subordinate was designated to write the petition. Prince Gong feared that the Board of Regents might detect the link with him when they saw the petition, so he left the Hunting Lodge before it arrived. On the eve of his departure for Beijing, he saw Cixi and Empress Zhen again. And this time the discussion was inescapably about what should be done if the Regents turned down the proposal.

It seems that Prince Gong agreed that force could be used to oust the Regents – but only as a last resort, and only after some unpardonable act on their part had been exposed, so that the coup would appear legitimate. The prince cared very much about his honour. What his role would be after the coup was still not decided, which suggests that Prince Gong thought it unlikely that the coup would happen soon, if at all.

Nothing would have happened, if there had been no further initiative from Cixi. As expected, the Regents rejected the petition unequivocally, on the grounds that the late emperor's will could not be altered, plus the cast-iron rule that women must be kept away from politics. Cixi now had to make the Regents do something inexcusable so that Prince Gong would agree to oust them. She and Empress Zhen set out to provoke an offence. Cradling the child emperor, they summoned the Regents and engaged them in a heated confrontation about the petition. The men grew angry and replied contemptuously that, as Regents, they did not have to answer to the two women. As they roared, the child became scared and cried and wet his pants. After a prolonged row, Cixi gave the impression that she bowed to their verdict. The petition was publicly rejected in the name of the child emperor.

Cixi had engineered a major offence by the Regents – that they dared to shout and behave disrespectfully in front of the emperor and had frightened him. Citing this event, she drafted by hand an edict in her son's name condemning the Regents. Her writing betrayed her lack of formal education. The text was littered with solecisms and inelegant sentences and was dotted with the wrong characters – errors that were all too easy to commit. Cixi knew her own shortcomings and wrote at the end of her draft edict: 'Please could the 7th brother revise it for me.'

The seventh brother was Prince Chun, the man who had married Cixi's younger sister, thanks to her manoeuvring. Now twenty years old, he had been through a rigorous classical education since the age of five and was able to write 'magnificent compositions and beautiful sentences', according to Grand Tutor Weng, who would become a tutor to two emperors and whose own scholarship was indisputable. A diligent pupil, the prince had imbibed the classics deep into the night and had, by his own account, clung to his teachers' words as if 'to sunshine in winter', and had followed their teaching in the same manner as 'sticking to an established path on the edge of a precipice, not daring to deviate by half a step'. This was a man who needed a guide, and Cixi was fulfilling the role.

Prince Chun had been devastated by the empire's defeat at the hands of the Westerners, the burning of the Old Summer Palace and the death of his half-brother. Before the court's flight from Beijing, he had pleaded with the emperor not to abandon the capital, and begged to be allowed to lead troops against the invaders. His entreaties had been refused by his half-brother, who did not want to send him to a certain death. Frustrated, the hot-blooded prince blamed his half-brother's advisers for mishandling events and longed to get rid of them. He was the first person after Empress Zhen whom Cixi took into her confidence about the coup.

Cixi's draft edict was delivered to Prince Chun by a eunuch she trusted. The next day he replied with a revised text, which ended by announcing the dismissal of the Regents. His wife, Cixi's sister, carried the revised edict to Cixi, and it was then stitched into the lining of Empress Zhen's robe. In his covering letter, Prince Chun pledged total support for Cixi. That she was about to act, he said, was 'indeed the good fortune of our country', and he would stand by her, 'come what may'.

Prince Chun's words reflected the prevailing sentiment among the princes, generals and officials. Cixi knew her action would be popular. With this conviction and the two seals representing the monarchical authority, she felt she could secure Prince Gong's commitment. As he was in the capital, Cixi's plan was to join him there ahead of the Regents, to coordinate with him and capture the men when they arrived. So Prince Chun steered the Regents into agreeing that the child emperor should take a shortcut back to Beijing and not go with the late emperor's enormous coffin, which would have to follow the main roads and move slowly, as it was carried by dozens of men and accompanied by the whole court. All accepted that the child must be spared this long and exhausting journey.

On an auspicious date two months after Emperor Xianfeng's death, the grand procession bearing his coffin set off from the Hunting Lodge. For the course of their journey, bridges had been repaired, roads levelled and broadened and covered with yellow soil as was required for all royal routes. Before the coffin was lifted, the child emperor knelt by its side in an act of farewell. He was scheduled to perform the same ritual to greet its arrival at a gate in the Forbidden City ten days later. Half the Regents travelled with the coffin, watched over by Prince Chun. The other half went with the child emperor, who, in strict accordance with court rules, sat with Empress Zhen in a sedan-chair with black curtains as a sign of mourning. Cixi was in another black-curtained sedan-chair. Travelling with all speed, they covered the distance to Beijing in six days, four days ahead of the coffin. As soon as she arrived at the outskirts of the capital, Cixi asked for Prince Gong and presented him with the coup edict, stamped with the two seals, one at the beginning and the other at the end. Prince Gong was now convinced, and felt able to convince others, that ousting the Regents was on the order of the new emperor.

He proposed a few changes to the coup edict, deleting his own name, which had been singled out for praise for bringing peace to the empire. The word referring to foreigners as 'foreign barbarians' was replaced with a neutral word meaning 'foreign countries' – *wai-guo*. The prince then set about getting ready the force needed for the coup.

On the last day of the ninth lunar month of 1861, while the coffin of Emperor Xianfeng was progressing towards the capital at a stately pace, Cixi ignited the fuse of her coup. She told Prince Gong to bring his associates to her and Empress Zhen, and when they arrived she had the coup edict declared to them. In a winsome show of grief, the Two Dowager Empresses denounced the Regents for bullying them and the child emperor. All present showed great indignation. In the middle of the denunciation, the Regents who had been travelling with Cixi rushed into the palace and shouted outside the hall that the women had broken a cardinal rule by calling the male officials into the harem. Cixi, looking mightily incensed, ordered a second edict written and stamped there and then: for the arrest of the Regents, on the grounds that they were trying to prevent the emperor from seeing his officials, which was a major crime.

The original edict had only ordered the Regents' dismissal from their positions. Now Prince Gong took the new decree and went to arrest the Regents who had been shouting. They bellowed: 'We are the ones who write decrees! Yours can't be proper since we did not write them!' But the two magic seals silenced them. Guards brought by the prince dragged them away.

Armed with yet another stamped decree, Prince Chun arrested those Regents who had been travelling with the coffin. He went in person for Sushun, their de facto leader. When the prince broke into the house where Sushun was staying the night, he found Sushun, a large man, in bed with two concubines. Sushun roared 'like a leopard', refusing to accept the 'arrest warrant'. This display of defiance to an imperial decree, and the fact that he had apparently indulged in sex when escorting the late emperor's coffin, gave Cixi grounds to have him executed. Sushun had been the only man on the Board who had had some idea of Cixi's intelligence, and he had wanted her killed. But having no inkling of her ambition and ability, he had allowed the others to persuade him to abandon his plan. On the way to the execution ground he howled with regret that he had underestimated 'this mere woman'.

The meting out of punishments followed a prescribed procedure. First Prince Gong headed a panel of princes and officials to ascribe precise crimes to each of the Regents and to propose appropriate punishments, in accordance with the penal codes. In order to topple the Regents, they had to be guilty of treason. But the offences that had been cited did not justify this charge. On the fifth day, as the deliberations ground to a halt, the two women intervened with a smoking gun: the eight men, they claimed, had forged their late husband's will. So grave was this new charge – and so improbable – that the men on the panel were hesitant to cite it, in case they were thought to be fabricating evidence. The two women then took full responsibility by allowing the panel to announce that the information had come from them. This enabled Prince

Gong and the panel to condemn the eight Regents for treason. The three main offenders were sentenced to death by a thousand cuts. In a calculated demonstration of magnanimity, Cixi greatly reduced the sentences, executing only Sushun, and by the much less painful decapitation.

Sushun's execution was greeted with cheering by the many who hated him. As the chief examiner for the Imperial Examinations, which selected officials, he had been extremely hard-hearted towards the literati candidates who had travelled to the capital, through considerable hardship, from every corner of the empire. He had treated them 'like slaves', commented Grand Tutor Weng, a fellow examiner. A sort of 'anti-corruption' zealot, Sushun had dished out disproportional punishments for minor offences, while he himself was more corrupt than most. He accused a subordinate of his, Junglu, of 'embezzling' and nearly had him beheaded. But according to Junglu, Sushun persecuted him because he had declined to give him his collection of choice snuff bottles and a first-rate horse. On the morning of Sushun's execution, Junglu rose early to be at the front of the crowds to see his enemy's head roll. Afterwards he went straight to a bar and got drunk. Junglu became a lifelong devotee of Cixi – a devotion that later gave rise to a rumour that they had been lovers.

Cixi ordered the other two main figures among the Regents, Prince Zheng and Prince Yee, to take their own lives, sending each a long white silk scarf with which to hang himself. This not-infrequently-used imperial order was called, rather poetically, *ci-bo*, 'bestowing silk'. It was considered a favour, as far as a death sentence was concerned: it would be suicide, not execution, and it could be carried out in private. The rest of the disgraced Regents were simply dismissed (one being sent to the frontier). Prompt edicts announced that no one else would be incriminated, and the papers confiscated from Sushun's house were swiftly burned, unread, in front of the Grand Council.

So, two months after her husband died, the twenty-five-year-old Cixi completed her coup with just three deaths, no bloodshed otherwise and no upheaval. The British envoy in Beijing, Frederick Bruce, was amazed: 'It is certainly singular that men, long in power, disposing of the funds of the state and of its patronage, should have fallen without a shot of resistance, and without a voice or hand raised in their defence.' This showed just how popular Cixi's coup was. As Bruce wrote to London, 'As far as I am able to ascertain, public opinion seems unanimous in condemning Su-shun [Sushun] and his colleagues, and in approving the punishments awarded to them.' Not only did the coup reflect people's wishes, but it had 'certainly been managed with great ability', causing no more 'confusion' than 'a change of ministry'. Word got out that it was Cixi who had brought off the coup, and she gained tremendous esteem. The Viceroy in Canton, 'in great spirits', praised her to the British consul, who reported his words to London: 'the Empress Mother is a woman of mind [*sic*] and strong will', the coup was 'well done' and 'there will be hopes now'. The famed military chief and later major reformer, Zeng Guofan, wrote in his diary when he learned the details of the coup from friends: 'I am bowled over by the Empress Dowager's wise, decisive action, which even great monarchs in the past were not able to achieve. I am much stirred by admiration and awe.'

Prince Gong was no less impressed. His camp called for her, not the prince, to take charge of the country – an idea that undoubtedly originated with him. Even though this was unprecedented in the Qing dynasty, these senior officials argued, precedents could be found in other dynasties going back more than 1,700 years. They produced a list of dowager empresses who had supervised their young sons. Omitted from the list, though, was Wu Zetian (AD 624–705), the only woman in Chinese history who had explicitly declared herself the 'Emperor' and ran the country in her own right – for which she had been much condemned. The support for Cixi was based on the understanding that her political role was transitional, pending her son's coming of age.

Cixi had considered making Prince Gong the Regent, but now she had a change of heart. She herself had pulled off the coup, with the prince very much the subordinate, and her self-confidence had soared. In the end, she gave him the title of Grand Adviser – *yi-zheng-wang* – which made clear that she was the boss. Prince Gong was showered with rare honours, which he insisted on declining, even bursting into tears. He may have sincerely felt undeserving. He would continue to serve Cixi and their common cause faithfully.

On the ninth day of the tenth moon 1861, the eve of Cixi's twenty-sixth birthday, it was proclaimed to the whole empire, in the name of the new emperor, that 'from now on, all state matters will be decided personally by the Two Dowager Empresses, who will give orders to the Grand Adviser and the Grand Councillors for them to carry out. The decrees will still be issued in the name of the emperor.' Cixi had become the real ruler of China. At the same time, she felt obliged to declare that it was not her wish, nor that of Empress Zhen, to rule. They were only bowing to the entreaties of the princes and ministers, who had implored them to do their duty in these difficult times. She begged the population to appreciate their dilemma, and promised that the young emperor would take over as soon as he entered adulthood.

The day before her birthday, overcast and with a drizzle hanging in the air, was the coronation day of her son, Zaichun, who was now crowned Emperor Tongzhi. This regnal name meant 'Order and prosperity', the Confucian ideal of what a good government should bring to society'.* At seven o'clock in the morning, the child was taken to the biggest hall in the Forbidden City, the Hall of Supreme Harmony, *Tai-he*. In a yellow brocade robe embroidered with golden dragons riding on colourful clouds, he was placed on a golden lacquered throne, which was adorned with nine splendidly gilded dragons. More dragons were carved on the screen behind, the pillars around and on the ceiling, where a coiled dragon at the centre had a large silver ball suspended from between its teeth. The idea was that the ball would fall on anyone who sat on the throne, if he did not have the mandate to be monarch. Everybody believed it. Cixi herself never sat on the throne.†

In front of the throne was a rectangular table, gilded and draped with yellow brocades of the auspicious-cloud pattern, standing on a yellow rug. On the table lay a rolled-up scroll, one that bore the imperial proclamation for the new reign. Written bilingually in Chinese and Manchu, the yellow scroll was several metres long and stamped with the new emperor's large official seal. To shroud it with mystery and solemnity, clouds of incense spread from four bronze burners, each on a tall stand. The hall was dark and mysterious, in contrast to the shiny white marble terraces outside, which, in three stately tiers, were made more magnificent by carved balustrades and sweeping stairs. Down below, in front, was a paved expanse of more than 30,000 square metres, now filled with senior officials and officers, who had gathered before dawn, lining up in orderly and hierarchical fashion. Under brilliantly coloured banners and canopies, accompanied by the

---

* It is commonly assumed that this regnal name referred to the 'joint rule' of the Two Dowager Empresses, as the word *Tongzhi* can mean 'joint rule' in modern Chinese. This is wrong. Their 'joint rule' was a temporary arrangement for which they felt obliged to apologise. It could not have been solemnised by being designated the name of the reign. The regnal name in fact comes from the Confucian teaching: 'There are many ways of being a good government, and they can all be summarised as order and prosperity; there are many ways of being an evil government, and they can all be summarised as chaos and mayhem.'

† Decades later, in 1915, when General Yuan Shikai made himself the new emperor, he had the throne moved back and away from the ball, apparently fearing that the ball might fall on him.

solemn music of bells and drums, they repeatedly went down on their knees and prostrated themselves before the new emperor.

When the ceremony was over, a procession escorted the scroll out of the Forbidden City to the Tiananmen Gate to the south. On top of the Gate, the scroll was opened and read out, first in Manchu and then in Chinese, to the gathered officials at the foot of the outer wall, all of whom were on their knees. When the declaration and the ritual of repeated prostration were over, the scroll was placed in the beak of a gold phoenix, slowly lowered on a rope along the outer wall and installed in a shrine, which was escorted away by a guard of honour. At the Ministry of Rites the proclamation was copied on special royal paper and delivered to the provinces, where it was read out to the officials, level by level, down to the grass roots. Notices were posted in towns and word spread to the villages. Along the routes that the copies were taken, all officials and ordinary people prostrated themselves.

Cixi was not at the coronation. The majestic main part of the Forbidden City was out of bounds to her – because she was a woman. She still could not set foot in it, even though she was now the de facto ruler. In fact, when her sedan-chair went within sight of it, she had to close the curtain and show humility by not looking at it. Virtually all decrees were issued in the name of her son, as Cixi had no mandate to rule. It was with this crippling handicap that she proceeded to change China.

PART TWO

Reigning Behind Her Son's Throne (1861–1875)

5 First Step on the Long Road
to Modernity
(1861–9)

THE signs of a new era were immediately apparent. Prince Gong now headed the Grand Council and the half-dozen new Grand Councillors were intelligent and sensible men like him. To Frederick Bruce, the first British minister to reside in Beijing, these were 'statesmen who understand our character and motives sufficiently to place confidence in us', and who 'are satisfied of our moderation, as well as of our strength'. He regarded the change of leadership as 'the most favourable incident that has hitherto taken place in the course of our relations with China'.

Indeed, through Prince Gong's reports, and the fact that the British-French troops had withdrawn from Beijing, Cixi had come to the conclusion that amicable relations with the West were possible, and she began to strive for such a relationship. She asked the most fundamental and clear-eyed questions: Are foreign trade and an open-door policy such bad things for China? Can we not benefit from them? Can we not use them to solve our own problems? This fresh way of looking at things heralded the Cixi era. She was pulling China out of the dead end into which it had been rammed by Emperor Xianfeng's all-consuming hatred and by the closed-door policy of 100 years. She was setting the country on a new course: opening it up to the outside world.

This Herculean process was presided over by Cixi, together with Empress Zhen, from the harem. They got up between five and six in the morning, sometimes even at four – which was always a struggle for Cixi – to be ready at the audience hall by seven o'clock. They would be splendidly dressed, in phoenix-patterned formal robes, pearl-studded shoes and bejewelled, gate-tower-shaped coiffure. In the hall they sat side by side, behind a yellow silk screen, through which they discussed business with the Grand Councillors. The Councillors would have been waiting for some time in their deliberately simple offices, with plain tables and chairs covered in cloth. When the meetings were over, the two women gave audiences to officials from around the empire. The child emperor, Tongzhi, now sat on a small throne in front of the screen facing the officials, while the women remained vaguely visible behind him. To attend these audiences, officials got up soon after midnight to travel to the Forbidden City, the rumbling of their mule-carts and the clatter of the mules' feet almost the only sounds in the deserted streets of Beijing. Throughout the audiences they prostrated themselves, their eyes cast down.

Cixi was the one who usually asked the questions. She was good at projecting authority. While in the harem, as many observed, she was vivacious and fond of laughing; but the moment a eunuch came to announce, on his knees, that her sedan-chair was ready to take her to the audience hall, she would switch off her smiles and assume a daunting air. Even with the screen separating them, the officials could feel her commanding presence – and she could assess their personality. Many who had audiences with her described how Cixi seemed to be able 'to read our thoughts', and that 'at a glance' she seemed able to 'see through the character of every one that appears before her'. Empress Zhen was quiet and retiring, willingly playing second fiddle.

After the audiences, back in their quarters, the women changed into less formal and more comfortable clothes, taking off some of the jewels that made their headdresses very heavy. They took the day's reports out of a yellow box and, using court conventions which they quickly picked up, they folded one corner of a page, or dented it with a finger nail, to indicate 'Report registered', 'Do as recommended', and so on. A lot of the daily work consisted of pure administration, such as approving official appointments. Empress Zhen dealt with these on her own, and most documents of this nature were stamped by her seal only. Policy was Cixi's domain. For two decades the two women were to work in perfect harmony, until Empress Zhen's death in 1881. The fact that they remained lifelong friends as well as political partners was a most remarkable feat – 'almost if not entirely unique in history', commented an American missionary.

It is commonly claimed that Prince Gong made all the decisions for Cixi, who, as a 'semi-illiterate' woman, was limited in knowledge and experience. The massive documented exchanges between them, and between Cixi and the officials, point to the contrary: that Prince Gong and all others in fact reported to Cixi, who was the decision-maker. She would, of course, always consult Prince Gong, and sometimes initiate debates among the top echelon. Her orders were then given verbally to the Grand Council, and the Councillors or their secretaries would write them up as decrees. Having approved them, she and Empress Zhen would stamp them with the seals. Following Qing rules, Grand Councillors (Prince Gong included) were prohibited from adding or changing anything in a decree.

As a check to its policies, the dynasty had the traditional institutionalised watchdog, the Censors, *yu-shi*, who were the official 'criticisers'. In addition to these, Cixi encouraged critical comments from other officials, starting a trend that led to the involvement of the literati in state affairs, a sharp break from the tradition that discouraged their political participation. These informal 'opposers' became a substantial force in the land and acquired a collective name, *qing-liu*, or 'clear stream', signifying that they were above self-interest. Their targets included Cixi herself. Over the years, members of the government would complain that these attacks hindered their work, but Cixi never tried to silence them. Instinctively she seems to have known that a government needs dissenting voices. Among those voices she spotted outstanding people and promoted them to high office. One such man was Zhang Zhidong, who became one of the most eminent reformers. Cixi took care not to go against majority opinion, but the final decision was always hers.

Running the empire needed more language skills and more knowledge of the classics than Cixi possessed. So she studied with educated eunuchs. Her lessons were like bedtime readings and took place before her after-lunch siesta or at night. She would sit cross-legged on her bed, with a book of poetry or one of the classics in her hand. The eunuchs would sit on cushions on the floor at a low table. They would go through the texts with her, and she would read after them. The lesson would go on until she fell asleep.

Under Cixi, China entered a long period of peace with the West. The British government, for instance, noted that 'China is now prepared to enter into intimate relations with foreigners instead of . . . endeavouring to prevent all intercourse whatever with them'. And 'since the policy of China is to encourage commerce with the nations of the world, it would be suicidal on our part not to endeavour to assist the enlightened Government of China . . .' Britain and other powers therefore adopted a 'co-operative policy'. 'Our present course,' said Lord Palmerston, now British Prime Minister, 'was to strengthen the Chinese empire, to augment its revenues, and to enable it to provide itself with a better navy and army.'

Prince Gong, leading China's first Foreign Office as well as the Grand Council, got on well with Western diplomats. He was a charming man. The Mitford grandfather, Algernon Freeman-Mitford, observed that he was 'full of jokes and fun', even appearing to 'have a flippant manner': 'My single eyeglass was a real boon to the Prince. Whenever he was getting the worst of an argument, and was at a loss for an answer, he would stop short, throw up his hands in amazement, and pointing at me cry out, "A single eyeglass! Marvellous!" By thus creating a diversion at my expense he gave himself time to consider his reply.'

The immediate benefit that Cixi gained from this new friendly relationship was the help of the Western powers in defeating the Taiping. At the time, in 1861, these peasant rebels had been waging ferocious battles in the heartland of China for a decade, and were holding large swathes of the country's richest land along the Yangtze River, together with some of the wealthiest cities, including Nanjing, their capital, next door to Shanghai. Because the rebels claimed to be Christians, Westerners had at first been rather sympathetic towards them. But disillusion eventually set in, when it became all too clear that the Taiping had little in common with Christians. Their leader, Hong Xiuquan, for a long time imposed total sexual abstinence on ordinary members and decreed the death penalty for those who broke the ban, even if they were husbands and wives; but he officially bestowed up to eleven wives on each of his chiefs and took eighty-eight consorts for himself. He wrote more than 400 crude 'poems' telling the women how to serve him – the Sun, as he called himself. And this was not the worst thing, as hordes of peasant rebels indulged in cruel and wanton slaughter of the innocent, burning villages and towns wherever they went. The area they devastated was as large as all Western and Central Europe combined. The English-language *North China Herald* came to the conclusion that the 'whole history' of the Taiping 'has been a succession of acts of bloodshed, rapine, and disorganisation; and [its] progress from the south to the north, and now in the east of this unhappy land, has been invariably attended by desolation, famine, and pestilence'. The rebels were not friendly to Western Christians, either: they turned down their request to leave Shanghai alone, and instead tried to seize the city, jeopardising Westerners' own business and security.

Some powers had offered help to fight the Taiping while Emperor Xianfeng was still alive. But he detested them as much as he did the Taiping themselves. Shortly after he died, the matter was raised again, and Cixi was enthusiastic. To those who suspected that Westerners were up to no good and might well occupy the land they took from the rebels, she reasoned: 'Since the treaties were signed, Britain and France have kept their word and withdrawn. It is in their interest to help us.' She was cautious, though, and declined to employ Western troops, taking note of the counsel of Thomas Wade, Secretary to the British Legation, that foreign troops on Chinese soil were not a good idea for China.★ That Wade should give advice with China's interest in mind was not lost on Cixi. She chose to have Western officers arming, training and leading local men, under overall Chinese command.

With her encouragement, Frederick Townsend Ward, a thirty-year-old American from Salem, Massachusetts, a tough adventurer and soldier of fortune with leadership qualities, organised an army of several thousand Chinese, with Western training and Western officers. Ward and his army won many battles, of which Cixi learned in glowing reports. She publicly conferred on him prominent honours, and named his force the 'Ever-victorious Army'. It was unheard-of that imperial decrees 'frankly and explicitly recognised' the merits of a foreigner, and Westerners saw this as 'a significant indication of the change in the Chinese attitude'.

Ward was fatally wounded in a battle in 1862 and Cixi ordered a temple built to commemorate him. Charles Gordon, an English officer, assumed the command of the Ever-victorious Army. Gordon felt strongly that 'the rebellion ought to be put down.' He wrote, 'Words cannot express the horrors these people suffer from the rebels, or the utter desert they have made of this rich province. It is all very well to talk of non-intervention; and I am not particularly sensitive, nor are our soldiers generally so; but certainly we are all impressed with the utter misery and wetchedness of these poor people.' Like Ward, Gordon had a penchant for bravado and would go into action armed only with a rattan cane. A hero to his men, he would become the

---

★ Wade was a pre-eminent sinologist, who pioneered the romanisation system for the Chinese language, later known as the Wade–Giles, a system that for much of the twentieth century was the tool for a non-native speaker to learn Chinese, and was an invaluable aid for the Chinese themselves to learn their own language. This author's name, Jung Chang, is spelt according to the Wade–Giles system.

famed 'Chinese Gordon' and played a key – and, some say, indispensable – role in defeating the Taiping and rescuing the Qing dynasty.

Although she had no direct contact herself with the Western warriors and envoys, Cixi was quick to learn about the West and to grasp ideas from the massive and detailed reports she received from Prince Gong and other officials who dealt with them. In one case, an imperial decree had thanked 'the English and French' for shelling Taiping troops. The French envoy complained, pointing out that only the French were involved, not the English. Cixi told her diplomats: 'You may say this is foreigners being petty-minded, but you must also see that they are being exact. In the future when you make a report, do not deviate an iota from the facts.' She had put her finger on a superannuated Chinese tendency to be imprecise.

One piece of information that made an impression on her was that individual Chinese lives mattered to the Westerners. This was often reported by Li Hongzhang, who was the commander of Ward and Gordon. With his manicured goatee and narrowed eyes that had seen a great deal, Li, who was an earl, was the classic Confucian gentleman, but he was to evolve into the most renowned of all China's reformers. At this early stage, through daily dealings with Westerners, he was already learning from them, when most of his colleagues still regarded them as aliens. Towards the end of 1863, Earl Li and Gordon laid siege to the city of Suzhou, famed for its silks and gardens and canals (some called it China's Venice), and strategically situated near Nanjing, capital of the Taiping. They persuaded eight defending Taiping chiefs to surrender the city, promising them safety and high office in return. In his camp outside the city gate, Earl Li gave a banquet for the chiefs, to which Gordon was not invited. Halfway through the drinking, eight officers came in, each carrying a mandarin's hat of honour, with a red button on top and a peacock feather sticking up. The officers moved on their knees to the chiefs and offered the hats to them. All at the banquet got to their feet and watched. The chiefs stood up, untied the yellow headscarves they were wearing and were about to take the hats and put them on when, in a split second, eight swords were drawn, and the eight heads were held by their hair in the grip of the officers. Earl Li, who had absented himself from the banquet just before the officers entered, in order not to be present at the killing, had the chiefs killed to prevent potential treachery, as had happened before. Afterwards, his army raced into Suzhou and massacred tens of thousands of Taiping troops who thought they were safe.

Gordon, who had given the murdered chiefs his word and personally guaranteed their lives, was filled with a righteous wrath and resigned his command of the Ever-victorious Army. Though he could, reluctantly, see Earl Li's point of view, he felt that as an English officer and Christian gentleman he had to disassociate his name from this act of 'Asiatic barbarity'.

Earl Li reported the strong reaction of Gordon to Cixi, as well as the outcry against the killings from the Western diplomats and merchants. Cixi did not comment on the matter, but she could not have failed to view the Westerners with a certain admiration. Confucian ideals also abhorred the killing of the innocent and of those who surrendered. And yet here were the imperial forces committing massacres and behaving no better than the despised Taiping – with the striking exception of the Ever-victorious Army. (Earl Li wrote to a colleague that Gordon's men 'can defeat the bandits but will not kill as many as possible, so my army has to be around to assist them'.) Cixi and her circle of officials were shedding the notion that Westerners were 'barbarians'. In fact, from this time on she seems to have developed a little defensiveness about her own country and its customs.

Gordon started to work with Earl Li to disband the Ever-victorious Army. This came as a relief to Cixi. She had been thinking about what to do with the Army once the war was over, as this invincible fighting force only followed Gordon and did not take orders from Beijing. In her letter to Prince Gong, Cixi said: 'If Gordon makes proper arrangements to disband the Army, and send the foreign officers home, then it proves that he is truly being good to us, and has been working for our benefit throughout.' Before his departure, Cixi publicly praised the Englishman in glowing language and offered him liberal rewards, including 10,000 taels of silver. Gordon declined the money on the grounds that he was not a mercenary, but an officer. Cixi asked Prince Gong, somewhat nonplussed: 'Is this really what he is thinking? Isn't it the case that foreigners only want money?' Earl Li and other officials were deputed to find out what would satisfy Gordon. At Earl Li's recommendation, Cixi awarded him a singular honour: a mandarin jacket in the royal yellow colour, of a kind that only the emperor was allowed to wear. Gordon had given Cixi much food for thought about Westerners.★

★ A statue of Gordon was erected in Trafalgar Square, London, and was later moved to the Victoria Embankment. Winston Churchill spoke in Parliament in 1948 in favour of the statue's return to its original location, calling Gordon 'a model of a Christian hero', and saying that 'very many cherished ideals are associated with his name'.

To defeat the Taiping, Cixi promoted Han personages in an unprecedented way: Earl Li for one, and also Zeng Zuofan, whom she made a marquis. It was Marquis Zeng's army that finally recaptured Nanjing in July 1864. This marked the end of the Taiping, the biggest peasant rebellion in Chinese history, which had caused the deaths of some twenty million people in fifteen years of war. Its leader, Hong Xiuquan, died of illness before the fall of Nanjing, and Hong's son and successor was caught and put to 'death by a thousand cuts', as prescribed by the Qing laws, even though he was aged only fourteen. Other captured Taiping chiefs were also subject to this form of execution. Reports of these bloody deaths, carried by newspapers like the *North China Herald*, complete with graphic photographs, horrified Westerners. Thomas Wade, now the British chargé d'affaires, wrote to Prince Gong to suggest that now that the rebellion had been destroyed, China should abolish this savage form of punishment. It was 'too cruel and deeply upsetting' to people in the West, Wade said, adding that its abolition would win the empire much goodwill and political advantage. His appeal was rejected by Prince Gong, who told Wade that this punishment was rarely used and that it was needed to scare off would-be rebels who might otherwise destroy countless lives. 'Without this punishment, I am afraid people in China would have nothing to fear . . . and before long, there would be more and more criminals, and it would be hard to ensure peace and stability.' The prince was plainly admitting that even death penalties such as decapitation would not deter rebels, and the empire could not survive without this cruellest of sanctions. Cixi did not contradict Prince Gong, but neither did she add a personal note, as Emperor Qianlong had done in 1774 when he wrote in his own hand about a rebel leader, Wang Lun: the man must be put to death by 'a thousand cuts, which must leave the skin of his body looking like fish scales', and his family members 'must all be beheaded, everyone of them, men, women, the old, the young'.

The humane side of Western culture was, to the Chinese, amazingly in tune with their own ideal, *ren*, or benevolence, which, according to Confucius, was the ultimate goal for all rulers. Prince Gong praised Wade for 'having the spirit of *ren*', although he lamented that this ideal could not be applied in China just yet.

With the end of the Taiping, other rebellions were also put down one after another. Within a few years of seizing power, Cixi had restored peace. This gave her indisputable authority in the eyes of the elite

– and minimised opposition to her forthcoming policies to revive the country, which was in a dire state.★ The wars had cost more than 300 million taels of silver. The streets of Beijing teemed with beggars; some were women who, normally hidden from public view, accosted passers-by, wearing little more than rags. And yet, with Cixi's leadership, China would make a stunning recovery in less than a decade and would begin to enjoy a degree of prosperity. One thing that helped crucially was a large new source of income: Customs revenues from the growing trade with the West, as a result of Cixi's open-door policy.

Cixi had noted the immense potential of international trade, whose centre was now Shanghai, where the Yangtze River, having originated in the Himalayas and having crossed the middle of China, flows into the sea. Within months after her coup, by the beginning of 1862, she had told Prince Gong: 'Shanghai is but a remote corner, and is imperilled [threatened by the Taiping] like piled-up eggs. And yet, thanks to the congregation of foreign and Chinese merchants, it has been a rich source for maintaining the army. I hear that in the past two months, it has collected 800,000 taels in import duty alone.' 'We must do our best to preserve this place,' she said. Shanghai showed her that opening up to the West presented a tremendous opportunity for her empire, and she seized it. In 1863, more than 6,800 cargo ships visited Shanghai, a giant leap from the annual 1,000 or so under her late husband.

The expansion of foreign trade obliged China to have an efficient – and uncorrupt – Customs service. At Prince Gong's recommendation, Cixi appointed a twenty-eight-year-old Ulsterman from County Armagh, Robert Hart, to be Inspector General of Chinese Maritime Customs, where Hart had already been working. Within a year of the appointment, she had given Hart an honour.

Born in the same year as she was, 1835, and educated at Queen's College in Belfast, Hart had come to China first as a bright, earnest and innocent nineteen-year-old interpreter-to-be in the British consular service. An outstanding linguist, he had also come with an armful of prizes in logic, Latin, English literature, history, metaphysics, natural history, jurisprudence and physical geography. His diaries show him to be a devout Christian, concerned with what was moral and just – and that he felt a deep sympathy for the Chinese. One entry shortly after his arrival in Hong Kong described an evening stroll to the waterfront with

★ In the places not despoiled or occupied by the rebels, the recovery was instant. Already in the mid-1860s, observed the English attaché, Freeman-Mitford, 'The prosperity of Canton is evident, and very striking.'

a Mr Stace: 'He rather surprised me by the way in wh[ich] he treated the Chinese – pitching their goods into the water and touching them up with his cane because they wd not row out from the Quay when he entered the Boat. Then it was supper time with them; and this Hour being sacred with them, they wd not work until supper was finished.'

A decade of work in China established Hart as a fair and remarkably able man, with a talent to mediate and to find acceptable compromises. He knew his strengths and was self-assured. On the morning that the official dispatch arrived announcing his appointment, he did not open it at once and recorded with more than a hint of self-satisfaction:

> I ate my breakfast in my usual way, and then, as usual, read my morning chapter and prayed . . . The despatch opened: first a very cordial letter from Sir F. Bruce begging me to accept the Inspectorateship, and assuring me of the support of the foreign ministers; 2nd a long letter . . .; 3rd a long Chinese letter . . .; 4th. a despatch from the [Chinese Foreign Office], appointing me to be Inspector General, &c. &c. &c . . .

Under Hart, Chinese Customs was transformed from an antiquated set-up, anarchical and prone to corruption, into a well-regulated modern organisation, which contributed enormously to China's economy. In five years, up to mid-1865, it delivered to Beijing duties of well over 32 million taels. The indemnities to Britain and France were paid out of the Customs revenue and were completely paid off by mid-1866, with minimal pain for the country at large.

With the new wealth, Cixi began to import food on a large scale. China had long been unable to produce enough food to feed its population, and the dynasty had always banned the export of grain. Systematic, duty-free imports were recorded by the Customs from 1867. That year the import of rice, the staple food, was worth 1.1 million taels. Food-sourcing and purchasing became a major job of the Customs under Hart, and the employee assigned to the job was honoured by Cixi.

Employing Hart and a large number of other foreigners caused resentment in the civil service. It was a courageous move.

The motto of Cixi's government was 'Make China Strong' – *zi-qiang*. Hart wanted to show Beijing how to achieve this through modernisation. His aim, as he put in his diary, was: 'to open the country to access of whatever Christian civilization has added to the comforts or well being, materially or morally, of man . . .' He wanted 'progress' for China. And progress in those days meant modern mining, telegraph and telephone, and above all the railway. In October 1865, Hart presented a memorandum to Prince Gong, offering his advice.

In his eagerness 'to get a fresh start out of the old dame' – China – Hart admonished and threatened. 'Of all countries in the world, none is weaker than China,' he asserted, blaming the country's military defeats on its rulers' 'inferior intelligence'. He wrote ominously that if China did not follow his advice, Western powers 'may have to start a war to force it'. These words reflected a common attitude among Westerners, who felt 'they know better what China wants, than China does itself', and they ought to 'take her by the throat' and 'enforce progress'.

Prince Gong did not pass on Hart's memorandum to Cixi for months. This uncharacteristic delay was most likely because he feared that the empress dowager might be so enraged that she would fire Hart, thus killing the goose that was laying the golden eggs. Although Cixi encouraged sharp criticisms and blunt advice from her officials, no one had shown such arrogance or used blatant threats. Prince Gong could not be sure how she would react. He decided to send Hart out of the country, so that if the empress dowager decided to sack him, at least the order would not be carried out straight away, and there would be time to persuade her to change her mind. It was then that Hart was offered a home leave to Europe, which he had been requesting for some time.

Hart departed at the end of March 1866 and his memorandum was presented to Cixi on 1 April, together with another piece of advice by the British chargé d'affaires Thomas Wade, which raised more or less the same issues, and in more or less the same tone – designed to 'frighten them', according to Hart. Having presented these documents, Prince Gong felt apprehensive. When the British attaché Freeman-Mitford came to see him to press 'Railroad, telegraphs' and 'all the old stories that have been trotted out a hundred times', he noticed that the prince 'was very nervous and fidgety. He twisted, doubled, and dodged like a hare.'

Prince Gong had underestimated Cixi. She read the memos carefully, and then sent them out to ten top officials who headed foreign affairs, trade and the provinces, inviting their opinions. In her cover letter there was no anger or any ill feeling towards Hart or Wade – unlike Prince Gong's own report, in which bitterness flared up here and there. She had taken Western arrogance in her stride, declining to allow it to cloud her judgement. Instead she looked for potential benefits in the proposals. Hart 'makes some good points', she found, 'in his evaluation of Chinese government, military, finance, and in his suggestions about adopting Western methods of mining, ship-building, arms production and military training . . . As for the matters to do with foreign relations, such as sending ambassadors to other countries, these are things we should be doing anyway.' She did not address the matter of the threatening language and tone, simply evoking her government's motto: 'Make China Strong is the only way to ensure that foreign countries will not start a conflict against us . . . or look down on us.' Perhaps she was also able to put the offence into perspective, knowing only too well that the Chinese talked about foreigners in a no less offensive manner. Nevertheless, Prince Gong warned Western envoys to watch their language. They obliged, and omitted offending expressions from subsequent correspondence.★

A few senior mandarins fumed against Hart, but the empress dowager never turned against him. Hart was honest, and ran the Customs efficiently and with great probity, which was a singular achievement in a country where corruption was endemic. That was enough for her. Never small-minded, she would invariably focus on the bigger picture and soon she would award Hart another honour for his service. Hart headed China's Customs for as long as her life and reign. For a foreigner to be in charge of a major fiscal channel for nearly half a century was an extraordinary phenomenon, and shows an astonishing lack of prejudice or suspicion on Cixi's part, as well as the shrewdness of her judgement. It was not blind faith. She was in no doubt that Hart's ultimate loyalty lay with his own country, Britain. A diplomat of hers reported to her that he had quizzed Hart on where his loyalty would lie, if there were a clash between China and Britain, and that Hart had replied: 'I am British.' And yet she had faith that Hart would be fair to China – and she strove to avoid presenting him with any conflict of interest. Few of the top echelon objected to Hart, which was also extraordinary. However anti–West some officials might be, they trusted their country's Customs to a Westerner. Hart did not let them down. He contributed not only significantly to China's financial well-being, but also to its general

---

★ Hart had at first been oblivious to the offence his memo had caused and, thinking he could force Cixi's government into industrialisation, had burst out into a 'Hurrah!' in his diary after submitting it. Then he registered his hosts' reserve after he had done another round of lobbying at the Foreign Office, selling telegraphs and railways. He wrote in his diary that the Chinese 'might think I was in foreign & not in Chinese pay', and he told them 'I shd. not again refer to the matters about which I had spoken . . .'

relationship with the outside world. He became somebody to whom Prince Gong turned for all sorts of services to do with the West. And the empress dowager learned about Western civilisation through dealing with him, even if the contact was indirect.

The modernisation projects proposed by Hart were, however, rejected by all those Cixi consulted. Even the most reform-minded man, whom Westerners came to regard highly, Earl Li, was vehemently against them, summing up their 'incalculable damages' thus: 'they deface our landscape, invade our fields and villages, spoil our *feng-shui* [geomancy], and ruin the livelihood of our people.' No one could think of any good that these expensive engineering projects would do, and Western representatives were unable to produce persuasive arguments in their favour. Prince Gong informed Cixi that Westerners had 'not said anything specific about how exactly these are going to be good for China'.

Instead, there seemed to be plenty of advantages for the West. China was near to paying off the war indemnities and had a huge trade surplus. It could afford these enterprises. Having set foot in the interior, Westerners found the place to be rich in unexploited natural resources. The British naval officer Henry Noel Shore noted that 'the coal-fields have been estimated by competent authorities at 419,000 square miles, or more than twenty times greater than those of Europe, while minerals, but especially iron ore of excellent quality, are said to abound in every province'. And mining required telegraphs and railways.

Among the many objections raised was that Westerners would have access to China's underground treasures and might seek to control them. Railways could carry Western troops into the heartland, if they wished to invade. Millions of people in the travel and communications business – the cart-drivers, goods-bearers, messengers, innkeepers and so on – would lose their jobs. No one seemed to regard a reduction in back-breaking labour as especially desirable, or foresee the creation of new forms of employment. The roaring noise and black smoke produced by machines were seen as a particular horror as they were deemed to interfere with nature – and, worst of all, disturb the dead souls in the numerous private ancestral tombs that defined the landscape of China.

In those days, in China, each extended family had its own burial lot. These grounds were sacred to the population. As Freeman-Mitford observed, 'in this place, the fairest spots are chosen for burying the dead'. Indeed, people believed that the tombs were their final destination where, after they died, they joined their deceased nearest and dearest. This comforting thought removed the fear of dying. The most deadly blow one could deal to one's enemy was to destroy his ancestral tomb, so that he and all his family would become homeless ghosts after death, condemned to eternal loneliness and misery.

Like most of her contemporaries, Cixi associated ancestral tombs with profound religious sentiment. Faith was essential in her life, and the only thing that frightened her was the wrath of Heaven – the mystical and formless being that was the equivalent of God to the Chinese of her day. Believing in Heaven was to them not incompatible with having faith in Buddhism or Taoism. Chinese religious feelings were not as well defined as those in the Christian world. To have more than one religious belief was common. Indeed at grand ceremonies, such as an extravagant funeral, which might last well over a month, prayers were said by both Buddhist and Taoist priests as well as the lamas of Tibetan Buddhism, alternating every few days. In this tradition, Cixi was both a devout Buddhist and a devotee to Taoist doctrine. Her most revered Bodhisattva was Guanyin, the Goddess of Mercy, the only female god in Buddhism, who was a Taoist Immortal as well. She frequently prayed in her personal chapels to a statue of Guanyin, with her palms together in front of her chest. The chapels were also her private sanctuaries where she went to be alone, to clear her mind before making critical decisions. As a Buddhist, she followed the ritual of setting captured creatures free. For her birthday, she would buy many birds – latterly as many as 10,000, according to her court ladies – and on the day, choosing the most auspicious hour, she would climb to the top of a hill and open the cages carried by the eunuchs one after another, watching the birds fly away.

It was mainly on account of the ancestral tombs that Cixi's government rejected the machine-age projects. The spirits of the dead simply must not be disturbed. Prince Gong told the foreign envoys that if this refusal meant war, then so be it. Cixi treated the threat of war seriously and issued a severely worded edict ordering provincial chiefs to resolve swiftly any outstanding disputes involving Westerners, so that no one had any pretext to start a war. Her government did its best to stick to the treaties. As Hart acknowledged, 'I do not know of any infraction of treaties.' After more futile lobbying, Western companies gave up. China's industrial age was delayed.

★

However, it was to creep in through another door. Cixi's court was united in favour of building a modern army and arms industry. Foreign officers were engaged to train troops, and engineers employed to teach the manufacture of weaponry. Technology and equipment were bought. In 1866, the building of a modern fleet started in earnest. Its chief foreign supervisor was a Frenchman, Prosper Giquel, who had first arrived in China serving in the British-French invading forces, and had stayed on. He had helped defeat the Taiping by leading a Franco-Chinese force named the Ever-triumphant Army, echoing the Anglo-Chinese Ever-victorious Army, before working in the Customs under Robert Hart. Cixi had faith in Giquel and authorised whatever money the enterprise required. There were many doubters who mistrusted a former French officer of an invading army, and others who were horrified by the astronomical cost. But Cixi was instinctively unsuspicious. She told her officials that Giquel and other foreigners 'must be treated extra well'. 'This fleet-building project is really fundamental to our goal to Make China Strong,' she declared excitedly.

In the space of just a few years, nine steamships were built, of a quality that apparently could hold its own against Western ships. No bottles of champagne were cracked open when they were launched; only solemn ceremonies offering apologies to the Celestial Queen, and the Gods of Rivers and of Soil, all of whom the steamers were about to distress. When the first ship sailed resplendently into the harbour of Tianjin in 1869, crowds of Chinese and foreign inhabitants gathered to witness the spectacle, and those who were involved in its building wiped away proud tears. For his services Giquel was richly rewarded with, among other things, a mandarin jacket in the royal yellow colour.

By the end of the first decade of her rule, Cixi had not only revived a war-torn country, but had also founded a modern navy and begun building a modern army and arms industry, with state-of-the-art equipment. Although full-scale industrialisation did not take off immediately in this ancient land, which had its own strong and deep-rooted traditions and religious sentiments, modern enterprises were appearing one by one: coal- and iron-ore mining, iron-mills building and machine manufacturing. Modern education was introduced to train the engineers, technicians, officers and crew. Railways and telegraphs were waiting just beyond the horizon. Medieval China had taken its first step towards modernisation under the empress dowager.

6 Virgin Journeys to the West
(1861–71)

O N the road to modernity Cixi had a kindred spirit, close adviser and dependable administrator in Prince Gong. Her decisions were formulated with the help of the prince, who then implemented them. Between them, the yellow silk screen barely existed.

Without such a man outside the confines of the harem, Cixi could not have ruled effectively. She showed the prince her appreciation by awarding him unparalleled honours – and, crucially, exempting him from having to prostrate before her. An imperial edict issued just after her coup, in the name of her son, specifically granted the privilege of not kneeling and kowtowing in everyday meetings to Prince Gong, together with Prince Chun and three other uncles of the child emperor. Prince Gong was the main beneficiary, as he saw Cixi every day. It eventually struck her that she really must withdraw this favour. Without the rigid etiquette, she realised, Prince Gong was too relaxed with her and was treating her in the patronising way he tended to treat all women, especially as she was young – still in her twenties. His behaviour irritated and angered her for some time, until one day in 1865 she exploded and in tremendous agitation fired him. She wrote a decree by hand, accusing him of 'having too high an opinion of himself', 'strutting about and giving himself airs' and, simply, being 'full of rubbish'. This was one of the few decrees Cixi wrote in her own hand. Her writing was still poor, and her text was littered with solecisms. That she threw caution to the winds and exposed her vulnerability – her lack of scholarship, which mattered so much to the elite – shows how furious she was.

Like most rocky moments in solid relationships, the storm passed. The grandees mediated. Cixi calmed down. Prince Gong apologised, prostrating at her feet (which remained behind the yellow silk screen), weeping and promising to reform his manners. Having made her point, Cixi rescinded her decree and restored Prince Gong to his former posts. She did, however, take away his title, Grand Adviser, although his role continued as before. She also told him to be deferential in court and stop behaving arrogantly. From now on Prince Gong, tamed, took care to humble himself, and to kneel and kowtow in her presence. This episode served as a warning to other grandees around her that Cixi was not to be patronised. She was the master. They all prostrated before her.

Her working relationship with Prince Gong remained close. In fact, they grew closer as they were thrown together as 'comrades' facing conservative opposition to their efforts to bring the empire into the modern age.

One major episode concerned the first modern educational institution, Tongwen College, the School of Combined Learning. It was set up in 1862, soon after Cixi's reign began, to train interpreters. At the time, it met with relatively little resistance – after all, China had to deal with foreigners. The school was housed in a picturesque mansion where, amidst date trees and groves of lilac and winter jasmine, a little bell tower announced class hours. Then in 1865, when, on Prince Gong's advice, Cixi decided to turn it into a fully fledged college teaching sciences, the opposition became frenzied. For two thousand years only the classics had been regarded as a fit subject for education. Cixi defended her decision by saying that the College only intended 'to borrow Western methods to verify Chinese ideas', and would 'not replace the teachings of our sacred sages'. But this did not assuage the officials who had risen to their present positions through imbibing Confucian classics, and they attacked the Foreign Office and Prince Gong as 'stooges of foreign devils'. Graffiti abusing the prince were pasted on city walls.

One source of outrage was that, in this college, foreigners would be made 'teachers'. By tradition, a teacher was a most revered figure, a mentor for life, who imparted wisdom as well as knowledge, and who must be respected like a parent. (The murder of a teacher was classified as parricide, which, like treason, was punishable by death of a thousand cuts.) Emperors and princes set up shrines in their homes to honour their deceased tutors. The most vocal opponent on this issue was a highly esteemed Mongol scholar, Woren, a tutor of Cixi's child, Emperor Tongzhi. He wrote to Cixi arguing that Westerners must not be accorded this exalted status, as they were enemies who had 'invaded our country, threatened our dynasty, burned our palaces, and killed our people'. And he reasoned: 'Today we are learning their secrets in order to fight them in future wars, and how can we trust them not to play evil tricks through fake teaching?'

While rebuking the abusive dissenters with strong words, Cixi was gentle with Woren, merely bidding him to find *Chinese* teachers to teach sciences. This put the Mongol tutor on the spot, and he had to concede that he had no one to nominate. Cixi told him to keep trying and come up with a solution to the country's problems. The tutor, who had been selected to teach the emperor on account of his deep-rooted Confucian principles, was convinced of his own arguments, but felt helpless and distraught in the face of reality. One day he burst into sobs while giving a lesson to the nine-year-old child emperor, who, having never seen the elderly teacher cry, was frightened and disconcerted. A few days later, the old man passed out while trying to mount a horse. He was ill and asked to resign. Cixi declined to accept his resignation, but gave him permanent sick leave. Woren left behind many sympathisers at the court, including his fellow tutor, Grand Tutor Weng, also a hater of the West. Weng had wept when the Old Summer Palace was burned down and called the Westerners in Beijing 'dirty animals' and 'wolves and jackals'.

Cixi pushed ahead in spite of tenacious opposition, and appointed a senior official, Hsü Chi-she, to head the college, announcing that Hsü had 'high prestige' and was 'a good model' for the students. Hsü's distinction, in the empress dowager's eyes, came from his book, the first comprehensive description of the world by a Chinese. Although he had never been abroad, Hsü had accomplished this major work with the help of an American missionary, David Abeel, with whom he had made friends while working on the southern coast in the 1840s. In the book, he placed China as just one country among many on Earth, contradicting the notion that China was the Middle Kingdom and the centre of the world. America seems to be the country he admired most, and he said of George Washington, 'Ah, what a hero!' Hsü wrote that after Washington fought victorious wars over a vast territory and people wanted to make him king, he 'did not ascend the throne, nor pass his position to his descendants. Instead, he created the system by which a person became the head of the country through election.' 'Washington was an extraordinary man!' he exclaimed.★ Hsü was most impressed by the fact that America 'has no royalty or nobles . . . In this brand new state, public affairs are decided

★ Hsü's words about Washington are engraved on a Memorial Stone in the Washington Memorial Monument, in Washington DC.

by the people. What a wonder!' To Hsü, America came closest to the Confucian ideal that 'everything under Heaven is for the people' (*tian-xia-wei-gong*), and was the place most similar to China's Three Great Ancient Dynasties, under the emperors Shun, Yao and Yu more than 4,000 years earlier. Under these dynasties, the Chinese believed, their country was a flourishing and kind place, where the emperors were voted into office on merit, and lived like everyone else. These dynasties were in fact mythical. But people imagined they were real, and quite a few Chinese who came into contact with the West expressed astonishment that China's legendary ancient practice appeared to be alive beyond the ocean. The British justice system was 'just like the one in our Three Great Ancient Dynasties,' one observed.

When Hsü's book was published back in 1848 under Cixi's late father-in-law, Emperor Daoguang, officials had been scandalised. They had accused him of 'inflating the status of foreign barbarians' and heaped invective on him. He had been dismissed from his job. Now, in 1865, his book reached Cixi, and she plucked him out of disgraced semi-retirement at his home on the Yellow River and promoted him to a key post in the Foreign Office. Hsü's appointment was seen by Westerners in Beijing as yet another sign of 'the beginning of a new era'.

In the next few years Hsü suffered continuous insults from other officials. He begged to retire, citing poor health, and eventually Cixi had to let him go. (He died in 1873.) After Hsü's retirement, Cixi appointed an American missionary, W. A. P. Martin, to head Tongwen College, at the recommendation of Robert Hart. As a foreigner, Martin was spared peer-group ostracism. But for Cixi, to put a Westerner at the helm of a Chinese educational institution was ground-breaking and extremely bold. The American was chosen because he had introduced Western legal concepts to China through his translation of Henry Wheaton's *Elements of International Law*, which was published with a subvention of 500 taels of silver from the Foreign Office, authorised by Cixi. He stayed in this post for decades, and trained many diplomats and other major figures. This Western-style college became a model for a new educational system in the empire.

To open people's eyes to the outside world, Cixi began to send travellers overseas. In spring 1866, when Hart was going on home leave, Prince Gong selected several students from Tongwen College to travel with him and tour Europe. A sixty-three-year-old Manchu named Binchun was assigned to lead the small group of young men. Sporting a scholarly goatee, he became, as he proudly wrote of himself, 'the first person to be sent to the West from China'.

Binchun was a clerk in the Customs office. For such a path-blazing mission, his rank was incredibly low, and his age far too advanced. The problem was that all who had been approached (whose rank could be no higher than Hart's, in order to be in his entourage) declined to accept the job. Binchun was the only man who volunteered. Many alarmists warned him that going to a foreign land would be like offering himself as prey 'to tigers and wolves in human form', and that he could be kept a hostage or possibly chopped into pieces. But Binchun had a strong sense of curiosity and was remarkably free of prejudice. He had learned enough about the outside world from his Western friends, one of whom was W. A. P. Martin, to know that the scary tales were baseless. In a poem he described how books from his foreign friends had broadened his horizon, so that he was no longer like the infamous frog that sat at the bottom of a well declaring that the sky was as big as the patch it could see.

Binchun travelled to eleven countries, visiting cities and palaces, museums and operas, factories and shipyards, hospitals and zoos, and met people from monarchs to the average man and woman. Queen Victoria noted down her audience with him in her diary on 6 June 1866: 'Received the Chinese Envoys, who are here without credentials. The head man is a Mandarin of 1st Class. They looked just like the wooden and painted figures one sees.' Binchun, whose status had been vastly inflated for this meeting, wrote in his own diary that Queen Victoria asked him what he thought of Britain and that he replied, 'The buildings and appliances are ingeniously constructed and made, and better than those in China. As for the way state affairs are run, there are very many advantages here.' To which Queen Victoria said she hoped that his tour would enhance the amicable relations between the two countries.

At a ball given by the Prince of Wales, Binchun was dazzled by the dancing, which, being non-existent in China, he described in some detail with obvious yearning. When the Prince of Wales asked for his impression of London, he said frankly that as the very first Chinese envoy abroad, he had the good fortune to be the first to know there was such splendour across the ocean.

He marvelled at the illuminated cities at night, and was amazed by the trains, which he rode on forty-two times. 'The sensation is like flying through the air,' he wrote, and he brought back home a working model of a train. He registered that machines could improve people's lives. In Holland, the use of water pumps to create fertile fields made him reflect: 'if these are used on peasants' land in China, we don't have to worry about drought or water-logging any more'. He liked European political systems and recorded with admiration his visit to the Houses of Parliament in London. 'I went to the great chamber of the parliament, which has a high vault and is grand and awe-inspiring. There, 600 people who have been elected from all parts of the country gather to discuss public affairs. (Different views are freely debated, and only when a consensus is reached will a decision be taken and implemented. Neither the monarch nor the prime minister can impose his will on decisions.)'

This inquisitive man was bowled over by everything he saw – even the fireworks, which had been invented in his own country. But while in China they remained firecrackers on the ground, here they were fired into the sky and produced ravishing explosions. Even his reservations were prefaced by praise: 'Westerners love being clean, and their bathrooms and toilets are immaculately washed. The only thing is that they throw newspapers and magazines into the faeces after they read them, and sometimes they use these to wipe the dirt. They don't seem to respect and treasure things that have writings on them.' Respecting the written word was a Confucian teaching.

Not least was Binchun smitten by European women and the fact that they could mingle with men, and dance with men, wearing gorgeous clothes. This kind of male–female relationship seemed to appeal to him. The way Western men treated their women particularly impressed him. On board a steamer, he noticed that 'the women walked arm-in-arm with men upon the deck, or rested on rattan couches while their husbands waited upon them like servants' – which was quite the opposite of how things were done in China, but which showed a kind of domestic intimacy that was attractive to him. He made a point of saying that in Europe women could be crowned monarchs just like men, one great example being Queen Victoria. About the queen, Binchun wrote admiringly: 'She was 18 when she succeeded to the throne, and everybody in her country sings in praise of her wisdom.'

Binchun's diaries, with their rhapsodic superlatives about the West, were delivered to Prince Gong upon his return to China, and the prince had them copied and presented to Cixi. This was the first eye-witness account that Cixi read of the outside world by one of her own officials, and it was bound to affect her deeply. In particular, the treatment of women in the West could not fail to attract her. While Western women could be monarchs in their own right, Cixi had to rule from behind her son's throne. She could not see her officials without a screen, and even with the screen she was still unable to receive foreign envoys, who had been requesting an audience to present their credentials. When she sought opinions from the grandees on this matter, their response had been cast-iron and uniform: the audience could not be granted while the emperor was a child; the envoys would have to wait until he formally assumed power. That *she* might receive the envoys was out of the question, so unthinkable that most officials did not address that possibility. It was impossible for Cixi not to be favourably disposed towards Western ways.

So her response after reading Binchun's diary was to promote him to a post in the Foreign Office and make him 'Director of Western Studies' at Tongwen College in early 1867, when Hsü, the admirer of Washington, was head of the college. The two men had been kindred spirits, and Hsü had given Binchun a copy of his world geography to take on his journey, during which Binchun had confirmed that Hsü was indeed right that China was not the centre of the world! Hsü wrote a preface to Binchun's diary when it was published, with Cixi's endorsement.

Just like Hsü, Binchun was attacked by the conservative grandees. Grand Tutor Weng mentioned him in his diary with loathing and contempt, calling him a 'volunteer to be a slave to the devils', aghast that he should 'refer to barbarian chieftains as monarchs'. It is unclear whether the pain Binchun endured for his broad-mindedness played any role in the deterioration of his health, which led to his death in 1871.

Sending ambassadors to Western countries had always been Cixi's intention. But no suitable men could be found to fill the posts, as no official spoke a foreign language or knew anything about foreign lands. In 1867, Anson Burlingame, US minister to Beijing, was leaving his post for home, and Prince Gong suggested that Burlingame be appointed Ambassador Extraordinary to Europe and America. In his recommendation, Prince Gong told Cixi that Burlingame was a 'fair and conciliatory' man, who had 'the interests of China at heart', and that he was 'always willing to help China solve its problems'. He could be trusted, just like the Briton, Robert Hart, with whom 'we have no barriers of communication'. America, the prince added, was also 'the most peaceful and unaggressive' country among the powers as far as China was concerned. Showing considerable imagination, Cixi approved the suggestion immediately and made Burlingame China's first ambassador to the West, providing him with official credentials and seals. Burlingame's brief was to present the new China to the world and explain its new foreign policy, to 'argue against and stop anything that is damaging to China's interests, and agree to anything that is beneficial'. He would have two young Chinese deputies, Zhigang and Sun Jiagu, and they should be consulted on all issues. Important decisions must be referred back to Beijing. In order that Britain and France would not feel put out, one diplomat from each country was invited to be a secretary to the mission.

The conservatives were annoyed. In his diary, Grand Tutor Weng contemptuously called Burlingame 'a foreign barbarian chieftain [*yi-qiu*]'. The foreign community was impressed by the idea – 'singular and unexpected,' wrote the English-language *North China Herald*. The paper could not believe that the 'Chinese mind' was capable of such an inspired initiative, and attributed it to 'Mr Hart's brain'. In fact, Hart was only told about it after it was conceived, and although he expressed support, his subsequent remarks were lukewarm and sceptical, if not downright critical. Perhaps he who was thought of as 'Mr China' was somewhat jealous.

The Burlingame mission travelled across America and Europe, attracting much attention wherever it went. It was received by the heads of all the states it visited, among them President Andrew Johnson in America; Queen Victoria in Britain; Napoleon III, Emperor of France; Bismarck in Prussia and Tsar Nicolas I of Russia. Queen Victoria wrote in her diary on 20 November 1868: 'to receive the Chinese ambassador, the 1st who has ever come here, but he is an American in European dress, a Mr Burlingham [*sic*]. His colleagues are however 2 real Chinese, – the 2 secretaries being English and French.'

Cixi could not have chosen a more suitable spokesman than Anson Burlingame. Born in New Berlin, New York, in 1820, Burlingame had been appointed by President Abraham Lincoln as his first minister to China in 1861. Fair-minded, with gentle manners, Burlingame believed in the equality of nations and never looked down on the Chinese. He would represent China to Western audiences most eloquently.

He was already known for his oratorical powers. After Harvard University Law School, he had entered the Massachusetts Legislature as a Senator, and then went into the Congress in Washington DC. There, in 1856, he delivered a powerful verbal thrashing of a fervid advocate of slavery, Congressman Preston Brooks, who had just savagely beaten up Senator Charles Sumner, an abolitionist, with a wooden cane. Burlingame was challenged to a duel by Brooks, and he accepted, naming the rifle as his weapon of choice, and Navy Island, above Niagara Falls, as the place for the meeting. The duel did not take place only because Brooks refused the conditions.

In Beijing, Burlingame was instrumental in getting Western countries to adopt the 'cooperative policy' and to substitute fair diplomacy for the doctrine of force. During the trip, his passionate speeches on behalf of China can be glimpsed from the following address to 'the citizens of New York' on 23 June 1868. This was how he introduced his mission: China 'now itself seeks the West . . . and confronts you with its representatives here tonight . . . she has come forth to meet you . . .' To loud cheers, he told his audience what Cixi's government had achieved, and how remarkable the achievements were:

> I aver, that there is no spot on this earth where there has been greater progress made within the past few years than in the empire of China. [Cheers.] She has expanded her trade, she has reformed her revenue system, she is changing her military and naval organ-isations, she has built or established a great school, where modern science and the foreign languages are to be taught. [Cheers.] She has done this under every adverse circumstance. She has done this after a great war, lasting through thirteen years, a war out of which she comes with no national debt. [Long continued applause and laughter.] You must remember how dense is her population. You must remember how difficult it is to introduce radical changes in such a country as that. The introduction of your own steamers threw out of employment a hundred thousand junk-men. The introduction of several hundred foreigners into the civil service embittered, of course, the ancient native employees. The establish-ment of a school was formidably resisted by a party led by one of the greatest men of the empire. Yet, in defiance of all these, in spite of all these, the present enlightened government of China has advanced steadily along the path of progress [cheers] . . .

Trade, Burlingame informed his audience, 'has, in my own days in China, risen from $82,000,000 to $300,000,000' – more than $4.5 billion in today's currency. These changes were truly impressive, Burlingame reminded politicians and the public, because they involved 'a third of the human race'. Challenging those who advocated 'coercing China' into quick industrialisation, he pointed out that the idea was 'born of their own interests and of their own caprice'. He condemned those who 'tell you that the present dynasty must fall, and that the whole structure of Chinese civilization must be overthrown . . .'

Burlingame did more than present the case for China. On behalf of the country, he signed an 'equal treaty' with America in 1868, different from any of the 'unequal' treaties signed between China and

Cixi was a devout Buddhist and revered Guanyin, the Goddess of Mercy. In 1903, she dressed as Guanyin to have photographs taken; here with the two eunuchs closest to her, Lianying (to her left) and Cui (to her right), in the costumes of characters associated with the Goddess.

Old Beijing streets. Visible in the foreground are mule-carts, taxis of the time. It was one of these that bore Cixi to the Forbidden City in 1852 to be inspected by Emperor Xianfeng, who chose her as one of his concubines.

A caravan of camels passing in front of a Beijing city gate. It was said that some five thousand camels came into Beijing every day.

When Emperor Xianfeng died in 1861, Cixi's five-year-old son succeeded to the throne. She launched a coup against the regents appointed by her husband and made herself the real ruler of China. She is carried to the regular morning audience, surrounded by eunuchs in richly-coloured robes. Cui, front left; Lianying, front right.

THE EMPRESS DOWAGER'S MEN
(THIS PAGE AND FACING PAGE)

(*Above*) Prince Chun, who was married
to Cixi's sister.

(*Above right*) Prince Gong, Cixi's right-hand
man and adviser.

(*Right*) Viceroy Zhang Zhidong,
major supporter of Cixi
and renowned moderniser.

(*Above*) Li Hongzhang (Earl Li), the most
important reformer to serve Cixi. In Britain in 1896,
with Lord Salisbury, British Prime Minister (on the left),
and Lord Curzon (on the right).

(*Left*) General Yuan Shikai,
later first President of the Republic of China.

Junglu (front centre), a fierce devotee of Cixi, entertaining Western female visitors.

CIXI'S WESTERN FRIENDS
(THIS PAGE AND FACING PAGE)
(*Above*) Anson Burlingame, President Lincoln's first Minister to China (1861–7), and afterwards China's first Ambassador to Western countries. Standing in the middle of his delegation, he is flanked by his two (seated) Chinese deputies, Zhigang and Sun Jiagu, and the two secretaries of the mission, one British, one French (seated).

(*Left*) Lieutenant-Colonel Charles Gordon ('Chinese Gordon'), who helped defeat the Taiping Rebellion. This victory paved the way for the Cixi era.

(*Above*) Sarah Conger (in dark dress), wife of the US Minister to China (1898–1905), holding hands with Cixi with other ladies of the American Legation.

(*Below*) Sir Robert Hart, with his Western band of Chinese musicians. He was Inspector General of Chinese Maritime Customs for the entire period of Cixi's political life.

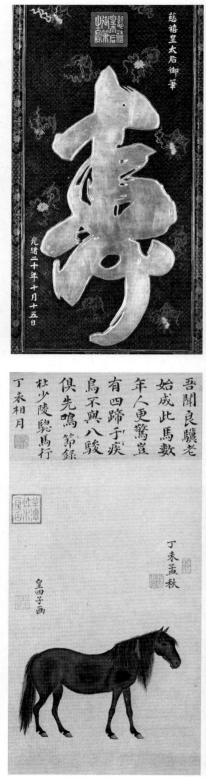

(*Above*) A painting by Cixi.

(*Above right*) Cixi learned to write characters as big as this (panel size 211 cm x 102 cm) in one single stroke. This was considered extraordinary, especially as she was small and elderly. This character reads *shou*, meaning 'longevity'.

(*Right*) Horse and calligraphy by Emperor Xianfeng when he was sixteen.

Western countries after the Opium War. It especially protected Chinese immigrants to America by giving them the status 'enjoyed by the citizens or subjects of the most favoured nation', and actively tried to stop the trade in slave labourers from China to South America, which was going on at this time.* In a 6,000-word article, Burlingame's friend and admirer Mark Twain vividly described the difference the treaty would make to the Chinese living in America: 'It affords me infinite satisfaction to call particular attention to this Consul clause, and think of the howl that will go up from the cooks, the railroad graders, and the cobble-stone artists of California, when they read it. They can never beat and bang and set the dogs on the Chinamen any more.' Before the treaty, the Chinese had no legal protection, as Mark Twain observed: 'I have seen Chinamen abused and maltreated in all the mean, cowardly ways possible to the invention of a degraded nature, but I never saw a policeman interfere in the matter and I never saw a Chinaman righted in a court of justice for wrongs thus done him.' Now, the Chinese became voters, and politicians could no longer ignore them. Twain wrote with relish, 'For at one sweep, all the crippling, intolerant, and unconstitutional laws framed by California against Chinamen pass away, and "discover" (in stage parlance) 20,000 prospective Hong Kong and Suchow voters and office-holders!' The Burlingame Treaty was ratified by Beijing the following year.

Burlingame's deputy, Zhigang, admired him for being 'open, understanding, fair' and for working 'with such dedication' to the country he was now representing. When things were not going as well as he wished, Burlingame was given to 'inconsolable despondency and frustration'. In Russia, China's neighbour with whom a border thousands of kilometres long boded potential trouble, the sense of responsibility seemed especially to weigh on him. Mental and physical exhaustion – for he had been on the road for two years – took their toll and Burlingame fell ill the day after his audience with the tsar, in the depths

---

* Article V: 'The United States of America and the Emperor of China cordially recognize the inherent and inalienable right of man to change his home and allegiance, and also the mutual advantage of the free migration and emigration of their citizens and subjects respectively from the one country to the other, for purposes of curiosity, of trade, or as permanent residents. The high contracting parties, therefore, join in reprobating any other than an entirely voluntary emigration for these purposes. They consequently agree to pass laws making it a penal offence for a citizen of the United States or Chinese subjects to take Chinese subjects either to the United States or to any other foreign country, or for a Chinese subject or citizen of the United States to take citizens of the United States to China or to any other foreign country, without their free and voluntary consent respectively.'

of a Russian winter. He died in St Petersburg in early 1870. Cixi had been kept informed about his tour, and she honoured and rewarded Burlingame with real feeling – before ordering Zhigang to take over, stressing that 'it is of utmost importance' that the mission continue.

Before he left Beijing at the beginning of 1868, Zhigang had been summoned to an audience with the empress dowager, who was seated behind the yellow silk screen, while Emperor Tongzhi, then eleven years old, sat on a throne in front of the screen. Zhigang went down on his knees as soon as he crossed the threshold and, taking off his mandarin hat and placing it on his left with the feather pointing towards the throne, as required by etiquette, he recited the prescribed greetings to the emperor, in the Manchu language (he was a Manchu himself), before touching his head on the ground. Then he straightened up, put his hat back on, stood up, moved forward and to the right, to a cushion closer to the throne, where he knelt again and waited for Cixi's questions. Cixi asked him about the route of the journey, to which Zhigang provided a list of the countries he was travelling to and through. It was clear that she had a good idea of the geography of the world – and was well informed about Western customs: she told Zhigang to get his entourage to watch their manners, and 'don't let them make a fool of themselves and be laughed at by foreigners'. Showing full awareness of the ostracism that her diplomats suffered at home, she said supportively to Zhigang, 'Working in foreign affairs, you have to be prepared to take all those snide remarks people make about you.' At this the young man answered: 'Even Prince Gong is subject to such things and he does not shy away. We small people can only do our utmost in our jobs.'

Zhigang was a diligent official, and his diary of the trip read very differently from that of the earlier traveller, Binchun. Rather than brimming with effusive enthusiasm for the West, his view was more detached. Some things would not work in China, he believed. Autopsies, for instance, horrified him, although he accepted that they served an important purpose. He felt that the children of the deceased could not possibly consent to their elders being cut up. Among the things he frowned upon were pleasurable pursuits in which men and women took part together, such as dancing, playing on the beach, swimming in the sea, skating on ice and going to the theatre. The Chinese valued sense, he claimed, the Europeans sensuality. He was averse to Christianity, which he thought was a good doctrine, but was hypocritical: 'Westerners preach the "love of God" and "love of man", and they seem really to believe it. And yet they wage wars with gunboats and cannons to conquer people by force, as well as imposing opium, a poison worse than plague, on the Chinese – all for profit.' 'It looks as though the love of God is less real than the love of profit,' he wrote.

And yet Zhigang also recorded that in London, at Madame Tussaud's, he was surprised to see a stately life-size wax figure of Commissioner Lin, the anti-opium crusader whose destruction of opium had led to the Opium War with Britain. Here Lin was, together with his favourite consort, dressed in resplendent costumes, standing majestically in what was effectively the Hall of Fame in London. Madame Tussaud's had commissioned the figures from a Cantonese artist and imported them at enormous expense. So it was far from the case that all British Christians were in thrall to 'the love of profit' or in favour of the opium trade. Other positive impressions ranged from the courtesy and hospitality of the kings and queens who entertained the mission, to the kindness and friendliness of fellow park strollers. Visiting George Washington's tomb, Zhigang was struck by its simplicity and paid homage to this 'very great man'. After witnessing a vote-rigging scandal in France, he ruminated that elections gave opportunities to immoral self-promoters. But Zhigang showed that he was on the whole an admirer of the Western political system. He described how the American Congress worked and commented, 'with this system, people's wishes can be expressed at the highest level and so the society is run fairly'. Of the countries he visited, America seemed to him the most sincere in wishing to be friendly with China, not least because its immense size and rich resources meant that it had no reason to covet anything from China. France he disapproved of, for imposing heavy taxation on its people in order to keep a large army for overseas wars. The young official was in favour of industrialisation. Writing in some detail about scientific inventions and modern enterprises, he evinced particular enthusiasm for the telegraph, regarding it as something that did not intrude on nature like the other projects (the machines involved were hardly visible), and could almost be part of nature. All in all, the mandarin concluded, 'If we are able to do what they are doing, there is no question we, too, can be rich and strong!'

Zhigang and his Chinese companions returned to China at the end of 1870, having travelled to eleven countries in nearly three years. Their diaries and reports were presented to Cixi. And yet no action followed on from the massive amount of knowledge gained or the goodwill generated. The only move was to send groups of young teenagers to America for education. But this project, whose objective was to produce future pillars of society who really knew the West and Western practices, had been in the pipeline for some time. Earl Li, who had been promoting this programme, was anxious that a comprehensive agenda should be set. He was then the Viceroy of Zhili, with his office in Tianjin, near the capital. In 1872 he asked to come to Beijing to see the empress dowager. But Cixi told him not to come. She had been in a most vulnerable position since late 1869, when some murderous events had occurred, leaving her struggling to survive and unable to launch major initiatives. Moreover, her son was about to take over, and her retirement to the harem was imminent. Zhigang lamented, 'Unexpectedly, the situation changed. Alas! There is nothing I can do but wring my hands.'

7 Love Doomed
(1869)

I N her first years as the ruler of the Chinese empire, Cixi, now a widow in her late twenties and early thirties, living in the harem surrounded by eunuchs, grew attached to a eunuch, An Dehai, known as Little An. In fact she fell in love with him. Eight years younger than she, Little An had come from an area near Beijing, Wanping, which traditionally supplied eunuchs for the court. His story was little different from that of most eunuchs. Poverty drove their parents to have them castrated as young children, hoping they would earn a better living at court. Usually the father would take the boy to a specialist castrator, who operated by the appointment of the court. After a contract was signed, absolving the castrator from any responsibility in case of death or failure (both highly likely outcomes), the unimaginably painful operation was performed. The castrator's fee was huge and had to be paid from future earnings. If the boy's rank stayed low, it could take him years to clear the debt. In order to save money, fathers would sometimes castrate their own sons.

Eunuchs were regarded with visceral disgust by most other men. Emperor Kangxi, who ruled for sixty-one years, called them 'the lowest and basest, more worms and ants than men'. Qianlong the Magnificent said that 'no one is smaller or lower than these stupid peasants', and that 'the court is extravagantly generous to allow them to serve here at all'. They lived like virtual prisoners in the palaces, from which they were rarely allowed out. The punishments to which they were subject did not have to follow the Qing legal procedure: all it needed to have a eunuch beaten to death was the emperor's whim. Ordinary folk sneered at them for the most common problem they suffered: incontinence, the result of castration, which became worse as they grew older and for which they had to wear nappies all the year round. Eunuchs were universally despised for having lost their manhood. Few men showed them compassion or considered that they had been driven to their wretched condition by desperate poverty. Pity and affection were usually felt only by the court women who lived in their company.

Little An, good-looking and sensitive, served Cixi for years and became indispensable to her. It was well known that he was her favourite. But Cixi's feelings towards him went far beyond fondness for a devoted servant. He turned her head. By summer 1869, courtiers had noticed that she was not working as hard as she had been and that there was a languidness about her, an air that pointed to 'indulgence in seeking pleasures'. She was clearly in love, and love made her do an extremely bold and dangerous thing that violated deeply entrenched dynastic precedent.

That year, Emperor Tongzhi, her son, was thirteen years old. Following tradition, Cixi started preparing for his wedding, which would signal his adulthood. The nationwide selection of his consorts was put in train in the spring. The wedding gowns were to be made by the royal dressmakers in Suzhou, the renowned silk centre near Shanghai. To this place, as famous for its beautiful canals and gardens as for its silk, Cixi dispatched Little An, to 'supervise the procurement'. This was unnecessary, as there was an established channel for the task. It was also unprecedented. No Qing emperor had ever sent a eunuch out of the capital on an errand. But all Cixi could think of was how excited Little An would be. He would get out of the Forbidden City, out of Beijing, and travel down the Grand Canal that linked north and south China. He could even celebrate his forthcoming birthday on the boat. Cixi would have loved the journey herself. She disliked the Forbidden City intensely, seeing it as a 'depressing' place with only walled-in courtyards and alleys. Heady winds from across the ocean that had been beating at the gates of the Forbidden City had also stirred up hitherto inconceivable aspirations.

In August, Little An set off in a party that included family members and other eunuchs. When he heard the news, Grand Tutor Weng wrote an alarmed entry in his diary, calling it 'a most bizarre thing'. Other grandees were similarly shocked, and then appalled, when it became known that Little An, with a sizeable retinue, was having a good time and attracting riveted attention. The public had never seen a eunuch before and were now greatly excited at the spectacle. When his barge appeared on the Grand Canal, crowds turned out to gape at him. The grandees were furious. When he got to Shandong, Governor

Ding Baozhen of the province, a stickler for established rules and practices, arrested Little An and the rest of the group. When Ding's report reached the court, Grand Tutor Weng exclaimed: 'How satisfying! How satisfying!'

All the grandees at the court said Little An must be executed, claiming that he had broken cardinal rules. Actually the young man had not broken any rule. The dynasty stipulated that eunuchs were 'forbidden to set foot outside the Royal City without authorisation'. But he had authorisation – from Cixi. What both of them had done was to break a tradition that imprisoned the eunuchs in the palaces. And this was unforgivable to the grandees. The man most insistent on the execution was Prince Chun, Cixi's brother-in-law, a like-minded friend of Grand Tutor Weng. They disapproved of so many things Cixi was doing, and this was the last straw. Even Prince Gong and his usually open-minded colleagues echoed the call for execution. Cixi, being an interested party, could play no part in the decision. Her friend, Empress Zhen, pleaded with the grandees, 'Can he be spared death on account of having served the Empress Dowager devotedly for so many years?' The grandees responded with a stony silence, which amounted to a resounding No. That settled it. A decree was written there and then, ordering Little An's execution on the spot.

To Cixi, it felt as though her world was collapsing. She managed to hold back the decree for two days, during which time she implored Empress Zhen to plead harder for Little An's life. But all efforts failed. Prince Chun arrived and pressured the women to release the decree instantly, probably warning Cixi that what she ought to do was distance herself from Little An, rather than otherwise. Empress Zhen was forced to allow the decree to be sent out.

Governor Ding was told to carry out the death sentence at once and not seek further confirmation from the court. Prince Chun and others were anxious that Cixi should have no more time to find a way to prevent it. Little An 'must not be allowed to defend himself with cunning explanations' and 'must not be interrogated' at all. It appears that the grandees suspected he had been having an affair with Cixi and wanted to cover up a scandal.

So Little An was beheaded. Also executed were six other eunuchs and seven hired bodyguards. Governor Ding reportedly had his corpse exposed on the execution ground for days, so the public could see that he had no male organs. Talk of his being Cixi's lover had been widespread. Back in the Forbidden City, Cixi ordered all Little An's belongings to be handed over to her and, once she got them, she gave them to one of her own brothers so that they were in the hands she trusted.

A close friend of Little An – another eunuch in the Forbidden City – complained to others that it was Cixi who had 'sent Dehai to his death' by first dispatching him out of Beijing and then failing to take responsibility. This remark hit a very raw nerve. In a fit of fury, she ordered the eunuch to be executed by strangulation. A chief secretary of the Grand Council, Zhu, wrote to a friend that the empress dowager was 'taking out her anger on the servants around her'. She was 'exuding bitter regret, brimming over with regret'. And, clearly hinting at her anger against Prince Chun, the chief secretary wrote that she was 'holding a deep hostility against some close princes and grandees' and 'refusing to be assuaged'.

Prince Chun and the other grandees not only killed Cixi's lover, but also sent out a warning about some of the startling changes she was introducing. Apart from giving eunuchs social status, she seemed to be allowing women to be seen publicly at a time when convention dictated they must stay in the home. (British diplomats found themselves assaulted with stones if there were ladies in their company, when otherwise they encountered bonhomie.) Little An had taken his sister, niece and some female musicians on the journey, and now they were all exiled to the northernmost wilderness to be slaves of the frontier guards. The grandees did not pursue Cixi herself. There was no wish to be rid of her. Her achievements had been monumental and were appreciated. Governor Ding said to his subordinates that her rule had brought China 'a boom, which has surpassed even the [glorious] dynasties like the Tang and the Song'. They were only warning her not to go too far. In any case, her retirement was in sight. Her son would take over after his wedding.

After all the executions were carried out, while Prince Chun and others expressed 'hearty delight', Cixi collapsed and was bedridden for well over a month. Unable to sleep, with ringing noises in her ears and her face badly swollen, she threw up constantly, often vomiting bile. Royal doctors diagnosed the Chinese equivalent of a nervous breakdown – 'the *qi* of the liver shooting upwards, in the opposite direction to the normal [downward] channel' – and kept vigil by her door. Among the medicines prescribed was blood of the Mongolian gazelle, which was said to reduce swellings. Towards the end of the year, although she started working again, the vomiting continued. This level of physical reaction was most unusual for her: after all, she was no shrinking violet; she had coolly brought off a coup without the smallest sign of physical or emotional stress, even though she was risking death by a thousand cuts. Now, it seemed, her heart had been wrung. Only love could wreak such havoc.

Her son prayed for her and visited her devotedly. But the child could not console his mother. She was inconsolable. Only music soothed her. For nearly a decade she had not been able to enjoy it as much as she would have liked. First, after her husband's death, in accordance with court rules, all entertainments had been banned for two full years. When that period was up, general pressure compelled Cixi to prolong the ban for another two years, until he was entombed. Even then, operas were only staged in the Forbidden City on a few festive occasions. Now, as if in defiance, Cixi had operas put on daily, and almost non-stop music played in her quarters. In her sick bed, with music to drown her sorrows, a thought churned: how to punish the man who had pressed most fiercely for Little An's execution and who was the leader of the baying pack – her brother-in-law, Prince Chun.

The executions of Little An and his companions were enough to put Cixi off taking a lover ever again. The cost was too high. It seems that her heart was now closed. The modernisation of China also suffered and was largely suspended in the coming years as she picked her way through a minefield.

8 A Vendetta against the West
(1869–71)

Prince Chun had been Cixi's earliest and staunchest ally when she launched the coup nearly a decade earlier. His motive had been to oust a group of incompetent fools whom he blamed for the empire's defeat and his emperor brother's death. Unlike Cixi, he had no intention of changing policy, but instead wanted the country to become stronger so that it could one day avenge itself on the Western powers. His support for Cixi in the coup, and his cooperation with her over the years, had been based on the assumption that this was also what she wanted.

But as the 1860s passed, Prince Chun began to see that revenge was not on Cixi's agenda and that she was actually attracted to Western ways. When, after the internal rebellions were quelled, many called for the expulsion of the Westerners, she had ignored them. At the beginning of 1869, Prince Chun decided he must act and presented Cixi with a memorandum. Reminding her of the burning of the Old Summer Palace and the death of her husband in exile, he wrote that the late emperor had 'died with an acute grievance in his heart', a grievance that was still tormenting the prince, making him feel he could not 'live under the same sky as the enemy'. Brushing aside the compelling fact that trade with the West had enriched the country, he demanded that she expel all Westerners and close China's door. Six things had to be done, he said. One was to boycott foreign goods, so that Westerners would have no incentive to come to the country; and he asked the court to set an example by publicly destroying all Western products in the palaces. The Foreign Office should compile a list of all the foreigners in Beijing, so that when the time came to break off relations, they could be 'wiped out' if need be, a job for which he volunteered his services. The prince wanted Cixi to 'issue a decree to all provincial chiefs telling them they are to encourage the gentry and the people . . . to burn foreign churches, loot foreign goods, kill foreign merchants and sink foreign ships', stressing that these actions must take place simultaneously 'in all provinces'. Ending his long memo, Prince Chun told Cixi bluntly that she 'must fulfil the dying wish' of her late husband, and that she 'must not let a day go by without thinking about revenge, never forget it for a minute'.

Cixi did not want to tie the empire to the chariot of retribution. 'Even if we do not forget the grievances for a day . . . grievances don't get addressed by killing people or burning houses,' she reasoned. She sent Prince Chun's memo to the grandees for discussion. They were all startled by the violence of his proposal, and told Cixi to keep it as 'top of all top secrets', not to be leaked out. To Prince Chun they made emollient noises, praising his sentiment and condoning such measures as shunning Western goods in the Forbidden City (except 'useful items like clocks and guns'). But they made clear that they opposed the aggressive thrust of his proposal, on the grounds that it could lead to war with the West, which China could not win. Sullenly Prince Chun accepted the grandees' verdict. But he was far from convinced.

It was soon after this exchange that Prince Chun insisted on the execution of Little An. Cixi was in no doubt that he was striking at her politically as well as personally. While she was waiting for her chance to hit back, Prince Chun plotted *his* next move.

At the time, the meeting of Western and Chinese cultures had resulted in many clashes. While Westerners branded China as 'semi-civilised', the Chinese called Westerners 'foreign devils'. But the focus of animosity was the Christian missions, which had established themselves in many parts of the country in the past decade. There had been riots against them from time to time, which had acquired a specific term in the language: *jiao-an*, 'cases to do with Christian missions'.

These did not spring from religious prejudice. As Freeman-Mitford, the attaché in Beijing, observed, the Chinese did not have strong religious antipathies:

> If it were otherwise, how is it that a colony of Jews has dwelt among them unmolested for two thousand years, and still remains . . . at Kai Feng in the province of Ho Nan? How is it that the

Mohammedans have flourished exceedingly in certain provinces . . .? On the walls of the Imperial palace at Peking there is a pavilion richly decorated with Arabic inscriptions from the Koran in honour of a Mohammedan lady who was a wife, or favourite, of one of the emperors. This does not look like persecution for religion's sake. And, more than these . . . Buddhism has been the popular religion . . .

Christianity was regarded as a teaching that 'persuades people to be kind': *quan-ren-wei-shan*. Even anti-Christian rioters were not averse to the doctrine. Their anger was directed at the missions themselves. Being foreign was always a cause for suspicion, but the major problem was that the missions had become a competing authority at the grass-roots level. There, local officials traditionally exercised absolute authority over all disputes and dispensed justice – or injustice – according to their judgement. The English traveller Isabella Bird once sat outside the gate of a county chief's office, the *yamen*, and observed its workings:

In the hour I spent at the entrance of the *yamen* of Ying-san Hsien 407 people came and went – men of all sorts, many in chairs, but most on foot, and nearly all well dressed. All carried papers, and some big *dossiers*. Within, secretaries, clerks, and writers crossed and recrossed the courtyard rapidly and ceaselessly, and *chai-jen*, or messengers, bearing papers, were continually despatched. Much business, and that of all kinds, was undoubtedly transacted.

The arrival of missionaries, backed by gunboats, introduced a new form of authority into society. In the numerous disputes, ranging from conflicting claims of ownership of water sources or properties to long-standing clan feuds, those who felt they did not or could not get justice from the local officials often sought protection from the church by becoming converts. In such a situation, a Chinese Christian might go to the priest, as Freeman-Mitford wrote:

swearing that the charge brought against him is a mere pretext, his profession of the Christian faith, in which he is protected by treaty, being the real offence. Full of righteous indignation and confidence in the truth of his convert, who, being a Christian, must necessarily be believed before his heathen accuser, the priest rushes off to the magistrate's office to plead the cause of his protégé. The magistrate finds the man guilty and punishes him; the priest is stout in his defence; a diplomatic correspondence ensues, and on both sides the vials of wrath are poured out. How can a priest who interferes, and the mandarin who is interfered with, love one another?

Some angry grass-roots officials therefore encouraged hostilities against Christians. The resentment was also fuelled by genuine misunderstandings. A major one concerned missionary orphanages. In the Chinese tradition only abandoned newborn babies were looked after by charitable institutions, registered with local authorities. Orphans and foundlings were the responsibility of their relatives, whose treatment of the children was their own business. It was incomprehensible to the Chinese that strangers should be able to take in boys and girls without the consent of their families and relatives, who were not even allowed to visit them, let alone take them away. This practice roused the darkest suspicions. Rumours abounded that missionaries kidnapped children and used their eyes and hearts as medical ingredients, or in photography – a mysterious phenomenon at the time. Isabella Bird wrote:

> Stories of child eating were current, and I am sure that the people believe that it is practised by the missionaries . . . I observed that when we foreigners entered one of the poorer streets many of the people picked up their infants and hurried with them into the houses; also there were children with red crosses on green patches stitched on the back of their clothing, this precaution being taken in the belief that foreigners respect the cross too much to do any harm to children wearing the emblem.

In June 1870, an anti-Christian riot broke out in Tianjin, seemingly triggered by just such a rumour that an orphanage run by the Sisterhood of Mercy, attached to the French Roman Catholic church, was kidnapping children and gouging out their eyes and hearts for photography and medicine. Several local Christians, accused of the actual kidnaps, were beaten up by crowds before being delivered to the magistrate's office. Although they were all found to be innocent (one was in fact taking a child home from the church school), thousands of men still crowded the streets, and bricks were hurled at local Christians. The French consul in Tianjin, Henri Fontanier, rushed over with guards and fired a shot that wounded one of the magistrate's servants. The roaring crowd beat the Frenchman to death and then killed between thirty and forty Catholic Chinese, as well as twenty-one foreigners. In three hours of lynching, plunder and arson, orphanages, churches and church schools were burned down. Victims were mutilated and disembowelled, and foreign nuns were stripped naked before they were killed.

Cixi's policy regarding incidents involving Christians had always been to 'deal with them fairly': *chi-ping-ban-li*. She did not believe the 'child-eating' rumour, which had surfaced time and again in other areas and had invariably been proved false. In no uncertain language she condemned the murders and the arson, and ordered Marquis Zeng, then Viceroy of Zhili, whose office was in Tianjin but who was at the time absent and ill, to go and intervene at once and 'arrest and punish the ring-leaders of the riot, so justice is done'. A decree expressed sympathy for the Christian victims, refuted the rumours and told all provincial chiefs to protect missionaries. Prince Gong set extra sentries to patrol outside Westerners' houses.

Marquis Zeng quickly established that the rumour in Tianjin was groundless. He found that this riot seemed to be different from the usual story of local officials going along with an anti-Christian mob – something more sinister seemed to lie behind it. During the investigation it emerged that the rumour had started with one Commander Chen Guorui, 'Big Chief Chen'. Arrested rioters confessed that they had learned about the 'eyes and hearts' from the Big Chief, who, they believed, had the organs in his possession. Chen had arrived in Tianjin by boat several days before the riot, at which point the rumour began to spread. Blacksmiths started to sell arms, which was prohibited by Qing laws, and thugs and hooligans were in and out of the Big Chief's dwelling, a temple-inn. On the day of the riot, crowds were assembled from street to street by men beating gongs. When the regional Imperial Commissioner, Chonghou, tried to prevent the mob from reaching the foreign settlement by having the pontoon bridge that led to it dismantled, Big Chief Chen ordered it reattached and, while the crowds were crossing, he called out to them from his boat: 'Good lads, wipe out the foreigners, burn their houses!' During the massacre, Chen, who had a foul temper and a habit of whipping underlings, was, by his own account, in the boat 'seeking pleasure with young boys'.

Big Chief Chen turned out to be a protégé of Prince Chun. After Chen was exposed, the prince wrote repeatedly to Cixi, telling her that 'I am extremely fond of this man and intend to use him for our cause against foreign barbarians.' Chen must be well treated, as all men of ideals in the empire would be watching what happened to him and would see whether the throne had any serious desire to 'avenge the country'. The mob must be 'encouraged', not punished, warned the prince. It was obvious that Chen had instigated the riot, and behind him stood Prince Chun.

It also became clear to Cixi that Prince Chun had intended the whole country to do as Tianjin did. During the massacre and its aftermath, unrest rippled throughout the empire, with the same eyes-and-hearts rumour circulating about the missionaries. In some places, posters were put up in the streets announcing that on a specified day all must come out to slaughter foreigners and destroy churches. Riots, though on a smaller scale, broke out in a number of cities. All this was exactly in line with the memorandum Prince Chun had sent Cixi a year earlier, and the conclusion was inescapable that the prince had taken it upon himself to put his scheme into action.

Realising Prince Chun's role, knowing how powerful he was and how popular his ideas were, Cixi became cautious. She had to refuse the demand to bring Big Chief Chen to justice from the French minister, who had learned about Chen's role from local Christians. To concede to the French demands would arouse unmanageable fury against her government and herself. There were already petitions calling for her to ride the wave of the Tianjin riot and ban Christian missions, destroy churches and drive out all Westerners. Grandees fumed against any punishment of the rioters, who were held up as heroes, admired by people like Grand Tutor Weng. Scenes of murder and arson were drawn on elegant fans and appraised by the literati as works of art. Marquis Zeng incurred much wrath for 'taking the side of the foreign devils' and was made to feel like an outcast. In front of the throne, in discussions about the riot, Prince Chun held sway, and no one dared to suggest that Big Chief Chen be punished. Arrogantly the prince denounced Cixi's government for having done nothing in the past ten years towards the goal of exacting retribution.

Cixi's position had already been drastically weakened by the Little An episode. Now she felt she had to ingratiate herself with Prince Chun by pretending to go along with him. She told him and the other grandees that she, too, regarded foreign barbarians as sworn enemies, but her problem was that her son was not of age and all she could do was keep things ticking over until he reached his majority. Perhaps feeling that she must use all her powers to charm and arouse sympathy, Cixi had the yellow silk screen removed and faced the grandees, quite possibly for the first time. Appearing appealingly helpless, she begged them to tell her and Empress Zhen what to do, as 'we don't have a clue'.

At this juncture, on 25 July 1870, Cixi's mother died. During her illness she had consulted not only Chinese doctors, but also the American physician Mrs Headland, who had become a trusted friend of many aristocratic families. Cixi sent people to her mother's house to pay last respects on her behalf, and prayed for her at a shrine that she had set up in her apartment. She arranged for her mother's coffin to be placed in a Taoist temple for a hundred days, during which time an abbot led a daily service. But she herself did not leave the Forbidden City. Security was much harder to guarantee in the Beijing streets. Perhaps some ominous instinct warned her. Around this time the court astrologer, who watched the stars and made interpretations in the European-equipped Imperial Observatory set up by the Jesuits, predicted that a major official would be assassinated. This was an extraordinary prediction, as assassinations were virtually unheard-of in Qing history. A month later, Viceroy Ma Xinyi was assassinated in Nanjing. He had exposed some rumour-mongers spreading false accusations against missionaries and had punished them. As a result he had prevented a Tianjin-like massacre in Nanjing.

Meanwhile, as the main victims of the Tianjin riot were French, including the consul, Henri Fontanier, French gunboats arrived and fired warning shots outside the Dagu Forts. War seemed to be inevitable. Cixi had to move troops and make preparations. Marquis Zeng, who had been sick, collapsed in a series of nervous fits and took to his bed. He wrote to Cixi: 'China absolutely cannot afford a war.' No one in the court, not even those who called most loudly for revenge, had any answer to the French show of force.

At this critical moment the man who gave Cixi most useful support was Earl Li, then the Viceroy of another region. (China was divided into nine viceroyalties.) He set off at once with his army to defend the coast, and produced practical advice on how to solve the crisis diplomatically. Convicted murderers must be executed, he counselled, but the number should be kept to a minimum in order not to inflame the population. The Foreign Office should explain to the legations who were pressing for the rioters to be punished that 'excessive executions would only create more determined enemies and would not be in Westerners' long-term interest'. Another argument he proposed for Beijing to say was that it understood that Westerners 'cherish the intention of treating ordinary Chinese with generosity and hold sacred the principle of not killing lightly'; it knew that missionaries preached kindness. 'All these sentiments ran counter to large-scale executions.' Appreciating his understanding of the West, Cixi made the earl the Viceroy of Zhili, which, being the region surrounding Beijing, was the most important viceroyalty. As the viceroyalty's capital was Tianjin, a Treaty Port inhabited by Westerners, the earl could deal directly with them. He was also, of course, close to Beijing. The earl succeeded Marquis Zeng who, after a long illness, died in 1872.

With advice from Earl Li, Prince Gong hashed out a conciliatory solution designed to satisfy the French while not further enraging the xenophobic Chinese. Twenty 'criminals' were sentenced to death and twenty-five were banished to the frontiers. Many of the men had no proper name – an indicator of the wretched lives they led. They were merely called 'Liu the Second Son', 'Deng the Old', and so on; the man heading the execution list was identified as 'Lame Man Feng'. On the day of the execution these men were feted like heroes by officials and bystanders alike, enjoying their only moment of glory. Two local officials who had been involved in the riots were punished, but only for dereliction ('not forceful enough in suppressing the mob') and were sentenced to exile to the northern frontiers. Their stay was short, as 'the whole empire is watching their fate', warned Marquis Zeng. As for Commander Chen, he was found to be 'totally innocent'. The mildest language was used in court correspondence about him, in case he should be riled.

Compensation was paid to the victims and to the churches for repairs. Chonghou, the official who had tried to protect the Westerners by having the pontoon bridge dismantled, was dispatched to France to declare Beijing's condemnation of the riot and to express its wish 'for conciliation and friendship'. This trip was (and is still) misrepresented as Cixi sending Chonghou to grovel. Prince Chun furiously denounced it.

France accepted this solution. It was at war with Prussia in Europe and could not embark on another in the East. The Chinese empire narrowly escaped a war.

Prince Chun was unrepentant about the crisis he had provoked and, sulking about the solution, claimed that he was suffering from 'sickness of the heart' and stayed in bed. There he wrote Cixi three long letters, trenchantly criticising her for not encouraging the Tianjin rioters and not getting people all over China to follow their example. She had let down her late husband, he implied. Cixi's response was all platitudes and avoided engaging with his point. Prince Chun would not let her off the hook: he immediately fired off a fourth letter, reiterating his accusation and alleging that, thanks to her, 'foreigners are running even more rampant'. He had noticed her evasiveness: 'What the decree says is not at all what I was talking about. There is not a word about the business of foreign barbarians. This is scary and worrying in the extreme.' Cixi was forced to address the issue, but she insisted that the expulsion of Westerners was 'not on the agenda' and China should still aim for 'peaceful co-existence with foreign countries'. Thanks to the support of Prince Gong and key officials like Earl Li, she managed to ignore Prince Chun.

The prince's bitterness continued to fester. At the beginning of the following year, 1871, he wrote again, going on and on complaining about the same thing: that Cixi was not seeking revenge against the West. Stopping short of denouncing her by name, he made Prince Gong and his colleagues the scapegoats and accused them of 'fawning over foreign barbarians'. The two half-brothers were not on speaking terms, while Cixi had to humour Prince Chun.

Obviously the prince was quite capable of instigating another Tianjin-style riot, which could well drag the empire into a catastrophic war. Yet Cixi was powerless to censure him. His anti-foreign stance was so popular with officials and population alike that to battle with him over this issue would be suicidal for Cixi. Prince Chun was thus a ticking time-bomb for the empire. As leader of the xenophobic faction, he was the main obstacle to Cixi's open-door policy; and, being the head of the Praetorian Guards, he was in a position to threaten her life. He had not done anything to her so far because, in addition to her being the emperor's mother and his wife's sister, it would not be long before her son assumed power and she returned to the harem. He would tolerate her for this short interim. But, for Cixi, the long-term safety of both the empire and herself meant that something had to be done about Prince Chun.

9 Life and Death of
Emperor Tongzhi
(1861–75)

A T the age of five Cixi's son, Tongzhi, was put on a rigid regime of formal schooling, which prepared Qing emperors and princes. He was moved out of his mother's quarters and started living in a separate dwelling. Most days he was in his study by 5 a.m., when teaching would begin. When he was carried over in a sedan-chair, the Forbidden City was still asleep, with a few servants moving about and occasionally leaning against pillars, dozing. The hand-held lanterns of his entourage would often be the only flickers of light in the darkness shrouding the alleys of the palace.

His tutors, by common consent, were of the highest repute in scholarship and morality and were approved and appointed by the Two Dowager Empresses. The curriculum focused on Confucian classics, which Tongzhi recited without comprehension. As he grew older, he understood more and learned to write essays and poetry. The syllabus also included calligraphy, the Manchu and Mongolian languages, plus archery and riding. Emperor Tongzhi did not take to the sacred Confucian texts like a duck to water. His main teacher, Grand Tutor Weng, moaned with immense exasperation day after day in the privacy of his diary: the emperor failed to concentrate, to read the texts out loud with any fluency, to write the correct characters – and he was always bored. When writing poetry, he showed little flair with ethereal themes such as 'Clear spring water flowing over a rock', although he seemed slightly more comfortable with topics to do with his royal duties, like 'On employing good people to govern the country well'. Cixi and Empress Zhen often enquired about his studies from the tutors. They were dismayed that the child seemed to 'get into a panic as soon as he sees a book', and they cried when this was still the case just before his assumption of power. They told his teachers simply to ensure a basic competence for his impending job, and Grand Tutor Weng reassured them that this would not be impossible, as the reports to His Majesty would not be as difficult as the classics, and his edicts would be drafted by other people. Then Cixi tested her son's ability in the context of an audience and discovered that he was unable to speak distinctly or coherently. Anxiously she urged the tutors to give him special coaching so that he was at least able to ask simple questions and give brief instructions.

One thing the emperor was interested in was opera, which his tutors regarded as an unworthy distraction: 'pleasure only to the senses'. He ignored them, and often even took part in acting. On such occasions he would put on make-up and perform in front of his mother, who did nothing to discourage him. As he was not a good singer, Tongzhi would play the parts that involved martial arts. Once, in the role of a general, he bowed to a eunuch who played the king. The eunuch hurriedly went down on his knees, whereupon he yelled, 'What are you doing? You can't do this when you are acting the king!' This made Cixi laugh. Emperor Tongzhi was also enthusiastic about Manchu dancing and would cheerfully dance for his mother.

He pursued other pleasures. In the emperor's early teens, Grand Tutor Weng noticed him 'giggling and fooling about' with his study companions. Once he seemed unable to control his giggles over a piece of the driest text, which greatly puzzled the tutor. 'How bizarre!' he exclaimed in his diary. But these were virtually the only moments when His Majesty seemed to have any energy; otherwise he tended to look exhausted and unable to rouse himself from listlessness. Once he owned up that he had not slept for quite a few nights. But he forbade his teachers to ask him what the matter was, and warned them sternly that no one was to say a word about this to his mother or Empress Zhen. Driven to his wits' end, Grand Tutor Weng even shouted at his royal pupil, but more often he confined his distress to his diary: 'What are we going to do! What are we going to do!'

The teenage emperor had tasted the joys of sex. The man who introduced him to this novel fun seems to have been a good-looking young scholar at court, Wang Qingqi, whom the emperor had taken a fancy to and installed in his study as his companion. Together they sneaked out of the Forbidden City to visit male as well as female prostitutes whenever they could.

While the emperor revelled in a wild boyhood, the court was preparing for his wedding. The process of selecting his consorts lasted nearly three years, interrupted by Little An's execution and Cixi's breakdown. By the beginning of 1872, before his sixteenth birthday, his consorts had been chosen – by the Two Dowager Empresses as well as by himself. The wedding was scheduled for later that year. Out of the hundreds of eligible young girls, a Miss Alute was designated to be empress.

A Mongol, this teenage girl was universally regarded by the elite families as an exemplary lady and peerless candidate. Her father, Chongqi, the only Mongol ever to come top in an empire-wide Imperial Examination, was an absolute devotee of Confucian values, which he instilled in the young mind of his daughter. She obeyed her father unconditionally, and could be depended on to be equally submissive to her husband. Perfectly mannered and very beautiful, she was also fluent in the classical texts, which her father had taught her himself. Empress Zhen set her heart on Miss Alute. So did Emperor Tongzhi himself. He had no wish to sleep with her, and he reckoned that she was someone who would tolerate that without a murmur of complaint.

Cixi had reservations. Miss Alute's maternal grandfather, Prince Zheng, had been one of the eight members of the Board of Regents formed by her late husband, and had been ordered to commit suicide after her coup, when she had sent him a long white silk scarf with which to hang himself. The man she had had beheaded, Sushun, who had hated her with a vengeance, was Miss Alute's great-uncle. Miss Alute's childhood had been marred by this family catastrophe, as her mother's family house, an elegant mansion famous in Beijing, had been confiscated according to the penal code, and the male members of the family had been barred from office. Underneath Miss Alute's impeccable conduct, her real feelings eluded Cixi. So she named another candidate, a Miss Fengxiu, saying that she liked the girl's quick wit. But eventually Cixi yielded to her son's pleading and accepted his choice: such was her love for him. She was willing to trust Miss Alute, and had faith that her father would not have put any unfit thoughts in her mind. After the matter was settled, Cixi ordered the confiscated mansion to be returned to Miss Alute's maternal family and restored the title to the male descendants.

The wedding followed the precedent set by Emperor Kangxi 200 years earlier in 1665, the last time that a ruling monarch married a girl chosen to be his empress. (Empress Zhen was not married as the empress; she was promoted to the position after she entered the court.) Although the occasion was called the 'Grand Wedding', *da-hun*, there was no nationwide celebration. It was only the business of the court. In the Forbidden City brightly coloured silk billowed around enormous red characters reading 'double happiness': *xi*. A similar display of silk was sported in the bride's mansion, particularly on top of the red pillars flanking the gate. From there to the Forbidden City, a route of several kilometres was selected for the bride to take: the dusty, rutted streets were made even and sprinkled with yellow soil, as required for a royal procession.

Along this route, every morning for a week before the marriage, porters in red tops with white spots carried the bride's trousseau to her new home: large cabinets as well as small jade dishes, practical hardwood washbasin stands as well as intricate pieces of art for connoisseurs. The smaller articles were displayed on yellow textile-covered tables, secured by stripes of yellow-and-red silk. To catch a glimpse of this exhibition of imperial house-furnishings, Beijing residents came out in droves at dawn, lining both sides of the route. This was their only involvement in the event. One morning, as the objects being carried were particularly precious, for security's sake the procession started before daybreak in order to miss the sightseers. After waiting in vain, they dispersed reluctantly, grumbling. Also disappointed were those who hoped to watch the training of the bridal chair-bearers. As the bearers must carry the chair perfectly steadily, and relieve each other quickly and without a jolt, they practised by carrying a vase filled with water inside the chair. But for some reason the chair never came out at the announced time.

The imperial astrologer selected 16 October 1872 to be the wedding day. Some time before midnight, under a full moon, Miss Alute was collected from her home by a large procession. She was dressed in a splendid robe embroidered with the pattern of a dragon (the emperor) and a phoenix (the empress) intertwined. A piece of red brocade of the same pattern was draped over her head. The road was empty. The few dogs that were running up and down, and the guards along the way, were the only ones permitted to gaze at this imperial pageant. The population had been told to stay away, and those who lived by the road were cautioned to stay indoors and not look out. At junctions where the royal route was joined by alleyways, blinds in bamboo frames had been erected to shut out any chance of a view. Foreign legations were told two days earlier that their nationals must keep within their own houses at this time – a request that generated outbursts of anger and frustration. What was the point of a grand state occasion, they asked, if nobody was going to see it?

Among the few people who did see it surreptitiously was an English painter, William Simpson, who sneaked into a shop on the route with a missionary friend. The shop was full of customers smoking opium, who took no notice of the foreigners, or of the royal to-do. The windows were made of thin paper, pasted over wooden frames, and could easily be poked through. Passing in front of the hole were princes and noblemen on white horses, preceded and followed by hoisted banners, canopies and giant fans. They appeared somewhat ghost-like in the dark, deserted Beijing streets, illuminated only by dimly lit paper lanterns, some hung and others hand-held. Even the moon was veiled by clouds, as if obeying the imperial directive. Silence accompanied the slow-moving column.

It was not a cheerful event, and could even be described as desolate. But this was thought to be what solemnity was all about. In this atmosphere, at a few minutes after midnight, Miss Alute, in her heavily gilded sedan-chair borne by sixteen men, crossed the threshold of the southernmost, front gate of the Forbidden City. She was the first woman in 200 years to go through this gate and enter the front section of the Forbidden City, which was off-limits to all women except the empress bride on her wedding day. Neither Cixi nor Empress Zhen had ever been there.

With this rarest honour, Miss Alute sat demurely, holding two apples. Inside the Forbidden City, when she got out of the sedan-chair, a prince's wife took the apples from her and placed them under two bejewelled saddles outside the door to her wedding chamber. The word for 'apple' contains the sound '*ping*', and the word for 'saddle' the sound '*an*'. Two apples and two saddles, '*ping-ping an-an*', alluded to the ever-present good wish: 'For safety and peace'. This seems almost too mundane to befit a new empress. And yet Miss Alute would step over those symbol-laden objects and enter her chamber, to find neither.

On that wedding night, when all the rituals were over, encased in a room decorated overwhelmingly in red, facing the giant character that means 'double happiness', the bridegroom made the bride recite Tang-dynasty poetry instead of making love. After this obligatory night together, he spent his nights in a separate palace a long way from her and his harem. Miss Alute felt it was her duty to go and offer herself to her husband, but he waved her away, and she – shy and having learned not to contradict him – dutifully left.

Miss Fengxiu, Cixi's preferred choice, was made the No. 2 consort. Just before the wedding day she was carried into the Forbidden City through the back gate, in a small sedan-chair borne by just four men with a tiny procession. The almost shabby ceremony had been prescribed for a concubine. She and another three imperial concubines fared no better than the empress, so far as their husband's affection was concerned. All five women were condemned to a life of loneliness.

After the wedding, in a ceremony on 23 February 1873, Emperor Tongzhi formally assumed office. He was sixteen. To be an absolute monarch so young was not unusual. Bizarre as it might seem, the first two emperors of the Qing dynasty, Shunzhi and Kangxi, took over the running of the empire at the age of thirteen. Emperor Tongzhi's assumption of power was also a court affair, like his wedding. The people at large learned about it from the imperial declaration, in a scroll lowered from the Tiananmen Gate, copied and distributed throughout the empire, in the same manner as the emperor's earlier coronation. From now on this teenager, and he alone, would make all decisions relating to the empire. As he would now write with his crimson-inked brush, the seals that had been stamped on decrees by the Two Dowager Empresses were no longer used. The yellow silk screen behind which Cixi and Empress Zhen had been sitting was folded away and they retired into the harem.

The emperor was determined to be worthy, and vowed to Grand Tutor Weng that he would 'not be lazy or negligent' and would 'not let my ancestors down'. The tutor was overjoyed. For about a year the young man was as good as his word, reading reports, authorising edicts and giving audiences. But he had none of his mother's initiative. His crimson-inked instructions were brief and routine. Cixi stuck to the rules and did not intervene in her son's work. There were no further projects, or attempts to modernise the empire.

There was one exception. Western legations had been requesting an audience with the throne to present their credentials ever since they entered Beijing. Hitherto, they had been told it was out of the question: the emperor was a child, and the Two Dowager Empresses, being female, could not be seen. The day after he took control, the legations sent a collective note applying for an audience. Furthermore, they insisted on seeing the emperor without going down on their knees and kowtowing. While Lord Macartney had reluctantly done so in 1793, for the sake of his trade mission, the second British envoy, Lord Amherst in 1816, had refused to go. Now the legations pooled their weight and demanded a kowtow-free audience. Most court officials were equally uncompromising, insisting that the kowtow had to be done.

Cixi had already made her decision on this issue: the envoys did not have to kowtow. A few years earlier she had discussed the matter with a small circle of open-minded officials like Prince Gong, Marquis Zeng and Earl Li, and they had all agreed that they could, and should, compromise. Emperor Tongzhi did what his mother told him to do. On 29 June 1873, he received the legation ministers without them kneeling, let alone touching their heads on the ground. This was a historic moment. The ministers stood, took off their hats and bowed at each stage as they advanced towards the throne. The dean of the diplomatic corps delivered a speech offering congratulations, and Emperor Tongzhi's response of goodwill was spoken by Prince Gong. The whole thing was over in half an hour. The court made no public announcement, not wanting to draw attention to the absence of the kowtow. Among those who heard about it, Grand Tutor Weng was troubled. Some, angered that the emperor had apparently succumbed to Western pressure, vowed to avenge this slight in the future.

Apart from this one tricky matter, the bureaucracy ran automatically. Traditional Chinese administration was a well-oiled machine, which, barring a crisis, would keep ticking over. Initiatives were not required and rarely offered. State policies depended almost entirely on the dynamism of the throne. While Cixi was full of innovative ideas, her son was entirely lacking in them. Nor was there any particular impetus for change. Cixi had brought peace, stability and a degree of prosperity to the empire. There was no peasant rebellion, or foreign invasion.

Nevertheless, even as a purely bureaucratic emperor, Tongzhi had at least to be hands-on, in order for the machine to run smoothly. Yet he grew tired of it. The tall, good-looking and fun-loving teenager stayed in bed later and later. The number of audiences decreased, until he saw just one or two people a day, and each time asked only a few stock questions. The ever-flowing reports often went unread and he would simply write on them the standard 'Do as you propose', whether there was actually a 'proposal' or not. Realising this, the ministries did as they saw fit, and the administration became lax.

This state of affairs had already disquieted the grandees when the emperor decided to rebuild part of the Old Summer Palace. He had visited the ruins with his mother and had been dejected by the sight of the remains of the formerly glorious buildings covered in weeds. In autumn 1873, he wrote an edict by hand, announcing his intention to restore the place, at least partially. The reason he gave was that the Two Dowager Empresses needed a home for their retirement. Some felt this was reasonable: Prince Gong donated 20,000 taels of silver towards the cost. Cixi gave enthusiastic support. The restoration was her dream. She longed to live there again. With her characteristic energy and attention to detail, she threw herself into the project, interviewing managers and architects, approving designs and mock-ups, even drawing some interiors herself.

The construction began the following spring, and the emperor inspected the site often, urging the builders to speed up, especially with his own quarters, so that he could move in, even before the dowager empresses. In fact, what the young monarch wanted most was a place where he would be free to pursue his sexual adventures. While he grew negligent with his royal duties, it was widely known that he spent his time 'revelling and frolicking with eunuchs'. He continued to sneak out of the Forbidden City in disguise to visit disreputable establishments. The Forbidden City was extremely inconvenient to him, as its gates had to be closed at sunset, after which not even the emperor was allowed out without a proper reason. At closing time, the duty eunuchs would cry out the 'sunset call' in their high-pitched voices, at which the heavy gates would be pushed shut one by one and locked with a loud clank. The immense compound would then fall into total silence, with only the occasional faint sound of the tap-tap-tap of the night watchmen's bamboo blocks as they did their rounds in the Beijing streets. Noiselessly, a club was passed from hand to hand by the sentries along the walls of the Forbidden City, to make sure that no guard was asleep or missing and that there were no gaps in the patrols. Emperor Tongzhi dreaded those sunset calls and tightly shut gates. The numerous immutable rules governing the emperor's life – from being woken up at the prescribed time to being shadowed by note-takers recording his every move – were a permanent irritation. He wanted the Old Summer Palace as a refuge. Vast, with no solid wall encircling it, this was the place where he could lead the life he wanted.

Very soon, however, a chorus of opposition burst out. This followed a tradition of reprimanding the monarch if he was seen to be indulging in excessive pleasure-seeking or embarking on an inordinately expensive undertaking. Petitioners pointed out that the country was not prosperous enough, and the Ministry of Revenue presented the emperor with a balance sheet which showed that the project was beyond the state's means. The emperor's uncle, Prince Chun, told him that the Old Summer Palace must only be a reminder of his father's death and of his duty to avenge him. But Emperor Tongzhi was set on fun, rather than revenge. He ignored his uncle, and threw the report from the Ministry of Revenue back at the prostrating minister. This was not a monarch who listened to his critics, and he wrote in crimson ink denouncing the petitioners, charging them with trying to prevent him from fulfilling his filial duties – a serious sin, according to Confucian ethics. Adopting the air of holding the moral high ground, the emperor fired one official 'as a warning' and told the rest 'there will be punishment for those who bring up the matter again . . .' Eventually Prince Gong, who had come to recognise that the project was not feasible, put his name to a petition entreating his royal nephew to change his mind. The young man snapped at him: 'Perhaps you want me to give up my throne to you!' One Grand Councillor, prostrating himself on the floor, was so shocked by the emperor's reaction and wept so hard that he passed out and had to be helped away.

Amidst the confrontation over the rebuilding of the Old Summer Palace, His Majesty's general lifestyle was raised disapprovingly, including his obsessive love of opera, his neglect of state duties and, in particular, his nights out in disguise. Tongzhi demanded to know from his two uncles who had been telling tales. Prince Chun cited the specific places of ill repute, and Prince Gong named his eldest son, who was a friend of the emperor, as a source of the information. In a fury, the emperor charged them with 'bullying' him, along with other accusations that amounted to high treason. The two princes kept knocking their heads on the floor, but it did nothing to reduce the emperor's wrath, and he penned a crimson-ink edict, stripping Prince Gong and his son of their titles, sacking Prince Gong from all his posts and placing him under guard in the Department of the Nobles. Another edict fired Prince Chun.

Luckily for the grandees, the emperor's mother was on hand. The grandees wrote to Cixi, imploring her to intervene. She came to her son's office with Empress Zhen and told her son to heed the majority. Tearfully she reprimanded him for his treatment of Prince Gong. While she talked, the young emperor stood and listened, and went down on his knees when his mother's rebuke became emotional. The emperor was obliged to show submission to his mother, according to the traditional code. He also loved her. All the sacking orders were rescinded – and Cixi had to abandon her dream of moving into the Old Summer Palace.

Emperor Tongzhi was unwilling to give up his sexual pursuits outside the Forbidden City and set his heart on the Sea Palace next door. Dominated by a vast man-made lake, this large estate housed no grand palaces, but quite a few temples and buildings of architectural distinction, screened off only by symbolic walls. The living quarters had fallen into disrepair as Emperor Tongzhi's father and grandfather had been hard up. The grandees agreed to the refurbishment, and work started straight away. The emperor became very attached to the place, and continued to visit it as summer turned into winter, until one day when he was out on the lake and caught a cold.

The emperor also caught something much more serious. His medical records from the Royal Clinic show that, on 8 December 1874, rashes appeared on his skin. The next day, doctors diagnosed smallpox. The diagnosis and the prescriptions were circulated among the Grand Councillors. Herbs and other ingredients were mixed and brewed, into which were added special items such as earthworms, which were considered useful in extracting poison. The doctors tasted the brew first, then eunuch chiefs did the same. The court began to observe all the rituals associated with smallpox. The way the Chinese dealt with a deadly force was – and in some ways still is – to appease it, even to put it on a pedestal, in the hope that it would be mollified and would leave them alone. So smallpox was ingratiatingly called 'heavenly flowers', *tian-hua*, and the emperor was said to be 'enjoying the heavenly flowery happiness'. Courtiers put on floral gowns, wore red (the colour of joy) silk scarves, and set up shrines to worship the Goddess of Blisters, the lady supposedly responsible for the pus-filled spots. On the ninth day of the illness, the blisters showed signs of maturity and release. The inner circle was invited in to see His Majesty.

By the side of the royal bed stood Cixi and Empress Zhen, with candles in their hands. They asked the grandees, on their knees some distance away, to come closer. The sick teenager lay with his face towards them and raised an arm for them to inspect. They saw, as Grand Tutor Weng described, that 'the flowers are extremely dense, from which his eyes are barely visible'. After a while they retreated from the chamber and were then summoned to the audience hall, where Cixi spoke to them at length. She was distraught and burst into sobs as she spoke. She said that her son might need some relaxation during his recovery, and if 'occasionally' he wanted music performed, she 'trusted' the grandees 'would not object'. With these words of obvious reproach, the grandees repeatedly banged their foreheads on the floor.

Cixi then discussed state affairs with them. Because he had been unable to work, she said, the emperor had grown anxious during recent days. He wished the grandees to find a solution. They proposed that the Two Dowager Empresses take charge, while the emperor was 'enjoying the happy event'. They then left to draft a petition to that effect. But Cixi had second thoughts; she recalled the grandees and told them to stop writing. It had occurred to her that a 'petition' might give the impression that the emperor was being asked to relinquish power. She decided that the request should come from her son, who, after she spoke to him, said that he was only too happy for her to step in. The following day, he summoned the grandees and, appearing to have more energy than the day before, told Prince Gong in a firm voice: 'I just have a few words to say. There mustn't be a day when state affairs are not taken care of. I plan to beg the Two Dowager Empresses to deal with all the reports on my behalf, and I myself will do my duty as before after this happy event . . .' Cixi then told him that the grandees had already 'requested' the same plan the previous day: everyone was of the same mind, so the emperor should stop worrying. The grandees left, feeling relieved and delighted that the reins of power were once again in Cixi's hands.

On the sixteenth day of the illness, the scabs on the young man's body began to flake off, and it seemed that he would be all right. The big shrine for the Goddess of Blisters that had been set up in one of the grand halls was lifted in an elaborate ceremony and, accompanied by a large brigade of guards of honour, was carried out of the Forbidden City.

But Emperor Tongzhi did not recover. His sores grew big and burst, suppurating unstoppably. On 12 January 1875, he died, not yet nineteen years of age. He had ruled for less than two years. There is an allegation that Cixi poisoned him. This is groundless. Many suspect that he died of syphilis; as this disease has very similar symptoms to smallpox (it is sometimes called the 'big pox'), and as modern methods of diagnosis did not exist, nothing definitive can be established. It seems that the court itself was not sure, and did suspect that the emperor's lifestyle had something to do with his illness. Wang Qingqi, his companion, was banished from the court and was banned permanently from official employment. Punishments were meted out to eunuchs close to the emperor – from caning to exile to the frontiers.

Smallpox remained the most likely cause. It was endemic in the capital at that time, and Emperor Tongzhi's only sibling, the Grand Princess, died of it soon afterwards, on 5 February. When she was delirious, she murmured that her late father had called on her to accompany her brother.

The person who chose to accompany the emperor in death was his wife, Miss Alute. For a woman to take her own life upon her husband's death was deemed a most illustrious virtue. In towns and villages, triumphal arches celebrated them.* Miss Alute, who had been selected for her virtues, lived up to those expectations. According to some eunuchs, when her husband expired, her father had a food box delivered to her, and when she opened it and found it empty, she knew that he was telling her to starve herself to death. She did as told, and was hugely admired for being a worthy daughter to her father. She died seventy days after her husband, on 27 March.

Miss Alute's death has been widely blamed on Cixi. The Chinese have accused her of ill-treating her daughter-in-law and driving Miss Alute to suicide. Westerners have asserted that she was pregnant with an heir to the throne and that Cixi murdered her to secure power. Neither charge is based on any evidence (although Cixi may have been severe to Miss Alute). In fact, Miss Alute had come from a family who seem to have embraced suicide as the supreme demonstration of honour. Later on, when Western troops invaded Beijing in 1900 and forced Cixi to flee, the entire family of fourteen people took their own lives to show their loyalty.

For a hundred days from Emperor Tongzhi's death, weddings and entertainments were banned in the capital. Throughout the empire, men were forbidden to shave or to have their hair cut. (In earlier days, Emperor Qianlong had imprisoned officials who had infringed the prohibition during the period of mourning for his wife.) All the bells in Beijing temples both big and small tolled 30,000 times. Minutely detailed guidance was issued on who was to wear what style of mourning clothes. The Chinese in those days were arguably the most ceremonious people on Earth. A book containing 3,000 rules of etiquette was required reading for the literati. One of the cardinal rules was that until the late

---

* One concubine of this author's maternal grandfather took her own life by swallowing opium upon his death in the early 1930s, when this was still considered the height of conjugal loyalty, and a plaque was put up in her honour.

emperor was buried, no music was allowed at court. So the Forbidden City was hushed again, with subdued figures moving silently about, trailed only by echoes.

The ban on music at court lasted four years, during which time Emperor Tongzhi's mausoleum was constructed. The emperor had not built a tomb for himself: he had not been on the throne long enough to begin such a project. After his death, his mother dispatched Prince Chun and Grand Tutor Weng, together with a team of *feng-shui* masters, to choose an ideal burial spot for him. Meanwhile, his giant coffin stayed in a hall in the Royal City, for senior officials to file past to pay their respects. The coffin was made of a precious wood, painted forty-nine times in a golden colour, adorned with Buddhist symbols and lined with thirteen layers of brocade decorated with countless dragons.

On the outskirts of Beijing there were two compounds of mausoleums for the Qing emperors, one to the west of the city and one to the east. There had been a rule that an emperor's mausoleum must be in the same compound as that of his grandfather, not that of his father. As Tongzhi's late father lay in the Eastern Mausoleums, he should be buried in the Western. But Cixi, who was destined to be buried with her husband in the Eastern Mausoleums, wanted to be near her son, so she buried him there. The grandees expressed understanding of her feelings and raised no objection to this deviation from tradition.

Both mausoleum compounds were enormous, and were places of serene natural beauty, in the embrace of hills, streams and woods. Each mausoleum had an underground chamber and an above-ground edifice that was a replica of a palace in the Forbidden City. At the front were carved white marble pillars, with lofty, wing-shaped crowns. The most awe-inspiring feature of a mausoleum was its approach: a long, straight avenue lined with giant stone statues of elephants, lions, horses and other big beasts on a vast area of open land. But there was no such avenue leading to Emperor Tongzhi's mausoleum. The budget would not stretch to it. Cixi had to choose between spending money on the avenue or on importing hardwood for the coffin and the burial buildings. China was short of top-quality wood, and her late husband's mausoleum had had to make do with wood left over from his father's tomb. Cixi, who believed in life after death, wanted the best material for her son in the next world, so she decided to sacrifice the glory of the approach. She bought from overseas the most expensive hardwood, a special kind of *nan-mu*, which was said to be so dense that it would sink rather than float in water.

More than four years after Tongzhi's death his mausoleum was finally ready, and on a day in 1879, picked by the court astrologer as the most auspicious, he and his empress, Miss Alute, were laid side by side in the underground chamber. Their coffins were weighed down with hundreds of pieces of gold, silver, jade and assorted precious jewels. Under Cixi's meticulous care, the entombment ceremony was as grand as it had ever been, involving the entire upper echelon of the Beijing bureaucracy trekking 120 kilometres from the capital; 7,920 men took turns to carry the coffin, each shift comprising 120 men. They had been professionally drilled, and had bathed carefully, before donning purple jackets made of sackcloth, the prescribed material for serious mourning. All officials working within 50 kilometres of the route went to specially constructed memorial halls to greet the coffin, in prostration, when it passed by. Each memorial hall was illuminated by thousands of large white candles.

Although all this was following established precedent, Cixi painstakingly attended to every detail. She really loved her son. Many years later, on an anniversary of his death, the American painter Katharine Carl, who was in the court painting Cixi's portrait, wore black. She wrote that Cixi realised she was wearing the mourning colour of the West and 'seemed much touched'. She 'took my hand in both hers, and said, "You have a good heart to think of my grief and to have wished to sympathize," and tears fell from her eyes on my hand, which she held in hers.'

PART THREE

Ruling Through an Adopted Son (1875–1889)

10 A Three-year-old is Made Emperor
(1875)

CIXI was by her son's side when he died on that January evening in 1875. Just before his death, the grandees had rushed in, having been informed by doctors of the emperor's impending demise, and they had found him barely breathing and Cixi too choked with tears to speak. After staying for a while, they left the room, leaving the last moments to the mother and son. Shortly after the emperor's death was announced, while they were all still crying, they were summoned by the empress dowager, who wanted to make arrangements for the future.

The instinctive reaction of the ever-prudent Prince Gong was to stay away. Knowing Cixi, perhaps he sensed that her arrangements would be irregular, and he hesitated to be involved. But he nevertheless went in with the rest of the grandees. Cixi frankly asked them whether they thought it was a good idea for her and Empress Zhen to continue at the helm 'behind the screen'. One man immediately answered 'Yes': could the empress dowager please, for the sake of the empire, name a new emperor and continue to rule as before? At this Cixi declared, on behalf of Empress Zhen as well: 'The two of us have made our decisions and we are in complete agreement. We are now giving you our definitive word, which may not be altered or modified. Listen, and obey.' This tremendously forceful language came from a position of strength. Emperor Tongzhi had left no heir, nor had he left a will dictating who should succeed him. And, just before he died, he had asked the Two Dowager Empresses to run the empire. It was now up to them to designate the next monarch.

Cixi announced that the two of them would adopt a son for their late husband – and themselves – a child who would be raised by them. It was obvious that Cixi intended to rule the empire again as the dowager empress and to do so for as long as possible. The normal and correct thing to do would have been to adopt an heir for her late son. But if that were to happen, it would be hard for Cixi, the grandmother, to justify her rule. Emperor Tongzhi's widow, Miss Alute, was still alive at that time and she would have become the dowager empress. And yet Cixi's irregular arrangement roused no objection. Most welcomed her return to power. She had done an outstanding job prior to her son's accession. In contrast, her son's brief reign promised only disaster. Indeed, nearly all of them had been wilfully rebuked, and quite a few dismissed, by the late emperor, and who knew what would have happened if Cixi had not been around to bring him to heel. That she would be holding the reins again came as a huge relief – especially for the reformers, who had been frustrated by the stagnation of the last few years.

Then Cixi named the new emperor: Zaitian, the three-year-old son of her sister and Prince Chun.

Prince Chun was in the room, and the announcement, far from delighting him, sent him into a terrified frenzy. Kneeling in front of the throne, he fell into convulsions, howling and knocking his head on the ground until he passed out – a heap of court gown and underclothing. The boy was his only son at the time, and was treasured by him and his wife almost with desperation, not least because their previous son had died. It seemed that he was losing his only son for ever. Cixi, looking utterly unmoved, ordered that the prince be taken out of the hall. According to an eye-witness, 'he lay in a corner, with no one paying him any attention. It was a wretched and desolate scene.'

The Grand Councillors withdrew to draw up the imperial decree proclaiming the new emperor. Shaking with tension, the man designated to write it out could not hold the brush steady. Watching this, Junglu, the then Lord Chamberlain, a man who was fiercely devoted to Cixi, became so anxious that an objection might be raised before the job was done that he grabbed the brush and started to write the decree himself – which was absolutely improper, as he was not a Grand Councillor. Junglu, apparently, had helped Cixi make up her mind to name the new emperor immediately after her son's death, so as to give no one the opportunity to speak or act against her decision.

Nothing went wrong for Cixi. In no time the formalities of establishing a monarch were completed and a procession was dispatched to fetch the new emperor. Before the first rays of dawn, the three-year-old had been woken up, separated from his mother, wrapped in a heavy court gown, put into a sedan-chair with an official by his side, carried into the Forbidden City amidst lanterns and candles and made to kowtow to Cixi and Empress Zhen in a dark hall. He was then taken to the bed where the dead Emperor Tongzhi was lying, to perform the obligatory wailing, which he did quite naturally as his sleep had been disturbed. Thus began the new life of Emperor Guangxu, Emperor of 'the Glorious Succession'.

This was Cixi's moment of revenge on Prince Chun. For the anguish she had suffered over Little An's execution, she now twisted a knife into the prince's heart by taking away his only son. And she did it in such a way that Prince Chun could hardly complain: after all, his son was being elevated to emperor.

Making the son the emperor removed Prince Chun's political role. As the emperor's biological father, but not the official Regent, the prince was compelled to resign all his posts to avoid any potential accusation that he was using his influence to meddle in state affairs – a crime tantamount to treason. The prince offered his resignation at once, couching it in extremely humble language. Cixi told the grandees to discuss it, and Prince Gong forcefully recommended its acceptance. Among the reasons he gave was a protocol conflict. As an official, Prince Chun had to prostrate himself in front of the emperor, but as a father to his son this was out of the question. Grand Tutor Weng, a conservative ally of Prince Chun, saw that with the prince gone there would be no one to resist the reformers, and argued for the prince to retain one key post, that of head of the Praetorian Guards. Cixi rejected the suggestion and accepted Prince Chun's wholesale resignation. She did keep one job for him, one that did not have any real power: he was to look after the mausoleums of the Qing emperors. And, of course, she showered him with honours.

By depriving Prince Chun of any serious position, Cixi effectively silenced him. Any protest from him against her policies would now be deemed interfering in state affairs and would invite condemnation. Prince Chun was clearly alive to Cixi's intentions. Fearing she might go even further and find an excuse to charge him with high treason, he wrote her an abject letter, assuring her that he had no intention of meddling. Prince Chun was finished as the champion of the xenophobic camp. The ticking time-bomb for the empire was thus defused.

★

The prince was to suffer yet more personal tragedy. Cixi's sister gave birth to two more sons, but one lived for only a day and a half, and the other died after a few years, the victim of too much anxious love, according to the servants. The couple were perpetually worried that he might overeat – a major problem for children in rich families – and as a result the child suffered malnutrition.

To the prince's surprise, Cixi did not actually want to destroy him. Having demonstrated that she could have finished him off, she bestowed favours on Chun. She gave him concubines, and the prince was able to have three more sons; the eldest, born in 1883, was given his name – Zaifeng – by Cixi. She also made the prince the supervisor of the child emperor's education, to give him access to his son. The prince's wife, Cixi's sister, was invited to stay in the palace from time to time, so that she too could see him. Neither parent felt fully able to relax with the child, now that he was the emperor and had been adopted by Cixi. But her treatment of him was beyond Prince Chun's expectations and he was overwhelmed with gratitude.

Cixi won over the prince's friends as well, by showing them that she bore no grudge, and by skilfully buying them off. She made Grand Tutor Weng the chief tutor for the new child emperor, for which the tutor felt eternally grateful. And she gave Governor Ding, the man who actually had Little An executed, the promotions and honours due to him as if nothing untoward had happened. When the governor was promoted to Viceroy, he followed the Qing practice and went to Beijing for an audience. Before his arrival, through Junglu, the Lord Chamberlain, Cixi gave him 10,000 taels to help him with his expenses in the capital, where there was much obligatory entertaining and present-giving. Ding was short of money: as an uncorrupt man, he had not taken advantage of his official positions to make money for himself. Junglu presented the gift as coming from himself, but Ding, who was not a particular friend of his, understood where it had come from. He not only accepted it, but wrote and asked to 'borrow' another 10,000 taels – which Junglu readily delivered. This was the old man's somewhat mischievous way of sending the message that he knew Cixi was the donor (he would not have asked another official for more) and that he was striking a deal with her. Although both Ding and Grand Tutor Weng retained their conservative views, they never again made trouble for the empress dowager.

And so Cixi removed all obstacles and steered the empire back on the course that she had first charted. This time, she would speed up the pace of progress. During her forced seclusion in the harem, her mind had not been idle, and she had learned much about the outside world from the reports and diaries of the travellers she had sent on those early journeys. Western-style newspapers in Hong Kong and the Treaty Ports had grown in number and were available to the court, where they had become an indispensable source of information. Compared with a decade ago, when she first came to power, Cixi now had a much better understanding not only of the West, but also of modernity. She was convinced that modernisation was the answer to the empire's problems – and she also knew that much time had been lost. Since the deadly warning conveyed by the execution of Little An, through the whole reign of her son, the country had stood still for five years. She was determined to make up for lost time.

11 Modernisation Accelerates
(1875–89)

IN early 1875, Cixi lost a son, but regained power. The year became an extraordinary milestone, packed with ground-breaking events. The first thing she did was to summon Earl Li to discuss an overall strategy for modernisation. The earl, who was based in Tianjin, had requested such a meeting in 1872, but at the time, feeling vulnerable and about to retire, she had turned him down. Now she saw him the day after he arrived, then the following day, and then for a third time a few days later. Her eagerness to resume her course and to regenerate the country was palpable.

The earl had by now emerged as the foremost moderniser of the country. He had surrounded himself with Westerners and made friends with many of them. Among their number was former US president Ulysses S. Grant, and the two men saw a great deal of each other in Tianjin in 1879. The missionary Timothy Richard described the earl thus: 'Physically he was taller than most, intellectually he towered above them all, and could see over their heads to the far beyond.' The earl became the key man in Cixi's modernisation drive. He and Prince Gong, who headed the Grand Council, and whose name was to Westerners 'synonymous with Progress in China', were now the empress dowager's right-hand men. With their assistance, Cixi steadily, yet radically, pushed the empire towards modernity. As Earl Li wrote to Cixi, expressing their shared aspiration, 'From now on all sorts of things will be introduced into China, and people's minds will gradually open up.' They did not exclude the conservatives. Cixi's style was to work with people like Grand Tutor Weng as well as the reformists, always using persuasion rather than brute force, and being prepared to let time and reason change people's minds.

Cixi had wanted to send diplomatic representatives abroad a decade earlier. Now they were dispatched. On 31 August 1875, she announced her first appointment: Guo Songtao as the minister to London. Guo was an exceptionally forward-looking man who advocated learning from the West and adopting projects such as railways and telegraphs. He was furiously assailed by the conservatives. Grand Tutor Weng, in his diary, dismissed him as 'perverse', and the literati from his province who were in Beijing taking Imperial Examinations talked heatedly at their gatherings about going and tearing down his house. Cixi comforted him, seeing him three times with Empress Zhen before his departure. The two women repeatedly told him not to be deterred by ridicule and slander: 'everyone working in the Foreign Office is a target of abuse,' they said. 'But the throne knows and appreciates you . . . you must take on this difficult job for the country.'

While Guo was abroad, his diary recording his impressions was published by the Foreign Office. In it he described the British adoringly: their legal system was 'fair'; the prisons were 'exquisitely clean, with polished floors, without foul air . . . one forgets this is a prison'; and their manners were 'courteous', which alone, he asserted, 'shows that it is not by accident that this country is so rich and powerful'. He even suggested that China's 2,000-year-old monarchical system was not as desirable as British parliamentary monarchy. Although some of his remarks – for example, that Chinese manners 'fall far short, far, far short' – were deleted for publication, the first instalment of the diary excited teeth-gnashing hatred from literati-officials, who accused Guo of trying to 'turn China into a British subordinate' and called on the throne to penalise him. Publication of the diary was forced to halt. But Guo was not rebuked. Instead, Cixi made him minister to France as well as to Britain, disregarding conservative officials' protestations. When Guo conducted a very public row with his traditionalist deputy in London, she transferred the deputy to Germany. Eventually, unable to get on with other mandarins, Guo asked to resign, and she accepted. She told his successor, Marquis Zeng Jr, son of the late Marquis Zeng Zuofan, that she knew that Guo was 'a good man, and did a remarkable job'.

Cixi may not have agreed with all of Guo's views, but she

appreciated his independent mind. And her style was to work with people of different persuasions. Her minister to Berlin, Hung Jun, was quite the opposite of Guo. He disliked European customs, especially those to do with male–female association. Outside official duties, he preferred to shut himself in his residence, carrying on with his research on Chinese history, going out only for walks in the Tiergarten. The consort he brought to Berlin, a concubine who had been a high-class call-girl by the professional name of 'Prettier Than Golden Flower', yearned for parties, but was not allowed to attend, even when Hung gave receptions at home. She would dress up exquisitely, sashay demurely downstairs to greet her guests and then retire upstairs for the rest of the evening. When on rare occasions she stayed at a party, she was unable to dance – not only on account of her husband, but also because of her crushed and bound feet, which made it painful for her to walk or even stand. She remembered bowing to the Kaiser and the empress, and being paid compliments about her beauty by a glowing-faced, silver-bearded, piercing-eyed and courteous but distant Chancellor Bismarck – and that was all. She had also lost most of her servants, who had refused to cross the ocean with them, except for two who gritted their teeth for what they were certain would be a 'journey of no return', and who were paid fifty taels a month each – far more than the monthly income of an average official in Beijing, and ten taels more than the German maids she hired in Berlin. She remarked that the German maids were 'extremely considerate and very good at looking after people. They were more loyal and far more obedient than Chinese servants.'

But even Hung Jun could not remain entirely resistant to his new surroundings. At first, he indignantly refused to wear European socks. Then, the realisation that they were immeasurably more comfortable than the rough cotton ones he had brought from home dissolved his resolution. By the time he left Berlin, he had bought an ice-sledge as a gift for the empress dowager.

By the mid-1880s, with Cixi constantly urging 'no foot-dragging', Beijing had geared up to dispatch groups of officials to travel round the globe and study Western institutions and cultures with a view to reforming their own system. And when applicants had been sought from the ministries, many scores had eagerly put their names forward – a far cry from a decade earlier. Dealing with the West was no longer regarded as a hardship or as shameful. Jobs that involved associating with foreigners were now coveted. Contemporary diaries and newspapers exclaimed how much society had changed. Even the sacred Imperial Examinations that had underpinned the political and social structures for well over 1,000 years were experiencing their first signs of modernisation. The applicants for the trips were told to write essays for their exams on such subjects as 'the railway', 'defence', 'trading ports' and 'the history of China's interaction with Western countries since the Ming dynasty'. These were mind-expanding subjects that spurred people on to learn new things and think new thoughts. Some candidates found the transformation unsettling and struggled to square the new with the old. One claimed that the essence of chemistry and steam engines could be traced to the teachings of Mozi, one of the Confucian sages in fourth- to fifth-century BC.

One group of people enjoyed immediate benefit from the regime's active diplomacy: the victims of the slave-labour trade, which had started from the late 1840s. Mainly in Cuba and Peru, they numbered hundreds of thousands. In 1873–4, the Qing government had dispatched commissions to investigate their conditions. The commission to Cuba reported:

> 8/10ths of the entire number declared that they had been kidnapped or decoyed; . . . on arrival at Havana they were sold into slavery, . . . the large majority became the property of sugar planters; . . . the cruelty displayed . . . is great, and . . . unendurable. The labour, too, on the plantations is shown to be excessively severe, and the food to be insufficient; the hours of labour are too long, and the chastisements by rods, whips, chains, stocks, etc., etc., productive of suffering and injury. During the past years a large number have been killed by blows, have died from the effects of wounds and have hanged themselves, cut their throats, poisoned themselves with opium, and thrown themselves into wells and sugar caldrons [cauldrons].

In Peru, they were found to be treated equally appallingly. Beijing was in negotiation with the two countries in an attempt to protect the labourers when Cixi resumed power in 1875. She stressed to her nego-tiators, headed by Earl Li: 'You must find ways to make absolutely sure that such abuse of the Chinese is strictly prohibited and discontinued.' The subsequent conventions freed the slave labourers and banned the trade. Cixi appointed one of her best diplomats, Chen Lanbin, who had been the chief investigator in Cuba, to be the minister to America, Cuba and Peru, with the major responsibility for looking after the emigrants.

★

In 1875, efforts redoubled to build a world-class navy – mainly because China's neighbour, Japan, was becoming increasingly aggressive and had just tried to take the island of Taiwan. Cixi and her inner circle had registered the rise of Japan before her retirement in early 1873, as they watched it learning from the West, buying machines and gunboats, building railways and making weapons. Her court now discussed how best to deal with this 'biggest permanent threat', and Cixi approved four million taels of silver a year – a huge budget – to build up the navy. It was the time when ironclad warships had just been invented in Europe, and her edict on 30 May authorised Earl Li to 'purchase one or two', given that they were 'astronomically expensive'. In the years following the edict, two ironclads and a group of other warships were purchased. Young men were sent to France to learn how to manufacture them and to Britain to train as naval officers. Germany was the destination for army cadets.

Finally, in 1888, Cixi approved the Western-style Navy Regulations. It was in endorsing these Regulations that she effectively unveiled China's first national flag. The country had had no national ensign, until its engagement with the West at the beginning of her reign neces-sitated a triangular-shaped golden yellow flag for the nascent navy. Now she endorsed its change into the internationally standard quadrangular shape. On the flag, named the Yellow Dragon, was a vividly blue, animated dragon, raising its head towards a bright-red globe, the sun. With the birth of this national flag, remarked contemporary Western commentators, 'China proudly took her proper place among the nations.'

In the autumn of the momentous year of 1875, Robert Hart, the Ulsterman and Inspector General of Customs, was commissioned to write a memorandum aimed at a wholesale expansion of foreign trade. He did so, following the explicit instruction that 'he must bear in mind how all-important it is that his proposals should be advantageous and not harmful to China'. Soon, more ports, mainly along the Yangtze River into the heartland, all the way up to Chongqing, were opened to international trade. These doors were not wrenched open by force. Cixi's government opened them willingly, in response to a request from Thomas Wade.★ In Philadelphia, USA, a Chinese official partici-pated in the world Expo for the first time, with the brief to record

---

★ The opening up of these new ports was written into the same convention (the Chefoo Convention) as the settlement for the murder in Yunnan of Mr Margary, a member of the British Legation. But the British did not demand it with any threat of force.

and report back on all his experiences. Among the modern institutions introduced by Hart was the Chinese Post Office, which issued the country's first set of stamps, 'Great Dragons', in 1878.

The meaning of the old adage 'Make China Strong' was expanded to incorporate 'Make the Chinese Rich' (*qiu-fu*). It was now the consensus in Cixi's circle that 'China's weakness lies with its long-standing poverty' and it could only become wealthy through Western-style industrial projects. 'We must gradually adopt the same things, so we can get out of poverty and become rich as well.' These projects had been proposed by Hart and Wade a decade earlier – but then the ancient land had not been ready for them. All those journeys to the West had opened eyes and minds. In 1875, Cixi ordered the installation of the telegraph, first in Fujian province, for communication with Taiwan, the island that Japan coveted and Cixi was determined to keep. The Imperial Telegraph Administration was founded, with one of the country's pioneering modern businessmen, Sheng Xuanhuai, as its managing director. At first, crowds pulled down the wires and poles. But as people saw how harmless they were, how miraculous communication could be and how many benefits it could bring to their lives, sabotage stopped, and telegraph lines began to extend all over the empire.

Also in 1875, Cixi decreed the beginning of modern coal-mining, by designating two trial areas. Resistance was strong and the fears numerous – not least that China's underground treasures were about to be stolen by foreigners. Addressing this concern, Cixi ordered specifically: 'We must keep decision-making power in our hands when we employ foreign personnel. Don't let foreigners control everything and make crucial decisions for us.' One of the two sites was on the island of Taiwan and the other was Kaiping, some 160 kilometres to the east of Beijing. Western technicians soon arrived with machinery, and Cixi appointed another outstanding pioneering businessman, Tong King-sing, as managing director. Tong had acquired his expertise while working for Western firms, and had founded China's first merchant-shipping company. Tong and Sheng, together with other first-generation industrialists and businessmen, heralded the rise of the middle class, while Kaiping became 'the cradle of modern Chinese industry'. A giant industrial centre, Tangshan, grew from here. Outside these state projects, individuals were given incentives to look for outcrops and open mines. To solve funding problems and to encourage entrepreneurs, Cixi decreed that private businessmen should be allowed to issue shares.

With coal came electricity. Cixi led the way by having electric lights installed in the Sea Palace by 1888. Generators were bought from Denmark and operated by the Praetorian Guards. These were the first electric lights outside the Treaty Ports, and stimulated the spread of electricity. In the next few years, seventeen electricity companies for civilian as well as military and commercial use were founded in Beijing and other big cities. By 1889, Beijing had seen its first tram.

Cixi also set her heart on replacing the country's outdated currency, silver ingots, with manufactured coins. These ingots put China at a huge disadvantage in international trade: because their silver content varied, they tended to be valued too low. Only modern minting could solve this problem, as well as make the Chinese currency compatible with the outside world. It was no small undertaking, especially as it required a sizeable initial investment. Facing stubborn resistance, Cixi was adamant and offered to pay the start-up costs out of the royal household allowance. The project took off, with a proviso that it would be reviewed in three years.

The most conspicuous project that Cixi did not launch in 1875, or in subsequent years, was the railway. It touched on something akin to religion. The numerous ancestral tombs dotted across the country, all lovingly built by their families in accordance with *feng-shui*, could not be moved. Nor could they be left where they were, if they were near a railway line: people believed that the dead souls would be disturbed by the roaring trains. Cixi wholeheartedly believed that the tombs were sacrosanct.

There was also the problem of funding. For three years after Cixi returned to power, between 1876 and 1878, nearly half the Chinese provinces and up to 200 million people were hit by floods, drought and swarms of locusts – the biggest succession of natural calamities in more than 200 years and one of the worst in recorded Chinese history. Millions died of famine and disease, especially typhus. Traditional ways of coping with famines included the court praying for good weather, opening the royal purse, exempting affected areas from tax, and providing the Chinese equivalent of 'soup kitchens': 'rice centres'. Now unprecedented sums were spent on importing food from overseas. In such circumstances the building of railways would have had to rely on foreign loans, something Cixi had no experience of. She was cautious. 'We would have to borrow tens of millions,' she said. 'And we could land ourselves in trouble.'

To showcase the railway, British merchants built a 20-kilometre line from Shanghai to its outer port, Wusong, in 1876 – the first to come into service in China. Villagers and officials were aghast. One day, when a train was running, a group of men, women and children stepped onto the track and forced it to a halt. When the train moved off, the group grabbed at the carriages in a futile effort to stop it again. Another day a man was run over by the train, and it looked as though this might spark a riot. Thomas Wade persuaded the British company to stop the service. Cixi's government bought the railway and had it dismantled, to satisfy both parties. It is often claimed that Cixi stupidly had this – China's first railway – thrown into the sea. In fact, it was wrapped up and shipped across the straits to Taiwan, with the intention of using it at the coal mine there. The indigenous people of Taiwan did not feel as strongly about their tombs as the mainland Chinese, and because the island was less densely populated, there were fewer tombs anyway. As it happened, the line was unsuitable and had to be shipped back to the mainland, in the hope that it might be used at Kaiping. Here, again, the area that the railway would cross was relatively barren and sparsely populated, with few tombs. It was only because Kaiping's English chief engineer, Claude W. Kinder, decided, far-sightedly, to adopt the standard gauge that the Wusong line, with its narrow gauge, was finally left to rust.

After the Kaiping line was laid, 10 kilometres long, some concern was expressed that the few dead souls in the vicinity might be disturbed. So the train was pulled by horses. Then, cautiously, the horses were replaced by a locomotive, built locally under the supervision of Kinder and named 'The Rocket of China'. Opposition went on and off, and finally died down.

But whether or not to build a more extensive system in China remained the most difficult decision for Cixi. For more than a decade she repeatedly invited debates among the elite. Views were sharply divided, and the usually decisive empress dowager was uncharacteristically hesitant. All the arguments in favour, championed by Earl Li, about how the railway would be good for defence, transportation, travel and communication, were not enough to convince her that a core belief of the population should be violated; or that the country should risk potentially crippling loans from the West.

In the end, Cixi decided to try the train herself. In 1888, she bought a train with six carriages and a 3.5-kilometre line from a French company, to be installed inside the Sea Palace. The whole thing, including packing and shipping, cost 6,000 taels, a fraction of the real price. Western manufacturers were competing with each other to win

Chinese contracts, and years earlier Britain had offered a similar train as a wedding present to her son, a gift that had been declined. Now Earl Li supervised the purchase. He reported to Cixi that while the price was symbolic, everything was beautifully made in Paris, including a most luxurious carriage for her. The railway was laid with the guidance of a court *feng-shui* master, who dictated when the construction could start and in which direction it should proceed. Digging towards the north, he said, was out of the question for that year, and so the northbound section had to wait until the tenth day of the first month of the following year, 1889. On that day, ground was broken between 3 and 5 p.m. When the line was operational, Cixi took a ride and got the feel of a real train, if only for a few brief moments. She tasted the speed and the comfort of travelling, although she also saw the black smoke and heard the clanking engine. The train was stored away, only to be taken out to show visitors; and, on those occasions, eunuchs pulled the carriages, using long yellow silks twisted into ropes.

Around the time of this personal experience, in April 1889, Viceroy Zhang Zhidong put forward a unique and powerful argument that finally made up Cixi's mind in favour of a railway network. The Viceroy, two years Cixi's junior at fifty-two, a short man with a long, flowing beard, was a major promoter of modernisation. Western contemporaries called him 'a giant in intellect and a hero in achievement'. Cixi had first noticed him years earlier, soon after her coup, during an Imperial Examination. His final essay, on current affairs, was bold and unconventional and had disconcerted the examiners, who slotted him at the bottom of the 'pass' grade. But when Cixi read the essay, she recognised a like-minded spirit and upgraded him to No. 3 of the whole empire. Over the years she adopted many of his proposals and promoted him to key posts, now a Viceroy governing two crucial provinces in the Yangtze Valley.

The Viceroy's clinching argument was that the railway could bolster exports, which, he pointed out, were the key to enriching the population and the country in the era of international trade. At the time, the main exports from China remained tea and silk, while imports were rising steeply, due largely to the modernising projects. The country's trade deficit stood at more than thirty-two million taels in 1888; and the future looked worrying, as the quantities of tea exported had begun to fall. In 1867, China had supplied 90 per cent of the Western world's consumption, but now teas from British India and elsewhere had entered the global market. It was imperative that the range of exports was expanded. With this need in mind, Viceroy Zhang proposed building a 1,500-kilometre trunk line from Beijing to the south, through inland provinces all the way to Wuhan, a major city connected to the sea by the Yangtze River. All the land-locked provinces in the catchment area would then be linked with the outside world. Local produce could be refined by imported machines, made exportable and then transported to the coast. Potentially this could transform China's economy and solve its most fundamental and disabling problem: poverty. This visionary proposal struck Cixi: here were the real benefits of the railways, and they would be worth all the sacrifices and the risks.

She kept the Viceroy's proposal for deliberation. After soliciting scrutiny from the top echelon, and receiving no objections, on 27 August 1889 Cixi finally issued a decree that heralded China's railway age with this north–south trunk line. The Beijing–Wuhan railway, subsequently extended south to Canton, became (and remains) the country's central transport artery, critical to its economy even today. Cixi seems to have foreseen this, for her decree rang like a manifesto: 'This project has magnificent and far-reaching significance, and is indeed the key component of our blueprint for Making China Strong. As we embark on this ground-breaking project, unavoidably there will be doubts and fears.' She went on to order the provincial chiefs, through whose territory the line would travel, to explain the enterprise to the local people and prevent them from obstructing it. 'All in all,' she said, 'I hope the court and country will be of one mind, the officials and the merchants will make concerted efforts, to achieve a complete success . . .' Viceroy Zhang was put in charge of the construction, together with Earl Li, and set up headquarters in Wuhan. There, associated with the railway, he initiated a host of modern industries, and made Wuhan one of the crucibles of China's industrialisation.

Cixi did not embrace industrialisation indiscriminately or unreservedly. In 1882, when Earl Li asked for permission to build textile factories, she objected, saying with unmistakable annoyance: 'Textile making is our basic domestic industry. Machine-produced fabrics take away our women's work and harm their livelihood. It is bad enough that we can't ban foreign textiles; we shouldn't be inflicting further damage on ourselves. This matter must be considered carefully.' In those days, 'textile making' was called *can-sang*, literally meaning 'silkworms and mulberry leaves', as silk production had been a major activity of Chinese women for thousands of years. To maintain this tradition, every year in spring, when the silkworms began their labour, Cixi led court ladies to pray in a special shrine in the Forbidden City to the God of the Silkworm, begging his protection for the little worms. She and the ladies would feed the silkworms four or five times a day, gathering leaves from the mulberry trees in the palace grounds. When a silkworm had finished spinning a silk thread and had enclosed itself inside the cocoon it had made with its silk, the cocoon would be boiled and the thread, which averaged many hundreds of metres, would be wound onto a spool, ready for weaving. All her life Cixi kept some of the silk she had woven as a young girl, to see if the new silk was as fine and lustrous as the old. She did not want to see the old ways disappear altogether. While she was determined to drive through change in some areas, in others she either resisted change or accepted it only reluctantly. Under her China's industrialisation did not move like a bulldozer out to destroy all traditions.

12 Defender of the Empire
(1875–89)

EVER since his son had been taken away and made emperor in 1875, Prince Chun's character had been changing. He had, for the first time, begun to fear his sister-in-law. The devastation of losing his only son had opened his eyes to a side of the empress dowager that he had not previously registered: that she possessed a deadly sting, even though she rarely used it. When he had backed the execution of Little An in 1869 and when, against her orders, he had spearheaded riots against missionaries in Tianjin in 1870, he had had no fear of retribution. Now he realised that she had not forgotten, or forgiven, what he had done: five years on, her revenge was served cold. The shock bewildered him. In a letter to Cixi after his son had been snatched away, he described how he had 'lost consciousness' when he heard her announcement, and had gone home 'trembling all over in the flesh and the heart, as if in a trance or a drunken stupor'. He collapsed, and took to bed 'in a vegetative state'. His former cockiness gone, he apologised for his past wrongs (without spelling them out), roundly castigating himself and begging her for mercy. 'You have seen right through me,' he wrote. 'Please grant me an undeserved favour' – to spare his life, 'the life of a dumb and useless idiot'.

Then he saw that Cixi did not destroy him when she could, but was rather kind to him; the prince was overcome with gratitude. Fear turned to awe. He spent much of his time in reflection and adopted the motto 'Step back and think how to make up for past wrongs' (*tui-si-bu-guo*), which was carved onto a plaque over the door to his study. His mansion was full of reminders of the sentiment, from the calligraphy in the scrolls on his walls, to the inscription engraved on an ivory paperweight on his desk. He came to recognise that his previous hostility to Cixi's approach to the West was 'prejudiced'; and he became one of her keenest supporters.

The prince's metamorphosis was also due to other, perhaps more important, causes. He came to be impressed by what Cixi had achieved for the empire – such as recapturing Xinjiang, a huge territory in Central Asia the size of Britain, France, Germany and Italy combined. The contemporary historian H. B. Morse remarked at the beginning of the twentieth century, 'This possession has been held by China for over two thousand years; held firmly when the central administration was strong, held laxly when the central power was relaxed, and let go in times of confusion . . . it has frequently broken away, only to be again subjected to Chinese rule.' The latest fracture came in the early 1860s, on the heels of the Taiping rebellion. Much of the breakaway land was controlled by a Muslim leader, Yakub Beg, described as 'a soldier of fortune' by Charles Denby, later American envoy to China. Cixi was determined to bring Xinjiang back under Beijing's control. This decision was made against the advice of Earl Li, who proposed letting the region go and allowing it to become one of the empire's vassal states, 'like Vietnam and Korea'.

The vassal states were small independent countries around China, which administered their own affairs, but recognised the overlordship of the Chinese emperor by periodically presenting tribute and by getting Chinese endorsement for each new ruler. Apart from Vietnam and Korea, the other vassal states included Nepal, Burma, Laos and the Liuqiu (Ryukyu) Islands. Earl Li counselled that Xinjiang be allowed to join their ranks. To the earl, Xinjiang was 'several thousand *li* of barren land', was 'not worth' recovering and, even if conquered, 'it could not be kept for long, as its neighbours all had designs on it: Russia to the north, Turkey, Persia and other Muslim countries to the west, and British India close to the south . . .' Recovering Xinjiang, said the earl, would involve a large army trekking a long way in the desert and fighting a protracted war that was 'beyond the means' of the empire. This had been the view of the late Marquis Zeng, a considerable strategist, and it was now also the view of Prince Chun himself.

But Cixi refused to let go of Xinjiang, and as soon as she returned to power in 1875 she dispatched General Zuo Zongtang to win it back. The expedition was a matter of urgency for her: Russia had occupied a key area in the region, Ili, for the past four years and, unless China acted now, Russian ownership would become a fait accompli.

In order to finance the expedition, Cixi squeezed money out of the provinces and authorised General Zuo to borrow five million taels from foreign banks. Following Zuo's journey through his detailed reports, she was at pains to meet his constant requests, mostly for funds. General Zuo, a rugged warrior now in his sixties, had a coffin carried with him as he embarked on the expedition into the desert – to signal his determination to fight for as long as it took. His campaign was successful and excruciatingly brutal. By the beginning of 1878 he had re-conquered most of Xinjiang. Mercy was not in his vocabulary and massacres were commonplace. In accordance with the Qing penal codes, the captured sons and grandsons of Yakub Beg (who had died) were castrated, before being given away as slaves. Westerners were horrified; but even moderate Chinese diplomats were insistent that such punishment was warranted, and they berated Westerners for 'minding other people's businesses'.

Cixi endorsed Zuo – and his methods. After reasserting Beijing's grip on Xinjiang, she took Zuo's advice and gradually made it a province, instead of allowing it autonomy. Troops were stationed there; they opened up virgin land to sustain themselves when not suppressing rebellions.

Cixi sent Chonghou to St Petersburg to negotiate for the return of Ili. Chonghou, an affable man, was the official who had tried to protect Westerners during the Tianjin massacre in 1870. He was not a tough negotiator, and after months of talks he signed an agreement that obliged China to cede a large hunk of Xinjiang to Russia in exchange for Ili. There was uproar in Beijing about the deal, and a council of grandees sentenced him to 'imprisonment awaiting execution', with Cixi's authorisation. Western envoys expressed strong disapproval: it was, they said, unworthy of 'China's new diplomacy' that a diplomat should be 'condemned to death by decapitation . . . charged, not with treason, but with failure'. Queen Victoria even addressed a personal appeal for clemency 'to the great empress dowager of China'. Cixi took the point and released Chonghou.

But she refused to recognise the treaty. Russia threatened war and moved 90,000 troops to the disputed territory. Chinese Gordon, the Englishman who had helped defeat the Taiping rebels, gave this advice: 'If you will make war, burn suburbs of Peking, remove the archives and emperor from Peking . . . and fight . . . for five years . . . If you want peace, then give up Ili *in toto* . . .' Neither of these extreme scenarios appealed to Cixi. War was out of the question, as China could ill afford it, while Russia might rather welcome it, in order to grab more land. But peace must not come at the cost of losing territory, either Ili or the land that Chonghou had signed away. Cixi gave every impression that China was 'ready for war – as ready as her rival', but dispatched a new representative, Marquis Zeng Jr, to Russia to renegotiate. She gave him detailed instructions, and the most important was the bottom line: if he was unable to get back all the territory in dispute, then he should settle for the pre-Chonghou status quo and leave Ili in Russian hands for the time being, while maintaining China's claim to it. The marquis went to the talks equipped with a marked-up Chonghou treaty making clear which items were absolutely unacceptable and which were negotiable. Throughout, he kept in telegram contact with Cixi.

A clear and precise strategy, as well as detailed preparations, paid off. China recovered most of the territory Chonghou had ceded, as well as Ili. The new treaty, a compromise,★ was hailed by Western observers as a 'diplomatic triumph'. Lord Dufferin, then British ambassador to St Petersburg, remarked: 'China has compelled Russia to do what she has never done before, disgorge territory that she had once absorbed.' For his country's first victory in modern diplomacy, Marquis Zeng Jr received numerous plaudits. But the pivotal role was played by Cixi.

At the height of the crisis, facing the prospect of war and loss of territory, Cixi collapsed under intense nervous strain. For days on end she could not sleep, felt depleted of energy and coughed blood. In line with tradition, the court sent out a request in July 1880 asking provincial chiefs to recommend doctors to help the royal physicians, and 'to have them escorted to Beijing in steamers so they arrive quickly'. A Dr Xue from Zhejiang province described his first session with Cixi. It began with his obligatory prostration before her, and her telling him to stand up and come to her bedside. She sat cross-legged inside the yellow silk curtains that fell around the bed. One of her lower arms was outside the curtain, resting on a little pillow on top of a small side-table. A plain handkerchief covered it, leaving only the part where the doctor could feel the pulse, a crucial diagnostic procedure. On his knees, Dr Xue pressed his fingers to the wrist. He diagnosed 'exceeding distress and anxiety' and informed the empress dowager that she would be all right soon, so long as she refrained from racking her brains. To this Cixi replied: 'I know, but it's just

---

★ China paid Russia for keeping Ili out of rebel hands and allowing trade to continue. This payment was not a war indemnity, although Chinese history books use the same term, *pei-kuan*, and treat them as though they were the same.

impossible to do.' Eventually she recovered, much helped by Marquis Zeng Jr's optimistic reports.

During the dispute, Prince Chun was involved. Having ensured his resignation from all posts, Cixi made a point of including him in the decision-making process, telling those who objected that the prince had 'begged to be excused, knocking his head on the ground over and over', and that it was she who had insisted on his participation. Cixi intended to win over the prince by letting him observe how she dealt with state matters. So the prince saw that Cixi was committed to the interests of the empire and defended it vigorously and ably. He was struck by her steeliness in launching the Xinjiang campaign and in facing down Russia, as well as by her ability to compromise and direct negotiations. By comparison, he who had bragged about 'revenge' against foreigners had no inkling of what to do when faced with real foreign threats. All this convinced the prince that he was serving a mistress who was a great asset to the empire, and he submitted himself as her humble servant.

Perhaps the event that most impressed Prince Chun and turned him definitively into Cixi's 'slave' was her handling of the war with France in 1884–5. France had started a military campaign in 1859 to colonise Vietnam, China's neighbour and a vassal state. As France annexed the south and was advancing north, the Qing government took no action – not least because the Vietnamese did not ask for help (which a vassal state was entitled to do). The only times Cixi sent troops into Vietnam were to round up *Chinese* bandits there, at the request of the Vietnamese. As soon as the jobs were done, the troops were pulled back.

By now, it seems, Cixi had formed a well-considered policy regarding the boundary of the empire. She was determined to preserve the territory that it regarded as its own, but was ready to let go of the vassal states, if and when she was forced to do so. A pragmatic woman, she knew that there were now stronger European forces and her empire was not in a position to keep the vassal states. So while she dispatched a large army to regain Xinjiang and made all efforts to hold on to Taiwan, she did no more than issue verbal protests when a vassal state, the Liuqiu (Ryukyu) Islands, was annexed by Japan by the end of the 1870s. Similarly, her action with regard to Vietnam was limited to securing the border, rather than retaining Vietnam. In August 1883, Vietnam was forced to become a protectorate of France. The French Prime Minister, Jules Ferry, aspired to acquire a colonial empire and initiated imperial adventures in countries as diverse as Tunis, Congo, Niger and Madagascar, as well as Indochina. And now French forces were moving steadily towards Vietnam's border with China.

Cixi began to prepare for war. Court and amateur astrologers saw signs of major battles coming, from the abnormally flaming sky that lasted for days, to the angle of a shooting comet. Cixi was a believer in astrology. To her, comets were warnings from Heaven. In the past, when comets appeared in the sky, she had reflected on what she might have done wrong and issued edicts soliciting comments on whether incompetent officials had been employed or the poverty of the population had been neglected. Now she was filled with apprehension. With a heavy cold that lasted for months, she coughed incessantly during her audiences. When officials tried to comfort her, she said: 'I can't but worry in this situation when I see those celestial signs.'

With the French pressing against the border, Cixi sent troops into Tonkin, the northernmost region of Vietnam, adjoining the Chinese provinces of Guangxi and Yunnan. The latter was particularly rich in mineral resources desirable to the French. Cixi's intention was to keep part of Tonkin as a buffer, if possible, but, if not, only to defend the border. From December to April the following year, 1884, Chinese troops fought French forces in this area and suffered repeated defeats. It looked as though the French might even penetrate into China itself.

Prince Gong, head of the Grand Council, was an appeaser by inclination. Fatalistic about winning a war with a Western power, he took no active part in helping Cixi conduct the fighting. According to Grand Tutor Weng's diary, the prince talked 'vaguely and offered no ideas'. 'He went on and on to the Empress Dowager for an extraordinary amount of time, all about nothing.' Sometimes he was listless; at other times he failed to turn up at his office. The fact that he had been in poor health did not help. Prince Gong had been suffering serious illnesses in the last few years, passing blood at times, and Cixi had given him long leaves. His energy had been sapped and his judgement blunted. And yet he did not offer to resign, and it was difficult for Cixi to dismiss him because of his status, and because he had been working with her since the very beginning. But she had been seething for some time.

The last straw came on 30 March 1884, when, right in the middle of a series of devastating defeats at the hands of the French, the prince insisted on discussing with Cixi her forthcoming fiftieth birthday★ in the autumn, in particular the arrangements for presenting the gifts. Prostrating himself before her, the prince talked for an hour and a half. An irate Cixi told him off: 'With the border situation like this, you are talking about birthday presents! It shouldn't be on the agenda at such a time; why are you bothering me with this business?' But the prince went on unabashed, kneeling for so long that he had difficulty standing up when he was finished. Grand Tutor Weng, who witnessed the scene, recorded it in his diary, with open contempt for the prince. The next day Prince Gong returned and resumed his blather, 'begging the Empress Dowager to be so kind as to accept birthday presents'. Cixi 'reproached him in words that showed a heavy heart', and yet her words seemed to make no impression. The Grand Tutor felt that he had to 'go above my station' and give the prince a piece of his mind. He told him to heed the empress dowager, and 'don't dwell any longer on trivialities'. In his diary, the Grand Tutor wrote scornfully: 'This highest nobleman has such low intelligence!'

Cixi made up her mind to dismiss Prince Gong. This was no small undertaking. By now he had been entrenched as the head of the Grand Council for a quarter of a century and was the most powerful person in the empire, after Cixi herself. She had to go about it with the utmost caution. With a suitable pretext, she sent Prince Gong out of Beijing for a few days and, while he was away, she summoned Prince Chun and made preparations, rather as if she was planning a coup. As soon as Prince Gong returned, on 8 April, Cixi threw him the crimson-inked decree that announced his dismissal and that of the entire Grand Council. With this surprise strike, the empress dowager parted with her political partner of more than two decades, the man who had stood by her side almost daily, sharing the challenges of reform with her. Perhaps because of the manner of his dismissal – more suited to a foe than to a close friend who had shown nothing but devotion and comradeship for her for so long – Cixi felt awkward and did not see the prince again for ten years. Prince Gong tried to reassure her that he held no grudge against her and quite understood that she had to take precautions. He begged to see her, even if only as one of the well-wishers on her birthdays, but she refused all entreaties.

Cixi appointed a new Grand Council and put Prince Chun in charge. As the emperor's biological father, he could not be the formal head and so he conducted business from home. This transfer of power

★ According to the Chinese system.

from one brother to another did not cause friction between the two princes. On the contrary, the brothers, who had formerly been at loggerheads because of their different attitudes towards the West, now became much closer. Prince Chun, who had changed fundamentally, frequently visited his disgraced half-brother. They had a bond: their shared adoration of their sister-in-law. They wrote poems to each other, and a recurring theme in Prince Gong's was that he found it 'hard to look back at all those bygone years'. The prince was expressing his nostalgia for the days of his collaboration with Cixi; he was also hoping to convey to her, via Prince Chun, that he cherished the memories and would always remain loyal to her.

Prince Chun had as little idea as his brother about how to resolve the crisis with France, but he executed Cixi's orders efficiently and unwaveringly. Westerners thought he was an uncompromising hawk, unlike Prince Gong. The replacement of Prince Gong with Chun was interpreted as an indication of Cixi's determination to pursue the path of war. Indeed she was resolved to fight a 'protracted war against the enemy' (*yu-di jiu-chi*), until the French, a long way from home, were exhausted and sought to end the conflict themselves.

Her real goal was peace, for which she was willing to let Vietnam go if necessary, provided its loss secured a commitment from France to respect the border with China. She appointed Earl Li as her chief negotiator. The earl was now her diplomatic ace as well as chief adviser. Vastly superior to Prince Gong, he worked with her in perfect harmony. They often thought alike and enjoyed a tacit understanding. Earl Li was at this time officially 'in mourning' for his deceased mother, which required him not to work for twenty-seven months. But Cixi told him to cut the period short, citing ancient sages who had specifically exempted those with military duties. During the negotiations, telegrams shuttled back and forth between them. They knew that France was deeply engaged in the scramble for Africa and had no wish for a prolonged war with China. Peace was achievable, and the earl was able to clinch a deal in Tianjin with Commandant Fournier, whom he already knew as a friend. The Li–Fournier convention embodied the minimum terms that Cixi was willing to settle for: France promised never to cross the southern boundaries of China and guaranteed to prevent anyone else from doing so; in return, China acquiesced to France taking control of Vietnam. Fournier had informed the earl that the French Foreign Ministry had asked for a war indemnity on the grounds that public opinion at home called for it. Cixi told Earl Li that the demand was 'totally unjust, totally unreasonable, and transparently against international convention'. The earl rejected the demand, and Fournier did not insist. When the draft agreement was sent to Cixi, she cabled back on 9 May 1884: 'Have read it carefully. None of the items does damage to the fundamental interest of our country. Endorsed.' The convention was signed on the 11th.

Cixi began to withdraw troops from Vietnam – cautiously, as she learned that Paris was unhappy about having not extracted any money, and that gunboats were on their way. On 12 July, France produced an ultimatum for a gigantic indemnity of 250 million francs, claiming that China had broken the agreement by starting an armed clash, which, in fact, was an accident and was judged by Western observers to have been 'an honest misunderstanding'. Cixi was incensed. Eye-witnesses were struck by her unusual severity in the audience, when she spat out her prohibition on anyone speaking in favour of negotiations over the indemnity. At the time, nearly everyone involved in this conflict, including Earl Li, was resigned to giving in to some extent to the French extortion, in order to avoid a war. But Cixi was firm: not a sou to the French. When her diplomats took it upon themselves to make an offer, suggesting a much lower sum, she reprimanded them sharply. Facing the prospect of war, she first sought mediation by America and, when France refused mediation, she gritted her teeth and proclaimed that 'war is unavoidable'. She told an official, Shi Nianzu, in an audience: 'When it comes to China's relationship with foreign countries, it is of course better to have peace. But before we can have real peace China must be ready to fight. If we give in to every demand, then the more we seek peace, the less likely we are going to get it.'

France initiated the Sino-French War on 5 August 1884, first attacking Taiwan, then annihilating the Chinese fleet at Fuzhou on the southeast coast, and blowing up the Fuzhou Navy Yard – which had been built under the direction of the Frenchman Prosper Giquel. On 26 August, in an outrage-filled treatise, Cixi declared that China was at war with France. A modern touch was added to the ancient warring rhetoric: foreign nationals were to be protected, including French citizens. When she learned that coastal officials were putting up posters calling on the Chinese inhabitants of the South Sea islands to poison the food supplied to stranded French ships, she immediately stopped them with an edict and reprimanded the officials in question, adding that overseas Chinese should stay out of the military conflict.

In the following months her army scored some victories and suffered many more defeats. But in late March 1885, they won a major battle at the Zhennan Pass on the border and, as a consequence, the French retreated from the strategically important city of Lang Son. Jules Ferry's government fell; his successor, Charles de Freycinet, promptly settled for peace. A treaty was signed on 9 June in Tianjin by Earl Li and the French minister Jules Patenôtre. This treaty was the same in essence as the Li–Fournier convention a year earlier. The French were back at square one, having failed to extract one single franc out of China. For the Chinese, the cost was heavy, but the fight was a tremendous morale-booster, which, in the words of Grand Tutor Weng, had 'swept away the country's meek acceptance that it was weak'.

Not only did Cixi demonstrate that she was capable of fighting a major war, but she had the acumen to stop it at the right moment. After the border victories, her commanders at the front had been eager to fight on. Even the usually sensible Viceroy Zhang Zhidong advocated keeping Lang Son and some other Vietnamese territory on the border as a buffer zone. Cixi sent them a succession of urgent and non-negotiable orders, telling them emphatically to cease fire and withdraw their troops. She told them that they could 'not be certain that there were going to be further victories; and even if there were, Vietnam doesn't belong to us in the end'. She knew that the Vietnamese had a long history of resisting Chinese domination (the Chinese name for the pass on the border, *Zhennan*, actually means 'Suppressing Vietnam') and that this time some Vietnamese were actively helping the French. Meanwhile, the French were blockading Taiwan and looked set to attack it if the war went on, in which case China might lose Taiwan. Her cables were written in the severest possible language, and they chastened the Viceroy and others, who obeyed. Later on, with hindsight, Prince Chun wrote: 'If it had not been for the Empress Dowager's farsightedness and decisiveness to settle for peace with France, we would have been embroiled in endless perilous wars, and would have seen our coffers emptied and our defence enfeebled. It does not bear imagining what might have happened.'[*]

Cixi's handling of the conflict won the empire respect. Robert Hart proclaimed, 'I don't think any one will say that China comes badly out of the year's trials . . .' At the banquet that followed the signing of the peace treaty, the French signatory Patenôtre enthused:

---

[*] Cixi is still criticised by some today for ending the Sino-French War after China won these battles. Her critics seem to suggest that China should have held on to Vietnam, a sovereign country.

I have every confidence that the diplomatic agreement we have just signed will do more than just put an end to our past disputes and — I hope — speedily efface them from our memory. By creating new links between France and China . . . the Treaty of 9 June will indubitably help to entrench and develop between the Chinese Empire and foreign countries that community of interests which has always most effectively cemented friendships between peoples.

Earl Li replied in kind: 'From now on, the friendship between our two countries will shine as brightly as the morning sun when it emerges from the gloom of night.'

After the war with France, Cixi focused on rebuilding and updating the navy, writing decrees in crimson ink to stress the significance of the enterprise. (She rarely wrote in crimson ink, the symbol of the authority of the monarch.) More gunboats were bought from Europe and crews trained by Western instructors. In spring 1886, she sent Prince Chun to inspect the newly equipped Northern Fleet off the coast opposite the Dagu Forts. The prince took with him Cixi's head eunuch, Lee Lianying, who was known to be extremely close to her. Standing by the side of the prince, carrying his water-pipe, Lianying became an eye-catching figure in the prince's entourage.

The prince brought him for a purpose. Seventeen years earlier, Little An, Lianying's predecessor, had been sent by Cixi to Suzhou to buy wedding robes for her son. Little An had been beheaded for leaving the capital, and Prince Chun had been the prime mover. Now the prince was making a gesture of repentance towards Cixi for the horrible wrong he had done. By inviting her current favourite eunuch to journey out of Beijing, to board a modern ship and sail out to sea, the prince was offering Cixi a belated, but sure-to-be-appreciated, apology.

Prince Chun made this extraordinary gesture because he really wanted to show Cixi his appreciation for her defence of the empire. During this period she completed treaties with European powers and extracted commitments from them to respect China's borders, which were formally drawn up at this time and largely remain in place to this day. The treaties included one with Russia (1881), with France (about the border with Vietnam, 1885) and with Britain (regarding Burma, 1886, and Sikkim, 1888). It is chiefly thanks to her that during those years, while the European powers were sweeping across the globe, gobbling up ancient kingdoms and carving up old continents, China was left alone.

At the beginning of 1889, at the height of her achievements, the empress dowager announced that she was going to retire and cede power to her seventeen-year-old adopted son. Under her reign China's annual revenue had doubled. Before she came to power, it had been around forty million taels, even at the most prosperous times under Qianlong the Magnificent. Now it stood at nearly eighty-eight million, of which as much as one-third came from Customs duties – the result of her open-door policy. Before returning to the harem she issued an honours list, thanking about 100 officials, living and dead, for their services. The second on her list was Robert Hart, Inspector General of Customs, for building up a well-organised and efficient fiscal institution, free of corruption, which had 'produced very considerable and ever increasing revenues for China'. Customs revenue helped save millions of lives. In the previous year, 1888, when the country was struck by floods, earthquakes and other natural disasters, it could afford to spend ten million taels of silver to buy rice to feed the population. The honour she conferred on Hart was the Ancestral Rank of the First Class of the First Order for Three Generations – the highest distinction because the title was bestowed on his *ancestors* for three generations, not his descendants. Hart wrote to a friend, 'from the Chinese, nothing could be more honourable; in any case it is extremely satisfactory to myself that the Empress Dowager should do this before retiring . . .'

One of Cixi's decrees thanked all foreign envoys for their help in forging amicable relationships between their own countries and China. She ordered the Foreign Office to select an auspicious day on which to give a grand banquet for the envoys and to present each envoy with a *ru-yi*, a good-wish sceptre made mostly of jade, as well as silks and brocades, which she personally selected. The banquet, which was held on 7 March 1889 and at which Western diplomats heaped praise on her, marked a high point of her reign.

One guest who spoke spontaneously that day was Charles Denby, the American minister to Beijing from 1885 to 1898. He later wrote of Cixi's 'splendid reputation' among Westerners at this time, and of her many achievements. Along with ending internal strife and maintaining the integrity of the empire:

a fine navy was created, and the army was somewhat improved. The electric telegraph covered the land. Arsenals and shipyards were located at Foochow [Fuzhou], Shanghai, Canton, Taku [Dagu], and Port Arthur. Western methods of mining were introduced, and two lines of railway were built. Steamers plied on all the principal rivers. The study of mathematics was revived, and the physical sciences were introduced into the competitive examinations. Absolute tolerance of religious faith existed, and the missionaries could locate anywhere in China . . . During the time covered by the rule of the empress many schools and colleges were established in China by our own countrymen . . .

Furthermore, Cixi's reign was the most tolerant in Qing history; people were no longer killed for what they said or wrote, as they had been under previous emperors. To alleviate poverty, she initiated large-scale food import and each year spent hundreds of thousands, even millions, of taels to buy food to feed the population. As Denby observed, 'To her own people, up to this period in her career, she was kind and merciful, and to foreigners she was just.' Foreign relations were fundamentally improved, and the relationship between China and the US stayed 'tranquil and satisfactory'. Most importantly, the American minister pointed out: 'It may be said with emphasis that the empress dowager has been the first of her race to apprehend the problem of the relation of China to the outside world, and to make use of this relation to strengthen her dynasty and to promote material progress.' Indeed, Cixi had ended China's self-imposed isolation and had brought it into the international community – and she had done so in order to benefit her country. 'At that time,' Denby summed up, 'she was universally esteemed by foreigners, and revered by her own people, and was regarded as being one of the greatest characters in history . . . Under her rule for a quarter of a century China made immense progress.'

The embryo of a modern China had taken shape. Its creator was Cixi. As Denby stressed, 'It will not be denied by any one that the improvement and progress above sketched are mainly due to the will and power of the empress regent.' With this impressive legacy, Cixi handed over the reins of the empire to her adopted son, Emperor Guangxu.

PART FOUR

Emperor Guangxu Takes Over (1889–1898)

13 Guangxu Alienated from Cixi
(1875–94)

BORN on the twenty-eighth day of the sixth lunar month of 1871, Emperor Guangxu succeeded to the throne at the age of three, when Cixi's own son, Emperor Tongzhi, had died without an heir. She adopted him and made him the next emperor, partly to elevate a member of her own family – her sister's son – and partly to punish his father, Prince Chun. She had no real love for the child, at least not of the kind she had felt for her own late son. Taken from his home and carried into the bitterly cold and impersonal Forbidden City in the depths of a wintry night, the child lost his parents – and his wet nurse, who was not allowed to join him. Instead, he was placed in the charge of eunuchs. Cixi told him to call her 'Papa Dearest' (*qin-ba-ba*) and, when he was older, he called her 'My Royal Father' (*huang-ba-ba*). It was a man's role that Cixi aspired to fill. As a mother, she was dutiful rather than warm. She had no instinctive fondness for children anyway. Once, at a party in the court for aristocratic ladies, a young girl started bawling and would not stop. An irate Cixi ordered the child's mother to take her away, telling her, as she fell to her knees in tears, 'I send you out of the Palace to teach you a lesson, which you must teach your child. I do not blame her; I blame you and pity her; but she must suffer as well as yourself.' The family was not invited again for some time.

Empress Zhen was more of a mother figure to the child emperor than Cixi. But she died when he was nine, on 8 April 1881, aged forty-three. He could not stop crying at her bier. It has been alleged that Empress Zhen was poisoned by Cixi, although no one has produced any evidence. In fact, she almost certainly died of a massive brain haem-orrhage, as doctors who studied her medical records have concluded. She had a history of what appeared to be strokes, of which Grand Tutor Weng's diary recorded at least three. The first happened as early as 1863, when she suddenly fainted and lost the ability to speak for nearly a month. Her reputation for 'speaking slowly and with difficulty' during audiences may have been a consequence. On the last occasion, she fell into unconsciousness and died within a couple of days.

Cixi mourned Empress Zhen's death as that of an intimate and superior family member – by wrapping her own head in a white silk scarf. This went beyond the prescribed mourning etiquette for the empress dowager and earned her 'immense admiration' from the traditionalists like Grand Tutor Weng. Although dynastic rules only required the period of mourning to be twenty-seven days, Cixi extended it to 100 days, during which time all joyful activities, like weddings, were prohibited. What was more, she decreed a twenty-seven-month ban on music in the court. This, just over a year after the four-year ban following the death of her son, and in the middle of an illness during which she craved music, was a real sacrifice. So starved of music was she that, months before the end of the ban, she started planning performances and selecting singers from outside the court. Within days after the ban was lifted, in summer 1883, she watched opera non-stop for ten hours. Thereafter there were continuous performances for days, one lasting twelve hours.

The death of Empress Zhen deprived Emperor Guangxu of a mother figure. It also left a vacuum as there was no one to act as conciliator between him and Cixi. When the child grew up and was increasingly alienated from his Papa Dearest, there was no one to bring them back together. No one was in a position to, and no one had the clout. Empress Zhen, senior to Cixi in rank, a friend from her teenage years and a comrade in launching their coup, for which both of them had risked death by a thousand cuts, had been the only person to whom Cixi displayed humility. Cixi had respected the empress's judgement in a working partnership that spanned two decades, and had deferred to her in domestic affairs – even in a matter as crucial as the choice of a wife for her son. Without Empress Zhen's help, Cixi was unable to halt the gradual worsening of her relationship with Emperor Guangxu, a deterioration that would result in disasters for the empire, as well as for themselves.

At this stage Cixi behaved like an 'absentee parent,' who, apart from receiving the child's daily ritual greetings, confined her involvement with him to his education. She engaged Grand Tutor Weng, who had taught her late son, to be the chief teacher. The fact that she and the conservative Weng had disagreed on so many issues did not prevent her from appointing him to the post. Weng was by consensus the most upright and acclaimed of scholars, and could be trusted to instil in the child all the qualities that a good emperor should possess. Cixi was firmly committed to Chinese culture, even though she was open to Western ideas. It was taken for granted that a Chinese monarch had to be brought up in the Chinese way. It does not seem to have occurred to her that this emperor should be educated differently, but, even if it did, no other way would have been approved by the grandees, who had a voice in how their emperor was educated. As a result, Emperor Guangxu was moulded like his ancestors: no part of his education would equip him to handle the modern world.

The child emperor began his lessons when he was four. On a sunny early spring day, he was taken into his study to meet his tutors. Sitting behind a low desk, facing south, he spread a large piece of paper on the desk and asked for a brush. He had already learned to write a little. Grand Tutor Weng dipped a brush into a well of ink and handed it to the child, who proceeded to write two phrases, each with four characters, in what his tutor called 'extremely symmetrical and pleasing' calligraphy. One phrase meant 'peace and stability under Heaven', and the other 'upright, magnanimous, honourable and wise'. Both were Confucian ideals to which a good monarch should aspire. With this delightful start, Grand Tutor Weng showed the child the word 'the Morality of the Emperor', *di-de*, which he repeated after the tutor four times. Next Weng opened a picture book, *Lessons for an Emperor*, in which the famously good and notoriously bad emperors were portrayed. As he explained to the child why they were good or bad, the boy's finger, following that of his teacher, paused over the portraits of the mythical Emperors Yao and Shun of the Three Great Ancient Dynasties, who were worshipped as exemplary monarchs. The four-year-old seemed to be attracted to them. After lingering over their images, he asked Grand Tutor Weng if he would again write down the word 'the Morality of the Emperor', which the Grand Tutor did. The child gazed at the word for some time before the first lesson ended.

This first session, recorded in Grand Tutor Weng's diary, provides a glimpse of Emperor Guangxu's education and the sort of pupil he would become. Quite the opposite of his cousin and immediate predecessor, Emperor Tongzhi, who dreaded the lessons, Guangxu seemed to take to them. At the age of five, to Cixi's amazement, he was reciting at all times – 'sitting, standing, walking or lying down' – what must have been to him incomprehensible classics. Such dedication may well have had something to do with the strong attachment he formed to his teacher, Weng. The boy wanted to please the old man. When he was six, Weng was away for some time, tending to the repairs of his family tombs. During his absence the child played like a normal boy, and did not do the homework the tutor had left him. Weng had asked him to recite some classical texts twenty times each, in order to learn them by heart, but Guangxu only read them once. The day Weng came back, the child threw himself into the old man's arms and cried: 'I have been missing you for such a long time!' Then he went to his desk and started reciting the texts, twenty times each. A eunuch in attendance commented: 'We haven't heard this sound for ages!'

With this powerful motivation to imbibe, and a good memory, Emperor Guangxu rapidly excelled. Grand Tutor Weng's diaries, which had been littered with exasperated outbursts about his former pupil, were now peppered with satisfied exclamations such as 'good', 'very good', 'extremely good' and 'brilliant!' By nine, the emperor was able to decorate fans with calligraphy that 'has a really artistic feel', said the delighted tutor, a renowned calligrapher himself. Barely into his teens, the boy could write 'utterly fluent' poetry and essays at speed, as if mature thoughts flew out of his young head 'with wings'.

The child's whole life was given over to his studies, which included the Manchu language, as well as some Mongolian, though Chinese classics remained the core subject. From the age of nine he began to practise reading reports and writing instructions on them in crimson ink. For this purpose, a copy was made of some reports for him to practise on. As the Chinese language had no punctuation marks in those days, the child first had to divide the sometimes very long texts into sentences by marking each pause with a crimson dot. The instructions he gave were sensible, though understandably limited to generalities. Sometimes, Cixi would sit with him while he practised, like a parent watching her child doing his homework today. One report came from a governor requesting a piece of calligraphy from the emperor, which would be carved on a plaque and mounted on the entrance of a temple to the God of Thunder. Apparently the god had been seen to make an appearance, which was interpreted by frightened locals to mean that there would be storms coming to destroy their crops. Royal reverence to the god could placate its wrath. The nine-year-old granted the request, in a reply that he had clearly absorbed from his readings. Cixi then showed him what he might say of a more specific kind, by writing an additional instruction to the effect that the official must not just count on the royal inscription for good harvests, and that the gods would be better pleased if he performed his duties conscientiously.

On another report, from Marquis Zeng Jr, suggesting allowing junior diplomats abroad to come home for vacation and paying for their extra costs, the then ten-year-old duly gave his consent. Cixi added the principle: 'The most important thing is to choose the right people. Once you have them, don't begrudge them expenses.'

So Emperor Guangxu was groomed, by the empress dowager as well as his Grand Tutors, to be a wise ruler. By the age of ten he was giving occasional audiences. When Cixi was ill, he stepped in and was able to talk to officials in this way: 'What are the crops like in Henan? Is there still a lack of rain? We in the capital are also suffering from drought. How we long for the rain!' These were the standard lines expected of a good emperor. And Grand Tutor Weng felt 'much rewarded and contented'.

Indeed Emperor Guangxu grew up to be a model Confucian monarch. From the Grand Tutor he learned to despise 'personal wealth', *cai*, and declared that he preferred 'thriftiness', *jian* – at which the old man exclaimed: 'What great fortune for all under Heaven!' His essays and poems, in their hundreds and well kept in envelopes of yellow silk in the Forbidden City archives, mostly expressed his thoughts on how to be a worthy emperor. 'Care for the people' (*ai-min*) was a constant theme. Writing about the moonlight over a palace lake, the emperor would think about far-away starving villagers, who shared the same moon, but not his luxury. In summer, on cooling himself in an open pavilion, nibbling ice-chilled fruits, his poems were about feeling pity for peasants toiling under a scorching sun. And in winter, on cradling a gilded charcoal burner in the heated palace while listening to howling winds, he imagined how the wind would be lashing at 'tens of thousands of families in inadequate homes'.

His sentiments and the language he used to express them conformed exactly to precedent, established over centuries, for a good Confucian emperor. And yet, for all the concerns he displayed for his subjects, the emperor had nothing to say about how to improve their lives through modern means. Nowhere in his writings did he mention industries, foreign trade or diplomacy. The emperor's young mind was frozen in the past.

Trained as a Confucian purist, he regarded fun as sinful. His holidays were mostly spent in the study, as were his birthdays. On his eighth birthday the court staged operas over several days. Each day he put in a brief appearance before returning to his study. He was a diligent pupil, but he had also been taught by Weng to dislike opera for its melodrama and tuneful melodies, which were deemed to be 'vulgar'. To the tutor's delight, the child said that he considered it to be something only for his attendants – that he preferred the 'elegant sounds of bells and drums', ancient music that was stately (if monotonous), designed not for pleasure, but for contemplation and ceremonies, approved of by Confucius.

The child shunned play, or any vigorous physical activity, including riding, which was on the curriculum for a Manchu emperor. To meet his obligation he had a wooden horse installed and sat on it for his lessons. But he did like to exercise his hands, and loved to take apart and reassemble watches and clocks. Eunuchs purchased these European imports from an enterprising Dane, who had a shop in the capital.

Guangxu was physically weak, timid and nervous, with a stutter, and he was easily frightened. The sound of thunder terrified him. When there was a storm, a crowd of eunuchs would gather around him, shouting at the top of their voices so as to drown out the thunder. Unlike his Papa Dearest, or his cousin, Emperor Tongzhi, Guangxu seemed to have no vitality. He expressed no desire to travel, not even to go beyond the Forbidden City: he was content in his isolation from the outside world.

Inside the Forbidden City, intense labour over the classics lasted for a decade – the time needed to produce a scholar. At the end of it, Emperor Guangxu's tutors pronounced that he had completed his studies 'with distinction'. In summer 1886, when he turned fifteen, he was deemed well qualified to be the ruler of China. Cixi felt obliged to issue an edict, bidding the imperial astrologer to select an auspicious date at the beginning of the following year for the young man to assume power.

The imminent departure of Cixi threw the modernisers into panic. Deprived of her energetic initiative and drive, the reform projects she had started were likely to peter out. For days Earl Li was 'unable to sleep or eat properly' and was 'in a constant state of trepidation'. In the end he wrote to Prince Chun, imploring him to think of a way for Cixi to stay on. The prince was well aware that his son could not fill Cixi's shoes, and so conducted a petition campaign pleading for

Cixi to act as the emperor's 'Guardian' for a few more years. He put pressure on his son to go down on his knees and beg the empress dowager not to retire. Cixi encouraged the campaign by having the Grand Council draft petitions for officials. One, singing her praises, proclaimed that she had 'brought the country into a brand new and glorious phase unprecedented in its long history' – an assessment that Grand Tutor Weng, who was most anxious that his pupil should take his rightful place, found 'inappropriate'. As always, Cixi considered every angle and anticipated the concern of some petitioners that, by calling for her to delay the handover, they might annoy the emperor: she let it be known that the emperor himself had begged on his knees for her to stay.

Eventually Cixi announced that she would 'continue to act as the Guardian for a few more years'. Earl Li was overjoyed. Prince Chun wrote: 'My heart, which has been in my mouth for days, has now returned to its proper place. This is really good fortune for all in the empire.' Earl Li commented: 'How extremely true.' Grand Tutor Weng was not pleased, but, as a seasoned courtier, he made no protest. When the empress dowager asked him whether his pupil was really ready to take over, he replied that, as the emperor's tutor, he could not boast that His Majesty had left no space for improvement; and that even if he had, 'the interests of the dynasty override all'.

Emperor Guangxu was disappointed. After being forced to perform the sham 'begging', he was unwell for days – 'under the weather, with a cold and a headache', Weng recorded. The emperor suspended the lessons, and when he next saw his tutor, he appeared so depressed that the old man, struggling to cheer him up, burst into tears. The normally placid young man became emotional. His tutor encouraged him to speak his mind to the empress dowager. But he did not. Of all the virtues extolled by Confucius, filial piety was foremost.* The concept had been drilled into the young man partly through ritual: every day, so long as they were staying in the same place, he never failed to go to his Royal Father to bid her 'good morning' and 'goodnight'. He had to remind himself constantly 'not to be disrespectful', but his heart grew bitter. As his mind was no longer on his studies, the previously joyful tutor now began to lament his pupil's lack of concentration.

An introverted man, Emperor Guangxu brooded. His health

---

* One of Grand Tutor Weng's heroes was an official who, after his parents died, declined to have treatment for his own illness and died himself.

deteriorated, and every few days he would take some sort of medicinal stew. He wrote later that it was from this time that he 'felt permanently cold around his ankles and knees, and would catch cold from the slightest draught' or if he was 'not tucked in extremely tightly at night'. His voice dropped to the level of a whisper and was unintelligible to officials in the occasional audiences he gave. Even his handwriting evinced signs of feebleness – the brush strokes trailing shakily, the characters dwindling to half their usual size, as if he were too weak to hold his brush.

Cixi was well aware of her adopted son's condition. She asked Grand Tutor Weng to persuade him to settle back into his studies, tearfully defending her delayed handover as doing her 'duty to the ancestors'. But the only remedy for his malaise was for her to release power, which she was unwilling to do.

Emperor Guangxu turned sixteen in summer 1887. This was the age at which Cixi's own deceased son was married, his wedding preparations having started when he was thirteen. Cixi had delayed her adopted son's marriage because it would signal his coming of age, after which she could hardly remain in charge. But the marriage could not be delayed indefinitely, and the nationwide selection of his consorts had to begin. The process took a long time and, one day in 1888, Emperor Guangxu exploded in frustration. He refused to go to a scheduled lesson and in tremendous agitation smashed the glass on a window. (The emperor was known to have a bad temper, and once, recorded his tutor Weng, 'in a fury he had three eunuchs from the Tea Department thrashed harshly, one of them to the verge of death, all for trifles'.) Now his anger towards his Papa Dearest could no longer be contained. Cixi was taken aback. Two days after this outburst, she announced that the wedding would take place at the beginning of the following year. Soon there was another decree declaring that she would retire immediately after the wedding – whereupon her adopted son issued his own decree dictating arrangements for her retirement ceremony, leaving no chance for anyone to intervene. Within days of these announcements, Cixi moved out of the Forbidden City into the Sea Palace, which was to be her retirement home. The paint in her new quarters was still wet, and she had to stay in a temporary apartment.

As the empress dowager, Cixi was entitled to help decide who should be her adopted son's wife. She wanted an empress who was totally obedient to her. After going through the obligatory selection process, she made clear her choice: a daughter of her brother, Duke Guixiang.★ She had always liked the girl, and had 'reserved' her as the empress for some years. Longyu was meek and good-natured, with beautiful manners. But she was very plain – a defect that was not compensated for by wit. And, being three years older than the emperor, she was twenty-one at the time of their marriage, well over the normal age for a royal bride. Even in the average family she would be considered an old maid. When Grand Tutor Weng recorded the choice of consorts, he omitted the new empress's age, mentioning only the ages of the two concubines, Pearl, twelve, and Jade, fourteen.

Emperor Guangxu disliked his empress – and liked her father still less. Duke Guixiang was a figure of scorn. He was an opium smoker, even though his sister, the empress dowager, detested the drug. Considered hopelessly incompetent, he never held any post of substance. As he had squandered much of his wealth, Cixi felt obliged to subsidise his family, not by giving him money, which might well go directly to the opium seller, but by giving him gifts from time to time. When the eunuchs came with a porcelain vase or a *cloisonné* jewellery box from the empress dowager, they expected handsome tips, which the duke had to raise by pawning some of his belongings. The eunuchs would time their arrival to give the family the opportunity to visit the pawn shop, and meanwhile would hang around the duke's house offering greetings to all members of the household, as well as paying endless compliments over tea to the duchess, who could not resist flattery. After receiving their tips, the eunuchs would lewdly ridicule the duchess among themselves. She and the duke were not the parents-in-law an emperor could feel proud of.

This arranged marriage betrayed Cixi's striking lack of sensitivity for her adopted son. In the case of her late son, she had allowed him to choose his own bride, even though she had misgivings about his choice, a girl whose grandfather had died at her hands and who might well harbour a hatred for her. But Cixi loved her son enough not to veto the choice. This time, she had chosen the empress for her adopted son without a shred of consideration for his feelings. Emperor Guangxu did not protest explicitly, observing the code of filial obedience – and his Papa Dearest was a formidable character to defy. But he had his

★ After making her sister's son emperor, Cixi was now making her brother's daughter empress. The marriage of first cousins was a common practice.

own way to retaliate and sprang a surprise immediately after his formal assumption of power on 4 March 1889.

The day after was his wedding day, on which 5.5 million taels had been spent. The occasion was predictably splendid, enhanced by sunny weather. Empress Longyu, carried in a golden sedan-chair, travelled along the central line in the Forbidden City, the line that only an emperor – and an empress on the single occasion of her wedding – was allowed to tread. Around her was the treeless immensity of the august front section of the Forbidden City, lined with red-uniformed Praetorian Guards carrying multicoloured banners, and officials in blue robes against a backdrop of crimson walls and golden roofs. Her sedan-chair passed through the Gate of Supreme Harmony, which had recently been burned down and was now a temporary paper-and-wood imitation, even though it looked as glorious as the real one. Like this gateway, Empress Longyu's marriage would be a sham.

Beyond the gateway stood the most magnificent hall of the Forbidden City, the Hall of Supreme Harmony, *Tai-he* – the location for the most important events of the dynasty. The grand banquet in honour of the bride's father, Duke Guixiang, was scheduled to be held there the day after the wedding. But that morning, according to Grand Tutor Weng, Emperor Guangxu got up, 'complained of feeling dizzy' and 'threw up water'. Royal physicians could find nothing wrong with him, but the emperor nevertheless declared that he must avoid draughts, and refused to go to the great hall. The banquet had to be cancelled and all the assembled grandees had to disperse. Such a cancellation was unheard of, and rumours started to fly at once throughout the capital. The emperor made sure that this snub to his bride's family was driven home by having the untouched food distributed to the officials on the invitation list, and specifically ordered that nothing was to be delivered to his father-in-law's house. It is easy to imagine Cixi's anger on learning about her brother's spectacular humiliation. In her Sea Palace, noted Grand Tutor Weng, 'opera shows did not stop' at the news that the emperor was unwell.

Thereafter Emperor Guangxu treated his wife, Empress Longyu, at best with coldness. Under the gaze of the court he would look right through her as if she did not exist. She tried to please him, which only annoyed him. It was widely known that when she 'came into his presence he not infrequently kicked off his shoes at her'. Cixi's desire to supervise her adopted son backfired and further strained her own relationship with him. Now that she was obliged to retire, the last thing Emperor Guangxu wanted to do was consult her about anything, least of all matters of state.

The emperor favoured Imperial Concubine Pearl, a lively young girl who, noticed the eunuchs, did not appear in front of him as a woman. She wore no make-up and sported a man's hairstyle (with a queue down her back), a man's hat, a riding waistcoat and flat black satin boots. As he later described to his doctors, including a French doctor, Dr Dethève, Emperor Guangxu had been experiencing involuntary ejaculations at night since early adolescence. He would feel aroused by the sound of percussion instruments in his dreams, which would give him sensual feelings and lead to nocturnal emissions. However, at other times, wrote Dr Dethève in his medical report, such ejaculations did not occur and 'there is no possibility of having an erection'. This suggests that Emperor Guangxu was unable to have conventional sex. People in China guessed as much at the time – and called it 'castration by Heaven'. Pearl, dressed like a man, thus put no pressure on him to have sexual intercourse, and he was able to feel relaxed with her. The emperor took up musical instruments such as gongs, drums and cymbals – all the ones that sexually aroused him – and became a rather good percussionist.

In spite of his physical problems, the emperor carried out his royal duties conscientiously, continuing, at the same time, with his study of the Chinese classics and the Manchu language. His life was spent exclusively in the Forbidden City, with excursions only to the adjacent Sea Palace and occasional trips to temples to pray for good harvests, or to the royal mausoleums to beg for his ancestors' blessings. He was as close as ever to Grand Tutor Weng, a father figure with whom he had spent all his formative years and whom he still saw virtually daily. There was another tutor, a modern-minded man named Sun Jianai, who urged him to think about reforms. But the young man was not interested. Nor did he have a rapport with this tutor. Only Weng was in a position to shape the policies of Emperor Guangxu's reign.

Weng remained disdainful of the West, although he was no longer filled with hatred and had become receptive towards some Western practices. From the descriptions of travellers abroad, as well as his own experience of passing through Shanghai, he recognised the benefits of industries such as 'iron mills, shipyards, and weaponry manufacturers'. He had his first photo taken in 1887. He even had approving things to say about a Catholic church that he visited. The church orphanage, he noticed, had separate male and female sections, standing on 'high and damp-free ground', and was 'tidy and orderly'. The church school had four classrooms, where children were reading out loud in a most pleasing fashion. His hosts were 'extremely courteous' and the servants 'declined tips'. All in all, the Grand Tutor was impressed. Still, in Shanghai, he felt a 'strong aversion' to Western buildings, and preferred to stay indoors alone rather than go out. He continued to oppose railway-building. When fire broke out in the Forbidden City just before the emperor's wedding, he saw it as Heaven's warning against having electric lights, motor boats and the little railway in the palaces.

Cixi was aware of his views and of his influence on her adopted son. But there was little she could do about it, especially as the young emperor had developed such an aversion for her, on top of his emotional attachment to the old man. Before the handover of power, she had had a meeting with the pair, and extracted from them a promise not to change the course she had set. But she could not stop them when, before long, they shelved the great north–south railway which she had decreed, and let the currency reform peter out. When the delegation of officials she had sent to tour the world returned home, both they and the knowledge they had gained were ignored. Anxious to steer her adopted son towards an appreciation of the West, Cixi 'ordered' him, noted Grand Tutor Weng, to learn English. As a parent, she had a say in his education, even though he was now an adult and had assumed power as the emperor. The English lessons started, to the Grand Tutor's dismay. 'What is this for?' he asked. In his diary he lamented: 'Foreign language books are now on the imperial desk. How sad this makes me!' Guangxu persisted, partly at Cixi's insistence and partly because he found the language intriguing. But his interest was purely academic and was not transferred into any modernising effort.

Emperor Guangxu did nothing to follow up Cixi's reforms, and let them lapse. He returned to the age-old way of running the empire: mere bureaucratic administration, writing brief minutes in crimson ink on the daily dispatches – 'Report received.' 'Do as you propose.' 'To the relevant office.' His audiences were routine and brief. It was widely known that the emperor 'has a hesitation in his speech . . . he speaks slowly and with difficulty'. Indeed his voice was barely audible, and he had a stammer. To spare him the obvious pain of having to speak, officials advised each other to produce a monologue after the emperor's first question and thus fill the obligatory minimum ten minutes. The emperor still fretted about the 'hard life of the people'. Once, when a flood burst a dyke, poured into Beijing and lashed at the walls of the Forbidden City, the distressed emperor worried about the numerous people living in the path of the flood. But he did no more than the traditional opening of the rice centres and praying to Heaven. It does not seem to have entered his mind that modernisation could provide some solutions. Food imports continued, as did foreign trade, but the country went into a 'period of slumber', noticed Westerners, 'in which the foreign traders alone were enterprising'.

No petitions were filed deploring this lethargy. Traditional watchdogs over the throne would cry out against deviations from precedent, royal extravagance or impropriety, or other offences to the precepts of Confucianism – but not inaction. The debates over policies that had enlivened Cixi's court were entirely absent, as the elite settled back into the old routine. Prince Gong was not in office, but even if he were, he was not a person to set the agenda or push for change. Prince Chun needed to work under a leader rather than lead himself. In any event, he was plagued by illness and died on the first day of 1891. Earl Li, whom many Westerners regarded as 'the greatest moderniser of China and a great statesman', was equally helpless without Cixi. Although he retained his posts, his hands were tied: his arch enemy and political adversary, Grand Tutor Weng, now had the emperor's ear.

Emperor Guangxu did not grant an audience to the diplomatic corps to receive their credentials for two years after his assumption of power. When he did, the occasion – his first contact with Westerners – went smoothly. It had been established in 1873, under Cixi's influence, that Western envoys need not kowtow. Following this precedent, the envoys bowed and Emperor Guangxu nodded in acknowledgement. Prince Ching, who had succeeded Prince Gong as the head of the Foreign Office, took from the ministers their written letters of congratulation and placed them on the yellow dragon altar, before going down on his knees to recite a sort of formal report. He then stood up and read out the royal reply to the envoys. This procedure was repeated each time a minister presented his credentials. 'Audience went off successfully,' wrote Robert Hart. The ministers might have been surprised if they had set eyes on the diary entry of Grand Tutor Weng. In the presence of His Majesty, Weng wrote, in language that had not been used in Cixi's court for decades, 'the foreign barbarian envoys were frightened and trembling, and so fell into performing proper obeisance'.

Westerners had had high hopes of the young emperor when he

took over. 'Railroads, the electric light, physical science, a new navy, an important army, a general banking system, a mint, all in the bud now, will soon be in full flower . . . The reign of the young emperor will be the most memorable epoch in Chinese history.' Many had dreamed this dream; but the buds so assiduously planted and nurtured by Cixi were not allowed to grow, let alone to flower.

Emperor Guangxu ambled along, a conscientious administrator with a penchant for scholarship, while Grand Tutor Weng indulged in leisurely appraisals of poetry and calligraphy. Both were reaping the benefits of peace and stability created by Cixi. They were to be rudely thrust into a whirlwind that would change everything for them – and the empire – when Japan, taking advantage of Cixi's absence, pounced in 1894.

14 The Summer Palace
(1886–94)

WHEN her retirement was mooted in 1886, Cixi's dream of restoring part of the Old Summer Palace, razed more than a quarter of a century earlier, came back to haunt her. The old splendour had only increased in allure as the years went by, and it was known in the court that her ultimate ambition was to restore it to some of its former glory. To finance her dream, she had been saving money from the royal household allowances. Eunuchs observed that she was 'extremely thrifty', and her ladies-in-waiting remembered her telling them to recycle gift wrappings and string. She decided that as the first step she would restore a palace called *Qing-yi-yuan*, the Garden of Clear Ripples, a landscaped estate around the enormous Kunming Lake, which she loved. There the buildings were relatively few and less damaged, and could be repaired without incurring enormous costs.

She knew the project was bound to arouse objections. More than a decade earlier, when her late son, Emperor Tongzhi, planned the project for her first retirement, the opposition had been so strong that she had felt compelled to call a halt. Now there would be the same chorus of disapproval, especially as there was already an official retirement home for her, the Sea Palace, adjacent to the Forbidden City. Even the renovation of that palace had brought criticism and was permanently short of funds. At one point the private contractors, who employed thousands of workers, failed to pay wages on time, and the workers went on strike – the modern word 'strike' thus entering court records for the first time in 1886–7.

Cixi was dissatisfied with the Sea Palace because it was in the middle of Beijing and would not give her the natural surroundings that she craved. Her heart was set on the Old Summer Palace. She tried to justify the building work in an imperial decree in which she, unusually, added a personal plea. Playing down the scale of the project ('very limited repair work'), she told the country that for a quarter of a century she had exhausted herself doing her duty 'day and night, fearfully as if standing over a precipice, worrying something might go wrong', and had brought 'some peace and stability' to the empire. In all those years she had never gone on 'pleasure trips like hunting, which previous monarchs had enjoyed to the full', because she was mindful of 'the hard life of the people'. She gave her assurance that the construction would 'not touch any funds from the Ministry of Revenue, so would not affect the livelihood of the people', and implored 'all in the empire to show understanding'.

Indeed, while Qianlong the Magnificent had often made two or three long trips a year, with his mother and consorts, each costing hundred of thousands of taels, Cixi had never indulged herself in any such journeys, however much she longed to travel. She was a devout Buddhist and yearned to visit the sacred Buddhist mountain of Wutai, to the southwest of Beijing, which had been a favourite destination for earlier emperors. But taking into account the cost of the journey, she had accepted the advice of Prince Gong and his fellow Grand Councillors and abandoned the idea. Now she told the grandees that, in exchange for forgoing expensive excursions, such as visiting the Hunting Lodge like previous emperors, or going to the coast to inspect the newly modernised navy — which she could legitimately do — she would build her dream retirement home. There was no loud protest; and so began the building of Cixi's own, new Summer Palace, the *Yi-he-yuan*, the Gardens of Nurturing Harmony.

Nowadays a major tourist attraction in Beijing, the Summer Palace has been the cause of much condemnation of Cixi. It has been claimed that its restoration cost tens of millions of taels, which Cixi stole from the navy, thus bankrupting it and leading to a devastating defeat by Japan. Visitors to the Summer Palace are more than likely to hear this denunciation from the guides. The truth about the cost and her diversion of funds is rather different. The Summer Palace did not cost *tens* of millions. The original Garden of Clear Ripples, developed by Emperor Qianlong in the mid-eighteenth century, had cost 4,402,852 taels. When Cixi rebuilt it, she added several buildings and modern comforts, so the expenditure certainly exceeded that sum. The initial costing by the project's Accounting Office covered fifty-six sites (about half the total) and came to 3,166,700 taels. According to Chinese historians who have since studied the court records extensively, the total cost of the restoration is estimated at a maximum of six million taels. This is slightly more than was spent on Emperor Guangxu's wedding – 5.5 million taels (an expenditure that came out of the Ministry of Revenue and gave rise to no complaints). Cixi put up three million from her savings from the royal household allowances. And some officials contributed 'donations'. But still she needed some government funding.

Although all state spending was authorised by the empress dowager, she could not simply take what she wanted. As she had promised in her decree that she would not use money from the Ministry of Revenue, Cixi devised a roundabout way of obtaining state funds. The navy was undergoing a process of modernisation, headed by Prince Chun, and was allocated a colossal budget of four million taels a year. Could not a small slice of this sum – perhaps a portion of *the interest* derived from the money deposited in a (foreign) bank – be used to help build her Summer Palace, a slice that would make no difference to the navy? This appears to be what she thought. She reckoned that the country need not know of her scheme if her devoted servant, Prince Chun, and the others involved covered up for her. Exactly how much she took is unclear. What is known is that in one year she was promised 300,000 taels, which seems to have been the usual annual amount. In just under a decade she may have siphoned off some three million taels – which tallies with the overall cost of the building works. This money did not come from the capital of the naval funds deposited in the bank, and leading Chinese scholars have concluded that the arrangement 'did not have a significant impact on the navy'.

While the impact was imperceptible, it was potentially corrosive. If she were to take the path of corruption, others would surely follow. Her strategem was bound to be detrimental to the navy, which was her own baby. It seems that Cixi was troubled by what she was doing. To make her feel better, as well as to mollify the population, who could see the building work and had begun to talk, the faithful Prince Chun suggested that, as Cixi was not going to the coast, the navy could train on Kunming Lake so that she could review their exercises. In this case, buildings could be legitimately repaired. Indeed, she watched some exercises, although they could hardly have been by gunboats. But she feared that Heaven could easily detect the fraud. When the big fire broke out in the Forbidden City at the beginning of 1889, just before Emperor Guangxu's wedding and her retirement, she started to panic, thinking this might be Heaven's wrath at her misdemeanour, and issued a decree halting the work. But soon passion for her beloved Summer

Palace conquered all other considerations, and Cixi cheated even Heaven. Construction resumed.

She oversaw the building work eagerly, going over the designs in detail, discussing them with the management, and having progress reported to her every few days. Three-quarters of the Summer Palace's grounds comprised water – Kunming Lake, 2.2 square kilometres in size, which was overlooked by the Longevity Hill, 60 metres in height. Along the lake meandered a long covered wooden corridor with vividly coloured pictures on its beams depicting Buddhist stories and folklore. Across the lake, visible in the distance, was an elongated stone bridge of seventeen arches, elegantly flung over a narrow stretch of water. The whole palace estate was a perfect ensemble of seemingly undisturbed nature and richly artful creation. Electric lights were fitted, with generators and lamps bought from Germany. Earl Li, who supervised the purchase, wrote to Prince Ching for the empress dowager that the lamps were 'the latest models in the West, and have not been seen in China . . . They are really extraordinarily beautiful.' The locals knew when she was in the palace: over the landing pier was a tall lamp post with electric lights, which would be lit whenever she was in residence. When shown around, Grand Tutor Weng commented that he had 'never seen such splendid buildings and such luxurious decoration'. It is generally considered to be the jewel of Beijing and a brilliant example of traditional Chinese landscape gardening.

15 In Retirement and in Leisure (1889–94)

BECAUSE the Summer Palace was still under construction when Cixi retired in 1889, she lived first in the Sea Palace, adjacent to the Forbidden City. There her adopted son had a villa, Yingtai, in the middle of the lake, where he often stayed. Seeing her almost daily for the routine greetings, Guangxu was totally silent about state business. He had long yearned to be in charge of his own affairs and wanted even less of Cixi's interference after she imposed a detested marriage on him.

Before her retirement, a set of rules, the Statutes, had been drawn up by Prince Chun and the grandees concerning her future political role, which she had accepted. The Statutes did not require Emperor Guangxu to consult her over policy, nor did they give her any say over the emperor's decisions – with the single exception of the appointment of senior officials, for which her approval had to be obtained before an announcement could be made. In addition, Emperor Guangxu was obliged to send her the titles of the reports he received, from which she could get a vague idea of what was going on in the empire, but no details. These copies were for information only. However much Prince Chun wanted Cixi to continue at the helm, and however much she wanted to be, this was as far as they could go. When, just before her retirement, an official petitioned for all reports that were destined for the emperor to be presented to her as well, she had no alternative but to reject the idea out of hand.

Emperor Guangxu followed the Statutes to the letter, and the first list was sent to Cixi on the very day after he assumed power. Simultaneously her contacts with the Grand Council and other officials were severed, including with Earl Li. At first, it seems, the woman who had been at the centre of historical action for nearly three decades found it hard to stay away. That summer she stepped in and announced the launch of the Beijing–Wuhan Railway in a decree that said specifically: 'His Majesty on the order of Her Majesty the Empress Dowager Cixi . . .' She was able to do this probably because Grand Tutor Weng was away attending to his family tombs, and the emperor bowed to her forceful intervention. But when the tutor was back and disapproved of the project, Guangxu shelved it. Early the following year, 1890, she seized the opportunity presented by a trip to pay homage at the Eastern Mausoleums, for which senior officials gathered, to meet with the Grand Council and Earl Li. They discussed railway projects and the latest situation in Korea, a vassal state of China's, where a crisis involving rivalrous foreign powers was looming. The meeting created such bad odour with the emperor that, it seems, he had it out with her, which in turn made Cixi furious. When she handed out fruits as a goodwill gesture to officials, she excluded the emperor's attendants. Similar moments of tension continued into 1891.

Cixi's formal move into the Summer Palace on 4 June 1891 put an end to this struggle, as she was now physically removed from the decision-making centre. Any further effort would involve nothing short of conspiracy. Emperor Guangxu made a point of marking her departure with an imperial decree and an elaborate ceremony attended by a large contingent of officials. That morning he led them all in formal garb to kneel outside the gate of the Sea Palace to see her on her way. After her sedan-chair set off, he went ahead, in order to greet her, again on his knees, upon her arrival at the Summer Palace. They had dinner together, after which he returned to the Forbidden City. Thereafter he visited the Summer Palace regularly, but only to bid her good health. These shows of etiquette kept her firmly away from politics. As Cixi later told a Viceroy, 'After my retirement, I no longer had anything to do with state affairs.'

Her royal duties were symbolic and prescribed. When harvests failed on a large scale, she would issue a public announcement, donating money from the court. When Prince Chun died in 1891, it was her responsibility to oversee all the requisite arrangements, from the interment to the construction of a temple dedicated to the prince. Otherwise, she spent her days with eunuchs and ladies of the court.

The person who looked after her and made sure things ran smoothly was her head eunuch, Lee Lianying – the man who had been taken by Prince Chun on his tour to inspect the navy. The trip had been Cixi's gift to the key figure in her daily life, as well as the prince's way of making amends to her. The American painter Katharine Carl, who met him some years later, described Lianying:

> In person he is tall and thin. His head is, in type, like Savonarola's. He has a Roman nose, a massive lean jaw, a protruding lower lip, and very shrewd eyes, full of intelligence, that shine out of sunken orbits. His face is much wrinkled and his skin like old parchment . . . He has elegant, insinuating manners, speaks excellent Chinese – having a fine enunciation, a good choice of words, and a low, pleasant voice.

Lianying's future as a eunuch was sealed when he was six by his poverty-stricken father, who took the child to a professional castrator. When he first entered the court, the boy preferred play to work and was considered 'lazy'. But strict training and severe punishments for 'dereliction' changed him and made him assiduous in serving his masters and obeying court rules. Exceptionally cautious and sensitive, he looked after Cixi to perfection. He was her taster – and also her best friend. Cixi was lonely. Some of her eunuchs recalled:

> Although the Empress Dowager had many matters to deal with, it appeared that her life was rather empty. When she was not working, she painted and watched operas, and so on, but she was often restless. The only person who could relieve her restlessness was the eunuch Lee Lianying. He knew how to look after her and became her indispensable companion. We could see that they were very, very close.

The eunuchs remembered that Cixi often dropped into Lianying's room and called out: 'Lianying, let's go for a stroll.' They 'would then walk together, and we would follow them from a distance. The empress dowager sometimes even called Lee Lianying to her bedchamber . . . and they would chat deep into the night.' When Lianying was ill – or pretended to be ill in order to stay in bed, according to the eunuchs – 'the Empress Dowager would worry and would summon the court doctors at once. She would stay with him until he took the medicine.' (Herbs and other ingredients took time to dole out, mix and brew.) In the court medical records Lianying had his own file, unique for a member of staff, who shared files. This medical privilege was unavailable even to lower-rank royal concubines. Cixi showered him with expensive gifts and promoted him to a high rank that was unprecedented for a eunuch in Qing history.

In the court Lianying's privileged position generated little malicious jealousy, as by consensus he was 'always respectful to his superiors, and always generous to his inferiors'. But in the country at large, because of his closeness to Cixi, and because he was a eunuch, officials were constantly accusing him of meddling in state affairs, although no one ever produced any proof. As a matter of fact Cixi never involved him in politics, following the Qing rules meticulously. But the accusations refused to die down. When he was taken on the navy inspection tour by Prince Chun, the news generated such a tempest that it almost overshadowed the inspection itself. One Censor wrote to reprimand Cixi, alleging that sending Lianying on the trip had caused floods that had ruined the crops in several provinces. Cixi broke her own rule of not punishing critics and accused the Censor of slander, on which basis she publicly and emphatically rejected his petitions ('threw them back at him'), and demoted the hapless man. When another official wrote to say that eunuchs should not be let out of the capital at all, she ignored the petition. Still there was widespread gossip that Lianying had attained his privileged position through his exceptional skill in dressing Cixi's hair – a baseless rumour that was charged with sexual innuendo. Even a later defeat by Japan during Cixi's retirement was blamed on her relationship with Lianying.

Lianying would get even in his own way. Often offered expensive gifts by officials hoping for a sinecure, he would accept them, but then do nothing. Cixi was well aware this was happening and acquiesced.

Trying all sorts of ways to reward Lianying, Cixi invited his sister to stay in the court. But her stay was short. As the relative of a eunuch she was in an awkward position. When other ladies rode in sedan-chairs, tired after a long walk, she had to trot, like her brother, alongside the chairs, which was excruciating for her bound feet. A palace maid observed that the empress dowager would have allowed her a sedan-chair for herself, but the prudent Lianying would never have accepted the favour. His sister's station was considered so low that the servants would not even take tips from her. 'We wouldn't accept her tips even if we were dying of poverty,' one of the maids snorted. Before long, the sister stopped appearing at court.

★

The court ladies around Cixi were mostly young widows. They had all had their marriages arranged by the empress dowager, which was considered the greatest of privileges, and all were prohibited by the traditional code of honour from marrying again after their husbands had died. Among them was a daughter of Prince Ching, Si Gege, who was clever and vivacious, fun-loving and popular, and who made Cixi laugh. Cixi said the girl reminded her of her younger self, and missed her whenever she was away. Another teenage widow was a Lady Yuan, who was not actually married in the normal sense: the man to whom she had been engaged, a nephew of Cixi, had died before the wedding. But before the funeral Lady Yuan dressed herself in a widow's garb, and in a sedan-chair draped with white sackcloth, a sign of mourning, went to his coffin and performed the ritual that established her position as his widow. This highly regarded act of spousal loyalty set her on a lifetime of chastity and loneliness. To an observer she was wooden and lifeless, and Cixi did not have much to say to her. But she took pity on Lady Yuan and always included her in the invitations.

Empress Longyu was a perennial fixture in Cixi's retinue. The emperor completely ignored her, even when they bumped into each other and she went down on her knees to greet him. People regarded her as 'sweet', 'charming' and 'lovable', 'but there is sometimes a look in her eyes of patient resignation that is almost pathetic'. Her life was empty and she was very bored. Some said she took out her frustration and bitterness on servants and pets, and that her cats always ran away after a few months. All the ladies would try to be cheerful when they were around Cixi, but there was little real happiness.

Cixi led a well-ordered life. In the morning she took her time getting up, no longer forcing herself to rise at five or six, but lingering sometimes until after eight. When she was ready for the day, signalled by the windows in her quarters being opened, the whole palace began to buzz. Eunuch messengers raced around to announce the 'news' and chief eunuchs congregated outside her apartment to await instructions.

In her room she put on a silk dressing gown, while a maid rushed to the kitchen to fetch hot water, which was poured into a silver bowl held aloft by a junior eunuch on his knees, with maids standing holding soap dishes and hand towels. Cixi attended to her face by covering it with a hot towel for a few minutes before patting it dry. Then she wrapped her hands in another towel and soaked them in the hot water for a rather long time – long enough for the water to be changed two or three times – which was said to be her secret for keeping her hands soft like a young girl's.

After rinsing her teeth, she sat on a chair facing south and a eunuch came in to dress her hair. According to the eunuchs, Cixi had begun to lose hair from the age of forty, and a jet-black toupee was placed over the thinned patch. It required considerable skill to keep the wig in position while combing her hair and fixing it in the complicated Manchu style, with jewelled pins. Her hairdresser would also supply her with the gossip of the previous day and she would slowly take her daily jelly of 'silver fungus' (*yin-er*), which was supposed to be good for one's health and looks. When the hairdressing was over, she placed ornaments in her hair. No Manchu lady's coiffure was considered complete without flowers, and Cixi preferred fresh flowers to jewels. She would deftly make flower arrangements on her hair, sometimes weaving the snowy blooms of jasmine into a diadem. (Her palace maids also wore flowers in their hair, and when they stood beside her, those on her right would have flowers on their right side and those on her left their left.)

There was not much she could do to her face: as a widow, she was not supposed to wear make-up. Otherwise, Manchu ladies painted their faces excessively white and pink, and had a vivid patch of red on their lower lip, to produce a 'cherry'-like small mouth, considered beautiful in those days when wide lips were deemed ugly. Longing to use a little make-up, Cixi would discreetly apply a touch of rouge on her cheeks and on the centre of her palms, even a little on her lips. The rouge used in the court was made with roses that grew in the hills west of Beijing. The petals of a certain red rose were put in a stone mortar and crushed with a white marble pestle. A little alum was added and the dark-red liquid thus produced was poured into a 'rouge jug' through fine white gauze. Silk wool was cut into small square or round pads and placed in the jug for days, to soak up the liquid. The silk pads were then dried, inside a room with a glass window to avoid catching dust, before ending up on the royal dressing table. Cixi would dab the pad with lukewarm water before applying it. For her lips she would roll up a pad, or twist one around a jade hairpin, to form a kind of lipstick, and daub the rouge in the centre of her lips – more on the lower lip than the upper. For perfume she mixed the oils of different flowers herself. (The Palace also made its own soap, under Cixi's direction. The maids would show her the paste that would eventually solidify into soap, and she would vigorously stir it herself.)

As a widow, Cixi could not wear brilliant colours like bright reds or greens. But even clothes that were considered discreet were colourful by European standards. Around the house she might put on a pale-orange robe with a pale-blue waistcoat, embroidered only along the hems, and for a special occasion one of her favourite outfits was a blue brocade robe embroidered with big white magnolias. Katharine Carl, the American painter who spent eleven months with her, observed:

> She is always immaculately neat. She designs her own dresses . . . has excellent taste in the choice of colors, and I never saw her with an unbecoming color on, except the Imperial yellow. This was not becoming, but she was obliged to wear it on all official occasions. She used to modify it, as much as possible, by the trimmings, and would sometimes have it so heavily embroidered that the original color was hardly visible.

Cixi's jewels were often set to her own designs, among which was a pearl mantle that she would wear over an official jacket. Diamonds were an acquired taste. The Chinese of her time considered their brilliance to be vulgar, and mostly used them as drill tips.

Dressing up was important to Cixi. She would examine herself at length in the mirror – for longer than seemed fitting, given her age, or so thought some of her maids and ladies-in-waiting. Cixi guessed what was in the young women's minds and one day told the lady-in-waiting, Der Ling, who recorded their exchange:

> 'It must seem to you quite funny to see an old lady like me taking so much care and pains in dressing and fixing up. Well! I like to dress myself up and to see pretty young girls dressed nicely; it makes you want to be young again yourself.' I told her that she looked quite young and was still beautiful, and that although we were young we would never dare compare ourselves with her. This pleased her very much, as she was very fond of compliments . . .

Before she left her dressing room Cixi would stand and take a last look at her shoes, which had a comfortable square-cut toe, quite unlike the sharply pointed ones worn by Han women. Her socks were made of white silk, and were tied at the ankle with a pretty ribbon, and she would look to see if the edges of the socks showing above the shoes were as they should be. Each pair was worn only once, so a constant supply was needed. Apart from a team of seamstresses, her family and other aristocratic households also made socks for her and presented them as gifts.

Her morning toilette completed, Cixi started towards the door to the outer hall, with her 'erect carriage and light swift walk'. A maid parted the curtains and at this movement, for which the eunuch chiefs outside had been waiting, their eyes fixed on the drapes, all dropped to their knees and cried out: 'Old Buddha [*lao-fo-ye*], all joy be with you!' She had adopted this nickname for herself, which, both illustrious and informal, was how she was addressed now in the court and was popularly known in Beijing.

While giving the eunuch chiefs their instructions for the day, Cixi took her first smoke from a water-pipe, which had an elongated stem and a small rectangular box to be held in the palm. Most of the time she did not hold her own pipe. This was the job of a pipe-maid, standing 'about two paving bricks' distance away from the Empress Dowager', according to one of them. When Cixi glanced at her, the pipe-maid's right hand that held the pipe would gently extend its tip to within an inch of the corner of Cixi's mouth, whereupon, with a slight turn of the neck, the firm lips would part to take it. The pipe remained in the hands of the maid while Cixi puffed on it. For this service the maids had been trained for many months, until their right palms could hold a cup of hot water for a long time without twitching.

After two pipes of tobacco, breakfast arrived. First came her tea. The Manchus drank tea with a lot of milk. In her case, the milk came from the breasts of a nurse. Cixi had been taking human milk since her prolonged illness in the early 1880s, on the recommendation of a renowned doctor. Several wet nurses were employed, and took turns to squeeze milk into a bowl for her. The nurses brought their sucking babies with them, and the woman who served her the longest stayed on in the palace, her son being given education and an office job.

While she sipped her tea, a team of eunuchs carried over her food in lacquered boxes wrapped in yellow silk with the dragon motif. Lianying, the head eunuch, took the boxes at the door and brought them himself to Cixi. She ate sitting cross-legged on a *kang* – a long, rectangular brick structure the height of a bed, which could be heated from underneath and was used all over north China as a bed or a seat. She liked to sit by a window, so that she could look out on the courtyard and enjoy the light and the sky. Her food was placed on a low table on the *kang* and extended to some small tables that would be folded away when the meal was finished. When the food boxes were properly arranged, they were opened in front of Cixi's eyes, as court rules dictated. They contained a large variety of porridges, rolls and cakes – steamed, baked and fried – and many kinds of drinks, ranging from soya-bean juice to beef-bone consommé. There were also plenty of savoury side-dishes, such as duck's liver cooked in soya and other spicy sauces.

The empress dowager had a hearty appetite and would go on to have another two sizeable meals and small snacks. The meals were taken wherever she happened to be: she had no fixed dining room. The scale and presentation of the meals followed court stipulations. They would only be reduced if there was a national disaster. As the empress dowager, Cixi was entitled to a daily allocation of 31 kilos of pork, one chicken and one duck. With these, as well as vegetables and other ingredients, the quantities of which were all specified, dozens of dishes were cooked and, for a main meal, would be set out in more than a hundred plates or bowls. Most of the dishes were never touched and were only there to amplify the presentation. She seldom drank with her meals, and mostly ate on her own, as anyone invited to join her had to do so standing – except the emperor. Often court ladies in attendance would be asked to eat at her table after she had finished and left, in which case they were permitted to sit down. Usually dishes from her table would be given to courtiers as tokens of imperial favour. The emperor would also receive her dishes if he was staying in the same palace complex. The vast quantities of leftover food from the court enabled a string of food stalls in the neighbourhood to do a brisk business, and at certain times each day ragged beggars were allowed to come to a particular gate to receive the remnants and sift through the rubbish before it was carted away.

Lunch was followed by a careful hand-washing, and then a siesta. Before she dozed off, Cixi would read the classics with her eunuch instructors, who would enliven the texts by weaving in jokes that amused Cixi. When she got up, there was another tremor in the palace, as an eye-witness described: 'when Her Majesty awakes, the news flashes like an eletric spark through all the Precincts and over the whole inclosure, and everyone is on the "qui vive" in a moment'.

Before she went to bed, at around 11 p.m., she often enjoyed a foot massage. Two masseuses first soaked her feet in a silver-plated wooden bowl, with wide rolled-back 'arms' as foot rests. The water in the bowl was boiled with flowers or herbs, as prescribed by her physicians, bearing in mind factors such as the climate and her physical condition. In summer, it might be dried chrysanthemum, and in winter it could be flowering quince. The masseuses pressed the various pressure points, especially on the soles – rather like a reflexology session today. If her toenails needed cutting, the masseuses would gently request permission to use scissors, which the chief maid then brought in. Sharp objects were normally forbidden in Cixi's quarters. A manicure meant tending to her long fingernails – extraordinarily long on the fourth and fifth fingers, as was common among aristocratic Manchu women. The exceptionally long nails were protected by shields made of openwork *cloisonné* or gold, set with rubies and pearls. As no lady of position would dress herself or comb her own hair, such nails did not present an insurmountable problem.

Her bed was a *kang* built into an alcove in the room, with shelves around the three enclosing sides, on which were placed ornaments such as small jade figures. Her bedside reading amounted to another session of studying the classics with her eunuch instructors, which sent her to sleep. As she slept, a maid sat on the floor of the room, as noiselessly as a piece of furniture. More maids and eunuchs were in the antechamber outside the apartment, and elsewhere in the building. The night-shifts would hear the snoring of a sound sleeper.

Cixi was now in her early fifties and in very good health. She played the game of kick-shuttlecock with more agility than her much younger entourage, and climbed hills fast, without any sign of fatigue. In Beijing's biting winter she normally declined heating, preferring nothing in her bedroom and only charcoal-burning copper braziers in the large halls. Picturesque though these were, they produced little more than curling blue flames and made little difference to the temperature. The doors of her apartment were left open and draped with padded curtains, which were constantly lifted for the passage of eunuchs and maids, so blasts of cold air swept in at every entry or exit. Everyone else felt frozen to the bone, and yet Cixi seemed impervious. She just wore silk-wool undergarments and a fur coat, at most with a big fur cloak on top.

Her mind was as sharp as ever, and so it was difficult for her to shut herself off completely from politics. What made it possible for her to endure the enforced isolation and leisure, day in, day out, was her wide range of interests. She was curious about all new things, and wanted to try everything. Having added a couple of steamboats to the lake, she asked to be flown in a hot-air balloon, which had been bought some years earlier for military use. But Earl Li gave her (via Prince

Ching, as the earl was no longer permitted to communicate directly with her) the disappointing news that the balloon was not in a fit condition and might explode.

The Summer Palace was a source of endless pleasure for Cixi, and she never tired of walking in its grounds. Strolling in the rain appealed to her the most. The eunuchs always brought an umbrella, but she would only use it in heavy downpours. A large retinue of eunuchs followed her, together with ladies-in-waiting and palace maids, bearing her 'clothes, shoes, handkerchiefs, combs, brushes, powder boxes, looking glasses of different sizes, perfumes, pins, black and red ink, yellow paper, cigarettes, water pipes, and the last one carried her yellow satin-covered stool . . .' – like 'a lady's dressing room on legs', according to one lady-in-waiting. Often Cixi and her ladies were carried in sedan-chairs to a picturesque spot of her choosing, where she would sit on her yellow satin stool, gazing for a long time into the distance. One scenic stop was the top of a high-arched bridge, which undulated in a soft, flowing way and was suitably named the Jade Sash. Another place she liked was a cottage built and furnished entirely of bamboo, where she often had tea. Her teas were the finest – the first leaves from all over the empire – which she drank from a jade cup, into which she would drop a few dried petals of honeysuckle, jasmine or rose. The dried blossoms were brought to her in a jade bowl, with two slender cherry-wood sticks, which she used to pick up the blossoms, drop them into her cup and stir the tea.

A favourite activity was boating on the lake, during which her barge was sometimes followed at a distance by eunuch musicians, playing the bamboo flute or bamboo recorder, or the *yue-qin*, a moon-shaped instrument like the mandolin. All would be silent when Cixi listened, 'as if entranced'. Sometimes, in moonlight, she would sing softly to the music floating over the water.

Nature was her passion and she adored plants. Chrysanthemums were among her best-loved flowers. During the season for propagation Cixi would lead the court ladies in taking cuttings and setting them out in flower pots, watering them religiously until they began to bud. The buds were then covered with mats so that they would not be damaged by heavy rain. For this she would even forgo her usual nap. Later on, when she returned to power, she broke with the old custom of allowing no plants in places of official duties and filled the audience hall with a profusion of potted flowers, arranging them in tiers. Officials coming for their audiences had to orient themselves before they went down on their knees, as her throne seemed to be hidden behind a 'flower mountain'.

She was devoted to her orchard, from which large baskets of fruits would be brought before her daily when they were in season. She would inspect their colour and shape, and would hold up a cluster of grapes against the light, for a long time. Apples, pears and peaches filled the huge porcelain pots in the halls, for their subtle fragrance. When the fragrance was gone, the fruits were divided among the servants. The scentless gourd also commanded her affection, and she would often stroke them on their trellises, sometimes in torrential rain. Her collection of gourds ran to several hundred, which an artistic eunuch sculpted into musical instruments, dinner sets and a variety of fanciful articles, adding miniature paintings and calligraphy to their surface. Cixi prepared some of the gourds to be carved by using a sharpened piece of bamboo to scrape off the outer skin.

Every few days, she would visit her large vegetable gardens and would be delighted if she could take away some fresh vegetables or other farm produce. Occasionally she cooked them herself in one of the courtyards and once she taught her ladies-in-waiting how to boil eggs with black tea leaves and spices.

Mosquitoes could be a nuisance in the Summer Palace, especially on summer evenings, but Cixi's eunuchs devised an ingenious solution. They erected giant marquees, each big enough to enclose a building and its courtyards completely. Roofed and curtained with reed matting and a system of ropes and pulleys that rolled and unrolled the top and hoisted and lowered the curtains, these works of art served as vast mosquito nets, in addition to shielding the large enclosures from the sun during the day. With lanterns hanging discreetly and candles flickering in the breeze, evenings were a scented pleasure, scarcely troubled by the insects. The same marquees were erected for the foreign legations.

Cixi loved birds and animals. She learned how to rear and breed them and engaged a eunuch who was a great expert to teach her. Birds in his care were not always confined, although there were hundreds of cages hanging in rows of bamboo frames in one of the large courtyards. Some flew freely, having made their home in the Summer Palace. To protect these rare species, young men with knowledge of birds were recruited into the Praetorian Guards to patrol the grounds with crossbows, ready to shoot down any natural predators or unwanted wild

A court painter's rendering of Cixi playing Go with a eunuch.

A photographic portrait Cixi sent to US President Theodore Roosevelt
in 1904, thanking him for his good wishes for her seventieth birthday.
Her face had been airbrushed in the photograph.

Emperor Xianfeng,
a standard portrait of
a monarch produced
after his death.
Xianfeng died in 1860
in self-imposed exile,
partly because the
Old Summer Palace
had been burned
down by the British.

From that palace, 'Lootie', a Pekinese,
was taken to Britain and presented to
Queen Victoria, who had it painted.

(*Left*) Cixi's son, who would become Emperor Tongzhi, playing with his half-sister.

(*Below left*) Emperor Guangxu who, upon Tongzhi's death in 1875, was put on the throne by Cixi when he was three.

(*Below right*) Zhen, Empress to Xianfeng, and lifelong friend of Cixi.

The harem, at the rear of the Forbidden City. Cixi found its high walls and closed-in alleys 'depressing'.

The front and main part of the Forbidden City, vast and grand – and out of bounds for women. Cixi never set foot in it, even when she was the supreme ruler of China.

As a woman, Cixi was not supposed to see her officials, who were all male.
So, during audiences, she would sit behind the throne and the yellow silk screen.
The child emperor was sometimes seated on the throne in front.

The Summer Palace, which Cixi loved passionately, by a foreign artist.

大清國慈禧皇太后

(*Above*) Portrait of Cixi by the American painter
Katharine Carl, for the St Louis Exposition in 1904.

(*Right*) Katharine Carl, in Chinese costume selected –
possibly designed – by Cixi.

birds that had the temerity to gatecrash. The demand for foods for Cixi's birds created a flourishing trade outside the Summer Palace, selling all sorts of caterpillars, grasshoppers, crickets and ant nests, each said to benefit a different avian attribute.

Some birds were trained to fly towards a high-pitched trill in order to receive their favoured foods. Wherever Cixi was whether climbing a hill or boating in the lake, eunuchs near her would sound the trill so that the birds would fly around her. Cixi herself was skilled at imitating birdsong and could entice birds to her outstretched fingertips. Her bird-taming ability later mesmerised Western visitors. One, her American portraitist Katharine Carl, wrote:

> She had a long, wand-like stick, which had been cut from a sapling and freshly stripped of its bark. She loved the faint forest odor of these freshly cut sticks . . . she held the wand she carried aloft and made a low, bird-like sound with her lips, never taking her eyes off the bird . . . He fluttered and began to descend from bough to bough until he lighted upon the crook of her wand, when she gently moved her other hand up nearer and nearer, until it finally rested on her finger!

Miss Carl was 'watching with breathless attention, and so tense and absorbed had I become that the sudden cessation, when the bird finally came upon her finger, caused me a throb of almost pain.'

Even fish were induced to jump onto her open palms – to her own childlike shrieks. It took buckets of a special kind of earthworm, red and about 3 centimetres long, to entice the fish to leap up towards a human hand at a quay where Cixi often disembarked for lunch.

She bred dozens of dogs. They lived in a pavilion furnished with silk cushions to sleep on and a large wardrobe of jackets, in brocades embroidered with chrysanthemums, crab-apple blossoms and other gorgeous patterns. To avoid undesirable couplings, only her dogs were allowed in the palace grounds. The hundreds of pet dogs belonging to the court ladies and eunuchs had to be kept in their owners' own courtyards. Some dog breeders considered that Cixi 'did more for the Pekingese than any other fancier since the origin of the breed'. One type of Pekinese whose breeding she discontinued was the 'sleeve-dog', a miniature that could be carried in the courtiers' ample sleeves that were used as pockets. The growth of the sleeve-dogs was said to be stunted by feeding them only on sweets and wine and making them wear tight-fitting wire-mesh waistcoats. Cixi told Katharine Carl that she detested such unnatural methods, and that she could not understand why animals should be deformed for man's pleasure.

The pets she was particularly fond of were a Pekinese pug and a Skye terrier. The latter could perform tricks and would lie completely still at Cixi's command, moving only when she told him to, no matter how many others spoke to him. The Pekinese pug had long and silky fawn-coloured hair and large, pale-brown, liquid eyes. He was not easily taught and was affectionately called Little Fool (*sha-zi*) by Cixi. Later she had their portraits painted by Katharine Carl, sitting behind the painter herself and taking 'the liveliest interest'.

In Beijing there was a large collection of birds and animals built up by the French missionary zoologist and botanist Armand David, who, since coming to China in the early years of Cixi's reign, had identified many hundreds of new species unknown in Europe, among them the giant panda. When Cixi heard about the collection she was intrigued and eager to see it. It so happened that the collection was attached to a Catholic cathedral, which overlooked the Sea Palace. After negotiations with the Vatican (through an English intermediary), her government paid 400,000 taels for another cathedral to be built elsewhere, and bought the old church along with the collection. Cixi visited it, but only once. She had scant interest in the dead creatures.

The only competitive games that tradition permitted her were parlour games. Cixi did not enjoy cards, or mah-jong, which she refused to allow at court. Dice-throwing was a popular pastime, and Cixi occasionally played. She invented a dice game not unlike 'Snakes and Ladders', except that the board was a map of the Chinese empire, with all the provinces marked in different colours. Eight carved ivory deities, representing the legendary eight Taoist Immortals, travelled round the empire attempting to reach the capital. In the process, they might be diverted to beauty spots like Hangzhou, or sent into exile, in which case they would have to drop out – all depending on the throw of the dice. The one who reached Beijing first was the winner and would receive sweets and cakes, while the losers had to sing a song or tell a joke. Gambling was not involved. In fact it was officially banned, with offenders being fined and caned.

Painting was a serious hobby, for which Cixi engaged a Lady Miao, a young widow, to be her teacher. Lady Miao was Han and was conspicuous in the court from her hair to her toes. Instead of the complicated and much-decorated Manchu headdress, she combed her hair in a neat coil on the back of her head and encircled the coil with strings of pearls. Rather than a full-length Manchu robe, she wore a loose upper garment that came down to just below her knees, over a long plaited skirt, which revealed a pair of 'three-inch golden lilies' – bound feet on which she teetered and swayed along in agony. Cixi, who as a Manchu had escaped foot-binding, would cringe at the sight of the deformed feet. Once before, when she had set eyes on the bare feet of one of the nurses who provided milk for her, she had said that she could not bear to see them, and had had them unbound. Now she asked Lady Miao to unbind her feet, an order that the painting teacher was only too happy to obey.

Under Lady Miao's tutorship, Cixi became a proficient amateur painter, wielding her brush 'with power and precision', according to her teacher. She achieved something much valued in calligraphy: to write in just one brush stroke a giant character that was as big as a human figure. These characters, denoting 'longevity' and 'happiness', were ritually given to top officials as gifts. Lady Miao's reputation as the empress dowager's tutor enabled her to sell her own paintings for high prices, to buy a large house and support her family.

Near the Summer Palace were many Buddhist and Taoist temples, which organised regular festivals, which women, if chaperoned, could attend, dressed in the most gorgeous colours. Folk artists came from far and wide, walking on stilts, bouncing in lion-dances, waving dragon-lanterns and performing acrobatic and magic tricks. As they passed by the Summer Palace, Cixi often watched from a tower above the walls. Knowing the empress dowager was there, the performers would show off their skills, and she would cheer and give generous tips. One bearded man, who gyrated in the disguise of a village woman, was for a while the recipient of the largest rewards: Cixi was a great fan of popular entertainments and never regarded them as beneath her.

It was in this spirit that she helped turn the genre of Peking Opera into the national opera of China. This genre had traditionally been for the 'average folk of the alleys and villages', as its music, stories and humour were easy to follow and enjoy. Considered 'vulgar', it had been shunned by the court, where only orthodox opera, with its restricted tunes and story lines, was staged. Cixi's husband, Emperor Xianfeng, began to patronise Peking Opera, but it fell to Cixi to mould it into a sophisticated art form, while retaining its playfulness. She extended royal approval by bringing in artists from outside the court to perform for her and to instruct the eunuchs in the Music Department. She demanded professionalism. Historically, Peking Opera was rather casual, with unpunctual opening times, slapdash make-up and costumes; actors would often hail friends from the stage or make impromptu jokes. Cixi addressed all these details with a series of specific orders. She made punctuality mandatory, threatening to cane repeated offenders. On one occasion a principal actor, Tan Xinpei, was late, and she, being a huge fan and feeling unable to have him caned, made him play a clownish pig in *The Monkey King*. Professional acting was handsomely rewarded. While previous emperors tipped the leading players one tael of silver each at most, Cixi habitually lavished dozens of taels on them – as much as sixty to a lead actor, for instance to Tan, who was also given presents as part of the dowry for his daughter's wedding. (In comparison, the chief of the Music Department at the court earned seven taels a month.) In one year her tips to all involved in the opera shows totalled 33,000 taels.

Being so well treated, Peking Opera actors became celebrities – like the film stars of a later age. The public could see how prestigious they were: in one case, 218 artists travelled in the royal procession from the Summer Palace to the Forbidden City, all on horseback, with twelve carts carrying their costumes and paraphernalia. A career in the opera became highly sought-after.

Cixi's opera houses were constructed with carefully designed artistry. In the Sea Palace, a pavilion-style theatre was built in the middle of the lake, where there were lotuses all around so that summer shows took place among their blooms. In the Forbidden City, a heated glass conservatory was erected, as a cosy warm theatre in the midst of winds and snows. In the Summer Palace, she restored a two-storey theatre in an area that attracted orioles: their call was said to go well with the arias. Then she built another, more magnificent three-storey opera house, with a stage 21 metres high, 17 metres wide and 16 metres deep, and a back-stage large enough to hold complicated sets. This was the grandest theatre in China. Both the ceiling and the floor could be opened during the performance, to allow gods to descend from Heaven and the Buddha to rise from the depths of the Earth sitting on an enormous lotus flower; snowflakes (white confetti) could shower from the sky, and water could spout upwards from the mouth of a giant turtle. A pool of water under the stage enhanced the acoustics. The theatre was situated next to the vast lake, so that the melody could travel unimpeded over its surface.

The Peking Opera repertoire was enormously expanded under Cixi. She revived a number of obsolete dramatic pieces by having their libretti dug up from the court archives and adapted to the tunes of

Peking Opera. In the process of adaptation, and trying to accommodate Cixi's own lines, one actor-composer, Wang Yaoqing, enlarged the Opera's musical range. With Cixi's rewards and encouragement, the actor-composer revolutionised Peking Opera by giving female characters (played by men, including him) proper acting roles. They had traditionally been confined to minor parts and could only sing stiffly, not act. Now, for the first time, Peking Opera had lead female roles.

In this undertaking, Cixi became intimately involved in the writing of a 105-episode work, *The Warriors of the Yang Family*, about a tenth- to eleventh-century family who took up arms defending China against invaders. In recorded history, the warriors were all men. But in folk legends the women of the family were the heroes, and this was reflected in a script in Kunqu, a disappearing drama form. Cixi knew the story and took it upon herself to make it a part of the Peking Opera repertoire. She summoned the literary men of the court, mainly doctors and painters, and read out to them her translation of the Kunqu script. The men were divided into groups, each being given some episodes to write for Peking Opera. Supervising them was a woman – a widow and a poetess – who had been sought out by Cixi at the same time as Lady Miao. Cixi herself remained the chief editor of the whole drama. Since then, episodes of *The Female Warriors of the Yang Family* have become some of the most-performed and best-loved Peking Opera numbers, and have been much adapted into other art forms. The names of the female warriors have entered everyday language as synonyms for brave and bright women who outshine men.

Cixi detested age-old prejudices against women. During one opera performance, when a singer sang the oft-repeated line 'the most vicious of all is the heart of a woman', she flew into a rage and ordered the singer off the stage. Her rejection of the traditional attitude was undoubtedly shaped by her own experience. No matter how successful her rule on behalf of her son and adopted son, she would always be denied the mandate to rule in her own right. Once the boys entered adulthood, she was obliged to give way and could no longer participate in politics. She could not even voice her opinions. Watching Emperor Guangxu shelving the modernisation projects she had initiated, Cixi could not fail to despair. And yet there was nothing she could do. Any attempt at changing the status quo would have to involve violent and extreme means, such as launching a palace coup – which she was not prepared to contemplate. Only one woman in Chinese history – Wu Zetian – had declared herself emperor and run the country as such. But she had had to do so in the face of mighty opposition, which she had quelled using hair-raisingly cruel means. On the long list of alleged bloody murders was that of her own son, the crown prince. Cixi was a different character and preferred to rule through consensus: winning over the opposition rather than killing them. As a result, she chose to observe the conditions of her retirement. But clearly she admired the female emperor, and would have liked to stake a similar claim — if the cost were not so high. Her feelings were known to Lady Miao, her painting teacher. The painter once presented her with a scroll that depicted Wu Zetian conducting state affairs as a legitimate sovereign. Cixi's acceptance of the painting says much about her aspirations and frustrations.

16 War with Japan
(1894)

JAPAN set about its miraculous transformation into a modern power during the reign of Emperor Meiji, who ascended the throne in 1867. With a population of forty million, it aspired to build a global empire. In the 1870s, it seized one of the China's vassal states, the Liuqiu Islands, and attempted to invade Taiwan, part of the Chinese Empire. Cixi's general policy was to keep the empire intact at all costs, while releasing the vassal states if she had to. She washed her hands of Liuqiu, by deeds if not by words, but made a determined effort to defend Taiwan, linking the island more closely to the mainland.

Japan also cast its eyes on Korea, another vassal state of China. In this case Cixi tried to prevent the Japanese from annexing the country as it shared a border with Manchuria, which was close to Beijing. As China was not strong enough to stop Japan by itself, Cixi sought to involve the West as a deterrent. She instructed Earl Li to persuade Korea to open up trade with the Western powers, so that they would have a stake in the country. In 1882, an internal strife broke out in Korea and the Japanese Legation was assaulted. Tokyo sent a gunboat to Korea to protect its nationals. As soon as she heard the news, Cixi told Earl Li her anxiety that Japan 'might exploit the situation to pursue its designs'. She immediately dispatched troops by both land and sea to the capital of Korea, today's Seoul, with Earl Li in overall command based in Tianjin. While the Chinese army helped end the riot, the Japanese refrained from getting involved in the fighting; they obtained some compensations – but, most importantly, their soldiers stayed on. In response, Cixi ordered some of her troops to be stationed in Korea for as long as there was a Japanese military presence.* Writing to Earl Li in her own hand in crimson ink, to stress the importance of her words, she said: 'Though a small country, Japan harbours big ambitions. It has already swallowed Liuqiu, and is now eyeing Korea. We have to prepare ourselves quietly. You must be extremely cautious about Japan, and do not lower your guard for a moment.' It was principally for this reason that she decided to spend enormous sums to build up the navy.

At the end of 1884, while China was at war with France on its border with Vietnam, a pro-Japanese coup broke out in Korea. From the information she gathered, Cixi was convinced that 'the Japanese were behind the coup', 'taking advantage of China's preoccupation' elsewhere. She sent over troops to help suppress the coup, but told them not to give the Japanese any excuse to start a war. As it turned out, when Chinese troops did clash with the Japanese in the Korean king's palace, the Chinese were victorious. On Cixi's instructions, Earl Li opened talks with Count Itō Hirobumi, soon to become Japan's first Prime Minister, and both sides agreed to withdraw troops from Korea. Cixi was pleased with the 'speedy and satisfactory conclusion'. So was Robert Hart, Inspector General of Customs, who wrote in a letter: 'The Japs were to sign yesterday at T'tsin [Tianjin]: so we win all round.'

Over the next decade, Japan accelerated the modernisation of its military, especially the navy. In China, Cixi laid down her guideline for naval development just before she retired at the beginning of 1889: 'Keep expanding and updating, gradually, but never slacken.'

But after Cixi's retirement, China stopped buying advanced warships. Emperor Guangxu was guided by Grand Tutor Weng, who was also in charge of the country's finance as the head of the Ministry of Revenue. Weng could not comprehend why huge sums of money should be spent on gunboats when there was no war. He did not see Japan as a threat. All his concerns were domestic. In 1890, natural disasters ravaged the country and millions were made homeless by floods. Hart wrote: 'We have had lakes in the city – a sea round it – rivers in the streets – swimming baths in the courtyard – shower

---

* The troops staying behind in Korea were under a Commander Wu Changqing, who seems to have succeeded in keeping his men strictly disciplined, which earned some goodwill from the Koreans. In 1884, he fell ill and returned to China. When it looked as though nothing could cure him, his despairing teenage son cut two slices of flesh from his own left chest, at a place near his heart, and cooked them with the medicine, in a desperate, but vain, hope that the love and sacrifice would move Heaven and revive his father. The son's idea had come from Confucian morality stories.

baths in the rooms – and destruction for roofs, ceilings . . .' Famine-stricken men and women depended on rice centres, to which Cixi as the empress dowager made donations. The government spent more than eleven million taels to buy rice from overseas that year.

When the disaster was over and rice imports halved, naval updating did not resume. On the contrary, in 1891, when Cixi moved into the Summer Palace and severed her ties with the government altogether, Emperor Guangxu decreed that all naval and army be discontinued, on the advice of Grand Tutor Weng ('there is no war on the coast'). This decision may have caused the rows at this time between Emperor Guangxu and Cixi, who was deeply concerned that Japan would now outstrip China in military material. Indeed, as Earl Li observed, Japan 'is concentrating the resources of the entire country to build its navy,' and 'is buying a gunboat every year . . . including first-class, latest ironclads from Britain'. As a result, in the ensuing years, the Japanese navy overtook the Chinese in its overall capacity, especially in faster and more up-to-date warships. The Japanese army also became better equipped.

At this time Earl Li was in charge of coastal defence. Emperor Guangxu had inherited and retained Cixi's old team after his takeover. Whatever resentment he felt for his Papa Dearest, he was not engaged in a power struggle with her. The emperor also had no interest in defence matters – in fact he preferred not to have to think about them and left everything in this field to Earl Li. But although the earl had this enormous responsibility, he had lost the unreserved trust that he had enjoyed with Cixi. At the emperor's side was his bitter foe, Grand Tutor Weng. The animosity of the arch-conservative royal tutor towards the major reformer went back a long way. The tutor had always suspected that some of the money allocated to the earl for building the navy had ended up in the earl's own pockets and those of his associates. This sneaking suspicion was behind his advice to the emperor to stop all purchases of gunboats. As soon as Cixi retired, the Grand Tutor started to check the earl's accounts, year by year, going back to 1884, when a major update of the navy began. The earl was required to present the financial records in detail, to answer endless queries and to justify himself – and to beg for such essentials as maintenance costs for the ships. The Grand Tutor remained suspicious, and the emperor appointed Prince Ching as the overlord of the navy, in a signal of distrust towards the earl.

The earl felt that the throne 'chooses to believe in groundless rumours and seems to want to take power away' from him. Under this pressure, he made it his priority to please the emperor and keep his job. After Emperor Guangxu halted the purchases for the navy, and knowing that His Majesty did not want to spend money on defence, the earl presented him with a glowing report about an impregnable coast. There was no mention of any problems, although the earl knew there were many. He wrote privately, 'Our ships are not up to date, and the training is not quite right. It would be hard to succeed in a sea battle.' Later he even said that he had known all along that the Chinese military was a 'paper tiger'. But to Emperor Guangxu he only said what His Majesty wanted to hear. Indeed, the emperor was pleased and praised him fulsomely for doing a brilliant job.

Naval chiefs repeatedly asked for new warships, but the earl did not pass on their requests to the throne. He was fearful that Grand Tutor Weng might accuse him of crying wolf in order to line his own pockets, and that the emperor might fire him.

The earl was in denial about Japan's ambitions. He did not seem to have any sense of unease, even though he could see that Japan's naval expansion was aimed at China: Japan was 'seeking to be one-up on us in everything: if our gunboat speed is 15 knots, they want theirs to be 16 knots . . .' 'That country will go far,' he remarked to a colleague. But he shut his mind to the inevitable fact that Japan could only 'go far' at the cost of the Chinese Empire.

If Cixi had been in charge, she would never have allowed Japan to become superior in military hardware. She knew that this was the only way to deter Japan. Before she retired, she had built up a navy that was the most powerful in Asia, far better equipped than that of Japan. And to keep that edge was by no means impossible, given that Japan had less total wealth at the time and could ill afford a gunboat race.

But Cixi in retirement had neither adequate information nor any say in international affairs. And the young emperor was not a strategic thinker. He simply left the whole business of defending the country to Earl Li, whose calculations were based on self-interest.

On 29 May 1894, after inspecting the coast, Earl Li presented the monarch with another optimistic report. This time, traces of apprehension crept in: he mentioned that Japan had been buying gunboats every year and that China was lagging behind. But he stopped short of spelling out the implications, which were consequently lost on Emperor Guangxu. His Majesty asked no questions, and once again praised the earl for doing a good job.

★

Just at this moment, Japan struck. In spring that year there had been a peasant uprising in Korea. On 3 June, the Korean king asked China to send in troops, and Beijing agreed. In keeping with Earl Li's agreement with Count Itō, China informed Japan. Tokyo claimed it needed its own soldiers in Korea to protect its diplomats and civilians, and dispatched a force. The uprising ended before the troops of either country could intervene, and the Koreans requested both countries to withdraw. The Chinese were prepared to do so. But the Japanese declined to leave.

The Prime Minister of Japan was now Count Itō, Earl Li's counterpart in the negotiations ten years earlier. An outstanding statesman, Itō had since that time helped draft the Meiji constitution (1889) and establish a bicameral national Diet (1890), which had laid the foundations of modern Japan. At the very time when he dispatched troops to Korea, his intention was that they should stay there – as a first step towards a very much more ambitious goal: to initiate a military contest with China, beat the massive empire and become the leader and master of East Asia. So, instead of withdrawing, he sent in more troops. His pretext for this act of invasion was that the Korean government must be forced to carry out modernising 'reforms'. The Chinese were told that they were welcome to join in this 'reformist' enterprise but, if they chose not to take part, Japan would carry it out alone. Prime Minister Itō's scheme put Japan in a win–win situation. If the Chinese troops left, Japan would occupy Korea – and challenge China at a time that suited Japan. If the Chinese stayed on, there would be numerous opportunities to create conflict between the two armies and spark off a war, again at a time of Japan's choosing. In fact Prime Minister Itō had made up his mind to take on China now.

No one in the Chinese government grasped Japan's intentions, not even Earl Li. While the Japanese military build-up in Korea gathered pace, it was business as usual in Beijing. Emperor Guangxu continued his classics lessons and planned banquets to mark his birthday at the end of July. Grand Tutor Weng wrote calligraphy on fans, a common scholarly pastime, and appraised his treasured stone-rubbing collections with visiting connoisseurs. Earl Li delayed reinforcing the Chinese troops in Korea, for fear of triggering a war. It does not seem to have occurred to him that Japan's goal was not confined to Korea – that it was actually seeking war with China. Thinking peace could be preserved, the earl busily lobbied European powers, especially Russia, which had its own designs on Korea (of which the earl was well aware), hoping that they would intervene and restrain the Japanese – a hope that proved futile. Robert Hart observed that the earl 'is calcu-lating with too much confidence on foreign intervention and infers too much from Japan's willingness to discuss'. 'The Powers are at work trying to induce Japan to withdraw and discuss, for they don't want war, but Japan is very bumptious and cock-a-hoop'; Japan 'thanks them for their kind advice, goes on her way, and would probably rather fight them all than give in!'

At the end of June, it finally dawned on Earl Li that Japan was 'not just threatening Korea', but wanted a decisive war 'with China, using everything it has'. This recognition came from news supplied by Robert Hart. 'Japan is mobilizing 50,000 troops, has ordered two up-to-date iron-clad gunboats from Britain and bought and hired many English commercial vehicles for transferring troops and arms.' When he reported this to the emperor, the earl's emphasis was now on the problems that beset his country's defence. This time he made clear that China was 'probably unable to win on the sea' and, moreover, that there were only 20,000 land troops defending the entire northern coast, from Manchuria to Shandong.

The emperor noticed the discrepancy between this and the earl's recent upbeat report, but he was not alarmed. He said that war between China and Japan over Korea was 'within our expectations', and he was sanguine. Grandly he talked about 'launching a punitive military action on a massive scale'. His Majesty's condescension towards Japan was shared by the vast majority of his subjects. Hart observed: '999 out of every 1000 Chinese are sure big China can thrash little Japan . . .'

On 15 July, while Japan moved 'in a really masterful way' (Hart's words), the Chinese emperor appointed his classics tutor as his key war adviser. The Grand Council could not have a meeting without Weng's presence. Teacher and pupil were blithely ignorant about just how bad the condition of their country's defence was. Hart wrote at the time that China would find that 'her army and navy are not what she expected them to be', and that if there was a war, 'Japan will dash gallantly and perhaps successfully, while China, with her old tactics, will have many a defeat to put up with . . .' Indeed, the Chinese military had slipped back into their old ill-disciplined and corrupt ways. Gunboats had been used for smuggling, and gun barrels, uncleaned, as laundry hangers. Nepotism had swelled the ranks with incompetent officers. No one was in the mood for war – while the Japanese military had been drilled into a superb war machine, primed for action.

Belatedly Earl Li started to transport troops to Korea by sea, for which three British ships were chartered. While the ferrying was under way, on 23 July, Japanese troops entered Seoul, seized the Korean king and set up a puppet government, which granted the Japanese army the right to expel Chinese troops. On the 25th, the Japanese navy launched a surprise attack on the ferries transporting Chinese soldiers and sank one ship, the *Kow-shing*. More than 1,000 men, including five British naval officers, died. News of the first military clash with Japan was withheld from Emperor Guangxu for two days by Earl Li. The earl was afraid that the poorly informed emperor might declare war at once, which he regarded as unwise. He was trying to use the sinking of a *British* ship to avert the war. 'Britain cannot allow this,' the earl reckoned; it would do something to check Japan. He clutched at his hopes like a handful of straws.

It quickly emerged that neither Britain nor the other powers wished to become entangled. China and Japan declared war on each other on 1 August. The burden of conducting China's first modern war – and its biggest war in more than 200 years – thus fell on the shoulders of a twenty-three-year-old who had led a totally secluded life. He had little knowledge of the world, only haphazard information about his own armed forces and none about his enemy, and relied almost exclusively for guidance on his backward-looking classics tutor. His military commander, Earl Li, laid all his bets on peace efforts and failed to prepare proper defences. Worse, the earl felt unable to share strategic planning with Guangxu – and often concealed the truth from him.

Facing this shambles was Japan's modern army and outstanding leadership. The outcome of the war was not hard to predict. The Chinese suffered one catastrophic defeat after another, on land in Korea as well as on the sea. By late September, the Japansese had captured the main city in northern Korea, Pyongyang, and had advanced to the Yalu River – the border with China.

During all this time, Emperor Guangxu did not involve Cixi beyond informing her when war looked inevitable, just before 16 July. She was living in her Summer Palace, cut off from the nerve-centre of policy decisions, with only a vague picture of the conflict. He had come to her for her confirmation that war must be fought, and she gave her full support. She also stressed that China 'must not do anything that gives the impression of weakness'. The way Earl Li conducted himself in pursuit of peace was an admission of weakness – even desperation. And yet there was no sign that the message was conveyed to the earl. Emperor Guangxu only mentioned it *en passant* to Grand Tutor Weng in his private study. Cixi herself had no contact with the earl and no way to give him, or anyone else, direct instructions.

After this brief consultation, Emperor Guangxu sought Cixi's views no more. Her role was purely symbolic. In her name an award was given to an army unit that was reported to have won China's first victory – which turned out to be phoney. There can be no doubt that Cixi was extremely anxious. She appears to have tried to get a couple of Grand Councillors to pass on information to her, through Prince Ching, but Emperor Guangxu learned about it and reprimanded the Councillors. At the urging of a group of friends close to him, the emperor kept Cixi out of the policy loop. Reports about the war were presented only to the emperor in sealed envelopes, and he only allowed her to glimpse their headings.

From the outbreak of war at the beginning of August until the eve of the fall of Pyongyang at the end of September, it seems that Emperor Guangxu only consulted Cixi once – when he wanted to sack Admiral Ting, head of the Northern Fleet that was fighting the war. He was bound by the Statutes drawn up governing his assumption of power to obtain Cixi's approval for major personnel changes. Presenting his case, the emperor accused the Admiral of being 'cowardly and incompetent', because he did not send his fleet out to the open sea. In fact the Admiral was adopting a defensive strategy, based on the fact that the Japanese had better and faster ships and their superiority would have been decisive on the open sea. By staying in its base, the fleet was afforded the protection of the forts. But the emperor heeded the advice of a cousin of Imperial Concubine Pearl, Zhirui, who insisted that as 'Japan was merely a tiny and poor country, our ships must parade on the open sea . . . and attack and destroy its gunboats. Our canons must fire first, the moment we encounter an enemy ship.' When Cixi saw the draft edict sacking the Admiral, she was incensed and said with palpable outrage: 'The Admiral has not been found to have committed any crime!' She refused to allow the edict to be issued. In a gesture of defiance, Emperor Guangxu gave a particularly harsh order condemning the Admiral and telling Earl Li to find a replacement. The earl wrote at length entreating the emperor to reconsider, explaining the defensive strategy, pointing out that there was no one to replace the Admiral, and arguing that sacking him would cause an upheaval in the navy. At last, the emperor grudgingly suspended the dismissal, but he continued to scold and berate the Admiral.

It was against this background that the Admiral conducted a major sea battle on 17 September 1894, in which four out of eleven of his warships were sunk. This event, together with the imminent fall of Pyongyang, forced Emperor Guangxu to involve Cixi, who had also just found an opportunity to leave the Summer Palace and go and stay in the Sea Palace adjacent to the Forbidden City. So, on the day of the devastating sea battle, and after two full months of disastrous warfare, Cixi saw the Grand Council for the first time in years. She still did not have a mandate to conduct the war. Her stay was initially supposed to be short, only ten days, after which she was scheduled to return to the Summer Palace on 26 September. But because of her status and her track record, she assumed a certain authority – especially in the eyes of those who had worshipped her. To brief her about the development of the war, Earl Li presented detailed reports attaching past telegrams that he had received. As a bleak picture began to emerge, Cixi announced that she was donating three million taels for the upkeep of the army. Then she extended her stay in the Sea Palace for another ten days, to 6 October – 'provisionally' – meaning it could be longer. Simultaneously she cancelled all celebrations for her sixtieth birthday,* which fell on 7 November.

The preparations for this birthday had started three years earlier, overseen by Grand Tutor Weng, amongst others. The sixtieth birthday was a milestone for the Chinese, and that of the empress dowager required glorious celebrations. One of the central responsibilities of the Ministry of Rites, a major government ministry, was to issue programmes for such occasions. The programme this time followed the precedent set by Qianlong the Magnificent for his own and his mother's sixtieth birthdays, and filled two booklets bound with red satin. The files of imperial decrees were thick with lists of honours to be bestowed, promotions to be made, criminals to be amnestied, and a thousand and one other things to be done. Along the route from the Forbidden City to the Summer Palace, sixty sites had been selected, where richly decorated arches, pavilions, marquees and stages for operas and dances were being constructed. These were now scrapped. Cixi would only receive congratulations in the Forbidden City, in a much-reduced ceremony.

For several days Cixi studied the history of the war, and she concluded that Earl Li had bungled China's position through a series of miscalculations – and misconduct, such as misleading the emperor. Given that the

---

* According to the Chinese method of calculation.

army had a personal allegiance to him, she felt that he could not be dismissed. To calls for his blood, she replied: 'Hold it for now. There is no one to replace him.' Prince Gong was reinstated and made the chief Grand Councillor. But the prince could conjure up no miracles. There were more defeats – and heroism. In one sea battle a captain called Deng Shichang sailed straight at a Japanese ship to try and ram it, and when that failed and his own ship was sunk, he refused to be rescued and drowned himself (apparently together with his pet dog).

By the end of September, all the Chinese troops had been driven out of Korea to their side of the Yalu River. Beijing knew, in the words of Robert Hart, that 'further fighting is unreliable and an early settlement the best step to be taken'. Two Grand Councillors approached Hart to ask Britain to broker a peace. The British suggested two terms as the basis for stopping the war: that Korea become a protectorate of the international powers, and that China pay a war indemnity to Japan. Under the circumstances, these terms were not at all bad. But they sent Grand Tutor Weng into a fury. Condemning the British minister who presented the proposal as 'vicious', he demanded that the Grand Councillors reject the terms. Cixi spent a long time trying to persuade him to agree to the British proposal, letting him know this was her wish. The courtier bowed to the will of the empress dowager with great reluctance, and the British put the proposal to the Japanese.

This episode showed Cixi that her current position was very different from what it had been in her pre-retirement days. She was now only a 'consultant', albeit one with clout. Indeed, she was not adequately informed, as the emperor only gave her access to some of the reports he received, which meant that her picture of the war was patchy. As a result, she entertained the illusion that, with the mediation of the British and the payment of an indemnity, settlement could be reached. She underestimated Japan's appetite, believing that at this stage it would be satisfied with gobbling up Korea. While waiting for Japan's response to the British proposal, she did something that was out of character with her as a statesman, but in character with another side of her, that of a woman avid for beautiful things. Earl Li had just sent her a list of his gifts for her birthday, and they consisted of nine sets of treasures:*
'Nine jade inlaid *ru-yi*, nine pure gold statues of the Buddha of Longevity,

---

* Nine was considered the most auspicious figure, because it is the highest single-digit number and has the same pronunciation as the word for 'long-lasting', *jiu*.

nine gold watches studded with diamonds, nine pairs of gold cups of "good fortune" and "longevity", nine diamond headdress flowers, nine bolts of pure yellow velvet, nine bolts of floral yellow brocade, nine gold incense burners inlaid with seven jewels, and nine gold vases inlaid with seven jewels.'

It was a magnificent list – even for the empress dowager of China. And it was particularly tempting for Cixi, who took much pleasure in art and luxury. The earl, who did not have fabulous wealth, was really desperate to ingratiate himself with Cixi, clearly in the hope that she would save his skin. He presented the gifts knowing that Cixi had actually issued a decree two years before announcing 'No presents, please' for her sixtieth birthday.

The earl's present-giving confirmed that he was an expert at pleasing his bosses through their weak spots. Indeed, Cixi found it hard to turn down this haul. And if she accepted the earl's gifts, she had to accept other people's. Birthdays celebrating a new decade were the chief gift-giving occasions, but her fiftieth birthday had been hit by the war with France, and she had had to veto all presents. Must she really forgo this opportunity again? The temptation proved too strong. After a few days' agonising, Cixi persuaded herself that accepting birthday presents was not incompatible with fighting the war. This was similar to her self-delusion in the past when she thought that taking a relatively small sum of money each year from the naval funds made no difference to the navy. Now she effectively rescinded her own decree, and sent eunuchs to announce that officials above a certain high rank could present gifts if they wished to do so.

Her words immediately caused disquiet among top officials in the court. Some, like Grand Tutor Weng, said that they had not prepared anything because they had been following the empress dowager's own decree, and their admiration for her could not be measured by material things anyway (as per a Confucian dictum). But the general flow was set: everyone began to rack their brains about what to give, and Weng and a few others employed an agent to scout for them. Realising she had made a mistake, Cixi quickly issued an edict attempting to explain herself, saying that she thought it would be wrong of her to spurn people's good will. But the damage had been done. The fighting spirit, which was already lacking in the court, was dissipating. Robert Hart wrote in a letter: 'Things look bad here. The officials have no fight in them and despair is generally settling down on all: it is a very bad lookout indeed, and if Japan will not accept "the olive leaf", I don't know how we'll get out of it . . .'

The Japanese did not accept 'the olive leaf'. Without replying to the British, they launched assaults on the Chinese border defences, which collapsed like a pack of cards. The Japanese were inside China itself by 27 October. Cixi belatedly tried to make amends. She offered to donate another two million taels to the war effort. But this gesture could not salvage either the war or her image. Her much-reduced birthday rituals were performed to the beat of a marching Japanese army. The ceremonies were a façade she simply had to preserve: cancelling them would have amounted to announcing a national catastrophe and would have caused bewilderment in the empire. But even the prescribed pomp could not dispel a bleak and dreary atmosphere.

Western powers were scandalised and contemptuous that the empire seemed incapable of one decent fight, and only capable of a birthday fanfare. Cixi's reputation plummeted. Robert Hart wrote ironically, his former reverence for the empress dowager now gone: 'we shall probably have the Emp. Dow.'s birthday (7 Nov.) celebrated by the capture of *Liao Yang* – I don't think [the Japanese] can march to Moukden by that date!' Liao Yang was right in the middle of the Liaodong Peninsula in southern Manchuria, close to Korea, and Moukden was the old capital of the Manchus, further north.

On 21 November, the Japanese seized the strategic fortress harbour of Port Arthur on the southern tip of the Liaodong Peninsula – the gateway to Manchuria by land, and to Tianjin and Beijing across a short stretch of water. This catastrophic development made Cixi see the full scale of Japan's ambitions and capabilities. She bitterly regretted the birthday-gifts fiasco, and the ceremony, however reduced in scale. Later on, she would declare no celebrations or gifts for any of her birthdays. Her seventieth birthday, a major occasion, would be no exception. On that occasion, calls for her to accept tributes echoed across the provinces, but she stood firm.

Back in November 1894, Cixi also blamed her misjudgement on her restricted access to information. She acted to break her adopted son's embargo on sharing with her the reports addressed to him. As his refusal had very much been on the advice of friends who had gained his ear through Pearl, Emperor Guangxu's favourite concubine, Cixi tackled her first.

Pearl was officially under her charge, as a member of the harem, and Cixi had shown no ill feelings towards her. In fact she had tried to be nice to Pearl, often inviting her and her sister, Jade, to stay in the Summer Palace. When Pearl expressed a wish to learn to paint, Cixi had made Lady Miao available to her. At the beginning of that year, as part of the celebrations for her sixtieth birthday, Cixi had promoted Pearl one rung up the royal consort ladder. Pearl, now eighteen years old, craved money. One not inconsiderable expense as an imperial concubine was tipping the eunuchs, in order to be served well, and Pearl was a lavish tipper. To make money, she sold official posts to the highest bidders. One post was Mayor of Shanghai, and she pleaded with the emperor to give the post to a certain Lu. When Emperor Guangxu ordered the Grand Council to appoint Lu – without telling the Councillors that the nomination had come from Pearl – they queried the appointment as they had not heard of Lu. The emperor was compelled to have Lu assessed by the Ministry of Officials. Lu was found undeserving of the job in Shanghai and was put on a reserve list, waiting for a far more junior assignment to become vacant. Word leaked out that Lu was illiterate and had bribed Pearl with a huge sum. There were other similar cases.

For an imperial consort to take advantage of her relationship with the monarch to sell official jobs was an offence punishable by death in the Qing court. The emperor would become a laughing stock and would be deemed stupid and unworthy if the scandal was exposed. Cixi knew about Pearl's misdeeds and Guangxu's involvement, and she decided to use them to force her adopted son to agree to her demands. She obtained confessions from Pearl and the eunuchs serving her – by having the eunuchs thrashed on their backsides with long flat bamboo bats, and by forcing Pearl to watch as their skins split and their screams weakened from howls to whimpers. Pearl herself was slapped across the face. In great pain, humiliated and terrified, she collapsed. A royal doctor found her 'unconscious, her teeth clenched, and her whole body twitching and shaking'. Blood trickled from her mouth and nose. She slipped in and out of consciousness for a fortnight.

Some years earlier, when Pearl had just been chosen as an imperial concubine, her mother had sensed an unhappy fate for the girl. Mrs Headland, the American doctor, had been called to see Pearl's mother and recalled that the aristocratic lady:

was suffering from a nervous breakdown due to worry and sleeplessness. On inquiry I discovered that her two daughters had been taken into the palace as concubines of the Emperor Kuang Hsu [Guangxu] . . . She took me by the hand, pulled me down on the brick bed beside her, and told me in a pathetic way how both of her daughters had been taken from her in a single day. 'But they have been taken into the palace,' I urged, to try to comfort her, 'and I have heard that the Emperor is very fond of your eldest daughter . . .' 'Quite right,' she replied, 'but what consolation is there in that? . . . I am afraid of the court intrigues, and they are only children and cannot understand the duplicity of court life – I fear for them, I fear for them,' and she swayed back and forth on her brick bed.

With Pearl's confession, Cixi compelled her adopted son to accept her 'deal'. She would allow his role in the scandal to be covered up, and in return Guangxu would give her full access to all the war reports. On 26 November, the emperor absented himself when Cixi told the Grand Council what Pearl had done, and then had a decree issued in her capacity as empress dowager overseeing the harem, announcing the transgressions committed by Pearl and her sister Jade and demoting them both. The decree portrayed the emperor as a monarch of impecable integrity. It said the two imperial concubines had 'begged the emperor' to give jobs to people they had recommended, but that he had felt 'deeply troubled by this behaviour' and had brought the case to the empress dowager, asking for his two consorts to be censured. When Grand Tutor Weng saw Emperor Guangxu the following day, His Majesty calmly raised the subject as if he had indeed been totally innocent. On that day, the 27th, Emperor Guangxu issued an edict ordering that all the reports addressed to him be presented to the empress dowager – and in their original form. It was only from this day on that Cixi had full access to information about the war.

Meanwhile, as a reminder of the gravity of the scandal, a severely worded reprimand was framed and hung in Pearl's apartment. A eunuch chief involved was executed. Cixi had wanted the execution to be in public, but was persuaded by Grand Tutor Weng that this would do damage to the dynasty; the death sentence was carried out inside the Forbidden City by the court's Judicious Punishment Department – using bastinado, namely, beating the eunuch to death with long wooden bats.

Cixi now resolved to separate Emperor Guangxu from his friends who had been urging him to exclude her from the decision-making process. She most wanted to shut out of the court Pearl's cousin, Zhirui, the man who had also tried to get the emperor to sack Admiral Ting and have him thrown into prison – even executed – all for no reason other than that the Admiral had taken up a (sensible) defensive position. In another petition Zhirui had advised the emperor to cut the pay of the troops defending Manchuria by 80 per cent – to save money, so he said. Why should he single out Manchuria, which borders on Korea, for cuts, when the Japanese were on the doorstep? Cixi could not but regard Cousin Zhirui's advice as toxic and of benefit to the Japanese. Deeply suspicious of him, she sent him to a post in the far north of the empire, well away from the court.

She also planned to eliminate the influence of Wen Tingshi, a family friend of Pearl. Wen had written to the emperor saying that Cixi had to be barred entirely from politics, because a woman playing a role in state affairs was like 'a hen crowing in the morning, which is bound to herald a disastrous day'. In addition, Wen had got a Censor, Weijun, to petition the throne and accuse Cixi of meddling, alleging that she was the puppet of her head eunuch, Lianying. Cixi was distraught by this allegation, which even some top officials tended to believe. One voiced his concern to her in an audience, and her anger was palpable as she interrupted him and told him to 'rest assured' that the allegations were untrue. Rumours began to circulate that she was an appeaser and had been 'putting pressure on the emperor not to fight Japan'. 'Historians are going to write it in this way. How am I to face the country? And what will the future generations think of me?' she cried. Emperor Guangxu felt compelled to punish the slanderous Censor and banished him to the frontier for several years. Such a harsh punishment for criticising Cixi was unheard of during her reign, and it caused a sensation. Many believed the accusations (it was – and still is – easy for women to be cast as scapegoats for failures), and feted the Censor as a hero. Much of the sympathy for him was stirred up by Wen, whose closeness to Emperor Guangxu gave him credibility. Wen collected tens of thousands of taels as a morale-boosting gift for the Censor as he went into exile. For all that Wen had done to her, Cixi's treatment of him was restrained. During the war she left him alone, and afterwards she made her adopted son send Wen out of the court and the capital. Two other friends of the emperor who had been whispering to him words such as 'Don't let the Empress Dowager butt in' were also sacked after the war, charged with 'setting the Two Majesties against each other'.

The major step Cixi took for now was to try and close the emperor's study, which was the one place where his friends could come and talk to him without arousing suspicion. This was also where the monarch continued to study the classics and the Manchu language – and even English – in the middle of a disastrous war. Cixi was entitled to close the study since, as a parent, she had overall responsibility for his education. Shutting down the study would also put a stop to the emperor's tête-à-têtes with Grand Tutor Weng, during which they framed war policy. Cixi wanted policies to be made with the Grand Council, and in her presence. She made Weng a Grand Councillor, so that he would have no reason to impart his advice in private.

Cixi's move to close the study was unsuccessful. Emperor Guangxu was very annoyed about losing his private world, and asked Prince Gong, now heading the Grand Council, to intervene. Weng was upset, too. So Cixi had to allow his classics lessons to continue, stopping only the language sessions. She had to reassure Weng that she regarded him as 'loyal and trustworthy', and shutting the study had not been aimed at him, but only at the likes of Zhirui. She apologised for her order being 'too blunt'.

Only as a result of this immense struggle did Cixi break into the decision-making process. This was near the end of 1894, months after the war had started, and when China was already doomed to defeat.

17 A Peace that Ruined China (1895)

AFTER taking Port Arthur, the Japanese declared that they were ready for peace talks. Two Chinese negotiators set off for Japan. On 5 January 1895, before they left, they saw Cixi and Emperor Guangxu. After the audience, Cixi put the key points of her instructions down on a sheet of royal yellow paper and had it delivered to the envoys, telling them emphatically not to sign anything without referring back to Beijing and, especially, not to make any promises that concerned territory or were beyond the country's means.

The day the two negotiators arrived in Japan the war took a drastic turn for the worse for the Chinese, with the Japanese poised to seize Weihaiwei, the headquarters of the Northern Fleet. The Fleet was under strict orders to break out and, as a last resort, to sink their ships to stop them falling into enemy hands. But officers and men refused to obey orders. Some went down on their knees and begged Admiral Ting not to destroy the ships because, if he did, the Japanese would certainly torture them ferociously before killing them. Under this pressure, Admiral Ting signed a letter of surrender and handed over the gunboats, ten in all, including one of the two ironclads, to the Japanese. The Admiral then committed suicide by swallowing opium. Thus in February 1895 the Northern Fleet – the backbone of the Chinese navy – was lost. While the Japanese warriors contemptuously compared their antagonists to 'dying swine lying on the ground to be slaughtered and cut up at will', Tokyo rejected the two negotiators, demanding instead a plenipotentiary with the highest position and prestige. It was clear they wanted Earl Li.

From the way Tokyo was dictating terms, Cixi felt it was impossible for the talks to produce any acceptable outcome. On 6 February, she told the Grand Council that Japan was bound to impose 'terms to which we can't possibly agree', and the government must recall the envoys, break the talks and fight on. The 'severity of her words and her demeanour' startled Grand Tutor Weng. The following day, when a top commander called Wang Wenshao had an audience with her, he was similarly struck, as he described in his diary:

> The Empress Dowager had outrage written all over her face and in her words. She bade me do everything possible to reignite the fighting spirit of officers and men. She told me to implement strict rules to award bravery and punish cowardice, and to do our utmost to salvage the situation . . . She instructed me long and hard, for three quarters of an hour, anxious that I should grasp her message. I could see how concerned she was for me to get it right, and so I lingered outside while she received the Grand Councillors, in case she had more directions for me.

Cixi gave the commander a decree to take to the troops. It was issued in her own name, and it called on them to fight on bravely.

She sent an order to Viceroy Zhang Zhidong, who was firmly opposed to peace talks based on unacceptable terms and had been cabling the court with ideas about how best to continue fighting. Her letter asked him to go beyond the remit of his viceroyalty and help plan an overall strategy. But when the Viceroy asked Beijing for more information about the war, the emperor, in a tone of displeasure, replied that it was none of his business.

It was clear that Cixi's words counted for little. The men at the top − Emperor Guangxu, Prince Gong and the rest of the Grand Council − did not want to fight and were willing to accept any Japanese terms. They were mortified by the prospect of their enemy marching on Beijing and overthrowing the dynasty. When he mentioned this possibility to Grand Tutor Weng, the emperor was in floods of tears, and the classics tutor was 'sweating and trembling'. Cixi was forced to agree to send Earl Li to Japan, but she asked the Grand Council to tell the earl to 'come and get instructions first'. Prince Gong was terrified that Cixi might impose conditions that would lead to the collapse of the talks, and intervened: 'But the emperor has said Li doesn't have to come. This is not in accordance with His Majesty's wishes.' Cixi snapped, 'Are you asking for my views or not? Do my words mean something or not?'

Earl Li did come for an audience. On 25 February, he and Prince

Gong informed Cixi of the Japanese demand that he should only go to Japan if he had a mandate to cede territory, in addition to paying a large indemnity. They also told her that Emperor Guangxu had decided to send the earl on those conditions. Cixi objected furiously – to no avail. In the end she said angrily: 'You do whatever you want to do. Don't ask me any more!' When Emperor Guangxu still sought her advice on what Earl Li should give away to Japan, she sent a eunuch to say that she was unwell, and could the emperor please make the decision himself.

As Earl Li did not want to take personal responsibility for the loss of territory – which mattered most for the Chinese – on 3 March Emperor Guangxu gave him written authorisation to 'cede territory'. This reflected the wishes of all the Grand Councillors, who wrote collectively to the empress dowager on the same day, entreating her to understand the emperor's dilemma, citing 'danger to the capital' as his main concern. Cixi did not reply. She turned her back on her adopted son, who in great distress tiptoed around her apartment trying to see her and get her endorsement.

On 8 April, Japan's full terms arrived. Apart from an astronomical indemnity, they demanded the cession of Taiwan, known to be a 'jewel' of the Chinese empire, and which, as Viceroy Zhang reminded the court, 'each year earns over 2 million taels for the state coffers, and dozens of times this amount for the merchants and population at large'. As well as Taiwan, Japan wanted the nearby islands of the Pescadores, and the Liaodong Peninsula in south Manchuria. An incensed Cixi told Emperor Guangxu: 'Cede no land, recall the negotiator and fight on!'

But of course there was no ace up her sleeve. What she had was a determination not to cave in, and a readiness to take risks. She was ignored by the men, who wanted no risks. Upon receiving an ultimatum from Prime Minister Itō, warning that 100,000 troops were on their way to Beijing, Emperor Guangxu, on 14 April, told Earl Li to accept the Japanese terms. On the 17th, the earl signed the Treaty of Shimonoseki with Itō. Japan got the territories it demanded, plus 200 million taels in indemnity.

During this period Cixi was consumed by outrage and despair, made worse by her powerlessness. So acute was her anguish that she would frequently pass out. A eunuch 'often spotted Cixi weeping when she thought she was alone'. He said that 'Cixi's private tears revealed untold agony in her heart . . . If one were to ask me to name one thing about Cixi, I would say she was the most tormented person on earth.'

★

Compared with the two previous indemnities, to Britain in 1842, and to Britain and France in 1860, the sum forced out of China in 1895 reveals the rising Asian power's unparalleled appetite and mercilessness. The European demands – sixteen million taels in the first case, and eight million to each country in the latter – had been more or less related to their war costs and the damages inflicted on non-combatants. The 200 million to Japan bore little relation to the costs incurred, as Japan had only thirty million taels in total in its state coffers at the beginning of the war, and the war bonds it had sold subsequently – eighty million – were only partially cashed. Prime Minister Itō did not dispute these figures when Earl Li cited them.

The treaty enraged the entire Chinese ruling elite. Many hundreds of officials in the capital signed petitions calling for its rejection, joined by more than a thousand members of the literati who were in Beijing from the provinces for the Imperial Examination. The scale of the 'No' campaign was unprecedented. Even though the treaty was not officially made public, word had got round. All petitioners implored the emperor to refuse to ratify it – some urging him to move the capital to the interior and settle for a protracted war. But their impassioned words were dismissed as 'a voice and nothing besides' (to quote Hart). Public opinion carried little weight with Emperor Guangxu, for whom the only domestic threat was armed peasant rebellion; otherwise, the only menace was Japan, which could topple the Great Qing.

Then, unexpectedly, some European powers came to the aid of Beijing. Russia, Germany and France stepped in and demanded that Japan return the Liaodong Peninsula to China, on the grounds that occupying it would 'put the Chinese capital in a permanently threatened position'. Europe feared a Japanese takeover of China. Robert Hart remarked: 'if Japan wins and takes China, the biggest empire the world ever saw – the most go-ahead and the most powerful . . . let 1900 look out!' Kaiser Wilhelm II of Germany coined the expression the 'Yellow Peril', to refer to what he saw as Europe's nightmare: Japan 'at the head of a consolidated Asia, the control of China by Japan'.

Seeing clear proof of Europe's concern, Cixi judged that it was highly unlikely that Japan would attack Beijing and finish off the Qing dynasty. Japan was not yet in a position to challenge the West. (As it happened, Japan eventually accepted the three European powers' demand and withdrew from the Liaodong Peninsula – albeit at a cost.) She hoped that Emperor Guangxu and the grandees could recognise that the capital and the dynasty were secure, and would then stand firm and refuse the Japanese terms. Of course Japan might go ahead and seize Beijing regardless, but Cixi reckoned that it was a risk worth taking. The terms of the treaty were too damaging to the empire for its leaders not to take that risk. In her calculation, pressured by Western powers and facing a China that showed a determination to fight a protracted war, Japan might well settle for a peace treaty that was far less fatal than the Treaty of Shimonoseki.

Hoping the court would think the same way as she did, on 26 April Cixi asked the Grand Council to reconsider the peace treaty thoroughly and give her their thoughts. But these men all agreed with the emperor that they must be certain that Europe would definitely intervene on their behalf before deciding to fight, and the emperor ordered cables sent to the three countries for a definitive commitment. Unsurprisingly, there was no immediate reply. While waiting, Emperor Guangxu became obsessed about meeting the deadline for the ratification of the treaty, petrified that once it had passed, the Japanese would march into Beijing. Stretched to breaking point, the twenty-three-year-old looked haggard beyond his years. No grandee advised against ratification: none wanted to be the one responsible for the fall of the dynasty. Grand Tutor Weng just groaned that he was ready to smash his head to smithereens if it were of any help. All eyes were on Prince Gong, even though he had in fact contributed little and was gravely ill. Characteristically, the prince advised endorsing the treaty. For all his qualities, he was essentially a weak man who was prone to buckle in a major crisis.

As neither the emperor nor the grandees expressed a resolve to fight, Cixi stopped trying to persuade them. But she refused to take part in endorsing the Treaty of Shimonoseki. The ratification was confirmed by Emperor Guangxu on 2 May, with Prince Gong and the Grand Council in attendance. The moment was accompanied by much 'trembling' and 'weeping'. Emperor Guangxu then cabled Earl Li, telling him to exchange the instruments of ratification at once. This was done on 8 May. The emperor even rushed the earl, as the young man could not wait to get the whole thing over and done with.

He had chosen 'the safest line to follow', Robert Hart remarked, 'it's an empire that is at stake!' But to Cixi the cost of 'peace' was just too high, and it would ultimately wreck rather than save the empire. She had foresight, defiance, and courage. What she lacked was a mandate.

The Treaty of Shimonoseki ruined China. Charles Denby, the American minister who had acted as an intermediary in the deal, who had witnessed the relatively good times before the war and the abysmal years afterwards, wrote: 'The Japanese war was the beginning of the end for China.' As well as the 200 million taels of indemnity, China was forced to pay Japan another thirty million for the return of the Liaodong Peninsula. These plus other 'costs' amounted to 231.5 million taels, more than four times Japan's annual revenue. There was also the booty of war in the form of arms and gunboats.

To make the payment Emperor Guangxu borrowed from the West. China's foreign debts had been forty-one million taels altogether over the past thirty years and had virtually been paid off by mid-1895. The country could have been cash-rich, with funds to carry out a wide range of modernising projects, not to mention raising living standards. But this splendid inheritance was thrown away and, instead, it was forced to borrow 300 million taels under crippling terms. Adding together the indemnity, the interest on the loans and China's own gigantic expenditure during the conflict, the war – and 'peace' – cost the country as much as 600 million taels, nearly six times its total revenue in 1895 (101.567 million). To exacerbate an already dire situation, the impatient Emperor Guangxu decided to pay off Japan in just three years. All the Customs' takings now went to Japan, and domestic taxes were increased. The provinces were given quotas to contribute, and they in turned squeezed the population. The life-blood was being pumped out of China.

As with many other false accusations, this disastrous war and 'peace' have often been blamed on Cixi. In a vague but categorical way, her accusers have asserted that she depleted the navy in order to build her Summer Palace, that she had been obsessed with her sixtieth birthday and neglected the war, and that she was a spineless appeaser. The truth is that it was she who had founded China's modern navy; the building of the Summer Palace did not deprive it of cash, even though she did take a small portion of the funds. She did not actively participate in the war for a long time, not because she was indulging in her birthday preparations, but because Emperor Guangxu barred her. And far from being an appeaser, she was the only person in the court who unambiguously advocated rejecting Japan's demands and fighting on.

Misappropriating naval funds before the war (even though she donated roughly the same amount during the conflict) and soliciting birthday presents were both massive misjudgements and were undoubtedly reprehensible. One sapped the discipline of the navy, the other damaged the morale of the court. She realised her mistakes, and would make amends in future years. In spite of these sins, she was liable neither for the defeat nor for the spectacularly harmful 'peace'. These were the responsibility of Emperor Guangxu (who has been undeservingly cast in popular myth as a tragic hero struggling to do his best) and, to a lesser extent, the Grand Councillors (though they were officially no more than advisers). Ultimately, the blame must lie in a system that deposited such heavy responsibility on such slight shoulders. Robert Hart lamented that 'there's no head – no strong man'. Indeed, there was only a strong *woman*, but she could not be the head at the moment of the crisis. Nor could her voice be heard outside a tiny circle in the court – a tragic situation that provided fertile soil for all the untrue allegations against her. Later a perceptive Frenchman said of Cixi, '*C'est le seul homme de la Chine.*' That was the real Cixi in the Forbidden City in 1895.

18 The Scramble for China
(1895–8)

A FTER the catastrophic war was over, Cixi returned to retirement. On 30 June 1895, a retinue formally accompanied her out of the Forbidden City to the Sea Palace, before she eventually moved back to the Summer Palace. With eunuchs in colourful costumes designed for special occasions, and court musicians playing trumpets, Prince Gong and the other grandees knelt on a stone path facing south, and banged their heads on the ground three times when Cixi's sedan-chair passed. Henceforth, whenever she visited the Forbidden City, there were elaborate rituals involving all the officials inside the palace wearing ceremonial robes. Such rituals highlighted the fact that she was not running the state.

Yet this new period of retirement was different from before. Since the Pearl affair, Cixi had been given sight of all key documents, and this continued. Her adopted son consulted her far more nowadays, and there was a marked increase in his visits to the Summer Palace. The young emperor and the Grand Councillors realised that signing the ruinous treaty against the wishes of the empress dowager was tantamount to 'drinking poison to quench thirst'. It had brought the empire anything but genuine peace. Viceroy Zhang, who had petitioned feverishly against signing the treaty and been ignored, now pointed out that the treaty only enriched Japan and whetted its appetite, and that it would be sure to seek to conquer a drastically enfeebled China at a future stage. In addition, the European powers were now all too aware how weak the empire was and would make endless demands backed up by the threat of war, knowing that China was unable to call their bluff.

Indeed, as far as the European powers were concerned, China was now exposed as a paper tiger. Hitherto they had regarded her with a certain respect, partly on account of her size. Now they knew the giant was 'filled with wind', to quote Charles Denby, and 'the Chinese bubble had burst'. They learned that 'she could not fight, and were prepared on the slightest pretence to seize her territory'. While the kinder-hearted excused her ('China is not a warlike nation – her antecedents, her civilization, her idiosyncrasies, all make for peace, and it's a pity that the rough world should disturb it . . .' wrote Robert Hart), the general attitude was undisguised contempt. Grand Tutor Weng noted: 'When the envoys of Western countries come to the Foreign Office, they no longer behave in a courteous manner; they shout abuse at the drop of a hat.' Witnessing one visit to the Foreign Office by some Westerners, a Chinese official felt his 'blood vessels were bursting from outrage'.

Emperor Guangxu felt defensive. It was noticed that he did not make a full public statement about the war, but only wrote to top officials, asking for their understanding – and telling them not to speak about the matter again, thus vetoing a post-mortem. The emperor offered no reflections on the lessons to be learned, or on specific plans for the future – apart from the platitude that they must do 'the two big things: train the army and find more money to fund it'. He was troubled, and tried to deflect responsibility in the most childish way, telling some officials that two of the Grand Councillors had 'forced me to ratify' the treaty. The main scapegoat was Earl Li. But rather than blaming him for the actual damage he had done – misleading the throne about the strength of China's defence before the war and mishandling the war when it broke out – the emperor went along with the widespread rumour that Earl Li had signed the treaty without his authorisation. At his first post-war audience with the earl, His Majesty berated Earl Li for handing over 200 million taels of silver, plus Taiwan and all the rest, when he himself had actually charged the earl to do so. The earl, who had just recovered from a pistol wound sustained in an assassination attempt while he was negotiating in Japan, could do nothing but bang his head on the floor again and again, saying: 'Yes, yes, Your Majesty, it is all my fault.' This charade was acted out in front of the Grand Councillors, all of whom were aware of the truth.

If a Chinese monarch were to receive the loyalty of his officials, he had to be seen to be fair. Cixi had a knack of being just with her officials. Her rewards and punishments were generally thought to be apportioned fairly. This was key to the fierce loyalty she commanded, from those who disagreed with her as well as those who agreed. But

Emperor Guangxu had none of her skills. During the war he had gravely mistreated Admiral Ting, which partially contributed to the sorry surrender of the Northern Fleet with its ten gunboats. An embittered Earl Li thought that the emperor did 'not even look like a monarch', and said so to his trusted subordinates. It became known even to officials outside the earl's camp that he wished for a change at court: that he wished Cixi to be in charge.

Cixi did not chide her adopted son or the Grand Councillors with an 'I told you so'. Rather, she decided that at such a moment the best thing to do was be gracious to the men. Indeed they were overcome with gratitude. Prince Gong had been the prime advocate for the signing of the treaty. But Cixi uttered not a word of reproach. Instead she invited him to stay in the Summer Palace, attending to such details as the furnishing of his quarters and the kind of food served to him. The prince was so grateful that he struggled from his sickbed to go to Cixi as soon as she asked for him, disregarding his son's entreaty that, given his condition, he should stay at home and rest and not subject himself to kneeling and other forms of demanding court etiquette. On one occasion, noted Grand Tutor Weng, Prince Gong was in the Summer Palace when the emperor arrived, but he did not come to greet His Majesty until a full day later, which seemed very like insolence to the tutor. Cixi was now a sort of mistress of the court. The grandees were at her beck and call, rushing to the Summer Palace when summoned and, if she so wished, staying on, accompanying her on her outings – which was most unusual. Sometimes they failed to turn up for the daily audience in the Forbidden City.

If Emperor Guangxu felt resentment, he did not show it. Instead he became more submissive to his Papa Dearest. This touched Cixi, who described him as 'an extremely nice person'. Cixi's feelings towards her adopted son acquired a new tenderness during the war, as she knew the weight of the burden on him and his limitations. Grand Tutor Weng saw that when the emperor fell ill, Cixi was gentle and kind to him, visiting his sickbed daily, and showing a degree of lovingness that he had never seen. To a Viceroy she said simply: 'I really love the emperor.' Now she spent more time with him, showing him round her Summer Palace and the beauty spots nearby. She reinstated the titles of Imperial Concubine Pearl and her sister, Jade. People noticed that mother and son got on really well during this period.

Cixi wanted no one around to disrupt their relationship. It was now that the emperor's friends who had urged him to shun her were cleared out of the court. Officials were warned that 'anyone doing this again will not get off so lightly, and will be punished severely'. The emperor's study was closed down altogether, so there was nowhere he could listen to secret whispers.

With Emperor Guangxu so compliant, Cixi took it upon herself to deal with what she regarded as the most pressing matter: the threat of Japan. Heavyweight strategists like Viceroy Zhang had strongly argued an alliance with Russia, China's northern neighbour and the only European power that was directly affected by Japan's rise. Cixi was conscious that Russia also had territorial designs on China: it had carved off a huge chunk in 1860, and tried again two decades later over Ili in Xinjiang, on which occasion Cixi had forced it to back off. But after spending months weighing up the pros and cons, she decided that seeking an alliance with Russia was still preferable to doing nothing and waiting for Japan to attack again. At the beginning of 1896, China began to try to secure a Russian commitment to fight on its side if the country was invaded by Japan. The Grand Council decamped and followed the empress dowager to the Summer Palace, setting up a temporary office in bungalows outside its eastern gate. Prince Gong moved into a mansion next door. No one cared where the emperor was.

Through the Chinese minister in St Petersburg, Cixi knew what China could offer Russia in return. The Trans-Siberian Railway that would connect Moscow and European Russia with the Russian Far East faced the choice of two routes before arriving at its terminus, the port of Vladivostok on the Pacific. If it stayed on Russian soil it would have to travel in a long arc, over difficult terrain, 500 kilometres longer than a straight line through northern Manchuria. The Russians wanted to build a shortcut through Chinese territory. After debate in the top circle, Cixi made up her mind to grant Russia its wish to construct the line, which later became known as the Chinese Eastern Railway (or the 'Siberian Railway'). The line actually made considerable economic sense to China. Linking Asia with Europe by land, it would be a money-spinner, as the huge volume of goods passing through could be taxed by Beijing. Since Russia offered to build it, its construction would be of minimal cost to China and, to ensure the empire would reap the benefits, Beijing put up part of the initial capital (five million taels), and became a shareholder (one-third), making the railway a joint venture. If ever the relationship with Russia soured, the railway was on Chinese land, and China could, theoretically, do what she liked with it. And all this was on top of a guaranteed powerful military ally in the event of a Japanese assault.

The drawback, so far as anyone could predict, was a dramatic increase in Russian influence in Manchuria, bringing unforeseen consequences. Cixi knew that Beijing had to be 'on guard against future perils', but shielding the empire against Japan overrode all such considerations.

Once decided on this approach, Earl Li was sent to Moscow to negotiate the pact. Cixi had turned against the earl for his role in the war with Japan, and was only employing him out of expediency – he was an unrivalled negotiator. It so happened that the coronation of Tsar Nicholas II would take place in May 1896, so the earl went as China's Minister Extraordinary for the coronation, while the real purpose of his trip was kept secret. When it became known that he would be visiting Russia, invitations arrived from other countries: Britain, France, Germany and the US. This was the very first trip abroad by a top-level dignitary – no less than 'China's leading statesman' in Western eyes. In order not to alienate these powers, and to conceal the real purpose of the trip, Earl Li toured the four other countries as well. The tour generated much fanfare, but little substance.★

The Russo-Chinese Secret Treaty was concluded successfully and signed on 3 June, days after the coronation of Tsar Nicholas II. Its opening line stated explicitly that Russia would use all its available armed forces to aid China, should it be invaded by Japan.

Earl Li was full of excitement when he was given the job. He took it as an indication that the empress dowager had forgiven him, and was willing to work with him again, now that she seemed to be very much in charge. And the earl was confident in his own abilities. Before departure, at a *bon voyage* banquet in a marquee, a high wind coated the dishes with dust. But the earl ate heartily, talking and laughing in high spirits. Told that the God of Wind had come to pay homage to him – and that after his grand tour he would return to the centre of state affairs and achieve even greater things – the earl smiled, nodded and basked in the flattery.

★ The only publicly announced objective that had any substance was to persuade Western powers to accept a higher customs tariff. Although the powers generally agreed that this was fair, no action followed and the tariff remained unchanged for the time being.

During the trip the earl was feted by the heads of the states he visited and hailed as the 'Bismarck of the East'. The *New York Times* carried this description of him: 'He walks and sits with his massive head inclined forward on his breast, recalling Browning's picture of Napoleon – "the prone brow oppressive with his mind."' But as soon as he set foot on Chinese soil again in late 1896, Earl Li realised that everything was not all right. He was made to wait for more than two weeks in Tianjin (where he disembarked), before being summoned to Beijing. In the capital he was given a mere half-hour audience with Emperor Guangxu, whose attention was almost exclusively given to the diamond-studded medal that Germany had presented to His Majesty. When the earl attempted to describe the strength of the West and the urgent need for China to reform, the young monarch told him to 'discuss these matters with Prince Gong and see what you can do'. As the earl did not have high expectations of the emperor in any case, he was not unduly disappointed. It was the next interview, with the empress dowager on the same day, that left him 'feeling really frightened'. Whatever Cixi said to the earl, of which there appears to be no record, it was certainly chilling, for the earl sank into a despondent torpor after the meeting. He was staying in a temple near her Summer Palace, and distractedly he wandered into the nearby ruins of the Old Summer Palace. Knowing who he was, eunuchs guarding the royal ruins allowed him entry. The earl's mind, as he himself wrote, continued to be 'in turmoil the whole night'. The next morning he tendered his resignation from all posts.

A curt imperial one-liner ignored his resignation, but implicitly made clear that he had been sacked, by announcing his new job: 'to work in the Foreign Office' – no longer as its overlord, but as an ordinary official. His two previous key posts, Imperial Commissioner for North China and Viceroy of Zhili, had already been transferred to somebody else and were not returned to him. The earl was allowed only to keep the title of Chief Administrator of the empire, which was largely honorific. As if this was not punishment enough, another edict publicly censured him for 'trespassing into a royal estate' and fined him a year's salary. These crushing blows were inflicted by the empress dowager, who wanted to punish the earl for his responsibility for China's ruin – although she was unable to spell this out publicly, as it was impossible to expose the precise nature of the earl's culpability without exposing that of the emperor. However, she left the complacent earl in no doubt that their close political relationship was over. And for the glory he had just enjoyed abroad, he would receive double punishment (hence fining him for 'trespassing' in addition to dismissing him). Later on, when Cixi returned to full power, and seemed to need a capable man by her side, the earl attempted to have himself reinstated. Cixi let him know that he deserved only further suffering, by sending the seventy-five-year-old on a hardship journey along the frozen Yellow River 'to conduct a geological study and propose ways to control flood'.

Thus Cixi ended her decades-long political partnership with Earl Li, an outstanding but gravely flawed statesman. With this, and the sense of relief that peace for the empire was secured for the foreseeable future by the pact with Russia, Cixi effectively turned her back on state affairs. The emotional roller-coaster during the war, with all its anxieties and frustrations and anguish, had exhausted her. She was shattered to see the fruits of her labour, over several decades, vanish. At sixty, she seems to have lost heart for a new beginning. The empress dowager was no longer her former self – she who had been so dynamic, presiding over debates, issuing decrees and launching policy innovations. She no longer seemed to care. After all, her adopted son was in charge. She could exercise control over one or two critical matters, but she could not interfere in daily affairs. Emperor Guangxu was in his usual state of inertia and cluelessness as far as reforms were concerned. When Viceroy Zhang presented a proposal for restarting modernisation, the emperor merely mouthed some clichés and did nothing. The railway programme, at least, did get restarted, including the Beijing–Wuhan Railway, which had been launched by Cixi, but shelved by the emperor. Now everyone recognised the railways' vital importance, even Grand Tutor Weng.

At this time, the budding Chinese bourgeoisie, rooted in shipping, mining and trade, and not affected by the war, was still active. Electricity had reached inland provinces like Hunan, where 'whole towns are bright with electric lights', an eye-witness exclaimed. Entrepreneurs were developing new ideas. Sheng Xuanhuai, the business pioneer who was entrusted with the building of the Beijing–Wuhan Railway, was calling for the founding of a state bank. If this idea had been put to her in the earlier years, Cixi would have adopted it eagerly. But now she appeared indifferent, and Emperor Guangxu told Sheng to form a bank himself through private investment. Foreign observers who had had high hopes of China carrying out reforms after Earl Li's tour of the West were disappointed. They saw that in more than two years since the end of the war, the country 'had done nothing to reform her administration or to reorganise her forces' and had learned no lesson from the defeat.

Cixi's multitude of interests outside politics made it easier for her to let go. And she concentrated on pursuing pleasure. On the occasion of the Moon Festival in 1896, which fell on 21 September, after the secret pact with Russia was wrapped up, she invited court grandees to the Summer Palace to celebrate. They were met at the Villa of the Jade Balustrade, the *Yu-lan-tang*, which sat right on the edge of the lake, with a panoramic view. It was the residence of the emperor, but Cixi acted as host. As Grand Tutor Weng recorded, she declared that the villa was 'full of light and air, better than the Forbidden City', and she was 'all praise and solicitude' for the grandees of their 'hard work' in concluding the Russian pact. Enquiring after a Grand Councillor who had been ill, she offered medical advice, telling Weng to warn him that he 'could take ginseng, but only with care'. State business was not discussed. The grandees were told to enjoy themselves. When night descended, a full moon rose in a rain-washed, now cloudless sky, magnificent over the Kunming Lake. Grand Tutor Weng drank with a few friends and enunciated poems. As the moon declined in size and brilliance, they wallowed in melancholy.

On that day there was no music. Emperor Guangxu's biological mother – Cixi's sister – had died on 18 June, and a 100-day mourning period was still in force, with the usual ban on all music. Three days later, when mourning came to an end, and Cixi and the emperor had discharged their final duties, the first notes were struck in a novel fashion. At dusk, decorated boats carried the grandees into the middle of the lake, where they stopped, gently swaying with the ripples sparkling under the moon. At a signal, all around the boats, red lanterns in the shape of lotus flowers lit up – powered by electricity – and a brilliantly illuminated platform floated silently into their midst. Opera was then performed on it, with modern lighting, the first ever witnessed by the grandees. This was followed by a firework display, dazzling against the dark silhouette of the nearby hill. Cixi was showing off her staging of the spectacle, disregarding the rising chill of the night on the water. Grand Tutor Weng, impressed though he was by the extravaganza, could not wait for it to finish, whereupon he rushed away to wrap himself up in a big padded coat.

The greater the joys the Summer Palace gave her, the more heartache Cixi felt. If that vast sum had not been given to Japan by those gutless men, how much she could have done to restore the Old Summer Palace! How much more beauty and splendour she could have created! And how many more modernisation projects could have been realised! As she restrained herself from berating the men, she was consumed by fury. One day, an irrepressible desire to lash out seems to have taken hold of her and she told the Ministry of Revenue, headed by Grand Tutor Weng, that she planned to start restoring the Old Summer Palace, and that she wished them to pass over to her all the tax collected from domestically grown opium. Large tracts of land had been used to grow this drug since its legalisation in 1860, and the revenue derived from it was sizeable.

The demand was insane, not only because it came at a time when the empire was crushed by colossal debts, but also because she was asking for the construction of a pleasure palace to be put on the state budget. She had made no such demand when she built her Summer Palace. In fact she had given a specific public assurance that it would not be funded by the state. Any public money she had used had been effectively stolen. Now, it was as if she were taunting the grandees: 'You had the money to give to the Japanese; I might as well have some for my use. It is you who have bankrupted the country and you have no right to deny me!' And, indeed, the grandees had forfeited the moral right to oppose her demand. Grand Tutor Weng sheepishly set out to explore ways to fulfil her wishes.

It took the Grand Tutor a year to arrive at a solution, such was his reluctance. In early summer 1897, he reported that he had consulted Robert Hart, and Hart reckoned that the output of domestically produced opium was substantially under-reported, and that taxation on the opium could be as much as twenty million taels per annum – considerably more than the state was receiving. Weng proposed to collect opium tax on the basis of Hart's estimated output, and hand over 30 per cent to Cixi 'for the building of royal palaces'. This would give her six million taels annually – an incredible sum. Cixi embraced the report with alacrity.

Opposition was immediately voiced: not by any grandee, but by Li Bingheng, the governor of Shandong, the coastal province southeast of Beijing. He argued that the new estimate of opium output was far too high, and that in the case of Shandong, taxation on that basis would be ten times what it currently was. 'Even exploitation to the limit may not be enough,' he wrote. As it was, in order to produce funds to help pay foreign debts, people in the provinces were already carrying an unbearable burden. Anything extra would be impossible, and could drive the people to rebellion. He urged the court to reject the report from the Ministry of Revenue, to 'abandon the desire to seek pleasure' and 'not to ruin our people'.

When she saw the argument, Cixi knew at once that she must forgo her dream. As she withdrew her request, the emperor referred the governor's petition to the Ministry of Revenue for reconsideration, and the ministry readily revoked what it called 'the scheme of the Inspector General'. No one in the government wanted his name to be associated with the scheme, and Robert Hart was thus made a convenient 'scapegoat'. Governor Bingheng, the plan's outspoken opponent, was promoted to Viceroy. The ruins of the Old Summer Palace remained ruins.

Cixi's pleasure-seeking period was in any case brief. Her nightmare scenario, articulated so eloquently by Viceroy Zhang in opposing the signing of the Treaty of Shimonoseki, materialised in late 1897. European powers, contemptuous and aggressive now towards China, began clamouring to grab a piece of the empire. Germany demanded Jiaozhou Bay in Shandong province, with its port Qingdao, as a naval station, claiming that it deserved this reward for helping force Japan to withdraw from the Liaodong Peninsula. As Beijing repeatedly rebuffed the demand, Kaiser Wilhelm II decided to use 'a little force'. German warships cruised up and down the coast, seeking what the Kaiser called 'a desired opportunity and pretext', which was soon found. On 1 November, two German missionaries were murdered in a village in Shandong. As Governor Bingheng acted at once to hunt down the criminals, the Kaiser was rejoicing: 'So the Chinese have at last given us the grounds and the "incident" which [the Germans] so long desired.' A German fleet, already prepared for action, arrived at Qingdao and gave the Chinese garrison forty-eight hours to vacate the port.

As soon as he received the ultimatum, Emperor Guangxu, fearing an invasion, acted like a scared rabbit and fired off a telegram 'absolutely forbidding' Governor Bingheng to resist by force, which the outraged governor had proposed to do. In a further telegram, the emperor declared: 'No matter how thuggishly the enemy behaves, the court will absolutely not resort to war.' According to Grand Tutor Weng, 'His Majesty forcefully insisted on two words: "No fighting [*bu-zhan*]."' Only after these exchanges was Cixi informed, when the reports and edicts were carried in person by Prince Gong to the Summer Palace. On his return to the Forbidden City the prince, much relieved, told the Grand

Council that she had 'accepted them'. The German demands were met more or less in full, with Prince Gong counselling 'yes to all', in order to get the German soldiers who had occupied the port out of the country. The Germans had made their demands in brutally blunt language: 'If you don't concede, we will start a war.' One of the demands concerned Governor Bingheng: he must 'be cashiered and dismissed from the public service'. The governor, who had been promoted after speaking out against Cixi's plan to rebuild the Old Summer Palace, was now forced out of office by the Germans. This personal experience turned him into a dedicated West-hater, and he would soon become a wholehearted promoter of the xenophobic Boxers. When the Boxer movement led to an invasion by Western armies, he volunteered to lead an armed force to fight them, and committed suicide when defeated.

Germany acquired the strategic port of Qingdao* and its bay 'by way of lease, provisionally for ninety-nine years'. The convention was signed in Beijing on 6 March 1898 by Earl Li and Grand Tutor Weng. The earl was by now a professional scapegoat, trotted out to sign anything that would give the signatory a bad name. The Grand Tutor had been appointed to the Foreign Office at the insistence of Prince Gong, who wanted the man full of verbal bravado to have his share of blame for signing treaties that amounted to 'selling out the country'. The Grand Tutor noted that when the German representative requested the signature of Prince Gong, the prince merely pointed at the tutor. He felt bitterly ashamed for his part in giving away Qingdao to the 'stinking beasts', torturing himself with the thought that he would now 'go down in history as a criminal'.

Although Cixi had played no part in recent events, but had simply accepted a fait accompli, her behaviour was remarkably consoling. Weng gratefully recorded that when the Grand Council upbraided themselves for doing a poor job, 'the Empress Dowager comforted us with kind words, and said that she understood completely our difficulties'. She only expressed grief at the fact that China was reduced to such a sorry state.

Things were tumbling from bad to worse. After the Germans came the Russians. Within a week of the German dash for Qingdao, Russian warships arrived at Port Arthur, on the tip of the Liaodong Peninsula.

* Hence the Qingdao beer of today, first made by German brewers.

Russia had been one of the powers that had forced Japan out of the peninsula – only to demand the port for itself now. 'If Germany occupies Qingdao, Russia must have Port Arthur,' said the Russians. Count Witte, Russia's negotiator of the secret deal with China the year before, regarded his country's conduct as 'the height of treachery and faithlessness'. Still he did what he could to achieve its object. When Beijing resisted the demand and Russia threatened war, Witte advised bribing the Chinese negotiators, Earl Li and Sir Chang Yinhuan, a suave diplomat. (Sir Yinhuan had been China's representative to Queen Victoria's Diamond Jubilee the previous year, and was knighted on the occasion, thus becoming the first Chinese official to be given a British knighthood.) According to Russian documents, they were offered half a million taels each, and both accepted. The Russians had also wanted to bribe Grand Tutor Weng, but the traditionalist gentleman refused to attend any secret meetings with them.

The earl received his half-million in person and 'expressed satisfaction' the day after he signed away Port Arthur – albeit 'only' on a twenty-five-year lease – on 27 March 1898. Actually, whether he took the money or not would not have made the slightest difference. Beijing's verbal resistance would have collapsed if Russia stepped up its threat of war, a war that Emperor Guangxu wanted to avoid at all costs. At court, the grandees could do nothing but weep together; 'what a pathetic sight,' lamented Weng. The earl also knew that he was the designated scapegoat. In an audience a few days before the signing, the emperor was already putting all the blame on him as he berated the earl: 'Now we have this trouble with Russia. What happened to that secret treaty of yours last year?' There was nothing the earl could say or do, except prostrate himself, panting. Eventually, when the emperor motioned for him to leave, he was unable to rise and had to be pulled up, after which he struggled to steady himself to catch his breath, before staggering out. After such treatment, perhaps the earl felt he deserved the money. His general frame of mind can be gleaned from his words to Sir Yinhuan when the latter complained of being made a signatory and having his reputation destroyed: 'It's not just you and I who are about to be destroyed. We [the whole empire] are all going down together.' For the moment Sir Yinhuan took just 10,600 taels, telling the Russians that he was already under a barrage of denunciations for bribe-taking. He had to wait, he said, for the storm to die down.

Cixi was not consulted about signing away Port Arthur. When Earl Li had asked the emperor: 'Has Your Majesty talked to the Empress

Dowager about this?' he replied that he had not. He also told Grand Tutor Weng that he had not even mentioned the business to Cixi, because she was already 'despondent with grief'. The Grand Tutor could 'imagine how much bottled-up anger and bitterness' the empress dowager was feeling. Clearly, Emperor Guangxu was afraid about being made to feel guilty again, even if only by Cixi's looks rather than her words. In any case, there would have been no point in telling her: as far as he was concerned, there was no alternative to leasing out Port Arthur.

Emperor Guangxu tried to avoid any act that might trigger Cixi's suppressed rage for his disastrous handling of the war with Japan, which had led to all these crises. Censor Weijun, who had made false accusations against her in order to keep her away from decision-making in the war, and who had been sent to the frontier, had served his term and was about to return to Beijing. When this came to the emperor's notice, Grand Tutor Weng recorded that he 'thought hard for a long time, and gave orders that the man stay where he was for another couple of years', adding, 'His Majesty really has the man's interests at heart.' Emperor Guangxu was concerned that if the Censor were to come back, he might well become a lightning conductor for the empress dowager's fury.

Following in the footsteps of Germany and Russia, Britain and France were keen not to miss out. Britain leased the former headquarters of the Northern Fleet, Weihaiwei, on the easternmost tip of the Shandong Peninsula – on the opposite coast from the Russian-leased Port Arthur. The British lease was to run as long as the Russian one: twenty-five years. The two countries were playing the Great Game, vying for power and influence in the East. Britain also added the Kowloon Peninsula and the New Territory to its Hong Kong colony – for a period of ninety-nine years. For the same length of time France leased Guangzhouwan, a small enclave on the south coast, as an outlier of French Indochina. Fujian province, across the sea from Taiwan, now a Japanese colony, became a Japanese sphere of influence. Thus by mid-1898 the strategic positions on the Chinese coast were more or less all in the hands of foreign powers, who could, if it suited them, do what they wished with China.

PART FIVE

To the Front
of the Stage
(1898–1901)

19 The Reforms of 1898
(1898)

H B. Morse, pre-eminent contemporary historian of China, . remarked, 'In the world's history no country, with so vast an extent of territory and so large a population, under one government, as China – no country with a tithe of its area or population – had ever been subjected to such a series of humiliations, or to so many proofs of the low esteem in which it was held, as China had been subjected to in the six months from November, 1897, to May, 1898 . . .' The need for reform was obvious. The empire might not otherwise survive for long. One petition after another was delivered to the Forbidden City. Even Emperor Guangxu was shaken out of his passivity and felt an 'urgent need' to do something.

Aged twenty-six, and having little knowledge of the real world, the emperor had no idea where to begin. Perhaps, like young people the world over, his instinct was to ditch restrictive forms of etiquette. In May 1898, Prince Heinrich of Germany paid a visit to his court. The brother of the Kaiser, the prince had in fact come as the admiral of a fleet reinforcing the German assault on Qingdao; but by the time he arrived, 'friendly relations' had already been restored, thanks to Beijing succumbing easily. The German minister negotiating his reception by the emperor asked for Prince Heinrich to be permitted to sit during the audience. This was unprecedented, as no one except Cixi sat in his presence. But Emperor Guangxu was more than willing to accommodate him. He even went further and volunteered to stand up while the German prince bowed to him, and to shake the prince's hand before inviting him to be seated. Grand Tutor Weng found this and some other violations of court protocol undignified and especially painful in light of the recent German outrage. He argued emotionally with His Majesty, but Emperor Guangxu did not share his tutor's agony and lost his temper with the old man. In the end, Cixi told off her adopted son: stop fighting over trifles when we have suffered such a disaster! She herself wanted to meet Prince Heinrich – this would be the first time she saw, and was seen by, a Western man – and she was unequivocal that the German prince had to stand before her. She had her way, and Emperor Guangxu had his. He even went to see the prince himself and personally brought a medal to award him. When the prince announced that he was presenting Emperor Guangxu with a medal on behalf of his royal brother, Guangxu went to extraordinary lengths to have one made for the Kaiser in return.

The young monarch had become fascinated by medals – just as he had fallen for European watches and clocks. He spent an inordinate amount of effort supervising the medal for the Kaiser, tirelessly discussing the colour, the size, the jewels, the craftsmanship, and innumerable other minute details with the Foreign Office and the project manager. The colour – gold, royal yellow or golden-red – was the subject of many a conference, and of much fretting. Then there was the question of what sort of pearl should be set on the medal. The emperor wanted a large one, and was disappointed that it would not fit. When he agreed to a smaller size, it turned out that no pearl of that size was of the finest quality. More discussions ensued before the right pearl and other design details were settled. The emperor himself took to wearing the medals given to him by foreign monarchs and on a whim awarded one each to Earl Li and Sir Yinhuan – although the earl was in disgrace and both were being bombarded with accusations of taking bribes. The emperor had seen medals being worn by Western diplomats.

While His Majesty's reformist initiatives extended no further, the grandees were at a total loss. When he asked them what to do, according to Grand Tutor Weng, 'Prince Gong was silent – and then said it must start with the administration. I said quite a few words, but the other Grand Councillors were all silent.' Prince Gong soon died, on 29 May 1898. On his deathbed he had nothing but tears for the shattered empire.

With the survival of his dynasty at stake, Emperor Guangxu turned to Cixi. Sir Yinhuan, who was very close to the emperor at the time, observed (and told the Japanese): 'The roller-coaster of events in the past few years has shaken the emperor very much and made him understand the need for reform . . . The Empress Dowager always likes reformers. So, given that the emperor has changed, and has come round to the idea of reform, he is becoming closer to the Empress Dowager. This inevitably increases her power.'

Emperor Guangxu now positively sought Cixi's guidance and she responded with affectionate enthusiasm. His office forwarded proposals about reforms to her, and she studied them, looking for ideas. Residing in the Forbidden City, he would travel in a sedan-chair for three hours each way to the Summer Palace every few days to consult her, and from time to time she would visit him in the Forbidden City. Altogether they spent more than two-thirds of their time together, when they would discuss state affairs. He was the pupil, and she was the teacher. It was after one such trip by the emperor to the Summer Palace that, upon returning to the Forbidden City, he announced a decree from Cixi to the Grand Council. Grand Tutor Weng recorded the moment in his diary entry of 11 June 1898:

> Today His Majesty relays a decree from the Empress Dowager [*shang-feng-ci-yu*]: what Censor Yang Shenxiu and Learning Companion Xu Zhijing said in the past few days is absolutely right. The fundamental policy of our state has not been made clear to all. From now on, we should comprehensively adopt Western ways. Make an unequivocal and unambiguous public announcement, etc. . . . The Empress Dowager is utterly determined. I ventured my view to His Majesty that of course Western ways should be adopted, but it is more important not to abandon our own sages' teachings in ethics and philosophy. Then I withdrew and drafted the imperial edict.

The subsequent edict, the 'Announcement of the Fundamental Policy of the State', drafted by Grand Tutor Weng according to Cixi's instructions, relayed by Emperor Guangxu and issued on that day, launched an historical movement, the Reforms of 1898. History books celebrate it as a milestone in Chinese history, but invariably credit it to Emperor Guangxu and condemn Cixi as an ultra-conservative opponent. The plain fact is that it was she who initiated the Reforms.

Drafting the Announcement was Grand Tutor Weng's last political act. Within days he was dismissed from the court by his pupil, Emperor Guangxu.

Breaking with the old man came at considerable personal cost to the emperor, as the Grand Tutor had been a father figure to him since his childhood: indeed, he had been closer to the tutor than to anyone else. The young monarch had relied on the older man for advice in all matters, especially during the war with Japan. After that disaster, as misfortune begot misfortune, the tutor's lustre dulled in his pupil's eyes. Then the relationship became intolerable as the emperor opted for reform while Weng stuck in the past. There had been many emotional disagreements. It was all too obvious that in a reformist court there was no place for the Grand Tutor, even though he was an outstanding scholar and calligrapher, and was upright and loyal. Emperor Guangxu wrote in his hand in crimson ink an edict ordering Weng to retire to his home. The old tutor was devastated and was heartbroken when the emperor refused to see him to say goodbye. Weng hurried to a gate inside the Forbidden City, which he had heard the emperor was about to pass through, in the hope of catching a glimpse of him. When the young man's sedan-chair went by, the elderly tutor prostrated himself, touching his forehead on the stone pavement. He later wrote: 'His Majesty turned round and gazed at me without a word. I felt as if I was in a nightmare.'

The decision undoubtedly had Cixi's approval. She had tried to reduce the emperor's dependency on Weng in state policy, but had had to tread gingerly, mindful of their intimacy. Now she could not but feel relieved and pleased. But she remained solicitous towards Weng. The day after the dismissal happened to be the occasion when the empress dowager routinely bestowed her summer gifts on the Grand Councillors. Weng declined his, saying to the eunuch bearing the special silk that he was no longer a Grand Councillor. Through the eunuch Cixi insisted, and he finally accepted it without writing a letter of thanks. His former colleagues thanked her on his behalf.

For the first time in their lives, Cixi and her adopted son collaborated remarkably well. From the palaces came a cascade of reformist decrees. Although issued in the emperor's name, all the decrees had Cixi's endorsement. They were based on proposals from officials throughout China. Top of the list for change was the educational system, which was central to producing the ruling elite. By focusing narrowly on esoteric Confucian classics, it left them ill equipped for the modern age, as well as ensuring that more than 99 per cent of the population remained illiterate. As the astute American missionary W. A. P. Martin remarked, 'The future of China depends on' its reform. As the system was the foundation of the state, its replacement by a Western one was nothing short of a seismic shift.

As a first step, the most arcane subjects in the Imperial Examinations were abolished, to be substituted the following year by tests in current affairs and economics. Emperor Guangxu edited the edict in his own hand, showing how keenly he felt about it. Western-style primary and secondary schools and universities, which taught Western-style natural and social sciences, were to be established across China. Their sites, funding, staff and teaching materials were carefully considered and planned. Beijing University was founded to lead the way.

Many of the projects either took up or developed Cixi's earlier modernising efforts. These included sending students abroad to study. It was announced that Their Majesties were going to take the train to Tianjin in the autumn to inspect the army, which had been receiving modern training. This was a symbolic gesture intended to demonstrate the importance they placed on railways and on up-to-date defence. The newer schemes embraced modern agricultural methods, Western-style commerce, new publications and technological innovations, for which patent regulations were being written. One precise and brand-new idea that would have far-reaching implications seems certain to have come from Cixi (she directed her loyal follower Junglu to carry it out): importing machines to process raw materials and turn them into manufactured goods for export. As an example, camel hair and lambswool, two traditional export items from north China, were to be made into fine textiles and blankets to increase their value. The prospect of expanding exports had been the clincher that had persuaded Cixi to build a railway network in the first place.

Their working relationship went smoothly for more than two months and the modernising zeal of the court was felt across the country. Support for it among the officials was estimated at 'six or seven out of ten, while those who stubbornly clung to the old ways are no more than one or two out of ten'. Some decrees were implemented at once, including the establishment of Beijing University. But before most could be carried out, a dramatic event forced the reform to an abrupt halt – an event brought on by a wily and unconventional man, Kang Youwei, nicknamed Wild Fox Kang.

A forty-year-old Cantonese from a family of officials, Kang grew up in an open port, Nanhai, where there was a strong Western presence. He acquired many reformist ideas, and was keen to put them into practice. He was a man of supreme self-confidence. In his manuscript, tellingly entitled 'The History of Me', he declared that he was already showing signs of greatness by the age of five. At twenty, one day as he was sitting alone he suddenly saw that 'the heaven and the earth and everything else became one with me, and this entity sent out spectacular rays of light. I knew I was the Sage, and I smiled joyfully.' The Sage was Confucius, of whom he believed he was the reincarnation. For some time he had tried to reach the throne so that his views would be known and acted on; indeed, he wished to direct the throne. As he was a very junior official, he met with many frustrations, but none deterred him.

Continuing to cultivate people of influence, Kang made a crucial friend who changed his fortunes: Sir Yinhuan, who was a fellow Cantonese and the principal official in the Foreign Office, and who had been taken on by the emperor as his confidant, in spite of accusations of bribe-taking. On 24 January 1898, through his machinations, Kang was interviewed by five of the empire's top grandees. Immediately after the interview he wrote a letter to the emperor, which Sir Yinhuan delivered. Thus the Wild Fox was introduced to the very highest circle and the throne.

Kang followed up by presenting other writings, which were all forwarded to Emperor Guangxu by Sir Yinhuan. The emperor sent them straight on to Cixi, not reading all of them himself. Cixi read the papers carefully and was impressed. She kept a pamphlet on the transformation of Japan and drew her adopted son's attention to it. Cixi had discovered a remarkable reformer with fresh ideas, who was also eloquent and fearless in expressing them. Soon she detected the same inspired thinking in the petitions of two officials, Censor Shenxiu and Learning Companion Xu – the two men she referred to in the decree that launched the Reforms on 11 June. Unbeknownst to her, these petitions had both been ghost-written by Kang. Evidently, Kang and Cixi were thinking very much alike.

As Learning Companion Xu was cited in the imperial decree, Kang ghosted another petition for him, which urged the emperor to install Kang 'as a close adviser on all new policies'. The ventriloquist then did the same for Kang's most-noted associate, a brilliant essayist called Liang Qichao. With Cixi's blessing, Emperor Guangxu gave Kang an audience in the Summer Palace on 16 June; the Wild Fox thus became one of the first very junior people interviewed by the emperor for a high-up position. Afterwards Kang was offered a post as a staff member in the Foreign Office, but he did not take up the job. Privately, he dismissed the offer as a 'humiliation' and 'ludicrous in the extreme'. He was intent on being by the emperor's side, making decisions for His Majesty. To this end he had, since the beginning of the year, advocated forming a kind of 'Advisory Board' to the throne that would be vested with some executive power.

Of all his ideas, this in fact seems to have been the one that really struck a chord with Cixi. There was no such body in the court, as the Qing dynasty explicitly ordained that the emperor alone should make all decisions: the Grand Council could advise, but could go no further. Kang thus identified a fundamental defect in the dynastic system – one that Lord Macartney had recognised 100 years earlier after visiting the eighty-year-old Emperor Qianlong. Macartney asked a prescient question: 'Who is the Atlas destined by him to bear this load of empire when he dies?' On 'whoever [*sic*] shoulders it may fall', he remarked, the shoulders had better be of superhuman strength. The Chinese empire was like a 'first-rate Man of War, which a fortunate succession of able and vigilant officers has contrived to keep afloat for these hundred and fifty years past . . . But whenever an insufficient man happens to have command on deck, adieu to the discipline and safety of the ship . . . she may drift some time as a wreck, and will then be dashed to pieces on the shore . . .' Emperor Guangxu was that 'insufficient' captain and needed some first-class minds to help him. Cixi knew this all too well. In fact, she was to observe that Britain was a world power not so much due to Queen Victoria herself, but to 'the able men of parliament' who collectively made decisions.

Cixi invited a number of top officials to debate the idea of an Advisory Board. They were against it. She told them to reconsider – to 'give the matter serious thought and detailed discussions', warning that 'no lip service is permitted'. After months of toing and froing, the consensus was still negative. The objection lay in an insurmountable problem: who should sit on the Board and share power with the emperor? There was no selection procedure and the fear was that 'evil' people could worm their way onto the Board through crooked ways like banding together to promote each other clandestinely, in which case the dynasty could well fall into their hands. Wild Fox Kang was foremost in the minds of the doubters. Word had gone round that Kang was paying for others to petition on his behalf – an accusation that was almost certainly true. A petition by Learning Companion Xu for Kang reportedly cost him 4,000 taels, and other petitioners were paid 300 taels a month as retainers. People in the capital were scandalised and called the Wild Fox 'shameless'. They also speculated about the source of his money, as his family was not wealthy. The emperor's old reformist tutor, Sun Jianai, argued that the Advisory Board could only succeed with a Western-style 'election' that subjected the candidates' characters to public scrutiny. As an 'election' was so absolutely unthinkable at the time, the idea of an Advisory Board was abandoned at the end of July.

In spite of all the unpleasant things said about the Wild Fox, and despite the fact that she herself was on guard against him, Cixi remained appreciative of Kang as a reformist and gave him key assignments. A decree told him to go and start the first modern government newspaper in Shanghai to publicise the new policies. He would also be responsible for drafting a press law based on Western models. Some of his friends regarded these occupations as ideal for him. It was very much Cixi's style to send a disaffected man out of the capital, to where he could not cause any harm, but still let him play a role, even an important one. She believed in creating as few enemies as possible. But Kang declined to leave. Nothing less than the throne would satisfy him. His right-hand man, Liang, was also not content with his assignment – which was to supervise new textbooks for the whole empire – even though it was an extraordinary promotion, given that he had never held any official post. Kang lingered in Beijing and, with Liang's assistance, plotted his next move.

He stayed with Sir Yinhuan, who was the key man in his plotting. The closest man to the emperor since the departure of Grand Tutor Weng, Sir Yinhuan was able to tell Kang a great deal about His Majesty. The young monarch was fragile and weak. His nerves had been over-stretched by his relentless workload, made worse by his obsessive habit of correcting the wrong characters and bad grammar in the innumerable reports that passed over his desk. Sir Yinhuan was also aware of the emperor's latent bitterness against his Papa Dearest. In addition to past animosities, in 1896 Cixi had initiated the Russo-Chinese Secret Treaty in the aftermath of the war with Japan, when Emperor Guangxu could not hold his head up in the court. She had made all the decisions, with no one even bothering to go through the motion of referring matters to him. This event had made the young man not only resent Cixi, but also hate Russia – quite unlike his feelings of indifference towards Germany or any other power. The Wild Fox was thus able to work on the emperor by pressing on these vulnerable spots, in writings that were delivered to the monarch by Sir Yinhuan clandestinely, bypassing the Grand Council and Cixi. In one key pamphlet, 'On the Destruction of Poland', Russia was cast as the bogeyman, 'the country of bloodthirsty beasts, which makes it its business to swallow up other countries'. Liberally stretching Polish history to produce a parable, Kang wrote that Poland had 'a wise and able king determined to carry out reform', but his efforts were 'obstructed by aristocrats and high officials', and so he missed 'a propitious moment to make the country strong'. Then, the Wild Fox claimed, 'Russian troops arrived . . . and the country perished in less than seven years.' The king himself 'went through the most cruel and most atrocious fate rarely encountered in history'. Kang declared that China was about to become another Poland as a result of 'the grandees blocking the Advisory Board' and that 'Russian troops will come once the Siberian Railway is completed in a few years'. The Wild Fox's reference to the Siberian Railway, a key part of the Secret Treaty, was designed to cause maximum upset to Emperor Guangxu.

This ominous and alarming fable was in the emperor's hands just after 13 August, his twenty-seventh birthday. He read it deep into the night, drops from the red candles seeping into the pages. His already-poor sleep became even more disturbed, and his brittle nerves snapped. As his medical records show, doctors started visiting him almost daily from the 19th. In this condition, between sobs, he ordered 2,000 taels of silver delivered to Kang as a token of his appreciation. Kang wrote a thank-you letter on the 29th, which was no ordinary missive of gratitude. Secretly handed to the emperor, it was exceptionally long: it retold the Polish horror story and emphasised that the only way to avoid the fate of Poland was to install the Advisory Board at once. It also heaped flattery on Emperor Guangxu that went far beyond the norm. It described the emperor as 'the wisest ever in history', with 'penetrating eyes sending off rays like the sun and the moon', and with abilities 'sublime and unparalleled even compared with the greatest emperors of all time'. It was 'the injustice of a thousand years' that China's troubles should be laid at his door. They had only happened because the emperor had not had the opportunity to exercise his 'supreme wisdom and mighty bravery, and his awesome thunderbolt-like force'. The emperor's potential had been obstructed by the 'old officials'. And the problem of all problems was that he had not had the right people at his side. All His Majesty needed was to rectify that and he would achieve greatness.

Nobody had ever said such things to Emperor Guangxu. The court had its formula of florid praise for the throne, but did not encourage extravagant compliments. A good emperor was supposed to embrace criticism and steer clear of flatterers. Moreover, Emperor Guangxu had always been made to feel inadequate, especially in comparison with his Papa Dearest. Suddenly he found someone who appeared fully to appreciate him. The impact of Kang's flattery on the insecure young man cannot be exaggerated. It hugely boosted his self-esteem. His sense of guilt since the war with Japan was expunged and the inferiority complex was much assuaged. Nothing, after all, had been his fault. The 'old officials' were the ones to blame. What was more, with Kang by his side, there was no limit to what he could achieve. It was thus that Emperor Guangxu fell under the spell of the Wild Fox, whom he had met only once. He immediately ordered all Kang's petitions to be collected into booklets for his personal study, and named the collection 'the Petitions of the Hero'.

As well as the long, flattering letter, Kang wrote separately, urging the emperor to dismiss his old officials and make new appointments. The emperor was so fired up that he instantly put pen to paper and sacked a host of officials, closing down a large number of offices. The decree, edited in his own hand, itched to 'get rid of the whole lot'. It appears not to have occurred to the emperor that, although many of these officials may have been incompetent, they were lowly clerks and administrators merely carrying out orders given by him.

When Cixi received the abolition edict before it was issued, she was alarmed. To accommodate her adopted son, however, she only restored a few crucial offices, such as the one in charge of shipping grain from south China to the north, and otherwise let it pass. To his face she forcefully objected to the wholesale dismissals, telling him it could lead to the 'loss of goodwill and support [*shi-ren-xin*]' for the Reforms, and could even cost him his throne. Indeed, as the edict suddenly deprived thousands of officials of their livelihood in the capital alone, administrators throughout the empire looked on appalled and fearful.

Knowing Cixi's disapproval, the emperor issued further edicts without showing them to her first, thus breaking the code of their working relationship. On 4 September, after Cixi had just left the Forbidden City for the Summer Palace, he sacked the minister and five other top officials from the Ministry of Rites in one wrathful crimson-inked edict. His anger seemed disproportionate to the offence: that the ministry had delayed passing on to him a proposal from a clerk named Wang Zhao. But the clerk was a friend of Kang. The emperor promoted him. He also appointed a new minister – another of Kang's friends, who had written to the throne in praise of the Wild Fox. The new vice-ministers included yet more of Kang's friends, such as Learning Companion Xu. Emperor Guangxu intended this to be the model for other ministries and offices. The next day he made four low-ranking men secretaries in the Grand Council, and two of them were also Kang's friends, each of whom he had met for no more than a few moments. But he regarded them and other such appointees as 'bright and brave men', in contrast to all those 'stupid and useless' old officials.

Cixi was only sent the emperor's edicts for information, after they were made public. When she next saw her adopted son, she told him that the sackings in the Ministry of Rites were unreasonable, and she refused to endorse some new appointees, including Learning Companion Xu, whom she now knew to be a member of the Wild Fox's clique. She then quietly made arrangements to ensure that edicts drafted by the new secretaries were shown to her first. Otherwise she did nothing regarding Guangxu's actions.

Now that Emperor Guangxu had established the precedent of firing and hiring on his own, the Wild Fox organised his cronies in a concerted petition campaign calling on the emperor to establish the Advisory Board – which he would lead. One of the four new secretaries who did not belong to Kang's coterie wrote in a private letter on 13 September: 'Every day, they are talking about the Advisory Board, and the emperor is being pushed towards it. Kang and Liang have not got the positions they want, and I am afraid the situation will become turbulent . . .' Indeed, on the same day Emperor Guangxu finally made up his mind to set up what was effectively the Kang Board. When the Wild Fox learned about it, he went at once to his small group of friends, his face beaming with delight. He told them that the Board would have ten members, who would have to be officially recommended to the throne. Then he handed out a list of ten men to those who were entitled to write to the throne direct, telling them each to recommend a few from the list. These included Kang himself, his brother Guangren, his right-hand man Liang, two sons of Learning Companion Xu and other cronies. And so the names of this cabal went forward to Emperor Guangxu.

On 14 September the emperor took the list to the Summer Palace. Cixi refused to authorise it and, in her forceful way, made it utterly clear that her decision was non-negotiable. The following day an anguished Emperor Guangxu summoned one of the four new secretaries and gave him a letter asking the new appointees whom the emperor referred to as his 'comrades' to find a way to form the Kang Board without antagonising his Royal Father. The secretary to whom he gave the letter, Yang Rui, was actually not a member of Kang's clique and did not even approve of what Kang was doing. But His Majesty was rather woolly about the different allegiances among the new appointees suddenly flooding the court, regarding them all as one progressive force.

The Wild Fox learned the contents of the letter and may have read it. The next thing he saw was a public edict from Emperor Guangxu, making an oddly personal plea for Kang to leave Beijing and go to Shanghai to take up his newspaper post. Thus the Wild Fox knew that his leap to the top had been blocked by the empress dowager. Cixi had never stood in the way of Kang's reformist policies – indeed, she agreed with them. She had actually been the first to appreciate Kang's talents and promote him. But she refused to hand over power to him.

Given that the Qing regime had brought such disasters to the country, the case for an alternative government was unanswerable. Whether Kang would have made a better leader is open to debate. But one thing is certain: he did not have a political programme to turn China into a parliamentary democracy, as is often claimed. He never advocated this; on the contrary, he argued in one of his articles that democracy, while good for the West, did not suit China. He wrote, 'An emperor is like the father of a family, and the people are like children. The Chinese people are all like toddlers and infants. May I ask how the family of a dozen babies can function if the parents don't have the exclusive right to make decisions, but instead let all the toddlers and infants make their own decisions? . . . I can tell you that in China, only the emperor must rule.'

Wild Fox Kang wanted to be the emperor, and had been trying to create a mandate for himself. First, he claimed that he was the reincarnation of Confucius. The assertion had indeed attracted attention, and even Westerners had heard him spoken of as 'the modern Sage' and 'the second Confucius'. Next, with his small but vocal band of disciples, Kang attempted to establish that Confucius had actually been crowned King of China, replacing the emperor of the time. To propagate the idea, they started a newspaper that used a 'Confucian Calendar', in which the year of Confucius's birth was Year One. As this strategy directly threatened Emperor Guangxu, the Wild Fox abandoned it when he began to ingratiate himself with the emperor. The moment he realised that the emperor was falling under his spell, Kang most anxiously explained to the monarch in one of his clandestine letters that he had been misunderstood and that he had never held the view that Confucius had been crowned king. Kang was eager to expunge any idea that he coveted the throne. With Emperor Guangxu seduced, Kang could fulfil his dream by first becoming the puppeteer behind the throne. This route was now blocked by Cixi with a will of iron, and the only way for the Wild Fox to achieve his goal was to remove her by force.

20 A Plot to Kill Cixi (September 1898)

WILD FOX Kang had been hatching plots to kill Cixi for some time, knowing that she stood between him and supreme power. For this purpose he needed an armed force, and he first thought of a commander named Nie. He asked Clerk Wang Zhao to approach Nie and persuade him to join them, but the clerk declined to go, telling Kang that the mission was a pipe dream. The army was firmly in Cixi's hands. The first thing she had done when she launched the Reforms was to make key military appointments, putting the man who had the most unwavering loyalty to her, Junglu, in charge of all the army in the capital and its surrounding area. Junglu's headquarters were in Tianjin.

Among those reporting to Junglu was General Yuan Shikai – the future first President of China when the country became a republic. Now he was an ambitious and outstanding officer. He noticed that incredibly high posts were being awarded by the emperor on the recommendation of Kang's men, and so made friends with them. Thanks to Kang, Emperor Guangxu gave General Yuan not one but two audiences, immediately after his altercation with Cixi on 14 September. His Majesty conferred on the General a promotion over the heads of his superiors, and practically told Yuan to detach himself from Junglu and to take orders directly from him. The emperor was doing what the Wild Fox had advised – establishing an army of his own.

After the audiences, one of Kang's fellow plotters, Tan Sitong, paid General Yuan a late-night visit on 18 September. Tan, one of the four newly appointed Grand Council secretaries, believed that reform could only be achieved through violence. 'There has been no reform without bloodshed since ancient times; we must kill all those deadbeats before we can start getting things done.' Known to General Yuan as a 'newly risen VIP close to the emperor', Tan claimed that he had come to express the emperor's wish. General Yuan was to kill Junglu in Tianjin and take his troops to Beijing; there he was to surround the Summer Palace and capture the empress dowager. After that, said Tan, 'to slay that rotten old woman will be my job, and need not concern Your Excellency'. Tan promised the General that the emperor himself would give him a crimson-inked edict to this effect in his third audience, in two days' time, on 20 September. Yuan, who thought Tan looked 'ferocious and semi-deranged', was non-committal, but said that such a big thing would take time to arrange.

Arrangements were actually being made by the Wild Fox, who had devised a way to transfer General Yuan's soldiers, numbering 7,000 and stationed outside Beijing, into the capital and position them next to the Summer Palace. He ghosted a proposal for another fellow plotter, Censor Shenxiu, to present to the emperor, claiming that a haul of gold and silver had been buried in the Old Summer Palace, which might now be dug up to help alleviate the state's financial crisis. The proposal was timed to arrive on the emperor's desk just before Yuan's third audience, so that the emperor could give the job of excavation there and then to the General, who could therefore legitimately move his army onto Cixi's doorstep.

As his diary later revealed, General Yuan was stupefied by Tan's proposal. He was faced with the dilemma of choosing sides between Emperor Guangxu and the empress dowager. As he said to Tan, if the emperor really issued a crimson-inked edict telling him to do away with the empress dowager, 'who would dare to disobey the slip of paper from the emperor?' And yet that very night he went directly to one of Cixi's trusted princes and denounced the plotters.*

Meanwhile, other events had been happening concerning a visitor in Beijing at the time, Itō Hirobumi, former Prime Minister of Japan, the architect of Japan's war against China four years earlier and of the calamitous Treaty of Shimonoseki. Recently out of office, Itō was making a 'private' visit to Beijing, and Emperor Guangxu was scheduled to receive him on the same day of General Yuan's third audience.

---

* Historians usually set Yuan's denunciation much later, after he saw the emperor for a third time. This could not have been the case. Any delay by him, on a matter of life and death for Cixi, would have been interpreted by her as hesitation and a lack of loyalty. He would never have been trusted again. The fact was that from this time General Yuan enjoyed unreserved trust from Cixi and a meteoric rise.

The mood among some educated Chinese in relation to Japan had swung from one of loathing to admiration and goodwill since the more recent encroachment by European powers in 1897–8. The Japanese actively cultivated influential men along this line: 'The war between us was a mistake, and we both suffered. Now that white men are bearing down menacingly on us yellow people, China and Japan must unite and resist them together. We must help each other.' Some officials were sympathetic to this argument and were eager for Japan to teach China how to become strong. There were petitions calling for the emperor to invite Itō to stay and be his adviser. The chorus was led by Wild Fox Kang, who ghosted several petitions for others to present. A widely read newspaper in Tianjin, the *Guo-wen-bao*, owned by a Japanese and with backing from the Japanese government, promoted the idea, claiming it would lead 'not only to good fortune for China and Japan, but also to the survival of Asia and the Yellow race'.

It was known that Emperor Guangxu intended to employ Itō as his adviser. The emperor had developed an extremely pro-Japanese attitude since falling under Kang's influence. On 7 September, he had written in his own hand a letter to the Japanese emperor, opening with intimate language unique in diplomatic documents: 'My dearest and nearest friendly neighbour of the same continent', and ending with a wish that the two countries would 'support each other to defend and secure the Great East'. Itō himself seems to have been expecting to work with the Chinese throne. When he arrived in Tianjin, he wrote to his wife: 'I am leaving for Beijing tomorrow, where the emperor seems to have been awaiting my arrival for some time . . . In Tianjin, I am busy with banquets the whole time. Many Chinese have come and asked me to help China, and it is really impossible to say no. I've heard that the emperor seems to be able and bright, and only 27 years old . . .' Indeed Emperor Guangxu would give an audience to Itō on 20 September and might well announce Itō's engagement immediately afterwards. (Appointments were often announced straight after the audience with the appointee.) To enable the decree of employment to be seen as a response to popular demand, the Wild Fox ghosted two petitions pressing the emperor to engage Itō – one to be on His Majesty's desk hours before Itō's audience, and the other the day after.

Wild Fox Kang so keenly promoted the employment of Itō out of personal calculations. He was not so naïve as to believe that Itō would be working for the interests of China, not Japan, and that China could maintain its independence under his stewardship. Japan had not wavered in its ambition to control China. During Itō's visit, Japanese newspapers were talking about 'the necessity' of China 'consulting the Japanese government' on all its policies. When he heard about the emperor's desire to employ Itō as his adviser, Earl Li wrote just one word in a letter: 'Ludicrous'. Viceroy Zhang, the famed moderniser who had conceived the strategic Beijing–Wuhan railway, was 'shocked' and 'rejected the idea outright'. The earl and the Viceroy were both ardent advocates of learning from Japan and employing Japanese advisers. But they knew that if Itō became the 'adviser' to Emperor Guangxu, there would be no way to prevent this former Japanese Prime Minister from becoming the puppeteer, and China from losing its independence.★

Wild Fox Kang was as shrewd as the two statesmen. And yet he was manoeuvring not only for the engagement of Itō, but also for creating a Sino-Japanese 'union' (*lian-bang*) or even a 'merger' (*he-bang*). The petitions he ghosted calling for Itō's appointment also urged Emperor Guangxu to opt for one or other course. It is unlikely that he was sincerely trying to deliver China to Japan. More likely, he and the Japanese had struck a deal to advance each other's interests. Indeed, ever since the Reforms began, the Japanese-owned newspaper in Tianjin had devoted much space to reporting Kang's opinions, which had hugely raised his profile and helped create the impression that the Reforms were entirely of his making. This impression was not restricted to readers of that particular paper. As its news items were copied by other papers throughout the Treaty Ports, Kang's name acquired such prominence that people thought he was the leader of the Reforms. The Tianjin paper also promoted the idea of the Advisory Board – while Kang suggested to Emperor Guangxu that the Board should include Itō. But the greatest service the Japanese did for Kang was to link him up with Emperor Guangxu in the first place – through Sir Yinhuan, who was almost certainly their agent and working for their interests.

One of the most Westernised officials, Sir Yinhuan was outstand-ingly able, and shone in foreign affairs. He was Cixi's flamboyant envoy to a string of countries (in Washington in the 1880s he was 'the first Chinese Minister to give a ball at the official residence', reported the *New York Times*), and was knighted in Britain, where he represented China at Queen Victoria's Diamond Jubilee. A confidential report to

---

★ This simple fact has not been recognised in the average history books, in which the planned employment of Itō is treated as a praiseworthy move that would have benefited China.

Tokyo by Yano Fumio, Japanese minister to Beijing in 1898, shows that he was the minister's regular source of top-secret information. When Grand Tutor Weng was dismissed, the minister went straight to Sir Yinhuan to find out the real reason, and he told the Japanese everything he knew. At the time some in the top echelon had brought impeachments against him for 'passing secret state policies to foreigners'. Grand Councillors had denounced him to the throne for 'acting secretively and suspiciously'. But in those days there was no mechanism to investigate spying charges, and with Emperor Guangxu indignantly defending him, nothing was done. Cixi had wanted to have Sir Yinhuan's house searched for evidence but, largely because of his close relationship with the emperor, her order was not carried out.

It was Sir Yinhuan who engineered Kang's initial entry into the top circle, through covert machinations rather than open recommendation. It was he who acted as the secret middle man between Kang and Emperor Guangxu. And it was he who enabled Kang to gain control over the emperor. He did so much for Kang not because they had a long-standing, close friendship – indeed the evidence suggests the contrary, as he later quite gratuitously ran the Wild Fox down. Sir Yinhuan acted as he did at Tokyo's behest – and he worked for Tokyo not out of a belief that China would benefit from Japanese domination. He knew how brutal the Japanese were, as he dealt with them in negotiations over the indemnity after the war. When China, crushed by crippling rates of foreign loans and struggling to cope with the Yellow River breaking its banks, requested that the three-year payment deadline be extended, Tokyo refused outright. Sir Yinhuan privately lamented that this showed 'the so-called Japanese desire to form a special relationship with China is only empty words'.

His most likely motive was money. A committed gambler, Sir Yinhuan was a well-known bribe-taker – to an extent that was deemed unacceptable even in this bribe-infested country. Accusations of him taking large kickbacks through foreign contracts that he'd negotiated were legion, and the bribes from Russia were on the record. The Japanese were shrewed and skilful bribers. Sir Yinhuan was also supremely cynical. When dealing with the German seizure of Qingdao, his indifference perplexed his colleague, Grand Tutor Weng, who himself felt as though he was being 'tortured in boiling water and flaming fire'. In his diary Weng wrote: 'When I go to his house [to discuss business], he is always lounging about and chatting and laughing as though nothing disastrous is happening. I really can't understand him.'

Cixi did not have a full picture of the skulduggery involving Sir

Yinhuan, Wild Fox Kang, the Japanese and her adopted son. She had been informed of Itō's visit, the calls for his engagement and his scheduled audience with Emperor Guangxu. Well aware of the perils of Itō's installation, she had in fact taken action: she made the emperor promise that Itō's advice, which he would invite, would not be given to him in person, but would be passed on to him through the Foreign Office. This way, she believed, no harm could be done.

But on the night of 18 September, an urgent letter was delivered to her and made her apprehensive. Written by a Censor, Chongyi, who was related to Earl Li by marriage, the letter emphatically drew her attention to the danger of Emperor Guangxu engaging Itō, as well as to Wild Fox Kang's extraordinary hidden access to the emperor. 'If the throne employs Itō,' it warned, 'it might as well be putting this country of our ancestors on a silver platter and offering it to [Japan] . . .' The Censor entreated Cixi to take back power at once to prevent disasters from happening.

Cixi was unsettled. What if her adopted son ignored their agreement and installed Itō at his side with an edict written in crimson ink? She decided to go to the Forbidden City the next day, 19 September, in time for Emperor Guangxu's audience with Itō on the 20th, to make sure this would not happen. After that, she planned to return to the Summer Palace. Having made this decision, she went to bed.

She was in her usual sound sleep in the small hours when General Yuan's denunciation of the plot arrived. Cixi was thunderstruck. It was true that her relationship with her adopted son was fraught, but that he should be connected with a plot to kill her was still inconceivable.

Although, from General Yuan's account, the emperor's role in the plot was far from clear, there could be no doubt that he knew something about it. Why else would he make General Yuan his own personal commander, separate from the army – the very general whom the plotters then approached to harm her? And why was he so surreptitious about his association with Wild Fox Kang? That her adopted son knew about Kang's plot, however tenuously, made him complicit and unforgivable – especially in a culture that put filial piety at the top of its ethical code.

In the morning Cixi left the Summer Palace as planned. Outwardly, everything was normal. She stepped onto a boat from the pier in front of her villa and was carried across the lake into the Imperial Canal that led to the city. Ten kilometres long, the canal was lined with willows and peach trees – and Praetorian Guards. At a sluice gate where a change of boat was necessary, she walked into the Buddhist temple on the bank and prayed. Where the canal ended, a sedan-chair bore her into the Sea Palace next to the Forbidden City. During that seemingly peaceful and leisurely journey her mind was in torment.

Emperor Guangxu learned of Cixi's unexpected arrival and hastily rushed to the palace gate to greet her on his knees. Whatever anger erupted inside her at the sight of her adopted son, the empress dowager maintained a calm exterior. She did not want to cause alarm, especially as the audience with Itō was scheduled for the following day: any complication with Japan had to be avoided. She may not have known the full story of Kang's relationship with Japan, but Itō's appearance at this moment seemed too improbable a coincidence.

The following morning, 20 September, it appeared to be business as usual. First Emperor Guangxu had his arranged third audience with General Yuan. He did not produce any crimson-inked edict, as the plotter Tan had promised the General – though this may not mean that he had not intended to. Cixi was within earshot. During the audience the General unmistakably alluded to the plot, saying that His Majesty's new friends were 'going about things in a careless and ill-thought-out manner', and 'if there was a slip, Your Majesty would be incriminated'. The emperor gazed silently at Yuan, looking as though something had touched him. That he understood what the General was talking about at all would have confirmed his guilt in Cixi's eyes.

Yuan returned to his troops in Tianjin. Cixi kept her unperturbed exterior when her adopted son, observing ritual, came to bid her good day before entering the grandest hall in the Sea Palace for his meeting with Itō. At the meeting he said nothing that went beyond the agreed text. Itō's counsel was solicited, but was to be given through the Foreign Office. As soon as the audience was over, Cixi placed her adopted son under house arrest, confining him to his villa at Yingtai, the islet in the middle of the lake in the Sea Palace, reachable only by way of a long bridge that could be opened and closed. When she went to the Summer Palace, she would take him with her. He had become her prisoner.

As such, on the following day he wrote in his own hand a decree in crimson ink, announcing that Cixi would be his Guardian. A formal ceremony was subsequently staged. Thereafter, Emperor Guangxu became Cixi's puppet, signing edicts with his crimson-inked brush according to her wishes. He continued to see officials and Grand

Councillors, but always with her. The silk screen that had been concealing her was removed: she stepped from behind the throne to the front of the stage.

Cixi quickly formed a clear picture of the Wild Fox's activities vis-à-vis her adopted son. The emperor had scarcely any secrets from his eunuchs, whom Cixi began to interrogate. Thus she established who had been seeing and influencing him. Sir Yinhuan was easily exposed, and became her second bête noire. She methodically rounded up the plotters, giving verbal rather than written orders. Arrests were not all made at once, as she wanted the whole process carried out as quietly as possible.

The first target for arrest was obviously Kang. But Cixi was two days too late. The Wild Fox had known the game was up as soon as he had heard that General Yuan had been non-committal – like another conspirator, who had been specially employed to kill Cixi, a man called Bi. Bi later described visiting Tan to enquire about his mission the following dawn. 'Mr Tan was combing his hair languidly' and told Bi that the General did not commit himself. Bi asked, 'Are you sure Yuan is the right man for the job?' Tan clearly did not trust Yuan and replied, 'I did argue with Mr Kang time and again, but he insists on using Yuan. What can I do?' Bi said, 'So you revealed the whole plot to Yuan?' Being told that Yuan knew everything, Bi exclaimed, 'We are done for. We are done for! Don't you know what sort of operation this is? You can't talk about it just like that! I'm afraid you and your families and clans are all going to the execution ground!' Bi promptly departed and abandoned the plotters.

The Wild Fox himself paid visits to two foreigners, the Welsh Baptist missionary Timothy Richard, who was his friend, and Itō himself – the day *before* Itō's audience with Emperor Guangxu. What Kang sought was safe haven. Richard had set out to cultivate the official class and the literati, and knew many powerful figures, including Earl Li. His dream was not only to 'establish the Kingdom of God' on Chinese soil, but also to run the country – 'reforming China, remodelling its institutions, and, in short, carrying on its government,' as Robert Hart noted, finding the idea 'too delicious!' British diplomats regarded Richard's grandiose plans as 'nonsense'. (Among his proposals was that 'two foreign governesses should be engaged for the Empress-Dowager'.) Kang had recommended him to Emperor Guangxu as one of the two foreign advisers on the Advisory Board, the other being Itō. Richard was grateful. He now rushed about to drum up assistance for Kang, but to little avail as the British minister, Sir Claude MacDonald, was, according to Richard, 'already prejudiced' against Kang.

Itō did not offer Kang sanctuary in the Japanese Legation. To use a bunch of amateurs to murder the empress dowager against insurmountable odds was almost certainly not part of their deal. Besides, Itō was going to see Emperor Guangxu the following day. It would be awkward if he were asked to produce Kang. So the Wild Fox had to flee Beijing. He did so swiftly and, by the time the arrest warrant was sent out, he had already reached and left Tianjin, on board a British steamship bound for Shanghai. At the Shanghai wharf, 'detectives and policemen' were waiting for the ship 'in a high state of excitement at the prospect of gaining the 2,000 dollars' – the award for Kang's arrest. Because of the newspaper reports promoting Kang as the principal author of the Reforms (and because of the court's secrecy, which concealed Cixi's role) the Acting British Consul-General, Byron Brenan, who recorded the scene, was determined to rescue Kang. As he could not openly do so, being an official representative of Great Britain, Brenan sent the correspondent for *The Times*, J. O. P. Bland, out to sea on a launch before the ship docked. Kang was intercepted and transported to Hong Kong on board a British gunboat. In the colony he was visited by the local Japanese Consul and invited to go and stay in Japan. Tokyo 'cherishes the aspiration to build a Great East Asia', to quote Kang. The Wild Fox soon arrived in Japan.

His right-hand man, Liang, sought asylum in the Japanese Legation the day after Itō's audience, and Itō helped him escape to Japan. Under Japanese protection and in disguise, with his queue cut off and wearing European clothes, he boarded a Japanese warship from Tianjin.

Tan, the violence-loving radical, was also offered sanctuary in Japan. But he declined. According to his friends, he again declared his reform-needs-bloodshed theory: 'Reforms in other countries have been successful all because there was bloodshed. In Chinese reforms, no blood has been shed, and that's why the country is not doing well. Let my blood be the first to be shed.' Indeed, he was beheaded on 28 September, together with five others: Guangren, Kang's brother; Censor Shenxiu, the petitioner for troops to be moved to the Summer Palace, ostensibly to dig for gold but really to kill Cixi; and the three other new secretaries of the Grand Council (in addition to Tan). At the place of execution, according to a newspaper report, Tan acted 'as if death was something delicious'. Kang's brother, on the other hand, did not seem to relish the prospect: he was seen to be 'wearing just socks and no shoes, his face the colour of ashes and dust'. The executions shocked the country: they were the first of Cixi's political enemies to die since she began her rule nearly four decades earlier.

Two of the four new secretaries, including Yang Rui, with whom the emperor had entrusted his agonised letter of 14 September, actually had nothing to do with Kang or his plot. In prison they had been light-hearted, certain that their innocence could be easily established at the trial, which Cixi had ordered in accordance with Qing procedure. But no sooner had the trial started than Cixi abruptly halted it and the two innocent men were carted off to the execution ground with the others, as fellow plotters. There they protested furiously. One refused to go down on his knees to listen to the imperial edict sentencing him to death, and the other, Yang Rui, insistently asked the official overseeing the execution what his crime was. Rumour has it that blood from his severed head spouted one metre in the air, such was his vehemence at the injustice. People were appalled by the peremptory executions. On learning the news, one courtier felt 'shocked and pained as though my heart was being stabbed' and he 'threw up violently'. Even the grandees who knew about the plot against Cixi's life were greatly upset about the flagrant disregard for the law – which was rare under her rule.

Cixi cancelled the trial when she realised that it would inevitably make public something that she had to conceal at all costs: her adopted son's involvement in the plot. A trial would reveal that Emperor Guangxu wanted her deposed, if not killed. The Wild Fox had started giving interviews to foreign newspapers claiming that the emperor had given him a 'secret edict', with instructions to raise support to free him and oust Cixi. This claim first appeared in Shanghai in the *North China Herald* on 27 September, the day before Cixi stopped the trial and ordered the executions. It may well have led to her decision. If Kang's assertion seemed to be confirmed officially through the trial, Cixi would be facing a dire prospect. The Chinese would be divided and forced to take sides, and the country could be thrown into upheaval. Foreign powers might decide to answer Kang's plea and send in troops. In particular, Japan could well try to prop up Emperor Guangxu as its puppet, on the pretext of rescuing him. Cixi could not allow the fatal breach between herself and her adopted son to be exposed.

Thus Cixi herself covered up the plot against her life. The decree about the plot and the executions, issued in the name of the prisoner emperor, was vague and evasive, and falsified the emperor's position. Kang and his accomplices were said to 'have attempted to surround and attack the Summer Palace, to kidnap the Empress Dowager and myself'. The other key figure, General Yuan, also had reason to suppress the truth: he did not want it known that he had betrayed the emperor. (He kept his diary about the event hidden during his lifetime.) As Cixi remained silent, Kang's was the only voice to be heard. When he adamantly denied there was ever a conspiracy to kill Cixi, claiming indeed that it was Cixi who had concocted a scheme to kill Emperor Guangxu, his version of events was widely accepted. Sir Claude MacDonald believed that 'the rumoured plot is only an excuse to stop Emperor Guangxu's radical reforms'.

So the story of Wild Fox Kang's attempted coup and murder of Cixi lay in darkness and obscurity for nearly a century, until the 1980s, when Chinese scholars discovered in Japanese archives the testimony of the designated killer, Bi, which established beyond doubt the existence of the plot. Meanwhile, the six men executed, four of them conspirators, have gone down in history as having died heroically for the Reforms, acquiring the household name of 'the Six Gentlemen'. Wild Fox Kang entered myth as the hero who lit the beacon of reform and even had a vision to turn China into a parliamentary democracy. Kang largely created the myth himself, by revising and falsifying his writings and petitions – deleting, for instance, his article that specifically rejected parliamentary democracy as a desirable political system for China. He was a first-rate myth-maker and propagandist. While promoting himself, he and his right-hand man, Liang, tirelessly vilified Cixi, inventing many repulsive stories about her in interviews, speeches and writings, some of which were carried in newspapers in the Treaty Ports, while others were produced as pamphlets in Japan and posted into China. In these, they charged Cixi with poisoning Empress Zhen, driving her son Emperor Tongzhi to death, forcing the son's widow to kill herself by swallowing a lump of gold, exhausting the naval funds to the tune of tens of millions of taels to build her Summer Palace, and causing China's defeat in the war with Japan. Almost all the accusations that have since shaped public opinion about Cixi, even today, originated with the Wild Fox.

It was he who first represented Cixi as a debauched despot, alleging that she had many male concubines and nightly orgies with eunuchs. People believed Kang largely because he implied that his source was Emperor Guangxu himself, who had given him the 'secret edict', smuggled out of the Forbidden City sewn into a belt. The emperor, Kang declared, did not regard Cixi as his mother, but 'merely as a concubine of a late emperor's' – and 'a licentious concubine' at that.

While Cixi's most deadly enemy was at large and shaping history's view of her for the next hundred years and more, her second most loathed foe, Sir Yinhuan, was taken off the original list for executions. The British and the Japanese lobbied on his behalf, the British especially persistently because they had given him a knighthood. His punishment was consequently commuted to exile in Xinjiang.* Cixi hated him with a vengeance because it was he who had turned her weak adopted son into a prey for the Wild Fox – and for the Japanese. Thanks to Sir Yinhuan, the empire came close to landing in Japan's lap.

Sir Yinhuan himself acknowledged that his relationship with Japan was the cause of his downfall. He told the guards escorting him to his place of exile that the empress dowager started to suspect him when she saw that he appeared intimate with Itō on the day of Itō's audience with Emperor Guangxu. Whether or not this was the precise moment, Cixi was certainly convinced that he was working for the Japanese. In fact, it may well have occurred to her that he had been a Japanese agent before 1898 – that he had even played a role in China's spectacular defeat in the 1894–5 war. At that time, Emperor Guangxu relied on Grand Tutor Weng to help make decisions. And the Grand Tutor, out of his depth, relied on Sir Yinhuan, sending him draft documents several times a day for comments. In addition, Sir Yinhuan was in charge of the vital telecommunication system between Beijing and the war front. In this capacity he had been denounced by a number of people for acting suspiciously. The charges included that he 'hid reports and cables, and changed some of their content'. Staff referred to him as a 'traitor', suspecting him of passing on military secrets to the Japanese. But like other charges against grandees, this critical one was not investigated. Grand Tutor Weng was his close friend, and would explain his actions away to the emperor. Since then, it has emerged that the Japanese had full knowledge of the telegraphic exchanges and knew 'like the fingers and palms of their hands' every move made by the Chinese military. Tokyo also knew, crucially, that

---

* Before he left, Sir Yinhuan sent a message to the Russians, asking for a further 15,000 taels from the bribes they had offered him. His guards for the journey ruthlessly tormented him, telling him that without the money, 'we can't change our faces from chilling winter frost to caressing spring breeze'. The Russians obliged, even if he was by then useless to them. They reckoned that future bribe-seekers needed to see that they honoured their deals.

Emperor Guangxu was willing to pay any price for peace, which allowed it to exact the wildly extortionate indemnity.

No matter how convinced she was of Sir Yinhuan's treachery, no matter how furious she felt, Cixi was, again, unable to expose him through a trial. In this case, she could not afford to offend Japan. As a result, when Sir Yinhuan was sentenced to exile, his 'crimes' listed in the imperial decree were outlandish: 'harbouring evil intentions, conducting himself in a secretive way, currying favour with the powerful and being unpredictable and unreliable'. This sounded like a grotesque fabrication and reinforced foreigners' abhorrence of Cixi. They kept pressing for Sir Yinhuan's release. Two years later, on the very day that she appealed for cooperation from Japan and Britain to cope with a foreign invasion, she ordered the execution of Sir Yinhuan in his place of exile, an order that she specified was to be delivered at the fastest speed. Sir Yinhuan had remained in the forefront of her mind and she wanted to pre-empt any demand from Britain and Japan for his release as a condition for agreeing to help.

Cixi ordered other executions, which did not need a trial and were at the discretion of the throne: those of the eunuchs. Four eunuch chiefs who had facilitated communication between Emperor Guangxu and the Wild Fox were put to death by bastinado inside the Forbidden City.★ This was not enough to quell her fury, and Cixi took the trouble to specify 'no coffins or funerals for them, just throw them into the mass burial pit'. Ten other eunuchs were first beaten and then forced to wear a cangue – a heavy wooden yoke, weighing between 13 and 18 kilograms, which sat on the wretched eunuch's neck and shoulders, in some cases for ever. Such punishments had not been practised for so long that the old cangues had rotted, and the court prison cells had partially collapsed. The court management had to have new cangues made and the cells repaired.

Compared with them, the officials implicated in the Kang case, but not directly involved in the plot to kill Cixi, got off rather lightly. Most were simply dismissed. Only one, Learning Companion Xu, was given life imprisonment. But he was released two years later. At that time Beijing was occupied by foreign invaders and the doors of the

---

★ Earlier in 1898 a eunuch, Kou Liancai, had been sentenced to death by the Ministry of Punishments and executed publicly. His death had nothing to do with the plot. He had written a petition, and the Qing absolutely prohibited the eunuchs from any form of political participation, with offenders strictly punishable by death.

prisons were opened. Rather than flee, he stayed on and was officially set free by Cixi. Another official was exiled to Xinjiang, but was allowed to return home after two years.

While dealing with her enemies, Cixi wished the Reforms to continue and issued decrees stressing her wish. She penned a long edict in her own hand, in which she extolled the West's 'ability to make their countries rich and strong', and vowed that China would 'learn from their good ways and apply them step by step'. But whilst many evolutionary changes did indeed go on, the Reforms as a movement inevitably stopped. Those decrees concerning Kang and his associates were cancelled; the hastily sacked officials were reinstated; the impracticable orders, such as giving *everyone* in the empire the right to write to the emperor direct and receive an answer, were rescinded; and the radical shake-up of the Imperial Examinations was put on hold. It did seem that the country was reverting to the old ways. Western observers, who had no idea that the Reforms had been launched and spearheaded by Cixi, and who thought instead that Kang was the leader through Emperor Guangxu, were unanimous in condemning her for killing the movement that had only lasted 100 days.

With Cixi cast as the villain, Kang tried to persuade foreign governments to use military force to overthrow her and reinstate Emperor Guangxu. In Japan, he started talks with the intelligence service the moment he arrived, urging them to help kidnap the emperor and set up a Japan-backed throne, ultimately 'forging a Great Asia merger'. One active member of these talks was Bi, the man chosen to kill Cixi. One intelligence officer, Kotaro Munakata, revealed Tokyo's official position: 'The Japanese government will not dispatch armed forces lightly, but if the right time comes, it will of course provide aid without you even asking for it.'

To prevent rescuers, or kidnappers, from reaching Emperor Guangxu, Cixi installed tight security around her prisoner. Large iron locks and bars, ordered from the royal ironsmith in the capital, were fixed onto his villa in the Sea Palace, Yingtai. Brick walls were erected, blocking the villa off from the surrounding lake. The big sluice gate that separated the lake from the waters outside was checked and strengthened, so that no swimmers could move in or out underwater. When winter came and the water froze, orders were given to break the ice, so as to prevent anyone from approaching the emperor on foot across the lake. Cixi even became paranoid that her adopted son's loud percussion instruments – his drums, gongs and cymbals – might be heard outside the palace walls and help his rescuers locate him and make contact.

She told the eunuchs who looked after his instruments to inform her before giving him the instruments.

Imperial Concubine Pearl had helped the emperor communicate with Kang, through her eunuch servants. Her villa was on the shore, looking out across the lake to the emperor's islet. Now the lakeside of her villa was blocked off by a brick wall, and she too became a prisoner.

The ugly grey walls even disfigured Cixi's own Summer Palace. Emperor Guangxu's residence there, the Villa of the Jade Balustrade, stood right on the edge of the lake and could potentially be reached by boat or underwater swimmers. The side facing the lake was therefore sealed off by a crudely erected pile of bricks, some of which still stand there today.

21 Desperate to Dethrone Her Adopted Son
(1898–1900)

CIXI had come to detest her adopted son: he had been involved in a plot to kill her and yet she was unable to expose him. He was widely regarded as a tragic reformist hero and she as a reactionary and vicious villain – and yet she was unable to defend herself. Her feelings of bitterness and frustration were only relieved when she watched an opera about a heartless adopted son, who drove his foster parents to death and then received his just deserts when he was struck dead by terrible lightning unleashed by the God of Thunderbolts. Cixi became very fond of this opera and watched it many times. She had the adopted son made up as a most despicable scoundrel and ordered the number of thunderbolts and shafts of lightning strikes to be increased fivefold. She also added the frightening Gods of Winds and Storms to the scene, so that the retribution looked and sounded even more horrendous. Unable to punish her adopted son sufficiently herself, Cixi wished the gods to punish him one day.

It may well have crossed her mind to kill Emperor Guangxu, but she did not seriously contemplate the idea. Apart from her fear of Heaven, she could not risk the national and international consequences. Indeed, she had to fight rumours that he was being murdered, or had already been murdered. The emperor, in poor health generally, had fallen seriously ill after his world turned upside down. As was traditional, the royal doctors' reports were circulated to top officials, and a public edict required the provinces to send their best doctors. These actions were seen as Cixi's moves to prepare the world for the announcement of his death. She had to dispatch Prince Ching, the head of the Foreign Office, to Sir Claude MacDonald to ask for the British minister's help to 'clear the air', and when Sir Claude suggested that a legation doctor be allowed to examine the emperor, Prince Ching agreed at once.

Dr Dethève from the French Legation entered the Forbidden City on 18 October 1898 to examine Emperor Guangxu. The doctor's report confirmed that the emperor was indeed very ill. His symptoms included nausea and vomiting, shortness of breath, buzzing noises in his ears and dizziness. His legs and knees appeared unstable, his fingers felt numb, his hearing was bad, his eyesight was failing and there was pain in the area of the kidneys. His urination pattern was abnormal. The doctor concluded that the twenty-seven-year-old was suffering from chronic nephritis – that his kidneys were damaged and could not properly filter waste and fluids from his blood. This helped quell the rumour of murder, but nobody felt Emperor Guangxu was too ill to rule the empire.

Cixi desperately wanted her adopted son to be off the throne. The daily routine of receiving his greetings and going to the morning audiences with him was a constant reminder of the conspiracy and his role in it, and left her no emotional peace. The routine began as soon as she got up, mostly between 5 a.m. and 6 a.m. The emperor, having washed and dressed and had his queue plaited, and having had a smoke and a quick breakfast, would soon arrive in his sedan-chair under a yellow canopy, carried by eight men. (His entourage brought everything he needed, including a chamber pot.) When his chair was set down in the courtyard outside Cixi's apartment and his arrival was announced, Cixi would sit erect and a eunuch would place a yellow brocade cushion on the floor. Emperor Guangxu would enter, kneel on the cushion, and perform the formal greetings from an emperor to a dowager empress, after which Cixi would say, 'Please get up, Your Majesty.' He stood up, stepped forward and enquired as a son to a parent, 'Did the Royal Father sleep well? And did he have a good dinner yesterday?' Affirmative answers from her were followed by her enquiries about him, until finally she could say, 'Your Majesty may go and have a rest.' At this, Emperor Guangxu went to another room, where he dealt with the reports that had been left for him by Cixi with her instructions. In the audience hall they sat side by side, flanked by special Praetorian Guards, authorised to be near the throne, one of them being Cixi's brother, Duke Guixiang. During the audiences the emperor seldom spoke, and when he did, he would only murmur a few bland, often inaudible questions.

This routine was repeated day after day. The sight of him elsewhere in the court would also annoy her. Famously fond of wearing much-patched cotton tunics as underwear, the emperor liked to don plain, modest, dark outer robes, which made him an incongruous figure among the brilliantly dressed court ladies and the bejewelled Cixi. Once he was spotted from a distance in the Sea Palace performing the Ploughing Rite – in which the emperor personally handled the buffalo and ploughed the first furrow of the year – in his instantly recognisable drab clothes, standing among his officials in their colourful formal court costumes. His living quarters were also known for their austerity. The lack of opulence was perhaps not entirely his own choice: the eunuchs may have neglected his comforts. Later, when Westerners frequented the court, they noticed that he was not treated like the Son of Heaven: 'no obsequious eunuchs knelt when coming into his presence . . . Never when in the palace have I seen a knee bend to the Emperor, except that of the foreigner when greeting him or bidding him farewell. This was the more noticeable as statesmen and eunuchs alike fell upon their knees every time they spoke to the Empress Dowager.'*

Emperor Guangxu never showed a trace of resentment – not even when eunuchs poked fun at him during parlour games, which he often played with them. This behaviour led many to believe that he was pretending to be an idiot and was biding his time. Others, like the American painter Katharine Carl, observed that the slender and delicate monarch had 'a Sphinx-like quality to his smile . . . Over his whole face there is a look of self-repression, which has almost reached a state of passivity.' Even Cixi with her sharp eye could not figure out what lay behind the passive, expressionless mask. In his prison villa, the emperor read translations of Western books as well as Chinese classics, practised calligraphy and played musical instruments. (He said he did not like sad tunes.) He continued to dismantle and reassemble clocks. Once he tackled a broken music box, and apparently not only brought it back to life, but also added a Chinese tune to it. What he was most fond of doing was drawing devil-like figures on pieces of paper, on the back of which he would always write the name of General Yuan, the man who had informed

---

* Emperor Guangxu did not have a taste for luxury. Katharine Carl observed that 'His Majesty was not much of an epicure. He ate fast, and apparently did not care what it was. When he finished, he would stand up near Her Majesty, or walk around the Throne-room until she had finished.'

on the plotters and caused his imprisonment. He would then paste the drawings on the wall, shoot at them with bamboo arrows and afterwards cut the tattered drawings to shreds.

Who knew the truth? Emperor Guangxu might indeed be waiting for the arrival of a rescue team – gathered by Wild Fox Kang and sponsored by the Japanese. This prospect made Cixi panic. In 1899, she even resorted to a ruse designed to neutralise the Japanese, by trying to give them the impression that she was as keen as her adopted son to form a close relationship. Two officials were dispatched to Japan, where they gave newspaper interviews and made public speeches, declaring that they were sent by the empress dowager to enter an alliance with Japan. They saw the Japanese emperor, and former Prime Minister Itō, who thought that his chance had come again and offered to go to China at once to be an adviser to the throne. To prevent the illusion from developing further, her messengers did their best to undermine their own credibility, so much so that the Japanese press found them 'weird'. The Europeans thought Cixi had 'made a mistake in the selection of her men, for these commissioners, unlike what we usually find [*sic*] the yellow man, revealed too much of the important mission . . .' A perplexed Tokyo did not respond to their proposal, although it seemed to think that Cixi did entertain the intentions. While these machinations seem to have confused the Japanese, they alarmed Russia, as well as public opinion, which reckoned that the government was doing some dirty deals with Japan. It was a clumsy manoeuvre far below Cixi's usual well-crafted standard, and the man who conceived it and talked Cixi into it, Censor Chongyi, offered to be publicly dismissed as a scapegoat. The whole enterprise suggests that Cixi was at her wits' end.

She feared all the time that her prisoner might flee and she would not allow him out of the palaces without accompanying him herself. There was, however, a place outside the Forbidden City where the emperor had to go, but which was forbidden to her as a woman: the Temple of Heaven. (Many considered it 'the most beautiful piece of architecture in China'.) The emperor had to go there regularly to pray to Heaven for good weather for the harvests, on which the nation's livelihood depended. The trip involved staying on the site overnight. All Qing emperors treated the ritual with the utmost seriousness. Emperor Kangxi, for example, attributed the five decades of relative good weather that had led to his successful reign to the sincerity of his praying at the Temple. Cixi believed in this wholeheartedly. But as she could not make the journey herself, and could not be sure that

Emperor Guangxu would not flee when he was beyond her reach, she sent princes in his place. Although the proxies were easy to arrange, praying by them was not the same as by the emperor himself. Cixi was permanently fearful that Heaven would interpret the sovereign's absence as irreverence and as a result would unleash catastrophe on the empire. It was with anguish and desperation that she yearned for a new emperor.

However, to dethrone Guangxu was unthinkable for the Chinese – even though public opinion on the whole welcomed Cixi taking charge. The plot against her life was leaked and was doing the rounds of the teahouses, and the emperor's involvement, blamed on Wild Fox Kang, was felt to be inexcusable. Many thought that 'His Majesty had shown deplorable judgment, and that the Empress Dowager was justified in resuming control'. But still, they wanted him to remain the emperor. He was deemed a sacred personage 'from Heaven', who was not even to be seen by his subjects (hence the screens that shielded his processions). People preferred to talk about Wild Fox Kang 'deceiving the emperor' and 'setting Their Majesties against each other'. Viceroys from the provinces, while supporting Cixi's takeover, wanted her to work with her adopted son. Earl Li, who had privately scorned the emperor, saying that he did 'not even look like a monarch', and wished Cixi were in charge, was uncompromisingly opposed to his removal from the throne. When Junglu, Cixi's closest confidant, sounded him out, the earl leapt to his feet before Junglu had finished talking and raised his voice: 'How can you possibly entertain the idea! This is treason! It would be disastrous! Western diplomats would protest, viceroys and governors would be up in arms, and there would be civil war in the empire. It would be a total calamity!' Junglu agreed with Earl Li. In fact he himself had privately been trying to dissuade Cixi from any attempt to dethrone her adopted son.

The legations had made it clear that their sympathy was entirely with Emperor Guangxu. Cixi knew that they regarded her adopted son as the reformer, and her as the anti-reform tyrant. In an attempt to correct this impression and to show that she was friendly towards the West, she invited the ladies of the diplomatic corps to a tea party in the Sea Palace on the occasion of her birthday in 1898. This would be the first time foreign women would enter the court. (The first Western man Cixi had met was Prince Heinrich of Germany earlier that year.)

Before they went, the foreign ladies reacted like girls playing 'hard to get'. Robert Hart wrote: 'first they were not ready the day H.M. wanted them to appear – then when the second appointed day came round they could not go because they could not decide on one interpreter . . . then another difficulty came up . . . so the visit is postponed *sine die* . . .'

The party eventually took place on 13 December, many days after her birthday. If Cixi felt put out, which she was bound to, she did not let her feelings mar the occasion. Sarah Conger, wife of the American minister, left a detailed description. At ten o'clock that morning, sedan-chairs were sent over for the ladies:

> We formed quite a procession with our twelve chairs and sixty bearers . . . When we reached the first gate of the Winter Palace [Sea Palace] we had to leave our chairs, bearers, mafoos, escorts – all. Inside the gate were seven red-upholstered court chairs in a line, with six eunuch chair-bearers each, and many escorts. We were taken to another gate inside of which was standing a fine railroad coach presented to China by France. We entered this car, and eunuchs dressed in black pushed and hauled it to another stopping place, where we were received by many officials and served with tea . . . After a little rest and tea-sipping, we were escorted by high officials to the throne-room. Our heavy garments were taken at the door, and we were ushered into the presence of the Emperor and Empress Dowager. We stood according to rank (longest time in Peking) and bowed. Our first interpreter presented each lady to Prince Ch'ing [Ching] and he in turn presented us to Their Majesties. Then Lady MacDonald read a short address in English on behalf of the ladies. The Empress Dowager responded through Prince Ch'ing. Another low bow on our part, then each lady was escorted to the throne where she bowed and courtesied [*sic*] to the Emperor, who extended his hand to each.

To Lady MacDonald, it was 'a pleasant surprise to us all to find [Guangxu] taking part in the Audience . . . A sad-eyed delicate-looking youth showing but little character in his face, he hardly raised his eyes during our reception.' After greeting the emperor, Mrs Conger went on: 'We then stepped before Her Majesty and bowed with a low courtesy [*sic*]. She offered both her hands and we stepped forward to her. With a few words of greeting, Her Majesty clasped our hands in hers, and placed on the finger of each lady a heavy, chased gold ring, set with a large pearl.'

The gift of rings, and the manner in which they were given, was common among women. This was an attempt by the empress dowager to claim sisterhood with the Western wives. Then the ladies were treated to a feast, hosted by Princess Ching and other princesses, wearing 'most exquisite embroideries, rich satins and silks, with pearl decorations', their fingernails 'protected by jewelled gold finger shields'. After the feast and tea, they were conducted back to Cixi. Sarah Conger recorded the scene:

> To our surprise, there on a yellow throne-chair, sat Her Majesty, the Empress Dowager, and we gathered about her as before. She was bright and happy and her face glowed with goodwill. There was no trace of cruelty to be seen. In simple expressions she welcomed us, and her actions were full of freedom and warmth. Her Majesty arose and wished us well. She extended both hands toward each lady, then, touching herself, said with much enthusiastic earnestness, 'One family; all one family.'

Next came a Peking Opera performance, after which Cixi bade them goodbye with a theatrical gesture: 'she was seated in her throne-chair and was very cordial. When tea was passed to us she stepped forward and tipped each cup of tea to her own lips and took a sip, then lifted the cup, on the other side, to our lips and said again, "One family, all one family." She then presented more beautiful gifts; alike to each lady.' Mrs Conger, who looks severe in the photographs, gushed after meeting Cixi:

> After this wonderful dream-day, so very, very unreal to us all, we reached home, intoxicated with novelty and beauty . . . Only think! China, after centuries and centuries of locked doors, has now set them ajar! No foreign lady ever saw the Rulers of China before, and no Chinese ruler ever before saw a foreign lady. We returned to the British Legation and in happy mood grouped ourselves for a picture that would fix in thought a most unusual day – a day, in fact, of historic import. December 13, 1898, is a great day for China and for the world.

Lady MacDonald took with her as translator Henry Cockburn, Chinese Secretary at the British Legation, 'a gentleman of over twenty years' experience of China . . . and is possessed of great ability and sound judgment'. She wrote, 'Previous to our visit, his opinion of the Dowager-Empress was what I may call the generally accepted one . . . On his return he reported that all his previously conceived notions had been upset by what he had seen and heard, and he summed up her character in four words, 'amiability verging on weakness!' Sir Claude reported to London: 'the Empress Dowager made a most favourable impression by her courtesy and affability. Those who went to the palace under the idea that they would meet a cold and haughty person of strong imperious manners, were agreeably surprised to find Her Majesty a kind and courteous hostess, who displayed both the tact and softness of a womanly disposition.' Others in the legations shared these views.

Cixi's image had improved. But the legation men only thought better of her because they had discovered that she had an unexpected 'womanly disposition'. It was far from the case that they would now favour her over Emperor Guangxu as the ruler of China. Over the following year she was weighed down by the strain of being a permanent prison warden. And the pressure became intolerable when she fearfully contemplated the potential consequence of the monarch persistently failing to pray at the Temple of Heaven. She leapt at a suggestion that an heir-apparent be adopted. The heir-apparent could fulfil the emperor's duties, and could, in due course, replace the emperor, who would then retire. The adoption had sufficient justification: Emperor Guangxu was in his late twenties and still had no children. It could be argued that he needed to adopt a son to continue the dynastic line. So the prisoner wrote in his own hand in crimson ink a humble edict announcing that his illness was preventing him from having a natural heir, and so, at his repeated entreaty, the empress dowager had kindly consented to designate an heir-apparent, for the sake of the dynasty.

The heir-apparent was a fourteen-year-old boy called Pujun. His father, Prince Duan, was the son of a half-brother of Emperor Xianfeng, Cixi's late husband, which provided the legitimacy.

This arrangement immediately set off speculation that Emperor Guangxu was unlikely to remain on the throne for much longer. Those who were dead-set against Cixi insisted that she would now murder him. 'The foreign ministers began again to look grave. They spoke openly of their fear that Kuang Hsu [Guangxu]'s days were numbered,' one eye-witness recorded. When Cixi announced the designation of

In snow in winter 1903–4. Slightly in the background is Cixi's close adviser,
Louisa Pierson, half-American, half-Chinese, whose two daughters,
Der Ling and Rongling, are on either side of Cixi.

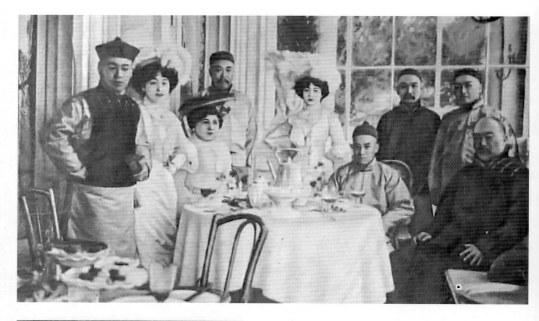

(*Above*) Louisa Pierson (seated), her husband, Yu Keng (far right), China's minister to France, their two daughters and son Hsingling (far left), here in a Paris restaurant entertaining Prince Zaizhen (seated in the middle), who had just attended the coronation of King Edward VII in London in 1902

(*Left*) Rongling, their daughter, studied dancing in Paris and has become known as 'the First Lady of modern dancing in China'.

(*Right*) Hsingling dressed as Napoleon at a fancy dress ball given by his parents to celebrate Chinese New Year in 1901.

(*Above*) A high class courtesan with a strong resemblance to Prettier Than Golden Flower, consort to Cixi's minister to Berlin in the mid-1880s.
(*Below*) As part of Cixi's modernisation programme, in the 1870s groups of young teenagers were sent to America to receive a comprehensive education.

In 1889, Emperor Guangxu took over the running of the empire whereupon Cixi retired. (*Above*) Guangxu's favourite concubine, Pearl. (*Right*) Grand Tutor Weng, a father figure to him.

Guangxu detested his empress, whom Cixi (centre, in cape) had picked.
Empress Longyu (second from left), was stooped and looked a pitiful figure in the court.
Far left: Cui, the eunuch; and far right: Louisa Pierson.

CIXI'S FOES
Sir Yinhuan (*above*), Emperor Guangxu's confidant and possibly Tokyo's biggest agent. He helped Kang Youwei (*above left*) to gain influence over Guangxu. Kang plotted to kill Cixi.

(*Left*) Liang Qichao, Kang's main disciple.

(*Right*) Former Japanese Prime Minister Itō Hirobumi, featured on a modern banknote, was the architect of Japan's war against China in 1894.

(*Above*) The xenophobic Boxers, who created mayhem in north China in 1900. Western powers invaded and Cixi was driven out of Beijing. The Allied forces entered the Forbidden City (*right*).

Cixi returned to Beijing at the beginning of 1902, travelling the last leg by train, with the imperial locomotive (*left*) provided by the Allies. A foreigner on the city wall snapped a picture of her (*above*) as she turned to wave at them, a handkerchief in hand.

(*Above*) Girls with bound feet. One of Cixi's first decrees upon her return to Beijing was to outlaw foot-binding.

(*Right*) Convicts in the cangues. The legal reforms started by Cixi abolished medieval forms of punishment like this – and 'death by a thousand cuts'.

the heir-apparent on 24 January 1900, the foreign legations pressed for an audience with Emperor Guangxu – unmistakably signalling their support for the imprisoned emperor and their snub for the heir-apparent. They were told that the emperor was in poor health and could not see them. When the diplomatic ladies asked for a repetition of that happy party a year earlier, they were turned down: the empress dowager was 'too busy with affairs of state'.

22 To War against the World Powers – with the Boxers (1899–1900)

T HAT the foreign legations took the side of her adopted son embittered the empress dowager. But she was more enraged by how the powers treated her empire after she sought their friendship at the reception for the diplomatic ladies. Soon after she reached out and proclaimed 'One family; all one family', she was dealt a nasty blow. At the beginning of 1899, Italy demanded the cession of a naval station on Sanmen Bay, a deep inlet on the east coast of Zhejiang province. This was not so much for some strategic reason as for Italy's desire to own a slice of China as a status symbol, to keep pace with other European powers.* As this acquisition presented no threat to the powers, Britain gave Italy its consent, as did most of the others. Italian warships then staged a demonstration off the coast near Beijing. It and other powers expected China to fall to its knees at this threat of war, as had hitherto been the case. Robert Hart, on China's side, was pessimistic: 'The Italian Ultimatum is in: China to say "yes" in four days or take the consequences! The situation is again critical . . . I fear we must go on from bad to worse. We have no spare money – we have no navy – we have no proper military organization . . . Other powers will follow suit and the *débacle* [*sic*] can't be far off. It is not China that is falling to pieces: it is the powers that are pulling her to pieces!' Hart lamented, as he had done during the war with Japan, 'there is no strong man . . .'

---

* This was at a time when Italy was asserting itself as a major sea power, and emphatically claimed that it had invented the compass, which had by common consent been invented in China. A statue of the supposed inventor, Flavio Gioja (who did not exist, as Italian historians have concluded), was erected in Amalfi in 1900.

But this time there was a different boss. Westerners saw that, to Italy's 'great surprise, as well as that of everyone else, China returned a stubborn refusal'. The Chinese Foreign Office sent back letters from the minister of the Italian Legation, De Martino, unopened. It explained to Sir Claude MacDonald that it, 'being unable to accede to this request, and considering that to argue the point with the Italian minister would mean a great expenditure of pen and ink, returned to Signore De Martino his despatches'. Cixi gave orders to prepare for war. 'There was a bustle of activity throughout the empire,' noted foreign observers.

In the middle of the crisis, Italy changed the minister at its legation. When the new minister, Giuseppe Salvago Raggi, arrived, he presented his credentials to Emperor Guangxu. Deviating from the protocol by which the head of the Foreign Office received the credentials on his behalf, Emperor Guangxu 'stuck out his hand to take the letter', noted Salvago Raggi, whereupon 'Prince Ching froze'. The Italians interpreted the emperor's hand as a very significant sign – that China was going out of its way to be nice to them, and that their gunboats had worked. They were deeply disappointed when Chinese officials arrived the following day to explain that what the emperor had done was only an anomaly, and that nothing should be read into it. On 20 and 21 November 1899, Cixi issued two decrees, in which she expressed her outrage and her resolve:

Now the situation is perilous, and the powers are glaring at us like tigers eyeing their prey, all trying to barge into our country. Considering the financial and military situation in China today, we will of course try to avoid a war . . . But if our powerful enemies try to force us to yield to demands to which we cannot possibly consent, then we have no alternative but to rely upon the justice of our cause and to unite and fight . . . If we are forced into a war, once the war is declared, all provincial chiefs must act together to fight those hateful enemies . . . No one is allowed to speak the word, *he* [appeasement], and no one must even think about it. China is a large country with rich resources and hundreds of millions of people. If the nation can be united in its devotion to the Emperor and Country, what powerful enemy is there to fear?

Italy, which in fact had no stomach for war, lowered its demands and eventually asked only for a concession in a Treaty Port. Cixi reportedly told the Italians: 'Not a speck of Chinese mud.' Italy climbed down and, by the end of the year, abandoned all its claims. A 'feeling of elation filled the hearts of patriotic Chinese', Westerners noticed. But the victory did not lessen Cixi's anxiety. She knew she was lucky, for Italy was 'a small and poor country' and did not really want a war. It was only bluffing, and she called its bluff. But the support given to Italy by major European powers destroyed her 'one family' illusion and deepened her bitterness. 'Foreign powers bully us too much, too much,' she kept saying. 'Foreign powers are ganging up on us' and 'I feel eaten up inside.'

Even the most open-minded and pro-Western members of the elite were enraged by the European powers' scramble for China. They were appalled that America, the only major power that did not take their territory, had introduced the Chinese Exclusion Act, discriminating against Chinese immigration.* Almost everyone had endured injury to their personal pride. One, Wu Tingfang, who had studied law in London, and headed China's mission to the United States, was much hurt by one incident: 'Western people are fond of horse-racing. In Shanghai they have secured from the Chinese a large piece of ground where they hold race meetings twice a year, but no Chinese are allowed on the grand-stand during the race days. They are provided with a separate entrance, and a separate enclosure, as though they were the victims of some infectious disease.'

Yung Wing, the first Chinese to graduate from Yale University, described an experience in a Shanghai auction room which marked him deeply: 'I happened to be standing in a mixed crowd of Chinese and foreigners. A stalwart six-footer of a Scotsman happened to be standing behind me . . . He began to tie a bunch of cotton balls to my queue, simply for a lark. But I caught him at it and in a pleasant way held it up and asked him to untie it. He folded up his arms and drew himself straight up with a look of the utmost disdain and scorn.' The matter ended in a fight when Yung Wing's blows 'drew blood in great profusion from [the Scot's] lip and nose'. 'The Scotsman, after the incident, did not appear in public for a whole week . . . but the reason . . . was more on account of being whipped by a little Chinaman in a public manner . . .' Yung Wing reflected:

---

* The federal law was signed in 1882, thus revising the Burlingame Treaty of 1868. This law was repealed in 1943. On 18 June 2012, the US Congress formally passed a statement of 'regret' for this discriminatory law against the Chinese.

since the foreign settlement on the extra-territorial basis was established close to the city of Shanghai, no Chinese within its jurisdiction had ever been known to have the courage and pluck to defend his rights . . . when they had been violated or trampled upon by a foreigner. Their meek and mild disposition had allowed personal insults and affronts to pass unresented and unchallenged . . . The time would soon come, however, when the people of China will be so educated and enlightened as to know what their rights are, public and private, and to have the moral courage to assert and defend them.

It was Yung Wing who initiated the scheme to send Chinese teenagers to America to be educated, while Wu Tingfang would in time become one of the drafters of a Western-style legal code. Both turned their hurt into an impetus to reform China on the model of the West, for which they retained a lifelong affection and admiration. Wu wrote about going to America:

When an Oriental, who, throughout his life, has lived in his own country where the will of his Sovereign is supreme, and the personal liberty of the subject unknown, first sets foot on the soil of the United States, he breathes an atmosphere unlike anything he has ever known, and experiences curious sensations which are absolutely new. For the first time in his life he feels he can do whatever he pleases without restraint . . . he is lost in wonderment.

For the average villagers and small-town people, anti-Western feeling was mainly directed at the Christian missions established among them. By now there were more than 2,000 missionaries living and working in China. Being foreign, they easily became targets of hate when times were bad. The inflexibility of some priests did not help. Animosity arose particularly when there was a drought, which inflicted protracted agony on the peasants. At such times, villagers often staged elaborate ceremonies and prayed to the God of Rain, in the desperate hope that they might survive the coming year. This was a matter of life and death, and all villagers were required to participate in order to demonstrate their collective sincerity. Many Christian missions held that they were praying to the wrong God and condemned the ceremonies as 'idolatrous' theatre. E. H. Edwards, for twenty years a medical missionary in China, wrote, 'It can scarcely be conceived by foreigners (to whom these theatrical displays are senseless and absurd) what a hold they have upon the people, and what immense sums are spent upon them every year.' Thus missionaries would forbid their converts to pay their dues or to take part. As a result, when the drought was prolonged, villagers blamed the foreigners and converts for offending the God of Rain – and causing them starvation. When mandarins explained this to the priests, the answer was unyielding, as Edwards observed: 'The officials further asked the missionaries to urge the Christians to pay such dues in order to prevent future troubles. To this request there was, of course, but one answer; and it was further explained to the officials that attendance at theatres was not only discountenanced by the Protestant Church in China, but that if any member was found to frequent them habitually he was disciplined.'

Backed as they were by gunboats, the missions had become a competing authority. As such they were able to protect their converts in numerous grass-roots disputes. The Rev. Arthur H. Smith, a missionary of the American Board in China for twenty-nine years, wrote (about the French mission):

> Whenever a Christian has a dispute with a heathen, no matter what the subject in question may be, the quarrel is promptly taken up by the priest, who, if he cannot himself intimidate the local officials and compel them to give right to the Christian, represents the case as one of persecution, when the French consul is appealed to. Then is redress rigorously extorted, without the least reference to the justice of the demand.

As a consequence, some non-Christians were convinced, justifiably or not, that the local official would always judge in favour of Christians, to avoid trouble for his government and problems for his own career. Their sense of grievance sparked many a riot against Christians. Cixi's order on dealing with disputes involving Christians was always 'be fair and even-handed'. Her government clamped down on anti-Christian riots and punished officials who failed to exert sufficient force to quell the riot – or, as sometimes happened, had a hand in stirring up the disturbance in the first place. The number of riots was thus restricted to a few dozen in four decades, and none of them resulted in the kind of massacre witnessed in Tianjin in 1870.

After Germany snatched parts of Shandong in late 1897 and established a significant presence there, many villagers converted to Christianity in order to receive protection. In a number of counties, as the local authorities saw it, people joined the Church to avoid being punished for 'owing debts and not wanting to pay them back . . . committing robbery or even murder.' And there was one man who sought the shelter of the Church so that he did not have to answer a subpoena after 'his father had filed a law suit against him for being seriously disobedient'. In one county, a Christian peasant was accused of taking wheat from his neighbour's field. In another, a relatively rich Christian, it was alleged, refused to lend grain to the starving during a drought (which was contrary to tradition). In both cases, as the local magistrates judged in favour of the converts, riots broke out that led to churches being burned. Yet another riot was triggered by Christians trying to turn a temple dedicated to the Celestial Emperor into a church. The violence usually ended with the local government punishing the rioters and paying hefty compensation to the Church – which produced even greater resentment among the non-Christians.

In spring 1899, in a bid to put an end to riots in Shandong, Germany sent an expedition into some villages, where the soldiers burned down hundreds of houses and shot dead a number of villagers. In the wake of these atrocities, a group that had been known for about a year as the Society of the Righteous and Harmonious Fists, the *Yi-he-quan*, gained immense popularity and acquired hundreds of thousands of followers. (Shandong was famous for the male population's fondness for martial arts, particularly a kind of fist-fighting similar to boxing.) This society blamed all the ills of the country and the hardship of their lives on foreigners, and vowed to drive them out. They were dubbed 'the Boxers' by the foreign press. People joined the Boxers for many different reasons. Some hated the Germans who had destroyed their homes – a hatred they now directed at all foreigners and local Christians. Others had scores to settle with neighbours who had converted. Still others sought release for their pent-up anxiety as the coming year's harvest looked likely to fail. 'On the whole . . . the Chinese is a fairly well-fed person,' observed the beady-eyed traveller Isabella Bird, who was in the country at this time. But as soon as the weather turned bad – as it was then in Shandong – that same person immediately faced a struggle for survival.

When violence against Christians broke out, Cixi ordered the perpetrators arrested and 'punished severely', and the Christians protected. The governor of Shandong, Yuxian, hated Western powers and was unwilling to protect the Christians effectively. Cixi replaced him with General Yuan Shikai. Shortly after General Yuan's arrival in Shandong, on 30 December 1899, the Rev. S. M. Brooks, a missionary of the Church of England, while travelling on a donkey on country paths, was murdered by a group of marauders who admired the Boxers. This was the first time in two years that a missionary had been murdered in China. An edict from Cixi declared that she was 'most deeply aggrieved', and commanded General Yuan to 'catch the criminals and punish them severely'. Yuan soon found the culprits and brought them to justice. Some of them were executed. General Yuan also reported to Cixi that in that year the Boxers had destroyed ten family houses used as churches, raided 328 Christian homes and killed twenty-three Christian converts. The General was determined to use force to suppress the Boxers, which Cixi endorsed, at the same time cautioning him that he must be 'extremely circumspect' in taking large-scale military action. His aim must be to 'disband' the gangs, punishing only those who had actually committed crimes. As Yuan conducted his campaign against the Boxers, they began to disperse – helped by a much longed-for snowfall that lasted for days, promising a better harvest in the coming year, and a full stomach. The life-saving snow was followed by thorough rain in the spring, further reducing the Boxer ranks.

Still, some Boxers became bandits, living on robbery, and roamed into the neighbouring Zhili province surrounding Beijing. On 19 February 1900, Cixi banned the Boxers in Zhili as well as in Shandong, ordering 'harsh punishment' for anyone engaged in violence. Following standard practice, the decree was copied out and pasted on the walls in the two provinces.

The foreign legations, which had found Cixi's edict about the Rev. Brooks's murder 'soothing', were dissatisfied with her ban on the Boxers. What they – mainly Britain, America, Germany, Italy and France – wanted was a nationwide imperial proclamation against the Boxers and any affiliated society, 'ordering by name [their] complete suppression'. They demanded that it must be 'distinctively stated in the decree that to belong to either of these societies, or to harbour any of its members, is a criminal offence against the laws of China'. They further insisted that the proclamation must be published in the *Peking Gazette*, the government news bulletin.

Cixi declined to do as told. Apart from feeling defiant, she did not want to broadcast her ban to the whole empire, given that the Boxers only existed in two provinces. She would only ban the Boxers where they were active, Shandong and Zhili. She would punish those who had committed violence and broken the law, but would not criminalise the average members. She especially loathed being perceived by the population to be heavy-handedly suppressing anti-Western sentiment, and hated to be taken for a puppet of the foreign powers. Besides, she felt the legations were being unfair and unreasonable. None of them had so much as raised a murmur against the offending German soldiers, while she was actively clamping down on the Boxers. Moreover, her approach was working: the Boxers in Shandong had largely been dispersed. The more the legations insisted on their demands, the more she dug in. No mention of the Boxers was made in the *Peking Gazette*. Sir Claude MacDonald, the British minister, wrote in frustration on 2 April: 'I have never known the [Chinese Foreign Office] so pigheaded or so pleased with themselves . . .' He blamed the Italian back-down: 'their ships came, looked, and went away and their Minister was recalled – the pigtails winning all along the line.' What Sir Claude did not know was that Cixi would have acted the same way with or without Italy's debacle.

On 12 April, Sir Claude and his colleagues, whilst deciding 'not to press further for a special Decree in the Gazette', gave the Chinese government two months to exterminate the Boxers. Otherwise, they threatened, their forces would enter China to do the job themselves. This threat was backed up by an emphatic parade of gunboats outside the Dagu Forts. Not wishing for a confrontation, Cixi made concessions. Two days later, a memorandum from the Viceroy of Zhili describing how government troops were dispersing the Boxers was published in the *Peking Gazette*, thus announcing to the country that the Boxers were illegal. On the 17th, a decree was carried in the *Gazette* condemning those who 'make a pretext to oppress converts . . . and involve themselves in crime'. The legations read the translation: 'the Throne sets no bounds to its principle of regarding all men with equal benevolence'; officials must 'take every opportunity of making it clearly known to all, that every man must attend to his own business and live continually at peace with his fellow men.' The decree did not mention the Boxers by name, and the tone was firm without being draconian.

That these items appeared at all in the *Peking Gazette* pleased Sir Claude and his colleagues, but the lack of desired severity in the decree left them far from satisfied. The gunboats remained outside the Dagu Forts, their presence sending a daily reminder that if Cixi did not wipe out the Boxers within two months, there would be an invasion. Western powers did not really want a war. As Mrs Sarah Conger, wife of the American minister, wrote, 'none of them wish to get into war with China'. But she also noted that 'there are many warships at Ta Ku [Dagu]'. These were part of the bluff. But as Britain's Prime Minister, Lord Salisbury, later remarked, 'I have passed some time in trying to persuade my countrymen that bluffing with the Chinese was a dangerous amusement: but I did not anticipate such a very striking confirmation of my views.' For Cixi, incensed, became more determined to defy the powers.

Ever since China's disastrous war and 'peace' with Japan five years earlier, a pattern had been established: foreign powers would make demands, then threaten force, and Beijing would instantly do as it was told. Cixi had just broken the pattern by calling Italy's bluff. She was committed to doing the same with the other, stronger powers. But if her challenge did lead to a war, how – and with what – could she fight? The navy had been destroyed and the army was weak. Defeat appeared inevitable. It was at this point, in desperation, that Cixi clutched at a straw: perhaps the Boxers would be able to fight a sort of 'people's war' against the invaders. The Boxers' hatred for foreigners would make them fierce and courageous soldiers, she thought.

Pragmatic men around Cixi, like Junglu, saw that a collision with the West was imminent and counselled accommodation with the legations in order to avoid it. Cixi turned a deaf ear. Fearing the worst, Junglu asked for sick leave, and stayed away from the court for sixty days. Her confidant, whose sensible advice she usually heeded, was thus absent when Cixi made her most fateful decision.

The man who had her ear now, Prince Duan, was the father of the newly appointed heir-apparent. Hating Westerners for snubbing his son, he vehemently promoted the idea of using the Boxers as soldiers. He and other like-minded princes and aristocrats tried to convince Cixi that the Boxers were loyal, fearless and 'disciplined'. They offered to organise the Boxers into a fighting force, prepared for invasion. Cixi's rational side told her that the Boxers were not remotely suited to such a conflict, but her emotional side desperately wanted to believe otherwise. They were her last resort. She may also have calculated that the Boxers could at least inflict some damage on the invaders, which could give her a chance to negotiate a compromise and so avoid a wholesale capitulation.

As she tilted towards using the Boxers as soldiers, her hand that was striking at them became hesitant. Although the army continued to try to disband the Boxers, Cixi's half-heartedness and ambivalence were felt by the troops, whose own ardour slackened. The Boxers, emboldened, increased their ranks and spread like wildfire, right in the area around Beijing.

In spring 1900, while Shandong was relieved by rainfall, the region surrounding Beijing was hit by a devastating drought. A contemporary missionary wrote: 'For the first time since the great famine in 1878 no winter wheat to speak of had been planted . . . Under the most favourable circumstances the spring rains are almost invariably insufficient, but that year they were almost wholly lacking. The ground was baked so hard that no crops could be put in, and at such times the idle and restless population are ready for any mischief . . .' Tormented by fear of starvation, the Boxers claimed that the God of Rain was not answering their prayers because he was bewitched by the 'foreign devils' – those inhuman creatures who had blue eyes! As the Chinese have black eyes, the colour of foreigners' eyes marked them out. There was a widely believed rumour that their multicoloured eyes could see through the surface of the Earth and spot underground treasures, which they proceeded to steal, leaving China poverty-stricken.

In May, the Boxers, mostly peasants hit hard by the bad weather, entered Beijing and crowded the capital's streets in their many tens of thousands. They wore red head-kerchiefs, red shirts, with a red sash around the waist, and they wielded large carving knives. Moving in gangs, they set up shrines worshipping a variety of deities – very often characters from popular theatre like *The Monkey King*. In the course of a ceremony the chief of the gang would act as though the spirit of a deity had entered him, thus making him and his words sacred. He would jump up and down, howling and dancing wildly as if in a trance: gestures that were also copied from Peking Operas. Members recited meaningless incantations after him and they learned *kung-fu* kicking. They were told that protective spirits had now entered their bodies and had made them immune to bullets and weapons, so foreigners' firearms could not hurt them.

Among them were some young women, who called themselves the Red Lanterners, and who had to be virgins or widows. Often carrying red lanterns as well as red-tasselled spears, the women wore red tops with short sleeves and tight trousers and paraded themselves in the streets. All this was a breach of tradition. And they went even further by waving to onlookers with their red handkerchiefs. These handkerchiefs were said to possess magical properties: place one on the ground and step on it and a Red Lantern girl would be carried to the sky (as in the theatre), where she could locate a foreign devil's head and sever it with a knife. She could also dust a tall building (such as a church) with a handkerchief, and the building would be set on fire and reduced to ashes. These women, most of whom led downtrodden lives, were now enjoying their moment of liberation, not least seeing crowds of men prostrating themselves on the ground in homage when they strode by.

On the walls in the Beijing streets, right next to the imperial edicts banning them, the Boxers' own eye-catching posters were defiantly displayed, calling for the 'killing of all foreigners in three months'. On 31 May, as the situation was running out of control, Cixi gave permission for 400 Western troops to enter Beijing from Tianjin, to protect the foreign legations. The legations did not feel this was sufficient, so on 10 June more than 2,000 troops under Admiral Edward Seymour, Commander-in-Chief of the British navy's China Station, set off for Beijing from Tianjin, 120 kilometres away, by railway. The expedition was not authorised by Cixi, who told her diplomats to persuade the legations to turn it back. The head of the Foreign Office, Prince Ching, was sympathetic to the coming of this foreign army, so Cixi in anger replaced him with the hardline Prince Duan. The legations refused to turn back the expedition.

Determined to halt a foreign army entering the capital unauthorised, Cixi endorsed the mobilisation of some Boxers along the railway line, in an attempt to stop it. The Boxers proved surprisingly effective. They thoroughly sabotaged the line and fought 'with the utmost courage', according to Captain Jellicoe, Admiral Seymour's Chief of Staff. Lieutenant Fownes Luttrell also remarked on the 'great bravery' of the Boxers. Soon joined by the imperial army with modern weapons, they managed to hold back the Seymour Expedition. This success raised Cixi's hope that the Boxers could indeed help repel invasion.

The fighting heightened tensions in Beijing. On 11 June, soldiers of a largely Muslim army defending the capital killed a chancellor of the Japanese Legation, Sugiyama Akira, while he was out on the street. Cixi publicly expressed 'deep regret' over the atrocity against a foreign diplomat, and promised punishment of the perpetrators. But when she gave the order to the commander of the army, Dong Fuxiang, he replied that if one single soldier from his army were executed for the murder, his forces would mutiny. After a long silence, Cixi said, 'Well, what's done is done . . .'

Supported by the Muslim army, the Boxers began to destroy railways, trains and telegraph lines. Telegraphic communication from Beijing to the provinces was broken, and the Viceroys from the south had to send their cables to Shangdong, to be relayed to Beijing on horseback. In Beijing, the Boxers started to burn churches and foreign properties, cheered on by large crowds. In an act of extreme hatred the mob raided foreign cemeteries, smashing tombstones and monuments, dragging out of their graves the bodies of foreigners, striking them with spears before burning them.

Foreigners were often referred to as 'Hairies' – *mao-zi* – because they have more body hair than the Chinese. Chinese Christians were called 'Secondary Hairies' – *er-mao-zi* – and they bore the brunt of the Boxers' ferocity. With their bodies horribly burned and lacerated, they fled into the legations for protection: 'more than flesh and blood could stand to see,' wrote a guard. Rescue parties were sent out in the hope of saving others, and they opened fire on the crowds, killing some 100 Boxers and other Chinese in a couple of days. Hatred overflowed. Frenzied men girt with red sashes and armed with swords, spears and knives crowded outside the Legation Quarter and laid siege to it.

Home to the representatives of eleven countries, the Legation Quarter, an enclave roughly 3 kilometres long and 1.5 kilometres wide, was situated right next to the southeastern walls of the Royal City, which cradled the Forbidden City. The south of the Quarter was bounded by the crenellated wall that separated the Manchu-inhabited Inner City from the Han-inhabited Outer City. A shallow canal running north and south roughly bisected it. Within the Quarter, 473 foreign civilians and thousands of Chinese Christians took refuge with 400 military guards, who constructed a labyrinth of barricades. The Boxer crowds, numbering tens of thousands, surged against the walls and the defending cordon, shouting 'Kill the foreign devils! Kill! Kill! Kill!' Those who listened to the blood-curdling nocturnal yells would 'never forget the suggestion of a pandemonium, a rehearsal of hell,' wrote the Rev. Arthur H. Smith.

Cixi sent the pro-Western Junglu, now back from 'sick leave', to lead his troops to protect the Legation Quarter. She issued many decrees intended to rein in the Boxers, and dispatched grandees whom the Boxers seemed to trust to try and talk them into disbanding and returning to their villages. If they did not stop destroying railways, churches and foreign residences, and stop assaulting – even murdering – foreigners and Chinese Christians, then they would be subject to an extermination campaign by government forces. Meanwhile, Cixi cabled Earl Li to come to Beijing to negotiate with the Western powers. The earl at that time was the Viceroy of Canton, governing two coastal provinces in the south. Considering Cixi's handling of the Boxers to be 'inconceivably preposterous', he had been exchanging cables with other dignitaries daily to discuss what to do. Burning with impatience to help, he wished he could 'fly with wings' to Beijing. But then, before he set off, events overtook all these efforts as Cixi learned that scores of Western warships were gathering on the coast, and many more thousands of troops were on their way. Invasion seemed inevitable.

Going to war meant gambling with the survival of the dynasty, and Cixi felt the need to be endorsed. On 16 June, she convened an unusually large meeting of more than seventy participants: the Grand Councillors and ministers of the government, who were – it was strikingly noticeable – overwhelmingly Manchu and undistinguished. An eye-witness recorded the scene. In a packed audience hall all attendants were kneeling before Cixi and Emperor Guangxu, who were seated side by side. Prince Duan led a chorus of heated voices calling for the Boxers to be given legitimate status and to be used as a fighting force. But a few spoke against the idea, asking instead for harsher measures to suppress the mob. As one of them was talking, Prince Duan cut him short sarcastically: 'Yours would be a very good way to lose the support of the people', at which point he stuck up his right thumb, a (universal) gesture for 'a very good idea'. When one attendant argued that the Boxers could not be relied on to fight a war, 'because much of their courage comes from the black arts which claim to shield them from bullets', Cixi herself replied indignantly, 'It's true that such arts cannot be relied upon, but can we not rely on the hearts and minds of the people? China has been weakened to an extreme degree, and all we have is the hearts and minds of the people. If we cast them aside, what do we have to sustain our country?' She proceeded to look furiously at those who persisted in arguing.

That same day, something ominous occurred. In the busiest shopping district in Beijing, just outside the Inner City and near the legations, the Boxers set fire to a pharmacy selling Western medicine and to other shops with foreign merchandise. As the flames leapt from store to store, devouring the best and rarest of silks, furs, furniture, jewels, antiques, art and other of the empire's most beautiful artefacts, a spark flew onto the Qianmen Gate tower nearby. Rising more than 30 metres above the ground, and nearly 15 metres above the wall on either side, this was the loftiest of all the city gates in Beijing, due south on a central axis from the Forbidden City. The gate would only be opened for the emperor, when he went to pray at the Temple of Heaven or the Temple to the God of Agriculture. The Boxers did not mean to destroy it and, as it was consumed by the flames, they dropped to their knees to beg the God of Fire to spare this sacred edifice. The gate tower was soon reduced to a huge pile of smouldering charcoal and rubble. The biggest fire in the capital for more than 200 years, it terrified all who learned about the destruction, who regarded it as a deadly omen.

Although she believed in omens, there was no retreat now for Cixi. On that very night, a joint force of eight countries – Russia, Japan, Britain, France, Germany, America, Italy and Austria-Hungary – attacked the Dagu Forts that guarded the sea entry to Tianjin and Beijing. After a fierce six-hour battle, the Forts fell. To Cixi, the fall of the Forts was associated with an enduring heartache: four decades earlier they had been seized by another allied, Anglo–French army, which had led to her fleeing with her husband, who died a bitter death outside the Great Wall. The invaders had then burned down the Old Summer Palace, leaving a vast ruin – and a gaping hole in her heart. Ever since then, it had been her dream to restore even a small part of the Old Palace, for which she had stolen from the navy and disobeyed Heaven – and attracted denunciation. At the fall of the Forts this time, nothing could stop her from fighting it out.

War was anticipated on all sides. In Britain, on that day, Queen Victoria wrote to Lord Salisbury: 'Should be glad to hear your views on the state of affairs in China which seem to me most serious: also please say what you propose to do . . .' From that day on, 'China Telegrams', in massive numbers, were typed out and presented to the queen, who sent out many messages, one of which read: 'Feel anxious for personal safety of Sir C. MacDonald. Have you considered possibility of removal of foreign Ministers from Peking. If one of them were killed war would be inevitable.'

All the reformers who mattered to Cixi – Junglu, Earl Li, Viceroy Zhang, among others – were opposed to the war and to her policy. In the previous conflict with Japan, there had been numerous impassioned petitions urging fighting. But now they were missing. Many felt that the foreigners had reason to send in troops to protect their own people, who were not being properly protected by the Chinese government. 'We are in the wrong', *li-qu*, Cixi was told. Grass-roots officials wanted the mob suppressed, as they were harassed and terrorised by the Boxers, who demanded food and shelter and exacted revenge for past grievances. But Cixi had made up her mind. At another top-level meeting she raised her voice and declared to the assembled dignitaries: 'Our choice is whether to put our country on a platter to hand over to the invaders, or to fight to the end. I cannot face our ancestors if we do not put up a fight. I would rather fight to the end . . . If the end comes, you gentlemen here are my witnesses and can testify that I have done my best.' Her passionate words and unusual agitation made a great impact on all present: they banged their heads on the floor, vowing to follow her.

On 20 June, soldiers of the Muslim army shot dead the German minister, Baron von Ketteler, when he stepped out of the barricades to go to the Foreign Office.★ Her bridge was now burnt – for Cixi knew, as Queen Victoria had spelt out, if one of the ministers 'were killed war would be inevitable'. The next day, 21 June, Cixi declared war on all eight invading countries.

★ According to his biographer, Andrew Roberts, Lord Salisbury told Betty Balfour that von Ketteler's death was 'poetical justice'. Salisbury said, 'It's all the fault of Germany. They began all this trouble.'

23 Fighting to a Bitter End
(1900)

AFTER Cixi declared war, the Boxers were given legal status and organised under the command of princes who were sympathetic to them. In the capital they numbered a quarter of a million, with Prince Duan in overall charge. They were formed into some 1,400 leagues, each with roughly 200 members. More than 100,000 of them defended the road to Beijing alongside the regular army, against an international force of more than 20,000. The regular army had received Western training and was armed with modern weapons. In their Western-style uniforms, its officers and men had been called 'Secondary Hairies' by the Boxers, who were now their comrades. Sarah Conger, wife of the American minister, recorded: 'The Boxers and soldiers combined made a strong army . . . The foreigners who have known the Chinese longest and best say that they have never before seen anything like it in their character . . . The battles at Tientsin [Tianjin] were terrific. The Chinese showed courage beyond the imagination of those who know them best. They were determined, fought bravely, and put the foreign armies to a bitter test.' The Rev. Arthur H. Smith wrote: 'There is no doubt that the Chinese armies . . . fought with a desperation for which nothing in the war with Japan afforded any parallel.'

Cixi announced her gratitude to the Boxers and rewarded them with silver from the court. She opened warehouses where old weapons from the now-updated regular army were stored, and had them distributed among the Boxers. Armed with these, which were rather primitive, and with their own even more primitive knives and spears, the Boxers threw themselves against modern technology with fanatical abandon. One of their adversaries wrote: 'Slowly they

271

came on, shouting, with their swords and pikes flashing in the sun, merely to be mowed down, whole ranks at a time by rifle and machine-gun fire.' Boxer leaders who believed in their own super-natural prowess died first. One British soldier described a scene: 'a well-dressed Boxer leader came impressively down alone towards the bridge of boats in front of the Russian infantry . . . He waved his sash and went through his ceremony, but of course he was a corpse in a few seconds.'

Seeing their leaders' magic overcome, some Boxers reckoned that foreigners must have mysterious powers and sought to block them by fouling, which was an ancient strategy. They laid out night-stools and binding cloth from women's feet – the two items that were considered the smelliest – on the battlements of the city walls, hoping vainly that the foreigners would be repelled by their stink. Cixi too was reduced to wild irrationality. She dictated two edicts asking a Buddhist monk who was said to be able to perform miracles through prayer to go to the front and help ward off gunboats. As Allied soldiers continued to pour in, it became plain that no magic, reek or divine intervention would work against them.

As they became crucial to the war effort, the Boxers ran wild. They did what they did most naturally: looting and pillaging cities and towns that were at their mercy. The losses in just one affluent street in Tianjin were estimated at tens of millions of taels, before the city fell to the invaders. Mobs ransacked people's homes, including those of some grandees. In Beijing, the mansion of the Imperial Princess, daughter of the late Prince Gong whom Cixi had adopted as her own, was plundered.

Not even the Forbidden City was immune. There, middle-aged princes took to wearing Boxer clothes – a short top and a red sash around the waist – as they strode around aggressively, 'jumping and yelling, behaving totally differently from their normal selves, as though they were crazy or drunk', Cixi later reminisced. One of them 'even quarrelled with me! Nearly overturning the imperial altar!' Even members of the Praetorian Guards (of which one branch was commanded by Prince Duan) joined the Boxers. Word went round that the Boxers intended to enter the Forbidden City and kill pro-Western grandees like Prince Ching and Junglu. One day, a request was put to Cixi that the servants in the Forbidden City should be sent out to be examined, to see if they were 'Secondary Hairies'. Cixi asked how this might be done, and received the answer that, after reciting certain incantations, the Boxers were able to see a cross on the forehead of anyone who had been baptised. Terrified eunuchs and maids begged Cixi to shield them, but she was forced to tell them to go and be examined – for fear that the Boxers might use this as an excuse to raid the Forbidden City. In the event, the Boxers did not make any accusations: they seemed sufficiently gratified by the fact that the empress dowager herself had had to oblige them. Cixi felt like a 'paper tiger'. As she explained to the Viceroys who opposed her handling of events, 'Suddenly in a matter of months there were more than a hundred thousand Boxers in the capital, from ordinary people to soldiers to princes and grandees . . . The capital would be plunged into unthinkable peril if I tried to use the army to crush them. I have to go along with them, to be treated as their leader, and manage to control them and salvage the situation somehow . . .'

Indeed, Cixi's control was less forceful than usual. Right under her nose, tens of thousands of Boxers, together with the Muslim army, were laying siege to the Legation Quarter. When the war started, they began to attack the Quarter. Cixi knew that it would be suicidal to harm more diplomats, and handed out no arms to the Boxers there. The fiercely anti-Western Muslim army was placed in just one section of the Quarter, and the rest faced the pro-Western Junglu. Junglu's assaults were full of sound and fury, but signified very little. Sarah Conger, within the legations, wrote about the attacks: 'The blowing of their horns, their yells, and the firing of their guns, are the most frightful noises I ever heard.' And yet, 'The Chinese often fire high, for which we give thanks.'

> The booming cannon send their shells right at us; they sometimes burst over our heads, sometimes they go beyond, but not a fragment touches us. When the enemy, after many attempts, gets the range to harm us, and a few shells would injure our buildings, then the hands of these Chinese seem to be stayed. Not once have they continued firing to the entire destruction of one of these buildings or walls. How could this be true if God did not protect us? His loving arm is round about us.

The truth was that Cixi had specifically given the cannon to Junglu, who then had the targeting gauge raised by many centimetres. Later

Cixi would say: 'If I had really wanted to destroy the legations, they could not possibly still exist.'*

After the siege had ground on for a month, Cixi became worried that those inside might die from a lack of fresh food and told Junglu to have fruit and vegetables delivered to the legations.

The siege lasted fifty-five days, from 20 June to 14 August, when the Allied force captured Beijing. Of the Westerners in the Legation Quarter, sixty-eight were killed and 159 wounded; the number of Chinese Christians killed or wounded was not counted. The Boxers, who charged with practically bare hands, suffered thousands of casualties – far more than the foreign enemies who were seemingly in their clutches.

Also under siege was the Catholic cathedral in Beijing, the Beitang, where nearly 4,000 foreign and Chinese Christians had taken refuge. Here Cixi ordered Prince Duan, the leader of the siege, 'not to use guns or other firearms'. Thus, when the Boxers launched attacks with their primitive weapons, against a solid edifice defended with superior arms, they fell in droves. As stocks of food in the cathedral dwindled, raiding parties would sporadically race out to seek new provisions. When Cixi learned of this, she at first gave a verbal order for 'the troops to put them down'; but she changed her mind and her edict read: 'If Christian converts fly out, do not harm them, but send troops to protect them.' As it happened, many Christians chose death by starvation inside the cathedral, rather than fall into the hands of the Boxers. This accounted for the majority of the 400 deaths among the besieged.

Cixi's ambivalent policies towards the Boxers sent many of them to certain death, while ensuring the survival of most foreigners trapped in China, often among murderous crowds.

In some other parts of China there were cases of missionaries and converts being murdered by officials. The worst atrocities took place in Shanxi province. Its governor, Yuxian, had been moved there from Shandong province because Cixi regarded him as too pro-Boxer – and there were no Boxers in Shanxi. Relations between the missions, the

---

* Katharine Carl remarked, after staying in the Legation Quarter: 'When I saw the position of the Legation quarter and especially that of the British Legation, where all the foreigners finally congregated . . . I felt convinced that had there not been some restraining force within their own ranks, the Chinese could have wiped out the foreigners in less than a week. Bad firing on their part could only have averted, for a short space, the inevitable result to the Legations. Had there not been some power that was acting as a check upon the Chinese, no European would have been left to tell the tale; and this restraining force I feel confident came from the Emperor and the Empress Dowager themselves.'

Shanxi authorities and the population at large had been amicable. But Yuxian brought his hatred for the West with him. Using mainly soldiers, he massacred 178 missionaries and thousands of Chinese converts, often in gruesome ways. One priest, Mgr Hamer, was taken 'for three days through the streets of To To, everybody being at liberty to torture him. All his hair was pulled out, and his fingers, nose, and ears cut off. After this they wrapped him in stuff soaked in oil, and, hanging him head downwards, set fire to his feet. His heart was eaten by two Beggars.'

Belatedly, Cixi put a stop to Yuxian's atrocities. She also vetoed a nationwide massacre, proposed by some grandees, including the father of her late daughter-in-law, Chongqi – the man who had almost certainly told his daughter to starve herself to death after her husband died, and who himself would soon commit suicide (as would the rest of his family) when Beijing fell into foreign hands. He and a few others petitioned Cixi for 'a decree to tell the whole country that every ordinary person is permitted to slay foreigners wherever he set eyes on them'. In this way, they advised:

> people will feel they can avenge their grievances which they have long bottled-up . . . For decades they have been poisoned by foreigners [with opium], bullied by Christian converts and repressed by officials, big and small, who made biased judgements against them – and they had nowhere to turn . . . Once the decree is known, people will feel so overjoyed and grateful to the throne that they will all rise up in arms to fight the invaders . . . The land of China will finally be purged of aliens and our people will be free from grief . . .

Cixi kept the petition to herself, and issued no such decree.

The Boxer mayhem under Cixi appalled and alienated all her old kindred spirits, especially Earl Li and Viceroy Zhang Zhidong. They wrote to rebuke her: 'If you continue to indulge yourself in this wilful manner and are only concerned to vent your anger, you will ruin our country. Into what deeper abyss will you plunge it before you are satisfied?' They pointed out that she was doing the Boxers no favours: 'Such huge numbers of them have been killed, and their corpses litter the fields . . . One can't help pitying them for their stupidity.' Besides, north China was by now reduced to 'a land of desolation' by the drought as well as by the Boxers: it was about time she paid some attention to the lives of her people.

The Viceroys across the country cabled each other daily, plainly agreeing that they would 'definitely not obey' her decrees. For the first time in her rule, most of the regional magnates, crucial to the vast empire, had apparently lost faith in Cixi. She had never been so friendless. When she launched her palace coup at the age of twenty-five; when she arbitrarily picked a three-year-old to place on the throne; when she ruled for decades without a mandate; and even when she made a prisoner of the emperor – at all those times they had always backed her. Now she was alone.

Isolation did not frighten her. A determined Cixi charged on single-handedly, gambling that she might find a way to deal with foreign invasions. But she had no wish to drag in the whole empire, and positively encouraged the Viceroys to stay out of her gamble. She told them that they must preserve their own territory and act in a 'totally realistic' way. It was with Cixi's implicit consent that the most import-ant Viceroys, led by Earl Li and Viceroy Zhang, signed a pact of 'neutrality' with the powers, which ensured peace in most of China, especially the south, restricting fighting to the area between the Dagu Forts and Beijing. Most provinces were spared Boxer-style violence.

As the Allies pressed closer to Beijing, Cixi was forced to sue for peace. She asked Earl Li, still in Canton, to come to the capital to be her negotiator, offering him as an inducement the job he wanted: to be Viceroy of Zhili. Having previously been eager to go the earl was now reluctant. He knew that surrender was the only option, but that the empress dowager was not ready to accept it and was hoping for better terms. Indeed, she was preparing to fight on even when the powers reached the walls of Beijing, moving in ammunition and troops for its defence. The earl went north only as far as Shanghai, where he paused, claiming to be sick. Meanwhile, Viceroy Zhang collected a long list of signatures, including six of the nine Viceroys of the empire, plus a number of governors and generals, asking Cixi to allow the earl to negotiate with the powers in Shanghai. Rarely had a petition been signed by so many powerful regional figures.

Cixi was convinced that without her direct supervision the outcome of the negotiation would not be acceptable, and she vetoed the proposal. Then she fired a warning shot at the petitioners, aiming particularly at Viceroy Zhang, their ringleader. On 28 July, she ordered the execu-tion of two men who were closely connected to him. One of them, Yuan Chang, a senior official in the Foreign Office, was known as the Viceroy's eyes and ears in Beijing. (The Viceroy had a sizeable information-gathering network in the capital, which Cixi was willing to condone.) The other man, Xu Jingcheng, had been China's minister to Berlin at the time when Germany was preparing to grab Qingdao. Documents from German archives have now revealed that he advised the German government, 'hinting – extremely secretly of course' – that the 'threat of military force' was the only way to get Beijing to hand over territory, and that Germany should 'simply go and occupy a harbour that suits it'. The Kaiser acted on his advice and abandoned the original plan for a less aggressive approach. The Kaiser told the German Chancellor, Prince Hohenlohe, that 'it is really shameful that we need a Chinese Minister to tell us stupid Germans how to act in China in our own interest'. Minister Jingcheng may well have been tormented by his conscience, for on the execution ground he appeared to welcome death: 'tidying up his hat and robe carefully, and then going down on his knees facing the north [direction of the throne], he put his forehead on the ground and expressed gratitude to the throne. There was not a look of grievance or complaint on his face.'

It seems that Cixi had got wind of Minister Jingcheng's treachery. The imperial decree announcing the executions charged the men with 'harbouring private agenda when dealing with foreigners'. Being vague about a charge that involved a foreign power was Cixi's style.

Viceroy Zhang understood that these executions were intended as warnings to him. He had indeed been plotting with foreign powers, especially Britain and Japan, which thought highly of him. He was famously a man of probity who preferred coarse cotton to fine furs and silks for his wardrobe, who invariably declined gifts and accumulated no personal wealth. When he died, there was not enough money in his family to pay for an appropriate funeral. His passions were nature and cats – of which he kept dozens and which he looked after himself. Westerners who dealt with him regarded him as being 'exceedingly honest and devoted to the welfare of his people', 'a true patriot'. He was one of the few officials the Japanese regarded as incorruptible and really respected. Former Prime Minister Itō said that the Viceroy was 'the only man' who could handle the monumental task of China's reforms; and the British considered him the most desirable man with whom to do business. Disappointed with Cixi, and thinking that once she was driven out of Beijing her government would collapse – a view shared by many – the Viceroy contemplated supplanting her. His representative in Tokyo, whose official job was to oversee the students from his viceroyalty, said to his Japanese contact that 'If the throne is forced to leave Beijing (probably to Xian) and the Qing empire is without a government', the Viceroy 'will be ready to step forward and form a new government in Nanjing together with two or three other Viceroys'. The same message was given to the British. To prepare for this eventuality, the Viceroy asked the Japanese to supply him with officers and arms. Cixi may not have known the exact details of these machinations, but she had her spies – and powerful instincts.

Giving notice to the Viceroys not to deal covertly with foreign powers, Cixi fought her war to the end. After a strategic defeat that exposed Beijing, her commander at the front shot himself. In his place she appointed Governor Li Bingheng, the man who had stopped Cixi from squeezing the population for the restoration of the Old Summer Palace – only to be promoted – and who had then been sacked under pressure from the Germans, as he was determined to resist their occupation. Loathing the invaders with all his heart, he vowed to Cixi that he would fight to his last breath; but he found the war a lost cause. The army had been thoroughly routed, and the soldiers 'simply fled without putting up any fight, blocking the roads in their tens of thousands. Wherever they passed, they plundered and torched the villages and towns,' Governor Bingheng reported to Cixi – before committing suicide.

On the day of his death, 11 August, all Cixi's hopes were finally extinguished: Beijing would be occupied by the powers in a matter of days. Three more high officials were executed, charged with being 'traitors'. One of them was her then Lord Chamberlain, Lishan, with whom she had been very close. Cixi believed that there were 'quite a few traitors' selling secrets to foreigners. Eunuchs remembered her muttering that 'there must be spies in the palace, otherwise how is it that whatever decision we make here is instantly known outside?' Her suspicion of Lishan may well have originated in 1898, when he had gone to great lengths to prevent a raid that she had ordered on Sir Yinhuan's house – a raid that could have found evidence of Yinhuan's liaison with the Japanese. But the executions were more to do with the present moment: Cixi wanted to stop senior officials from collaborating with the victorious Allies who were about to enter Beijing.

Finally Cixi's mind turned to flight. She enquired about transport, and learned that 200 carriages and horses had been on standby, but that they had been snatched by retreating troops, and it was now impossible to buy or hire replacements as everyone was running away.

The fact that Cixi did not have these 200 lifelines well guarded shows that fleeing had been very far from her thoughts. At the news of the loss of the transport, she sighed, 'Then we'll stay.' And she stayed. It seems that she was prepared to die right there in the Forbidden City. But at the eleventh hour she changed her mind. On the early morning of 15 August, while the Allies were pounding at the gates of the Forbidden City itself, at the urging of a prince Cixi left in a mule-cart that he had brought from his house.

As there were only a few mule-carts available, most of the court had to be left behind. Cixi took with her Emperor Guangxu, Empress Longyu, the heir-apparent, a dozen or so princes and princesses and grandees, and the emperor's concubine, Jade. The other concubine, Pearl, who had been living under house arrest for the past two years, presented a problem for Cixi. With transport at a premium, Cixi did not want to make room for her, but neither did she want to leave Emperor Guangxu's favourite concubine and accomplice behind. She decided to use her prerogative, and ordered Pearl to commit suicide. Pearl declined to obey and, kneeling in front of Cixi, tearfully begged the empress dowager to spare her life. Cixi was in a hurry, and told the eunuchs to push her into a well. As no one stepped forward to do this, she shouted angrily for a young and strongly built eunuch, Cui, to carry out her order at once. Cui dragged Pearl to the edge of the well and threw her into it, as the girl screamed vainly for help.

24 Flight
(1900–1)

HER hair twisted into a bun, and in an informal blue cotton gown that she often wore at home, Cixi began her flight in a mule-cart. It was the height of summer and the clothes she wore stuck to her wet body. The sweating animals and their load attracted swarms of flies and insects. Soon it began to rain, and although she was not soaked like her unprotected entourage of about 1,000 people, who rode and trudged through the mud, the cart jerked violently, throwing her this way and that. Later someone found a chair borne by two mules, one in front and one at the back, and she had a little more comfort, but the chair still swung around on the bumpy roads. Crossing a flooded river with no bridge, her guards lifted the bottom of her chair. The floods were swift, and she was nearly swept away.

She was fleeing to the west, into the interior. In front of her lay a wasteland of smouldering villages and towns, pillaged by the Boxers and by the shattered imperial army. Hardly a door or a window was intact and the walls were scarred by bullets. Not an inhabitant was in sight. She was desperately thirsty, but when eunuchs went to draw water from a well, they found human heads floating in it. So she had to chew plant stems for their moisture. No matter how hungry she felt, there was no food. And there was no bed, either. She and the emperor sat throughout the first night on a bench with their backs against each other, staring at the roof. Near dawn, a chill rose from the ground and seemed to penetrate her bones. Famously immune to the cold, the sixty-four-year-old now found it hard to bear – as she would later describe. On the second night, the emperor slept in a mosque, on a prayer mat, with a rattan dustpan and a handleless broom wrapped in a grey chair-cover as his pillow. In the morning, His

Majesty rolled up his precious bedding into a bundle, which he clutched to his chest, not trusting it to the eunuchs. Many eunuchs lagged behind and sneaked away: they were unused to long-distance walking on stone-strewn country roads in their cotton-soled shoes, which, soaked in mud, made every step agony for them.

The emperor, also holding on tight to his pure-gold water pipe, was dressed in a thin silk gown and shivered uncontrollably once the sun set and the temperature plummeted. Lianying, the head eunuch, offered His Majesty his own padded jacket, which he presented on his knees, with tears streaming down his cheeks. Later the emperor would often say that without Lianying he would not have survived the journey, and that he was forever grateful. Thereafter he treated the eunuch as his friend.

After two nightmarish days and nights, Cixi arrived at a town where the local chief was still in place to greet her. County Chief Woo Yong had received notification of their arrival on a piece of dirty, crumpled paper without an envelope. It gave a long list of the court that he was ordered to provide for – and provide for in style. In keeping with imperial pomp, a Full Banquet of Manchu and Han Dishes (*man-han-quan-xi*) was to be laid out for the empress dowager and the emperor. After that, a Grade One Feast was to be served to each of the dozen princes and grandees. The note said that the number of officials and servants was unknown, and that he should prepare as much food and horse-feed as possible. This was a tall order in a county town that had been emptied by the Boxers and soldiers. County Chief Woo's staff had advised him to ignore the piece of paper and to pretend not to have received it – or just to get out of the place, like other officials on the royal route. But Woo was a loyal and kind-hearted subject, so rather than dismissing the demands as ludicrous, he fretted about how best to fulfil them.

County Chief Woo's best was pitiful. His cook had gathered some food, but was robbed on his way to the kitchen by soldiers from the retreating army, who simply grabbed the donkey that carried the provisions. When the cook resisted, he was slashed on the right arm. He eventually succeeded in making three woks of mung-bean and millet gruel, but two were wolfed down by starving soldiers, who reluctantly left one for the royals. Woo placed sentries around the remaining wok, ready to open fire on anyone who came close.

He then tidied up a room in a deserted inn for the empress dowager to rest in, managing to put cushions on the chairs and curtains on the doors, even paintings on the walls and some ornaments on the tables.

When she arrived and set eyes on this luxury and on the County Chief prostrating himself on the floor, Cixi burst into tears. Between loud sobs she told Woo that she had never thought things would become as bad as this. After describing the misery of the journey, she brightened up at the news of the mung-bean and millet gruel, and was about to order it brought in when she suddenly remembered the emperor, and told Lianying to take the County Chief to greet His Majesty. Woo saw a shabby man, unshaven and unwashed, wearing an old padded jacket, which hung loosely about him. Emperor Guangxu did not say a word and Woo withdrew to fetch the gruel. It then emerged that he had forgotten chopsticks, so Cixi told the servants to bring some sorghum stems. As Woo retreated outside the room, he heard Their Majesties sucking eagerly at the gruel. After a while Lianying came out and gave an approving thumbs up, saying how pleased the empress dowager was. He also said that 'the Old Buddha' longed for an egg. Thereupon Woo searched the town, at last finding five eggs in an empty drawer inside an abandoned store. Having lit a fire and boiled the eggs himself, he served them in a coarse bowl with a few pinches of salt. Lianying carried them in to Cixi and, on his return a few minutes later, smiled to Woo: 'The Old Buddha loved them. She ate three, and left two to the Master of Ten Thousand Years. No one else got to touch any. This is good news. But now the Old Buddha would love to have a puff of her water pipe. Do you think you could find some spills?' Woo improvised by rolling up some rough paper on the windowsill. Shortly afterwards, the empress dowager stepped out of the room onto the terrace, parting the curtain on the door herself (a job always done by servants). Lighting the pipe herself as well, she puffed at it and seemed the picture of perfect contentment.

Looking around her, she caught sight of Woo and began to speak to him, which obliged the County Chief to go down on his knees in the muddy yard. She asked him if he could find some clothes for her. Woo said that his wife had died and her clothes were all in Beijing, but he had some clothes that his late mother had left behind, and 'if the Empress Dowager did not mind their coarseness . . .?' At this Cixi said, 'Anything that can keep me warm. By the way, it would be just wonderful if you could also find some clothes for the emperor and the princesses, who brought no changes either.' Woo went home and opened his late mother's trunk. He found a wool coat for the empress dowager, a long waistcoat for the emperor and a few robes for the princesses. From his sister-in-law he took a dressing-table set, which had a mirror, a comb and face powder. Wrapping everything into a large bundle, he delivered it to a eunuch. Later on, when the royals came out of their quarters, they were all dressed in his family's clothes. This was the first time Cixi was seen wearing Han Chinese attire.

The imperial party stayed in County Chief Woo's town for two nights. Cixi learned from him that the Boxers had not only wrecked his county, but also came close to killing him during the time they occupied the town. On one occasion, they had seized him and told him they wanted to satisfy themselves that he was not a 'Secondary Hairy'. The verdict, fortunately in his favour, hinged on whether the ashes from a piece of paper they burned went up or down. On another occasion, a letter from him to a good friend in which he complained about the Boxers had been intercepted, and he only escaped retribution after vehemently denying it was his handwriting. On the most recent occasion, when he was actually trying to get out of the town in order to greet the royal company, the Boxers refused to open the gate, but snorted: 'They are fleeing and don't deserve to be on the throne!' But the mob feared the approaching Praetorian Guards after all, and took to their heels.

Disapproving though he was of her backing for the Boxers, County Chief Woo loyally found the empress dowager a sedan-chair and another for Emperor Guangxu. Cixi took Woo along with them, making him a manager for the onward journey. She told him: 'You have done a very good job, and I am deeply grateful. I will not forget your loyalty, and will show my gratitude. The emperor and I appreciate how difficult it will be for you to manage the logistics . . . We would not dream of being difficult or demanding. Please be at ease, and don't have any misgivings.' These words brought tears to Woo's eyes, and he took off his hat and touched his forehead on the floor. Then Cixi enquired gently, 'That cook of yours, Zhou Fu, is really good. The noodles he just served are quite delicious, and the stir-fried shredded pork is very tasty. I am thinking of taking him with me on the journey, but I wonder whether he would be willing?' To this delicately put command Woo naturally answered affirmatively on the cook's behalf, adding that it was his honour too. Having lost his cook, he had to eat at a friend's house that evening. The cook was promoted to the Royal Kitchen and was given an impressive title.

Cixi had fled the capital and Western Allies had occupied it. The Chinese defences had disintegrated, and yet Cixi's rule did not collapse, as most had anticipated. In flight, and in a sorry state, she showed that she was still the supreme leader. Eye-witnesses seeing her climbing onto the mule-cart said that she did so as if it were the imperial throne. From then on, wherever she was became the nerve centre of the empire. The orders she sent to the provinces, using the same language and tone as always, conveyed absolute authority. Reports from all over China found their way to her. She asked for troops to escort the royal group, and troops rushed over as fast as their horses or legs could carry them. She asked for money, food and transport, and these poured in quickly and abundantly. She was well provided for during the rest of her journey, which covered more than 1,000 kilometres and lasted for more than two months. In late October, in western China, as she settled in the ancient city of Xian, capital of more than a dozen Chinese dynasties from 1100 BC, she received more than six million taels from all over the empire. When the court returned to Beijing a year later, 2,000 carts were loaded with tributes as well as paperwork. This miraculous display of loyalty in an unprecedented crisis spoke volumes for the general stability of the empire, rooted in a deep faith in the empress dowager by the population, the grass-roots leaders and the provincial chiefs – a deep faith that overrode their recent disenchantment.

That she was still alive and very much in command stopped in their tracks those who had thought of jumping ship. One straw in the wind concerned the fate of her bête noire, Sir Yinhuan. When she had ordered the governor of Xinjiang, where Sir Yinhuan was in exile, to execute him, the governor chose not to do so. He was hedging his bets: the invaders were marching on Beijing and Sir Yinhuan was their friend. The order was only carried out fifty days later, on 20 August, when the governor learned that Cixi had left the capital and was safe.

That she was evidently still at the helm and her government had not collapsed changed the mind of Viceroy Zhang, who abandoned his plan to set up a separate regime in Nanjing. The people he had envisaged joining him in his new government – who in fact had not been told about his plan – had affirmed their allegiance to Cixi. Earl Li left Shanghai for Beijing to act as her negotiator. And when the British approached Viceroy Liu Kunyi, his closest colleague, telling him that London looked to him and Viceroy Zhang to take control and negotiate with the Allies, Liu was horrified. He cabled Viceroy Zhang and asked him whether he had received the same bizarre message. He also reminded Zhang that the man the British should be dealing with was Earl Li, who took instructions from the empress dowager. So, when Tokyo was still talking about 'setting up a new government', implying that there would be a key role for him, Viceroy Zhang flew into a panic and fired off a cable marked with an unusual 'thousand times urgent' to his representative in Japan, telling him to 'stop this at once at all costs'. He sent a follow-up the next day, explaining that any such move now 'would most definitely ignite internal strife and throw the whole of China into warring chaos'.

Zhang proceeded to lobby Western powers to protect Cixi. Indeed, her safety had always been one of his priorities, even when he contemplated forming a new government. He and Viceroy Liu had told the British Acting Consul-General in Shanghai, Peiham L. Warren, who reported to Lord Salisbury, that 'unless it is guaranteed that her person shall be protected they will be unable to carry out the agreement of ·neutrality' (which the Viceroys had signed with the powers, promising to maintain peace and protect foreigners in their provinces). When he heard that Allied troops had entered Beijing, Viceroy Zhang repeated his request that Cixi must not suffer 'the slightest alarm'. And when he learned that Cixi had fled, he cabled the Chinese minister in London, asking him to see Lord Salisbury and request 'the same assurance once more'.

The unequivocal support for Cixi by the Viceroys dashed Westerners' hopes of pursuing and toppling her. Many had advocated replacing her with Emperor Guangxu. Sir Claude MacDonald, the British minister, was one of them. But he was warned off by Lord Salisbury: 'There is great danger of a long and costly expedition which, at the end, would not succeed.' The Prime Minister rejected the idea of a joint occupation of conquered territory: 'The attempt to undertake the maintenance of order in Northern China would be hopeless even if we stood alone. But as it would certainly produce a collision between ourselves and our allies, it could only end disastrously.' No occupation would work without a high-ranking Chinese collaborator. But the powers realised that all the most senior Chinese 'ranged themselves solidly' on the side of the empress dowager. They had thought that 'the empire was in the hands of the Viceroys', who were furiously opposed to Cixi; but now, when the crunch came, they found that these men were still in thrall to her. Not one of them was willing to step forward to challenge her. It was all too clear that Cixi was the only person who could hold the empire together. Her demise would result in civil war, which for Westerners would mean especially the collapse of trade, the default of loans and the emergence of more Boxers. And so, for these overwhelming reasons, the Allies decided not to pursue the empress dowager. On 26 October 1900, confident of her safety, Cixi took up residence in Xian. Her representatives, Prince Ching and Earl Li, opened negotiations with the powers.

Meanwhile, Viceroy Zhang, the only man in the regime who had contemplated replacing her and who had enlisted foreign powers' assistance, was anxious to explain himself to her. From the shots she had fired across his bows, he knew Cixi was conscious of his machinations, which could be deemed treason by many a monarch. Although she did not punish him, he reckoned she could not have been pleased. He wanted to explain to her in person that his had only been a contingency plan in the case of her government's demise, and he had never wanted to overthrow her. He wrote and asked for an audience, saying that he had not seen Her Majesty for well over a decade and, filled with regret and a sense of guilt, he longed to come to a place on her route ahead of her, to 'welcome Your Majesty on my knees'. Cixi's reply was a curt 'No need to come'. Her displeasure was transparent. The Viceroy then asked a close associate to intercede on his behalf when the man had an audience with Cixi. The Viceroy had 'not seen Your Majesty for eighteen years,' said the man, 'and since Your Majesty's journey to the west, he has been so concerned and worried about Your Majesty, and missed Your Majesty so much that he has been unable to eat or sleep properly. Dare I ask why Your Majesty declines to receive him?' Cixi gave an excuse: 'he can't leave his post at the moment as things have not quite settled down', and she promised to 'ask him to Beijing once we are back'. But when eventually she returned to the capital at the beginning of 1902, she found another pretext and postponed the audience again. Another year later, the Viceroy could not wait any longer and wrote to announce that he was coming to Beijing in the spring of 1903 anyway as he would be free of duties then, and he just had to see Her Majesty, whom he had been 'missing for twenty years'. This time, he received a positive one-liner: 'You may come for an audience.'

In May that year, Viceroy Zhang arrived in Beijing and at last had his meeting. According to the Grand Council secretary who escorted him in the Summer Palace, and the eunuchs outside the audience hall, he and Cixi said virtually nothing to each other. The moment he went in, she burst into tears, at which he too began to cry. She went on sobbing and did not ask him any questions, so Zhang was unable to talk. The audience protocol was for the official to speak only when the monarch addressed him. And Cixi gave Viceroy Zhang no chance to open his mouth. They sobbed for a while, before Cixi told him to go and 'have a rest', upon which he withdrew. The silence was by design. For Cixi, what the Viceroy had done was best left unsaid. Spelling it out and trying to explain would only upset and alienate her – she had already decided to accept his action, which she judged to be of decent motive. She further demonstrated to Zhang that she held nothing against him by having delivered to him the next day a painting by her own hand – of a pine tree, symbol of uprightness, next to a plant, *zi-zhi*, to which a man of integrity and wisdom was often compared. The meaning was eloquent and the Viceroy was relieved and overjoyed. Immediately putting pen to paper, he wrote: 'Like a withered old tree touched by the most gracious winds / Overnight, the colour of black returned to the greyed hair on my temples.'

Viceroy Zhang composed fifteen similar Poems of Gratitude. They described his time with the empress dowager, and noted all her little tokens: dishes from her own table, fruits from her orchards, ravishing silks, brocades and a long coral necklace to wear on official occasions, and so on. One day, in her presence, some sweet melons grown in the palace grounds were brought for him. She pronounced that they were not beautiful enough, and servants were dispatched to town to search for better-looking melons. Another day, he heard from an official that the empress dowager had compared him to a great historical figure who had been the pillar of his dynasty. These 'Celestial words', as he wrote, sent the Viceroy into a grateful frenzy and made him more humbly devoted than ever. When he left Beijing, Cixi gave him various farewell presents, including 5,000 taels of silver, which he used to start a modern school. When he reached home, three lots of gifts from her were already awaiting him. The Viceroy was overcome and wrote another of his poems of gratitude.

Thus Cixi conquered the hearts of her subjects and earned herself phenomenal loyalty. When she was fleeing Beijing in 1900, Junglu, another devotee, took it upon himself to lead an army in a different direction, aiming to lure away potential pursuers. Among the voluntary decoys was Chongqi, the father of Cixi's late daughter-in-law. When the pursuers did not materialise, and in despair that he was not able to do more to help, Chongqi hanged himself with the sash of his robe, leaving behind a few poignant lines: 'I fear that I am powerless to be of any service to the throne. I only have my life to offer, and I hereby offer it.' When the Allies entered the capital, his wife had two huge pits dug in their house and conducted the whole family, children included, to sit in them in an orderly manner, before she told the servants to fill the pits with earth and bury them alive. When the servants refused and fled in horror, her son set the house on fire, killing all thirteen of them. This was not an exceptional case. Scores of families committed suicide by setting their houses on fire, in addition to individuals drowning or hanging themselves.*

Cixi also had determined enemies – who saw their chance in 1900. Wild Fox Kang set about raising an army and occupying a number of major cities, with arms supplied from Japan. Many Japanese took part in his venture, while he himself stayed overseas. An assassination squad was formed, comprising more than thirty sea pirates. Recruited from the south coast around Hong Kong, it was led by a Japanese, and was ready to go north with the twin objectives of assassinating Cixi and restoring Emperor Guangxu. Hoping to persuade Britain and other powers to help them achieve their goal, the Wild Fox's men wrote to Acting Consul-General Peiham L. Warren in Shanghai, stating, as Warren cabled to Lord Salisbury, 'that, unless the Emperor was restored to the Throne, they were prepared to stir up the Secret Societies throughout the country with the object of compelling foreign powers to intervene. It was pointed out in this communication that grave injuries would be inflicted on foreign trade by popular risings, which they regarded as inevitable, and . . . destruction of missionary property was to be anticipated.' Clearly, this line of argument was unlikely to be persuasive. It merely confirmed to the British that Kang's force was no better than the Boxers. Not surprisingly, Britain lent them no support. The Wild Fox had been dreaming of being collected, protected and conveyed to Beijing by a British gunboat. The dream was dashed. Instead, the powers fully backed Viceroy Zhang as he rounded up Kang's men who gathered in his territory, Wuhan, the moment their uprising began. Britain supported the Viceroy's execution of the main rebels, as the British representative there reported to Warren (who forwarded the cable to Lord Salisbury):

Peace of Yang-tsze [*sic*], otherwise secure, is imperilled by Reform party [Kang's group], which is actively fomenting a rebellion;

---

* In one case, while the family waited for the fire to devour them, at the last moment they allowed their two young children to escape the burning building.

they [? give – *sic* in original] out that they have our support . . .
Arms and ammunition have been smuggled from Japan, and
incendiary Proclamations have been posted up everywhere. It is
no longer a question of reform, but of anarchy and pillage. There
are many Japanese among confederates of Kang. Viceroy [Zhang]
requests that you will confer secretly with the Japanese Consul-
General [to stop Japanese participation].

Tokyo reined in the Japanese in Kang's camp. The demise of the
empress dowager and internal strife across China were not in Japan's
interest at this time, when there were the armies of other powers on
Chinese soil, all with territorial ambitions of their own. The Japanese
leader of the assassination squad pulled out, claiming illness, and was
replaced by a Chinese, Shen Jin. But before it set off, Kang's rebellion
had collapsed.

Also hoping to take advantage of Cixi's troubles was one Sun
Yat-sen, an early proponent of Republicanism. A dark-moustachioed
Cantonese, who had long shed his queue and Chinese costume in
favour of a European-style haircut and clothes, he was dedicated to
the overthrow of the Qing dynasty by force. In 1895, in the aftermath
of the disastrous war with Japan, he launched an armed uprising in
Canton. It failed, but made his name known to the court. He fled
overseas, eventually to London, where he was seized by the Chinese
and detained in their legation in Portland Place. The British government, which had refused to extradite him, intervened and secured his
release. Later on, in Japan, he sought a collaboration with Wild Fox
Kang, but Kang refused to have anything to do with him. Undeterred,
Sun worked doggedly for his Republican ideal through armed insurrections, and acquired a Japanese following as well. In 1900, according
to one of his Japanese comrades who reported to Tokyo, Sun's plan
was to carve away six provinces on the south coast and 'found a
Republic, before gradually expanding to all eighteen provinces of China,
toppling the Aisin-Gioros, and finally establishing a Great East Asia
Republic'. In spite of his flirtation with Japan, the Japanese gave him
only limited and intermittent support. Sun also got nowhere.

The empress dowager, exiled in Xian, remained the unshakable ruler
of China. And she was adept at turning her plight to her advantage.
She would sometimes burst into tears when she received her officials.
A picture of vulnerability, she made the men feel protective and

forgiving, happy to rise to the occasion and help a woman in need. But anyone stepping over a line would see a very different person, as County Chief Woo witnessed. As he had given her crucial service at her most difficult time and she never forgot a favour, he had been treated with intimacy, so much so that he felt bold enough to offer her some advice. One day he told her she should not have executed the officials before her flight, especially the former minister to Berlin, Jingcheng, the man who, unbeknownst to the County Chief, had given the Germans critical advice that had done China untold harm. 'In the middle of a sentence, the Empress Dowager's face suddenly fell, her eyes were like shooting daggers, her jaws set tightly, the veins in her forehead bulged, and she gnashed her teeth, hissing in the sternest voice . . .' She told Woo that his criticism was unfair and born of ignorance of what had really happened. 'I had never seen the Empress Dowager in anger, and all of a sudden her wrath crashed down on me and scared the soul out of me.' Woo felt 'sweat trickling down my back'. He kowtowed and apologised, and 'the Empress Dowager calmed down, and in an instant all her angry expressions vanished, and her face was relaxed and unclouded again . . .' The shift was like 'the mightiest storm of thunder and lightning changing into a clear blue sky in a blink without leaving any trace'. The County Chief remarked that he had not imagined that 'the Empress Dowager's wrath had such force. People said that great figures like Marquis Zeng and Earl Li were so awed by the Empress Dowager that they lost their composure in her presence. I now believe it.' Cixi had a gift of simul- taneously inspiring protectiveness and fear – although not hate.

In exile and a less rigid environment, more people had access to Cixi and Emperor Guangxu. They never failed to be struck by the contrast between the two. The hardship of the long journey left her unmarked by any sign of fatigue or fragility, while her adopted son looked permanently on the verge of collapse. At audiences, sitting side by side, the emperor always kept his mouth shut, no matter how long and awkward the silence, until Cixi turned to him: 'Your Majesty, do ask some questions.' Even then, he rarely asked more than two or three: 'Is everything all right outside?' 'Is the harvest good?' County Chief Woo, who saw him many times, remembered that he only asked two identical questions. 'His voice was extremely tiny, like the buzz of a fly or a mosquito. You could hardly make out what he was saying.' In contrast, Woo observed, 'the Empress Dowager talked most eloquently, quoting classical stories with ease, while at the same time being totally down to earth, familiar with the ways of people and society. She could read your mind after a few words, so the grandees were afraid of her. With an Empress Dowager so smart and strong, and the emperor so odd and weak, no wonder he was under her thumb . . .' Eventually, the officials who noted down their audiences often simply referred to Cixi as '*Shang* (the Monarch)' – a designation usually reserved for the emperor. Cixi herself was well aware of the shift of status. In Xian, for formal audiences, she had a throne set up for herself, behind and above the emperor's, thus presenting herself quite literally as superior to the emperor. When they returned to Beijing, Cixi would sit on a centrally placed throne during an audience, while Emperor Guangxu was seated lower down on the dais to her left.

The ordeal of the invasion, rather than damaging Cixi's authority, had enhanced it and brought her a new sense of security and confidence.

25 Remorse
(1900–1)

THE last thing Cixi did before fleeing the Forbidden City was to
give the guardians of the palaces a handwritten note, stamped
with her seal, telling them that only someone bearing an authorisation
from her which was marked with the same seal could remove anything
from the precinct. The treasures in the palaces preoccupied her as she
set out on her journey.

Within days she was cheered by reassuring news from the guardians.
Instead of wantonly looting or burning the palaces, the invaders had
actually placed guards on them. The heavy gates were shut and fixed
with notices addressed to the occupying army that all men were 'politely
requested not to kick the Chinese attendants because they declined to
open doors . . .' With palpable relief, the guardians informed Cixi that
'foreign troops are now guarding the Royal City and everywhere
within . . . all the palaces and government offices are intact . . . All
palaces and temples are safe.'

The guardians continued to keep Cixi informed. She was told that
foreigners had been visiting the Forbidden City but, apart from a
handful of objects, most things were undisturbed. Later, when the
foreign troops withdrew, and the guardians checked the inventory of
all the objects in the palaces, they found that relatively few valuables
had gone. The biggest loss was from the Royal Kitchen, where sixty-
eight gold and fifty-four silver items were missing. Otherwise, forty
vases and 200 plates and bowls had been stolen from the porcelain
warehouse – more likely by local robbers, as access had been obtained
by digging through the walls. The Summer Palace, where the Italians
and British stayed, was left as it had been, with only minor damage.
(The ruins of the Old Summer Palace next door, however, were picked

bare – by the locals – who sneaked in and thoroughly dismantled all the buildings that had been left standing after the fire, stealing everything from timber to bricks.) Unlike the situation under Lord Elgin in 1860, looting was strictly forbidden this time. When the Western Mausoleums – in which a number of Qing emperors were buried – lost some ceremonial vessels made of gold, silver and bronze, a complaint was made to the French minister, and the French army, which had been stationed there, handed back the ones they had taken.

What did disappear was silver bullion. Millions of taels were seized from the Forbidden City and from various ministries in both the capital and Tianjin, and were shipped abroad. There were also losses from wealthy homes, forcibly entered at the beginning of the occupation by foreign soldiers demanding silver. But such incidents lasted only a few days, after which the guardians had a meeting with Robert Hart, who helped stop them. According to their report to Cixi, the guardians told Hart that 'the most urgent and the most important thing is to protect the dynastic temples, the Eastern and Western Mausoleums, and all the palaces including the Forbidden City and the Royal City; the next thing is to protect the lives of millions of people . . .' To this Hart replied, not without irony, 'In the West, we regard the lives of the people as of primary importance, and the dynasty comes second. Still, your request is not hard to meet . . .' Hart produced two posters, one in various foreign languages and one in Chinese, and told the guardians to print thousands of copies and paste them all over the city. The first poster forbade foreign soldiers from disturbing the local people. And the second one ordered the Boxers and other bandits to go home and resume their normal life, threatening 'extermination' if they disobeyed. Most Boxers did scatter. Cixi wrote to Hart to express her gratitude: 'For decades Your Excellency has lent your talents to a land that is not your own, and today your sincere devotion to it is clear to all. I cannot be more appreciative.'

A small number of Boxers made futile attempts to resist the foreigners. One Allied officer remembered being led by local Christians to round up a group in their hiding place: 'The place was evidently securely held and refused to surrender. Grouped all round, and armed with choppers, bars of iron and long poles, the crowd of native rapscallions waited in a grim silence for the denouement. It was an extraordinary scene. Everything and every one was so silent . . . Such things never happen twice in a lifetime.'

Beijing soon returned to normal and people who had braced themselves for the conquering army to 'plunder, burn, rape and slaughter' were immensely relieved. Cixi was told that 'there was no slaughtering' and no arson.★ No rape was reported. The aristocrats were mortified, however, when they were treated like the common people and required to carry the bodies of those killed by the Boxers out of Beijing. In a drive to clean up the capital, they also had to pull carts, like draught animals, and anyone resisting was whipped by foreign supervisers.

Nevertheless, the Allies were considered a vast improvement on the Boxers. They even took care of hygiene in the streets, which at the time were like a giant public toilet. The new authorities ordered all shop-owners and householders to clean up the area immediately in front of them. Thus the streets of Beijing were transformed, much to the satisfaction of the residents – and of Cixi, when she returned to the capital. This policy of being responsible for the area immediately outside one's front door was adopted by future Chinese governments.

Two months after Beijing was occupied, a large German contingent arrived, even though the war had virtually ended before it left Germany. Field Marshal Count von Waldersee was, through the lobbying of Kaiser Wilhelm II, appointed Commander-in-Chief of the Allies. The Field Marshal dreamed that he would 'return home as the Conqueror of the Chinese' and sent out his men on punitive expeditions outside Beijing, during which, as he recorded, many Chinese were shot. They were Boxers and 'deserved their fate', he wrote. In one city, the Germans executed six officials who they said had slaughtered missionaries. One man's severed head was hoisted on a pole, in the Chinese style, but flexing German muscle. Whilst subjecting the region around Beijing to continual violence, Count von Waldersee, in his reports to the Kaiser, substantially exaggerated the extent of destruction and looting by the Allies before his arrival, so as to portray himself as the restorer of order: 'I believe I may say that except in a few individual cases there have been no excesses since I have been here . . .'

★ The Imperial Library, housing numerous invaluable books, was situated next to the British Legation, and had been set on fire by the Boxers during the siege in a bid to burn down the British Legation. But rumour blamed the British for the fire, and a report to Cixi presented this as fact. As the report was published in the *Peking Gazette*, the British minister protested, pointing out that the Westerners under siege in the legation had in fact fought the fire and tried to save the books. The man who made the report apologised – to Cixi as well as publicly – for giving her misleading information.

The post-war violence created by the Germans eventually came to an end, while the Commander-in-Chief set up his HQ in Cixi's quarters in the Sea Palace. The beauty of the place captivated the count, who found Beijing on the whole 'the dirtiest city in the world'. He wrote in his diary:

> Yesterday evening late I returned from the city to my palace. Never in my life have I seen such a beautiful starry sky as on this occasion. Just as I had made my way through the great white empty courtyard of the Imperial Palace, and reached the bank of the Lotus Lake, strains of music broke out . . . the band of the 1st East Asiatic Infantry Regiment was playing in the Island Palace, wherein the Emperor had been held a prisoner . . . here, within the great heathen city, ringing over the countless Buddha temples, it made the most powerful impression on me. I stood still until the last notes died out.

Not without a sense of decorum, the count ordered that 'the bedroom and the sitting-room of Her Majesty the Empress are not to be used by us'. But one night the whole splendid building, lovingly created by Cixi over many years, was razed to the ground. A fire had broken out, caused by a large iron stove which the Germans had installed in the pantry. The destruction was heart-rending to Cixi, but there was consolation: the damage done to the palaces, and to Beijing on the whole, turned out to be far less serious than she had feared, for which she was grateful. The local people found this so unexpected that they credited a courtesan who claimed this was due to her wheedling pillow-talk with Count von Waldersee. The woman, Prettier Than Golden Flower, had gone with her husband to Berlin as his consort when he was posted there as China's minister in the 1880s. After they returned home and he died, she picked up her old profession. During the Allied occupation, she made use of her past as the minister's consort and the little German she had learned, and did brisk business with German officers, with whom she was often seen out riding through the streets of Beijing. She persuaded the German officers in her circle to take her into the Sea Palace to Count von Waldersee's quarters, clearly hoping to be introduced to him or at least to catch his eye. Whether or not she succeeded is unclear. But her claim of having 'saved the people of Beijing' by enchanting the German Field Marshal caught the popular sentimental imagination, and Prettier Than Golden Flower has become a household name, regarded by many as something of a tragic heroine.*

The Boxer Protocol, the concluding document of the war, was not signed until 7 September 1901, a year after the Allies entered Beijing. The Chinese negotiators, Prince Ching and Earl Li, did little negotiating but waited for the powers to agree among themselves what they would demand from China.

They decided not to hold Cixi responsible for the Boxer atrocities. Instead, Prince Duan, the father of the heir-apparent and the main sponsor of the Boxers, was named as the primary culprit and sentenced to death with a proviso that the throne, if it wished, could spare his life, on the grounds that he was a key member of the royal family. He was sent to Xingjiang for life imprisonment. Six grandees and officials were given unconditional death sentences, and more were punished in other ways. The throne dispatched representatives to Germany and Japan to express 'regret' for the murder of their diplomats. The Dagu Forts were dismantled. And it was prohibited by law to set up or join xenophobic societies.

The clause that really made a difference to the lives of the Chinese people concerned the indemnity. It came to a staggering 450 million taels. This figure was arrived at by adding up all the claims from all the countries involved, for the cost of their military expeditions and the damage done to their persons. America had argued that the indemnity 'should be within the ability of China to pay'. It urged the powers to scale down their claims accordingly and initially suggested an overall sum of forty million. But Germany 'saw no reason why the powers should show excessive generosity', and most others concurred. Count von Waldersee wrote that the Kaiser had told him 'as big a war indemnity as possible should be imposed on the Chinese, as he was needing money urgently for the Fleet'. There was no authority to examine the validity of each country's claim, and no common principle to assess the amounts claimed. It was up to each country to decide how reasonable it should be. Many were not. The biggest claimant was Russia, whose railway in Manchuria had been attacked by mobs, and whose claims accounted for

---

* In the 1930s, a play was staged about her. The soon-to-be Mme Mao, Jiang Qing, wanted to play her, but the role went to another actress, Wang Ying. Mme Mao bore a grudge so deep and poisonous that it became one of the factors in her personal vendetta against the actress in the Cultural Revolution three decades later, ending with the death of the actress in prison.

29 per cent of the total indemnity. Next came Germany at 20 per cent; then France and Britain, which, after first agreeing with America's suggestion, soon wanted more. They were followed by Japan, which showed relative restraint compared with 1895. Even America changed course and finally made what a later investigation found to be an excessive claim.★ The total sum of 462,560,614 taels was then slightly rounded down to 450 million. As the Chinese population at that time was roughly the same number, the Chinese mistakenly assumed (and still do) that the sum symbolised the penalisation of the entire population.

Robert Hart and others argued that 'the country is not in a position to meet it'. But some insisted that it was. The French bishop, Pierre-Marie-Alphonse Favier, alleged 'that the Imperial Family are in possession of treasure of the value of 300 million marks'. But even Count von Waldersee found this assertion fantastic: looking at the Forbidden City 'gives one the impression of former greatness but of a gradual decay . . .' Reporting to the Kaiser, he said, 'I cannot believe a Court which puts up with such a state of decay can own great wealth. I do not know where any such treasure could have been stored.' One solution advanced was that 'Every power must indemnify itself and occupy a portion of Chinese territory.' Count von Waldersee wanted 'to take part of Shan-tung [Shandong]'. This was the dream the Kaiser had cherished and wished the count to fulfil. But other powers, Britain and America in particular, objected to any form of partition. Count von Waldersee remarked that America 'seems to desire that nobody shall get anything out of China'. Sarah Conger, wife of the American minister, wrote with feeling:

★ The claims by all countries, whether or not part of the Allied force, were as follows (in taels; one tael was calculated at three English shillings or 0.742 American dollars):

Russia:	133,316,000
Germany:	91,287,043
France:	75,779,250
Great Britain:	51,664,029
Japan:	35,552,540
USA:	34,072,500
Italy:	27,113,927
Belgium:	8,607,750
Austria-Hungary:	3,979,520
Netherlands:	800,000
Spain:	278,055
Sweden:	110,000
Portugal:	no claim
Total:	462,538,116 [*sic*]

(H. B. Morse, *The International Relations of the Chinese Empire*, vol. 3, pp. 352–3)

I have much sympathy for the Chinese . . . China belongs to the Chinese, and she never wanted the foreigner upon her soil . . . The Chinese seemed willing to make untold sacrifices to accomplish this end . . . To divide China among the nations would mean wars and a standing army large and strong. The bitterness of the Chinese would grow deeper and more active, and they would sting their venom into the foreigner with a poison not yet calculated.

So the idea of a carve-up was shelved. Some countries then wanted to force China to take out more foreign loans. Robert Hart demurred: China was already using a quarter of its annual revenue to pay old debts, and any increase could lead to bankruptcy. Deeply sympathetic to the misery of the Chinese people, Hart and a group of foreign experts busied themselves with finding new sources of revenue. In the end, they persuaded the powers to agree to China raising customs tariffs on imports to 5 per cent (from 3.17 per cent or less), and to levy taxation on hitherto tax-free imports: goods for consumption by foreigners, such as European wines, liquor and cigarettes. So the burden of the Boxer indemnity was partially shared by Westerners.* Hart estimated that the new revenues could raise up to eighteen million taels annually.

Cixi also thought of this new source of revenue and calculated that the increase in import tax would generate roughly twenty million taels a year. Raising customs tariffs had been Beijing's goal for years, and when Earl Li toured America and Europe in 1896, one of his main objectives had been to persuade the Western governments to agree to it. He had failed on that occasion. This time, Cixi told her negotiators to try again – and enlist the help of the British. Britain had the most commercial interest in China and would suffer if China went bankrupt. Cixi also had faith in the British sense of restraint and moderation – and she may have heard about Hart's proposal. Britain, as well as America, supported the scheme. It would appear that the empress dowager's judgement of a nation was as astute as her judgement of an individual. She further instructed Prince Ching and Earl Li to negotiate appropriate terms of payment, so that the new income 'would be enough to pay the indemnity and even if it were not enough, the difference would

---

* Hart also took over some of the internal customs run by often corrupt officials, who routinely kept some of the taxes they collected. As he described, 'the former occupants had merely to pay nominal sums to the treasury and pocketed the rest. T'tsin, e.g., collected over *400,000* taels and of this only 90,000 went to the treasury . . .'

not be too hard to raise'. In the end, the payment term was fixed at thirty-nine years, so that the annual payment would be around twenty million taels. (In addition to the indemnity itself, there were also the interests to pay.)

The new duties did indeed pay a large part of the Boxer Indemnity and helped reduce the unbearable burden imposed on the Chinese. By identifying these new sources of income, at the expense mainly of foreigners and corrupt officials, and by persuading the powers to accept the increase of import tax, Robert Hart did China a sterling service. In a letter at the time he wrote that 'I have been of some use I think, but that will be recognised more easily later than now.' Cixi deeply appreciated his work and bestowed on him a title that had just been conferred on the two very top men in the empire, Viceroy Zhang and General Yuan: Junior Guardian of the Heir Apparent. And yet, for more than a hundred years since her death, no recognition or credit has been given to Hart by the country for which he arguably did more than any other foreigner – and most natives. Today he is virtually unknown to the average Chinese, while the Boxer Indemnity is in all the text-books, constantly invoked to condemn 'the imperialists' and denounce Cixi for pawning her country.

America has fared better than Hart, in that its behaviour has been given due credit: after receiving payment for a few years, it wrote off the rest, specifying that the money was to be used in education. This enabled the top Chinese university, Tsinghua, to be founded, and a large number of young people to receive scholarships and study in the States. America was also the only country to return to China the silver bullion it had seized during the invasion: in 1901, American soldiers had captured 500,000 taels in the office of the Salt Commissioner in Tianjin, and its equivalent, US $376,300, was restored to China six months later.

When Cixi received the draft of the Boxer Protocol near the end of 1900, she was 'overcome with a multitude of feelings', one of which was relief. Her main fears had been the loss of sovereignty or being forced to retire in favour of Emperor Guangxu. Neither materialised. The demands were not entirely unreasonable and, compared to Shimonoseki, the indemnity was not so outrageous. As a result, and because the Allies had largely protected the palaces and the capital, Cixi warmed up to the West.

Throughout her exile, Cixi had been reflecting on past events. She saw that her policies had led to war and atrocities, with hundreds of thousands of casualties – missionaries and Chinese Christians, Boxers and soldiers and ordinary civilians. She still felt that 'foreigners had bullied us too much' when she recalled how she had come to be associated with the Boxers in the first place; but she acknowledged that 'as I am the one responsible for the country, I should not have let things deteriorate so disastrously. It was my fault. I let down our ancestors and I let down our people.' It was in this state of mind that early in the new year, she issued a decree, which she called 'the Decree of Self-reproach' (*zi-ze-zhi-zhao*). In it she said that she had been 'ruminating on past events, and felt pierced by emotions of shame and outrage at the wrongs that had been done'. She condemned 'the cruel and ignorant mob' that had attacked Christian missions and the lega-tions, and expressed her gratitude that the Allies did not conduct tit-for-tat retribution, and that they 'did not infringe our sovereignty nor carve away our land'. Mostly, she reflected on the damage she had done: 'The dynasty has been brought to the precipice. The spirits of our ancestors have been devastated, and the capital has been ravaged. Thousands of families of scholar-officials have been made homeless, and hundreds of thousands of soldiers and civilians are dead or wounded . . .' Although she attempted to explain herself and apportion some blame to others, such as the Boxer-promoting grandees, she mainly blamed herself: 'What position am I in to reproach others when I cannot reproach myself enough?' Her emphasis was on her own 'remorse over the catastrophe' (*hui-huo*) that she had caused.

Cixi knew remorse and articulated it many times. The Boxer episode became a watershed event, and life would be referred to in the court as 'before' or 'after' it. It was with contrition that she vowed to change. On 29 January 1901, still in Xian, she issued a decree that signalled the start of a new phase of her reign. Its essence was 'learning from the West': 'The Empress Dowager enjoins her people that only by adopting what is superior about the foreign countries can we rectify what is wanting in China.' Similar sentiments had been expressed in the past, but on the agenda for change this time were 'all the fundamentals that have made the foreign countries rich and strong', encompassing 'dynastic rule, national traditions, governing methods, people's livelihood, educa-tional systems, the military, and financial affairs'. She announced in yet another decree: 'Making these changes is a matter of life or death for our country, and it gives our people the chance to live a better life. The emperor and I are determined to make the changes for the sake of our dynasty and for the sake of our people. There is no other way.'

Her initiatives enjoyed widespread support – in spite of the Boxer mayhem, or because of it. Foreign occupation of Beijing and Tianjin brought home to the people in the north, as Hong Kong and Shanghai had done to the south, what Western-style governance could achieve, and how it could improve their lives. The impact was even more striking here, as the two southern cities had been fishing villages and swampland when the Europeans took over in the early 1840s after the Opium War. Beijing and Tianjin, on the other hand, were large cities with millions of inhabitants and concentrations of mandarins, all of whom now experienced life under a clean and efficient system. Tianjin in particular benefited, as the occupation lasted two years, and a provisional government had been set up by the Allies. The city was being transformed from medieval to modern. By the end of its administration, the provisional government had collected from taxation 2,758,651 taels and spent 2,578,627, with every penny of the expenditure counted for and the results on show: for the first time residents enjoyed running water, trams, street lamps and telephones. The city was effectively spring-cleaned and an infrastructure for sanitation was being put in place. Piles of garbage were disappearing from the streets. The novelty of public toilets was introduced. And public order was enforced by Western-style policing.* The consensus emerged that the West was a desirable model. Viceroy Zhang, the pre-eminent reformist, remarked:

> Unlike 30 years ago, people now admire the wealth of the West and lament the poverty of China; stare awestruck at the power of the Western armies and scorn the cowardice of the imperial troops; enjoy the fairness and ease of the Customs [under Robert Hart] and detest the fault-finding of China's own tax collectors; praise the orderly governance of the Western-administered cities and resent the harassment of our officials, big and small.

The provincial Viceroys gave Cixi their full backing – as did the reformists who now staffed central government, the xenophobic grandees having been disgraced or marginalised. Although there were still West-haters and reactionaries, they were at least silenced and did not dare sabotage her course. W. A. P. Martin, the American missionary who

---

* Modernisation brought heartache as well. Perhaps the greatest for many was the dismantling of the stately walls that encircled the city 'for military and hygiene purposes'. Tianjin was the first city to see its walls go, and to most people a city was not a city without those lofty corrugated walls – even though convenience and ease of moving around were also appreciated.

lived in China for several decades, felt that 'the spirit of reform was abroad in the land, and that the heart of the people was with her'.

Western governments recognised Cixi as the indisputable leader, and began to view her as someone who 'ranks with Catherine of Russia and Elizabeth of England, with the Egyptian Queens Hatshepsut and Cleopatra, as one of the great women rulers in history.' They resolved to cooperate with her. Buoyed up by this wide-ranging support, Cixi embarked on a course of such massive and profound change in the following years that it deserves to be described as the 'real revolution of modern China'.

PART SIX

The Real Revolution of
Modern China
(1901–1908)

26 Return to Beijing
(1901–2)

THE great, sweeping changes that China underwent in the first decade of the twentieth century began when Cixi was still in exile in Xian. There, in April 1901, she formed a Political Affairs Office to manage the whole programme under her. She left Xian for Beijing on 6 October, after the Boxer Protocol was signed and the occupying armies had withdrawn (though they were still in Tianjin). She did not feel safe with foreign troops in the capital and her anxiety was reciprocated by the Western community. There was 'some uneasiness' in the legations when the date of her return was announced, wrote Robert Hart, and 'the Legation guards are to be kept ready lest anything should happen . . . I don't think the Court will be so foolish as to try a *coup*, but . . . if anything does happen we'll be eaten up, and in that case this may be my last letter!'

At seven o'clock on the morning of the departure from Xian, local officials gathered outside the gate of the palace where the court had been staying, to say their farewell. After the luggage carts, the mounted guards, the eunuchs and the princes and grandees on horseback had started on their way, there came a brief pause. A eunuch stepped forward and waved a giant whip, 10 metres long. It was made of hard-braided yellow silk soaked in wax, with a golden dragon carved on the handle, and he cracked it three times on the ground. This signalled the descent of the monarch and called for all to be still. Cixi and Emperor Guangxu emerged in yellow sedan-chairs, followed by a large retinue. This colossal column then meandered along Xian's streets and exited by the city's South Gate, before heading east and joining the road for Beijing. Actually, it could have gone straight out of the East Gate, but for geomantic reasons the throne had to start all journeys from the South.

Along the way, shops and houses were decorated with colourful silks and lanterns, and as the procession passed by, the residents were on their knees. According to tradition, no one should look at Their Majesties' faces, so some prostrated themselves, while others lowered their heads and eyes and clasped their hands in front of them in a Buddhist gesture of homage. There was a sincere surge of gratitude. When Cixi arrived in Xian, the area was suffering from the aftermath of a disastrous harvest, and people were starving. With the supplies sent to her from other provinces, she was able to feed the population. Soon the weather turned fine, and this year's harvest was excellent. The locals credited this to the royal sojourn, and crowds along the streets wept and cried, 'Long Live the Old Buddha! Long Live the Emperor!' At the places where the crowds were densest, in a dramatic departure from tradition, Cixi ordered her sedan-chair curtains to be parted so that people could see her. She had learned from travellers to the West that European monarchs were seen in the streets. Eunuch chiefs handed out silver coins, and the elderly were given silver cards in the shape of the character for 'longevity'. In the hope of receiving more silver, some locals followed Cixi for days.

The officials who turned out to bid the royals farewell had arrived with their own banners, which added yet more colour to the scene. Some, though, had not wanted to come, but had been informed that failure to turn up could result in their chance of promotion being blocked for two years. Similarly, along the royal route through several provinces, local officials were instructed to come out and greet the throne, in addition to providing food and refreshments, for which they were given generous allowances. However, on the very next stop after leaving Xian, the local chief failed on all counts, even though he had been given 27,000 taels. Apparently he had got himself the job by using his connection with the provincial governor, in order to lay his hands on the handsome royal allowance. But he was really incapable of organising a proper reception for such a huge party, with its complicated royal protocols, and so, instead, he went into hiding, burying his head in the sand. When Cixi learned this, in a villa without candles for the night, she ordered that he should be spared – not even sacked. Her entourage told each other that the Old Buddha really had mellowed.

En route, Cixi visited sacred mountains and beauty spots, travelling along narrow tracks on valley bottoms under towering cliffs, making up for all the years when she had been yearning to travel, but had been unable to do so. A month into the journey, news came that Earl Li had died, on 7 November 1901, before his eightieth birthday – and a month after signing the Boxer Protocol. His death deprived Cixi of a first-rate diplomat, but made no difference to the unfolding of her revolution. The earl's reputation as 'the greatest moderniser of China' is an overstatement.

The earl's last letter to Cixi – written with intense feeling – soon arrived by cable. He said he felt immensely grateful that he had been the man 'appreciated and trusted the earliest and the deepest' by her; he had been reading her decrees on the forthcoming reforms and, knowing that this would make China strong, felt he could now 'die without regret'. On her part, Cixi issued a personal decree in addition to an official one, saying, 'Reading the letter by the late Earl, I was overcome with grief.' The wake for the earl was under way in the capital, with numerous white banners, a large mourning hall shrouded in white, and mourners wearing white coarse sackcloth streaming in and out to the sound of wailing music. The earl's coffin, a giant cata- falque borne by scores of men, was then escorted by his family back to his birthplace more than 1,000 kilometres down south in Anhui province. Cixi ordered the officials along the route to facilitate the arrangements, and shrines and resting pavilions were erected all the way. Sarah Conger said that 'in magnitude and splendor' the proces- sion 'surpassed all that I could extravagantly imagine'. Cixi made sure that the earl was appropriately honoured, and his family well looked after. Above all, she formally retracted all the censure to which he had been subjected by the throne.

She was then in Kaifeng, one of China's old capitals, where the accommodation was suitably royal. A month after she received the late earl's last letter she was still there, and issued another decree, heaping further honours on him and his family. Clearly, the earl meant a very great deal to her. Their working relationship went back four decades, and for many years he had been her right-hand man – the person who understood her best. Together they had achieved a great deal and had dragged the empire out of its isolation and into the world. And yet they had both made fatal mistakes that cost the country dearly, and which had resulted in their own estrangement. In her heart she could not forgive him for his role in the war with Japan – and in China's decline; and he was angry at her handling of the Boxers. Now she needed him, not least to protect her from possible humiliation, and even harm, from Westerners (with whom he got on) once she returned to Beijing. Hesitating, she lingered in Kaifeng – until the day a cable arrived from General Yuan Shikai, who had succeeded the earl as Viceroy of Zhili and Imperial Commissioner for North China. These distinguished appointments had been Cixi's reward for his denunciation of the plotters against her life in 1898, but his ability also amply matched his loyalty. His cable informed Cixi that the foreign armies would not leave Tianjin, which they were still occupying, unless she returned to Beijing. She set off from Kaifeng at once.

While still in Kaifeng, in anticipation of returning to the capital, Cixi annulled the title of the heir-apparent and sent him away from the court. The teenager's father, Prince Duan, had been designated the chief culprit responsible for the Boxer atrocities. Cixi knew that everything done by the prince in relation to the Boxers had in fact been approved by her, and that she should bear the ultimate responsibility. Feeling indebted, she had preserved the heir-apparent's position at court – although officials had been urging her to repeal his title. She herself was aware that the heir-apparent could not possibly have made a decent emperor. He showed no aptitude for state affairs and lacked the bearing of a monarch-to-be. His interest lay in caring for his many pets – dogs, rabbits, pigeons and crickets – and he was fond of playing practical jokes. On one occasion he caused Emperor Guangxu, his uncle and the Son of Heaven, to fall sprawling on the ground. His Majesty tearfully complained to Cixi, who ordered twenty (largely symbolic) lashes for the heir-apparent. Eunuchs despised and poked fun at him as he played with them in ways judged to be beneath him. But Cixi waited for a whole year to go by before revoking his title: she did not want to 'heap frost onto snow', as the old saying went. Now the time had come to act, but her decree mentioned none of his defects. It said that he himself had begged to be relieved, citing his problematic circumstances. The young man left the court as a prince, with his old nanny, to be reunited with his father in exile.

It was also the moment to say farewell to County Chief Woo. Cixi gave him a post in the coastal province of Guangdong, telling him that she was sending him to a prosperous area because she knew he had been out of pocket while serving her. She meant that there would be opportunities for him to make money there. Such corrupt practice was a way of life. The Chinese knew it was a problem and that Westerners despised them for it, but they despaired of ever changing it. Cixi herself, for all her radical reforms past and future, never attempted to tackle it. She went with the flow – and, in doing so, inevitably helped maintain it.

During the audience, repeatedly wiping away tears, Cixi told Woo how grateful she was to him, that he had been a friend in need; she said that she was sad at parting and that she would always miss him. Leaving the audience with the empress dowager's presents, silver taels and scrolls of calligraphy written in her own hand, the County Chief was overwhelmed with gratitude.

Woo then worked non-stop for a day and a night to attend to the details of Cixi's crossing of the Yellow River upon leaving Kaifeng. A snowstorm had swept the ancient capital the day before her scheduled departure, but the weather had cleared by the time she set out and the crossing was perfectly smooth. With her departure attended by officials and local people on their knees, Cixi prayed in a riverside marquee, and paid homage to the God of the River. Then she stepped onto a boat decorated in the shape of a dragon, and the massive flotilla, all colourfully kitted out, rowed to the north in water as still as glass, disturbed only by the oars cutting the surface. Cixi was delighted. She saw this 'extraordinarily smooth' crossing as a sign of the gods' protection – and approval of the course she had chosen. But she also rewarded the boatmen handsomely for their work.

The last leg of Cixi's three-month journey was by train – travelling on the northern section of the great Beijing–Wuhan Railway, whose history was almost as chequered as Cixi's own. The year before, the tracks outside Beijing had been uprooted by the Boxers and a number of stations torched. The railway was repaired by the foreign invaders, who then handed it over to her government, with a royal carriage for her use. She rode to Beijing in style on 7 January 1902, and entered the city through the southern gates, which had hitherto been reserved for the emperor: first the Qianmen, whose massive gate-tower had caught fire during the Boxer chaos, but had since been rebuilt; then, further north, the Gate of the Great Qing. But she stopped short at the front gate to the Forbidden City itself, and turned to go round and enter the harem through the back gate. For a woman to enter the front section of the Forbidden City would have been seen as such a shocking afront to the sacredness of the monarch that Cixi made sure she did not break this rule.

Inside the Forbidden City, one of her first acts was to pray to the ancestors of the Qing dynasty. And as soon as arrangements were made, she took the court to the Eastern Mausoleums to pay homage to the buried ancestors and to beg their protection. While there, she spotted a little pet monkey that belonged to an official and was hopping on his tent. She expressed affection for the monkey and got herself a 'tribute'. It was soon leaping about wearing a beautiful yellow silk waistcoat.

But before all else, the day after she returned from exile Cixi honoured Imperial Concubine Pearl, whom she had had drowned in a well just before she fled. This was an act of contrition. It was also an attempt to make amends to her adopted son, who had given her his cooperation over several years, especially during the exile. Above all, perhaps, Cixi was making a gesture to the Western powers, who had been appalled by the murder. She was determined to win their goodwill. It would make an enormous difference to the country, and to the way she herself would be treated. The yearly payment of the Boxer Indemnity could vary considerably, depending on the exchange rates, and, with goodwill, the foreign powers could adopt the method of calculation that was advantageous to China. Besides, her transformation of the empire needed the cooperation of a friendly international community.

27 Making Friends with Westerners
(1902–7)

FOR her entry into Beijing, Cixi broke with tradition and announced that foreigners were welcome to watch the royal procession. Diplomats were invited to a special building, which allowed a good view of the proceedings. And others stood on the city walls. One of them took a photograph of the empress dowager outside her sedan-chair, about to enter a hall. In the picture she is turning round to wave at them from below, a handkerchief in her hand, her heavily embroidered robe twirling. Waving to spectators was unprecedented: Cixi had encountered it in the descriptions of foreign monarchs written by the travellers she had dispatched abroad.

Twenty days after her return, on 27 January 1902, the diplomatic corps had an audience with Cixi and Emperor Guangxu. There was no silk screen and she sat on a throne. The reception was, in the words of Sarah Conger, 'dignified, and most respectful'. A few days later, Cixi gave another reception for the diplomats' families. As she was unable to socialise with men, her effort to make friends focused on Western women. 'The Court is over-doing it in civility,' wrote Robert Hart in amusement; 'not only will Empress Dowager receive Ministers' wives, but also Legation *children!*'

On the day of the reception the sky was unusually clear, free of the frequent blinding sandstorms. Before the audience, Sarah Conger, the doyenne of the diplomatic ladies and a devout and forgiving Christian, gathered up the women and requested them to be courteous. Inside a hall of the Forbidden City, Cixi sat behind a long altar-like table, upon which lay a coral sceptre. She smiled in recognition at Sarah Conger, who had been at her previous reception three years earlier and had subsequently been caught up in the siege of the legations.

Throughout the Boxer turmoil, America had shown most understanding to China and to Cixi. Now Mrs Conger addressed Cixi in a friendly manner, and Cixi replied in the same spirit, with a written speech read out by Prince Ching, who had stepped up to the throne and, on his knees, taken it from Cixi's hand. All the ladies and children were presented to Cixi, who treated them each with a sort of handshake. They were then presented to Emperor Guangxu, who took the hand of each lady.

After the formal presentations were over, as soon as the group was ushered into another hall for an informal reception, Cixi asked for Sarah Conger, who wrote: 'She took my hands in both of hers, and her feelings overcame her. When she was able to control her voice, she said, "I regret, and grieve over the late troubles. It was a grave mistake, and China will hereafter be a friend to foreigners. No such affair will again happen. China will protect the foreigner, and we hope to be friends in the future."' This was both a performance and a sincere declaration. At the banquet that followed, a reconciliation ritual was enacted. Mrs Conger described the scene: Cixi 'took her glass of wine, and we did likewise. She placed her glass in my left hand, gracefully pressed my two hands together, so that the glasses touched, and said, "United." She then took my glass, leaving me hers, and raised the glass to all, and all responded.' Cixi 'again and again assured me that such troubles as those of the past two years should never be repeated. Her manner was thoughtful, serious in every way, and ever mindful of the comfort and pleasure of her guests. Her eyes are bright, keen, and watchful that nothing may escape her observation. Her face does not show marks of cruelty or severity; her voice is low, soft, and attractive; her touch is gentle and kind.' Clearly, Cixi had made the intended impression.

Cixi and her foreign guests then sat down to eat, which was something extraordinary, as court rules required her fellow diners to stand. Her experiment, however, proved to be unpleasant. On one side of her was seated the 'first lady' of the British Legation, Lady Susan Townley – the wife of the First Secretary, as the legation minister, Sir Ernest Satow, was unmarried. Lady Townley had come to China in the aftermath of the Boxer unrest with 'a decided aversion from the thought of being surrounded by Chinese servants – I imagined they would be dirty and smelly, with repulsive hands'.* She now leaned

---

* A view she later revised. 'Looking back, I often regret them and wish I had them now. They were the cleanest people imaginable, and the quietest in their service. They never gave the slightest trouble and never wanted an evening off!'

towards Cixi and asked her for a gift, the bowl from which the empress dowager was eating. Lady Townley knew well that court etiquette prescribed that no one should share a sovereign's dishes. Her request could only be perceived as an insult. Later Cixi told a lady-in-waiting: 'These foreigners seem to have the idea that the Chinese are ignorant and that therefore they need not be so particular as in European Society.' But Cixi was also aware that many Westerners hated her because of the Boxers. She swallowed the insult and obliged Lady Townley (who later boasted of her 'unique present'). Cixi continued to be amiable to the lady, who described herself as the empress dowager's 'Prime Favourite'. The affability did not diminish even after Lady Townley was caught trying to help herself to more treasures from the palace. A fellow Westerner who had seen her asking Cixi for the bowl wrote, 'On another occasion the lady referred to above took an ornament from a cabinet and was carrying it away when the palace maid in attendance asked her to put it back, saying that she was responsible for everything in the room and would be punished if it was missing.' Cixi showed no ill feelings towards Lady Townley, partly, of course, because she was a representative of Britain. But perhaps the empress dowager also discerned something more sympathetic in Townley. On her way to China in a steamer, Townley had seen a young girl being subjected to foot-binding and was full of pity for 'the poor little children'.

The banquet was the only one Cixi attended, but it marked the beginning of her frequent socialising with Western women. As she told the diplomatic wives at the end of the meal: 'I hope that we shall meet oftener and become friends by knowing one another better.' As gift-giving (especially gifts of a personal nature) was an essential way of expressing goodwill in China, Cixi showered the wives with presents. On this occasion, she took Sarah Conger's hands in hers and, 'taking from one of her fingers a heavy, carved gold ring set with an elegant pearl, she placed it upon one of mine; then from her wrists she took choice bracelets and placed them upon my wrists. To each lady she presented gifts of great value. The children and the interpreters were also kindly remembered.'

Back in the legations, the men decided that Cixi was trying to bribe their women, and requested the court not to give gifts in the future. Robert Hart remarked: 'The Audiences have all gone off so well that the critics consider them too sweet and so suspect insincerity.' They accused Cixi of trying 'to wheedle the foreigners, and curry favour, so that she might receive better treatment at the hands of the Powers'.

This was undoubtedly one of her motives. But, as Sarah Conger put it: 'This historic day cannot do harm . . .'

Other goodwill gestures followed, not least invitations to the Western and Eastern Mausoleums, the Summer Palace and even the Forbidden City. When visitors came to her quarters, gifts from their countries would be prominently displayed. Portraits of the Tsar and Tsarina of Russia stood on a table when the wife of the Russian minister called. And two steel-engravings of Queen Victoria, one of her in regal array, and the other with Prince Albert, surrounded by their children and grandchildren, hung on the wall to catch the eyes of the British, alongside a music-box and other ornaments from the queen. Lots of European clocks would replace her usual display of white and green jade statues of Buddha.

Cixi's second meeting with the diplomatic wives was, for Sarah Conger, 'full of womanly significance'. The empress dowager took the most extraordinary step of inviting the foreign ladies into the privacy of her bedroom. 'When we were taken into the most private room, Her Majesty seemed greatly pleased and waved her hand toward a richly draped and cushioned *k'ang* that reached across one end of the long room.' The *k'ang* – a heated brick bed and seat – was Cixi's favourite place to sit. There, as if out of mischief, she gave the women more presents:

> Her Majesty got upon the *k'ang* and motioned for me and others to do the same. She took a small jade baby boy from the shelf, tucked it into my hand, and with actions interpreted her unspoken words, "Don't tell." I took the dear little thing home, and I prize it. It showed good will, and I do not intend to let go of that thought . . . I was truly grateful that I could see the good spirit manifested in that woman whom the world has so bitterly condemned.

More gifts were to come. Knowing Mrs Conger's fondness for the Pekinese, a 'beautiful little black dog' arrived in the American Legation in a 'basket with red satin pad', complete with 'a gold-mounted harness with a long silk cord and gold hook'. For Mrs Conger's newborn granddaughter, Cixi sent over 'yellow silk boxes containing two beautiful jade ornaments . . . her first gifts sent to a foreign little one'.

Every now and then potted peonies and orchids from her gardens, baskets of fruits from her orchards, boxes of cakes and balls of tea would arrive at the legations, bearing Cixi's good wishes. For the Chinese New Year, fish – a most auspicious symbol as it shares its sound with 'abundance' – would be delivered to the diplomatic families. The American Legation received a colossal specimen: almost 3 metres long and weighing 164 kilos. In her very Chinese way, Cixi tried to build good relations, and in Sarah Conger she made one most valuable friend, who undoubtedly eased her dealings with the foreign powers. The friendship helped to generate sympathy for China in America, and facilitated America's return of the Boxer Indemnity.

In her goodwill offensive, Cixi encouraged other Chinese women to make friends with Westerners. Soon after the first reception, Sarah Conger, who was sympathetic to the Chinese ('While there is much that I find undesirable, I also find in their characters much to admire . . . I really wish to know them. I like the Chinese'), invited some court ladies to the American Legation for dinner. Cixi's adopted daughter, the Imperial Princess, acted as her representative and headed the guest list of eleven. Known to be 'plain in appearance, dignified in bearing' and noted for 'making the most graceful courtesy of any lady in the court', she arrived in a yellow sedan-chair. The other princesses were in red chairs, and those of lesser ranks were in green, with the interpreter in an official mule-cart. They came with 481 servants, including eight eunuchs each and sixty soldiers at the gate. For the Chinese, the more senior a person was in rank, the larger the number of servants. Mrs Conger exclaimed: 'What a sight!' The Imperial Princess brought greetings from Cixi, who 'hopes that the pleasant relations that now exist between America and China will always continue as they now are'. When the ladies left, 'the grand procession passed from under the American flag and into the streets of the Dragon flag . . . all Chinese were kept from the streets through which the procession passed, but thousands were standing elsewhere enjoying the sight.'

Before long the ladies of the court invited the foreign ladies in return, and Mrs Conger went with nearly 100 servants 'to conform to Chinese custom'. Thereafter the women began to mingle and became friends. In early 1903 Mrs Conger wrote about her recent life to her daughter, who had been with her in China earlier:

Do you note the departure from old-time customs and the opening, little by little, of the locked doors? I detect and appreciate it . . . the wives of high officials, both Manchu and Chinese, are opening their doors to us, and I am entertaining them in return. My former ideas of Chinese ladies are undergoing a great change . . . I find that they are interested in the affairs of their own country and also in the affairs of other countries. They study the edicts and read their newspapers. At times I refer to items and events to bring out their ideas and I find that they have much information to give.

'I find that we have many thoughts and ideas in common,' Mrs Conger discovered. The Chinese women had read books translated by missionaries. They 'spoke of Columbus's discovery of America, of the landing of the Pilgrims, of our troubles with England, the seceding of the colonies, of our Declaration of Independence . . .' One was 'greatly interested in Professor Jenks' monetary system' – a system that the professor of Cornell University, Jeremiah Jenks, was proposing for China that year. The American minister, Edwin H. Conger was as impressed as his wife. When an American admiral asked Mrs Conger, 'What do you ladies talk about – dress and jewels?', he replied, 'Quite the contrary. They talk about the Manchurian troubles, political questions, and many things pertaining to their Government.' At least some of the court ladies must have been told to do their homework, as Cixi knew Westerners respected women with intelligence and opinions.

Sarah Conger and Cixi met often and had long conversations. Cixi told the American about her experiences in 1900, relating 'in a vivid way the incidents of her flight and that of the Court; she told me of their trials and privations . . . Her Majesty cited to me many things of which I thought her totally ignorant.' Cixi listened as well as talked: she was 'deeply interested in hearing of her China as I really saw it'. When they met after Conger had travelled extensively in the country in 1905, the American lady described her impressions: 'The Chinese are reaching out for foreign ideas as never before . . . The whole world detects the dawn of broader thoughts . . .' Sarah Conger was giving Cixi something most valuable to the empress dowager: feedback from a Westerner about the monumental reforms she had put in train.

Conger felt 'indignant over the horrible, unjust caricatures' of her friend in the foreign press, and 'a growing desire that the world might see her more as she really is'. So she gave interviews to American newspapers and described Cixi 'as I have many times seen her'. The American's portrayal of Cixi and the fact that they had become close friends created a new, sympathetic image of the empress dowager, especially in the United States. The press began to acknowledge her reforms, although they habitually gave credit to Mrs Conger, claiming that 'Through Mrs Conger's influence numerous changes have taken place . . .' 'China's Woman Ruler Americanizing Her Empire' read one headline. However grudgingly, the papers began to present Cixi as a progressive, one sketch even showing her in a fighting posture with a captain reading: 'She orders women's feet unbound.' (The unbinding of women's feet was one of Cixi's first edicts when she returned to Beijing.) Sarah Conger was instrumental in bringing Cixi a better press in the West.

Cixi was appreciative and felt genuine friendship for the American lady. In 1905, the Congers had to leave China for another post. Sarah was decorated with a most exalted title and was presented with beautiful farewell presents. Before departure, she called on the palace to say goodbye to Cixi and, after the formalities, 'we were seated and as one woman with another, the Empress Dowager and I conversed'. Then, 'Our good-byes were said, and as I was leaving Her Majesty's presence I was asked to return. Her interpreter placed in my hand a "good-luck stone" – a blood jade, with these words: "Her Majesty has taken the good-luck stone from her person and wishes to give it to you to wear during your long journey across the great waters, that you may safely arrive in your honorable country."' Unremarkable in appearance, this piece of jade had been passed down through generations of the Qing dynasty, and had been worn by Cixi herself during her reign, as a talisman that would protect her in her tribulations. To part with such an object was no small thing. To do so impulsively showed Cixi's real feelings. The Congers continued to receive her messages after they were gone.

In her effort to improve Cixi's reputation in the West, Sarah Conger conceived the idea of having the empress dowager's portrait painted by an American artist for the St Louis Exposition in 1904. Cixi agreed, at considerable psychological cost. Traditionally, portraits were only painted of *dead* ancestors (although there were watercolours depicting daily life), and Cixi, for all her departures from convention, was superstitious. But she did not want to turn down her friend's kindness – and she also welcomed the chance to promote her image.

Katharine Carl, whose brother worked in the Chinese Customs, was recommended, and came into the court in August 1903. Cixi had only committed to one sitting, and for this she was splendidly decked out, as befitted the empress dowager of China. She wore a brocade gown of imperial yellow, richly embroidered with threads of pearls in a wisteria pattern. Hanging from the top button on her right shoulder was a string of eighteen enormous pearls separated by pieces of jade. Also suspended from the button was a large ruby, with yellow silk tassels that terminated in two immense pear-shaped pearls. A pale-blue embroidered silk handkerchief was tucked under one arm and a scent-bag with long, black silk tassels under another. The headdress was packed with jewels of different kinds, as well as large fresh flowers. Her arms and hands were adorned with bracelets and rings and, as if to extend the area for more decoration, bejewelled nail-protectors capped two fingers on each hand. The feet were not neglected: the square-fronted embroidered satin shoes were covered with small pearls, leaving bare only the centimetres-high soles. Walking on those impossible soles, Cixi advanced animatedly towards Miss Carl and asked where the Double Dragon Throne, her seat, should be placed. And so the painter began work, in a hall where she counted eighty-five clocks ticking and chiming, and feeling the eyes of her sitter 'fixed piercingly upon me'.

Those eyes judged Miss Carl to be a straightforward person with an open and strong character. Cixi liked her. After the sitting, wrote Carl, she 'asked me, looking straight into my eyes the while, if I would care to remain at the palace for a few days, that she might give me sittings at her leisure'. The artist, who had very quickly warmed to Cixi, was overjoyed. 'The reports I had heard of Her Majesty's hatred of the foreigner had been dispelled by this first Audience and what I had seen there. I felt that the most consummate actress could not so belie her personality . . .'

Carl stayed on for nearly a year. Through her, Cixi was allowing the outside world into the mysterious Chinese court. She also enjoyed Carl's company. The painter lived in the palaces, saw Cixi practically every day and mingled with people in the court. With an observant and sensitive eye, she came closer to Cixi than most. She noticed her awesome authority, not least through the fact that her portrait was treated 'with the respect a reverent officiant accords the Holy Vessels of the Church'. Even the artist's painting materials were invested with a sort of semi-sacred quality. 'When Her Majesty felt fatigued, and indicated that the sittings were finished, my brushes and palette were taken by the eunuch from my hands, the portrait removed from the easel and reverently consigned to the room that had been set aside for it.' The brushes and palette were gingerly placed in specially made large flat boxes, which were locked and the keys entrusted to the head eunuch.

Katharine Carl saw how Cixi got her way, in this case by presenting her requests about the painting diffidently, as if asking for a favour. 'She took my hand in hers, and said in an almost pleading way, "There is a bit of trimming that is not well finished. You will arrange it for me, will you not . . .?"' She would apologise for her requests: 'I am giving you a great deal of trouble, and you are very kind.' One request most tentatively and anxiously made concerned the date when the portrait would be finished. It had to be an auspicious one: the painter could not simply finish when she wished. The almanacs were consulted, and it was decided that 19 April 1904 was the right day, and four o'clock in the afternoon the ideal time. Miss Carl readily accepted and Cixi looked hugely relieved.

Carl was very struck by Cixi's passion for her gardens: 'however careworn or harassed she might be, she seemed to find solace in flowers! She would hold a flower to her face, drink in its fragrance and caress it as if it were a sentient thing. She would go herself among the flowers that filled her rooms, and place, with lingering touch, some fair bloom in a better light or turn a jardiniere so that the growing plant might have a more favorable position.'

The painter also shared Cixi's love of dogs. The empress dowager had a large and luxurious kennel, which Carl often visited. Noticing this, Cixi gave her a pet of her own. One day 'some young puppies were brought to be shown the Empress Dowager. She caressed the mother and examined critically the points of the puppies. Then she called me up to show them to me, asking me which I liked best . . . she called my attention to their fine points and insisted upon my taking each of them up.' As Carl felt awkward about taking one, Cixi had one delivered to her as a present: 'a beautiful white-and-amber-colored Pekingese pug'. This was in fact Carl's favourite puppy, in which she had shown particular interest when she visited the kennel. Cixi had clearly made it her business to find out.

Carl experienced the most thoughtful side of Cixi, in a personal and feminine way. One day they were out walking: 'As the day was fading and as I was thinly clad, Her Majesty thought I was cold, and, seeing I had no wrap, she called to the Chief Eunuch to bring me one of hers. He selected one from the number that were always brought along for these promenades, and gave it to Her Majesty, who threw it over my shoulders. She asked me to keep it and to try to remember to take better care of myself in the future.' When the cold season was coming, Cixi sent a maid to Carl's apartments to get one of her tailor-made European dresses, and had the palace tailors copy this in padded silk. She gave Carl a long, soft sash to tie at the side, which she said made it look more graceful. As the weather got colder still, Cixi designed for Carl a long fur-lined garment, a hybrid of European and Chinese styles, which the painter thought not only pretty, but comfortable to paint in. The empress dowager also picked a sable hat for Carl, choosing a colour that she felt would complement Carl's blonde hair, and a design that she said would bring out her strong character.

These non-European outfits were presented to the painter delicately, as Cixi was mindful that the American lady might not like the costume of another culture. Cixi's own clothes were expressions of her ethnic identity. The only time she did not wear Manchu dress was during her flight, when she wore the clothes belonging to County Chief Woo's family, which were Han. She told Carl that her new clothes were only for practical purposes and would not violate her personality. Showing the same sensitivity, when she gave a garden party for the diplomatic ladies, Cixi would arrange for Carl to be taken out of the palace to join Mrs Conger and re-enter with the American Legation ladies – in case Carl might be embarrassed to appear as though she were a member of the empress dowager's entourage. Going for walks in the gardens, Cixi would pick small flowers and tuck them behind Carl's ears, in a gesture of intimacy that Carl realised was 'to insure a similar treatment of me by the Ladies and eunuchs'. Cixi also saw to it that Carl was included in all enjoyable activities. The beginning of the kite-flying time in spring was one such, when grandees and literati ran around like children. It was customary for the first kite to be sent up by the empress dowager. On that day Cixi invited Carl to the garden and, after letting out the string and expertly handling the kite, handed it to Carl and offered to teach her how to fly it.

Cixi behaved to Miss Carl like a girlfriend. They had a lot in common. No one appreciated Cixi's gardens as keenly as the American painter: 'The exquisite pleasure the contemplation of this glorious view gave me made me tremble with delight.' They laughed together. One day Cixi went to see her chrysanthemums, which were in full bloom, while Carl remained at her work. When she returned, the empress dowager brought Carl a new variety and said, 'I will give you something nice if you guess what I have named this flower.' Carl thought the curious bloom, with hair-like petals and compact centre, resembled the bald head of an old man, at which a delighted Cixi exclaimed, 'You have guessed. I have just given it the name of the Old Man of the Mountain!' There was a casual intimacy between them. At one of her garden parties, Cixi scanned Carl's grey dress, and took a pink peony from a vase and pinned it on her, saying that a little colour would be nice. They chatted about clothes. Cixi praised European fashions for their 'pretty colors', but said that while 'the foreign costume was very becoming to well-made and well-proportioned people', 'it was unfortunate for any one who was not so blessed'. The Manchu costume, on the other hand, 'falling in straight lines from the shoulder, was more becoming to stout people, for it hid many defects'. (The empress dowager refrained from criticising Western corsets to the American painter. She apparently responded to a court lady, who had lived abroad and told her about this fashion item with some exaggeration, 'It is truly pathetic what foreign women have to endure. They are bound up with steel bars until they can scarcely breathe. Pitiable! Pitiable!')

Staying with Cixi for almost a year, seeing her virtually daily in her own milieu, Katharine Carl felt that she 'had come to really love' Cixi. The feeling was mutual. Cixi invited Carl to stay on for as long as she wanted and suggested that she paint other ladies in the court – and maybe even spend the rest of her life in Beijing. Carl gently declined, feeling that 'The world beyond the Palace gates called me.'

Her painting of Cixi was an unremarkable one. Western portraits have shadows on the face, but in the Chinese tradition a face with black shadows was a 'Yin-Yang Face', which pointed to a dubious character – a double-crosser. Heavy pressure, however tactfully exerted, was put on Miss Carl to iron out the face. 'When I saw I must represent Her Majesty in such a conventional way as to make her unusually attractive personality banal, I was no longer filled with the ardent enthusiasm for my work with which I had begun it, and I had many a heartache and much inward rebellion before I settled down to the inevitable.' However, she wrote a book about her unique experience, *With the Empress Dowager*, published in 1906, which painted a memorable picture of Cixi. The empress dowager had made another loyal Western friend.

Meanwhile, Carl's portrait was presented to the US government after the St Louis Exposition. In the Blue Room of the White House on 18 February 1905, the Chinese minister to Washington told President Theodore Roosevelt and the assembled company that the empress dowager's gift was intended to show her appreciation of America's friendship for China and 'her abiding interest in the welfare and prosperity of the American people'. In accepting the portrait 'in the name of the Government and people of the United States', President Roosevelt said, 'It is fitting this mutual friendship should exist and be maintained and strengthened in all practicable ways, whether in the larger field of international relations or by pleasing incidents like that which brings us together today.' The portrait, he said, 'will be placed in the National Museum as a lasting memorial of the good-will that unites the two countries and the strong interest each feels in the other's well-being and advancement.'

A third woman, similarly involved with Cixi's efforts to build ties with the West, became close to her from 1903. This was Louisa Pierson, the daughter of a Boston-born American merchant in Shanghai and his local Chinese wife. At the time, the 1870s, there were many Eurasian liaisons, and their children were invariably looked down on as half-casts. Robert Hart had 'a Chinese girl kept by me', he wrote. He lived with her for years, until he discarded her to marry a British girl. Their three children were sent to England to be raised by the wife of a bookkeeper, and neither parent set eyes on them again. His behaviour was deemed 'generous in the extreme, almost quixotic', by the standards of the day, as other foreigners tended simply to desert their mixed-race children. How Louisa Pierson was treated by her American father, who died in Shanghai, is unknown, but she was married as a proper wife by an unusual Chinese official, Yu Keng, who did not take her as a concubine or treat her as a kept woman. Their liaison was not an easy one. The Chinese called Louisa 'quasi foreign devil' (*gui-zi-liu*), and the foreign community shunned them. But the pair lived happily together with their children, completely unashamed and unapologetic about their union. Somewhat grudgingly Hart acknowledged that 'the marriage, I believe, was a *love* affair', while remarking, 'The *Yu Keng* family are not well thought of anywhere, but the old man himself has powerful backing – I don't know why.'

The backing came from unprejudiced sponsors, not least Cixi herself. Yu Keng had been working under Viceroy Zhang, who put him in charge of dealing with clashes between the local population and Christian missions in his provinces. The bilingual Louisa Pierson was able to talk to both sides, helping to smooth out misunderstandings and resolve disputes. Viceroy Zhang thought highly of the couple and recommended them to Beijing. There Yu received rapid promotion, first as minister to Japan, then as minister to France. While Hart grumbled ('I don't like the appointment!'), Yu Keng and Louisa Pierson went to the hub of Europe with their 'noisy family of English speaking children'.

In Paris, they led a cosmopolitan life. According to the Western press, who were fascinated by the couple, Louisa Pierson 'speaks French and English perfectly, with a slight accent, which recalls the Bostonian twang, together with something indefinable which is doubtless purely Chinese. She is a most wonderful artist, drawing on silk in the fashion of the old Chinese masters with a skill and a certainty of metier which makes French painters open their mouths wide with astonishment.' She 'presides over the embassy receptions with exceeding charm and refinement'. At a fancy-dress ball the couple gave to celebrate the Chinese New Year in 1901, one of their sons, Hsingling, dressed up as a convincing Napoleon. A Catholic, he went on to marry a French piano teacher in a church in Paris. The wedding, for which the bridegroom wore a Manchu sky-blue robe with red coral buttons, was attended by the American Ambassador to France, General Horace Porter, and was widely reported in the press, described as 'the most picturesque and interesting marriage recently seen here' and 'a Novel Event'. (The marriage did not survive their subsequent return to China.) The two daughters, Der Ling and Rongling, wrote the *New York Times*, 'are adorably pretty, and they dress in the European style with a finish and skill to which something of Oriental charm is added which makes them the cynosure of all eyes when they enter a drawingroom [*sic*]'. Louisa and her husband gave their daughters unheard-of freedom to enjoy Paris to the full. They socialised, frequented the theatre (where they were mesmerised by Sarah Bernhardt) and took dancing lessons with the famed Isadora Duncan. They performed at their parents' parties and danced European-style ballroom dancing with close body contact with foreign men. The family's lifestyle, including Louisa letting a Frenchman kiss her hand, raised not only eyebrows but also rancour: the family was denounced to the throne by outraged mission officials.

But Cixi liked what they were doing and waited impatiently for their return. After Yu Keng's term ended, and after a whirlwind tour of major European cities, the family arrived back in Beijing in early 1903. At once, Cixi invited Louisa Pierson and her daughters to the palace to be her ladies-in-waiting, and placed them ahead of most other court ladies. The two daughters, both speaking English and French, interpreted for Cixi in her increasingly frequent contacts with Westerners. When she heard that the younger daughter, Rongling, had studied music and dance in Paris, Cixi was enthusiastic. She said that she had always felt it a tremendous pity that Chinese dancing had almost disappeared, and that she had tried unsuccessfully to find someone to research court records and revive it. 'Now Rongling can do it,' said the empress dowager. So Rongling began a career that established her reputation as 'the First Lady of modern dancing in China'. Urged on by Cixi, she studied court and folk dances and, combining them with ballet and other types of Western dancing, choreographed a series of dances, which she performed in front of a greatly delighted Cixi. Accompanying her was a Western-style orchestra set up by General Yuan, as well as the court ensemble.

Louisa Pierson was Cixi's most-valued general consultant about the outside world. At last having someone close to her who had first-hand knowledge of Europe and Japan, and whose views she respected, Cixi sought her advice daily. One early interpreter, a girl who had been to Germany with her father, an attaché in the Chinese Mission, had told Cixi that the German court was 'very simple'. Trying to gauge how extravagant her own court was by international standards, Cixi asked Louisa, who said that although she had not been to any German palaces, she understood that they were in fact quite grand. Cixi was reassured. Intelligent and competent, Louisa Pierson was far more than a source of information or adviser on diplomatic etiquette. Even international politics fell within her orbit. When Japan and Russia looked set to go to war in Manchuria in late 1903, Cixi often talked to her about Japan, where Louisa had been stationed with her husband. One day the wife of the Japanese minister, Uchida Kōsai, requested a visit. Cixi was very fond of the lady and had given her a Pekinese puppy, as she had to Mrs Conger. Such friendly gestures were of course also for the benefit of Tokyo. Cixi knew the lady's visit at this moment had a political agenda, and that Tokyo wanted to sound out her real thoughts about Japan, which she had no wish to divulge. Louisa Pierson helped Cixi decide to have Rongling as the interpreter, who, on her mother's instruction, mistranslated the Japanese lady's probing and politically charged questions, turning them into harmless chatting. Louisa was so indispensable to Cixi that when she occasionally went away to see her sick husband, Cixi would urge her, however tactfully, to hurry back. It was with reluctance and resignation that Cixi let Louisa leave the court altogether when her husband was extremely ill – indeed dying – in 1907.

28 Cixi's Revolution
(1902–8)

CIXI carried out her revolution over seven momentous years: from her return to Beijing at the beginning of 1902 until her death in late 1908. Milestone changes defined the era, during which China decidedly crossed the threshold of modernity. Modernisation enabled the country's annual revenue to more than double in this period, from just over 100 million taels to 235 million. And as revenues grew, so it became possible to fund further rounds of modernisation. The reforms in these years were radical, progressive and humane, designed to improve people's lives and to eradicate medieval savagery. Under her measured stewardship, Chinese society was fundamentally transformed, thoughtfully and bloodlessly, for the better, while its roots were carefully preserved and suffered minimum trauma.

One of Cixi's first revolutionary decrees, proclaimed on 1 February 1902, was to lift the ban on Han–Manchu intermarriage, a ban as old as the Qing dynasty itself. In a family-oriented society the ban had meant that there was little social intercourse between the two ethnic groups. Even if officials were close colleagues, their families hardly ever met. The American physician Mrs Headland described one occasion when two Manchu princesses and the granddaughter of a Han Grand Councillor encountered each other in her house. For a while, getting them to converse was 'like trying to mix oil and water'. Now the Manchu–Han segregation was to be dismantled.

The same decree required the Han Chinese to abandon their tradition of foot-binding, stressing that the practice 'harms creatures and violates Nature's intentions' – an argument that appealed to a deeply held belief: respect Nature's creation. Aware of the tenacity of the custom that had been in place for a thousand years, and anticipating resistance that could lead to violent collisions, Cixi approached the implementation of her injunction with characteristic caution. She bid grass-roots leaders make all households aware of her message and use example and persuasion to convince the families, explicitly and emphatically forbidding the use of brutal coercion. Cixi's style was not to force through drastic change, but to bring it about gradually through perseverance. When her American friend Sarah Conger asked her if her edict would have an immediate effect in the empire, she replied, 'No; the Chinese move slowly. Our customs are so fixed that it takes much time to change them.' Cixi was prepared to wait. Her emphasis on gradual change contributed to the fact that many young girls (including this author's grandmother) still had their feet broken a decade later. But they were the last generation to be subjected to this suffering.

Again using persuasion and promotion rather than force, Cixi began to release women from their homes and from male–female segregation, breaking a fundamental Confucian tradition. Women started to appear in public, and to go to theatres and cinemas, enjoying undreamed-of pleasures. She particularly espoused modern education for women, repeatedly urging Viceroys, high officials and aristocrats to lead the way and set up and fund girls' schools. She herself set an example by personally founding a School for Aristocratic Women, to which she appointed her adopted daughter, the Imperial Princess, as headmistress. Another of her plans was to open an institute of higher education for women and, as an incentive for applicants, it was announced that each graduate would have the honour of being referred to as a Personal Pupil of the Empress Dowager. In 1905, a female sponsor of a girls' school, Madame Huixing, used self-immolation (a traditional and not uncommon way to draw attention to a cause) to appeal for regular funding for the school. The flourishing press of the time made her a national heroine. Men and women gathered for her memorial services, and a Peking Opera was written to tell her story. Cixi gave her full support by publicly selecting a star-studded cast to perform the opera in the Summer Palace. She also chose another new play to be performed on the same occasion: *Women Can Be Patriots* – aimed at awakening women's political consciousness. In spring 1907, a Regulation for Women's Education was decreed, which made it official that women should receive education.

A champion in women's education was Viceroy Duanfang, who had impressed Cixi with his reformist ideas and his ability during her exile in Xian, where he had been the acting governor. Elevated to key posts in the Yangtze Valley, this new political star was responsible for many modernising projects, including China's first nursery school. It was he who dispatched the country's first female students abroad, in 1905. They went first to Japan to study teacher training, and then to America. Among the teenage girls who were awarded government scholarships for Wellesley College in Massachusetts was one Song Qinglin (Qingling), later Mme Sun Yat-sen and, later still, Honorary President of Communist China. With her was her younger sister Meiling, then a child, who later attended Wellesley as well, and became Mme Chiang Kai-shek, First Lady of Nationalist China.

Many prominent women in the future benefited from the opportunities created by Cixi. One was the first female editor of a major paper, the *Ta Kung Pao*, in 1904, in which capacity she attracted teams of adoring young men. Educated women launched some thirty journals to promote women's liberation, and one, *Women's Daily*, was apparently the only women's daily in the world at that time (even though the paper itself did not last long).

In the first decade of the twentieth century the expression 'women's rights' – *nü-quan* – was in vogue in China. An influential booklet proclaimed as early as 1903: 'The 20th century will be the era of revolution for women's rights.' In a civilisation that had treated women with unparalleled cruelty, their emancipation had begun.

Another key component of Chinese society, the traditional educational system through which the empire's ruling elite had been selected, was finally scrapped. This hindrance to modernisation – and to Chinese thought as a whole – had been on Cixi's agenda for some years, and during that time she had gradually established an alternative educational system – and alternative routes to a career, in government as well as in private sectors. So when the final push came, in 1905, this giant pillar in China's political infrastructure for well over a thousand years collapsed with extraordinary ease. The new educational system was based on Western models, with a whole range of subjects introduced, although Chinese classics remained on the curriculum. That year, after visiting one of the new schools, with English-speaking teachers and uniformed pupils in European-style classrooms, library and athletics room, Sarah Conger pondered in amazement, 'What will be the future of China when these hundreds and hundreds of educated young people go out from these schools as a leaven into its vast population?' Three years later, the number of such schools, not all of them so well equipped perhaps, was in five figures.

Young people studying abroad received either scholarships or incentives such as the promise of desirable jobs when they returned with satisfactory qualifications. At the beginning, many were reluctant to go, especially the sons of elite families, who found life without troops of servants unimaginable. But anyone who aspired to be an official was told to go, to travel if not to study, and in 1903 being abroad for at least several months was made a mandatory qualification for future posts. An edict from Cixi also ordered existing officials to travel abroad, which, she said, was something that had 'only advantages and no drawbacks'. The number of students studying overseas soared. In Japan alone, in the early years of the century, they were estimated at something approaching 10,000.

With new education and new thinking, young Han Chinese began to question and reject the Manchu rule, and their publications were full of outcries in this vein: 'The Manchus are foreigners who invaded China and have dominated us Hans for 260 years! They conquered us by slaughtering, and brought us disasters for which we had to pay the price! They force us to wear "pig tails", and make us a laughing stock in London and Tokyo . . .' After the list of grievances came the inevitable battle cry: 'Drive out the Manchus! China for the Han Chinese!' In 1903, a devastatingly anti-Manchu essay, *The Revolutionary Army*, by one Zou Rong, appeared in a newspaper in Shanghai. Calling Cixi 'a whore', the essay vehemently advocated the overthrow of the Manchu government. 'Expel all Manchus who live in China, or kill them for revenge,' it cried; not least: 'Slay the Manchu emperor!' The essay infuriated the Manchu grandees, including the most open-minded reformers, and quite possibly Cixi herself. By the Qing legal code, these incitements amounted to high treason, punishable by some gruesome form of death. Even the dedicated reformist Viceroy Duanfang, who was a Manchu, wanted the author 'extradited' from Shanghai (which, as a Treaty Port, was governed by Western laws) and punished with life imprisonment, if not death. Shanghai turned down the request for extradition, and Zou was tried *in situ* by a largely Western panel, with the Chinese government represented by a lawyer. Judged against a Western law to do with sedition by word and not by deed, in mid-1904 the author was sentenced to two years' imprisonment and hard labour in a Western-style jail. The newspaper was banned.

This cause célèbre was a lesson to all. Extremist writers felt the need to tone down their language. The prison in Shanghai, though not a hell-hole like most in China, was far from pleasant, and Zou, in poor health and unable to sleep, died within a year. For Cixi, the case provided much food for thought. She was faced with a new challenge: how to deal with hitherto unthinkable expressions akin to blasphemy in the rapidly expanding press. To treat them as treason and to deal with them by the old laws would be to turn back the clock, and she rejected the option. She refused to listen to those who advised suppression or recommended stopping sending students abroad, where they learned all manner of heresy. She chose instead to regulate the press with laws and regulations based on Western and Japanese models – and these were gradually introduced. As a result, the new century witnessed an explosion of Chinese-language newspapers and journals. Hundreds of titles sprang up in more than sixty locations around the empire. Anyone could start a newspaper, if they had the funds, and no one could silence them. General Yuan, as the Viceroy of Zhili based in Tianjin, was mercilessly assailed by the most influential newspaper there, the *Ta Kung Pao*, and, much as he hated it, he was unable to shut it up. All he could do was order government employees not to buy the paper, and the post office not to deliver it. Both measures were unsuccessful and only served to increase the paper's circulation. Cixi's tolerance of attacks on her government – and on herself – as well as her willingness to permit a diversity of viewpoints were unmatched by any of her predecessors – or, arguably, her successors.

Along with the introduction of unimagined freedoms, Cixi began to revolutionise China's legal system. In May 1902, she decreed a wholesale review of 'all existing laws . . . with reference to the laws of other nations . . . to ensure that Chinese laws are compatible with those of foreign countries'. With a legal reform team headed by a remarkable mind, Shen Jiaben, who had a comprehensive knowledge of traditional laws and had studied several different Western codes, a brand-new legal structure based on Western models was created in the course of the decade, covering a whole range of commercial, civil, criminal laws and judicial procedures. Cixi approved the team's recommendations and personally decreed many landmark changes. On 24 April 1905, the notorious 'death by a thousand cuts' was abolished, with a somewhat defensive explanation from Cixi that this horrific form of execution had not been a Manchu practice in the first place. In a separate decree, torture during interrogation was prohibited. Up to that point it was universally regarded as indispensable to obtain confessions; now it was deemed 'only permissible to be used on those whom there was enough evidence to convict and sentence to death, but who still would not admit guilt'. Cixi made a point of expressing her 'loathing' for those who had a penchant for torture, and warned that they would be severely punished if they failed to observe the new constraints. Prisons and detention centres were to be run humanely; the abuse of inmates would not be tolerated. Law schools were to be set up in the capital and provinces, and law studies were to be made a part of general education. Under her a legal framework began to be constructed.

In a less obviously groundbreaking development, commerce was made respectable. Although paradoxically the Chinese loved making money, the culture traditionally held commerce in distaste and ranked it at the bottom of the professions (the order of prestige being: scholar-officials, peasantry, craftsmen, and – lastly – merchants). In 1903, for the first time in its history, China had a Ministry of Commerce. A series of imperial decrees offered precisely defined inducements for aspiring entrepreneurs to 'form companies', whose registration local governments were told to grant 'instantly, without a moment of delay'. One such incentive ran: 'Those who raise 50 million yuan worth of shares are to be appointed First-grade Adviser to the Ministry, with First-grade official status, and be awarded the special Imperial Double-dragon gold medal, with their male descendants inheriting a Third-grade Advisory post in the Ministry for three generations.' Further incentives were given for merchants to attend expositions abroad and to identify new products for export.

The many other developments included the establishment of the state bank in 1905, followed by the birth of a national currency, with the 'yuan' as the unit. The system is still in use today. The great north–south artery, the Beijing–Wuhan Railway, was completed in 1906. An embryo network of railways was in place. The army and navy acquired new HQs, two grand European-style turn-of-the-century edifices with oriental features. Designed by a Chinese architect, they are among the most interesting buildings in Beijing. It is said that Cixi footed the bill herself. Perhaps she was atoning for having taken money from the navy in the past.

As the Chinese were adopting a whole range of new ways to live, the old habit of opium-smoking finally started to decline. Half a century had gone by since the country was forced to legalise the drug, and a large part of the population – officially estimated at 'nearly 30 or 40%' – was taking some opium. A stereotypical image of the Chinese in the West was filthy and contemptible faces in foul opium dens: a most unfair portrayal, considering the origin of their addiction. Chinese anxious about the state of their country had been tirelessly advocating a ban; so had Western missionaries. Foreign opium imported into China was chiefly produced in British India and shipped solely from British ports. Public opinion on both sides of the globe was overwhelmingly in favour of prohibiting the trade. In mid-1906 the British Parliament debated the issue, and the mood of the country so excited the Chinese minister in London that he wrote home at once: 'If we show we are serious about prohibition, I am certain Britain will be deeply sympathetic and will act in collaboration with us.' Seizing this opportunity, Cixi announced her intention to eradicate opium production and consumption in China within ten years. In the decree she expressed her revulsion towards the drug, and described the damage it was doing to the population. A detailed ten-point plan was drawn up, to enable all people in the empire under the age of sixty to kick the habit. (Those over sixty were deemed to lack the physical strength needed for this strenuous process.) The effect of the edict 'on the nation', observed H. B. Morse, who was in China at the time, 'was electrical'. Farmers stopped cultivation with little resistance. 'Smokers abandoned the habit by millions; it became unfashionable to smoke in public; and the young were constrained not to acquire the habit. Many millions continued, of course, to smoke, but a generation of Chinese is growing up of whom few have acquired this habit . . .'

A request was put to Britain to bring the opium trade to an end. And the British government readily responded. In line with Cixi's ten-year programme, it agreed to restrict opium export from India by one-tenth each year. Both Britain and China regarded this as a 'great moral movement', and each willingly bore a considerable loss of revenue. At the end of ten years the eradication of opium-smoking and production in China had made astounding progress, and the British export of opium had come to a complete stop.

Great changes chased after one another like ocean waves. Chinese who did not live in the Treaty Ports enjoyed many a 'first' in their lives: the first street lighting, first running water, first telephone, first colleges of Western medicine (to one of which Cixi donated 10,000 taels), first sporting event, first museums, first cinemas, first zoo and public park (a former royal park in Beijing) and the first government experimental farm. Many read their first newspapers and magazines, and a pleasurable habit of reading the daily paper was being formed.

Cixi experienced quite a few 'firsts' herself. One day in 1903, she asked Louisa Pierson whether her daughters knew how to take photographs, as it would cause a storm 'to allow a male photographer into the Palace'. Louisa Pierson informed Cixi that one of her sons, Xunling, had studied photography while abroad and had brought back good equipment from Europe – and perhaps he could take pictures of Her Majesty. Although a man, Xunling was Louisa's son and could be treated as 'family'. He became the only photographer ever to take photographs of Cixi.

Later, the Dutch-American painter Hubert Vos claimed to have photographed Cixi, in addition to painting her – a claim that is generally assumed to be true. In fact, there is no record of any kind to support his vaguely told story. Nor does it seem likely, given that he was an adult man, and a foreign man at that. Even Robert Hart, who had served the empress dowager for decades, only had a few formal meetings with her, the longest of which, in 1902, lasted twenty minutes. It was a memorable occasion and Hart recorded it:

> The old lady talked in a sweet feminine voice, and was very complimentary: I said there were others quite ready to take my place, but she rejoined that it was myself she wanted. Among other things she referred to the Coronation [of King Edward VII] and said she hoped His Majesty would enjoy all happiness. Apropos of railway travelling she said with a laugh that she began to think she would enjoy even a foreign tour!

Given her love of travelling and her intense curiosity, Cixi would have liked nothing better than a foreign tour. But she never seriously contemplated the idea, as she judged it unfeasible. Similarly, even though she was the supreme ruler of the empire, she never set foot in the front section of the Forbidden City, or entered the palace through its front gates. She would not challenge such enormously controversial conventions for the sake of gratifying her own desires. Although she must have wished to mix freely with men, and would not have minded at all having a foreign man paint or photograph her,

Cixi would have resisted doing so.* Her restraint and her discrimination were key qualities that enabled her to change the empire as well as rule it. Her judgement as to what should be changed – and when and how it should be done – was crucial to the fact that there was little upheaval throughout her revolution.

When Xunling came to take Cixi's photographs, he had to do so on his knees at first: everyone was obliged to kneel when they engaged the empress dowager's attention. But in this position he was unable to reach the camera on its tripod. Lianying, the head eunuch, brought him a stool to kneel on, but he could not balance himself while handling the camera. Cixi said, 'All right, exempt him from kneeling while he takes the photographs.'

Cixi, now in her late sixties, looked her age in the photographs. These realistic pictures would have made her frown, so before they were presented to her, they were touched up, which was not uncommon in those days. Her face was airbrushed, with the wrinkles erased and puffy bags under her eyes smoothed away. Many years were expunged, leaving the images of a beautiful woman in her bloom. This 'facelift' is unmistakable when comparing the prints in Xunling's own collection (now in the Freer Gallery, Washington DC), which were not worked on, with the prints of the same photographs in the Forbidden City archives.

These touched-up images were not what her mirrors had been telling her for quite some time. Cixi was thrilled when she saw them, and there followed a frenzy of photo-taking. She posed in various postures – in one, putting a flower in her hair, like a coquettish young girl. She changed clothes, jewels and surroundings, and had complicated sets constructed, as if for the stage. She had long wanted to act in an opera, and courtiers had spotted her singing and dancing in the palace grounds when she thought no one was watching. Now she dressed up as Guanyin, the Goddess of Mercy, had court ladies and eunuchs clothed in the costumes of the characters associated with the Goddess, and posed with them on the sets. Her favourite pictures were then enlarged to as big as 75 by 60 centimetres, tastefully coloured and framed, and mounted on the

---

* Hubert Vos's portrait of Cixi, on the other hand, shows more of her character than Katharine Carl's painting. His portrait was most likely based on a photograph of Cixi, taken by Xunling.

walls of her palace, so excited was Cixi by her own younger and prettier looks.

Some large, framed prints were later presented to foreign heads of state, who had written to congratulate her on her seventieth birthday in 1904. These were delivered to the legations with considerable solemnity. American newspapers commented: 'The picture gives her the appearance of forty years instead of seventy.'

The touching-up, enlargement and framing of the pictures were done by the oldest and best-known photographic studio in Beijing, owned by one Ren Jingfeng, who had studied photography in Japan. Ren was soon invited to the court, where he was put in touch with the great Peking Opera actor, Tan Xinpei, a member of the court's Music Department. The actor's biggest fan was the empress dowager, who not only rewarded him handsomely, but also enabled him to command huge fees when he performed outside the court. Now Tan was directed by Ren in China's first film, *The Dingjun Mountain*, showing an episode in a Peking Opera of the same name. This was 1905, and Cixi could reasonably be credited as China's first movie 'executive producer'.

The film was shot in spite of an earlier accident. The British had given Cixi a projector and some silent movies for her birthday the year before. After three reels in the first screening, the motor had exploded. Cixi does not seem to have taken to films. Their appeal to her was limited as there was no soundtrack, which meant no music. But Ren and others went on to make other films, and cinemas showing their work as well as foreign films, including short detective stories, blossomed and percolated into the vast interior.

The news that Cixi had photographs taken with eunuchs in stage costume – at a time when no woman could appear on stage, and to be playful with eunuchs was considered 'improper' – soon became known to her enemies, who seized upon it in an attempt to damage her reputation. From late 1904 to the end of 1905, *Shi-bao*, a newspaper set up by Wild Fox Kang (with his right-hand man, Liang, as the main contributor writing from Japan), carried daily advertisements offering photographs of Cixi for sale. The advertisements, in the name of the paper's sister publishing house owned by a Japanese, Takano Bunjiro, highlighted the fact that she was dressed up in theatrical costume and 'sitting side by side' with her two favourite eunuchs, one being Lianying. This was calculated to arouse public disgust. In addition, the prints were being offered at exceedingly low prices and were marked as discount goods, so as to maximise the insult.

Cixi did nothing about the advertisements, or the publishing house, which had an office in Beijing, a stone's throw from the Forbidden City, as well as in Shanghai. Rather, she turned the table on her enemies by giving a photo of herself with Lianying as a present to a Japanese diplomat.

The impact of the advertisements seems to have been non-existent. Cixi was enjoying considerable popularity. Pearl Buck, the Nobel Laureate for literature, was then living in China among peasants and other ordinary people (her parents were missionaries), and she observed that they 'loved her'. For her seventieth birthday Cixi had decreed that there would be no celebrations. But many still celebrated. In Beijing, outside the Qianmen gate, numerous lanterns of different colours and shapes illuminated the whole area, attracting crowds of spectators and revellers. In Shanghai, Sarah Conger wrote:

> In driving through the streets in the foreign concession of Shanghai, we saw many beautiful decorations in honor of Her Majesty's birthday. The Chinese stores were aglow with brilliant colors; even the Chinese flag was waving, a most unusual thing, as the flag, in China, is used only officially. I never before saw such a departure from old customs . . . Myriads of beautiful lanterns in their almost endless varieties added brilliancy to the many other decorations. The Chinaman proclaimed his loyalty to China and her rulers in such a way that the foreigner could understand that loyalty . . .

For all the dramatic reforms sweeping across China, Cixi introduced very few at court. Rules did relax for the eunuchs, who were allowed to visit bars and theatres outside the palace. But the medieval practice of keeping eunuchs remained – and so, consequently, did the castration of boys for this purpose. There was a moment when Cixi considered abolishing eunuch-keeping, but the eunuchs reacted with a campaign of weeping to get her to change her mind, and she suspended the move. On the whole the court stuck to the old rules, with rigid etiquette and formality. Prescribed costumes for different occasions remained sacrosanct. Arriving at a gathered court, Cixi would with a glance take in all the details of the clothes being worn and would address any errors. In her presence, people continued to stand, if not kneel. On the only occasion when she dined with the ladies of the diplomatic corps, she and the foreign diners were seated, while the Chinese princesses stood. As the banquet proceeded, Sarah Conger asked if the princesses might not be seated, too. Cixi felt obliged to turn to them and, with a wave of her hand, tell them to sit. This was the only time any Chinese (except the emperor) sat down to eat with her. But they did not really eat. An eye-witness observed, 'They sat down in a timid, rather uncomfortable way on the edge of the chair, but did not presume to touch any of the food.' During the dinner, China's minister to Britain interpreted for her, on his knees.

Cixi was especially strict about officials observing etiquette. Every time she travelled between her palaces, designated officials had to kneel at the arrival and departure points to greet her or see her off – even in the rain. One day the rainwater dripping from a kneeling figure was bright red and green, and it turned out that the official was too poor to own a real formal robe for the occasion and had had to wear a painted paper one. On another occasion, after she had bestowed gifts on a large number of officials, they gathered and waited to thank her by going down on their knees. Because of their numbers, they had to perform the ritual in the courtyard where it was raining hard. They waited for more than an hour, while Cixi watched the rain from behind a curtain. When the rain subsided, she ordered the ritual to proceed, during which the officials knelt on the wet ground, spattered with mud.

The obligation to kneel was a nuisance for everyone. Grandees found it unbearable if the audiences were protracted. Eunuchs had knee pads permanently sewn into their trouser legs, as they had to drop to their knees whenever she addressed them, at all places, whether it was on stone floors or rocks. Arthritis of the knees was a common problem for eunuchs.

Cixi understood that it was painful to kneel and would usually curtail the time people had to do so. Once, for the benefit of Katharine Carl, some court painters were summoned to draw chrysanthemums in the fields. As the empress dowager was watching, the painters had to kneel while drawing. Their discomfiture was visible to Cixi, and she told them to pluck some flowers and go and paint at home. For one reception she gave, the Foreign Office official presenting the diplomats, Wu Tingfang, was supposed to kneel. This would have put him in an embarrassing position, as the foreign diplomats he presented would be standing. He would 'look like a dwarf next to foreigners', he complained to Louisa Pierson.

On her advice Cixi exempted him: 'In that case, he doesn't have to kneel.'

Wu was then posted as China's minister to Washington, and led a life of heady freedom, acquiring a reputation as the 'man who enjoyed making blandly insolent remarks at dinner parties'. Upon returning to Beijing, he interpreted for Alice Roosevelt, daughter of President Theodore Roosevelt, when she visited China in 1905 and had an audience with Cixi. Having got used to the American way of treating himself as an equal to anyone, Wu seems to have forgotten that he had to be on his knees to Cixi, or ask beforehand for permission not to kneel. He stood and chatted, quite at ease. Alice wrote:

He stood between us, a little to the side, but suddenly, as the conversation was going on, the Empress said something in a small savage voice, whereat he turned quite gray, and got down on all fours, his forehead touching the ground. The Empress would speak; he would lift his head and say it in English to me; back would go his forehead to the ground while I spoke; up would come his head again while he said it in Chinese to the Empress; then back to the ground would go his forehead again . . . One literally had the feeling that she might at any moment say, 'off with his head,' and that off the head would go.

This was in fact the time when Wu was co-heading the empire's legal reforms – and enjoying Cixi's esteem. In those years, with her blessing, even rather conservative governors banned kneeling as part of the etiquette in their provinces. But Cixi retained it in the court. At stake for her was the god-like sacredness of the throne, which was the one thing that gave the throne its hold over the vast empire. Kneeling was the manifestation and reinforcement of that sacredness, without which – without all those bent knees – the throne, and even the empire, might falter.

To hold on to this symbol of total submission in an increasingly enlightened empire, Cixi sacrificed her curiosity and never rode in a car. She had been presented with one by General Yuan, who had stepped into Earl Li's shoes in ways more than one. Not only had he inherited the earl's jobs and role as a close adviser to the empress dowager, but, like the earl, he was a talented gift-giver. The car he bought for her was lacquered in imperial yellow, with a dragon motif and a throne-like seat within. Cixi longed for a ride, particularly as she had just had fun riding a tricycle, also a present from the General.

But with a car there was an insurmountable problem: it was impossible for the chauffeur to operate the wheel while kneeling, or even standing. The chauffeur would have to sit down, right in front of her. The car remained the only modern device that was interesting and available to the empress dowager which she did not try.

29 The Vote!
(1905–8)

C IXI was aware that the throne could not be sustained for long by symbols. Something more solid was needed to ensure its survival. There was the option of shutting down her revolution and winding back the clock, but she rejected it and chose to press forward. In 1905 she set the ball rolling for the most fundamental of all her reforms: to turn China into a constitutional monarchy (*li-xian*) with an elected parliament. She hoped that a constitution would set in concrete the legitimacy of the Qing dynasty, while enabling a large part of the population – most of all Han Chinese – to participate in the affairs of the state. This historic move, involving an election with as wide an electoral base as in the West, meant the introduction of the vote into China.

Cixi was convinced that China was unable to do as well as Western countries because there was not the same sense of connection between the ruled and the rulers. 'In foreign countries,' she remarked, 'the ruled [*xia*] feel connected with the ruling [*shang*]. This is why they are so formidable.' Only the vote could produce this connection. From her vantage point, she saw clearly the benefit of a parliamentary monarchy such as Britain. Once, talking about Queen Victoria, Cixi observed, 'England is one of [the] great powers of the world, but this has not been brought about by Queen Victoria's absolute rule. She had the able men of parliament back of her [*sic*] at all times and of course they discussed everything until the best result was obtained . . .' In China, 'I have 400,000,000 people, all dependent on my judgment. Although I have the Grand Council to consult with . . . anything of an important nature I must decide myself.' Proud though she was of her own abilities, she conceded that even she had made

339

a disastrous mistake, in the case of the Boxers. Her adopted son had been calamitous. Indeed, she could think of no one at court remotely capable of succeeding as an absolute monarch, especially in the modern world.

At the time, the idea of a constitutional monarchy was very much in the air and some newspapers were promoting it. Among them was the mainstream paper in Tianjin, the *Ta Kung Pao*, whose editor was a Manchu who had married an Aisin-Gioro. As a member of the royal family, the editor's wife was in and out of the court and wrote a lively column about court life. (It is an indication of Cixi's tolerance that the editor was a Catholic, and the paper professed allegiance to Emperor Guangxu and urged Cixi to retire.) An 'Opinion' article in 1903 remarked that 'the process of political reform has always gone from absolute monarchy to constitutional monarchy and then on to democracy . . . If we want to reform China's political system, a constitutional monarchy is our only route.' In April 1905, the newspaper invited essays on the theme 'What must we do most urgently to revive China?' Many contributors contended that they must 'end autocracy and build a constitutional monarchy'. Endorsing this view and addressing other proposed priorities like 'developing industry, commerce and education', an editorial argued that 'without changing our political system, all these, even if developed, would not have a solid foundation to rest on, and there would still be the chasm between the ruling and the ruled . . .' In reaching her decision, Cixi may well have taken heed of press comment.

On 16 July 1905, Cixi announced that a Commission would be sent to a number of Western countries to 'study their political systems'. She stressed to the Commissioners that their job was to study how the different parliamentary governments were organised, 'so we can put a suitable system into practice when you come back'. By seizing the initiative and commencing the mammoth task 'from the apex of the pyramid', as a contemporary Western observer put it, Cixi was able to protect the interests of her dynasty. Heading the Commission was Duke Zaize, a direct descendant of the Aisin-Gioro family, who was married to another daughter of Cixi's brother, Duke Guixiang. He and other grandees involved in the project would ensure that no harm would come to the Manchus in the new system. They would also help Cixi to convince other Manchus, who feared for their future.

The Commission was divided into two groups, and would travel to Britain, France, Germany, Denmark, Sweden, Norway, Austria, Russia, Holland, Belgium, Switzerland and Italy, as well as Japan and

America. On 24 September, Duke Zaize and his large entourage of carefully selected assistants boarded a train at Beijing railway station to begin their journey. At that moment, Wu Yue, a Republican dedicated to overthrowing the Manchu dynasty, detonated a bomb in the duke's carriage, wounding him and more than a dozen other passengers. Three were killed, including the bomber himself. Wu Yue was China's first suicide bomber. Cixi, in tears when she comforted members of the Commission, reaffirmed her determination to continue the enterprise. The men departed later that year, having been told that they carried her 'high hopes' with them. While they were away, a Constitution Office was set up to research the different kinds of parliamentary monarchy, with the goal of devising the constitution best suited to China.

The Commissioners returned from their travels in summer 1906. Knowing how eagerly the empress dowager was waiting, Duke Zaize went straight from the train station to the Summer Palace and presented his application for an audience. Cixi saw him at the crack of dawn the following morning, and the audience lasted for two hours. In addition to seeing him again, she had audiences with other Commissioners. They wrote reports, which extended over many dozens of volumes and were presented to the Constitution Office. In an epoch-making proclamation on 1 September 1906, in her own name, Empress Dowager Cixi announced her goal of establishing a constitutional monarchy, with an elected parliament, which would replace the existing absolute monarchy. Western countries, she said, were rich and strong because of this political system, in which 'the public participate in state affairs' and 'the creation and spending of the country's wealth, together with the planning and execution of its political affairs, are open to all'. She made it clear that, in the Chinese version, 'the executive power resides with the court, while the public has its say in state affairs'. She asked the population to 'be public spirited, pursue the road of evolution' and make the transition in an 'orderly, conservative and peaceful manner'. She bid them strive to become 'qualified citizens': the people were now 'citizens of the country': *guo-min*.

The proclamation generated tremendous waves. Newspapers printed special editions devoted to the subject. When he read about it in Japan, Liang Qichao, Wild Fox Kang's closest colleague, felt that a new epoch had arrived and immediately set about organising a political party – one of many political organisations that began to spring up. Cixi's government engaged in a huge amount of preparatory work: drafting laws, spreading educational opportunities, informing the public about the new political system, founding the police and training them in how to keep order the modern way, and so on. Two years later, on 27 August 1908, a draft outline of the constitution was published with Cixi's endorsement. This historic document combined the political traditions of the East and the West. Continuing the age-old oriental custom, it gave real political power to the monarch, who would still head the government and retain the final say. Parliament would draw up laws and proposals, but all were subject to the approval of the monarch, who would then issue them. The inviolable power of the throne was stressed in the draft outline, not least through its opening line: 'The Qing dynasty shall rule over the Qing empire for ever, and shall be honoured through all ages.' Drawing from Western practices, the people were guaranteed a number of fundamental rights, including the 'freedoms of speech, writing, publication, assembly and association' – and the right to be 'members of parliament as long as they were qualified by law'. A parliament was to be founded, where elected representatives of the people would have a significant say in state affairs, including the budget. The draft outline omitted to say what would happen in the inevitable event of a clash between the throne and parliament. But the drafters' letter to Cixi indicated a solution: 'the monarch and the people would both make concessions'.

A Preliminary Assembly, *Zi-zheng-yuan*, had been set up in 1907 to act as a transitional parliament. It spent ten months working out a draft regulation for the founding of the future parliament, including the composition of its members. The document was approved and announced by Cixi on 8 July 1908. Roughly half of the members would sit in an Upper House and would be appointed by the throne from these sections of society: Manchu princes; Manchu and Han aristocrats; Mongolian, Tibetan and Hui (Muslim) aristocrats; medium-rank officials, eminent scholars and the highest taxpayers. The other half, in the Lower House, would be elected by members of the Provincial Assemblies, which were being set up across China, and whose members would themselves be directly elected by the provinces' citizens. A draft Electoral Regulation, for the election of the Provincial Assemblies, was made public by Cixi with her endorsement on 22 July 1908.

In this great historical document, the franchise was based on contemporary Western practice. In Britain, for instance, the vote was extended to adult males who owned property or paid at least ten pounds in rent a year, so the electorate comprised about 60 per cent of the British adult male population. For the Chinese electorate (male and over twenty-five), the property qualification was defined as owning 5,000 yuan in business capital or property. Alternative qualifications were added: men who had run public projects for more than three years with distinction; graduates of modern secondary schools or higher institutions; literati from the old educational system; and so on. All these people could vote, even if they were poor and without property. Mentioning their deviation from the current Western models, the writers of the Regulation argued that if property-owning were the sole qualification, people would be encouraged only to seek profit and wealth.

The eligibility of parliamentary candidates also largely followed Western practice, except that they had to be at least thirty years old (as in Japan), which, according to Confucius, was the age of full maturity. One group of men excluded from standing was unique to China: primary school teachers. The argument was that they, of all people, bore the responsibility for training citizens. Their energy must therefore be totally devoted to this worthiest cause. Among those disqualified from voting (and standing) were officials of the province and their advisers, as they were the administrators, who had to be separated from the legislators in parliament, in order to prevent corruption. Military men were also ruled out, because the army must not be involved in politics.

Cixi approved the Electoral Regulation and asked for a timetable to be set for elections and the calling of parliament. Prince Ching, head of the Grand Council, who oversaw the drafting of the Regulation, argued against a specific schedule. Their task was unprecedented and daunting, and unforeseen problems were bound to emerge, he advised – not least the danger of leaving open loopholes that would enable bad characters to seize power. Cixi vetoed Prince Ching's recommendation. Without a time frame, there would be no momentum and the whole thing might not even happen. Many officials feared and opposed this particular change, finding it impracticable, and unthinkable, in so vast and populous a country, where levels of education were so low. Without a deadline they would simply be paying lip service. Only a timetable could spur them on and bring the venture to fruition.

A nine-year timetable was drawn up and endorsed, together with a list of work to be done and objectives to be achieved in each of the years. The list included preparations for the elections; law-making; a census; a taxation programme – and the specification of the rights, duties and financing of the throne. Literacy was a prominent issue. The percentage of the population who could read and write (in Chinese) at the most elementary level at the time was below 1 per cent. The writing of new textbooks, together with a drive for modern education, would begin in the first year. By the end of the seventh year, 1 per cent of the population must qualify as 'literate', and by the end of the ninth the target was 5 per cent. The fulfilment of each objective was made the responsibility of a specific ministry, and Cixi had the time-table inscribed on plaques and hung in government offices. In her decree she invoked 'conscience' and the 'omnipotent Heaven' to warn sluggish officials. Her passion and determination were in no doubt. If all went according to plan, in the ninth year after 1908 millions upon millions of Chinese would be able to vote. (Voters in Britain in 1908 numbered more than seven million.) The Chinese would for the first time in their history have a say in state affairs. W. A. P. Martin, the American missionary who had spent decades in China, exclaimed, 'What a commotion will the ballot-box excite! How suddenly will it arouse the dormant intellect of a brainy race!'

In Cixi's version of constitutional monarchy, the Chinese electorate did not have the same power as their Western counterparts. But she was bringing the country out of unquestionable autocracy and opening the business of government to the ordinary people – citizens, as they were now called. She was restricting her own power and introducing a negotiating forum into Chinese politics, where the monarch and the representatives of the people, including different interest groups, would confer, bargain and, doubtless, fight verbal battles. While Cixi lived, given her sense of fairness and her penchant for consensus, there was every chance that the wish of the people would continue to gain ground.

Conceding that 'it is premature to speculate' on the outcome of the empress dowager's initiative, Martin had faith in her. 'During her lifetime she could be counted on to carry forward the cause she had so ardently espoused. She grasped the reins with a firm hand; and her courage was such that she did not hesitate to drive the chariot of state over many a new and untried road.' All in all, he remarked: 'It is little more than eight years since the restoration, as the return of the Court in January, 1902, may be termed. In this period, it is safe to assert that more sweeping reforms have been decreed in China than were ever enacted in a half-century by any other country, if one except Japan, whose example the Chinese profess to follow, and France, in the Revolution, of which Macaulay remarks that "they changed everything – from the rites of religion to the fashion of a shoe-buckle."'

Cixi's 'important innovations or ameliorations', wrote Martin, went all the way back to the moment she seized power, and they 'made the reign of the Empress Dowager the most brilliant in the history of the Empire. The last eight years have been uncommonly prolific of reforms; but the tide began to turn after the peace of Peking in 1860. Since that date every step in the adoption of modern methods was taken during the regency of that remarkable woman, which dated from 1861 to 1908.' Out of those forty-seven years, Cixi effectively ruled for thirty-six (her son for two and her adopted son for nine). Given how much she had achieved during her period in power, and the colossal odds she had faced – and overcome – it does not seem far-fetched to expect that suffrage would have been introduced into China in 1916, if·the empress dowager had lived.

30 Coping with Insurgents, Assassins and the Japanese (1902–8)

A contemporary Han official remarked that Cixi's revolution was 'advantageous for China, but hugely disadvantageous for the Manchu government'. Indeed, many Manchus were anxious about what was happening. It was only Cixi's authority that made them put their faith, and fate, in her hands. She herself was seeking to preserve her dynasty – not least by introducing her version of constitutional monarchy. But in the end, the exclusively Manchu throne proved to be her Achilles heel. Although she took many steps to dismantle Han–Manchu segregation, she wished the throne to remain Manchu. The decree that lifted the ban on intermarriage in 1902 had added that the imperial consorts should still only be chosen from among the Manchus (and the Mongols). There were signs that she would eventually bow to the inevitability of an ethnically inclusive throne, but she never quite reached that point in her lifetime.

Cixi had a strong sense of Manchu identity, made stronger by the fact that the Manchu were such a small minority, always at risk of being overwhelmed by the Han. To her court ladies, mostly Manchu, she always talked of 'we Manchu'. Although she could not speak the Manchu language she compensated by sticking religiously to other outward signs of belonging: Manchu customs were unfailingly observed in the court, and Manchu clothes and hairstyles were worn without exception. Her diplomats, mostly Han, wished they could swap their Manchu costume for Western suits, but their request was rejected. Their desire to be rid of the queue was not even mentioned. Cixi was not prejudiced against the Han; indeed, she promoted Han officials in an unprecedented way, appointing them to key positions previously reserved for the Manchu. Nor did the Han have fewer privileges or lower standards of living. It was simply the Manchu throne that she desperately wanted to preserve.

It was for this reason that for a long time Cixi resisted allowing first-rate Han statesmen into the heart of the court. Earl Li, for all his unique relationship with Cixi and his singular importance to the empire, was never a member of the Grand Council. Indeed, the Council did not have the cream of Han officials until as late as 1907, when Cixi finally appointed General Yuan and Viceroy Zhang. She had, on several occasions, not least in spring 1898 when her Reforms began, contemplated appointing Viceroy Zhang to the Grand Council, but had always decided against the idea, fearing that the throne itself might be lost to this supremely able man. By clinging to the notion that the throne must be occupied by a Manchu, Cixi undermined the desirability of a parliamentary monarchy and made Republicanism an attractive alternative.

Sun Yat-sen, loosely the leader of the Republican movement, was the most persistent advocate of military action to overthrow the Manchu dynasty. He had tried to organise an armed uprising in 1895 and had been active in the new century with a series of insurrections. Their scale was small, but Cixi treated them with the utmost seriousness. She berated provincial chiefs for underestimating 'these flames that could spark off a prairie fire', and cable after cable urged them to 'extinguish them; do not let them spread'.

Assassination was very much a part of Republican tactics, as demonstrated by the suicide bomber on the train in 1905. Two years later a local police chief in Zhejiang province in eastern China, Xu Xilin, gunned down at close range the governor of the province, a Manchu named Enming, who had come to inspect the police college. Enming had regarded Xilin as a kindred reformist spirit and had plucked him out of obscurity and entrusted him with the police force. By the traditional ethical code, Xilin ought to be grateful to his benefactor; but he killed him instead – because the governor was Manchu. After his arrest, Xilin declared in his testimony, which was published in the newspapers, that his goal was 'to slaughter every Manchu, to the last one'. He was beheaded. Troops loyal to the dead governor ripped out his heart as a sacrificial offering – a grisly old ritual symbolising ultimate revenge. Decades earlier, the assassin of Viceroy Ma had been subjected to the same treatment.

The killing of the governor was part of a planned insurrection, one of whose leaders was a woman. Once a student in Japan and now a teacher in a girls' school back in the province, Miss Qiu Jin was beautiful and elegant – and was one of the pioneers of feminism in China. Defying prescribed behaviour for women, she paraded herself in public, dressed in men's clothes and sporting a walking stick. She started a feminist newspaper and gave public speeches that won applause 'like hundreds of spring thunders', wrote admiring journalists. Violent action appealed to her, and she attempted to make bombs for the insurrection, in the process of which her hands were injured. Miss Qiu was arrested, and executed in a public place – but before dawn.

If this had happened just a few years earlier, the average man would not have raised an eyebrow. Summary execution of armed rebels was taken for granted. But this time a barrage of press condemnation greeted the execution. They asserted that the weapons found with Miss Qiu had been planted and her confession that had been made public was faked. Even the most moderate newspapers described her as being completely innocent, a victim of a vendetta by local conservative forces. They heaped eulogies on her, credited beautiful poems to her and turned her into a heroine – an image that has lasted to this day. Her comrade, the police chief, also enjoyed almost unqualified sympathy. The press asked how it came about that his heart had been cut out, given that barbaric forms of execution had been outlawed and torture in interrogation banned. The press flexed its muscles and shaped public opinion: its naming and condemning of the officials involved in the Miss Qiu case turned those involved into hate figures. When some were transferred to other regions, the authorities there declined to accept them. The county chief who sentenced Miss Qiu to death hanged himself under the pressure.

The newly gained influence and confidence turned the press into an awesome force, especially as a watchdog over the government. Cixi never attempted to suppress it, in spite of its overwhelmingly anti-Manchu sentiment (it had not a word of sympathy, for example, for the slain Manchu governor). However, she responded to violent actions with utter ruthlessness. After receiving detailed reports about the case of Miss Qiu, which showed unmistakably that she had been one of the insurrection leaders, Cixi endorsed the handling of her case, and continued with other tough measures to do with stamping out insurgency. As a result, while she was alive, the *New York Times* reported in 1908: 'no general disorders are apprehended. China is quieter now than at any time since 1900.' Still, Republicanism remained potent, waiting for the moment when she was gone.

Fending off the Republicans with one arm, with the other Cixi wrestled with Wild Fox Kang. After his failed plot to kill her in 1898, Kang had fled to Japan. Under heavy pressure from the Qing government and, in particular, from Viceroy Zhang, whom the Japanese were keen to cultivate, Tokyo soon had to ask him to leave. But the Wild Fox was not cast into the wilderness. He left Japan to travel the world, accompanied by a Chinese-speaking Japanese intelligence man, Nakanishi Shigetaro, who had trained in Japan's espionage institute, which was specifically targeting China. He now acted as Kang's interpreter and bodyguard – and contact man with Tokyo. Kang left behind in Japan his disciple and right-hand man, Liang Qichao, who carried out Kang's orders. Overseas, Kang continued to pursue the restoration of Emperor Guangxu. This was also what Japan wanted, as it was the easiest way to control China. The Wild Fox thus worked in conjunction with, if not entirely on behalf of, Japan.

Wild Fox Kang now organised repeated attempts on Cixi's life, and a series of assassins sailed from Japan to Beijing. One of them was Shen Jin, who had embarked on such a mission in 1900 with a pirate gang. But then their whole enterprise had failed and he had gone into exile. In 1903, he arrived in the capital to try again, and made friends with senior policemen and eunuchs. News of the would-be assassin got to the ears of Cixi's devotees and he was arrested.

A public decree charged Mr Shen with involvement in an armed rebellion and ordered his immediate execution. As Emperor Guangxu's birthday fell within that month, and a Qing convention enjoined that the birthday month should be free of public executions, the decree instructed the Ministry of Punishments to carry out the death sentence in prison by bastinado. This medieval form of execution, which meant beating the convicted to death, was normally reserved for offending eunuchs behind the thick gates and walls of the Forbidden City, and the state prison did not possess the required equipment or expertise. Long wooden bats had to be specially made, and inexperienced executioners took quite some time to end the life of Mr Shen, who was a big man with a tough constitution. The story reached the newspapers, and the horrific detail revolted readers, especially Westerners. The English-language

North China Herald called the execution 'a monstrous perversion of even Chinese justice' and denounced Cixi directly: 'only she whose word is law would have dared to do it'. The British Legation boycotted Cixi's reception that autumn.★

Cixi had issued the decree without a second thought, just as she had ordered other bastinados to punish eunuchs over the years. Now she recognised that this cruel punishment was unacceptable in modern times, and she learned a lesson. Legal reforms soon banned the bastinado, and she publicly declared that she loathed (*tong-hen*) torture, including beating with wooden bats. In the following year, June 1904, she amnestied all those who had been involved in Wild Fox Kang's 1898 plot and 1900 armed revolt. Those in prison were released, and the exiles could now return home. Political offenders were officially reduced to three people, all of them in exile: Wild Fox Kang, Liang Qichao and Sun Yat-sen. There were discussions about pardoning Liang.

She tightened her security, and the places frequented by eunuchs were closely watched. In November 1904, Wild Fox Kang sent over a high-level assassination group from Japan, one key member of which, Luo, was a bomb operator. (He also practised hypnotism, which he seemed to think might be of some use.) Their plan was to plant bombs in places frequented by Cixi, ideally in the little steamer in which she travelled between the city and the Summer Palace. As the pilot of the steamer was the only person on board who was employed from outside the palace, they tried to secure that post for the bomb operator. But while he was perfecting the bombs, which involved travelling between China and Japan, Luo was captured on the coast in July 1905 and was swiftly executed on the spot. The incident was successfully hushed up. Cixi had learned to have her assassins eliminated in secret, and this was easier to achieve in the provinces, where there was less press

★ It is often claimed that Mr Shen was executed because he was an outspoken journalist. In fact, there is no sign that he wrote anything for any newspaper or other publication. His role in journalism was restricted to obtaining a document that has been referred to as the 'Sino-Russian Secret Treaty', which was then published in Japanese newspapers. This was actually a list of demands made by Russia to Beijing in the aftermath of the Boxer mayhem, in exchange for withdrawing troops from Manchuria. Beijing never accepted the demands, and there was no treaty, 'secret' or otherwise. (The only treaty had been in 1896.) The Japanese wanted this document to stoke anti-Russian fervour. Even so, passing this document to the Japanese was not the cause of Mr Shen's execution. His 'crime' was his role in the armed rebellion of 1900. Cixi wanted him dead urgently because she knew he was in Beijing to try to kill her again.

Putting a flower in her Manchu-style coiffure. Cixi took great care of her appearance. She designed her clothes and jewellery and supervised the making of cosmetics such as rouge, perfume and soap. In the background, apples from her orchard were on display for their subtle fragrance.

(*Above*) The only photo in which Cixi is smiling. She actually liked laughing, but would switch off her smiles and assume a serious air when she went to work − or faced the camera.

(FACING PAGE)
On a barge on the lake of the Sea Palace, amidst lotus flowers.
(*Above*) With court ladies and eunuchs. Louisa Pierson far right; fifth from right Imperial Concubine Jade, Pearl's sister. All had to stand in Cixi's presence, who alone was sitting.

(*Below*) Wearing opera costumes. Cixi was passionate about music, and helped make Peking Opera the national opera of China.

(*Above*) Leading the first group of court ladies to the American Legation for dinner in 1902 was Cixi's adopted daughter, the Imperial Princess, acting as her representative. Seated in the middle, with Sarah Conger next to her.
(*Below*) The courtyard outside the dining-room of the Congers. In the summer, the open-air court and the whole building were covered by a giant 'mosquito net', made of reed matting by ingenious eunuchs. Sarah Conger wrote:
'The air is fresh, and the beautiful trees, potted plants, shrubs, many flowers, and delightful guests make the day truly a happy one.'

Cixi among four young, good-looking eunuchs, Lady-in-waiting Der Ling to the side.
Such physical intimacy was bound to lead to sexual desires in her younger years. In fact
she fell in love with a eunuch, An Dehai, when she was in her early thirties. He was beheaded
in 1869, and she suffered a breakdown.

(*Left*) On her deathbed in 1908, Cixi made her two-year-old great-nephew, Puyi (standing), the next emperor, and his father, Zaifeng (seated holding Puyi's brother), the Regent.

(*Above*) Sun Yat-sen (centre), known as the 'Father' of Republican China, had tried repeatedly to overthrow the Manchu dynasty by military means.

(*Above*) Cixi's funeral. Brooke Astor, American philanthropist, was a child in Beijing and watched the procession with her family from the city wall: 'All day it passed beneath us through the gate. There were Buddhist and Taoist priests in white robes and Buddhist lamas in yellow with red sashes. There were endless bands of eunuchs dressed in white, who tossed paper money in the air (for the Empress's use on her way to heaven) ... There were twenty-four white camels, with yellow brocade tents on their backs ... and a whole company of white ponies ... there were papier-mâché replicas of all the Empress's palaces ... All this passed accompanied by the cries of the mourners, who tore their hair and beat their chests to the clashing of cymbals.'
The colossal palanquin was covered with yellow brocade embroidered with phoenixes.
When it passed by, all Westerners rose and took off their hats.

The Eastern Mausoleums of the Qing monarchs outside Beijing, where Cixi was buried with her husband and her son. In 1928, an unruly Republican army unit broke into her tomb to plunder the jewels that were buried with her. Her corpse was left exposed.

scrutiny than in the capital. The Wild Fox helped her cover it up, as he did not want it known that he was masterminding assassinations.

The death of Luo the bomb operator was a major setback for the Wild Fox. But the rest of the group continued to work under his old friend and bodyguard, Tiejun. In summer 1906, Tiejun and a fellow conspirator were arrested. He admitted straight away that he was in Beijing on the order of Kang to assassinate Cixi. The two men were not delivered to the Ministry of Punishments, as they should have been, according to legal procedure. In that case information about them would be open to the public – and to the press. So instead they were taken to General Yuan's garrison in Tianjin, where they could be court-martialled away from the public eye. Cixi feared that, in an open trial, the men would simply defend themselves by pronouncing that they were only doing what the emperor wanted them to do.

In Tianjin the two captives were escorted to separate barracks, not in shackles and not tortured, according to eye-witnesses. The barracks were under orders to treat them like VIPs, decorating their rooms with silk brocade and supplying them with lavish meals. Tiejun, a fine-looking man in his forties, wore European-style clothes: a white suit and a matching white hat. As he sweltered in the summer heat, the garrison arranged for tailors to work overnight to make him a change of clothes. The officer in charge asked him what sort of material he would like for his outer garments. He specified a kind of expensive silk, of which one side was black and shimmering and the other brown and matt.

There was a tradition that people about to be executed were given special treatment. The day before the execution they were customarily given a lavish meal. On the execution ground, as Algernon Freeman-Mitford (grandfather of the Mitford sisters) observed when he was residing in Beijing: 'Nothing could exceed the kindness of the officials, one and all, to the condemned men. They were giving them smokes out of their pipes, tea, and wine; even the wretched murderer, who was struggling and fighting between two soldiers, was only asked to "be quiet, be quiet," in spite of all provocation . . . I was specially struck by the excessive kindness of the soldiery to the criminals.'

Tiejun knew that his treatment was a prelude to execution. But he chatted and joked, showing not a hint of unease. The sentence of death arrived on 1 September in the form of a coded cable from General Yuan, who had gone to Beijing after interrogating his prisoners. The cable ordered the barracks to execute the men immediately and then confirm by return cable within one hour. In Tiejun's case, the court-martial judge showed him the cable and offered him the option of taking his own life. Tiejun asked for poison and died a painful death. He was buried in a nearby unmarked mass grave for executed criminals. The barracks were told to say to anyone who enquired that he had died of a sudden sickness.

Ironically, it was on the same day that Cixi proclaimed her intention to establish a constitutional monarchy. General Yuan had gone to Beijing to help draft the proclamation, and his order for the conspirators to die followed several audiences with the empress dowager. There is little doubt that it was Cixi who authorised the death sentences.

The death of Tiejun was only reported in one newspaper and drew little attention. As in the case of the bomb operator, Tiejun's own master, Wild Fox Kang, had as much incentive to keep the whole thing secret as General Yuan or Cixi did. The fact that Tiejun took his own life made a difference. He had been cooperative because he had actually changed his mind about his mission. In a letter to Kang before his arrest, he had asked the Wild Fox to stop pressing him to carry out his task, saying that they should abandon assassination and, instead, try to assist Cixi in her reforms. On the day before his capture, he had written to friends: 'Don't make any move . . . use peaceful means from now on . . .' But he was not reprieved. Perhaps he would not collaborate and inform on his co-conspirators? Or perhaps Cixi was unwilling to take chances.

She was not paranoid, though. The route she took between the palaces remained the same. One snowy day, travelling in a sedan-chair from the Summer Palace to the city, one of her chair-bearers slipped and threw her to the ground. Alive to rumours of assassins, her entourage was panic-stricken, fearing this was part of some deadly plot. 'See if she is still alive,' cried terrified court ladies, and her lady-in-waiting, Der Ling, rushed to her side. She found Cixi 'sitting there composedly giving orders to the chief eunuch not to punish this chair-bearer, for he was not to blame, the stones being wet and very slippery'.* There

---

* Der Ling went on to describe the scene more fully: head eunuch Lianying advised that the chair-bearer must be seen to be punished, as this was the rule. 'After saying this, he turned his head to the beaters (these beaters, carrying bamboo sticks, went everywhere with the Court, for such occasions as this) and said: "Give him eighty blows on his back." This poor victim, who was kneeling on the muddy ground, heard the order. The beaters took him about a hundred yards away from us, pushed him down and started to do their duty. It did not take very long to give the eighty blows and, much to my surprise, this man got up, after receiving the punishment, as if nothing had happened to him. He looked just as calm as could be.' Clearly, the beaters just went through the motions, knowing that the empress dowager was not angry with him. Eunuchs who made mistakes punishable by thrashing were not always so lucky. Many took to wearing rubber mats around their backsides, just in case.

is no evidence that Cixi ever punished anyone purely on suspicion that they were involved in an assassination conspiracy.

Japan, where the assassins were based, was the focus of Cixi's mistrust. Her dread intensified after 1905, when Japan emerged victoriously in the Russo-Japanese War.

Russia had occupied parts of Manchuria during the Boxer turmoil in 1900, taking advantage of the fact that mobs had assaulted some Russians there. According to the Russian politician and diplomat, Count Witte, 'On the day when the news of the rebellion reached the capital, Minister of War Kuropatkin came to see me at my office in the Ministry of Finances. He was beaming with joy.' And he proceeded to tell the count, 'I am very glad. This will give us an excuse for seizing Manchuria.' After the Boxer Protocol was signed, foreign troops withdrew from China, but the Russians refused to leave Manchuria − which Count Witte called 'treacherous'. Japan had long coveted the place itself and went to war against Russia. During the war, fought on Chinese soil by two foreign powers, Cixi declared China to be neutral. It was a humiliating position, but she had no better alternative. She prayed for minimal damage to her empire, in her private chapel accessed by way of hidden stairs behind her bed. When Japan won the war, many Chinese felt elated, as though Japan's victory were theirs. A 'small' Asiatic state had defeated a big European power and shattered the assumption that Europeans were superior to Asians, and the White race to the Yellow. Japan was glorified to an unprecedented degree. But for Cixi, Japanese victory only raised the spectre that, with its new confidence and strength, Japan would soon turn a predatory eye on China. This sense of impending crisis gave her an added impetus to transform the country into a constitutional monarchy, and her mind was made up right after the Japanese win in 1905. She hoped that the population would be more patriotic as *citizens*.

Her apprehensions about Japan were well justified. Japan quickly embarked on a series of diplomatic offensives to gain the powers' connivance in its designs on China, and signed deals with Britain, France and even Russia. Japanese diplomats intensified their persuasion campaign among Chinese officials and newspaper owners and editors, selling the notion that the two Asian countries should really form a 'union'. Many listened favourably, even though Japan was bound to dominate such a union, in reality if not in name. Chinese who had been to Japan were impressed by what they saw: 'the tidiness of the streets, the wellbeing of the people, the honesty of the merchants, and the work ethic of the average man'. It was also well known among European diplomats that Japan was spending the equivalent of six to eight million German marks a year (roughly two to three million taels) cultivating useful people, with 'the ultimate goal of moving the emperor of Japan to Beijing', at least figuratively. Confidently, some Japanese asked the rhetorical question: 'Why can't 50 million Japanese do what 8 million Manchus had done [to the Chinese]?'

Cixi had no desire to allow Tokyo to dominate her empire. Nor did she have any illusion that Japanese domination would make China a better place. In Korea, which Japan had put under its 'protection' after it defeated China in 1894–5, Japanese rule was brutal. At a time when the Chinese press was enjoying unfettered freedom, the Korean press was strictly censored to eradicate any hint of anti-Japanese sentiment. An outspoken newspaper editor, Yang Ki-Tak, who was editing a British-owned Korean-language paper, was arrested and confined to a cell that was 'so crowded that he could not lie down yet whose ceiling was too low that he could not stand up'. After a few weeks he had been reduced to a skeleton. The British Consul-General in Korea, Henry Cockburn, was shocked and went to protest to a senior Japanese official. The official was wholly unmoved and told Cockburn that if he 'persisted in dwelling on so trivial a side issue, it must be because [he] was inspired by an unfriendly wish to interpose obstacles in the Japanese path'. Outraged by the incident and appalled that Britain was ignoring the brutality of Japanese rule, Cockburn resigned, cutting short a promising diplomatic career.

Cixi had no automatic preference for the yellow Japanese over the white Europeans. Skin colour did not preoccupy her and she was not given to racial prejudice. Her foreign friends included white Americans – Sarah Conger and Katharine Carl – the half-American, half-Chinese Louisa Pierson, and Uchida Kōsai, the wife of the Japanese minister.

Her wariness towards Japan did not push the empress dowager into the arms of any other power, as it might have done. Her government declined to have any foreign adviser for the throne, although it employed many Japanese and Western advisers in the ministries and provinces. In 1906, the German Kaiser, Wilhelm II, sent her a message via the departing Chinese minister in Berlin, offering to form 'an *Entente Cordiale*, which would *guarantee* the most important parts of China' in the event of a Japanese attack. Cixi did not reply. After experiencing Russia's treachery she had no illusion about any such guarantees. Least of all did she have any trust in the Kaiser, who had, after all, spearheaded the scramble for China. The Kaiser's expression of concern was itself offensive to her, as he called a Japan–China union the 'yellow peril'. The Kaiser would soon declare to a *New York Times* journalist: 'the control of China by Japan . . . is sharply and bitterly antagonistic to the white man's civilization. That would be [the] worst calamity . . . The future belongs to [the] white race; it does not belong to the yellow nor the black nor the olive-colored. It belongs to [the] blond man . . .'*

Cixi's total silence perplexed and frustrated the Kaiser – 'It's a year now. But nothing has been done. We must start working now! At once! Hurry up! . . . I explained to them a year ago . . . Obviously, their time is not money.' And 'China is so slow. They put everything off and then put it off again . . .' The Kaiser tried to get America to sign up to his plan – and America was the only foreign country in which Cixi entertained a little hope. In late 1907, she received two pieces of encouraging news. America was returning the outstanding part of the Boxer Indemnity, and it was dispatching a major fleet into the Pacific. Seeing the proof of America's friendliness towards China and its obvious intention to rival Japan, Cixi decided to send an emissary to America to explore possibilities to forge closer links, while conveying thanks for the return of the indemnity. The emissary would then visit Germany and other European countries. But the return of the indemnity was delayed and the emissary did not depart for a year. The fact that Cixi neither instructed her minister in Washington to talk about the Kaiser's proposed *Entente*, nor dispatched a special emissary for this purpose, suggests that she did not regard it as a real possibility. America would not go to war with Japan on behalf of China; it was more likely to sacrifice China's interest for its own. Indeed, before long, America also signed a deal with Japan, the Root–Takahira Agreement, by which America endorsed Japan's dominance in southern Manchuria, in return for Japan's acquiescence to America's occupation of Hawaii and the Philippines.[†]

★

---

* The italics and square brackets in the Kaiser's comments are in the original quotes. The journalist also wrote that during the interview, 'His Majesty's face flushed and he lifted his arm, his fist clinched [clenched] in air [*sic*]. Between set teeth with his face close to mine, he exclaimed . . .'

† Just over three decades later, with its wings fully fledged, Japan launched a surprise strike on the US base in Pearl Harbor, Hawaii, before invading the Philippines.

In summer 1907, Japan all but completely annexed Korea. The Korean king was forced to abdicate in favour of his son: he had not been quite obedient enough to his Japanese 'adviser' – none other than former Prime Minister Itō Hirobumi. A new agreement between Korea and Japan now made Itō the Resident-General, and spelt out that the Korean king could not make any decision without his authorisation. Itō was to be assassinated by a Korean nationalist two years later, as he 'won the hatred of the natives by harsh rule', wrote the *New York Times* at the time of his death. Now his elevation to overlord of Korea only reminded Cixi that in 1898 this 'principal figure in Japan's rise as world power' had come very close to controlling Emperor Guangxu, and that China had been in danger of becoming another Korea. In addition, now that Korea had effectively become Japanese territory, Japan had secured a land border with China, which its army could quite easily cross if it wished.

Against this background, Cixi made a determined effort to clear her court of suspected Japanese agents. Her principal target was an army officer called Cen Chunxuan, who had escorted the court when it fled from Beijing in 1900. Cixi had been grateful and allowed him easy access to her. It had subsequently emerged, however, that Officer Cen, whose army was stationed far away from the capital, had raced to the court's aid in defiance of his superior's order; and that he had done so at the behest of Wild Fox Kang, with whom he had maintained clandestine ties, in order to protect Emperor Guangxu. She also learned that Officer Cen had had meetings in Shanghai with the Wild Fox's associate, Liang, who had come over specially from Japan – meetings that Kang himself had planned to attend. Cixi gave Officer Cen 'sick leave'. She also transferred his close friend, Grand Councillor Lin Shaonian, out of Beijing to Henan province to be its governor. On 'sick leave' in Shanghai, Officer Cen continued to meet senior Japanese politicians, including Inukai Tsuyoshi, the future Prime Minister who led Japan in the invasion of Manchuria in 1931 – and who was now the most active supporter of both Wild Fox Kang and Sun Yat-sen.

Cixi reorganised the Grand Council and appointed three new Grand Councillors, who, she was sure, would not be Japanese stooges. One was General Yuan, whom Cixi made the head of the Foreign Office, even though he was described by a foreigner as having 'less poise than other Chinese dignitaries'. The General was one of Japan's biggest fans and had ordered all new officials reporting to him to travel there for three months before taking up their posts. But he was also tough and astute in his dealings with the Japanese, and had long been vigilant against Japan's ambitions towards China. As such, he had been a thorn in the side of Tokyo, and Wild Fox Kang made him the prime target for assassination after Cixi.*

The second new Grand Councillor was Viceroy Zhang, another admirer of Japan. In spite of his dalliance with Tokyo in 1900, Cixi trusted his commitment to an independent China, and his strong character which meant he would not be anyone's puppet. His incorruptibility also meant that he was bribery-proof.

The third new Grand Councillor was Zaifeng, the son of her old devotee Prince Chun. Cixi was in fact grooming him to be her successor. When the Boxer Protocol demanded that a Chinese prince be sent to the German court to apologise for the murder of Baron von Ketteler, Zaifeng was chosen for the task at the age of eighteen. He handled the difficult mission well and showed quiet dignity when he delivered China's apology, having rejected Berlin's demand that he and his suite perform the kowtow to the Kaiser – a demand that Berlin eventually withdrew. After his return to Beijing, Cixi arranged a marriage for him to the daughter of Junglu, one of the men closest to her.† She gave Zaifeng as much exposure to foreign affairs as possible, sending him at every opportunity to represent the government at public functions involving foreigners. He knew the diplomatic corps and the missionaries better than most Chinese. Westerners liked him, and he mixed easily with them. Cixi had faith in him and believed that he would not be a Japanese collaborator – and he did not let her down. When Zaifeng eventually took over as Regent, after Cixi died and his son, Puyi, became the emperor, he resisted all Japanese overtures.‡ When his son was crowned Emperor of Manchukuo, the Japanese puppet state in Manchuria, Zaifeng visited him only once in the fourteen years of Manchukuo's existence. He stayed for a month and steered clear of politics. (He died in 1951.)

One of Japan's key agents was Prince Su, a scion of the ruling Aisin-Gioro family. Around forty years old at this time, the prince was the most Japanised grandee, and a supporter of Emperor Guangxu. In his mansion he set up a school for his daughters and other women of the household, and had them taught by a Japanese. As the prince appeared

---

* General Yuan was flamboyant as well as formidable. His guards, selected for their size, wore leopardskin-patterned uniforms, and looked like 'tigers and bears', commented gawking onlookers.
† Junglu died in 1903.
‡ Puyi's story is immortalised in Bernardo Bertolucci's film, *The Last Emperor*.

to be an able and open-minded man, Cixi made him Chief of Police. The adviser to the police was a Japanese, Kawashima Naniwa, who had demonstrated considerable effectiveness when policing the capital during its occupation by foreign troops in the aftermath of the Boxer mayhem. The two men became good friends, and Kawashima later adopted one of Prince Su's daughters. Growing up in Japan, she became a star spy for the Japanese during their invasion of China in the Second World War, and acquired the sobriquet Eastern Jewel. She would be executed for treason after the war.

Prince Su was to promote a Japanese takeover of China as fanatically as his daughter would. For now, though, he lay low. In 1903, Cixi was warned about his true colours. The revelation came from Qing Kuan, a court painter (whose panoramic depiction of the Summer Palace and Emperor Guangxu's wedding are today among China's national treasures). Fiercely devoted to Cixi, the painter had been instrumental in the capture of the assassin Shen Jin. Afterwards he had written to Cixi confidentially to say that the arrest had only been possible because it was kept secret from those closest to Prince Su. Cixi confronted the prince, who was reduced to mumbling, unconvincingly, in his own defence. She removed him from his post as Chief of Police, on the pretext that his duties had become too onerous, and had him closely watched. He told a liaison man from Wild Fox Kang that even his favourite concubine was working for Cixi and that he felt as though he was permanently 'sitting on a blanket of needles'.

With the prince now under surveillance, Cixi reappointed him, in June 1907, as head of the newly established Ministry of Public Services, under which the police force came. This move was a smokescreen for the benefit of Tokyo: as she was clearing Officer Cen and others out of the court, she wanted to avoid giving the Japanese the impression that the expulsions were connected with them. Meanwhile she ensured that the police force was firmly in the hands of the prince's deputy, a man she trusted.

Still, the capital's fire brigade was the responsibility of the prince's ministry. He told Clerk Wang Zhao, a member of the 1898 conspiracy, who had been released from prison in Cixi's amnesty: 'I have armed the fire brigade and drilled it like an army. When the time of drastic change comes, I will use it to storm the palaces on the pretext of putting out a fire, and the emperor will be restored to the throne.' Wang Zhao totally agreed: 'The moment we get hold of the information that the Empress Dowager is ill and bed-ridden, Your Highness can take the fire brigade into the Sea Palace to secure the emperor, sweep him into the grandest hall in the Forbidden City and place him on the throne. Then the grandees can be summoned to take orders from him. Who would dare to disobey?'*

The Summer Palace was too far away from the city for Prince Su's fire brigade to reach it. So, it seems, another scheme was devised for it. The Japanese government offered the empress dowager a present: a steamer, to be tailor-made for the Kunming Lake. This was a gift Cixi could not refuse. So Japanese engineers were let into the Summer Palace, where they made a full-scale survey of the lake, together with the canal that linked it to the city, noting down exactly how deep and wide the waters were and how best to manoeuvre in them. They inspected her other boats, to make sure theirs was superior. The steamer was manufactured in Japan and shipped over to the Summer Palace to be assembled in its dock – by more than sixty Japanese technicians, who took to walking around the grounds, peering at the villas. Finally, at the end of May 1908, the steamer was presented to the empress dowager, complete with its own Japanese crew. She was requested to name it, which she did: *Yong-he*, Forever Peace. The dedication ceremony took place in the Summer Palace and was attended by officials from both countries – but no Cixi, or Emperor Guangxu. Only eventually did the last Japanese engineers and crew leave. There is no record of Cixi ever setting foot on the 'gift'.

A Grand Council secretary expressed dismay in his diary at the time. 'The security of the imperial residences is a grave matter,' he wrote, 'and even the average officials cannot enter the grounds. And yet these foreigners are wandering round day and night. This does not seem right. I have also heard that the Japanese are often drinking and yelling. I wonder what will happen if they barge into forbidden places by force.' It was impossible for Cixi not to share the secretary's misgivings. The steamer (which actually resembled a warship in appearance) was like a Trojan Horse within her palace grounds and could be used to reach Emperor Guangxu, whose villa was right on the waterfront.

The Trojan Horse entered the Summer Palace just as Cixi was

---

* Wang Zhao tried to persuade Prince Su to act straight away, but the prince was cautious and wanted to wait for the right moment. He said: 'The rules of our dynasty are especially strict concerning us princes. We can't enter the palaces without being summoned. One foot wrong and I am a dead man.' As Wang Zhao urged him to take the plunge, he countered: 'This is not something that risk-taking can achieve. Look what taking risks got you, straight into the prison of the Ministry of Punishments. What use was that?'

becoming ill. For a while her strong constitution had sustained her, and on a visit to the country's first modern experimental farm in May, she walked several kilometres, while Emperor Guangxu was carried in a chair by two bearers. But from the beginning of July she really had to struggle to carry on with her work, as she felt feverish and dizzy all the time, with a metallic ringing in the ears.

Worrying news also crashed in on Cixi from her Manchurian Viceroy about problems at the border with Korea, now in Japanese hands. The Japanese were building ferry points on the Korean side and laid a railway line up to the river bank. They had even been constructing a bridge, which had reached the middle of the river before they were forced to dismantle it as a result of fierce protests from Beijing. As all this was taking place, the Japanese minister to Beijing presented a diplomatic note, threatening that their force would cross the border to strike an anti-Japanese Korean gang that was making trouble for them. It seems that Tokyo could use any excuse to send in troops – as backup for what might be happening in the palaces.

On 18 July, Japan's legendary military-intelligence gatherer, Lieutenant-General Fukushima Yasumasa, arrived in China and went straight to Hunan province to visit Officer Cen, whom Cixi had appointed provincial governor. Perhaps prompted by a sense of foreboding, Cixi told General Yuan and Viceroy Zhang to inspect the confiscated files containing the correspondence of Wild Fox Kang and his associates. It was an order unusual enough for a Grand Council secretary to note it in his diary with surprise. Cixi normally took care to avoid doing things that were likely to incriminate those who had connections with her political foes; now she seemed to feel the need to find out whether there were other as-yet-unexposed Officer Cens.

It was in the middle of this nerve-racking tension that Emperor Guangxu's thirty-seventh birthday was celebrated on 24 July. Cixi chose an opera to be performed for the occasion – and it was about the death of a king, Liu Bei, in AD 223. Cixi, who loved this particular opera, had had all the costumes and props made in the colour of mourning: white. On the stage the cast wore white brocade, with the dragon pattern on the king's robe embroidered in stark black thread. The armour and banners were also brilliantly white. As a rule, the colour white was taboo on an imperial birthday: courtiers would not even wear robes with sleeves that showed white linings – to avoid bad luck. But Cixi was begging for her adopted son to have bad luck. Only his death could halt the Japanese machinations to use him as their puppet.

31 Deaths
(1908)

A T this time Emperor Guangxu was in fact gravely ill, and doctors from the provinces were summoned to Beijing. In notes to his doctors, His Majesty complained that he was hearing noises, 'sometimes distant wind and rain and human voices and drum beating, other times cicadas chirping and silk being torn. There is not a moment of peace.' He described 'great pains from the waist down', difficulty in lifting his arms to wash his face, deafness and 'shivering from cold even under four quilts'. He berated his doctors for not curing him or making him feel better. But he hung on tenaciously to life.

The emperor had acquired a little more freedom since the court's return from exile, and had resumed the most important duty: visiting the Temple of Heaven on the winter solstice and praying for Heaven's blessing on the harvests in the coming year. Since he had first been imprisoned, this ritual had been performed in his stead by princes, and Cixi had been frightened of Heaven's wrath. Now, confident that the guards and officials would obey her rather than the emperor, she finally allowed him out of the palace grounds without her.

Yet she still lived in constant dread that he might be spirited away, and was always vigilant, especially when there were foreign visitors. On one occasion Cixi spoke to a group of foreign guests and one of them later recalled:

The Emperor, probably becoming weary of a conversation in which he had no part, quietly withdrew by a side entrance to the theatre which was playing at the time. For some moments the Empress Dowager did not notice his absence, but the instant she discovered he was gone, a look of anxiety overspread her features, and she

361

turned to the head eunuch, Li Lienying [Lee Lianying], and in an authoritative tone asked: 'Where is the Emperor?' There was a scurry among the eunuchs, and they were sent hither and thither to inquire. After a few moments they returned, saying that he was in the theatre. The look of anxiety passed from her face as a cloud passes from before the sun – and several of the eunuchs remained at the theatre.

It seems that Emperor Guangxu did make several attempts to get away. One day he walked towards a gate of the Sea Palace, before eunuchs dragged him back by his long queue. On another occasion a Grand Council secretary saw him outside their office, tilting his head to the sky as if praying, before heading for a gate out of the Forbidden City. His way was instantly barred by a dozen or more eunuchs.

It was forbidden to visit him in his villa, and only a trusted few had conversations with him. When Louisa Pierson first joined the court, her young teenage daughter, Rongling, used to chat with him when they bumped into each other. One day, the eunuch who was always at the emperor's side came to her room and showed her a watch. A character in crimson ink was written on its glass surface. The eunuch told the girl that His Majesty wanted to know where the man with this surname was. Having grown up abroad, Rongling could hardly read Chinese and did not recognise the character. The eunuch grinned, 'You don't know this? It's Kang.' It dawned on her that it referred to Wild Fox Kang, whose name even she knew was unmentionable in the court. Scared, she said that she really did not know where Kang was and that perhaps she should go and ask her mother. At this, the eunuch told her to forget the whole thing. Given that the eunuchs around Emperor Guangxu had all been selected by Cixi with the utmost care, it seems unlikely that the character 'Kang' had really been written by the emperor. More likely, Cixi was testing the girl, whose chats with the emperor had doubtless been reported to her, and she needed to be sure that Rongling was not being used as a messenger between the Wild Fox and Emperor Guangxu.

From summer 1908, Cixi began to suffer from diarrhoea, which depleted her. She carried on with her mountainous workload, only occasionally delaying her morning audience until nine o'clock. Most of the decrees she issued in this period were to do with creating a constitutional monarchy. She endorsed the draft constitution, authorised the Election Regulations and specified the nine-year time frame for establishing the parliament.

She also concentrated her declining energy on an upcoming visit of the thirteenth Dalai Lama. The Qing empire had incorporated Tibet into its territory in the eighteenth century. Since then, Tibet had been running its own affairs while accepting Beijing's authority. An Imperial Commissioner was stationed in Lhasa acting as the link, and Beijing rubber-stamped all Lhasa's decisions. On this basis, in 1877, Cixi (in the name of Emperor Guangxu) had approved the Tibetan Regent's identification of the child Thubten Gyatso as the reincarnated thirteenth Dalai Lama. Her subsequent edicts had endorsed the educational programme drawn up for the child, whose teachers were all Tibetans. There was nothing Han or Manchu on the curriculum. The Tibetans were cooperative with her, and she left them completely alone. She was, however, always well informed: since the telegraph came to China, the Imperial Commissioner in Lhasa had been equipped to conduct cable communications with Beijing.

In 1903–4, a British military expedition, led by Major Francis Younghusband, invaded Tibet from British India. The Tibetans fought the invaders and suffered heavy casualties. The Dalai Lama fled, and Younghusband pressed on to Lhasa. There he signed a treaty with the remaining Tibetan administration before withdrawing. The treaty imposed a war indemnity of £500,000, and required Tibet to open more centres for trade. It went on: 'As security for the payment of the above-mentioned indemnity and for the fulfilment of the provisions relative to trade marts . . . the British Government shall continue to occupy the Chumbi Valley . . .' It told the Tibetans to 'raze all forts and fortifications and remove all armaments which might impede the course of free communication between the British frontier and the towns of Gyangtse and Lhasa'. Tibet could not make any foreign-policy decision 'without the previous consent of the British Government'.

When the Qing Imperial Commissioner cabled her the terms of the treaty, Cixi saw that her empire's 'sovereignty' over Tibet was in jeopardy. In an edict on 3 October 1904, she announced: 'Tibet has belonged to our dynasty for 200 years. This is a vast area rich in resources, which has always been coveted by foreigners. Recently, British troops entered it and coerced the Tibetans to sign a treaty. This is a most sinister development, and . . . we must prevent further damage and salvage the present situation.' She dispatched representatives to India to negotiate with the British and to establish the principle that Britain had to deal with Beijing over Tibet. 'No concession over sovereignty,' Cixi instructed her negotiators.

Britain agreed to renegotiate with Cixi's representatives. It signed a treaty with Beijing in April 1906, which basically (though not unambiguously) recognised Tibet as part of the Chinese empire.

Cixi held a strong card: the fleeing thirteenth Dalai Lama. A good-looking man in his late twenties, wearing a monk's habit, he travelled northeast, finally arriving at Urga, now Ulan Bator, capital of Outer Mongolia and, at that time, part of the Qing empire. The Dalai Lama was the spiritual leader of the Mongols as well as the Tibetans. Cixi immediately dispatched officials to attend him and ordered local officials to look after him. She also cabled her sympathies for his arduous journey. She urged him to return to Lhasa as soon as the British were gone and to run Tibet as before.

The thirteenth Dalai Lama did not return for some time, but asked to go to Beijing and meet the empress dowager. During his absence a Han official, Chang Yintang, was running Tibet (though not as Imperial Commissioner – a post traditionally specified not to be given to a Han). Yintang attempted to implement 'reforms', with the intention of making Tibet more like a Han province. Having been in India negotiating with the British, and having seen how they ran things there, he advised Beijing to adopt the British method: to send in a sizeable army, make the Imperial Commissioner a 'governor-general', appoint the administration and treat the Dalai Lama and Panchen Lama like the Indian maharajas, taking away their political power and paying them off handsomely. Cixi did not endorse Yintang. After receiving reports that his plans were hugely unpopular among the Tibetans, she transferred him to another post, effectively aborting his programme. It seems she understood that the Tibetans' desire to be left alone was non-negotiable, and came to the conclusion that only by respecting it could she keep Tibet in the empire. Her approach was registered by the Dalai Lama, who regarded it as his best option, and so repeatedly asked to see her – in order to nail down an agreement. Eventually Cixi issued the invitation, and on 28 September 1908 the thirteenth Dalai Lama arrived in the capital.

Cixi had been reluctant to make the invitation, most likely because a visit by the Dalai Lama posed potentially explosive protocol problems. The biggest dilemma was whether the Dalai Lama should kneel to her and the emperor. As a spiritual leader, people knelt before him. But he was also a political leader, and as such he would be expected to kneel to the throne. If the Dalai Lama was not required to kneel, given that only foreigners were exempt, this would imply that Beijing did not regard Tibet as part of China. The problem would be particularly acute on the occasion of the state banquet in his honour, when political leaders from Mongolia, for instance, would go down on their knees as Emperor Guangxu arrived and departed. The banquet was a 'public' affair, and Cixi was well aware that it would be the focus of attention: while Western powers would be watching for signs that Tibet was not treated as part of her empire, the Tibetans needed to be reassured that their God was not humiliated. The protocol office asked Cixi what to do, and she pondered the problem for several days. Finally she decided that the Dalai Lama would kneel, like all others at the banquet, except that he would do so at his seat – a low throne on which he sat cross-legged – rather than at the entrance to the hall like everybody else. This way, his kneeling would be inconspicuous, especially with his ample robe. The Dalai Lama did not object, clearly regarding this as a worthwhile price to pay for Tibet to maintain its self-governing status, which both he and the empress dowager wanted.

For Cixi, it was vital to keep Tibet in the empire, in a mutually acceptable and amicable way. She deliberated over the most appropriate symbol-laden gifts and, when conferring a new title on the Dalai Lama, made a point of adding words to the effect that he was 'sincerely loyal' to the empire. But she would not use a heavy hand to assert her authority. Earlier that year she had appointed a new Imperial Commissioner to Tibet, Zhao Erfeng, but Lhasa rejected him, disliking his record as the administrator of a neighbouring region inhabited by Tibetans. Rather than send Zhao in by force, Cixi held him back, which was an unprecedented concession in Qing history. This was 'in order not to lose the goodwill of the Tibetans', as she spelt out in her decree. The imperial troops were further told not to engage in clashes with the Tibetan army. In Beijing, she and the Dalai Lama agreed that he would return to Lhasa as soon as possible and continue to run Tibet as before.

During the whole of the Dalai Lama's stay, Cixi was struggling to cope. Their first meeting after his arrival had had to be cancelled as she had felt too ill to go ahead. She had sobbed with frustration when she gave the order. It was not possible to set another date in advance, as her condition fluctuated daily. They only managed to meet when she got up one morning and felt strong enough.

The Dalai Lama's visit coincided with Cixi's seventy-third birthday, the tenth day of the tenth lunar month – or 3 November 1908. She very much wanted to entertain the Tibetan Holy Man, and so felt she really must sit through the endless performances and rituals, even though she had constant diarrhoea and a high fever. Her doctors recorded that she was 'exceptionally exhausted'.

Four days after her birthday she sensed that death was breathing down on her, and sent Prince Ching to the Eastern Mausoleums to check out her burial ground, near her late husband's and son's. This last resting place was of paramount importance to her, and she had had it constructed in splendour. During her burial a large quantity of jewels would be placed in the tomb with her, as befitted an empress dowager.

Meanwhile, she started to put the empire's affairs in order. The moment had come to deal with Emperor Guangxu. Bedridden and seemingly on the verge of death, he refused to die and could pull back, as he had done before. If he survived and she was gone, the empire would fall into the hands of the waiting Japanese. It was in these circumstances that Cixi ordered the murder of her adopted son, by poisoning. That Emperor Guangxu died from consuming large quantities of arsenic was definitively established in 2008, after forensic examination of his remains. His murder would have been easy to arrange: Cixi routinely sent him dishes as tokens of a mother's affection for her son. At 6.33 p.m. on 14 November, Emperor Guangxu was pronounced dead by the royal physicians.

His empress, Longyu, had been with him at the end. They had apparently wept in each other's arms – embracing as they had so rarely done in nearly twenty years of marriage. During those last hours Empress Longyu was seen rushing between her dying husband and her dying mother-in-law with swollen eyes. After Emperor Guangxu died, she dressed his body. According to court tradition, the finest pearl available must be placed in the emperor's mouth to accompany him to the next world. Empress Longyu wanted to pluck the pearl from the emperor's crown, but a eunuch stopped her, saying that they did not have the empress dowager's permission. So Empress Longyu removed the pearl from her own crown and put it in her dead husband's mouth.

Emperor Guangxu died in a bed that was 'unadorned like an average folk's', observed one of the provincial doctors. There was no outer curtain to encircle it, and the footstool on which he stepped to get into it was covered only with a blanket, rather than silk brocade. Doctors and court officials were with him in his final hours, but none of the Grand Councillors was present. His last words were not officially recorded. The Grand Council gathered at Cixi's bedside while he lay dying, and again after they learned of his death, to hear Cixi make arrangements for the succession. Zaifeng, whom Cixi had been training for years, was designated Regent, and his two-year-old son, Puyi,

Cixi's great-nephew, was named as the successor to the throne. The appointment of the child emperor ensured that the father would take charge as Regent – and furthermore Cixi was able to remain in control for as long as she was alive. Her decree made clear that 'all key policies are to be decided by myself'. She was determined to hold on to the reins of the empire until her last breath.

Zaifeng was not the ideal choice, but Cixi regarded him as the best there was. She trusted that he would not deliver China to Japan, and that he could deal with Westerners in a friendly and dignified manner. There were serious limitations about him, of which she was well aware. Once, at a dinner party at the American Legation, he was asked, 'What does Your Highness think of the relative characteristics of the Germans and the French?' and he replied, 'The people in Berlin get up early in the morning and go to their business, while the people in Paris get up in the evening and go to the theatre.' Clearly he was recycling a cliché.

Cixi was fading; but she still managed to oversee the myriad things to be done after the passing away of a monarch, including the writing of Emperor Guangxu's official will, to be announced to the empire. The will referred to the establishment of a constitutional monarchy in nine years' time. This, it declared, was the emperor's 'unfulfilled aspiration', and this, once accomplished, would give him untold joy in the other world.

A night passed while Cixi dealt with one matter after another, conscious all the time that she had just murdered her adopted son. She was forced to stop working at about eleven o'clock in the morning, as death was imminent. She died less than three hours later.

A Grand Council secretary drafted Cixi's own official will according to her wishes, 'with my hand and heart trembling, everything seeming unreal', he recorded in his diary. This will recalled her involvement in China's state affairs for nearly fifty years and her efforts to do what she regarded as her best. It reiterated her determination to transform China into a constitutional monarchy, which, the will stated with much regret, she was now unable to see to completion. The two wills made unmistakably clear that it was Cixi's dying wish that the Chinese should have their parliament and their vote.

During the last three hours of her life Cixi's mind was still restless. She now dictated her very last political decree, one that would seem bizarre to any observer. 'I am critically ill, and I am afraid I am about to pass away,' she said, in direct and personal language. 'In the future, the affairs of the empire will be decided by the Regent. However, if he comes across exceptionally critical matters, he must obey the dowager empress.' The 'dowager empress' referred to here was Empress Longyu, who had just been given the title on her husband's death and the appointment of the heir. To stress that the Empress Longyu's wishes were final, Cixi unusually used the word *must* in her decree – an apparently redundant term. It was with this added emphasis that Cixi made the fate of the empire ultimately the responsibility of Empress Longyu.

The empress was by all accounts a pitiable figure. Foreigners who had met her described her as having 'a sad, gentle face. She is rather stooped, extremely thin, her face long and sallow, and her teeth very much decayed.' From the day of her wedding, her husband treated her at best with disdain. Kinder-hearted observers found her full of pathos, and the less generous despised her. Rarely venturing a remark on her own initiative, she was accustomed to (and meekly accepted) being denigrated. Mrs Headland, the American physician who frequented the court, remembered, when hearing about her new role:

> At the audiences given to the [foreign] ladies she was always present, but never in the immediate vicinity of either the Empress Dowager or the Emperor . . . she always stood in some inconspicuous place in the rear, with her waiting women about her, and as soon as she could do so without attracting attention, she would withdraw . . . In the summer-time we sometimes saw her with her servants wandering aimlessly about the court. She had the appearance of a gentle, quiet, kindly person who was always afraid of intruding and had no place or part in anything. And now she is the Empress Dowager! It seems a travesty on the English language to call this kindly, gentle soul by the same title that we have been accustomed to use in speaking of the woman who has just passed away.

The grandees held Empress Longyu in such disregard that no one troubled to inform her of her new title as dowager empress. Fearful of being overlooked, she tentatively asked the Grand Councillors about her status as they gathered in the bedchamber of the now-deceased Cixi, whom she had just been dressing. One Grand Councillor ignored her, pretending he was too deaf to hear what she was saying. When she learned about her new title, Empress Longyu was overjoyed. Although it was her due, she had not dared to expect it. In spite of the fact that it was Cixi who had chosen her as empress, and that she had been attending to Cixi all those years, Cixi had rarely addressed a comment to her and never sought her opinion. And yet Cixi's last political act was to place the burden of the empire's destiny on her narrow and bowed shoulders.

Earlier that year, Cixi was strolling round in the garden of the Forbidden City, contemplating the many Buddhist statues there. Somehow, she felt the statues were not ideally placed and ordered the eunuchs to rearrange them. As the statues were being moved, a large pile of soil was exposed. With a frown, Cixi ordered the soil to be swept away. Head eunuch Lianying went down on his knees and implored her to leave it untouched. The soil had been there for as long as anyone could remember, and the strange thing about it was that it had remained a neat and tidy pile, with not a speck of earth out of place. Birds, it seemed, had never perched on it and the rats and foxes that prowled the palace grounds had evidently avoided it. Word had been handed down for generations that this was a mound of 'magic earth', there to protect the great dynasty. Cixi was famously superstitious, but she seemed to be annoyed by this explanation and snapped, 'What magic earth? Sweep it away.' As the pile of soil was being levelled, she repeatedly murmured to herself, 'What about this great dynasty? What about this great dynasty?!' Listening to her, one eunuch said he and his fellow attendants felt sad: it seemed the empress dowager was expecting that the Qing dynasty was nearing its end.

Indeed, Empress Dowager Cixi had foreseen that her reforms, drastically changing China, could in the end bury her own dynasty. As long as she lived, the Manchu throne would be secure. But once she was gone, her successor might not have the same strength, and the constitutional monarchy she had tried to create might come to nothing. Chinese and Western observers were already predicting anti-Manchu uprisings after her death. The fate of the Manchu, her own people, preoccupied the empress dowager in her last hours. If Republican uprisings did inundate the empire, the only option for the vastly outnumbered Manchu would have to be surrender, if a bloodbath was to be avoided. Only surrender could save her people – as well as spare the country civil war. She was quite certain that, faced with Republican uprisings, the men at court would choose to defend the dynasty and fight to the death. No man would counsel surrender, even if he wanted to. This is why Cixi gave the decision-making power in such an 'exceptionally critical' crisis to Empress Longyu. Cixi could depend on the empress to surrender the dynasty in order to ensure her own survival, as well as that of the Manchu people. Empress Longyu had lived in surrender all her life. She did not care about humiliation and was the ultimate survivor. As a woman, she was also not required to demonstrate macho bravado.

Cixi's far sight was borne out exactly three years later, when long-anticipated uprisings and mutinies broke out in 1911. Triggered by a disturbance over the ownership of a railway in Sichuan, and followed by a major mutiny in Wuhan, upheaval spread to a succession of provinces, many of which declared independence from the Qing government. Although these events had no unified leadership, most shared a common goal: to overthrow the Qing dynasty and form a Republic.★ Manchu blood began to flow: the reformist Viceroy Duanfang was murdered, and in Xian, Fuzhou, Hangzhou, Nanjing and other cities Manchu men and women were being slaughtered. The idea of surrender, in the form of abdication by the emperor, was mooted. As Cixi had foreseen, Manchu grandees vehemently resisted, vowing to defend the dynasty to the last man. Again as she had foreseen, the Regent himself also spoke publicly against abdication, even though privately he was in favour. He knew that it was futile to fight (in spite of the substantial support the court still enjoyed), but he did not want to be the person responsible for his dynasty's downfall. Cixi's deathbed decree solved this excruciating dilemma. On 6 December, Zaifeng resigned his position as Regent and referred all decisions to Empress Longyu. The empress, gathering the grandees around her,† declared through her tears that she was prepared to take responsibility for ending the dynasty through the abdication of the five-year-old Puyi. 'All I desire is peace under Heaven,' she said.

Thus, on 12 February 1912, Empress Longyu put her name to the Decree of Abdication, which brought the Great Qing, which had ruled for 268 years, to its end, along with more than 2,000 years of absolute monarchy in China. It was Empress Longyu who decreed: 'On behalf of the emperor, I transfer the right to rule to the whole country, which will now be a constitutional Republic.' This 'Great Republic of China will comprise the entire territory of the Qing empire as inhabited by the five ethnic groups, the Manchu, Han, Mongol, Hui and Tibetan'. She was placed in this historic role by Cixi. Republicanism was not what Empress Dowager Cixi had hoped for, but it was what she would accept, as it shared the same goal as her wished-for parliamentary monarchy: that the future of China belong to the Chinese people.

★ Sun Yat-sen, travelling overseas, was not the leader of the uprisings. But he had been the earliest and most persistent promoter of Republicanism and is rightly seen as the 'father' of Republican China.
† Viceroy Zhang Zhidong was not among them; he had died in 1909.

Epilogue: China after Empress Dowager Cixi

EMPRESS Dowager Cixi's legacy was manifold and towering. Most importantly, she brought medieval China into the modern age. Under her leadership the country began to acquire virtually all the attributes of a modern state: railways, electricity, telegraph, telephones, Western medicine, a modern-style army and navy, and modern ways of conducting foreign trade and diplomacy. The restrictive millennium-old educational system was discarded and replaced by Western-style schools and universities. The press blossomed, enjoying a freedom that was unprecedented and arguably unsurpassed since. She unlocked the door to political participation: for the first time in China's long history, people were to become 'citizens'. It was Cixi who championed women's liberation in a culture that had for centuries imposed foot-binding on its female population – a practice to which she put an end. The fact that her last enterprise before an untimely death was to introduce the vote testifies to her courage and vision. Above all, her transformation of China was carried out without her engaging in violence and with relatively little upheaval. Her changes were dramatic and yet gradual, seismic and yet astonishingly bloodless. A consensus-seeker, always willing to work with people of different views, she led by standing on the right side of history.

She was a giant, but not a saint. Being the absolute ruler of one-third of the world's population and the product of medieval China, she was capable of immense ruthlessness. Her military campaigns to regain Xinjiang and to quell armed rebellions were brutal. Her attempts to use the Boxers to fight invaders resulted in large-scale atrocities by the Boxers.

For all her faults, she was no despot. Compared to that of her predecessors, or successors, Cixi's rule was benign. In some four decades of absolute power, her political killings – whether just or unjust – which are recorded in this book, were no more than a few dozen, many of them in response to plots to kill her. She was not cruel by nature. As her life was ending, her thoughts were about how best to prevent bloody civil war and massacres of the Manchu people, whose survival she ensured by sacrificing her dynasty.

She also paid a heavy personal price. Cixi was a devout believer in the sanctity of the final resting place, but her own tomb ended up being desecrated. The leaders of the first few Republican administrations, starting with General Yuan (who died in 1916), observed the agreed terms of the abdication and protected the Qing mausoleums. In 1927, the more radical Nationalists, led by Chiang Kai-shek, drove these men out and established a new regime. A year later, and twenty years after Cixi's death, an unruly army unit broke into Cixi's tomb to plunder the jewels that were known to have been buried with her. Using dynamite, officers and men blasted a breach in the wall and, with bayonets and iron bars, forced open the lid of her coffin. After seizing the jewels around her, they tore off her clothes and pulled out her teeth, in search of any possible hidden treasure. Her corpse was left exposed.

When Puyi, the last emperor, heard about the sacrilege, he was devastated, as he later described. Now in his twenties, Puyi had been summarily expelled from the Forbidden City in 1924 (which had been a breach of the abdication agreement) and had since been living in Tianjin. He sent members of the former royal family to rebury Cixi's remains, and protested to the Chiang government. As the robbery became a national scandal, there was an investigation, but it petered out and no one was punished – thanks, it seemed, to handsome bribes all round. When Puyi heard a widely believed rumour that the pearl in Cixi's mouth had been plucked out and used to decorate Mme Chaing's shoe, he became filled with bitter hatred. The outrage cemented his resolve to throw in his lot with the Japanese, who made him the Emperor of Manchukuo, the puppet state set up in Manchuria, which they occupied in 1931. Japan then invaded China proper in 1937.

Cixi had struggled to thwart Japan's attempts to turn China into part of its East Asian empire, and had murdered her adopted son to prevent it. Ironically, if she had delivered China to Japan, it is almost certain that her last resting place – and her remains – would have been respected.

Chiang Kai-shek, a true heir to Cixi, fought Japan throughout the Second World War. The Japanese devastation of Chiang's state paved the way for Mao to seize power in 1949, although the pivotal role in his rise was played by Stalin, Mao's sponsor and mentor. While post-war Japan metamorphosed into a flourishing democracy, China was plunged into an unprecedented abyss by Mao's twenty-seven-year rule, which swallowed the lives of well over seventy million people in peacetime – until his death in 1976 put a stop to his atrocities. For his misrule Mao offered not a word of apology, unlike Cixi, who publicly expressed remorse for the damage she had done – which, though grave, was a fraction of what Mao inflicted on the nation. Pearl Buck, the Nobel Prize-winner for literature, who was born in 1892 and grew up in China when Cixi was in power, and who then lived under, or observed, the subsequent regimes, described in the 1950s 'how the Chinese whom I knew in my childhood felt about her': 'Her people loved her – not all her people, for the revolutionary, the impatient, hated her heartily . . . But the peasants and the small-town people revered her.' When they heard she was dead, villagers felt 'frightened': '"Who will care for us now?" they cried.' Pearl Buck concluded, 'This, perhaps, is the final judgment of a ruler.'

The past hundred years have been most unfair to Cixi, who has been deemed either tyrannical and vicious or hopelessly incompetent – or both. Few of her achievements have been recognised and, when they are, the credit is invariably given to the men serving her. This is largely due to a basic handicap: that she was a woman and could only rule in the name of her sons – so her precise role has been little known. In the absence of clear knowledge, rumours have abounded and lies have been invented and believed. As Pearl Buck observed, those who hated her were simply 'more articulate than those who loved her'. The political forces that have dominated China since soon after her death have also deliberately reviled her and blacked out her accomplishments – in order to claim that they have saved the country from the mess she left behind.

In terms of groundbreaking achievements, political sincerity and personal courage, Empress Dowager Cixi set a standard that has barely been matched. She brought in modernity to replace decrepitude, poverty, savagery and absolute power, and she introduced hitherto untasted humaneness, open-mindness and freedom. And she had a conscience. Looking back over the many horrific decades after Cixi's demise, one cannot but admire this amazing stateswoman, flawed though she was.

Notes

Chapter 1   Concubine to an Emperor (1835–56)

Page

3   **'the woman of the Nala family'**: First Historical Archives of China (ed.) 1998, vol. 4, no. 164; Wang Daocheng 1984, p. 213; Yu Bingkun et al., p. 56; **footnote**: Professor Wang argued convincingly that *Lan* was not Cixi's maiden name: Wang Daocheng 1984, pp. 216–18. Also: Yehenala Genzheng & Hao Xiaohui 2007, p. 13

5   **Cixi's family**: Wang Daocheng 1984, pp. 195–208; **Huizheng**: Yu Bingkun et al., pp. 7–43

6   **Manchu translated into Chinese**: Weng Tonghe 2006, vol. 1, p. 148; Jin Liang 1998, p. 161; **Daoguang against extravagance**: Xin Xiuming, p. 1; Forbidden City Publishing House (ed.), p. 39; **the state coffer incident**: Yu Bingkun et al., pp. 13–31; Yehenala Genzheng & Hao Xiaohui 2007, pp. 17–18

8   **'Limping Dragon'**: Xin Xiuming, p. 2; **consort selection**: Wang Daocheng 1984; Yu Bingkun et al.; Shan Shiyuan 1990, pp. 1–23; Wang Shuqing, 1980, no. 1; Li Guorong, pp. 216–19; **Maugham mused**: Maugham, p. 2

9   **'After ten hours'**: Freeman-Mitford, pp. 151–2

10   **'a high nose'**: Carl, p. 19

11   **'I don't know why'**: Xin Xiuming, p. 14

12   **For food**: Wang Shuqing, 1983, no. 3; Wang Daocheng 1984; **Xianfeng sex life**: Wang Daocheng 1984, p. 196; Mao Haijian 2006, p. 148; cf. Forbidden City Publishing (ed.), pp. 22–3; Li Guorong, pp. 260–1; Tang Yinian, pp. 23–4; **footnote**: Jin Liang 1933, p. 27

13   **Xianfeng wept**: Mao Haijian 2006, p. 75

14   **Imperial Apology**: Qing History Institute, Renmin University (ed.), vol. 9, p. 69; **silver reserve etc.**: Archives of Ming and Qing Dynasties (ed.) 1979, vol. 1, pp. 1–80; Mao Haijian 2006, p. 106; **admonitions**: Palace Museum (ed.) 2002, vol. 10, p. 276; **her father**: Yu Bingkun et al., pp. 14–22

15   **'crafty'**: Woqiu Zhongzi, p. 2; **'exterminated'**: Yun Yuding, vol. 2, p. 782; **Empress Zhen mediated**: Xue Fucheng 1983, p. 25; **'Younger Sister'**: Xin Xiuming, p. 10; **named *Yi***: First Historical Archives of China (ed.) 1998, vol. 4, no. 164; Ding Ruqin, p. 229

Chapter 2 **From the Opium War to the Burning of the Old Summer Palace (1839–60)**

17 **palace file**: Yu Bingkun et al., pp. 63–70

18 **second son**: First Historical Archives of China (ed.) 1998, vol. 11, no. 1856; **sister marries Prince Chun**: Pujia, Pujie et al., p. 209; **Headland . . . noted**: Headland, p. 264; cf. Carl, p. 82

19 **wet nurse**: Yu Bingkun et al., pp. 67–8; Tong Yue and Lü Jihong, pp. 15–16

20 **Macartney visit**: Macartney's diaries in Helen H. Robbins; First Historical Archives of China (ed.) 2001, pp. 130–6; Rockhill, p. 31; **1.1 million taels**: Li Guorong, p. 338

21 **fifty years of good weather**: Kangxi to his sons and officials, in Forbidden City Publishing (ed.), p. 239; **population explosion**: Jiang Tao 1993, pp. 30–4; Li Zhiting, pp. 475–7

22 **'tell the fishes'**: Association of Chinese Historians (ed.), *The Opium War*, vol. 2, pp. 107–8; **Daoguang approved Lin's letter**: Qing Government (ed.), *Daoguang*, pp. 492–504

23 **Gladstone speech**: Hansard, 8 April 1840; **footnote 2**: Ridley, p. 259; Hansard, 4 August 1843

24 **Wu Tingfang wrote**: Wu Tingfang, pp. 246–7

25 **Daoguang agony**: Qing Government (ed.), *Daoguang*, pp. 4746, 4807; Palace Museum (ed.) 2002, vol. 9, p. 8; **Daoguang writing will**: Archives of Ming and Qing Dynasties (ed.) 1979, vol. 4, pp. 273–8; First Historical Archives of China (ed.) 2001, p. 150

26 **Qiying denounced, ordered to commit suicide**: Mao Haijian 2006, pp. 44–6; Association of Chinese Historians (ed.), *The Second Opium War*, vol. 3, pp. 449–50

27 **'I am so awed'**: First Historical Archives of China & History Department of Fujian Normal University (eds), vol. 1, p. 44; **'ships of war'**: Morse, vol. 1, p. 417; **'pistol at the throat'**: Morse, vol. 1, p. 573

28 **Xianfeng exchanges with officials**: Association of Chinese Historians (ed.), *The Second Opium War*, vols 3 & 4, *passim*. The English translation of the emperor's endorsement in Parkes Papers 28/10, Department of Manuscripts and University Archives, Cambridge University Library, Cambridge.; **Wolseley commented**: Wolseley, pp. 16, 57, 92–3, 113,

29 **a bounty**: Association of Chinese Historians (ed.), *The Second Opium War*, vol. 5, p. 92; *kao-niu*: Lin Keguang et al., p. 150; **court exchanges over Parkes**: Association of Chinese Historians (ed.), *The Second Opium War*, vol. 5, pp. 64, 67–8, 80, 94–5, 101–3, 111

30 **'tied their feet'**: Grant, pp. 133–4; **'My dearest'**: Hurd, p. 234; **Grant wrote**: Grant, p. 203

31 **Montauban wrote**: Morse, vol. 1, p. 606; **'Indiscriminate plunder'**: Wolseley, pp. 224–7; **'What a terrible scene'**: Swinhoe, p. 305

32 **'One room only'**: Grant, p. 129; **'Lootie'**: Royal Archives, Windsor, PPTO/PP/QV/MAIN/1861/7469; Millar, pp. 130–1; **French refused**: Morse, vol. 1, p. 611; **'On 18th October'**: Grant, pp. 204–5

33 **'ruined nothings'**: Wolseley, p. 280; **Gordon wrote home**: Boulger, p. 31; **Victor Hugo wrote**: *UNESCO Courier*, November 1985

34 **Backhouse forgery**: Bland & Backhouse, pp. 14–29; Trevor-Roper; Association of Chinese Historians (ed.), *The Second Opium War*, vol. 2, pp. 66–9

Chapter 3 Emperor Xianfeng Dies (1860–61)

36 **'what phrenologists would describe'**: Thomson, p. 252

37 **'returned him a proud'**: Grant, p. 209; **'Both of the national'**: Wolseley, p. 295; **Elgin friendly letter**: Association of Chinese Historians (ed.), *The Second Opium War*, vol. 5, p. 264; **Xianfeng to Prince Gong**: Association of Chinese Historians (ed.), *The Second Opium War*, vol. 5, pp. 225–6, 264; **One diarist**: Association of Chinese Historians (ed.), *The Second Opium War*, vol. 2, p. 42; **Ignatieff to Gong, Gong to Xianfeng**: Association of Chinese Historians (ed.), *The Second Opium War*, vol. 5, pp. 235, 246, 261; vol. 4, p. 463

38 **'With this treaty'**: Ignatieff, pp. 44–5; **Xianfeng refused to receive credentials**: Association of Chinese Historians (ed.), *The Second Opium War*, vol. 5, pp. 239, 260–1, 269–70

39 **operas in last days**: Ding Ruqin, pp. 221–7; Li Guoliang, p. 95; **Xianfeng death**: Archives of Ming and Qing Dynasties (ed.) 1979, vol. 1, pp. 82–3; Anon., p. 13; Wu Xiangxiang, pp. 49–55; First Historical Archives of China (ed.) 1998, vol. 11, nos 877, 881

Chapter 4 The Coup that Changed China (1861)

41 **unnamed 'others'**: Wu Xiangxiang, p. 56; **emotional row**: Anon., p. 13

42 **two women plotted**: Xue Fucheng 1983, p. 25

43 **seals established**: First Historical Archives of China (ed.) 1998, vol. 11, nos 886–91; Archives of Ming and Qing Dynasties (ed.) 1979, vol. 1, p. 85; **'all is in harmony'**: Anon., pp. 13–14; **'If we saw'**: First Historical Archives of China (ed.) 1998, vol. 11, nos 338, 882

44 **Allowing Gong to visit**: Weng Tonghe 2006, vol. 1, p. 131; **'no one had shown'**: Anon., p. 8; **Gong first meeting with Cixi**: Xue Fucheng 1983, p. 19; Anon., pp. 8–9

45 **'one or two'**: Archives of Ming and Qing Dynasties (ed.) 1979, vol. 1, pp. 91–2; **Cradling the child emperor**: Wu Xiangxiang, p. 62

46 **'Please could the 7th brother'**: First Historical Archives of China (ed.) 2001, p. 176; **Prince Chun as pupil**: Lin Keguang et al., p. 441; Pan Xiangmin 2006, no. 2; **Chun pleaded with the emperor**: Qing Government (ed.), *Tongzhi*, pp. 5940, 7286; **Chun's reply**: First Historical Archives of China (ed.) 2001, p. 176; Li Ciming, p. 539

47 **the coup**: Archives of Ming and Qing Dynasties (ed.) 1979, vol. 1, pp. 96–118; Weng Tonghe 2006, vol. 1, pp. 143–7; Xue Fucheng 1983, p. 21; Sato, p. 177

49 **Sushun hated**: Xue Fucheng 1983, pp. 17, 23; Weng Tonghe 2006, vol. 1, p. 54; vol. 5, p. 2889; Chen Kuilong, p. 96; Aisin-Gioro Puyi, p. 11; **no one else incriminated**: First Historical Archives of China (ed.) 1998, vol. 11, no. 1533; Archives of Ming and Qing Dynasties (ed.) 1979, vol. 1, pp. 120, 139; **Bruce wrote**: Bruce to Earl Russell, 12 November 1861, F.O. 17/356, National Archives, London

50 **'the Empress Mother'**: Robertson to the British Foreign Office, 30 November 1861, F.O. 17/360, National Archives, London; **'I am bowled over'**: Zeng Guofan, vol. 1, p. 690; **had considered making Gong Regent**: original letter to Prince Chun, First Historical Archives of China (ed.), 2001, p. 176; **Gong title and reaction**: Archives of Ming and Qing Dynasties (ed.) 1979, vol. 1, pp. 106, 119–21; **'from now on'**: Archives of Ming and Qing Dynasties (ed.) 1979, vol. 1, p. 123; **obliged to declare**: Archives of Ming and Qing Dynasties (ed.) 1979, vol. 1, p. 137

51 **footnote 2**: Lin Keguang et al., p. 16

52 **close the curtain**: Shan Shiyuan 1997, pp. 452–3

Chapter 5   First Step on the Long Road to Modernity (1861–9)

55   **'statesmen who'**: Bruce to Earl Russell, 12 November 1861, F.O. 17/356, National Archives, London

56   **as many observed**: Carl, p. 51; Rongling 1994, pp. 13, 20; Der Ling 2004 pp. 69, 78, *passim*. (For an assessment of the writings of Rongling and Der Ling, who were both important eye-witnesses, see Zhu Jiajin 1982, no. 4.); **'to read our thoughts'**: Headland, p. 71; **Zhen in audience**: Guo Songtao, p. 16; Xue Fucheng 1983, pp. 25–6; **Zhen seal only**: Yu Bingkun et al., p. 116; **'almost if not entirely'**: Headland, p. 28

57   **Cixi's lessons**: Xin Xiuming, pp. 35–6; **'China is now'**: Palmerston, in Hake, pp. 86–7; Morse, vol. 2, p. 119

58   **'full of jokes'**: Freeman-Mitford, p. 72; **crude 'poems'**: Yang Tianshi, pp. 6–7; **'whole history'**: Morse, vol. 2, p. 63

59   **'Since the treaties'**: Qing Government (ed.), *Tongzhi*, pp. 293–306; **She was cautious**: Qing Government (ed.), *Tongzhi*, pp. 298, 352–8, 403–4, 417–18, 485–7. For more information about Wade, see Cooley, Jr.; **imperial decrees 'frankly'**: Morse, vol. 2, p. 76; **'Words cannot express'**: Gordon, pp. 49–50

60   **'You may say'**: Qing Government (ed.), *Tongzhi*, p. 353

61   **'Asiatic barbarity'**: Morse, vol. 2, pp. 102–4; **'can defeat'**: Li Hongzhang, vol. 29, p. 157; **Cixi re Gordon**: Qing Government (ed.), *Tongzhi*, pp. 2461–2, 2526–9; Morse, vol. 2, p. 105

62   **Wade to Gong**: Qing Government (ed.), *Tongzhi*, pp. 3894–3900; Hart, *Journals, 1863–1866*, p. 167; **Qianlong on Wang Lun**: Zuo Buqing

63   **'Shanghai is'**: Qing Government (ed.), *Tongzhi*, p. 301; **6,800 cargo ships**: Li Yunjun (ed.), p. 243; **footnote**: Freeman-Mitford, p. 29

64   **'He rather surprised'**: Hart, *Journals, 1854–1863*, p. 15; **'I ate'**: Hart, *Journals, 1854–1863*, pp. 317–18; **well over 32 million**: Hart, *Journals, 1863–1866*, p. 343; **indemnities paid out**: Morse, vol. 1, p. 570; vol. 2, p. 33; Qing Government (ed.), *Tongzhi*, p. 3615; **import of rice**: Li Wenzhi (ed.), pp. 770, 773; Qing Government (ed.), *Tongzhi*, pp. 6032–4

65   **Hart writings**: Hart, *Journals, 1863–1866*, pp. 282–8, 326–46; Qing Government (ed.), *Tongzhi*, pp. 3764–87; **'like a hare'**: Freeman-Mitford, pp. 240–1

66   **'makes some good points'**: Qing Government (ed.), *Tongzhi*, pp. 3767–70; **watch their language**: Mi Rucheng (ed.), pp. 29–31; **'I am British'**: Guo Songtao, p. 15

67   **'incalculable damages'**: Qing Government (ed.), *Tongzhi*, p. 5157; **'not said anything'**: Qing Government (ed.), *Tongzhi*, p. 3765; **Shore noted**: Shore, p. 394; **'in this place'**: Freeman-Mitford, p. 158

68   **Gong told the foreign envoys**: Mi Rucheng (ed.), p. 30; **severely worded edict**: Qing Government (ed.), *Tongzhi*, pp. 3817–18; **'I do not know'**: Hart, *Journals, 1863–1866*, p. 298

69   **Cixi on ship-building**: Qing Government (ed.), *Tongzhi*, pp. 4469–72

Chapter 6   Virgin Journeys to the West (1861–71)

70   **granted no kneeling**: First Historical Archives of China (ed.) 1998, vol. 11, no. 1349; **'having too high'**: Wu Xiangxiang, p. 10

71   **Grand Adviser title taken away**: First Historical Archives of China (ed.) 1998, vol. 15, nos. 293, 378; **'to borrow Western methods'**: Association of Chinese Historians (ed.), *The Movement to Learn from the West*, vol. 2, p. 30; **'stooges of'**: Weng Tonghe 2006, vol. 1, pp. 519, 521

72   **Cixi-Woren**: Qing Government (ed.), *Tongzhi*, pp. 4557–616; Weng Tonghe 2006, vol. 1, pp. 527–44; **Weng against the West**: Weng Tonghe 2006, vol.

I, pp. 78, 93, 429; Kong Xiangji 2008, pp. 29–32; **Cixi on Hsü**: Qing Government (ed.), *Tongzhi*, pp. 4523–5; Weng Tonghe 2006, vol. I, p. 515

73   **'just like the one'**: Zhang Deyi, p. 520; Hsü Chi-she, on America; **'inflating the status'**: Gu Hongming, p. 54; **Cixi appoints Hsü**: Qing Government (ed.), *Tongzhi*, p. 3503; Shan Shiyuan 1990, pp. 68–9; Association of Chinese Historians (ed.), *The Movement to Learn from the West*, vol. 2, p. 28; Freeman-Mitford, pp. 181–2; **appoints Martin**: Qing Government (ed.), *Tongzhi*, pp. 2701–4

74   **Binchun's travels**: All quotes in Binchun; **Queen Victoria noted**: Royal Archives, Windsor, VIC/MAIN/QVJ/1866

75   **Binchun diaries to Cixi**: Qing Government (ed.), *Tongzhi*, pp. 4443–5

76   **Binchun promotion**: Hart, *Journals, 1863–1866*, p. 360; Weng Tonghe 2006, vol. 2, p. 684; **Weng mentioned him**: Kong Xiangji 2008, p. 31; Weng Tonghe 2006, vol. 2, p. 684; **Gong to Cixi on Burlingame**: Qing Government (ed.), *Tongzhi*, pp. 4899–917

77   **The conservatives**: Weng Tonghe 2006, vol. I, p. 568; **'Mr Hart's brain'**: Morse: vol. 2, pp. 188–9; **In fact, Hart**: Morse: vol. 2, pp. 190, 194, 203; **Queen Victoria diary**: Royal Archives, Windsor, VIC/MAIN/QVJ/1868

78   **'the citizens of New York'**: Burlingame speech in Schrecker; in Shore, p. 408–9

79   **'It affords me'**: Schrecker

80   **'it is of utmost importance'**: Qing Government (ed.), *Tongzhi*, p. 6640; Zhigang, p. 361; **Zhigang quotes and audience:** Zhigang, pp. 244–380

81   **Madame Tussaud's commission**: 1845 edition of Madame Tussaud's catalogue, in Arthur, p. 11; **diaries presented to Cixi**: Li Hongzhang, vol. 4, pp. 363–5

82   **Cixi told Li not to come**: Li Hongzhang, vol. 5, p. 183; **'Unexpectedly'**: Association of Chinese Historians (ed.), *The Movement to Learn from the West*, vol. 8, p. 270

Chapter 7   Love Doomed (1869)

83   **Emperors against eunuchs**: Li Guorong, p. 184

84   **'indulgence in seeking pleasures'**: Weng Tonghe 2005, vol. I, p. 1; Weng Tonghe 2006, vol. 2, p. 703; **'depressing' place**: Carl, p. 203; **Weng comments**: Weng Tonghe 2006, vol. 2, pp. 705, 711

85   **Prince Chun insistent on execution**: Xue Fucheng 2004, vol. I, p. 42; Xue Fucheng 1983, p. 83; **'Can he be spared'**: Xue Fucheng 2004, vol. I, p. 42; **'must not be allowed'**: First Historical Archives of China (ed.) 1998, vol. 19, no. 526; **corpse exposed for days**: Woqiu Zhongzi, p. 52; Xue Fucheng 1897; **An's belongings**: First Historical Archives of China (ed.) 1998, vol. 19, no. 548; Tang Yinian, p. 153

86   **friend of An strangulated**: First Historical Archives of China (ed.) 1998, vol. 19, no. 632; Woqiu Zhongzi, p. 52; Yuan Xieming; **'taking out her anger'**: Xue Fucheng 2004, vol. I, p. 43; **women allowed to be seen**: Ding Baozhen, vol. 2, pp. 801–2; First Historical Archives of China (ed.) 1998, vol. 19, no. 631; **'a boom'**: Xue Fucheng 1897; **Cixi collapsed**: Weng Tonghe 2006, vol. 2, pp. 721–30

87   **operas put on daily**: Ding Ruqin, pp. 231–2

Chapter 8   A Vendetta against the West (1869–71)

88   **Chun memorandum**: Qing Government (ed.), *Tongzhi*, pp. 5927–41; Weng Tonghe 2006, vol. 2, p. 671

89   **'Even if we do not'**: Zeng Jize, p. 334; **grandees' reaction**: Qing Government (ed.), *Tongzhi*, pp. 5941–50; **'If it were otherwise'**: Freeman-Mitford, pp. xii–xiii

90   **Isabella Bird observed**: Bird, p. 257; **'swearing that the charge'**: Freeman-Mitford, pp. xlii–xliii

91   **'Stories of child eating'**: Bird, p. 346; **1870 Tianjin riot**: Daily communications, including Cixi's detailed instructions, in First Historical Archives of China & History Department of Fujian Normal University (eds), vol. 1, pp. 775ff.; Weng Tonghe 2006, vol. 2, pp. 776ff.; Morse, vol. 2, p. 246.

92   **'deal with them fairly'**: First Historical Archives of China & History Department of Fujian Normal University (eds), vol. 1, pp. 778–9; First Historical Archives of China (ed.) 1998, vol. 11, no. 1538

93   **Chun held sway**: Weng Tonghe 2006, vol. 2, pp. 784–5; **screen removed**: Weng Tonghe 2006, vol. 2, p. 784

94   **Ma Xinyi**: Weng Tonghe 2006, vol. 2, p. 793; First Historical Archives of China & History Department of Fujian Normal University (eds), vol. 1, pp. 814–17; **'excessive executions'**: Li Hongzhang, vol. 4, p. 76

95   **Chun to Cixi**: Qing Government (ed.), *Tongzhi*, pp. 7285–336; Wu Xiangxiang, vol. 1, pp. 121–7; Weng Tonghe 2006, vol. 2, p. 824

Chapter 9   Life and Death of Emperor Tongzhi (1861–75)

97   **Tongzhi starts schooling**: First Historical Archives of China (ed.) 1998, vol. 11, no. 343; **his education and life**: Weng Tonghe 2006, vol. 2, *passim*.

98   **Cixi–son relationship**: Weng Tonghe 2006, vol. 2, pp. 839, 849–50, 862, 882, 1068; Yu Bingkun et al., p. 240; **Wang Qingqi**: Wu Xiangxiang, vol. 1, pp. 218–25; Weng Tonghe 2006, vol. 2, pp. 1067, 1073; Gao Shu, p. 156

99   **Miss Alute**: Xue Fucheng 1983, pp. 26–7

100   **the bride's route and procession**: Simpson, Chapter XV; Morse, vol. 2, pp. 265–6

101   **Foreign legations**: Morse, vol. 2, p. 266; **the wedding**: Zhang Shiyun

102   **No. 2 consort**: Zhang Shiyun; **After the wedding**: Xue Fucheng 1983, pp. 26–7; **seals no longer used**: Yu Bingkun et al., p. 116; **'not be lazy'**: Weng Tonghe 2006, vol. 2, p. 849; **Tongzhi's rule**: Wu Xiangxiang, vol. 1, pp. 214–25; Qing Government (ed.), *Tongzhi*, *passim*; **arguments over kowtow**: Qing Government (ed.), *Tongzhi*, pp. 8226–353

103   **Cixi had already made her decision**: Qing Government (ed.), *Tongzhi*, pp. 8287–8; **Weng troubled**: Weng Tonghe 2006, vol. 2, pp. 983–4

105   **Over Old Summer Palace**: Wu Xiangxiang, vol. 1, pp. 206–25; **Chun: Tongzhi duty to avenge father**: Qing Government (ed.), *Tongzhi*, pp. 8527–32; **Tongzhi against opposition**: Weng Tonghe 2006, vol. 2, pp. 1059, 1062; Wu Xiangxiang, vol. 1, pp. 208–9, 219–26; Wu Rulun, vol. 1, p. 314; **Cixi intervenes**: Weng Tonghe 2005, vol. 1, p. 2; Tonghe 2006, vol. 2, p. 1063; Wu Rulun, vol. 1, p. 314

106   **Tongzhi's medical records, his illness**: *Tongzhi jinyaobu*, in Archives of Ming and Qing Dynasties (ed.) 1979, vol. 7, pp. 265–92; Weng Tonghe 2006, vol. 2, pp. 1073–86

107   **Cixi stands in for son**: Weng Tonghe 2006, vol. 2, pp. 1076–7; Weng Tonghe 2005, vol. 1, p. 3; **Wang Qingqi banished**: First Historical Archives of China (ed.) 1998, vol. 24, no. 1119; Weng Tonghe 2006, vol. 2, p. 1089

108   **Grand Princess died**: Weng Tonghe 2006, vol. 2, pp. 1092–3; **Miss Alute's death**: Xin Xiuming, p. 26; Xue Fucheng 1983, p. 27; **family deaths**: First Historical Archives of China (ed.) 2003, vol. 3, pp. 891–2; Qing History Institute, Renmin University (ed.), vol. 12, p. 226; Yun Yuding, vol. 2, p. 789

109   **burying her son**: Weng Tonghe 2006, vol. 3, pp. 1096–112; Li Yin, pp. 238–52; Qu Chunhai, pp. 39–40, 79–81

110   **'You have a good heart'**: Carl, p. 243

Chapter 10   A Three-year-old is Made Emperor (1875)

113   **Cixi after son died**: Weng Tonghe 2006, vol. 2, pp. 1086–7; Chen Kuilong, p. 100

114   **Chun terrified**: Weng Tonghe 2006, vol. 2, p. 1087; **only son at the time**: Aisin-Gioro Puyi, p. 29; **'he lay in a corner'**: Chen Kuilong, p. 100; **Junglu**: Chen Kuilong, p. 100

115   **Guangxu into palace**: Weng Tonghe 2006, vol. 2, p. 1087; Zhu Shoupeng, vol. 1, p. 2; **Chun resignation**: Weng Tonghe 2006, vol. 2, pp. 1088–9; Zhu Shoupeng, vol. 1, p. 3

116   **Chun's more personal tragedy**: Aisin-Gioro Puyi, pp. 29–30; **Cixi favours and Chun grateful**: Pujia, Pujie et al., pp. 209–14; Zhu Shoupeng (ed.), vol. 2, p. 1470; Zhu Jiajin, 1982, no. 4; **10,000 taels**: Chen Kuilong, p. 197, cf. pp. 120–1

117   **newspapers available to the court**: Qing Government (ed.), *Tongzhi*, pp. 4549–56

Chapter 11   Modernisation Accelerates (1875–89)

118   **Earl Li meetings**: Li Hongzhang, vol. 31, p. 166; **US President Grant**: Packard, p. 711; **'Physically he was'**: Richard, p. 298; **'synonymous'**: Carl, p. 256; **'From now on'**: Zhu Shoupeng (ed.), vol. 1, p. 336

119   **Guo minister to London**: Tang Jiaxuan (ed.), p. 780; Guo Songtao, *passim*; **'perverse'**: Kong Xiangji 2008, p. 32; **Guo's three audiences with Cixi**: Guo Songtao, pp. 2–21; **'a good man'**: Zeng Jize, p. 335

120   **Hung Jun**: Liu Bannong et al., pp. 11–14, 71–2; **'no foot-dragging'**: First Historical Archives of China (ed.), 1996, nos 1020, 1021; **officials to travel**: Wang Xiaoqiu & Yang Jiguo, pp. 1–34

121   **commission to Cuba report**: Cuba Commission, p. 3; **'You must find ways'**: Li Hongzhang, vol. 6, pp. 327–8; **banned slave trade**: Tang Jiaxuan (ed.), pp. 75, 277, 439; **Chen Lanbin**: Cuba Commission, p. 5; Zhu Shoupeng (ed.), vol. 1, p. 85

122   **'biggest permanent threat'**: Li Hongzhang, vol. 4, pp. 216–17; **build up the navy**: Zhu Shoupeng (ed.), vol. 1, p. 74; vol. 2, p. 1977; Wang Daocheng 1994, no. 4; **endorsing first national flag**: First Historical Archives of China (ed.), 1996, vol. 14, no. 848; Zhang Xia et al. (eds), pp. 470–505; Palace Museum (ed.) 2002, vol. 11, pp. 16–17; **'China proudly took'**: Morse, vol. 2, p. 393; **'he must bear in mind'**: Morse, vol. 2, Appendix D

123   **'Great Dragons'**: Palace Museum (ed.) 2002, vol. 12, p. 379; **'China's weakness'**: Mi Rucheng (ed.), vol. 1, p. 78, cf. p. 7; **installation of telegraph**: Association of Chinese Historians (ed.), *The Movement to Learn from the West*, vol. 6, p. 325ff.; Sheng Xuanhuai, vol. 1, p. 107; **modern coal-mining**: Association of Chinese Historians (ed.), *The Movement to Learn from the West*, vol. 1, pp. 153–5; vol. 7, pp. 20, 23–4, 26, 103, 128, 138, *passim*; Sun Yutang (ed.), vol. 1, no. 2, pp. 612–47; **electricity**: Huang Xi, pp. 33–4; Huang Xing, 2009, vol. 38, no. 3

124   **Beijing's first tram**: Huang Xi, p. 35; **replacing outdated currency**: Weng Tonghe 2006, vol. 4, p. 2032; Association of Chinese Historians (ed.), *The Movement to Learn from the West*, vol. 7, p. 540; **'We would have to borrow'**: Li Hongzhang, vol. 9, p. 259

125   **the Wusong line**: Mi Rucheng (ed.), vol. 1, p. 39ff.; Sun Yutang (ed.), vol. 1, no. 2, p. 612; **railway in the Sea Palace**: Association of Chinese Historians (ed.), *The Movement to Learn from the West*, vol. 6, pp. 221–2; Yang Naiji; Carl, p. 290; Weng Tonghe 2006, vol. 5, p. 2561; Yu Bingkun et al., p. 173

126   **'a giant in intellect'**: Martin 2005, p. 219; **trade deficit**: Zhu Shoupeng (ed.), vol. 3, p. 2556; **Viceroy Zhang proposal**: Zhang Zhidong, vol. 1, pp. 661–7

127   **Cixi deliberation**: Zhang Zhidong, vol. 1, p. 667; **'This project has**

magnificent': Association of Chinese Historians (ed.), *The Movement to Learn from the West*, vol. 6, p. 262; **'Textile making'**: First Historical Archives of China (ed.) 2005, vol. 1, p. 74

Chapter 12   Defender of the Empire (1875–89)

129   **'lost consciousness'**: Zhu Shoupeng (ed.), vol. 1, p. 3; **Chun change**: Pujia, Pujie et al., pp. 210–14; Aisin-Gioro Puyi, pp. 7–8; Association of Chinese Historians (ed.), *The Movement to Learn from the West*, vol. 6, p. 186

130   **Morse remarked**: Morse, vol. 2, pp. 328–9; **'a soldier of fortune'**: Denby, vol. 1, p. 242; **Earl Li's view**: Qing Government (ed.), *Tongzhi*, pp. 9136–8; **Marquis Zeng**: Qing Government (ed.), *Tongzhi*, p. 9137; **Chun's view**: Association of Chinese Historians (ed.), *The Movement to Learn from the West*, vol. 1, p. 116

131   **'minding other people's business'**: Zeng Jize, p. 382; **Cixi endorsing Zuo**: Zhu Shoupeng (ed.), vol. 1, pp. 804, 917–19; vol. 2, p. 1838; **'China's new diplomacy' and Queen Victoria**: Morse, vol. 2, p. 333; **Gordon advice**: Morse, vol. 2, pp. 334–5

132   **'ready for war'**: Morse, vol. 2, p. 338; **Cixi conducting negotiations**: Zeng Jize, pp. 41–7; Zhu Shoupeng (ed.), vol. 1, pp. 855–6, 870, 896–7; **'diplomatic triumph'**: Morse, vol. 2, p. 338; **Lord Dufferin**: Morse, vol. 2, p. 339; **Cixi illness**: Zhu Shoupeng (ed.), vol. 1, p. 936; Xue Baotian, pp. 50–116

133   **'begged to be excused'**: Zhu Shoupeng (ed.), vol. 2, pp. 1679–82; **Cixi approach to Vietnam**: Zhu Shoupeng (ed.), vol. 1, p. 1213; vol. 2, pp. 1399–400, 1685–6, 1729–30, *passim*; Zhang Zhenkun, vol. 1, pp. 30–1, 44–5, 54–5

134   **'I can't but worry'**: Weng Tonghe 2006, vol. 4, pp. 1787–8; **Prince Gong**: Weng Tonghe 2006, vol. 4, pp. 1732 , 1737, 1775–7, 1787, 1790, 1811–15; **30 March 1884**: Weng Tonghe 2006, vol. 4, p. 1816

135   **dismissing Gong**: Weng Tonghe 2006, vol. 4, pp. 1817–18; He Gangde, p. 9

136   **'hard to look back'**: Dong Shouyi, pp. 433–40; **'protracted war'**: Li Hongzhang, vol. 10, pp. 331–3; **'totally unjust'**: Zhu Shoupeng (ed.), vol. 2, p. 1699

137   **'Have read it'**: Li Hongzhang, vol. 21, p. 150; **Cixi withdrew troops**: Zhu Shoupeng (ed.), vol. 2, pp. 1744–5; **France demands indemnity**: Morse, vol. 2, p. 355; Li Hongzhang, vol. 21, p. 181; **not a sou**: Li Hongzhang, vol. 21, p. 199; Kong Xiangji 2001, pp. 344–8; **'war is unavoidable'**: Zhu Shoupeng (ed.), vol. 2, pp. 1766–7; **'When it comes to'**: Kong Xiangji 2001, p. 329; **overseas Chinese**: Zhu Shoupeng (ed.), vol. 2, pp. 1804–5

138   **'swept away'**: Kong Xiangji 2001, p. 348; **Cixi orders ceasefire**: Zhang Zhidong, vol. 3, pp. 1917–22; Zhu Shoupeng (ed.), vol. 2, pp. 1912–14; **Vietnamese helping French**: Zhu Shoupeng (ed.), vol. 2, pp. 1729–30; Li Hongzhang, vol. 10, p. 418; Archives of Ming and Qing Dynasties (ed.) 1979a, vol. 1, p. 60; **'If it had not been'**: Kong Xiangji 2001, p. 352

139   **Patenôtre and Earl Li**: http://history.cultural-china.com/en/34History6627.html; **Cixi writes in crimson ink**: First Historical Archives of China (ed.) 1995, vol. 64, pp. 818, 821, 823, 840

140   **annual revenue had doubled**: Shen Xuefeng; **ten million taels**: Li Wenzhi (ed.), p. 773; **Hart's honour**: Zhu Shoupeng (ed.), vol. 3, p. 2570; Hart, *Letters, 1868–1907*, vol. 1, pp. 737–8; **the banquet**: Kong Xiangji & Murata Yujiro 2004, pp. 48–58; **Charles Denby**: Denby, vol. 1, pp. 241–8

Chapter 13   Guangxu Alienated from Cixi (1875–94)

145   **'I send you out'**: Carl, pp. 192–3

146   **Empress Zhen's strokes**: Weng Tonghe 2006, vol. 1, p. 259; vol. 2, p. 735; vol. 3, p. 1555; see the historian Xu Che's investigation, in Xu Che, pp. 345–7; **mourning**

ban: Zhu Shoupeng (ed.), vol. 1, pp. 1065, 1244; vol. 2, p. 1450; Hart, *Letters, 1868–1907*, vol. 1, p. 371; Weng Tonghe 2006, vol. 4, p. 1751; Ding Ruqin, p. 242

147 **Guangxu's first lesson**: Weng Tonghe 2006, vol. 3, p. 1191

148 **'sitting, standing'**: Weng Tonghe 2006, vol. 3, p. 1266; **'I have been missing you'**: Weng Tonghe 2006, vol. 3, p. 1327; **Guangxu's education**: Weng Tonghe 2006, vols 3 & 4 *passim*; First Historical Archives of China (ed.) 2005, vol. 1, pp. 69–75; **report from a governor**: from the First Historical Archives of China, Beijing, archive number: 04-01-14-0080-001; First Historical Archives of China (ed.) 1995, vol. 1, p. 73

149 **'don't begrudge them expenses'**: from the First Historical Archives of China, Beijing, archive number: 04-01-12-0528-062; **essays and poems**: Society of Manchu Studies (ed.), pp. 178–201

150 **wooden horse**: Society of Manchu Studies (ed.), p. 195; **enterprising Dane**: Headland, p. 116; **stutter**: He Gangde, p. 16; **thunder**: Xin Xiuming, p. 31; Weng Tonghe 2006, vol. 5, p. 2452

151 **Cixi postpones retirement**: Zhu Shoupeng (ed.), vol. 2, pp. 2119–27; Weng Tonghe 2006, vol. 4, pp. 2028–31; **Earl Li and Prince Chun**: Li Hongzhang, vol. 34, pp. 42, 47, 50; **Weng reaction**: Weng Tonghe 2006, vol. 4, pp. 2030–1; **Guangxu reaction**: Weng Tonghe 2006, vol. 4, pp. 2029–31, 2089–92, 2103; Lin Keguang et al., p. 27; **health deteriorated**: Zhu Jinfu & Zhou Wenquan 1982, no. 3; Weng Tonghe 2006, vol. 4, pp. 2068, 2125; First Historical Archives of China (ed.) 2005, vol. 1, pp. 75–6

152 **'duty to the ancestors'**: Weng Tonghe 2006, vol. 4, p. 2103; **smashed glass and Cixi reaction**: Weng Tonghe 2006, vol. 4, pp. 2201–2, 2211–2; Lin Keguang et al., p. 39; **'in a fury'**: Weng Tonghe 2006, vol. 5, p. 2503; cf. Headland, p. 202

153 **'reserved' as empress**: Yehenala Genzheng & Hao Xiaohui 2008, p. 4; Weng Tonghe 2006, vol. 4, p. 2231; **Duke Guixiang figure of scorn**: Pujia, Pujie et al., p. 94; Xin Xiuming, p. 85; Yehenala Genzheng & Hao Xiaohui 2007, pp. 164, 170–4; Jin Yi & Shen Yiling, pp. 295–8

154 **5.5 million taels**: Weng Tonghe 2006, vol. 4, p. 2255; Weng Tonghe 2005, vol. 2, p. 1051; **The grand banquet**: Weng Tonghe 2006, vol. 4, p. 2261; **how Guangxu treats Longyu**: Rongling, p. 21; Headland, p. 202

155 **Pearl**: Pujia, Pujie et al., p. 187; Xin Xiuming, p. 23; **French doctor**: Franzini; **Weng in Shanghai**: Weng Tonghe 2005, vol. 2, p. 1052; **Weng on church orphanage**: Weng Tonghe 2006, vol. 4, p. 2311

156 **Heaven's warning**: Weng Tonghe 2006, vol. 4, p. 2249; **Cixi's meeting with the pair**: Weng Tonghe 2006, vol. 4, p. 2256; **shelved the railway**: Association of Chinese Historians (ed.), *The Movement to Learn from the West*, vol. 6, pp. 274–6; Li Hongzhang, vol. 34, p. 634; **currency reform ditched**: Association of Chinese Historians (ed.), *The Movement to Learn from the West*, vol. 7, pp. 548ff.; Weng Tonghe 2006, vol. 4, p. 2032; **ordered Guangxu to learn English**: Weng Tonghe 2005, vol. 2, p. 1056; Li Hongzhang, vol. 35, p. 324; **Weng's dismay**: Weng Tonghe 2006, vol. 5, pp. 2481, 2484; **speech problem**: Seagrave, p. 175; He Gangde, p. 16

157 **'period of slumber'**: Morse, vol. 2, p. 394; **'Audience went'**: Hart, *Letters, 1868–1907*, vol. 2, p. 837; **'The foreign barbarian'**: Weng Tonghe 2006, vol. 5, p. 2428

158 **'Railroads'**: Seagrave, p. 175

Chapter 14   The Summer Palace (1886–94)

159 **ultimate ambition**: Xin Xiuming, pp. 47–8; **'strike'**: Yu Bingkun et al., pp. 158–68

160 **'all in the empire'**: First Historical Archives of China (ed.), 1996, no. 80; Zhu Shoupeng (ed.), vol. 3, pp. 2414–15; **abandoned visiting Wutai**: He Gangde, p. 17;

told grandees: Weng Tonghe 2006, vol. 4, p. 2060; **Summer Palace cost**: Wang Daocheng 1994, no. 4; Ye Zhiru & Tang Yinian, pp. 1027–31; cf. Xin Xiuming, p. 47

161 **some three million taels**: Association of Chinese Historians (ed.), *The Movement to Learn from the West*, vol. 3, p. 141; Wang Daocheng 1994, no. 4; Ye Zhiru & Tang Yinian, pp. 1029–30

162 **'the latest models'**: Li Hongzhang, vol. 35, p. 213; **'never seen such'**: Weng Tonghe 2006, vol. 5, pp. 2879–80

Chapter 15   In Retirement and in Leisure (1889–94)

163 **the Statutes**: First Historical Archives of China (ed.), 1996, vol. 14, no. 1164; cf. Mao Haijian 2005, p. 11; **reject an official's petition**: First Historical Archives of China (ed.), 1996, vol. 15, no. 85; **first list sent to Cixi**: *Junjichu suishou dengjidang (Files of Documents that Passed through the Grand Council)*, 5 March 1889 ff.

164 **stepped in over the railway**: First Historical Archives of China (ed.), 1996, vol. 15, no. 813; Zhu Shoupeng (ed.), vol. 3, p. 2646; **Weng against it**: Zhu Shoupeng (ed.), vol. 3, p. 2552; Weng Tonghe 2006, vol. 4, p. 2323; **Guangxu shelved it**: Association of Chinese Historians (ed.), *The Movement to Learn from the West*, vol. 6, p. 274–6; Li Hongzhang, vol. 34, p. 634; **met with Grand Council**: Weng Tonghe 2006, vol. 5, p. 2353; Li Hongzhang, vol. 35, p. 324; **tension with Guangxu**: Weng Tonghe 2006, vol. 5, pp. 2353, 2446; **move into Summer Palace**: Weng Tonghe 2006, vol. 5, p. 2447; **'After my retirement'**: to Liu Kunyi, in Association of Chinese Historians (ed.), *The Reforms of 1898*, vol. 4, p. 301; Xin Xiuming, pp. 18, 21

165 **'In person'**: Carl, p. 125; **eunuchs recalled**: Pujia, Pujie et al., pp. 189–90

166 **Censors wrote to reprimand**: Zhu Shoupeng (ed.), vol. 2, pp. 2149, 2151; Weng Tonghe 2006, vol. 4, p. 2049

167 **Longyu**: Carl, p. 43; Rongling, p. 22; Jin Yi & Shen Yiling, p. 150

168 **jet-black toupee**: Xin Xiuming, p. 13; **daily routine**: Der Ling 2004; Rongling; Jin Yi & Shen Yiling; Xin Xiuming; Carl; Headland; Yehenala Genzheng & Hao Xiaohui 2007

170 **'Old Buddha'**: Jin Liang 1998, p. 163; Headland, p. 85; **taking human milk**: Xin Xiuming, p. 41; Forbidden City Publishing (ed.), pp. 200–2; Carl, p. 48

171 **daily allocation of food**: Kong Xiangji 1998, p. 110; **seldom drank**: Carl, ·p. 190; Rongling, p. 19; **'when Her Majesty awakes'**: Carl, pp. 23–4

172 **hot-air balloon**: Li Hongzhang, vol. 35, pp. 502–3

173 **'clothes, shoes'**: Der Ling 2004, p. 26; **'as if entranced'**: Jin Yi & Shen Yiling, p. 165; Der Ling 2004, p. 128

174 **'flower mountain'**: Gao Shu, p. 176; Carl, p. 40; **collection of gourds**: Rongling, p. 15; Xin Xiuming, p. 3; Carl, p. 115; **cooked food herself**: Der Ling 2004, p. 95; **giant marquees**: Carl, p. 60, Conger, pp. 261–2; Jin Yi & Shen Yiling, pp. 146–7

175 **'She had a long'**: Carl, p. 140; **dog-breeders considered**: Hubbard, p. 220; **against 'sleeve-dog'**: Carl, pp. 53–5

176 **'the liveliest interest'**: Carl, p. 173; **visiting collection in church**: Yu Bingkun et al., p. 172; First Historical Archives of China (ed.) 2005, vol. 2, pp. 920–1; **invented a dice game**: Der Ling 2004, pp. 76–7; **against gambling**: Rongling, p. 32

177 **hated foot-binding**: Carl, p. 48; Headland, pp. 88, 233; **watched village performers**: Xin Xiuming, p. 71; Gao Shu, p. 157

178 *The Monkey King*: Rongling, p. 9; **tips to performers**: Ding Ruqin, pp. 255–7

179 *The Warriors of the Yang Family*: Ding Ruqin, pp. 267–8; Zao Yang; Xin Xiuming, p. 38; **'The most vicious'**: Forbidden City Publishing (ed.), p. 377

180 **Lady Miao scroll**: Yu Bingkun et al., p. 157

Notes

Chapter 16   War with Japan (1894)

181   **On Japan in 1882**: Li Hongzhang, vol. 10, pp. 74–6, 277; First Historical Archives of China (ed.) 1995, vol. 64, p. 821

182   **on Japan in 1884**: Li Hongzhang, vol. 10, pp. 640–1, 684; **'speedy and satisfactory'**: Li Hongzhang, vol. 11, p. 60; **Hart wrote**: Hart, *Letters, 1868–1907*, vol. 1, p. 592; **Cixi guideline for navy**: Li Hongzhang, vol. 12, p. 531; First Historical Archives of China (ed.) 1995, vol. 65, pp. 33, 45; **stopped buying warships**: Li Hongzhang, vol. 15, p. 335; **'We have had lakes'**: Hart, *Letters, 1868–1907*, vol. 1, p. 803; **footnote**: Li Hongzhang, vol. 10, pp. 497–8

183   **rice imports**: Li Wenzhi (ed.), p. 773; **naval/army purchases discontinued**: Association of Chinese Historians (ed.), *The Sino-Japanese War*, vol. 3, pp. 177–8; **'is concentrating the resources'**: Li Hongzhang, vol. 35, p. 562; **Japan better equipped**: Li Hongzhang, vol. 15, pp. 423–4; vol. 35, p. 562; Jiang Ming, pp. 328–9; **checking Earl Li accounts**: Li Hongzhang, vol. 13, pp. 74–7, 207–9, 249–50, 351–4, 364–8, 391–2, 420, 546–53; vol. 14, *passim*; vol. 35, p. 587

184   **'chooses to believe'**: Wang Daocheng 1994, no. 4; **glowing report**: Li Hongzhang, vol. 14, pp. 94–6; **'Our ships are not'**: Li Hongzhang, vol. 35, p. 252; **'paper tiger'**: Wu (Woo) Yong, p. 107; **navy requests not passed on**: Li Hongzhang, vol. 15, p. 406; **'seeking to be one-up'**: Li Hongzhang, vol. 35, p. 562; **Li 1894 report**: Li Hongzhang, vol. 15, pp. 333–6

185   **Ito made up mind to take on China**: The memoirs of Mutsu Munemitsu, *Kenkenroku*, in Wang Yunsheng, vol. 2, p. 35

186   **'calculating with too much'**: Hart, *Letters, 1868–1907*, vol. 2, p. 976; **'not just threatening'**: Li Hongzhang, vol. 15, pp. 371–4; **'within our expectations'**: Li Hongzhang, vol. 15, p. 372; **'launching a punitive'**: Li Hongzhang, vol. 15, p. 383; Weng Tonghe 2005, vol. 1, pp. 117–18; **'999 out of'**: Hart, *Letters, 1868–1907*, vol. 2, p. 979; **'in a really masterful way'**: Hart, *Letters, 1868–1907*, vol. 2, p. 976; **'her army and navy'**: Hart, *Letters, 1868–1907*, vol. 2, pp. 974–5

187   **'Britain cannot allow'**: Li Hongzhang, vol. 24, p. 168

188   **Cixi gave full support**: Weng Tonghe 2006, vol. 5, p. 2708; **'must not do anything'**: Weng Tonghe 2006, vol. 5, p. 2708; **reprimanded Councillors**: Weng Tonghe 2006, vol. 5, p. 2720; **Cixi out of policy loop**: Weng Tonghe 2005, vol. 2, p. 1108; **'cowardly and incompetent'**: Li Hongzhang, vol. 15, p. 406; **Zhirui insisted**: Qi Qizhang (ed.), vol. 1, p. 41; **Cixi, Guangxu and Earl Li over Admiral Ting**: Weng Tonghe 2005, vol. 2, p. 1091; Li Hongzhang, vol. 15, pp. 405–7

189   **Cixi saw Grand Council**: Weng Tonghe 2006, vol. 5, pp. 2730–1; **scheduled to return to Summer Palace**: Weng Tonghe 2006, vol. 5, p. 2732; **Li presented detailed reports**: Li Hongzhang, vol. 15, pp. 415–36; **donating three million taels**: Li Hongzhang, vol. 15, p. 424; **sixtieth birthday celebrations cancelled**: Weng Tonghe 2006, vol. 5, p. 2732; First Historical Archives of China (ed.), 1996, vol. 20, nos 1011–12

190   **'Hold it for now'**: Weng Tonghe 2005, vol. 2, p. 1096; **'further fighting'**: Hart, *Letters, 1868–1907*, vol. 2, p. 991; **Cixi trying to persuade Weng**: Weng Tonghe 2006, vol. 5, p. 2738; Weng Tonghe 2005, vol. 2, p. 1098

191   **Earl Li's gifts**: Li Hongzhang, vol. 15, p. 452; **'No presents, please'**: Weng Tonghe 2006, vol. 5, p. 2740; **tell officials to present gifts**: ibid.

192   **attempting to explain**: First Historical Archives of China (ed.), 1996, vol. 20, no. 1117; **'Things look bad'**: Hart, *Letters, 1868–1907*, vol. 2, pp. 991–2; **'we shall probably'**: Hart, *Letters, 1868–1907*, vol. 2, p. 992; **no gifts for seventieth birthday**: First Historical Archives of China (ed.), 1996, vol. 30, no. 370; Zhu Shoupeng (ed.), vol. 5, p. 5071; Hu Sijing, pp. 28–9. For other birthdays: Wu (Woo) Yong, p. 99; Zhu Shoupeng (ed.), vol. 5, pp. 5093, 5575, 5745, etc.

193 **Pearl sold posts**: Weng Tonghe 2006, vol. 5, p. 2754; Xin Xiuming, p. 24; Kong Xiangji 1998, pp. 89–95; First Historical Archives of China (ed.), 1996, vol. 20, no. 803; also nos 446, 459; **obtained confessions from Pearl**: Kong Xiangji 1998, pp. 84–7

194 **Headland recalled**: Headland, pp. 203–4; **26 November decree**: First Historical Archives of China (ed.), 1996, vol. 20, no. 1301; **Guangxu reaction to decree**: Weng Tonghe 2006, vol. 5, p. 2754; **Cixi had full access to information**: First Historical Archives of China (ed.), 1996, vol. 20, no. 1304ff.; Weng Tonghe 2005, vol. 2, p. 1108; Weng Tonghe 2006, vol. 5, p. 2797

195 **Zhirui petitions**: Qi Qizhang (ed.), vol. 1, pp. 41–5; **'a hen crowing'**: Kong Xiangji & Murata Yujiro 2004, pp. 290–1; **distraught by allegation**: Weng Tonghe 2006, vol. 5, pp. 2756, 2764; **'rest assured'**: to Liu Kunyi, in Association of Chinese Historians (ed.), *The Reforms of 1898*, vol. 4, p. 300

196 **Two other friends**: Weng Tonghe 2006, vol. 5, p. 2856; Mao Haijian 2005, p. 468; Zhu Shoupeng (ed.), vol. 4, p. 3685; **tried to close Guangxu's study**: Weng Tonghe 2006, vol. 5, pp. 2757–9

Chapter 17 A Peace that Ruined China (1895)

197 **Cixi key points, 5 January 1895**: Weng Tonghe 2005, vol. 2, p. 1116; **'dying swine'**: Kong Xiangji 2001, p. 16; **6 February, told Grand Council**: Weng Tonghe 2005, vol. 2, p. 1125; Weng Tonghe 2006, vol. 5, p. 2776

198 **'Empress Dowager had outrage'**: Wang Wenshao, p. 870; **called on troops to fight on**: Zhu Shoupeng (ed.), vol. 4, p. 3539; **Viceroy Zhang**: Zhang Zhidong, vol. 3, pp. 2036, 2047; **Guangxu and Council willing to accept Japanese terms**: Weng Tonghe 2005, vol. 2, pp. 1125–6; Weng Tonghe 2006, vol. 5, pp. 2776–7; **'come and get instructions'**: Weng Tonghe 2006, vol. 5, p. 2778

199 **Cixi objected to ceding territory**: Weng Tonghe 2006, vol. 5, p. 2782; Weng Tonghe 2005, vol. 2, pp. 1134–5; **Guangxu authorised 'cede territory'**: Li Hongzhang, vol. 16, p. 31; Weng Tonghe 2005, vol. 2, p. 1137; **Councillors wrote to Cixi**: Li Hongzhang, vol. 16, p. 31; **Guangxu tiptoed**: Weng Tonghe 2006, vol. 5, p. 2787; **'each year earns'**: Zhang Zhidong, vol. 3, p. 2041; **8 April, Cixi: 'Cede no land'**: Weng Tonghe 2006, vol. 5, p. 2792; **14 April, Guangxu told Li to sign**: Li Hongzhang, vol. 16, p. 56; **Cixi frequently passed out**: Association of Chinese Historians (ed.), *The Reforms of 1898*, vol. 4, p. 300; **eunuch 'often spotted'**: Xin Xiuming, p. 16

200 **Itō did not dispute figures**: Wang Yunsheng, vol. 2, pp. 260, 268–9; **'a voice and nothing besides'**: Hart, *Letters, 1868–1907*, vol. 2, p. 1009; **'if Japan wins'**: Hart, *Letters, 1868–1907*, vol. 2, pp. 992, 1006; **Kaiser Wilhelm II**: the Kaiser's interview with Dr William Hale, 19 July 1908, in Rohl, Appendix 2

201 **Cixi asked Grand Council to reconsider**: Weng Tonghe 2006, vol. 5, p. 2798; **Cixi stopped trying to persuade**: ibid.; **'trembling'**: Weng Tonghe 2006, vol. 5, pp. 2799–800; **Guangxu rushed ratification**: Weng Tonghe 2006, vol. 5, pp. 2801–2, cf. p. 2791; Weng Tonghe 2005, vol. 2, p. 1062; **'the safest line'**: Hart, *Letters, 1868–1907*, vol. 2, p. 1017

202 **'The Japanese war'**: Denby, vol. 2, p. 147; **foreign debts**: Jin Pushen, 2000, no. 1; Qi Qizhang, p. 504

203 **'there's no head'**: Hart, *Letters, 1868–1907*, vol. 2, p. 992; **'C'est le seul homme'**: Carl, p. 101

Chapter 18 The Scramble for China (1895–8)

204 **Cixi continued to receive documents**: Weng Tonghe 2006, vol. 5, p. 2889; First Historical Archives of China (ed.), 1996, vols 21–4, *passim*; **marked increase**

in **Guangxu visits**: Mao Haijian, 2010, no. 4; Zhu Shoupeng (ed.), vol. 4, pp. 3637, 3648–9, 3652, 3656, 3662, 3670–726, *passim*; **Viceroy Zhang pointed out**: Zhang Zhidong, vol. 2, pp. 989–90; cf. Sheng Xuanhuai, vol. 1, pp. 472–3, 476, 479; **European powers regarded China**: Denby, vol. 2, pp. 147–8; Morse, vol. 3, p. 101; Hart, *Letters, 1868–1907*, vol. 2, p. 998

205   **'When the envoys'**: Weng Tonghe 2005, vol. 2, p. 1063; **'blood vessels'**: Wu (Woo) Yong, p. 130; **Guangxu to top officials**: Weng Tonghe 2006, vol. 5, p. 2803; Zhu Shoupeng (ed.), vol. 4, pp. 3595–6; **'forced me to ratify'**: Tsinghua University History Department (ed.), p. 44; **Guangxu berated Li**: Weng Tonghe 2006, vol. 5, p. 2829

206   **'not even look'**: Mao Haijian 2010, no. 4; **Gong from sickbed**: Mao Haijian 2010, no. 4; Tsinghua University History Department (ed.), p. 180; **mistress of the court**: Mao Haijian 2010, no. 4; Weng Tonghe 2006, vol. 5, pp. 2837, 2844, 2878, 2890; **Cixi on Guangxu**: Association of Chinese Historians (ed.), *The Reforms of 1898*, vol. 4, pp. 300–1; Weng Tonghe 2006, vol. 5, p. 2742; **got on really well**: Mao Haijian 2010, no. 4; **officials were warned**: Weng Tonghe 2006, vol. 5, p. 2856; Wang Wenshao, pp. 919–20

207   **study closed down**: Weng Tonghe 2006, vol. 5, p. 2878; **Viceroy Zhang for alliance with Russia**: Zhang Zhidong, vol. 2, pp. 1002–3; **Grand Council decamped**: Weng Tonghe 2005, vol. 2, p. 1064; Weng Tonghe 2006, vol. 5, p. 2883

208   **'on guard against future perils'**: Tsinghua University History Department (ed.), p. 197; ***Bon voyage* banquet**: Wu (Woo) Yong, p. 113; **footnote**: Morse, vol. 3, pp. 103–4; Sun Ruiqin (tr.), vol. 1, p. 116

209   *New York Times* **description**: *New York Times*, 3 September 1896; **Guangxu audience**: Weng Tonghe 2006, vol. 5, p. 2944; Li Hongzhang, vol. 26, p. 275; **after seeing Cixi**: Li Hongzhang, vol. 16, p. 84; vol. 26, p. 275; Weng Tonghe 2006, vol. 5, p. 2944; Zhu Shoupeng (ed.), vol. 4, pp. 3876–7; Mao Haijian 2010, no. 4

210   **journey to Yellow River**: State Archives Bureau, Ming and Qing Archives (ed.), pp. 466–7; Mao Haijian 2011, no. 1; Li Hongzhang, vol. 36, pp. 199–226; **Zhang proposal**: Zhang Zhidong, vol. 2, pp. 989–1001; Zhu Shoupeng (ed.), vol. 4, p. 3631ff.; **'whole towns'**: Zhang (Chang) Yinhuan, p. 533; **'had done nothing'**: Morse, vol. 3, p. 108

211   **Moon Festival**: Weng Tonghe 2006, vol. 5, pp. 2934–6

212   **Cixi planned to restore Old Summer Palace**: Weng Tonghe 2006, vol. 5, p. 2891; **Weng to collect opium tax**: Zhu Shoupeng (ed.), vol. 4, pp. 3963–5; **Li Bingheng argued**: Zhu Shoupeng (ed.), vol. 4, pp. 3972–3

213   **'the scheme of the Inspector General'**: *Qing shilu*, vol. 57, p. 301; Zhu Shoupeng (ed.), vol. 4, p. 3973; **Germany grabbing Qingdao**: Sun Ruiqin (tr.), vol. 1, pp. 106–47; Qingdao Museum et al. (eds.), pp. 121ff. Dugdale, E. T. S. (ed. & tr.), XIV, p. 69; Morse, vol. 3, pp. 106–7; **'No fighting'**: Weng Tonghe 2005, vol. 2, p. 1069; Wang Yunsheng, vol. 3, pp. 173–4; **Cixi informed afterwards**: Weng Tonghe 2005, vol. 2, p. 1069

214   **'stinking beasts'**: Weng Tonghe 2006, vol. 6, p. 3099; Weng Tonghe 2005, vol. 2, p. 1072; **'the Empress Dowager comforted us'**: Weng Tonghe 2005, vol. 2, p. 1071; Weng Tonghe 2006, vol. 6, p. 3081

215   **'the height of treachery'**: Witte, p. 100; **bribing Chinese negotiators**: Zhang Rongchu (tr.), pp. 203–12; **'what a pathetic sight'**: Weng Tonghe 2006, vol. 6, p. 3104; **Guangxu audience with Earl**: Zhang (Chang) Yinhuan, p. 519; **'It's not just you'**: ibid.; **Cixi not consulted**: Zhang (Chang) Yinhuan, pp. 519–20; Weng Tonghe 2006, vol. 6, p. 3104

216   **Censor Weijun**: Weng Tonghe 2006, vol. 6, p. 3103

Chapter 19   The Reforms of 1898 (1898)

219   **'In the world's history'**: Morse, vol. 3, p. 127; **'urgent need'**: Weng Tonghe 2006, vol. 6, p. 3081; Association of Chinese Historians (ed.), *The Reforms of 1898*, vol. 2, p. 430; **receiving Prince Heinrich**: Weng Tonghe 2006, vol. 6, pp. 3118–28; Weng Tonghe 2005, vol. 2, p. 1072; Zhang (Chang) Yinhuan, p. 530

220   **stop fighting over trifles**: Zhang (Chang) Yinhuan, p. 522; **prince had to stand before Cixi**: Weng Tonghe 2006, vol. 6, p. 3118; **Guangxu and medals**: Mao Haijian 2005, pp. 428–35; **'Prince Gong was silent'**: Weng Tonghe 2006, vol. 6, pp. 3081, 3114; **'The roller-coaster'**: Kong Xiangji & Murata Yujiro 2004, pp. 252–3

221   **Cixi launches reforms**: Weng Tonghe 2006, vol. 6, p. 3132

222   **Guangxu orders Weng to retire**: Weng Tonghe 2006, vol. 6, p. 3134; **Cixi's summer gifts**: Weng Tonghe 2005, vol. 2, p. 1074; Weng Tonghe 2006, vol. 6, p. 3134; **collaborated remarkably well**: Mao Haijian 2005, pp. 31–3; **all decrees had Cixi's endorsement**: Mao Haijian 2005, pp. 16–18, 33–5; **'The future of China'**: Martin 1896, p. 327

223   **Junglu to carry it out**: Zhu Shoupeng (ed.), vol. 4, p. 4135; **'six or seven out of ten'**: Kong Xiangji 1988, p. 369

224   **'I knew I was the Sage'**: Kang Youwei, p. 8; **writings sent on to Cixi**: Mao Haijian 2005, p. 382; Weng Tonghe 2006, vol. 6, p. 3112; First Historical Archives of China (ed.), 1996, vol. 23, no. 1107; **Cixi drew Guangxu's attention to Kang**: Guangxu asked Weng to give him another copy of Kang's pamphlet on Japan most likely because Cixi, who kept the pamphlet, talked to him about it and he had not read it. Weng Tonghe 2006, vol. 6, p. 3128; Mao Haijian 2009, p. 382; **'as a close adviser'**: Kong Xiangji (ed.) 2008a, p. 231; **With Cixi's blessing**: Kong Xiangji (ed.) 2008a, pp. 234–5

225   **'humiliation'**: Kang Youwei, p. 44; Mao Haijian 2009, p. 441; **Macartney question**: Cranmer-Byng, p. 238; Robbins, p. 386; **'the able men'**: Der Ling 2004, p. 277; **Debates on Advisory Board**: Mao Haijian 2009, pp. 576–88; Zhang (Chang) Yinhuan, p. 547; State Archives Bureau, Ming and Qing Archives (ed.), pp. 6–11; **4,000 taels**: Zhang (Chang) Yinhuan, p. 562; Kong Xiangji (ed.) 2008a, p. 142; Liang Dingfen, in Tang Zhijun, p. 67

226   **Sun Jianai**: Mao Haijian 2009, pp. 582–3; **friends regarded Kang's occupations**: Kong Xiangji & Murata Yujiro 2009, no. 1; **writings delivered to Guangxu clandestinely**: Kong Xiangji (ed.) 2008a, pp. 355, 432; Mao Haijian 2009, p. 721 ; Liang Dingfen, in Tang Zhijun, p. 67

227   **Guangxu read Poland fable and fell ill**: Kong Xiangji (ed.) 2008a, p. 433; Mao Haijian 2005, p. 131; Zhang (Chang) Yinhuan, p. 553; **'the wisest ever in history'**: Kong Xiangji (ed.) 2008a, pp. 351–5

228   **Kang petitions collected into booklets**: Kong Xiangji (ed.) 2008a, p. 360; bound booklets in the library of the Palace Museum, Beijing; **'get rid of the whole lot'**: Kong Xiangji 1988, pp. 373–5; **'loss of goodwill'**: Kong Xiangji 1988, p. 380

229   **four secretaries**: Mao Haijian 2005, pp. 35, 65, 81; **'Every day'**: Mao Haijian 2005, p. 73; **Kang Board**: Association of Chinese Historians (ed.), *The Reforms of 1898*, vol. 4, p. 332; Mao Haijian 2009, p. 709

230   **'An emperor is like the father'**: Kong Xiangji 1988, p. 62; **'the modern Sage'**: Morse, vol. 3, p. 132; **Confucius crowned King**: Sun Jianai, in Mao Haijian 2009, pp. 42, 534; Liang Dingfen, in Tang Zhijun, pp. 63–4

231   **Kang anxiously explained**: Kong Xiangji (ed.) 2008a, pp. 350–1

Chapter 20   A Plot to Kill Cixi (September 1898)

232   **Wang Zhao to approach Nie**: Wang Zhao, in Cen Chunxuan, Yun Yuding et al., p. 84; **Tan to Yuan**: Yuan Shikai, pp. 550–3; Bi Yongnian, p. 28

233   **a haul of gold**: Kong Xiangji (ed.) 2008a, pp. 402–3; Mao Haijian 2009, p. 774; **Kang ghosted petitions re Japan**: Kong Xiangji (ed.) 2008a, pp. 399–401, 404–5, 443–5

234   **newspaper in Tianjin**: Kong Xiangji & Murata Yujiro 2011, pp. 107–95; Tsinghua University History Department (ed.), p. 958; **'My dearest and nearest'**: Mao Haijian 2005, pp. 440–2; **Itō wrote to wife**: Wang Xiaoqiu, p. 122

235   **Japanese newspapers**: Wang Xiaoqiu, p. 129; **'Ludicrous'**: Li Hongzhang, vol. 36, p. 193; **Viceroy 'shocked'**: Zheng Xiaoxu, vol. 2, p. 671; **Tianjin paper promotes Kang**: Kong Xiangji & Murata Yujiro 2011, pp. 148–53; Liang Dingfen, in Tang Zhijun, p. 69; **'the first Chinese Minister'**: *New York Times*, 13 May 1897; **confidential report to Tokyo**: Kong Xiangji & Murata Yujiro 2004, pp. 251–4

236   **Sir Yinhuan denounced**: Kong Xiangji 1988, p. 252; Zhang (Chang) Yinhuan, p. 540; **nothing was done**: Zhang (Chang) Yinhuan, pp. 539–41; Mao Haijian 2005, p. 38; **secret middle man**: Kong Xiangji 2008, pp. 230–3; Kong Xiangji (ed.) 2008a, pp. 144, 188, 422; Ma Zhongwen 1998; Mao Haijian 2009, p. 721; Liang Dingfen, in Tang Zhijun, p. 67; **'so-called Japanese desire'**: Zhang (Chang) Yinhuan, p. 510; cf. Kong Xiangji & Murata Yujiro 2009a, p. 83; **'When I go to his house'**: Weng Tonghe 2006, vol. 6, p. 3068; Weng Tonghe 2005, vol. 2, p. 1071

237   **'If the throne employs Itō'**: State Archives Bureau, Ming and Qing Archives (ed.), p. 461

238   **'going about things'**: Yuan Shikai, p. 553

239   **Bi later described**: Bi Yongnian, p. 28; **The Wild Fox visited Richard, 19 Sept**: Kang's letter to Timothy Richard, in Association of Chinese Historians (ed.), *The Reforms of 1898*, vol. 3, p. 528; **Richard's words**: Richard, dedication, pp. 258, 263, 266; **'too delicious!'**: Hart, *Letters, 1868–1907*, vol. 2, p. 1044; **'nonsense'**: National Archives, London, P.O. 17/1718, p. 191

240   **'detectives and policemen'**: Brenan to MacDonald, in Seagrave, p. 244; **'cherishes the aspiration'**: Kang Youwei, p. 66; **reform-needs-bloodshed theory**: Liang Qichao 1964, p. 109; **newspaper report**: Mao Haijian 2009, p. 822

241   **The two innocent men**: Chen Kuilong, p. 37; Wang Xiagang, pp. 240–4; **people were appalled**: Yun Yuding, vol. 1, p. 170; Mao Haijian 2011, no. 1; **Kang claim first appeared**: Tang Zhijun, p. 39

242   **'have attempted'**: First Historical Archives of China (ed.), 1996, vol. 24, no. 1399; cf. Mao Haijian 2005, p. 133; **Yuan diary hidden**: Yuan Shikai, pp. 554–5; **'the rumoured plot'**: Association of Chinese Historians (ed.), *The Reforms of 1898*, vol. 3, p. 542; **Kang charged Cixi**: Tang Zhijun, pp. 57–63

243   **Sir Yinhuan acknowledged**: Zhang (Chang) Yinhuan, p. 562; **Weng to Yinhuan**: Weng Tonghe 2006, vol. 5, *passim*; Wu (Woo) Yong, pp. 21–2; Kong Xiangji 2001, pp. 199–200; Ma Zhongwen 1996, no. 4; **'traitor'**: Weng Tonghe 2005, vol. 2, p. 1084; **'like the fingers'**: Zhang Shesheng, p. 156; **footnote**: Zhang (Chang) Yinhuan, p. 561; Zhang Rongchu (tr.), pp. 211–12

244   **'harbouring evil intentions'**: First Historical Archives of China (ed.), 1996, vol. 24, no. 1411; **Ordered execution of Yinhuan**: First Historical Archives of China (ed.), 1996, vol. 26, no. 662; cf. nos 679, 681; **punishments of eunuchs**: Mao Haijian 2005, pp. 142–6; **Learning Companion Xu**: Mao Haijian 2009, p. 859; **footnote**: Xin Xiuming, p. 33

245   **Reforms to continue**: First Historical Archives of China (ed.), 1996, vol. 24, nos 1376, 1399, 1754, *passim*; Mao Haijian 2005, pp. 136, 547–8; **'forging a Great Asia merger'**: Yang Tianshi, pp. 188–90; **'The Japanese government'**: Yang Tianshi, p. 159; **imprisoning Guangxu**: Mao Haijian 2005, pp. 149–53, 160; **percussion instruments**: Ding Ruqin, p. 272

246   **Pearl a prisoner**: Wang Daocheng, in Society of Manchu Studies (ed.), vol. 2, p. 223; Mao Haijian 2005, pp. 143, 152

Chapter 21   Desperate to Dethrone Her Adopted Son (1898–1900)

247   **opera about a heartless adopted son**: Ding Ruqin, pp. 269–70

248   **'clear the air'**: Royal Archives, Windsor, VIC/MAIN/Q/16, no. 116; Association of Chinese Historians (ed.), *The Reforms of 1898*, vol. 3, p. 538; **Dr Dethève's report**: Franzini; **daily routine**: Xin Xiuming, pp. 12–14; Jin Liang 1998, p. 14; Rongling, p. 12

249   **Guangxu's modest living**: Yun Yuding, vol. 1, p. 405; Wang Zhao, pp. 103–4; Carl, pp. 191, 292; **'no obsequious eunuchs'**: Headland, pp. 165–8; **eunuchs poked fun**: Wu (Woo) Yong, p. 74; **'a Sphinx-like quality'**: Carl, pp. 66–7; **read translations, etc.**: Ye Xiaoqing 2007, no. 2; Rongling, p. 22; Wang Zhao, pp. 102–3; **devil-like figures**: Wu (Woo) Yong, p. 74

250   **a ruse**: Kong Xiangji & Murata Yujiro 2004, pp. 123–209; **'made a mistake'**: Headland, p. 65; **Emperor Kangxi attributed**: Forbidden City Publishing (ed.), p. 239

251   **'deceiving the emperor'**: Tsinghua University History Department (ed.), pp. 1198, 1205; Liu Kunyi, vol. 3, pp. 1112, 1415; **Junglu and Earl Li**: Chen Kuilong, p. 23

252   **Hart wrote**: Hart, *Letters, 1868–1907*, vol. 2, p. 1180; **Cixi's tea party and impressions**: Conger, pp. 40–3; Lady Ethel MacDonald, 'My Visits to the Dowager Empress of China', *Empire Review*, April 1901, in Seagrave, pp. 259, 261

254   **the prisoner wrote**: First Historical Archives of China (ed.), 1996, vol. 25, no. 1512

255   **legations pressed to see Guangxu**: First Historical Archives of China (ed.), 1996, vol. 25, nos 43–4; Headland, p. 161; **'too busy'**: Headland, p. 161

Chapter 22   To War against the World Powers – with the Boxers (1899–1900)

256   **powers gave Italy consent**: Royal Archives, Windsor, VIC/MAIN/Q/16, no. 121; Morse, vol. 3, pp. 124–5; **'The Italian Ultimatum'**: Hart, *Letters, 1868–1907*, vol. 2, p. 1190; Hart, *Journals, 1863–1866*, p. 1192

257   **'great surprise'**: Headland, p. 61; **'being unable to'**: Xiang, pp. 87–8; **'There was a bustle'**: Morse, vol. 3, p. 125; **'stuck out his hand'**: Salvago Raggi, pp. 148–9; **Cixi's decrees**: First Historical Archives of China (ed.), 1996, vol. 25, nos 1207, 1220; **'Not a speck'**: Xiang, p. 95

258   **'feeling of elation'**: Morse, vol. 3, p. 125; **Italy only bluffing**: Xiang, p. 101; **Li Hongzhang**, vol. 36, p. 250; **'Foreign powers bully'**: Sheng Xuanhuai, vol. 2, pp. 652–6; First Historical Archives of China (ed.), 1996, vol. 25, nos 1247–8; Wu (Woo) Yong, p. 89; **'Western people'**: Wu Tingfang, p. 254; **'I happened to be'**: Yung Wing, pp. 70–3

259   **'When an Oriental'**: Wu Tingfang, p. 181

260   **Edwards quotes**: Edwards, pp. 53–4; **'Whenever a Christian'**: Smith, p. 54; **'be fair and even-handed'**: Archives of Ming and Qing Dynasties (ed.) 1979a, vol. 1, p. 44; First Historical Archives of China (ed.), 1996, vol. 25, no. 1451, *passim*

261   **'owing debts'**: Archives of Ming and Qing Dynasties (ed.) 1979a, vol. 1, p. 13; **German expedition**: Archives of Ming and Qing Dynasties (ed.) 1979a, vol. 1,

pp. 21–32; First Historical Archives of China & History Department of Fujian Normal University (eds.), vol. 5, pp. 588–92; **'On the whole'**: Bird, p. 298; **'punished severely'**: Archives of Ming and Qing Dynasties (ed.) 1979a, vol. 1, pp. 19–21, 38

262   **replacing Yuxian**: Archives of Ming and Qing Dynasties (ed.) 1979a, vol. 1, pp. 38, 44–5; **'most deeply aggrieved'**: First Historical Archives of China (ed.), 1996, vol. 25, no. 1423; Morse, vol. 3, p. 179; **Boxers had destroyed**: Archives of Ming and Qing Dynasties (ed.) 1979a, vol. 1, p. 57; **'extremely circumspect'**: Archives of Ming and Qing Dynasties (ed.) 1979a, vol. 1, pp. 46–8; **Cixi banned Boxers**: First Historical Archives of China (ed.), 1996, vol. 26, no. 53; **legations dissatisfied and demanded**: National Archives, London, P.O. 17/1412; Morse, vol. 3, p. 187

263   **'I have never known'**: National Archives, London, P.O. 17/1412; **On 12 April**: National Archives, London, P.O. 17/1412; Association of Chinese Historians (ed.), *The Boxers*, vol. 3, p. 169; **published in the *Peking Gazette***: National Archives, London, P.O. 17/1412; Archives of Ming and Qing Dynasties (ed.) 1979a, vol. 1, p. 80

264   **'none of them wish'**: Conger, p. 91; **Lord Salisbury remarked**: Roberts, p. 773; **Junglu sick leave**: Ronglu (Junglu), p. 405; Hou Bin; **'disciplined'**: Wu (Woo) Yong, p. 86; Kong Xiangji 2008, p. 168; Qing History Institute, Renmin University (ed.), vol. 12, p. 180

265   **'For the first time'**: Smith, p. 169; **blue eyes!**: Qing History Institute, Renmin University (ed.), vol. 12, p. 175

266   **'killing of all foreigners'**: Qing History Institute, Renmin University (ed.), vol. 12, p. 179; **permission for 400 troops**: Archives of Ming and Qing Dynasties (ed.) 1979a, vol. 1, pp. 110–11; Conger, p. 92; **not authorising Seymour**: Conger, pp. 97, 100; MacDonald, Sir Claude et al., p. 49; Archives of Ming and Qing Dynasties (ed.) 1979a, vol. 1, pp. 142–4; Qing History Institute, Renmin University (ed.), vol. 12, p. 182; **mobilisation of some Boxers**: Archives of Ming and Qing Dynasties (ed.) 1979a, pp. 145, 157–8; **'with the utmost courage'**: Xiang, p. 261; **'deep regret'**: Archives of Ming and Qing Dynasties (ed.) 1979a, vol. 1, p. 133

267   **'Well, what's done'**: Qing History Institute, Renmin University (ed.), vol. 12, p. 183; **Rescue parties**: Morse, vol. 3, p. 204; Fleming, p. 95; Xiang, pp. 269–70; **'never forget'**: Smith, p. 240; **Junglu to protect**: Archives of Ming and Qing Dynasties (ed.) 1979a, vol. 1, pp. 144–5; **decrees to rein in Boxers**: Archives of Ming and Qing Dynasties (ed.) 1979a, vol. 1, pp. 136–41

268   **Earl Li and other dignitaries**: Li Hongzhang, vol. 27, *passim*; **An eye-witness recorded**: Yun Yuding, vol. 2, pp. 785–6

269   **Queen Victoria to Salisbury**: Royal Archives, Windsor, VIC/MAIN/Q/16, no. 133; **'China Telegrams'**: Royal Archives, Windsor, VIC/MAIN/Q/16, nos 135–851; **'Feel anxious'**: Royal Archives, Windsor, VIC/MAIN/Q/16, no. 130

270   **'We are in the wrong'**: Li Hongzhang, vol. 27, p. 74; **Grass-roots officials**: Wu (Woo) Yong, p. 28ff.; **'Our choice is'**: Yun Yuding, vol. 2, p. 786; **Queen Victoria had spelt out**: Royal Archives, Windsor, VIC/MAIN/Q/16, no. 130; **footnote**: Roberts, p. 771

Chapter 23   Fighting to a Bitter End (1900)

271   **1,400 leagues**: Kong Xiangji 2008, p. 170; **'The Boxers and soldiers'**: Conger, pp. 116, 199; **'There is no doubt'**: Smith, p. 577; **Cixi rewarded Boxers**: Archives of Ming and Qing Dynasties (ed.) 1979a, vol. 1, pp. 161–2; First Historical Archives of China (ed.), 1996, vol. 26, nos 587–8; Li Hongzhang, vol. 27, p. 97; **opened warehouses**: Archives of Ming and Qing Dynasties (ed.) 1979a, vol. 1, p. 176; **'Slowly they came'**: Xiang, p. 261

272　**'a well-dressed'**: Xiang, p. 301; **laid out night-stools**: Liu Bannong et al., p. 75; **asking a Buddhist monk**: First Historical Archives of China (ed.) 2003, vol. 2, pp. 476, 478; **mansion of Imperial Princess**: Headland, p. 206; **Forbidden City not immune**: Wu (Woo) Yong, p. 87; Chen Kuilong, p. 39; Ronglu (Junglu), p. 404; Kong Xiangji 2008, p. 169; **request put to Cixi**: Wu (Woo) Yong, p. 87

273　**'Suddenly in a matter'**: Archives of Ming and Qing Dynasties (ed.) 1979a, vol. 1, p. 187; **Sarah Conger wrote**: Conger, pp. 114–17, 129–30; **cannon gauge raised**: Chen Kuilong, p. 52

274　**'If I had really'**: Wu (Woo) Yong, p. 89; **Cixi told Junglu to deliver fruit**: Li Hongzhang, vol. 27, p. 154; **thousands of casualties**: Li Hongzhang, vol. 27, p. 117; **Cixi's orders re Catholic cathedral**: Archives of Ming and Qing Dynasties (ed.) 1979a, vol. 1, p. 414; **footnote**: Carl, p. 266

275　**massacred 178**: Morse, vol. 3, p. 242; **Mgr Hamer**: Edwards, pp. 106–7; **Cixi put a stop**: Archives of Ming and Qing Dynasties (ed.) 1979a, vol. 1, pp. 327–8, 421–3; **vetoed nationwide massacre**: First Historical Archives of China (ed.) 2003, vol. 1, pp. 253–4; **'If you continue to indulge'**: Archives of Ming and Qing Dynasties (ed.) 1979a, vol. 1, pp. 415–7

276　**Viceroys would not obey her**: Li Hongzhang, vol. 27, *passim*; **'totally realistic'**: Archives of Ming and Qing Dynasties (ed.) 1979a, vol. 1, pp. 156–7; vol. 2, p. 946; **Cixi not ready to surrender**: Archives of Ming and Qing Dynasties (ed.) 1979a, vol. 1, pp. 401, 404, 411–12, 414; **Viceroy Zhang petition**: Archives of Ming and Qing Dynasties (ed.) 1979a, vol. 1, pp. 386–7; **Yuan Chang**: Kong Xiangji 2008, pp. 166–71

277　**Zhang information-gathering network**: Mao Haijian 2011, no. 1; **Xu Jingcheng**: Sun Ruiqin (tr.), vol. 1, pp. 106, 121–45; **'tidying up his hat'**: Association of Chinese Historians (ed.), *The Boxers*, vol. 2, p. 496; **'harbouring private agenda'**: Archives of Ming and Qing Dynasties (ed.) 1979a, vol. 1, p. 392; **foreigners regarding Zhang**: Morse, vol. 3, p. 362; Martin 1896, p. 238; Kong Xiangji 2008, p. 213; Liu Kunyi, vol. 6, p. 2586; **Zhang – Britain and Japan**: Royal Archives, Windsor, VIC/MAIN/Q/16, no. 628; Kong Xiangji & Murata Yujiro 2011, pp. 408–9; Liu Kunyi, vol. 6, p. 2586

278　**'simply fled'**: Archives of Ming and Qing Dynasties (ed.) 1979a, vol. 1, p. 469; **'quite a few traitors'**: Sheng Xuanhuai, vol. 2, p. 656; **Eunuchs remembered**: Xin Xiuming, p. 37; **Lishan in 1898**: Mao Haijian 2005, p. 38; **200 carriages**: Chen Kuilong, pp. 57–9

279　**early morning of 15 August**: Natong, vol. 1, p. 350; Pujia, Pujie et al., pp. 90–1; **Pearl drowned**: Pujia, Pujie et al., pp. 187–8; Xin Xiuming, pp. 24–5

Chapter 24　Flight (1900–1)

280　**beginning of flight**: Pujia, Pujie et al., pp. 90–3; Cen Chunxuan, in Cen Chunxuan, Yun Yuding et al., pp. 14–15; Wu (Woo) Yong, p. 51; Xin Xiuming, pp. 33–4; Wang Zhao, p. 100

281　**with County Chief Woo**: Wu (Woo) Yong

283　**first time in Han attire**: Pujia, Pujie et al., p. 93

284　**Eye-witnesses seeing her**: Pujia, Pujie et al., p. 90; **orders to provinces**: Archives of Ming and Qing Dynasties (ed.) 1979a, vol. 1, p. 489, *passim*; First Historical Archives of China (ed.) 2003, vol. 2, *passim*; **six million taels**: First Historical Archives of China (ed.) 2005, vol. 1, p. 37; **2,000 carts**: Wu (Woo) Yong, p. 95; **Sir Yinhuan execution**: First Historical Archives of China (ed.) 1996, vol. 26, no. 662; Ma Zhongwen 1996, no. 4; **Liu Kunyi to Zhang**: Liu Kunyi, vol. 6, p. 2586

285　**'thousand times urgent'**: Kong Xiangji 2008, pp. 162–3; **lobby Western powers to protect Cixi**: Royal Archives, Windsor, VIC/MAIN/Q/16, nos 592,

Notes

806; **'There is great danger'**: Royal Archives, Windsor, VIC/MAIN/Q/16, no. 843; **'ranged themselves solidly'**: Morse, vol. 3, pp. 330, 342

286   **Zhang to Cixi re audience**: Zhang Zhidong, vol. 2, pp. 1453–4; vol. 3, pp. 1526, 1580; Li Xizhu, pp. 116–17; **silent audience**: Gao Shu, p. 148

287   **Poems of Gratitude**: Zhang Zhidong, vol. 12, pp. 10566–8; **Junglu as decoy**: Archives of Ming and Qing Dynasties (ed.) 1979a, vol. 1, p. 484; **Chongqi and family**: Archives of Ming and Qing Dynasties (ed.) 1979a, vol. 1, pp. 484, 532; First Historical Archives of China (ed.) 2003, vol. 3, pp. 891–2; Qing History Institute, Renmin University (ed.), vol. 12, p. 226; Yun Yuding, vol. 2, p. 789

288   **suicides**: Natong, vol. 1, p. 352; Yun Yuding, vol. 2, p. 789; **assassination squad**: Yang Tianshi 2011, no. 5; Sang Bing, pp. 334–5; Yang Tianshi, pp. 157–61; **Warren cabled Salisbury**: National Archives, London, P.O. 17/1718, p. 372; **'Peace of Yang-tsze'**: Royal Archives, Windsor, VIC/MAIN/Q/16, no. 859; **footnote**: Liu Bannong et al., p. 31

289   **'found a Republic'**: Tang Zhijun 1997, p. 337; **burst into tears**: Wu (Woo) Yong, pp. 50, 89; Cen Chunxuan, Yun Yuding et al., p. 18; Xu Che, p. 486

290   **'In the middle of a sentence'**: Wu (Woo) Yong, p. 83; **'Your Majesty'**: Wu (Woo) Yong, p. 74

291   **throne set up for herself**: Wu (Woo) Yong, p. 81; Roosevelt Longworth, p. 99; Carl, p. 71; Townley, p. 89

Chapter 25   Remorse (1900–1)

292   **The last thing Cixi did**: interview with Prof. Wang Daocheng, who has seen the note, 21 October 2010; **'politely requested'**: Smith, pp. 529–30; **guardians informed Cixi**: Archives of Ming and Qing Dynasties (ed.) 1979a, vol. 1, pp. 496–7, 551–2; vol. 2, pp. 1152, 1214, 1321, 1328–9, 1340–1; cf. Zhang Zhidong, vol. 3, p. 2168

293   **Millions of taels seized**: Morse, vol. 3, p. 367; Chen Kuilong, p. 44; First Historical Archives of China (ed.) 2003, vol. 8, p. 604; Zhang Zhidong, vol. 2, p. 1451; **losses from homes**: Natong, vol. 1, p. 350; Archives of Ming and Qing Dynasties (ed.) 1979a, vol. 1, p. 498; **Hart helped stop looting**: Archives of Ming and Qing Dynasties (ed.) 1979a, vol. 1, pp. 496–7; **'For decades'**: Archives of Ming and Qing Dynasties (ed.) 1979a, vol. 1, p. 513; **'The place was'**: Weale, p. 342

294   **'there was no slaughtering'**: Archives of Ming and Qing Dynasties (ed.) 1979a, vol. 1, p. 552; **hygiene in the streets**: Liu Bannong et al., p. 36; **'return home as the Conqueror'**: Von Waldersee, p. 205; **'deserved their fate'**: Von Waldersee, pp. 252–3; **'I believe I may say'**: Von Waldersee, pp. 216–21; **footnote**: Archives of Ming and Qing Dynasties (ed.) 1979a, vol. 2, pp. 1155–6

295   **'Yesterday evening'**: Von Waldersee, pp. 241–2; **'the bedroom'**: Von Waldersee, p. 221; **Prettier Than Golden Flower**: Qi Rushan, in Liu Bannong et al., pp. 253–63

296   **'should be within the ability'**: Morse, vol. 3, pp. 346–7, 350; **footnote**: Chang & Halliday, Chapter 56

297   **German demands**: Morse, vol. 3, p. 350; Von Waldersee, p. 210; **America's claim excessive**: Hunt; **Chinese population at that time**: Jiang Tao 1993, pp. 78–9; **arguments over indemnity**: Von Waldersee, pp. 224, 233, 239–40; People's Bank of China (ed.), pp. 888–98

298   **'I have much sympathy'**: Conger, pp. 188–9; **raising customs tariffs**: Boxer Protocol of 1901, in National People's Congress Standing Committee Secretariat (ed.), p. 205; People's Bank of China (ed.), p. 892; **up to eighteen million**: Morse, vol. 3, p. 351; **Cixi on new source**: Archives of Ming and Qing Dynasties (ed.) 1979a, vol. 2, p. 1075; **raising customs tariffs Beijing's goal**: Morse, vol. 3, pp. 103–4; Sun Ruiqin (tr.), vol. 1, p. 116; **Cixi on payment terms**: Archives of Ming and Qing Dynasties (ed.) 1979a, vol. 2, p. 1075; **footnote**: Hart, *Letters, 1868–1907*, vol. 2, p. 1282; Morse, vol. 3, p. 351

299   **'I have been of some use'**: Fairbank et al., p. 167; **Cixi bestowed on Hart**: First Historical Archives of China (ed.), 1996, vol. 27, no. 751; Hart, *Letters, 1868–1907*, vol. 2, p. 1294; Morse, vol. 3, p. 470; **500,000 taels**: Morse, vol. 3, p. 367; **'overcome with'**: Archives of Ming and Qing Dynasties (ed.) 1979a, vol. 2, p. 853

300   **'as I am the one responsible'**: Wu (Woo) Yong, p. 89; **'the Decree of Self-reproach'**: Archives of Ming and Qing Dynasties (ed.) 1979a, vol. 2, pp. 944–7; **'before' or 'after'**: Carl, p. 269; **29 January 1901 decree**: Archives of Ming and Qing Dynasties (ed.) 1979a, vol. 2, pp. 914–16; **'Making these changes'**: Archives of Ming and Qing Dynasties (ed.) 1979a, vol. 2, p. 1328

301   **Tianjin provisional government**: *Procès-verbaux des Séances du Gouvernement Provisoire de Tientsin*, vol. 1, Introduction, pp. 1–16; **2,758,651 taels**: Morse, vol. 3, p. 365; **'Unlike 30 years ago'**: Zhang Zhidong, vol. 2, p. 1428

302   **'the spirit of reform'**: Martin 2005, p. 198; **'ranks with Catherine'**: Roosevelt Longworth, p. 95; **'real revolution'**: Reynolds, p. 1

Chapter 26   Return to Beijing (1901–2)

305   **'some uneasiness'**: Hart, *Letters, 1868–1907*, vol. 2, p. 1299; **departure from Xian**: Wu (Woo) Yong, pp. 95–6

306   **'Long Live'**: Xin Xiuming, p. 30; **not even sacked**: First Historical Archives of China (ed.) 2003, vol. 8, p. 532; Wu (Woo) Yong, pp. 95–7

307   **'appreciated and trusted'**: Wang Yanwei (ed.), vol. 4, pp. 4275–6; **Cixi on Earl Li**: Wang Yanwei (ed.), vol. 4, p. 4276; **'in magnitude'**: Conger, pp. 212–15; **heaping further honours**: Wang Yanwei (ed.), vol. 4, p. 4283

308   **Yuan Shikai cable**: ibid.; **heir-apparent's title**: First Historical Archives of China (ed.), 1996, vol. 27, no. 712; Wu (Woo) Yong, pp. 80, 121; Zhang Zhidong, vol. 10, p. 8654; **farewell to Woo**: Wu (Woo) Yong, pp. 123–4

309   **'extraordinarily smooth'**: First Historical Archives of China (ed.), 1996, nos 768–9; **to Beijing by train**: Wang Yanwei (ed.), vol. 4, p. 4287; First Historical Archives of China (ed.) 2003, vol. 8, pp. 536–7; Conger, pp. 215–16; **stopped short**: cf. First Historical Archives of China (ed.) 2003, vol. 8, p. 618; Shan Shiyuan 1997, pp. 452–3

310   **pet monkey**: Gao Shu, p. 130; **honoured Pearl**: First Historical Archives of China (ed.), 1996, vol. 27, no. 824

Chapter 27   Making Friends with Westerners (1902–7)

311   **foreigners welcome to watch**: First Historical Archives of China (ed.) 2003, vol. 8, p. 586; Conger, pp. 215–16; **'dignified'**: Conger, p. 217; **'The Court'**: Hart, *Letters, 1868–1907*, vol. 2, p. 1301; **reception for diplomatic ladies**: Conger, pp. 217–23

312   **Lady Townley**: Townley, pp. 80–1, 100–2; Headland, p. 100

313   **'These foreigners'**: Der Ling 2004, p. 286; **'The Audiences'**: Hart, *Letters, 1868–1907*, vol. 2, p. 1303; **'to wheedle'**: Carl, p. 232

314   **Other goodwill gestures**: Sarah Conger's Diary, the Jewell Collection, Museum of Fine Arts, Boston, 19 March 1904, 14–15 June 1904; Conger, p. 315; Carl, p. 209; First Historical Archives of China (ed.) 2005, vol. 2, p. 1261; Rongling, p. 23; Der Ling 2004, p. 148; **further relationship with Conger**: Sarah Conger's Diary, the Jewell Collection, Museum of Fine Arts, Boston, 1902–4, *passim*; Conger, p. 223ff.

315   **'While there is'**: Conger, pp. 236, 290; **dinner at American Legation**: Conger, pp. 226–9; **'plain in appearance'**: Headland, p. 206; **Before long**: Conger, p. 232ff.

316 **Conger and Cixi met often**: Conger, p. 236ff.

317 **'Through Mrs Conger's'**: *Boston Daily Globe*, 1 January 1905; **'China's Woman Ruler'**: *Chicago Daily Tribune*, 23 October 1904; **'She orders women's feet'**: *Chicago Daily Tribune*, 23 October 1904; **'we were seated'**: Conger, pp. 352–3; **The Congers continued to receive**: Sarah Conger interview, in *Washington Post*, 17 November 1908; **Katharine Carl with Cixi**: Carl

321 **'Pitiable!'**: Headland, p. 32; **In the Blue Room**: *New York Times*, 19 February 1905; *The Washington Post*, 19 February 1905

322 **Louisa Pierson's parents**: Hart, *Letters, 1868–1907*, vol. 2, pp. 1200, 1328; Zheng Xiaoxu, vol. 1, p. 505; **'a Chinese girl kept by me'**: Hart, *Journals, 1863–1866*, p. 363; **Hart's three children**: ibid.; **Pierson and Yu Keng, promotion**: Zheng Xiaoxu, vol. 1, p. 505; Hart, *Letters, 1868–1907*, vol. 2, pp. 1200, 1328

323 **'speaks French'**: *New York Times*, 9 November 1902; **'presides over'**: *Boston Globe*, 26 October 1902; **fancy-dress ball**: *Boston Daily Globe*, 29 April 1901; **son's marriage**: *Boston Globe*, 26 October 1902; *Chicago Daily*, 17 October 1902; *Chicago Daily Tribune*, 2 November 1902; *Atlanta Constitution*, 21 June 1908; **The two daughters**: *New York Times*, 9 November 1902; Der Ling 1948

324 **'now Rongling can'**: Rongling, p. 11; **'very simple'**: ibid.; **visit of Uchida Kōsai**: Rongling, pp. 32–5

Chapter 28   Cixi's Revolution (1902–8)

325 **100 million taels to 235 million**: Shen Xuefeng 2002, no. 1; **decree on inter-marriage and foot-binding**: First Historical Archives of China (ed.), 1996, vol. 27, no. 960; **'like trying to mix'**: Headland, p. 231

326 **'No; the Chinese'**: Conger, p. 254; **espousing education for women**: Xia Xiaohong, pp. 228–51; Zhu Shoupeng (ed.), vol. 5, pp. 5627, 5637–8; Zhang Hailin, p. 344; Shu Xincheng (ed.), p. 4

327 **first nursery school**: Zhang Hailin, p. 559; **Wellesley College**: Zhang Hailin, pp. 354–5; **female editor**: Fang Hanqi et al., pp. 66–8; **some thirty journals**: Zhao Guangjun; **Women's Daily**: Headland, p. 225; **'The 20th century'**: Jin Yi, p. 79; **'What will be the future'**: Conger, p. 336; **in five figures**: First Historical Archives of China (ed.) 2005, vol. 2, p. 1367; Morse, vol. 3, p. 416

328 **incentives for studying abroad**: Zhang Zhidong, vol. 2, pp. 1430–1; vol. 3, pp. 1593–4; Shu Xincheng (ed.), pp. 231–5; Kong Xiangji & Murata Yujiro 2004, pp. 308–13; Kong Xiangji 1998, p. 76; **In Japan alone**: First Historical Archives of China (ed.) 2008, vol. 2, p. 1526; Yang Tianshi, p. 262; **Revolutionary Army**: Association of Chinese Historians (ed.), *The 1911 Revolution*, vol. 1, p. 331ff.; Huang Hu, p. 89

329 **She refused to listen**: Fang Hanqi et al., p. 21; Association of Chinese Historians (ed.), *The 1911 Revolution*, vol. 1, p. 481; **hundreds of titles**: Huang Hu, pp. 85, 89; **Yuan assailed**: Fang Hanqi et al., pp. 42–4; **'all existing laws'**: First Historical Archives of China (ed.), 1996, vol. 28, no. 402; **'death by a thousand cuts' abolished**: First Historical Archives of China (ed.), 1996, vol. 31, no. 192; **torture prohibited**: First Historical Archives of China (ed.), 1996, vol. 31, no. 197; Zhu Shoupeng (ed.), vol. 5, pp. 5328–32, 5342–3, 5356–9

330 **Ministry of Commerce**: First Historical Archives of China (ed.), 1996, vol. 29, nos 314, 1294; Zhu Shoupeng (ed.), vol. 5, pp. 5015–6, 5091, 5122–3; Sun Yutang (ed.), vol. 2, no. 1, p.637ff.; **'50 million'**: Sun Yutang (ed.), vol. 2, no. 1, pp. 640–2; **expositions abroad**: Zhu Shoupeng (ed.), pp. 5015–16; **Cixi footed the bill**: Lin Keguang et al., p. 362

331 **'nearly 30 or 40%'**: Zhu Shoupeng (ed.), vol. 5, p. 5593; **'If we show'**: Song Yanli; **decree to eradicate opium**: Zhu Shoupeng (ed.), vol. 5, pp. 5593–6; **observed Morse**: Morse, vol. 3, p. 437; **Britain readily responded**: Morse, vol. 3, pp. 437–9

332   **Cixi had photos taken**: Dan; Rongling, pp. 16–7; **Hubert Vos claim**: *New York Times*, 17 December 1905; **Hart meeting with Cixi**: Hart, *Letters, 1868–1907*, vol. 2, pp. 1304–5

333   **75 by 60 centimetres**: Lin Jing, p. 25

334   **to foreign heads of states**: *Los Angeles Times*, 13 November 1904; Natong, vol. 1, pp. 518–19, 535, 539, 547; **'forty years instead of seventy'**: *Washington Post*, 26 February 1905; *Atlanta Constitution*, 26 February 1905; **Ren Jingfeng**: the name of the laboratory – Fung Tai Photographer – was written on the frames, in the archives of the Freer Gallery, Washington; Cheng Jihua et al. (eds), vol. 1, pp. 13–4; www.china.com.cn/chinese/2005/dybn/1052350.htm; **Tan Xinpei**: Xu Baoheng, vol. 1, p. 141; Ding Ruqin, pp. 245–6, 255; **China's first film**: Cheng Jihua et al. (eds), vol. 1, p. 14; **British had given a projector**: Cheng Jihua et al. (eds), vol. 1, p. 10; **Takano Bunjiro**: Kecskes; **'sitting side by side'**: *Shi-bao*, fourth day of the twelfth lunar month, 1905, Library of the Institute of Modern History, Chinese Academy of Social Sciences, Beijing

335   **photo to Japanese diplomat**: Kong Xiangji & Murata Yujiro 2011, p. 270; **'loved her'**: Buck, Foreword; **lanterns outside Qianmen**: Xu Baoheng, vol. 1, p. 152; **'In driving through'**: Conger, p. 319; **Cixi considered abolishing eunuch-keeping**: Kong Xiangji & Murata Yujiro 2011, p. 276

336   **'They sat down'**: Headland, p. 98; **minister interpreted on knees**: Conger, p. 221; **One day the rainwater**: Rongling, p. 39; **Cixi watched the rain**: Du Zhongjun, p. 432; **court painters**: Rongling, p. 38

337   **'In that case'**: Rongling, p. 13; **'blandly insolent remarks'**: Roosevelt Longworth, p. 100; **'He stood between us'**: Roosevelt Longworth, pp. 99–100

338   **riding a tricycle**: Rongling, p. 42; **did not try a car**: Rongling, p. 42; Carl, pp. 290–1

Chapter 29   The Vote! (1905–8)

339   **'In foreign countries'**: Sheng Xuanhuai, vol. 2, p. 653; **'England is'**: Der Ling 2004, p. 277

340   *Ta Kung Pao* **articles**: Fang Hanqi et al., pp. 31–2; **'study their political systems'**: Archives of Ming and Qing Dynasties (ed.) 1979b, vol. 1, p. 1; **'from the apex'**: Morse, vol. 3, p. 441

341   **'high hopes'**: Dai Hongci, p. 314; First Historical Archives of China (ed.), 1996, vol. 31, no. 722; **Zaize audience**: Zaize, p. 685; **epoch-making proclamation**: Archives of Ming and Qing Dynasties (ed.) 1979b, vol. 1, pp. 43–4; **Liang Qichao**: Liang Qichao 2008, p. 240

342   **draft outline of constitution**: Archives of Ming and Qing Dynasties (ed.) 1979b, vol. 1, pp. 54–67; **the future parliament**: Archives of Ming and Qing Dynasties (ed.) 1979b, vol. 2, pp. 627–37; **draft Electoral Regulation**: Archives of Ming and Qing Dynasties (ed.) 1979b, vol. 2, pp. 667–84; **the franchise**: Archives of Ming and Qing Dynasties (ed.) 1979b, vol. 2, pp. 671–3

343   **Cixi asked for a timetable**: Archives of Ming and Qing Dynasties (ed.) 1979b, vol. 2, pp. 683–4; **Prince Ching against schedule**: Kong Xiangji 1998, p. 78; **Officials opposed vote**: Archives of Ming and Qing Dynasties (ed.) 1979b, vols 1 and 2, *passim*; **nine-year timetable**: Archives of Ming and Qing Dynasties (ed.) 1979b, vol. 1, pp. 61–7

344   **timetable inscribed on plaques**: Archives of Ming and Qing Dynasties (ed.) 1979b, vol. 1, p. 68; Kong Xiangji 1998, p. 79; **'conscience'**: Archives of Ming and Qing Dynasties (ed.) 1979b, vol. 1, p. 68; **Martin's comments**: Martin 2005, pp. 197–9

346   **'advantageous for China'**: Yun Yuding, in Kong Xiangji 2001, p. 387; **Her diplomats**: First Historical Archives of China (ed.) 2008, vol. 2, pp. 1466–78

347   **contemplated appointing Zhang to Grand Council**: e.g. Mao Haijian 2005, pp. 186–209; **'these flames'**: Association of Chinese Historians (ed.), *The 1911 Revolution*, vol. 2, pp. 501–22, 554–8; vol. 3, pp. 221–5, 272ff.; **'to slaughter every Manchu'**: Xu Zaiping & Xu Ruifang, p. 188; photograph of the testimony in Palace Museum (ed.) 2002, vol. 11, p. 179

348   **Qiu Jin**: Xu Zaiping & Xu Ruifang, pp. 191–9; Association of Chinese Historians (ed.), *The 1911 Revolution*, vol. 3, pp. 37–46, 92–7, 187–214; Xia Xiaohong, pp. 289–302; Fu Guoyong; **press not suppressed**: cf. Xu Zaiping & Xu Ruifang, pp. 191–9; Xia Xiaohong, p. 294; Zhejiang 1911 Revolution Study Association & Zhejiang Provincial Library (eds.), p. 393; **Cixi endorsed Qiu handling**: Association of Chinese Historians (ed.), *The 1911 Revolution*, vol. 3, pp. 187–214; **'no general disorders'**: *New York Times*, 16 November 1908

349   **Nakanishi Shigetaro**: Tōten Miyazaki, pp. 220, 223; **A public decree charged Shen**: First Historical Archives of China (ed.), 1996, vol. 29, no. 697; **Shen death by bastinado**: Kong Xiangji 1998, p. 58; **newspapers' readers revolted**: Fang Hanqi et al., p. 45; **Western outrage**: Hart, *Letters, 1868–1907*, vol. 2, pp. 1374–5; Association of Chinese Historians (ed.), *The 1911 Revolution*, vol. 1, pp. 432, 478

350   **declared that she loathed**: Zhu Shoupeng (ed.), vol. 5, pp. 5329–32; **amnestied**: Zhu Shoupeng (ed.), vol. 5, p. 5191; **Discussions about pardoning Liang**: Li Yongsheng; **Luo, bomb operator**: Liang Qichao 2008, p. 224; Li Yongsheng. (cf. Jin Liang 1998, p. 20); **footnote**: Association of Chinese Historians (ed.), *The 1911 Revolution*, vol. 1, pp. 286–307; First Historical Archives of China (ed.), 1996, vol. 29, no. 697; Kong Xiangji 1998, pp. 54–7; Sang Bing, p. 335

351   **Tiejun**: Liang Qichao 2008, pp. 206, 225, 241; Sang Bing, pp. 338–40; Kong Xiangji 1998, pp. 68–71; Li Yongsheng; **'Nothing could exceed'**: Freeman-Mitford, pp. 193, 198

352   **'Don't make any move'**: Li Yongsheng; **'See if she is alive'**: Der Ling 2004, pp. 234–5

353   **Count Witte**: Witte, pp. 107–9; **prayed privately**: Carl, pp. 207–8; Der Ling 2004, p. 269

354   **'the tidiness of the streets'**: Fang Hanqi et al., pp. 15–16; **'the ultimate goal'**: Sun Ruiqin (tr.), vol. 3, pp. 28, 35; **Yang Ki-Tak**: Cockburn; **Kaiser sent a message**: Sun Ruiqin (tr.), vol. 3, p. 39; cf. Rohl

355   **'yellow peril'**: the Kaiser's interview with Dr William Hale, 19 July 1908, in Rohl, Appendix 2, pp. 345–7; **'It's a year now'**: Sun Ruiqin (tr.), vol. 3, pp. 38, 48; the Kaiser's interview with Dr William Hale, 19 July 1908, in Rohl, Appendix 2, p. 347; **emissary to America**: Sun Ruiqin (tr.), vol. 3, pp. 44–9

356   **'won the hatred'**: *New York Times*, 27 October 1909; **Officer Cen**: Cen Chunxuan, Yun Yuding et al., pp. 12–13; Yun Yuding, vol. 1, pp. 351–2; Zheng Xiaoxu, vol. 2, p. 1100; Kong Xiangji 2001, pp. 219–26; Kong Xiangji 2008, pp. 195–7; Sang Bing, pp. 266–70; Yang Tianshi, p. 178; Hu Sijing, p. 24; Zhu Shoupeng (ed.), vol. 5, p. 5713; **Grand Councillor Lin**: Zhu Shoupeng (ed.), vol. 5, p. 5713; Kong Xiangji 2008, p. 197; **'less poise'**: Roosevelt Longworth, p. 102; **Yuan ordered all new officials**: Sato, pp. 363–4

357   **target for assassination**: Yang Tianshi, p. 173; Sun Ruiqin (tr.), vol. 3, p. 28; Sato, p. 48; **Zaifeng to Berlin**: Wang Yanwei (ed.), vol. 4, pp. 4233–45; Rockhill, p. 53; **Prince Su relationship with Japan and Guangxu**: Liang Qichao 2008, p. 293; Pujia, Pujie et al., pp. 81, 88, 100, 304–15; Shanghai Cultural Relics Committee (ed.), p. 158; Jin Liang 1998, p. 24; Kamisaka, pp. 202–3, 214; **footnote 1**: Gao Shu, p. 158

358   **court painter**: Kong Xiangji 1998, pp. 54–5; **Cixi confronted Su**: Jin Liang 1998, p. 24; **removed Su as Chief of Police**: Zhu Shoupeng (ed.), vol. 5, p. 5147; **'sitting on a blanket of needles'**: Liang Qichao 2008, p. 293; **reappointed Su**: Zhu Shoupeng (ed.), vol. 5, p. 5681; **police force in hands of**: Zhang Kaiyuan, p. 328; **Su to Wang Zhao**: Wang Zhao, p. 108

359   **Japanese steamer**: Liu Ruoyan; Wang Daocheng, in Lin Keguang et al., pp. 484–7; Palace Museum (ed.) 1932, vols 73–4, no. 5474; **'The security'**: Xu Baoheng, vol. 1, p. 183; **Cixi becoming ill**: Zhu Jinfu & Zhou Wenquan 1985, no. 1

360   **experimental farm**: Ma Zhongwen 2006, no. 5; Xu Baoheng, vol. 1, p. 190 **from Manchurian Viceroy**: Palace Museum (ed.) 1932, vols 73–4, no. 5472ff.; **Japanese minister to Beijing**: Palace Museum (ed.) 1932, vols 73–4, nos 5506–7; **Fukushima to Hunan**: Palace Museum (ed.) 1932, vols 73–4, nos 5504–5; **Cixi told Yuan and Zhang**: Xu Baoheng, vol. 1, p. 193; **opera for Guangxu birthday**: Ding Ruqin, pp. 273–6

Chapter 31   Deaths (1908)

361   **'distant wind'**: Zhu Jinfu & Zhou Wenquan 1982, no. 3; Xu Baoheng, vol. 1, p. 186; **'The Emperor'**: Headland, pp. 165–8

362   **Guangxu attempts to get away**: Gao Shu, p. 154; **Rongling and the watch**: Rongling, pp. 10–11, 21–2, 31, 41; **From summer 1908**: Zhu Jinfu & Zhou Wenquan 1985, no. 1; Xu Baoheng, vol. 1, p. 197

363   **in 1877**: First Historical Archives of China & Centre for Tibetan Studies in China (eds.), p. 8; **endorsed educational programme**: First Historical Archives of China & Centre for Tibetan Studies in China (eds.), p. 18; **'As security for'**: Tibet Justice Center, www.tibetjustice.org/materials/treaties/treaties10.html; **'Tibet has belonged'**: First Historical Archives of China (ed.), 1996, vol. 30, no. 609; **'No concession over sovereignty'**: Zhu Shoupeng (ed.), vol. 5, pp. 5234–5; Zhang Xiaohui & Su Yuan, pp. 48–9

364   **Cixi cables to Dalai Lama**: First Historical Archives of China & Centre for Tibetan Studies in China (eds.), p. 82ff.; cf. Hart, *Letters, 1868–1907*, vol. 2, p. 1432; **Dalai Lama asked to meet Cixi**: First Historical Archives of China & Centre for Tibetan Studies in China (eds.), p. 118ff.; **Yintang's programme aborted**: Guo Weiping; Talo (Draklo); **problem about kneeling**: First Historical Archives of China & Centre for Tibetan Studies in China (eds)., pp. 156–60

365   **'sincerely loyal'**: First Historical Archives of China & Centre for Tibetan Studies in China (eds.), p. 169; Xu Baoheng, p. 214; **'in order not to lose goodwill'**: Tsewang Dorje, p. 66; Xu Baoheng, vol. 1, pp. 201, 214, 217; **She and the Dalai Lama agreed**: First Historical Archives of China & Centre for Tibetan Studies in China (eds.), p. 169; **Their first meeting**: Xu Baoheng, vol. 1, pp. 205–7; First Historical Archives of China & Centre for Tibetan Studies in China (eds), pp. 151–3; **birthday with the Dalai Lama**: Rongqing, pp. 140–1; Zhu Jinfu & Zhou Wenquan 1985, no. 1

366   **Prince Ching to Mausoleums**: Xu Baoheng, vol. 1, p. 217; **Guangxu poisoned**: Dai Yi; forensic examination findings in *Qingshi yanjiu (Studies in Qing History)*, 2008, no. 4; **Empress Longyu**: Xin Xiuming, p. 34; Yun Yuding, vol. 1, p. 405; **bed 'unadorned'**: Du Zhongjun, p. 435; **Grand Councillors**: Lu Chuanlin, 1994, no. 3; Xu Baoheng, vol. 1, pp. 217–18; **Zaifeng Regent and Puyi emperor**: First Historical Archives of China (ed.), 1996, vol. 34, nos 922–3

367   **'all key policies'**: First Historical Archives of China (ed.), 1996, vol. 34, no. 935; **'What does Your Highness'**: Headland, pp. 175–6; **Guangxu's official will**: First Historical Archives of China (ed.), 1996, vol. 34, no. 936; **A night passed**: First Historical Archives of China (ed.), 1996, vol. 34, nos 926–45; Xu Baoheng,

vol. 1, p. 218; **'with my hand'**: Xu Baoheng, vol. 1, p. 218; **Cixi's will**: First Historical Archives of China (ed.), 1996, vol. 34, no. 951; **'I am critically ill'**: First Historical Archives of China (ed.), 1996, vol. 34, no. 946

368   **Longyu made 'dowager empress'**: First Historical Archives of China (ed.), 1996, vol. 34, no. 938; **'a sad, gentle face'**: Headland, p. 202; **'At the audiences'**: Headland, pp. 202–3; **councillor ignored her**: Lu Chuanlin 1994, no. 3

369   **'magic earth'**: Xin Xiuming, p. 97

370   **Regent against abdication**: Pujia, Pujie et al., p. 83; **Zaifeng resigned**: Xu Baoheng, vol. 1, p. 381; **'All I desire'**: Xu Baoheng, vol. 1, pp. 385–6; **Decree of Abdication**: First Historical Archives of China (ed.) 2001, p. 234

Epilogue

372   **agreed conditions for the abdication**: Yu Bingkun et al., p. 287; **broke into Cixi's tomb**: Yu Bingkun et al., pp. 288–91; **Puyi devastated**: Aisin-Gioro Puyi, pp. 230–1

373   **'Her people loved her'**: Buck, Foreword; **'more articulate'**: ibid.

Archives Consulted

Bodleian Library, Chinese Collection, Oxford, UK

Cambridge University Library, Department of Manuscripts and University Archives, UK

First Historical Archives of China, Beijing, China

Freer Gallery of Art and Arthur M. Sackler Gallery Archives, Washington DC, USA

French Ministry of Foreign Affairs, Centre des archives diplomatiques de Nantes, France

Isabella Stewart Gardner Museum Archives, Boston, USA

Italian Ministry of Foreign Affairs Archives, Rome, Italy

Library of Congress, Washington DC, USA

Museum of Fine Arts Archives, Jewell Collection, Boston, USA

National Archives, London, UK

National Palace Museum Archives, Taipei, Taiwan

Royal Archives, Windsor, UK

Royal Collection, Royal Library and Print Room, Windsor, UK

Wellcome Library, Iconographic Collections, London, UK

Bibliography

Aisin-Gioro Puyi, *Wo de qianbansheng (The First Half of My Life)*, Qunzhong chubanshe, Beijing, 1964

Anon., 'Rehe mizha' (Secret Letters from Rehe), in *Jindaishi ziliao (Modern History Documents)*, no. 36

Archives of Ming and Qing Dynasties (ed.), *Qingdai dangan shiliao congbian (Collections of Archive Documents of the Qing Dynasty)*, Zhonghua shuju, Beijing, 1979

Archives of Ming and Qing Dynasties (ed.), *Qingmo choubei lixian dangan shiliao (Archive Documents on the Preparations to Establish a Constitutional Monarchy)*, Zhonghua shuju, Beijing, 1979b

Archives of Ming and Qing Dynasties (ed.), *Yihetuan dangan shiliao (Archive Documents on the Boxers)*, Zhonghua shuju, Beijing, 1979a

Association of Chinese Historians (ed.), *Dierci Yapian zhanzheng (The Second Opium War)*, Shanghai renmin chubanshe, Shanghai, 1978

Association of Chinese Historians (ed.), *Wuxu bianfa (The Reforms of 1898)*, Shanghai shudian chubanshe, Shanghai, 2000

Association of Chinese Historians (ed.), *Xinhai geming (The 1911 Revolution)*, Shanghai shudian chubanshe, Shanghai, 2000

Association of Chinese Historians (ed.), *Yangwu yundong (The Movement to Learn from the West)*, Shanghai shudian chubanshe, Shanghai, 2000

Association of Chinese Historians (ed.), *Yapian zhanzheng (The Opium War)*, Shanghai shudian chubanshe, Shanghai, 2000

Association of Chinese Historians (ed.), *Yihetuan (The Boxers)*, Shanghai renmin chubanshe, Shanghai, 1960

Association of Chinese Historians (ed.), *Zhongfa zhanzheng (The Sino-French War)*, Shanghai shudian chubanshe, Shanghai, 2000

Association of Chinese Historians (ed.), *Zhongri zhanzheng (The Sino-Japanese War)*, Shanghai shudian chubanshe, Shanghai, 2000

Astor, Brooke, *Patchwork Child*, Weidenfeld and Nicolson, London, 1963

Bi Yongnian, in Tang Zhijun, *Chengfu xinhuo (New Discoveries from Japan)*, Jiangsu guji chubanshe, Nanjing, 1990

Binchun, 'Chengcha biji, shi erzhong' (The Travel Diaries and Poems of Binchun), in Zhong Shuhe (ed.), *Zouxiang shijie congshu (Collected Diaries of the Early Envoys to the West)*, Yueli shushe, Changsha, 1985

Bird, Isabella, *The Yangtze Valley and Beyond*, Virago Press, London, 1985

Bland, J. O. P. & Backhouse, E., *China under the Empress Dowager*, William Heinemann, London, 1910

Borel, Henri, *The New China: A Traveller's Impressions*, T. Fisher Unwin, London & Leipsic, 1912

Boulger, Demetrius Charles, *The Life of Gordon*, Volume I, The Project Gutenberg e-book

Brown, Arthur Judson, *New Forces in Old China: An Inevitable Awakening*, http://infomotions.com/etexts/gutenberg/dirs/etext99/ldchn10.htm, 1904

Buck, Pearl S., *Imperial Woman*, Moyer Bell, Mount Kisco, New York & London, 1991

Carl, Katharine A., *With the Empress Dowager of China*, Eveleigh Nash, London, 1906

Cen Chunxuan, Yun Yuding et al., *Lezhai manbi; Chongling chuanxin lu; Wai erzhong (The Memoirs of Cen Chunxuan and Yun Yuding; Two Additional Memoirs)*, Zhonghua shuju, Beijing, 2007

Chang, Jung, *Wild Swans: Three Daughters of China*, Simon & Schuster, New York, & HarperCollins, London, 1991

Chang, Jung & Halliday, Jon, *Mao: the Unknown Story*, Random House, London & New York, 2005

Chen Kuilong, *Mengjiaoting zaji (Jottings of Chen Kuilong)*, Shijie zhishi chubanshe, Beijing, 2007

Chen Pokong, 'Bainian fansi: Sun zhongshan shi wenti renwu' (Reflections on the Past Hundred Years: Sun Yat-sen is a Problematic Character), in the *Open* magazine, Hong Kong, 2011, no. 11

Chen Pokong, 'Toward the Republic: A Not-so Distant Mirror', in *China Rights Forum*, 2003, no. 4

Cheng Jihua et al. (eds.), *Zhongguo dianying fazhanshi (A History of Chinese Cinema)*, Zhongguo dianying chubanshe, Beijing, 1981

Cockburn, Patrick, 'A Prehistory of Extraordinary Rendition', in *London Review of Books*, 13 September 2012

Conger, Sarah Pike, *Letters from China*, Hodder & Stoughton, London, 1909

Cooley, James C., Jr, *T. F. Wade in China, 1842–1882*, E. J. Brill, Leiden, Netherlands, 1981

Cranmer-Byng, J. L. (ed.), *An Embassy to China. Being the journal kept by Lord Macartney during his embassy to the Emperor Ch'ien-lung, 1793–1794*, Longmans, London, 1962

Crossley, Pamela Kyle, 'The Late Qing Empire in Global History', in *Education about Asia*, 2008, vol. 13, no. 2

Cuba Commission, *Chinese Emigration: Report of the Commission Sent by China to Ascertain the Condition of Chinese Coolies in Cuba*, Imperial Maritime Customs Press, Shanghai, 1876

Dai Hongci, 'Chushi jiuguo riji' (The Diaries of Dai Hongci as an Envoy to Nine Countries), in Zhong Shuhe (ed.), *Zouxiang shijie congshu (Collected Diaries of the Early Envoys to the West)*, Yueli shushe, Changsha, 1986

Dai Yi, 'Guangxu zhisi' (The Death of Guangxu), in *Qingshi yanjiu (Studies in Qing History)*, 2008, no. 4

Dan, Lydia, 'The Unknown Photographer: Statement Written for the Smithsonian', Freer Gallery of Art and Arthur M. Sackler Gallery Archives, Washington D.C., 1982

Denby, Charles, *China and Her People*, L. C. Page & Company, Boston, 1906

Deng Zhicheng, *Gudong suoji quanbian (A Collection of Miscellaneous Historical Anecdotes)*, Beijing chubanshe, Beijing, 1999

Der Ling, *Princess, Two Years in the Forbidden City*, 1st World Library, Fairfield, Iowa, 2004

Der Ling, *Tongnian huiyilu (Memoirs of My Childhood)*, Baixin shudian, Shanghai, 1948

Ding Baozhen, *Ding Wenchenggong yiji (Writings of Ding Baozhen)*, edited by Luo Wenbin, Wenhai chubanshe, Taipei, 1967–8

Ding Ruqin, *Qingdai neiting yanxi shihua (A History of Opera Performing in the Qing Court)*, Zijincheng chubanshe, Beijing, 1999

Dong Shouyi, *Gongqinwang yixin dazhuan (A Biography of Prince Gong, Yixin)*, Liaoning renmin chubanshe, Shenyang, 1989

Du Maizhi et al. (ed.), *Zilihui shiliaoji (Historical Documents on the Zili Association)*, Yueli shushe, Changsha, 1983

Du Zhongjun, 'Dezong qingmaiji' (Memories of Treating Emperor Guangxu), in Deng Zhicheng, *Gudong suoji quanbian (A Collection of Miscellaneous Historical Anecdotes)*, Beijing chubanshe, Beijing, 1999

Bibliography

Dugdale, E. T. S. (ed. & tr.), *German Diplomatic Documents, 1871–1914*, Harper & Brothers, New York, 1930

East Asia Common Culture Association (ed.), *Duihua huiyilu (Memoirs of Personal Experiences in China)*, Shangwu yinshuguan, Beijing, 1959

Edwards, E. H., *Fire and Sword in Shansi*, Oliphant Anderson & Ferrier, Edinburgh & London, 1907

Fairbank, John King, Coolidge, Martha Henderson and Smith, Richard J., *H. B. Morse: Customs Commissioner and Historian of China*, University Press of Kentucky, Kentucky, 1995

Fang Hanqi et al.,*Dagongbao bainianshi (A History of Dagongbao in the Past Hundred Years)*, Zhongguo renmin daxue chubanshe, Beijing, 2003

Feng Erkang, *Shenghuo zai qingchao de renmen (The People Who Lived in the Qing Dynasty)*, Zhonghua shuju, Beijing, 2005

Feuchtwang, Stephan, *Popular Religion in China: The Imperial Metaphor*, Curzon Press, Surrey, Britain, 2001

First Historical Archives of China (ed.), *Gengzi shibian qinggong dangan huibian (Archive Documents on the Incident of 1900)*, Zhongguo renmin daxue chubanshe, Beijing, 2003

First Historical Archives of China (ed.), *Guangxuchao shangyudang (Imperial Decrees of the Reign of Emperor Guangxu)*, Guangxi shifan daxue chubanshe, Guilin, 1996

First Historical Archives of China (ed.), *Guangxuchao zhupi zouze (Imperial Decrees Written in Crimson Ink during the Guangxu Reign)*, Zhonghua shuju, Beijing, 1995

First Historical Archives of China (ed.), *Mingqing dangan yu lishi yanjiu – zhongguo diyi lishi danganguan liushi zhounian jinian lunwenji (Ming and Qing Archives and History Studies – Papers to Mark the Sixtieth Anniversary of the First Historical Archives of China)*, Zhonghua shuju, Beijing, 1988

First Historical Archives of China (ed.), *Mingqing dangan yu lishi yanjiu lunwenji (Essays on Ming and Qing Archives and History Studies)*, Xinhua chubanshe, Beijing, 2008

First Historical Archives of China (ed.), *Mingqing dangan yu lishi yanjiu lunwenxuan (A Selection of Papers on Ming and Qing Archives and History Studies)*, 1994.10–2004.10, Xinhua chubanshe, Beijing, 2005

First Historical Archives of China (ed.), *Xianfeng tongzhi liangchao shangyudang (Imperial Decrees of the Reigns of Emperor Xianfeng and Emperor Tongzhi)*, Guangxi shifan daxue chubanshe, Guilin, 1998

First Historical Archives of China (ed.) (chief editors Qin Guojing and Zou Ailian), *Yubi zhaoling shuo qingshi (Key Archive Documents in Qing History)*, Shandong jiaoyu chubanshe, Jinan, 2001

First Historical Archives of China & Centre for Tibetan Studies in China (eds),*Qingmo shisanshi dalai lama dangan shiliao xuanbian (Selected Archive Documents on the Thirteenth Dalai Lama in Late Qing)*, Zhongguo zangxue chubanshe, Beijing, 2002

First Historical Archives of China & History Department of Fujian Normal University (eds), *Qingmo jiaoan (Cases to Do with Christian Missions in Late Qing)*, Zhonghua shuju, Beijing, 1996

Fleming, Peter, *The Siege at Peking*, Rupert Hart-Davis, London, 1959

Forbidden City Publishing (ed.), *Mingqing gongting quwen (Interesting Stories from the Courts of Ming and Qing)*, Zijincheng chubanshe, Beijing, 1995

Franzini, Serge (ed.), 'Le docteur Dethève appelé en consultation par l'empereur Guangxu', in *Etudes chinoises*, 1995, vol. XIV, no. 1

Freeman-Mitford, Algernon B., *The Attaché at Peking*, Elibron Classics, www.elibron.com, 2005

Fu Guoyong, 'Qiu jin beishahai zhihou' (After Qiu Jin Was Murdered), www.artx.cn/artx/lishi/40096.html

Gao Shu, *Jinluan suoji (Scraps of Memory in the Qing Court)*, in Cen Chunxuan, Yun Yuding et al., *Lezhai manbi; Chongling chuanxin lu; Wai erzhong (The Memoirs of Cen Chunxuan and Yun Yuding; Two Additional Memoirs)*, Zhonghua shuju, Beijing, 2007

Ge Bin, 'Guangxudi zhupi shuping' (On the Instructions in Crimson Ink by Emperor Guangxu), in First Historical Archives of China (ed.), 2005, vol. 1

Gong Pixiang, 'Qingmo fazhi gaige yu zhongguo fazhi xiandaihua' (Legal Reforms in Late Qing and the Modernisation of China's Legal System), in *Jiangsu shehui kexue*, 1994, no. 6

Gordon, Henry William, *Events in the Life of Charles George Gordon*, Kegan Paul, Trench, London, 1886

Grant, James Hope, *Incidents in the China War of 1860*, Elibron Classics, www.elibron.com, 2005

Gu Hongming, *Gu hongming de biji (The Notes of Gu Hongming)*, Guomin chubanshe, Taipei, 1954

Guo Songtao, *Lundun yu bali riji (Diaries of London and Paris)*, Yueli shushe, Changsha, 1984

Guo Weiping, 'Zhang yintang zhizang zhengce shibai yuanyin chutan' (A Study of the Causes for the Failure of Zhang Yintang's Policy in Tibet), in *Qinghai minzu xueyuan xuebao (Journal of Qinghai University for Nationalities)*, 1988, no. 1

Hake, A. Egmont, *Events in the Taeping Rebellion, Being Reprints of MSS. Copied by General Gordon, C. B. in His Own Handwriting*, W. H. Allen & Co., London, 1891

Hansard, edited verbatim report of proceedings of both the House of Commons and the House of Lords, London

Hart, Robert, *Entering China's Service: Robert Hart's Journals, 1854–1863*, edited by Katherine F. Bruner, John K. Fairbank & Richard J. Smith, Council on East Asian Studies, Harvard University, Cambridge (Mass.) & London, 1986

Hart, Robert, *Robert Hart and China's Early Modernization: His Journals, 1863–1866*, edited by Richard J. Smith, John K. Fairbank & Katherine F. Bruner, Council on East Asian Studies, Harvard University, Cambridge (Mass.) & London, 1991

Hart, Robert, *The I.G. in Peking: Letters of Robert Hart, Chinese Maritime Customs, 1868–1907*, edited by John King Fairbank, Katherine Frost Bruner & Elizabeth MacLeod Matheson, The Belknap Press of Harvard University, Cambridge (Mass.) & London, 1975

Hayter-Menzies, Grant, *Imperial Masquerade*, Hong Kong University Press, Hong Kong, 2008

He Gangde, *Chunming menglu (The Jottings of He Gangde)*, privately printed and photocopied by Shanghai guji shidian, Shanghai, 1983

Headland, Isaac Taylor, *Court Life in China*, Fleming H. Revell Company, New York, 1909

Hogge, David, 'The Empress Dowager and the Camera: Photographing Cixi, 1903–1904', http://ocw.mit.edu/ans7870/21F/21f.027/empress_dowager/cx_essay_03.pdf

Hou Bin, 'Nalashi, ronglu yu yihetuan yundong' (The Woman Nala, Junglu and the Boxer Movement), *Yihetuan yanjiuhui huikan (Journal of the Association for the Study of the Boxers)*, 1983, no. 2

Hsü Chi-she, *Yinghuan zhilue (A Brief Description of the World)*, privately printed in 1848

Hu Sijing, *Guowen beicheng (The Jottings of Hu Sijing)*, Zhonghua shuju, Beijing, 2007

Huang Hu, *Zhongguo xinwen shiye fazhanshi (A History of the Press in China)*, Fudan daxue chubanshe, Shanghai, 2009

Huang Xi, *Zhongguo jinxiandai dianli jishu fazhanshi (A History of Electric Power Technology in Modern China)*, Shandong jiaoyu chubanshe, Jinan, 2006

Huang Xing, 'Wanqing dianqi zhaomingye fazhan jiqi gongye yicun gaishu' (A Brief Account of the Development of Electric Lighting and Industry in the Late Qing), in *Neimenggu shifan daxue xuebao (Journal of Inner Mongolia Normal University)*, 2009, vol. 38, no. 3

Huang Xingtao, 'Qingmo minchu xinmingci xingainian de "xiandaixing" wenti' (The 'Modernity' of New Words and New Concepts in the Late Qing and Early Republican Period), in *Zhongguo jindaishi (Modern Chinese History)*, 2005, no. 11

Huang Zhangjian, *Wuxu bianfashi yanjiu (A Study of the History of the 1898 Reforms)*, Shanghai shudian chubanshe, Shanghai, 2007

Hubbard, Clifford L. B., *Dogs in Britain*, Macmillan and Co., London, 1948

Hunt, Michael H., 'The American Remission of the Boxer Indemnity: A Reappraisal', in *Journal of Asian Studies*, 1972, vol. 31, no. 3

Hurd, Douglas, *The Arrow War*, Collins, London, 1967

Ignatieff, Michael, *The Russian Album*, Chatto & Windus, London, 1987

Bibliography

Jia Yinghua, *Modai taijian sun yaoting zhuan (A Biography of the Last Eunuch, Sun Yaoting)*, Renmin wenxue chubanshe, Beijing, 2004

Jiang Ming, *Longqi piaoyang de jiandui (The Fleet of the Dragon Flag)*, Sanlian shudian, Beijing, 2008

Jiang Tao, 'Wushinianlai de wangqing zhengzhishi yanjiu' (The Studies of Late Qing Political History over the Past Fifty Years), in *Modern Chinese History Studies*, 1999, no. 5

Jiang Tao, *Zhongguo jindai renkou shi (The Population History in Modern China)*, Zhejiang renmin chubanshe, Hangzhou, 1993

Jiang Weitang et al., *Weixin zhishi, aiguo baoren peng yizhong (Peng Yizhong, Determined Reformist and Patriotic Journalist)*, Dalian chubanshe, Dalian, 1996

Jin Liang, *Guangxuan xiaoji (The Jottings of Jin Liang about the Reigns of Emperor Guangxu and Emperor Tongzhi)*, Shanghai shudian chubanshe, Shanghai, 1998

Jin Liang, *Qinggong shilue (A Brief History of the Qing Court)*, privately printed in 1933

Jin Pushen, 'Zhongri jiawu zhanzheng yu zhongguo waizhai' (The Sino-Japanese War of 1894 and China's Foreign Debts), in *Dongnan xueshu (Southeast Academic Research)*, 2000, no. 1

Jin Yi, *Nüjie Zhong*, 1903; new edition edited by Bernadette Yu-ning, Outer Sky Press, New York, 2003

Jin Yi & Shen Yiling, *Gongnü tanwanglu (Memoirs of a Palace Maid)*, Zijincheng chubanshe, Beijing, 1992

Jin Zhong (ed.), *Open Magazine*, Hong Kong

Junjichu suishou dengjidang (Files of Documents that Passed through the Grand Council), in First Historical Archives of China (ed),

Kamisaka Fuyuko, *Nanzhuang nüdie chuandao fangzi zhuan (A Biography of Kawashima Yoshiko)* translated by Gong Changjin, Jiefangjun chubanshe, Beijing, 1985

Kang Youwei, *Kangnanhai zibian nianpu (The Chronology of Kang Youwei as Edited by Himself)*, Zhonghua shuju, Beijing, 1992

Kecskes, Lily, 'Photographs of Tz'u-hsi in the Freer Gallery Archives', *Committee on East Asian Libraries Bulletin*, no. 101, The Association for Asian Studies, Inc., December 1993

Keswick, Maggie (ed.), *The Thistle and the Jade*, Francis Lincoln, London, 2008

Kong Xiangji (ed.), *Kang youwei bianfa zouzhang jikao (A Complete Collection of Kang Youwei's Petitions for Reforms)*, Beijing tushuguan chubanshe, Beijing, 2008a

Kong Xiangji, *Qingren riji yanjiu (A Study of Diaries from the Qing Dynasty)*, Guangdong renmin chubanshe, Guangzhou, 2008

Kong Xiangji, *Wanqing yiwen congkao (A Study of Miscellaneous Late Qing Anecdotes)*, Bashu shushe, Chengdu, 1998

Kong Xiangji, *Wanqingshi tanwei (Exploring Some Details of the Late Qing History)*, Bashu shushe, Chengdu, 2001

Kong Xiangji, *Wuxu weixin yundong xintan (A New Study on the Reforms of 1898)*, Hunan renmin chubanshe, Changsha, 1988

Kong Xiangji & Murata Yujiro, *Cong dongying huangju dao zijincheng (From Japanese Imperial Palace to the Forbidden City)*, Guangdong renmin chubanshe, Guangzhou, 2011

Kong Xiangji & Murata Yujiro, *Hanweirenzhi de zhongri jiemeng ji qita (The Rarely Known Story of an Attempted Sino-Japanese Alliance and Others)*, Bashu shushe, Chengdu, 2004

Kong Xiangji & Murata Yujiro, 'Yige riben shujiguan jiandaode kang youwei yu wuxu weixin' (Kang Youwei and the Reforms of 1898 in the Eyes of a Japanese Secretary), in *Guangdong shehui kexue (Social Sciences in Guangdong)*, 2009, no. 1

Kong Xiangji & Murata Yujiro, *Zhongdao xiong qiren yu 'wangfu wenxin mulu (Nakajima Yuu and His 'List of Official Correspondence')*, Guojia tushuguan chubanshe, Beijing, 2009a

Kwong, Luke S. K., *T'an Ssu-t'ung, 1865–1898: Life and Thought of a Reformer*, E. J. Brill, Leiden, The Netherlands, 1996

Lei Chia-sheng, *Liwan kuanglan: wuxu zhengbian xintan (Turning the Tide: A New Study on the Coup of 1898)*, Wanjuanlou, Taipei, 2004

Li Ciming, *Yuemantang guoshi riji (The Political Diaries of Li Ciming)*, edited by Wu Yuting, Wen Hai Press Company, Taipei, 1977

Li Guoliang, 'Qingdai bishushanzhuang yanxi suotan' (Scraps of Information on the Opera Performances in the Hunting Lodge), in *Gugong bowuyuan yuankan (Palace Museum Journal)*, Beijing, 1984, no. 2

Li Guorong, *Qinggong dangan jiemi (Revelations from the Archives of the Qing Court)*, Zhongguo qingnian chubanshe, Beijing, 2004

Li Hongzhang, *Li hongzhang quanji (The Complete Works of Li Hongzhang)*, edited by Gu Tinglong, Dai Yi et al., Anhui jiaoyu chubanshe, Hefei, 2008

Li Wenzhi (ed.), *Zhongguo jindai nongyeshi ziliao (Documents on the History of Modern Agriculture in China) 1840–1911*, Sanlian shudian, Beijing, 1957

Li Xizhu, *Zhang zhidong yu qingmo xinzheng yanjiu (A Study of Zhang Zhidong and the New System in Late Qing)*, Shanghai shudian chubanshe, Shanghai, 2009

Li Yin, *Qingdai diling (The Mausoleums of the Qing Emperors)*, Zhongguo xiju chubanshe, Beijing, 2005

Li Yongsheng, 'Wuxuhou kangliang mouci cixi taihou xinkao' (A New Study on the Assassination attempts on Empress Dowager Cixi by Kang and Liang after 1898), www.docin.com/p-335080067.html

Li Yunjun (ed.), *Wanqing jingji shishi biannian (A Chronicle of the Late Qing Economy)*, Shanghai guji chubanshe, Shanghai, 2000

Li Zhiting, *Qing kangqian shengshi (The Great Eras of Kangxi and Qianlong)*, Jiangsu jiaoyu chubanshe, Nanjing, 2005

Liang Qichao, *Liang qichao nianpu changbian (Detailed Chronological Record of Liang Qichao)*, edited by Ding Wenjiang & Zhao Fengtian, Shanghai renmin chubanshe, Shanghai, 2008

Liang Qichao, *Wuxu zhengbian ji (The Coup of 1898)*, Zhonghua shuju, Beijing, 1964

Lin Jing, *The Photographs of Cixi in the Collection of the Palace Museum*, Forbidden City Publishing House, Beijing, 2002

Lin Keguang et al., *Jindai jinghua shiji (Historical Sites and Stories in Beijing)*, Zhongguo renmin daxue chubanshe, Beijing, 1985

Liu Bannong et al., *Sai jinhua benshi (The Extraordinary Story of Sai Jinhua)*, Yueli shushe, Changsha, 1985

Liu Kunyi, *Liu Zhongchenggong yiji (The Writings of Liu Kunyi)*, Zhonghua shuju, Beijing, 1959

Liu Ruoyan, 'Fengyu bainian yonghe lun' (Yonghe Steamer in Its Hundredth Year), in *Yiheyuan gengzhitu jingguan wenhua zhuankan (Journal on the Scenes in the Garden of Ploughing and Weaving of the Summer Palace)*, no. 4

Lovell, Julia, *The Opium War*, Pan Macmillan, London, 2011

Lu Chuanlin, 'Lu chuanlin riji' (The Diaries of Lu Chuanlin), in *Wenwu chunqiu (Heritage Spring and Autumn)*, 1992, no. 2–1994, no. 3

Lu Di, *Men Shi Tan Shi (A Collection of Essays on Chinese History)*, personal communication, ludi666_45@hotmail.com

Ma Zhongwen, 'Shiren riji zhongde guangxu, cixi zhisi' (The Deaths of Guangxu and Cixi in the Diaries of Their Contemporaries), in *Guangdong shehui kexue (Social Sciences in Guangdong)*, 2006, no. 5

Ma Zhongwen, 'Zhang yinhuan liufang xinjiang qianhou shiji kaoshu' (A Study of Chang Yinhuan's Exile to Xinjiang), in *Xinjiang daxue xuebao (Journal of Xinjiang University)*, 1996, no. 4

Ma Zhongwen, 'Zhang Yinhuan yu wuxu weixin' (Chang Yinhuan in the Reforms of 1898), in Wang Xiaoqiu & Shang Xiaoming (eds), *Wuxu weixin yu qingmo xinzheng (The Reforms of 1898 and the New System in Late Qing)*, Beijing daxu chubanshe, Beijing, 1998

MacDonald, Sir Claude et al., *The Siege of the Peking Embassy, 1900*, The Stationery Office, London, 2000

Mao Haijian, *Cong jiawu dao wuxu: Kang youwei 'woshi' jianzhu (From 1894 to 1898: A Critical Appraisal of 'the History of Me' by Kang Youwei)*, Sanlian shudian, Beijing, 2009

Mao Haijian, *Kuming tianzi: xianfeng huangdi yizhu (The Unfortunate Emperor Xianfeng, Yizhu)*, Sanlian shudian, Beijing, 2006

Bibliography

Mao Haijian, *Wuxu bianfa shishikao (A Detailed Study of the Historical Facts of the Reforms of 1898)*, Sanlian shudian, Beijing, 2006

Mao Haijian, 'Wuxu zhengbian qianhou zhang zhidong yu jing jin hu de midian wanglai' (The Secret Telegram Exchanges between Zhang Zhidong and His Men in Beijing, Tianjin and Shanghai around the Time of the Coup in 1898), in *Zhonghua wenshi luncong (Journal of Chinese Literature and History)*, 2011, no. 1

Mao Haijian, 'Zhang zhidong yu yangrui de guanxi' (The Relationship between Zhang Zhidong and Yang Rui), in *Zhonghua wenshi luncong (Journal of Chinese Literature and History)*, 2010, no. 4

Martin, W. A. P., *A Cycle of Cathay*, Oliphant Anderson and Ferrier, Edinburgh & London, 1896

Martin, W. A. P., *The Awakening of China*, The Project Gutenberg e-book, produced by Robert J. Hall, 2005

Maugham, W. Somerset, *On a Chinese Screen*, Vintage, London, 2000

Mi Rucheng (ed.), *Zhongguo jindai tielushi ziliao (Historical Documents on the Early Railway Building in China)*, Zhonghua shuju, Beijing, 1984

Millar, Oliver, *The Victorian Pictures in the Collection of Her Majesty the Queen*, Cambridge University Press, Cambridge, 1992

Morse, H. B., *The International Relations of the Chinese Empire*, first published in 1910; this edition reprinted by Cheng Wen Publishing Company, Taipei, 1971

Naquin, Susan, *Shantung Rebellion*, Yale University Press, New Haven (Conn.), 1981

National People's Congress Standing Committee Secretariat (ed.), *Zhongguo jindai bupingdeng tiaoyue huiyao (A Collection of the Unequal Treaties in Early Modern China)*, Zhongguo minzhu fazhi chubanshe, Beijing, 1996

Natong, *Natong riji (The Diaries of Natong)*, edited by the Beijing Archives, Xinhua chubanshe, Beijing, 2006

Packard, J. F., *Grant's Tour Around the World*, Forshee & McMakin, Cincinnati (Ohio), 1880

Palace Museum (ed.), *Qingguangxuchao zhongri jiaoshe shiliao (Historical Documents on Sino-Japanese Relations during the Reign of Emperor Guangxu)*, Beiping gugong bowuyuan, Beijing, 1932

Palace Museum (ed. and chief editor Zhu Chengru), *Qingshi tudian (A Pictorial History of the Qing Dynasty)*, Zijincheng chubanshe, Beijing, 2002

Pan Xiangmin, 'Lun cunqinwang yixuan' (On Prince Chun, Yixuan), in *Qingshi yanjiu (Studies in Qing History)*, 2006, no. 2

Parkes Papers 28/10, in the Department of Manuscripts and University Archives, Cambridge University Library, Cambridge

People's Bank of China (ed.), *Zhongguo qingdai waizhaishi ziliao (Documents on the Foreign Debts of China's Qing Dynasty)*, Zhongguo jinrong chubanshe, Beijing, 1991

Procès-verbaux des Séances du Gouvernement Provisoire de Tientsin, Liu Haiyan et al. (trs.), Tianjin shehui kexue chubanshe, Tianjin, 2004

Pujia, Pujie et al., *Wanqing gongting shenghuo jianwen (Eye-witnesses' Accounts of the Late Qing Court)*, Wenshi ziliao chubanshe, Beijing, 1982

Qi Qizhang, *Jiawu zhanzhengshi (A History of the 1894 Sino-Japanese War)*, Shanghai renmin chubanshe, Shanghai, 2005

Qi Qizhang (ed.), *Zhongri zhanzheng xubian (Sequel to 'Archive Documents on the Sino-Japanese War')*, Zhonghua shuju, Beijing, 1989

Qiao Zhaohong, 'Lun wanqing shangpin bolanhui yu zhongguo zaoqi xiandaihua' (On Expos in Late Qing and Early Modernisation of China', in *Journal of Humanities*, Shanghai, 2005

Qing Government (ed.), *Chouban yiwu shimo (Papers Relating to Foreign Affairs)*, Palace Museum, Beijing, 1929–30

Qing History Institute, Renmin University (ed.), *Qingshi biannian (A Chronological Record of Qing History)*, Zhongguo renmin daxue chubanshe, Beijing, 2004

Qing shilu (Comprehensive Records of Qing), Zhonghua shuju, Beijing, 1987

Qingdao Museum, First Historical Archives of China & Qingdao Social Science Institute (eds.), *Deguo qinzhan jiaozhouwan shiliao xuanbian (Selected Historical Documents on German Occupation of Jiaozhouwan)*, Shandong renmin chubanshe, Jinan, 1987

Qu Chunhai, *Qinggong dangan jiedu (A Study of the Archives of the Qing Court)*, Huawen chubanshe, Beijing, 2007

Reynolds, Douglas R., *China, 1898–1912: The Xinzheng Revolution and Japan*, Council on East Asian Studies, Harvard University, Cambridge (Mass.) & London, 1993

Richard, Timothy, *Forty-five Years in China*, Frederick A. Stokes Company, New York, 1916

Ridley, Jasper, *Lord Palmerston*, Constable, London, 1970

Robbins, Helen H., *Our First Ambassador to China*, Elibron Classics, www.elibron.com, 2005

Roberts, Andrew, *Salisbury: Victorian Titan*, Weidenfeld & Nicolson, London, 1999

Rockhill, William Woodcille, *Diplomatic Audiences at the Court of China*, Luzac & Co., London, 1905

Rohl, John, *Wilhelm II: Der Weg in den Abgrund 1900–1941*, C. H. Beck Verlag, Munich, 2008

Rongling, *Qinggong suoji (Scraps of Memory in the Qing Court)*, in Wang Shuqing & Xu Che (eds), *Cixi yu wo (Cixi and I)*, Liaoshen shushe, Shenyang, 1994

Ronglu (Junglu), *Ronglu cunzha (The Letters of Junglu)*, edited by Du Chunhe et al., Qilu shushe, Jinan, 1986

Rongqing, *Rongqing riji (The Diaries of Rongqing)*, Xibei daxue chubanshe, Xian, 1986

Roosevelt Longworth, Alice, *Crowded Hours*, Charles Scribner's Sons, New York & London, 1933

Salvago Raggi, Giuseppe, *Ambasciatore del Re: Memorie di un diplomatico dell'Italia liberale*, Le Lettere, Firenze, 2011

Sang Bing, *Gengzi qinwang yu wanqing zhengju (The Actions to Rescue Emperor Guangxu in 1900 and the Political Situation of Late Qing)*, Beijing daxue chubanshe, Beijing, 2004

Sato Tetsujiro, *Yige riben jizhe bixiade yuan shikai (Yuan Shikai as Described by a Japanese Journalist)*, edited by Kong Xiangji & Murata Yujiro, Tianjin guji chubanshe, Tianjin, 2005

Schrecker, John, 'For the Equality of Men – For the Equality of Nations: Anson Burlingame and China's First Embassy to the United States, 1868', in *Journal of American–East Asian Relations*, 2010, vol. 17

Seagrave, Sterling, *Dragon Lady*, Vintage Books, New York, 1993

Shan Shiyuan, *Gugong zhaji (Jottings about the Forbidden City)*, Zijincheng Chubanshe, Beijing, 1990

Shan Shiyuan, *Wo zai gugong qishinian (Seventy Years in the Forbidden City)*, Beijing shifan daxue chubanshe, Beijing, 1997

Shanghai Cultural Relics Committee (ed.), *Kang youwei yu baohuanghui (Kang Youwei and the Emperor Protection Association)*, Shanghai renmin chubanshe, Shanghai, 1982

Shen Xuefeng, 'Qingdai caizheng shouru guimo yu jiegou bianhua shulun' (A Study of the Changes in Scale and Composition of the Qing Revenues), in *Beijing shehui kexue (Social Sciences of Beijing)*, 2002, no. 1

Sheng Xuanhuai, *Sheng xuanhuai nianpu changbian (A Detailed Chronological Record of Sheng Xuanhuai)*, edited by Xia Dongyuan, Shanghai jiaotong daxue chubanshe, Shanghai, 2004

Shi-bao, in the Library of the Institute of Modern History, Chinese Academy of Social Sciences, Beijing

Shimura Toshiko, 'Wuxu bianfa yu riben: jiawu zhanzheng houde baokan yulun' (The Reforms of 1898 and Japan: The Press and Public Opinion after the Sino-Japanese War of 1894), in *Guowai zhongguo jindaishi yanjiu (Modern Chinese Studies Abroad)*, vol. 7, Zhongguo shehui kexue chubanshe, Beijing, 1985

Shore, Henry Noel, *The Flight of Lapwing*, Longmans, Green & Co., London, 1881

Shu Xincheng (ed.), *Zhongguo xinjiaoyu gaikuang (Essays on Modern Education in China)*, Zhonghua shuju, Shanghai, 1928

Simpson, William, *Meeting the Sun*, Longman, London, 1874

Smith, Arthur H., *China in Convulsion*, Fleming H. Revell Company, New York, 1901

Society of Manchu Studies (ed.), *Qingdai diwang houfei zhuan (Short Biographies of Qing Emperors and Consorts)*, Zhongguo huaqiao chuban gongsi, Beijing, 1989

Song Yanli, 'Qingmo xinzheng shiqi de zhongying yapian jiaoshe' (The Negotiation between China and Britain on Opium in the New-Policy Period of the Late Qing Dynasty), in *Tangdu xuekan (Tangdu Journal)*, 2003, no. 4

Spence, Jonathan D., *The Search for Modern China*, W. W. Norton & Co., New York & London, 1990

State Archives Bureau, Ming and Qing Archives (ed.), *Wuxu bianfa dangan shiliao (Archive Documents about the Reforms of 1898)*, Zhonghua shuju, Beijing, 1958

Sun Ruiqin (tr.), *Deguo waijiao wenjian youguan zhongguo jiaoshe shiliao xuanyi (Translations of Selected German Diplomatic Documents on Dealing with China)*, Shangwu yinshuguan, Beijing, 1960

Sun Xiaoen & Ding Qi, *Guangxu zhuan (A Biography of Guangxu)*, Renmin chubanshe, Beijing, 1997

Sun Yat-sen, *Sun zhongsan nianpu changbian (A Detailed Chronological Record of Sun Yat-sen)*, edited by Chen Xiqi, Zhonghua shuju, Beijing, 1991

Sun Yutang (ed.), *Zhongguo jindai gongyeshi ziliao (Documents on the History of Modern Industries in China)*, Kexue chubanshe, Beijing, 1957

Swinhoe, Robert, *Narrative of North China Campaign of 1860*, Elibron Classics, www.elibron.com, 2005

Talo (Draklo), 'Qingmo minzu guojia jianshe yu zhang yintang xizang xinzheng' (Nation Building and Zhang Yintang's New System in Tibet), in *Minzu yanjiu (Ethno-National Studies)*, 2011, no. 3

Tang Jiaxuan (ed.), *Zhongguo waijiao cidian (Dictionary of China's Diplomacy)*, Shijie zhishi chubanshe, Beijing, 2000

Tang Yinian, *Qinggong taijian (Eunuchs of the Qing Court)*, Liaoning daxue chubanshe, Shenyang, 1993

Tang Zhijun, *Chengfu xinhuo (New Discoveries from Japan)*, Jiangsu guji chubanshe, Nanjing, 1990

Tang Zhijun, *Kang youwei zhuan (A Biography of Kang Youwei)*, Taiwan shangwu yinshuguan, Taipei, 1997

Thomson, John, *Through China with a Camera*, A. Constable & Co., London, 1898

Tong Yue & Lü Jihong, *Qinggong huangzi (The Princes of the Qing Court)*, Liaoning daxue chubanshe, Shenyang, 1993

Tōten Miyazaki, *Sanshisan nian zhimeng (My Dreams of Thirty-Three Years)*, translated by Chen Peng Jen, Shuiniu chubanshe, Taipei, 1989

Townley, Lady Susan, *The Indiscretions of Lady Susan*, D. Appleton and Co., New York, 1922

Trevor-Roper, Hugh, *Hermit of Peking*, Macmillan, London, 1976

Tsewang Dorje, 'Lun qingmo chuanjun ruzang he shisanshi dalai lama waitao' (A Study of the Sichuan Army Entering Tibet at the End of the Qing Dynasty and the Thirteenth Dalai Lama Fleeing Abroad), in *Zangzushi lunwenji (Essays on the History of the Tibetans)*, Sichuan minzu chubanshe, Chengdu, 1988

Tsinghua University History Department (ed.), *Wuxu bianfa wenxian ziliao xiri (Documentary Chronology of the Reforms of 1898)*, Shanghai shudian chubanshe, Shanghai, 1998

UNESCO Courier, November 1985

Varè, Daniele, *The Last of the Empresses*, John Murray, London, 1936

Von Waldersee, Count Alfred, *A Field Marshal's Memoirs: From the Diary, Correspondence and Reminiscences of Alfred, Count Von Waldersee*, Hutchinson & Co., London, 1924

Waley, Arthur, *The Opium War Through Chinese Eyes*, Routledge, London, 1958

Wang Daocheng, 'Beijing zhengbian yuzhi tanxi' (A Study of the Decrees in the Beijing Coup), in *Shoudu bowuguan congkan (Capital Museum Journal)*, 2004, no. 18

Wang Daocheng, 'Cixi de jiazu, jiating he rugong zhichu de shenfen' (Cixi's Clan, Family and Status at the Time She Entered the Court), in *Qingshi yanjiu ji (Collections of Studies in Qing History)*, vol. 3, Sichuan renmin chubanshe, Chengdu, 1984

Wang Daocheng (ed.), *Yuanmingyuan chongjian dazhengbian (The Great Debate on the Rebuilding of Yuanmingyuan)* Zhejiang guji chubanshe, Hangzhou, 2007

Wang Daocheng, 'Zhongri jiawu zhanzheng yu cixi taihou' (The Sino-Japanese War of 1894 and Empress Dowager Cixi), in *Qingshi yanjiu (Studies in Qing History)*, 1994, no. 4

Wang Junyi, *Qingdai xueshu tanyan lu (An Exploratory Study of the Qing Academic Ideas)*, Shehui kexue chubanshe, Beijing, 2002

Wang Lixiong, *Tianzang (Sky Burial)*, Dakuai Publishing, Taipei, 2009

Wang Shuqing, 'Qingdai gongzhong shanshi' (Food in the Qing Court), in *Gugong bowuyuan yuankan (Palace Museum Journal)*, 1983, no. 3

Wang Shuqing, 'Qingdai houfei zhidu zhongde jige wenti' (Some Issues in the Qing System of Imperial Concubines), in *Gugong bowuyuan yuankan (Palace Museum Journal)*, 1980, no. 1

Wang Shuqing & Xu Che (eds), *Cixi yu wo (Cixi and I)*, Liaoshen shushe, Shenyang, 1994

Wang Wenshao, *Wang Wenshao riji (The Diaries of Wang Wenshao)*, Zhonghua shuju, Beijing, 1989

Wang Xiagang, *Wuxu junji sizhangjing hepu (A Combined Chronology of the Four Secretaries of the Grand Council in 1898)*, Zhongguo shehui kexue chubanshe, Beijing, 2009

Wang Xiaoqiu, *Jindai zhongguo yu riben (China and Japan in Modern Times)*, Kunlun chubanshe, Beijing, 2005

Wang Xiaoqiu & Shang Xiaoming (eds), *Wuxu weixin yu qingmo xinzheng*, Beijing daxu chubanshe, Beijing, 1998

Wang Xiaoqiu & Yang Jiguo, *Wanqing zhongguoren zouxiang shijie de yici shengju (A Splendid Move towards the World in Late Qing China)*, Liaoning shifan daxue chubanshe, Dalian, 2004

Wang Yanwei (ed.), *Qingji waijiao shiliao (Historical Documents on the International Relations of Qing Dynasty)*, Shumu wenxian chubanshe, Beijing, 1987

Wang Yunsheng, *Liushinianlai zhongguo yu riben (China and Japan in the Last Sixty Years)*, Sanlian shudian, Beijing, 1979

Wang Zhao, 'Fangjiayuan zayong jishi' (The Jottings of Wang Zhao), in Cen Chunxuan, Yun Yuding et al., *Lezhai manbi; Chongling chuanxin lu; Wai erzhong (The Memoirs of Cen Chunxuan and Yun Yuding; Two Additional Memoirs)*, Zhonghua shuju, Beijing, 2007

Warner, Marina, *The Dragon Empress*, History Books Club, London, 1972

Weale, B. L. Putnam, *Indiscreet Letters from Peking*, Dodd, Mead and Co., New York, 1907

Weng Tonghe, *Weng tonghe ji (A Collection of Works by Weng Tonghe)*, edited by Xie Junmei, Zhonghua shuju, Beijing, 2005

Weng Tonghe, *Weng tonghe riji (The Diaries of Weng Tonghe)*, edited by Chen Wenjie, Zhonghua shuju, Beijing, 2006

Westad, Odd Arne, *Restless Empire: China and the World Since 1750*, Basic Books, New York, 2012

Witte, *The Memoirs of Count Witte*, Doubleday, Page & Co., Garden City, New York & Toronto, 1921

Wolseley, Garnet Joseph, *Narrative of the War with China in 1860*, Elibron Classics, www. elibron.com, 2005

Woqiu Zhongzi, *Cixi chuanxinlu (A Collection of Stories about Cixi)*, Chongwen shuju, Shanghai, 1918

Wu Rulun, *Tongcheng wuxiansheng riji (The Diaries of Mr Wu of Tongcheng)*, edited by Song Kaiyu, Hebei jiaoyu chubanshe, Shijiazhuang, 1999

Wu Tingfang, *America: Through the Spectacles of an Oriental Diplomat*, Nankai daxue chubanshe, Tianjin, 2009

Wu (Woo) Yong, *Gengzi xishou congtan (Memoirs of the Westward Journey of 1900)*, Yueli shushe, Changsha, 1985

Wu Xiangxiang, *Wanqing gongting shiji (Records of the Qing Court)*, vol. 1, Zhengzhong shuju, Taipei, 1952

Xia Xiaohong, *Wanqing nüxing yu jindai zhongguo (Women in Late Qing and Early-Modern China)*, Beijing daxue chubanshe, Beijing, 2004

Xiang Lanxin, *The Origins of the Boxer War*, RoutledgeCurzon, London, 2003

Xiang Si, *Xiang si tan cixi (Xiang Si Talking about Cixi)*, Zhongguo gongren chubanshe, Beijing, 2010

Xin Haonian, 'Qingmo de dalunzhan yu lishi de zhongyao qishi' (Great Debates in Late Qing and Important Revelations from History), http://jds.cass.cn/Item/6032.aspx

Xin Xiuming, *Laotaijian de huiyi (Memoirs of an Old Eunuch)*, Beijing yanshan chubanshe, Beijing, 1987

Xu Baoheng, *Xu baoheng riji (The Diaries of Xu Baoheng)*, Zhonghua shuju, Beijing, 2010

Xu Che, *Yige zhenshide cixi taihou (A True Empress Dowager Cixi)*, Tuanjie chubanshe, Beijing, 2007

Xu Zaiping & Xu Ruifang, *Qingmo sishinian shenbao shiliao (Historical Documents on Shen Bao during Its Forty Years in Late Qing)*, Xinhua chubanshe, Beijing, 1988

Xue Baotian, *Beixing riji (Diaries of a Journey to the North)*, Henan renmin chubanshe, Zhengzhou, 1985

Xue Fucheng, *Xue Fucheng riji (The Diaries of Xue Fucheng)*, edited by Cai Shaoqing & Jiang Shirong, Jilin wenshi chubanshe, Changchun, 2004

Xue Fucheng, *Yongan biji (Jottings of Xue Fucheng)*, Jiangsu renmin chubanshe, Nanjing, 1983

Xue Fucheng, *Yongan xubian (Additional Jottings of Xue Fucheng)*, privately printed, 1897

Yang Naiji, 'Xiyuan tielu yu guangxu chunian de xiulu dalunzhan' (The Railway in the Sea Palace and the Debates on Whether or Not to Build Railways during the Early Years of the Reign of Guangxu), in *Gugong bowuyuan yuankan (Palace Museum Journal)*, 1982, no. 4

Yang Tianshi, 'Gemingpai yu gailiangpai de liangci wuli changshi' (The Two Armed Attempts by the Revolutionaries and the Reformists), in *Wenshi caikao (Historical Reference)*, 2011, no. 5

Yang Tianshi, *Wanqing shishi (Miscellaneous True Stories of Late Qing)*, Zhongguo renmin daxue chubanshe, Beijing, 2007

Ye Xiaoqing, 'Guangxu huangdi zuihou de yuedu shumu' (The Books Emperor Guangxu Read in the Last Period of His Life), in *Lishi yanjiu (Historical Research)*, 2007, no. 2

Ye Zhiru & Tang Yinian, 'Guangxuchao de sanhai gongcheng yu beiyang haijun' (The Refurbishment of the Sea Palace and the Qing Navy), in First Historical Archives of China (ed.), 1988, pp. 1015–33

Yehenala Genzheng & Hao Xiaohui, *Wosuo zhidaode cixi taihou (The Empress Dowager Cixi I Know About)*, Zhongguo shudian, Beijing, 2007

Yehenala Genzheng & Hao Xiaohui, *Wosuo zhidaode modai huanghou longyu (The Last Empress Longyu I Know About)*, Zhongguo shudian, Beijing, 2008

Youtai, *Youtai riji (The Diaries of Youtai)*, manuscript in the Beijing Library, Beijing

Yu Bingkun et al., *Xitaihou (The Empress Dowager of the Western Palace)*, Zijincheng chubanshe, Beijing, 1985

Yu Zuomin, 'Congxin renshi wanqing jidu jiaomin' (Re-analysing Chinese Christians in Late Qing), in *Journal of Yantai University*, 2005, no. 3

Yuan Shikai, 'Wuxu riji' (My Diaries of 1898), in Association of Chinese Historians (ed.), *The Reforms of 1898*, vol. 1, 2000, pp. 549–55

Yuan Shuyi, *Li hongzhang zhuan (A Biography of Li Hongzhang)*, Renmin chubanshe, Beijing, 2004

Yuan Weishi, 'Ershishiji zhongguo shehui biange de kegui kaiduan' (A Valuable Beginning of the Changes in Twentieth-Century Chinese Society), www.cuhk.edu.hk/ics/21c/issue/articles/063_001112.pdf

Yuan Xieming, 'An dehai shengping shiji kaoyi' (A Critical Study of the Life and Death of An Dehai), in *Shilin (Historical Review)*, History Institute, Shanghai Academy of Social Sciences, 2006, no. 6

Yun Yuding, *Yun yuding chengzhai riji (The Diaries of Yun Yuding)*, Zhejiang guji chubanshe, Hangzhou, 2004

Yung Wing, *My Life in China and America*, Henry Holt & Co., New York, 1909

Zaize, 'Kaocha zhengzhi riji' (The Diaries of the Tour to Study Political Systems), in Zhong Shuhe (ed.), *Zouxiang shijie congshu (Collected Diaries of the Early Envoys to the West)*, Yueli shushe, Changsha, 1986

Zao Yang, 'Qingdai gongting xiqu huodong zongshu' (On the Opera Performances in the Qing court), www.mam.gov.mo/showcontent2.asp?item_id=20081213010301&lc=1

Zeng Guofan, *Zeng guofan riji (The Diaries of Zeng Guofan)*, Zongjiao wenhua chubanshe, Beijing, 1999

Zeng Jize, *Zeng jize yiji (A Collection of the Writings of Zeng Jize)*, edited by Yu Yueheng, Yueli shushe, Changsha, 1983

Zhang (Chang) Yinhuan, *Zhang yinhuan riji (The Diaries of Zhang Yinhuan)*, edited by Ren Qing & Ma Zhongwen, Shanghai shudian chubanshe, Shanghai, 2004

Zhang Dechang, *Qingji yige jingguan de shenghuo (The Everyday Life of a Qing Official in Beijing)*, Xianggang zhongwen daxue, Hong Kong, 1970

Zhang Deyi, 'Hanghai shuqi' (The Travel Diaries of Zhang Deyi), in Zhong Shuhe (ed.), *Zouxiang shijie congshu (Collected Diaries of the Early Envoys to the West)*, Yueli shushe, Changsha, 1985

Zhang Hailin, *Duanfang yu qingmo xinzheng (Duanfang and the New System in Late Qing)*, Nanjing daxue chubanshe, Nanjing, 2007

Zhang Kaiyuan, *Xinhai geming yu jindai shehui (The 1911 Revolution and the Early Modern Society)*, Tianjin renmin chubanshe, Tianjin, 1985

Zhang Rongchu (tr.), *Hongdang zazhi youguan zhongguo jiaoshe shiliao xuanyi (Translations of Selected Historical Documents on Dealing with China from the Magazine the Red File)*, Sanlian shudian, Beijing, 1957

Zhang Shesheng, *Jueban li hongzhang (Rare Pictures of Li Hongzhang)*, Wenhui chubanshe, Shanghai, 2008

Zhang Shiyun, 'Tongzhi dahun liyi' (Records of the Grand Wedding of Tongzhi), in *Gugong bowuyuan yuankan (Palace Museum Journal)*, 1992, no. 1

Zhang Xia et al., *Qingmo haijun shiliao (Archive Documents on the Navy in Late Qing)*, Haiyang chubanshe, Beijing, 2001

Zhang Xiaohui & Su Yuan, *Tang shaoyi zhuan (A Biography of Tang Shaoyi)*, Zhuhai chubanshe, Zhuhai, 2004

Zhang Zhenkun, *Zhongfa zhanzheng xubian (Sequel to 'Archive Documents on the Sino-French War')*, Zhonghua shuju, Beijing, 1996

Zhang Zhidong, *Zhang zhidong quanji (The Complete Works of Zhang Zhidong)*, Hebei renmin chubanshe, Shijiazhuang, 1998

Zhang Zhiyong, 'Qingmo xinzheng shiqi de zhongying jinyan jiaoshe' (The Negotiation between China and Britain on Banning Opium in the New-Policy Period of the Late Qing dynasty), www.qinghistory.cn/qsyj/ztyj/zwgx/2007-05-14/25650.shtml

Zhao Erxun et al., *Qingshi gao (Draft History of Qing)*, Zhonghua shuju, Beijing, 1976

Zhao Guangjun, 'Qingmo baokan dui shijie funü yundong de baodao jiqi dui zhongguo funü yundong de qimeng zuoyong' (The Reports about World Women's Movements in Late Qing Press and Their Enlightening Impact on Chinese Women's Movement), in *Funü yanjiu luncong (Essays of Women Studies)*, 2006, no. 3

Zhejiang 1911 Revolution Study Association & Zhejiang Provincial Library (eds), *Xinhai geming zhejiang shiliao xuanji (Selected Historical Documents on the 1911 Revolution in Zhejiang)*, Zhejiang renmin chubanshe, Hangzhou, 1982

Zhejiang Social Science Academy & Zhejiang Provincial Library (eds), *Xinhai geming zhejiang shiliao xuji (Sequel to 'Selected Historical Documents on the 1911 Revolution in Zhejiang')*, Zhejiang renmin chubanshe, Hangzhou, 1987

Zheng Xiaoxu, *Zheng xiaoxu riji (The Diaries of Zheng Xiaoxu)*, edited by Zhongguo guojia bowuguan (China National Museum), Zhonghua shuju, Beijing, 2005

Zhigang, 'Chushi taixi ji' (The Travel Diaries of Zhigang as an Envoy to the West), in Zhong Shuhe (ed.), *Zouxiang shijie congshu (Collected Diaries of the Early Envoys to the West)*, Yueli shushe, Changsha, 1985

Zhong Shuhe (ed.), *Zouxiang shijie congshu (Collected Diaries of the Early Envoys to the West)*, Yueli shushe, Changsha, 1984–6

Zhu Jiajin, 'Deling rongling suozhushu zhong de shishi cuowu' (Factual Errors in the Books by Der Ling and Rongling), in *Gugong bowuyuan yuankan (Palace Museum Journal)*, 1982, no. 4

Zhu Jinfu & Zhou Wenquan, 'Cong qinggong yian lun guangxudi zaitian zhisi' (On Emperor Guangxu's Death in Light of the Medical Archives of the Qing Court), in *Gugong Bowuyuan yuankan (Palace Museum Journal)*, 1982, no. 3

Zhu Jinfu & Zhou Wenquan, 'Lun cixi taihou nalashi zhisi' (On the Death of Empress Dowager Cixi), in *Gugong Bowuyuan yuankan (Palace Museum Journal)*, 1985, no. 1

Zhu Shoupeng (ed.), *Guangxuchao donghualu (A Detailed Chronological Record of the Reign of Guangxu)*, Zhonghua shuju, Beijing, 1984

Zhu Yong, 'Qingmo xinzheng: yichang zhenzhengde falü geming' (The New System in Late Qing: A Real Legal Revolution), in *Jining shizhuan xuebao (Journal of Jining Teachers' College)*, April 2002

Zuo Buqing, 'Qianlong zhenya wanglun qiyi houde fangmin jucuo' (Measures Adopted by Qianlong against the Population after the Wang Lun Uprising Was Suppressed), in *Gugong bowuyuan yuankan (Palace Museum Journal)*, 1983, no. 2

Acknowledgements

I am indebted to the many historians and specialists in China who have given me generous and invaluable help in my research on Empress Dowager Cixi: Professor Wang Daocheng, Professor Wang Junyi, Professor Dai Yi, Professor Kong Xiangji, Professor Mao Haijian, Professor Jiang Tao, Ma Zhongwen, Professor Yang Tianshi, Xiang Si, Professor Huang Xingtao, Professor Zhu Chengru, Professor Wang Rufeng, Professor Li Zhiting, Professor Huang Aiping, Professor Xu Che, Professor Guan Jialu, Professor Yang Dongliang, Professor Pan Xiangming, Qiu Zhihong, Wang Lixiong and Yehenala Genzheng.

I wish to thank Her Majesty the Queen for permission to quote material from the Royal Archives at Windsor. In accessing this wealth of information, I had the advice of Sheila De Bellaigue and benefited from the professionalism of Pamela Clark, Senior Archivist, and her colleagues. Kate Heard and her colleagues at the Royal Library and the Print Room were most helpful and I am deeply appreciative. Indeed, I am thankful to all the archivists who assisted me; I am only sorry not to be able to name them all here, but would like to stress that they made my research not only fruitful, but also pleasurable. In particular, working with David Hogge, Head of Archives at the Freer Gallery of Art and the Arthur M. Sackler Gallery in Washington DC, was a joy.

I thank Professor John Röhl for answering my questions to do with Germany; Professor Guido Franzinetti for help with the Italian documentation; and Dr Ngo Minh Hoang for research in the French archives.

Prince Nicholas Romanov and James Reeve separately urged me to write this book. The following people kindly made suggestions, sent material, facilitated research and opened their collections of books for me: Professor John Adamson, Bao Pu, Professor Chen Peng Jen, Chen

Pokong, Patrick Cockburn, the Dowager Duchess of Devonshire (née the Honourable Deborah Freeman-Mitford), Edmund Fawcett, Professor Roy Foster, David Halliday, Charles W. Hayford, Professor Michael Ignatieff, Kazuo Ishiguro, Jia Yinghua, Jin Zhong, Fang-Ling Jong, Sir Henry and Lady Keswick, Professor Gavan McCormack, Professor Roderick MacFarquhar, Derry and Alexandra Moore, Lady Ritblat, Lady Roberts, Lord and Lady (John) Sainsbury, Lady Selborne, Sir David Tang, Professor Q. Edward Wang, Lisa and Stanley Weiss, Lady Wellesley, Guorong Xu, Joe Zhang and Pu Zhang.

My agent, Gillon Aitken, read the manuscript and made perceptive comments – for which I am immensely grateful. My gratitude also goes to Dan Franklin, my editor at Cape; to Clare Bullock, the assistant editor; to Mandy Greenfield, my copy-editor; and to Suzanne Dean, who designed a most gorgeous cover. I owe a special thank-you to Will Sulkin, who did a superb job of editing the manuscript. My assistants, Alexandra Adamson and Kristyan Robinson, were indispensable to the writing of the book.

I am lucky to have Jon Halliday, my husband and co-author of *Mao: The Unknown Story*, by my side. His wise and constantly sought counsel has given my writing a real lift. I dedicate this book to him.

Picture Credits

Photograph nos. 1, 4, 13, 31, 39, 50, 51, 52, 53, 56, Freer Gallery of Art and Arthur M. Sackler Gallery Archives, Smithsonian Institution, Washington, DC: Photographer: Xunling; 2, 6, Courtesy of Wellcome Library, London: Photographer: John Thomson; 3, © *The Siege at Peking* by Peter Fleming, Birlinn Ltd., Edinburgh, 2001; 5, From *Qingshi tudian* (*A Pictorial History of the Qing Dynasty*), ed. Zhu Chengru, vol. 11, Zijincheng chubanshe, Beijing, 2002; 7, 32, 33, 36, 41, 42, 46, 48, Every effort has been made to trace copyright holder; 8, From *Memoirs of Li Hung Chang*, edited by William Francis Mannix, Houghton Mifflin Company, Boston, 1913; 9, 10, 15, 54, From *Court Life in China* by Isaac Taylor Headland, Fleming H. Revell Company, New York, 1909; 11, Courtesy of the Stephan Loewentheil collection of Chinese Photography; 12, From *Events in the Taeping Rebellion*, by Charles Gordon, W. H. Allen, London, 1891; 14, From *Old China and Young America* by Sarah Pike Conger, F. G. Browne & Company, Chicago, 1913; 16, Courtesy, Richard Nathanson Fine Art, London; 17, 18, 23, 57, Provided by the Palace Museum: Photographer: Liu Zhigang; 19, Courtesy of Blair House, The President's Guest House, United States Department of State; 20, 26, Provided by the Palace Museum: Photographer: Feng Hui; 21, Royal Collection Trust/© Her Majesty Queen Elizabeth II 2013; 22, 24, Provided by the Palace Museum: Photographer: Liu Mingjie; 25, 60, © Jung Chang; 27, Provided by the Palace Museum: Photographer: Hu Chui; 28, © The Trustees of the British Museum; 29, Arthur M. Sackler Gallery, Smithsonian Institution, Washington, DC: Gift of the Imperial Chinese Government, S″011.16.1–2a-ap; 30, From *With the Empress Dowager* by Katharine A. Carl, The Century Company, New York, 1905; 34, Courtesy of George Eastman House, International Museum of Photography and Film; 35, Courtesy of Howard and Jane Ricketts; 37, Provided by the Palace Museum: Photographer unknown; 38, Photographer unknown; 40, From *American Democrat: The Recollections of Perry Belmont*, Columbia University Press, New York, 1941; 43, Courtesy of the Embassy of Japan, London; 44, Library of Congress/The Whiting View Company © 1901 by The Whiting Bros; 45, Library of Congress/Underwood & Underwood, 1901; 47, Courtesy of Marcelo Loeb, Buenos Aires; 49, Detail from page 49, China Travel Album 1883, Isabella Stewart Gardner Museum, Boston, Massachusetts; 55, From *Letters from China* by Sarah Pike Conger, A. C. McClurg & Company, Chicago, 1909; 58, © Topical Press Agency/Getty Images; 59, Photographer unknown. Additional editing by Frances Nutt Design.

Index